Lorne Pierce, c. 1955: The public face of Ryerson Press's editor, hearing aid in place. Courtesy of Beth Pierce Robinson

BOTH HANDS

BOTH HANDS

*A Life of Lorne Pierce
of Ryerson Press*

SANDRA CAMPBELL

McGill-Queen's University Press
Montreal & Kingston · London · Ithaca

© McGill-Queen's University Press 2013

ISBN 978-0-7735-4116-0 (cloth)
ISBN 978-0-7735-8864-6 (ePDF)
ISBN 978-0-7735-8865-3 (ePUB)

Legal deposit second quarter 2013
Bibliothèque nationale du Québec

Printed in Canada on acid-free paper that is 100% ancient forest free
(100% post-consumer recycled), processed chlorine free

This book has been published with the help of a grant from the
Canadian Federation for the Humanities and Social Sciences,
through the Awards to Scholarly Publications Program, using funds
provided by the Social Sciences and Humanities Research Council
of Canada. Funding has also been received from the Faculty of Arts
and Sciences at Carleton University.

McGill-Queen's University Press acknowledges the support of the
Canada Council for the Arts for our publishing program. We also
acknowledge the financial support of the Government of Canada
through the Canada Book Fund for our publishing activities.

LIBRARY AND ARCHIVES CANADA
CATALOGUING IN PUBLICATION

Campbell, Sandra
Both hands : a life of Lorne Pierce of Ryerson Press /
Sandra Campbell.

Includes bibliographical references and index.
ISBN 978-0-7735-4116-0. – ISBN 978-0-7735-8864-6 (PDF). –
ISBN 978-0-7735-8865-3 (EPUB).

1. Pierce, Lorne, 1890–1961.   2. Publishers and publishing – Canada
– Biography.   3. Editors – Canada – Biography.   4. Ryerson Press –
Employees – Biography.   I. Title.

Z483.P53C34 2013   070.5092   C2013-900362-2

Set in 11/13.5 Adobe Caslon
Book design & typesetting by Garet Markvoort, zijn digital

For DUNCAN

and in memory of my parents,

BARBARA VAN ORDEN
(1917–1986)

and

CORNELIUS J. CAMPBELL
(1904–1989),

who both,
whatever the vicissitudes of life,
loved books and reading

"Henceforth, listen as we will,
The voices of that hearth are still ..."
– John Greenleaf Whittier, "Snow-Bound"

CONTENTS

ACKNOWLEDGMENTS

As Virginia Woolf wrote with respect to fiction, a biography is attached to life at all four corners. Many people and several institutions helped me to make connections between my research on Lorne Pierce and Canadian life and culture, and I am grateful to all of them.

The staff of the Queen's University Archives, home of the voluminous Lorne Pierce Papers (whose comprehensiveness has been both a blessing and a burden), have been very helpful through the tenure of several archivists – the late Shirley Spragge, the late Donald Richan, and Paul Banfield. I have particularly warm memories of the helpfulness of, first and foremost, archivists George Henderson and Stewart Renfrew – both now enjoying a productive retirement – as well as Gillian Barlow, Heather Holmes, Jeremy Heil, Susan Office, and other staff of that incomparable reading room. Thanks are also due those at the Edith and Lorne Pierce Collection of Canadiana at the Queen's Library, including its retired head, W.F.E. Morley (who generously presented me with now dog-eared copies of the Frank Flemington bibliography and the Wallace bibliography of Ryerson Press when I began my research), and Barbara Teatero.

Elsewhere, I was helped by Carl Spadoni and his staff at the William Ready Archive at McMaster University, by Lorna Knight, then at the National Library of Canada, and by Anne Goddard and Charles MacKinnon (my former Grade 12 teacher at Noranda High) at the National Archives of Canada (now Library and Archives Canada). Phebe Chartrand, then an archivist at the McGill University Archives, shared knowledge and laughter. I also benefited from the personnel and resources of the United Church Archives, Victoria University; the University of Toronto Archives; the Victoria University Archives in the E.J. Pratt Library and the Fisher Rare Book Library at University of Toronto; and the archives at the University of Ottawa.

Many individuals took an interest in my work on Lorne Pierce and variously provided most welcome encouragement, hospitality, advice, or information. Any errors or omissions are mine: the largesse is theirs.

Thanks to: Kerry Abel, D.M.R. Bentley, Michael Bliss, Anna Chester, Lorne Chester, Gwen Davies, Susan Thomson Dewar, Gwyneth Evans, David and Joan Farr, Paul Fritz, Michael Gnarowski, Joan Gordon, Debby Gorham, Norman Hillmer, Ed Horn, Heather Jamieson, Peggy Kelly, Kelly House Bed and Breakfast, Marianne Keyes, John Lennox, Glenn J Lockwood, Roy MacSkimming, Brian McKillop, Hon. John Matheson, Seymour Mayne, Mary O'Brien, Brian Osborne, Jeremy Palin, Michael Peterman, Susan Pollak, Pauline Rankin, Anne Richard of Rose Cottage Bed and Breakfast, Brian and Gillian Robinson, Mary Rubio, David Russo, Marianne Scott, David Staines, John Taylor, Clara Thomas, Frank Tierney, Collett Tracey, Marie Tremblay-Chenier, Glenna Uline, Pamela Walker, Tracey Ware, and Elizabeth Waterston. Sadly, some generous souls are no longer here to be thanked: the late Mary Beesly, C.H. Dickinson, Robin Farr, John Webster Grant, Pearson Gundy, A.C.H. Hallett, Marshall "Padre" Laverty, Rob McDougall, Lorraine McMullen, Mary Mott, the incomparable Jacqueline Neatby, J.D. "Jack" Robinson, and D.W. Thomson. Marie Tappin expertly formatted the manuscript through waves of WordPerfect.

Charlotte Gray generously critiqued all of my chapters in draft form. She unfailingly asked, "And what news of Mr. Pierce?" and, even more crucially, listened to the answer, often over afternoon tea at Zoe's at Ottawa's Chateau Laurier, its marble halls a balm and a refuge. Janet Friskney, expert on the Methodist Book and Publishing House, now at York University, did a stint of invaluable follow-up research for me in the Board of Publication Papers at the United Church Archives. My colleagues at the Pauline Jewett Institute of Women's and Gender Studies at Carleton University were warm and encouraging, especially its two most recent directors, Virginia Caputo and the stalwart Katharine Kelly. Faculty of Arts and Science Dean John Osborne, himself an art historian, was interested in Pierce and Canadian art history, and the Faculty generously gave a publication grant for the book.

Above all, this biography was made possible by the courage and candour of Lorne and Edith Chown Pierce's two children, Beth Pierce Robinson and the late L. Bruce Pierce – the remarkable offspring of remarkable parents. It is not easy to have a biographer rummaging through your family tree. Beth and Bruce were magnanimous and forthcoming, even when the topic was painful or poignant. Beth's generosity of spirit has meant much to literary history in so many ways.

It is not easy to have two writers in a household: accordingly, I want to thank my husband, historian Duncan McDowall, who has shared me with Lorne Pierce for many years. Thanks also to the successive spaniels who slept under my desk – in town and at our cottage, where much of this book was written: Phaedra, Miss Black, McNab, Maud, Paget (who in puppyhood chewed through my computer cord one dramatic day), and Lily.

I am grateful to all of those who skilfully shepherded the manuscript through the publication process at McGill-Queen's University Press, including senior editor Donald Akenson, editors Joan Harcourt and Ryan Van Huijstee, and my patient and gifted copy editor, Curtis Fahey. I am particularly grateful to the Press's two anonymous readers of the manuscript, who made many helpful suggestions for revision. This project was made possible by a SSHRC Research Grant, awarded while I was teaching as a sessional lecturer with the equivalent of a full-time load in the Department of English, University of Ottawa.

Earlier versions of some material in this biography were published in the *Journal of Canadian Studies*, *Papers of the Bibliographical Society of Canada*, and *Canadian Poetry*, as a book chapter in *Canadas of the Mind* (McGill-Queen's University Press 2007), edited by Norman Hillmer and Adam Chapnik, and on the website on Canadian publishing history sponsored by McMaster University, the University of Toronto, and Queen's University Archives. I am grateful to all of the above for permission to include revised material in the biography, effected through the kind offices of Kerry Cannon, Eli MacLaren, David Bentley, Adrian Galwin, and Carl Spadoni respectively.

Sandra Campbell
Pike Lake, Ontario
April 2012

CHRONOLOGY

This listing includes milestones in the life of Lorne Pierce (hereafter abbreviated as LP) as well as key publications by him. All titles were published by Ryerson Press unless otherwise indicated.

1864 — Births of Harriet Louise Singleton (14 May) and Edward Albert Pierce (28 June), parents of LP.

1886 — Marriage of Harriet Singleton and Edward Pierce (1 March).

1890 — Birth of LP in Delta, Ontario (3 August).

1892 — Birth of LP's sister, Sara, in Delta (27 February).

1904–07 — LP attends Athens High School, then stays at home for a year assisting in the family hardware business as his father recuperates from surgery.

1908–12 — Attends Queen's University as a member of the Arts 1912 class.

1909/10 — Summer teaching in the west, near Moose Jaw, Saskatchewan.

1912–14 — LP becomes a ministerial probationer in the Methodist Church of Canada, serving in Saskatchewan – at Colonsay, Plunkett, and Fillmore.

1914 — Enters the Bachelor of Divinity program at the Methodist Victoria College, Toronto. Invalided out by Christmas, he is later granted an *ad eundem* Victoria BD (1917).

1915 — Begins his diary while convalescing in Delta (16 June).

1915–16 — Attends Union Theological Seminary, New York City, on scholarship. With courses at New York University (NYU),

                receives a BD (1916) from Union as well as an NYU MA
                (1916).

1916   – Marries his former Queen's classmate Edith Chown
                (b. 1890) in Kingston, Ontario (19 September).

1916–17   – Assistant pastor at St Paul's Methodist Church, Ottawa,
                after ordination in Smiths Falls on 8 June 1916. Symptoms
                of hearing loss, first noticed when he was a Saskatchewan
                probationer, become marked.

1917   – Enlists (9 April), ultimately serving in the Queen's Field
                Ambulance after working as a recruiting officer in eastern
                Ontario. Officiates at Sara's marriage to his Victoria and
                Union classmate Rev. Eldred Chester, Delta (12 June).

1917–18   – Military Service in Kingston, first on infantry course,
                then as acting sergeant major at Ongwanada Military
                Hospital. Medical discharge from service with suspected
                tuberculosis (March).

1918–20   – Minister in the eastern Ontario hamlet of Brinston,
                serving the three-point rural Matilda Circuit. Becomes
                known for community projects.

1920   – Birth of Elizabeth Louise Pierce to Edith and LP,
                Kingston (22 July).
              – LP hired as literary critic and adviser for the Ryerson
                Press division of the Methodist Book and Publishing
                House; begins work at the House's Wesley Building,
                Queen Street, Toronto, on 3 August.

1921   – Publication of LP's pamphlet *Everett Boyd Jackson Fallis*
                about the death of House Book Steward Samuel Fallis's
                son in the First World War. LP's disseminated lupus
                diagnosed about this time.

1922   – Awarded doctorate in systematic theology (STD) from
                United Theological College, Montreal, with a thesis on
                Russian literature (done by correspondence).
              – Conceives Ryerson's bicultural Makers of Canadian
                Literature series.
              – Co-edits the anthology *Our Canadian Literature* with
                poet Albert Durrant Watson.

1923   – Birth of Edith and LP's son, Bruce (5 January).
        – *Primitive Methodism and the New Catholicism* and *Albert Durrant Watson: An Appraisal* published.

1924   – Blanche Hume, LP's long-time secretary and confidante, comes to work for LP at Ryerson Press (January).
        – LP makes textbook sales trip to western Canada.
        – LP begins to set up Canadiana Collection of books and manuscripts at Queen's University (later known as the Edith and Lorne Pierce Collection of Canadiana).
        – LP authors *Fifty Years of Public Service: A Life of James L. Hughes* (Oxford University Press), *Albert Durrant Watson* (privately printed), and *The Beloved Community.*

1925   – Launches the Ryerson Chapbook Poetry series.
        – *Marjorie Pickthall: A Book of Remembrance.*
        – Publishes Frederick Philip Grove's controversial novel *Settlers of the Marsh.*

1926   – Death of Albert Durrant Watson (3 May), LP's friend and mentor.
        – Elected to the Royal Society of Canada (26 May) after the awarding of the Society's first Lorne Pierce Medal, donated by LP the previous year.
        – The Pierces move to 233 Glengrove Avenue from their first Toronto home, 56 Wineva Avenue (June).
        – Writes five booklets for Ryerson Canadian History Readers series: *John Black, James Evans, John McDougall, Sieur de Maisonneuve,* and *Thomas Chandler Haliburton.*

1927   – Begins to personally edit and issue *The Ryerson Books of Prose and Verse,* first in a very successful series of textbooks.
        – *In Conference with the Best Minds* (Nashville, TN: Cokesbury Press).
        – *An Outline of Canadian Literature* (Montreal: Carrier).
        – Edits William Kirby's *Annals of Niagara,* published by Macmillan.

1928   – Awarded Honorary LLD by Queen's University.

1929   – Death of Edward Pierce, Delta (4 January), during the
           near-fatal illness of LP's son, Bruce.
        – Death of Bliss Carman (8 June).
        – Ryerson and Macmillan initiate a highly successful
           joint reader series, *The Canada Books of Prose and Verse*
           (elementary and high school texts).
        – Begins publication of *The Canadian Treasury Readers*
           (elementary school texts).
        – *Toward the Bonne Entente.*
        – *William Kirby: The Portrait of A Tory Loyalist* (Macmillan).
        – Edits *The Chronicle of A Century, 1829–1929, The Story of
           Canada*, and the Canadian section of the empire literary
           anthology *The New Countries* compiled by Hector Bolitho
           (London: Jonathan Cape).

1930   – On medical leave from House after collapse from
           overwork and the pressures of a copyright controversy
           over one of his textbooks (February–March).

1931   – *New History for Old.*
        – Edits *Bliss Carman's Scrap-Book* and Carman's *The Music of
           Earth.*

1932   – Death of Book Steward Samuel Fallis, who is succeeded
           by Donald Solandt.
        – LP awarded an honorary D.LITT by Laval University.
        – *Unexplored Fields of Canadian Literature.*

1933   – *Three Fredericton Poets.*

1934   – LP and Edith move to 5 Campbell Crescent in York Mills
           (which they christen "La Ferme") and tour Europe in July
           and August.

1935   – LP edits *The Complete Poems of Francis Sherman* and the
           poetry anthology *Our Canadian Literature* (new edition,
           co-edited with Bliss Carman, who had worked on the
           poetry section before his death in 1929).

1936   – Death of Book Steward Donald Solandt, who is
           succeeded in June 1937 by Rev. C.H. Dickinson.

1937   – *Master Builders*, LP's booklet on freemasonry.

1938	– LP and his sister, Sara Chester, compile *In an Eastern Window: A Book of Days*, a tribute to their mother, Harriet Pierce.
1938–39	– LP assumes ownership of the magazine *The Canadian Bookman*.
1939	– Co-founder of Queen's Art Foundation. – *J.E.H. MacDonald: A Postscript, 1873–1932*.
1940	– Death of Harriet Louise Pierce, Delta (9 January). – Co-founder of Canadian Society for the Deaf (now the Canadian Hearing Society). – Establishes Ryerson Fiction Award.
1942	– *Thoreau MacDonald*.
1943	– Booklet *Jacques De Molay*. – *The Armoury in Our Halls*. – Death of Sir Charles G.D. Roberts (26 November). – Plagued by writers' cramp and chronic fatigue, LP ceases keeping a diary around this time.
1944	– *Queen's University Art Foundation*. – *Prime Ministers to the Book*.
1945	– *A Canadian People*.
1946	– Member, with his friend Harold Innis, of the United Church's Commission on Christianity and Culture (reported 1950).
1947	– *Christianity and Culture in Our Time*.
1949	– *E. Grace Coombs, Artist*.
1951	– *The Royal Tour in Canada, 1951*. – *On Publishers and Publishing*.
1953	– *Canada at the Coronation*.
1954	– Death of Edith Chown Pierce (23 April) after a four-year battle with breast cancer. – *The House of Ryerson*.

— Anthology *Canadian Poetry in English* (co-edited with Bliss Carman and V.B. Rhodenizer).
— Edits *The Selected Poems of Bliss Carman.*

1955 — LP moves to apartment 309, 49 Glen Elm Avenue, his last address.

1957 — LP to Caribbean (March).
— Edits *The Selected Poems of Marjorie Pickthall.*
— Booklet *Memorial Windows: St. George's United Church* (privately printed).

1958 — *Early Glass Houses of Nova Scotia* (privately printed).

1959 — LP to Caribbean (March).

1960 — LP retires in January as general editor of Ryerson Press.
— LP in Mexico (March).
— *A Canadian Nation.*

1961 — LP dies of lupus-related heart disease, Toronto (27 November) and is interred beside his wife, Edith, in Mount Pleasant Cemetery, Toronto.

1970 — Sale of Ryerson Press to McGraw-Hill Canada by the United Church of Canada.

BOTH HANDS

INTRODUCTION

The problems of publishing in this country are economic ones, but the importance of publishing in the life of Canada is cultural before it is anything.

Ontario Royal Commission on Canadian Publishers and Canadian Publishing, 1971[1]

No one involved in the production or reception of literary texts – from the writer to publisher to bookseller to reader – is free of the boundaries that get drawn by editors in privileged positions.

Canadian writer Roy Miki[2]

Near the end of his long and illustrious career as editor of Ryerson Press, Lorne Pierce summed up the sense of mission that had always driven him. His editorial desk, he declared in a letter to a prospective successor, was "a sort of altar at which I serve ... as one very much concerned about the entire cultural life of Canada." His mission, he believed, was one of "planning a high destiny for our people" – with French-English entente always in view. Pierce was frank about the power of the post and about his commitment to his self-appointed mission. He emphasized to his prospective successor: "You would choose the spokesmen and interpreters best equipped to write for you. You would look back as I now do, and thank God that this power was placed in your hands for so much good."[3] Dramatic words. Canadians need to understand better the influential figure who wrote them.

Scholar Maria Tippett has emphasized that "culture is made as much by the critics and the scholars who write about it, the galleries who collect and exhibit it, and the patrons who buy it, as by the artists themselves."[4] Tippett was writing about Canadian art, but her insight also illuminates the crucial role of the country's editors and publishers in the shaping of Canadian book culture from its beginnings to the present, a power emphasized in the two quotations that begin this Introduction.

As Roy Miki so vividly phrases it, in the production and reception of literary texts, no one is free of the boundaries that get drawn by editors in privileged positions. However, as the Ontario royal commission on Canadian publishing pointed out, the role of Canadian publishers in shaping Canada's culture has in fact been little appreciated – and, until recently, even less analyzed.

That is to say, the men (and usually they have been men) who have been major players in Canadian publishing have not to date received scholarly attention commensurate with their importance, for better and for worse. Lorne Pierce (1890–1961), unquestionably one of the most influential publishers in Canadian literary history, is no exception.

Pierce, from 1920 to 1960 editor of Ryerson Press, a division of the United Church Publishing House (before 1925 the Methodist Book and Publishing House), was Canada's leading publisher for four decades. Contemporaries recognized his importance. Historian Donald Creighton characterized Ryerson Press under Pierce as one of the most important Canadian publishing companies active between the two world wars and beyond. Creighton observed: "Ryerson Press [was] ... the very liberal and catholic descendant of the old Methodist Book and Publishing House ... [its] chief editor, Lorne Pierce, was a man of strongly independent views and wide sympathies."[5] Yet today, almost four decades after Creighton's provocative verdict, few Canadians remember Lorne Pierce. Not many even recognize the name of Ryerson Press. Moreover, Pierce has received little attention from Canadian literary historians, despite honourable exceptions in the work of scholars George L. Parker, Janet Friskney, Laura Groening, and a few others.

In other words, time has clouded our cultural memory. As Pierce himself ruefully observed, "time ... dims, and gives everything a feathery edge."[6] Even in works devoted to the book trade, Pierce is often sketched as a more simplistic figure, or a more grandiose one, than he really was – often both at once. In *The Perilous Trade: Publishing Canada's Writers* (2003), for example, Roy MacSkimming's history of the Canadian book trade during the post-1960 period, the evidence presented suggests that, some fifty years after Pierce's death, his image has been distorted into stereotype. For example, MacSkimming writes that Jack McClelland, Pierce's younger competitor in the 1950s, damned Pierce with faint praise: "[Pierce's] successor a generation later in promotional zeal, Jack McClelland, remembered Pierce as 'a sort of wild, strange fellow' who 'always seemed to be in a hurry' but was 'a very good publisher.'"[7]

McClelland's appraisal, made in an interview decades after Pierce's death, offers a construct of Lorne Pierce – not for the first time by any means in modernist and postmodernist chronicles – as a hyperactive and uncritically patriotic church publisher. In other words, Pierce as a publisher was, as MacSkimming puts it, a "Methodist scholar with [five] university degrees," an earnest man of the cloth. *The Perilous Trade* touches upon Pierce's career in the course of an analysis whose main focus is the post-1960 publishing scene, which, it is emphasized, was a more libidinous and sophisticated age. MacSkimming writes of forerunner Pierce: "Pierce nurtured a notion called Canadian literature. He published copious amounts of it, commissioned critical studies of it, edited school readers bursting with it, and wrote, lectured, and pamphleteered about it. There was an evangelical industry about the man."[8]

Happily, MacSkimming chooses exactly the right quote from Pierce himself to crystallize Pierce's significance. Looking back at his career, Pierce situated himself as a major cultural nationalist, an ardent patriot with ideals similar to those of two of his major Canadian publishing contemporaries, John McClelland (1877–1968) of McClelland and Stewart and Hugh Eayrs (1894–1940), long-time president of Macmillan of Canada. Pierce recalled the orientation of this de facto triumvirate during the 1920s, the first decade of his Ryerson editorial career: "We were at the beginnings of things as a nation and we felt under obligation to assist as many spokesmen of our time as we could … It was simply that a birth, and then possibly a rebirth, of Canadian letters had to begin somewhere, and it might as well begin with us."[9]

This biography of Pierce examines his life and work. Its title, *Both Hands*, is taken from Pierce's favourite complimentary closing in letters to kindred spirits in Canadian cultural nationalism, a sign-off adopted from the correspondence of William Withrow, his eminent nineteenth-century predecessor at the Methodist Book and Publishing House (hereafter "the House"). The "both hands" image captures Pierce's unstinting energy and heartfelt (dare one say "two-fisted"?) enthusiasm for cultural nation making throughout his editorial career. Nevertheless, this biography is mindful – like all responsible biography – of the variable degree to which posterity can and cannot accept its subject at his own estimate, or that of his friends and rivals.

Pierce was both a product of and a maker of his era in Canada, a duality this study addresses by studying the social and cultural forces that shaped Pierce's values both inside and outside the publishing world.

The value-shaping contexts of Pierce's seventy-one years of life began
with his staunchly Methodist upbringing in the eastern Ontario hamlet
of Delta and his secondary education in the nearby village of Athens.
Pierce's post-secondary education was formidable, especially for the day:
he obtained degrees from Kingston's Queen's University (BA, 1913), Toronto's Victoria College (BD, 1917), New York City's Union Theological
Seminary (BD, 1916) and New York University (MA, 1916), and Montreal's United Theological Seminary (STD, 1922). He was ordained into
the Methodist ministry in 1916 after circuit riding as a ministerial probationer in pioneer Saskatchewan on the eve of the First World War.
His wartime military service was bracketed by urban and rural Ontario
pulpits before he changed careers to spend forty years in the editorial
chair at Ryerson Press.

In this biography, the image Pierce projected of himself as an impassioned cultural nationalist will be both qualified and deconstructed.
There can be no doubt of the importance of Pierce's work as editor and
publisher, a field in which he won prominence as the influential proponent of a certain very particular version of Canadian cultural nationalism –
an idealistic, bicultural, whiggish, assimilative, and dynamic nationalism
rooted in elements of Methodism and the idealism of Queen's University philosopher John Watson. Moreover, in terms of both reach and longevity, Lorne Pierce was unquestionably *primus inter pares* among such
publishing contemporaries as Hugh Eayrs and John McClelland. For
one thing, unlike either of the latter, Pierce consistently functioned as
a hands-on book editor throughout his career, personally editing scores
of seminal Ryerson publications – many with a nationalist agenda.[10] He
also personally developed and edited hugely successfully elementary and
high school readers, series that dominated the English textbook market
for over three decades from about 1930, perhaps his most overlooked
major achievement as a cultural nationalist. Additionally, Pierce published and championed Canadian writers and artists, including Harold
Innis, C.W. Jefferys, the early E.J. Pratt, Donald Creighton, J.E.H. Mac-
Donald, and many others, thereby indelibly shaping the book and art
culture of his times.

Of course, publishers like Eayrs and the McClellands, father and son,
also championed Canadian writers. Yet, in his Ryerson career, Pierce differed from his peers in another important respect, one that makes him an
even more significant cultural figure of mid-twentieth-century Canada.
Pierce never functioned as the administrative head of his publishing

house; this role was filled by the book steward (during Pierce's tenure, the reverends Samuel Wesley Fallis, Donald Solandt, and C.H. Dickinson successively). As a result, he was able to devote himself more intensively to the literary/intellectual aspect of publishing in a way that his peers at other publishing concerns could not. Pierce began his editorial career in 1920 resolved, as he confided to his diary, to take on the "real he-man's task" of making Ryerson Press "the cultural mecca of Canada."[11]

Pierce faced daunting challenges, however. The story of his life is also the story of his relentless adult struggle against the depredations of disseminated lupus and of profound hearing loss. Lupus meant Pierce battled lung infections, exhaustion, heart disease, joint pain, and other ailments throughout his career, periodically collapsing from illness and overwork. His deafness limited his ability to socialize and give speeches, networking activities that are usually key to a publisher's success. Especially in light of his health challenges, Pierce's editorial energies were prodigious. But his achievements were costly in terms of both his well-being and his family life, as his colleagues, as well as his wife, Edith Chown Pierce (1890–1954), and their two children were well aware.

Pierce differed from his contemporaries in publishing in another respect. Unlike Eayrs and the McClellands, Pierce himself was a prolific author. During his Ryerson career, he was the author of a score of biographies and monographs, including works on poet Marjorie Pickthall and novelist William Kirby as well as an influential early (1927) study of Canadian literature and a spate of booklets on Canadian nationalism. Uniquely, he became well known as an advocate and critic of Canadian nationalism in the period 1920 to 1960 as both author and publisher. Above all, for forty years, Lorne Pierce shaped the book lists of Ryerson Press according to his vision of Canadian literature and culture. Moreover, the House was throughout Pierce's tenure Canada's largest publisher, and the only one with an in-house printing and production plant. Thanks to such a platform, Pierce speedily became a powerful and influential Canadian cultural figure.

Moreover, whatever the liabilities for Pierce and Ryerson Press of being part of a church publishing house (for example, a prim public image, and the requirement to print in-house, often economically disadvantageous), the benefits of Ryerson's status as part of the publishing arm of a large and prosperous church were considerable. Pierce enjoyed a blend of security and autonomy as publisher that free-standing rivals like McClelland and Stewart or branch-plant operations like Macmillan of Canada lacked. Thanks to church backing and informal cross-subsidization made possible by his own successful textbook series, Pierce orchestrated the country's largest Canadian trade book lists during his career.

From the creation of the imprint in 1919, "The Ryerson Press" (as it was formally designated on the title page of Ryerson publications) formed part of a large printing and publishing operation. Located within the so-called trade division of the House, Ryerson Press, with Pierce as its general editor, published the House's original Canadian imprints, that is, both educational and mass-market books written and edited in Canada. Undoubtedly, compared to the large volume of agency titles for which the House imported or printed Canadian editions under the Ryerson imprint (an area that was never Pierce's responsibility), the proportion of Ryerson's original Canadian titles to the total number of books issued by the House was small (about 10 per cent). However, the influence of that list in the small Canadian book world was disproportionately large. (By the 1940s, a Canadian novel might sell on average about 2,500 copies, a best-seller about 5,000 copies.[12])

Overall, for most of its existence, Ryerson Press *was* identified with Lorne Pierce, and vice versa. In 1920 Pierce was recruited from a rural pastorate in eastern Ontario to be the Press's "Literary Critic and Advisor" (he was formally named editor in 1922), a year after "The Ryerson Press" imprint was created by House Book Steward Samuel Fallis.[13] Pierce's arrival almost coincided with Ryerson's creation and it did not long survive him. In 1970, amid nationalist controversy, the United Church of Canada sold Ryerson to the Canadian subsidiary of American publisher McGraw-Hill. Ryerson Press effectively disappeared, but for forty years Pierce had done much to make it a major force in Canadian publishing.

Given Pierce's major importance as publisher of Canadian books, an understanding of his life – boyhood, education, early experiences, and literary career – is vital to understanding the evolution of Canadian culture in the period 1920 to 1960. His values shaped Ryerson's policies and influenced its authors and publications through a blend of editorial and personal power.

A biography of Pierce is therefore needed. The charismatic, eloquent, well-dressed man so long seated in the editor's chair, disarmingly fiddling with his hearing aid and wittily satirizing his own Irish heritage or his "Continuing Methodism," has become in the twenty-first century an éminence grise. We need to turn up the lights and examine what manner of man Lorne Pierce was and how he helped shape key parts of Canadian culture during the Roaring Twenties, the Depression of the 1930s, the Second World War, and the 1950s, as well as two successive waves of cultural modernism from the 1920s to the 1960s. How do questions of class, gender, ethnicity, race, and historical moment figure in the life of Lorne Pierce, in his publishing policies and loyalties, and in his relations with readers and authors? How did Pierce's beliefs and policies shape the making of the Canadian literary canon between the First World War and the beginning of the 1960s, a period that embraced the first and second waves of modernism in Canada? *Both Hands* addresses these important questions. To do so, it examines Pierce's life and values, and analyses the background, impact, and career of a man whose ideological involvement with Canadian literature, art, publishing, and education played a key role in fostering the strong sense of cultural nationalism that emerged in English-speaking Canada between the First World War and the 1967 Centennial of Confederation.

Lorne Pierce's life and values were in fact shaped by several major factors: the spiritual and ethical training inculcated by his parents, Edward and Harriet Pierce (especially his mother), in particular their zealous Methodist faith, which he absorbed during an eastern Ontario village boyhood at the beginning of the twentieth century. He was also shaped by the freemasonry into which he was initiated by his father on the eve of the First World War. For Pierce father and son, the Masonic brotherhood constituted a fraternal organization which emphasized moral idealism and community involvement, one rooted in white Protestant male solidarity. Pierce also absorbed the nationalism and idealism that infused the Queen's University undergraduate arts program in the early twentieth century. That dynamic set of values was reinforced in his struggles as student teacher and Methodist probationer to effect social cohesion via the establishment of churches and schools amid the immigrant polyglot of the Saskatchewan prairie before the Great War.

Pierce's outlook was also shaped by the ecumenism and excitement of his 1915–16 studies at New York City's Union Theological Seminary, as well as by the rigours – present to some degree even on the home front, where he served – of military service during the First World War. Pierce was both haunted and inspired by Canada's role in the war, including the legacy of the Battle of Vimy Ridge, where he lost a beloved cousin in a battle which, like many of his contemporaries, he came to see as seminal to the forging of Canadian national consciousness. Furthermore, Pierce's ordination to the Methodist ministry in 1916 imbued him with a sense of mission and "set-apartness" which never left him, even when he turned from the active ministry to a crusade in Canadian publishing at Ryerson Press. He was convinced, as he told one correspondent, that his editorial work "extend[ed] [my] mission as an ordained man beyond anything you can imagine."[14]

The Toronto of the 1920s – the era when Pierce arrived to take up his post in the House's imposing red brick headquarters on Queen Street – resonated with currents of theosophy as well as with the cultural nationalism of the Group of Seven. Both ideologies animated circles in which Pierce moved, for example, the Arts and Letters Club. Pierce's involvement with poet and physician Albert Durrant Watson and with Group of Seven member J.E.H. MacDonald – both leading theosophists and nationalists – helped inspire his early patriotic publishing ventures like the landmark Makers of Canadian Literature series of the 1920s.

All of these forces, physical, spiritual, and intellectual, animated Pierce's policies as publisher. In a similar manner, his family life – graced by the devotion of his wife, Edith, who functioned as an "angel in the house" wife and mother while Pierce relentlessly toiled for success as editor and cultural nationalist – is intertwined with his mission in the publishing world. Pierce himself recognized this link, writing in 1956 (not without guilt) at the end of his official account of his years at Ryerson Press: "Every decision made from 1916 on, every major move of any sort, and all my work of every description owes so much to the inspiration, wisdom and loyalty of my wife, that she must be regarded as a silent partner in everything done or attempted. I owe more than I can say to the mind and heart, the affection and devotion, the integrity and stamina and vision of Edith Chown Pierce."[15] Of course, the relationship between Pierce's career and his family was even more complex than that. For example, Pierce's mother's idealism and boundless ambition for him fostered her son's relentless drive, while his wife's domestic and social skills made it possible for him to devote his energies to his career to an astonishing degree.

Arguably, a detailed appreciation of Pierce's commitments – to country, to church, to family, to freemasonry, to alma mater – are vital to an understanding of his achievements as editor and publisher. It is necessary to assess where Lorne Pierce triumphed and where he fell short in his goals and ideals, as every human being inescapably does. Pierce himself understood the importance of biography to an understanding of human endeavour and cultural genesis. As he put it, biography "sums up an age for you ... [its] atmosphere [and] standards."[16]

In fact, Pierce himself assembled and donated the comprehensive collection of documents which makes the writing of a full biography possible. The rich and voluminous Lorne Pierce Papers at Queen's University Archives – most deposited by Pierce himself – includes extensive records relating to his family, his education, his career, his associations, his friendships, and his own writing and editing projects. The Lorne Pierce Papers and related collections encompass dozens of boxes of diaries, personal and business correspondence, manuscripts, speeches, sermons, articles, books, photographs, scrapbooks, memorabilia, and other material. Such a formidable trove has been both a blessing and a burden for this biographer. The archival bounty is rich, but, given its bulk, it is not surprising that earlier would-be biographers found it too daunting. The biography of a pack-rat workaholic publisher with a finger in every Canadian cultural pie over four decades is a challenge to research and write.

A Pierce biography is a prospect the subject himself viewed with ambivalence. At the end of his life, troubled by how, in his view, he had neglected the emotional needs of his family in favour of his career, Pierce declared that he wanted no biography to be written.[17] But, with the subtlety and ingenuousness so typical of him (qualities beautifully captured in the Wyndham Lewis pastel portrait[18]), he made sure to preserve extensive records of his life and work, perhaps the most complete we have for any cultural figure in Canadian history. He apparently destroyed little (though he did have his former assistant Blanche Hume go through all his correspondence before it was sent to Queen's[19]). Thus, even as he protested that no biography should be written, Pierce secured for posterity a comprehensive and tantalizing record of a major career in Canadian letters.

Accordingly, this biography – made possible by the gracious and unstinting cooperation of Lorne and Edith Pierce's daughter, Beth Pierce Robinson, and their son, the late L. Bruce Pierce – delves into Pierce's life and work, analyzing the light and shadow of a major Canadian life in the context of the cultural and social milieu of the day. Of course, responsibility for the portrait penned here is mine alone.

Pierce's life records and the vast Edith and Lorne Pierce Collection of Canadiana housed at Queen's in fact constitute an important gift to posterity as a record of the literary and publishing scene in Canada, the more so because, until recently, Canadian publishing history has been a sadly anaemic field. During the last decade, with the publication of the weighty three-volume *History of the Book in Canada*, completed in 2007, and Roy MacSkimming's *Perilous Trade*, our picture of Canadian publishing has been fleshed out somewhat, building on George L. Parker's seminal *The Beginnings of the Book Trade in Canada* (1985) as well as material in *The Literary History of Canada* (1965) and the background papers prepared for the Ontario Royal Commission on Canadian Publishers and Canadian Publishing in the early 1970s. Valuable studies by such scholars as Carl Spadoni, Bruce Whiteman, Ruth Panofsky, Janet Friskney, Jack King, Michael Gnarowski, Carole Gerson, and others in the last two decades have also helped illuminate the world of Canadian publishing, as have memoirs by such key figures in the book trade as Jack Gray, head of Macmillan of Canada from 1946 to 1973, and Marsh Jeanneret, head of University of Toronto Press from 1953 to 1977.[20]

However, the aforementioned books, articles, and memoirs relating to Canadian publishing are still only nebulae in a dark sky. We have few studies of major Canadian publishing companies, and even fewer biographies of publishers. For one thing, the relevant records, despite the joys of publishing-related collections such as those at Queen's and McMaster universities, tend to be either dauntingly voluminous or frustratingly absent. Moreover, to the extent that Canadian scholars have devoted attention to our writing culture, we have understandably, until recent years, tended to focus on the publishing history of *individual* writers rather than on the editors and publishers who make publication possible and whose tastes and priorities have so greatly affected the shaping of the Canadian literary canon.

However, in a country where book publishing has always faced both the formidable supply and marketing challenges attendant on great geographical size and scattered population and same-language foreign competition from two imperial anglophone cultures (Britain and especially the United States), the role of a relatively small number of Canadian editors and publishers has been crucial. The roster includes, in the nineteenth century, John Lovell of Montreal and the Reverend Egerton Ryerson of Toronto's Methodist Book and Publishing House, as well as, at the turn of the twentieth century, William Briggs of the Methodist Book and Publishing House and, a little later, John McClelland and his contemporaries, Samuel Gundy of Oxford University Press and Hugh

Eayrs and John Gray of Macmillan of Canada. Pierce is one of this pantheon of influential publishers.

Whether planning a nationalistic art or literature series, or bending over books of illustrations of Canadian art with C.W. Jefferys or Thoreau MacDonald, or scheming with Harold Innis to publish seminal Canadian historical works by Innis, Donald Creighton, or Arthur Lower, or debating with E.J. Pratt, Northrop Frye, E.K. Brown, or Earle Birney over literary manuscripts, Lorne Pierce was a seminal figure over forty years of Canadian cultural publishing. Not only that, Pierce's own elementary and high school textbooks, best-sellers in Canadian schools from the late 1920s to the 1960s, laid the groundwork for the explosion of interest in Canadian culture in the mid-twentieth century.

Lorne Pierce was thus inescapably a "Maker of Canada," the creator and promoter of a potent construct of the nation. He acted on the basis of mid-twentieth-century conceptions of nation, gender, ethnicity, and class, ones that exalted a Protestant male construct of nation which valorized French-English entente and immigrant assimilation to a precisely defined national ideal. Pierce's life and work constitute a key thread in the shaping of the culture of twentieth-century Canada. Providing answers to how, why, and to what end Lorne Pierce became such a key figure in our cultural history lies at the heart of this biography. He – and the country – deserve no less.

I

Lorne, Mother, and Methodism

Delta, Athens, and Off to Queen's, 1890–1908

Lorne's first words were "mother" and "Jesus" and at eighteen months … Lorne began to preach.

Harriet Pierce, early 1892, childhood journal kept for her son[1]

[A mother's love] never loses its faith, never loses sight of a child's perfectability.

Lorne Pierce, in an article about mothers for the Christian Guardian, *10 May 1922, inscribed "For my Mother" in his clipping book*

In the eastern Ontario village of Delta, on gables and eaves atop the rosy brick of the old buildings, sheets of patterned tin siding sold by Edward Pierce's hardware business still gleam in the sun. The sheeting was installed long ago, some of it by the merchant's son Lorne well before the First World War.

The former storefront of the Pierce hardware business, which the elder Pierce sold to his neighbour Austin Sweet in 1923 – its handsome facade and white-framed windows little altered, although the premises are shabby now – can still be seen. The storefront is part of the most substantial commercial edifice on Delta's winding Main Street – the two-storey brick Jubilee Business Block, erected in 1897.[2] Delta lies in the verdant, rolling mixed farmland of Leeds County, along the St Lawrence River just northwest of Brockville – in the former Bastard Township (now part of Rideau Lakes Township).

Lithographs of Queen Victoria and other long-dead worthies still look down sombrely from the walls of the meeting room of Delta's town hall,[3] beneath the pressed tin ceiling of the room. Nearby lies a brace of churches and the substantial old stone grist mill, now a museum. During

Lorne Pierce's boyhood in the 1890s, the mill machinery filled the gravel streets of the village with humming. Not far away is the red-brick Methodist church – since 1925, Delta United Church – the centre of spiritual and social life for Lorne Pierce's mother, Harriet Singleton Pierce, and her family from the 1880s.[4] Stained-glass windows, pulpit, and communion table, all the gift of Lorne and his sister, Sara, in honour of their parents, grace the interior of the present structure, which dates from 1888–89.

Beyond Delta's meandering Main Street is Lower Beverley Lake, where Lorne Pierce summered all his life. On Main Street, a creek a stone's throw wide once flowed beneath a solid stone bridge, connecting Upper and Lower Beverley Lake and turning the old mill wheel. The swampy upper lake was actually created by the dam for the grist mill. The dam flooded 2,000 acres above the town in 1815: hence the name Delta for a settlement first called Stevenstown by its Vermont pioneers, then Stone Mills (1807) and Beverly (1823).[5] In summer, the village can still suggest a sunshine sketch of late-nineteenth-century Ontario reminiscent of Stephen Leacock's *Sunshine Sketches of a Little Town* (1912).[6]

The Mariposa air of Delta is augmented by a frame grandstand at the old dirt racetrack on the village fairgrounds – its venerable wooden buildings still home to one of Ontario's oldest country fairs, founded in the 1830s. Late in Queen Victoria's reign and into Edward VII's, the Delta Fair, with its horseracing and drinking, was anathema to Methodist wives and mothers like Harriet Pierce.

At the close of the nineteenth century, Delta was a hamlet of about five hundred people, in an area with an economy based on mixed farming, cheese and maple-syrup production, and lumbering. Its heyday as a bustling hamlet with tanneries, a working grist mill, and a small foundry was slowly coming to an end. Its modest pretensions (for it had no high school) were soon to be further eclipsed by the advent of the automobile and the economic synergy of the more dominant farming centre of Athens to the east and the nearby county seat of Brockville, a rail and water centre on the St Lawrence. But, in the 1890s, Delta was one of those well-rooted, distinctly defined villages that were the pride of late-nineteenth-century Ontario, even if the flow of migration to the opening west from the played-out farmland of eastern Ontario was underway.

In adult life, Lorne Pierce, Delta's most famous son, never forgot either its homogenous sense of community or the attendant narrowness.

Edward Pierce and his wife, Harriet Singleton Pierce, not long after their marriage in 1886. Courtesy of Beth Pierce Robinson

He returned regularly to the "quaint hamlet" to visit his parents and to holiday at the cottage.[7] But, after both of his parents were dead, Pierce evoked Delta's more repressive aspects, wryly labelling it "Sleepy Hollow immersed in [both] pious Victorianism" and "embalmed Puritanism."[8]

Lorne Pierce was born in Delta on 3 August 1890. Delta and his family shaped him in important ways. There his mother and father gave him a particular sense of community, a distinct identity, a sense of the nation, and a strong spiritual faith. Above all, his upbringing instilled in him a drive and work ethic that formed the nucleus of his being. That drive was at once his blessing and his curse, and the engine of his future contributions to the culture of Canada as editor and man of letters.

IN DELTA, the respectable red-brick house trimmed in dark-painted wood on Mathew Street where Lorne Pierce was born is just a short stroll from Main Street. Lorne was the elder of two children born to Edward Albert Pierce (1864–1929) and his wife Harriet Louise Singleton (1864–1940). Both parents came from large families with strong roots in eastern Ontario, roots put down by sets of grandparents from Ireland's County Wexford who had settled in Leeds County early in the nineteenth century. Born on 28 June 1864, three years before Confederation, Edward Pierce had grown up some thirteen miles west of Delta, in the hamlet of Newboro, a lock station on the Rideau Canal about halfway between Ottawa and Kingston. Harriet Singleton was born on 14 May of the same year to John Singleton and his wife, Sara Donahue. Hattie, as she was nicknamed, was the youngest of a large family. She grew up a couple of miles away from her future husband – just outside Forfar near the crossroads at Crosby – then called Singleton's Corners. At the crossroads, one can turn toward Ottawa, Brockville, Kingston, or West-port – and on the Brockville Road lies Delta, a lesser centre, some ten miles away, just west of the village of Athens. John Singleton had an ample home for his large family, one of Upper Canada's classic Georgian stone farmhouses. Such a dwelling was in the 1860s the pride of a well-established farmer of the second generation of Irish settlers.

The Singleton house (which still stands) was set in the rolling fields around Crosby, shaded by an elm or two, with an ample verandah. There were many relatives to welcome to its wide rooms. Little Hattie had two Singleton uncles who had similar stone houses nearby. Her father and her mother, who was John Singleton's second wife, nurtured their large brood of fifteen children (Hattie's nine half-siblings and five full siblings) with ample servings of farm produce and Methodism.

Both John and Sara Singleton were staunch Methodists – leaders in a congregation that also numbered Edward Pierce's family – and usually boarded the minister. John Singleton was a powerful personality, a contrast to his more reserved, refined, and high-minded wife. Lorne remembered his grandfather vividly, writing in his diary: "He was a short, thick set Irishman, rosy face, blue eyes, ready wit. A great Bible student, [he] made phrenology [a craze of the day] his hobby, boasted that he could throw any man in the county, had tossed every minister on the circuit over his shoulder ... Each of his children he saw well established, each son with a farm."[9]

Harriet's mother, Sara Singleton – Lorne's lone grandparent with Scottish blood in this Hibernian family tree – was dignified and, Lorne remembered, "quiet yet at times very jolly. Her presence was a benediction. Falsehood could not exist in her presence, sham shunned. Her church was her home, her home a sanctuary ... My mother [Harriet] was the nearest like her of all her children." Harriet Pierce's behaviour in married life was to suggest, however, that she combined her mother's devoutness and dignity with her father's dynamism. She had an interest in moulding character that left her father's phrenology far behind. Rather than feel her children's skulls for clues to their destiny, she implanted her values *in* their skulls for the same purpose. (For his part, phrenologist Grandfather Singleton loftily assured young Lorne that he had the "mouth of an orator" and "the nose of a general or a bishop."[10])

A web of Singletons and Pierces had settled throughout eastern Ontario by the late nineteenth century. It was a family tree that Lorne Pierce later exuberantly, if with slight exaggeration, described as "all Irish – four generations untainted."[11] His overwhelmingly Irish heritage was to be ideologically significant to him as a publisher in a country whose anglophone culture often tended to kowtow to the British tradition or to be framed in terms of the Loyalist myth. (In 1932, in Toronto, when asked by a snobbish interviewer about his ancestry, Pierce startled her by chortling: "Irish, thank God."[12]) Lorne Pierce grew up on the margins of Loyalist myths and ideologies and usually viewed them skeptically (Loyalism was strong among the numerous "U.E.L." descendants of Leeds County). Instead, he was weaned on great draughts of John Wesley, a dash of John Ruskin, and a generous dollop of the cultural glories of Ireland.

For her part, as she matured in a newly created and expanding Canada, Harriet Singleton displayed a wit and verve that bespoke her Irish ancestry, qualities she was to pass on to her son. Lorne found her tales of her maternal grandfather, Thomas Singleton, secretary to an Anglo-Irish baronet, whatever their accuracy, especially spellbinding. The latter had allegedly eloped to the bush of British North America about 1817 with Sarah Anne Butler, his pupil and the daughter of Sir Pierce Butler.[13] The first church built at Singleton's Corners had been a Methodist Church, and scores of Harriet Pierce's letters (she wrote two letters a week to each of her children for over a generation[14]) attest that the little girl's mind and soul had been shaped for life in that first frame church.[15]

Edward and Harriet Pierce – Ed and Hattie, as their circle called them – knew each other all their lives, growing up as they did in adjoining hamlets (Newboro was the post office for Singleton's Corners until 1890).[16] Both families attended the little Methodist church at Crosby. In fact, Harriet Singleton's older sister Lucinda lived in Newboro after her marriage – to Ed Pierce's brother John.[17] Ed and Hattie Pierce were married in Crosby's wood-frame Methodist Church on 1 March 1886 (they now rest side by side in its cemetery). Their married life began in neighbouring Delta, a village close enough to Crosby that the nearby Canadian National Railways station at Forfar served both Crosby and Delta.

By the time he chose a wife, Ed Pierce had begun to establish himself in Delta as a hardware and tin merchant – a business bought from William Singleton, a connection of his future wife's – and as a pillar of Delta Methodist Church.[18] The proud husband brought his bride there after their wedding trip to Niagara Falls, already a popular honeymoon destination.[19]

When the minister, the Reverend William Barnett, looked out at the congregation on the Sunday the Pierces made their debut as newlyweds, his glance might have lingered on bride and groom. He would already have taken twenty-two-year-old Ed Pierce's measure – reliable, devout, quiet, upright, yet with a twinkle in his hazel eyes. A man of "infinite patience, sweet temper and few words,"[20] Ed Pierce was known as a good businessman, stalwart member of the Masonic Order, and staunch Conservative, a merchant coping with the financial uncertainties and nerve-wracking business cycles which were the lot of a village businessman in late-nineteenth-century Ontario. A good citizen as well as a good Methodist, Ed Pierce also played in the town band.[21] Calm, fair-skinned, and handsome in a quiet way, he had already displayed thrift, probity, and sobriety in the course of building a business and selecting a wife. Certainly, Ed Pierce was representative of the aspiring middle-class Methodists whom the church sought to serve in the Ontario of the day. Moreover, Delta was in the heart of an area where "flatout" Methodism camp meetings with dramatic conversion experiences attended by struggling pioneers in the semi-wilderness were becoming a memory as Methodism adapted itself to the emerging middle classes and vice versa.[22]

For her part, Mrs Barnett, the minister's wife, might have been struck by the diminutive frame, upright carriage, and determined air of twenty-two-year-old Hattie Pierce. The new bride was black-eyed, dark-haired, vivacious, intelligent, principled, religious, artistic, and bookish. She was speedily to prove a power to be reckoned with in Delta. In fact, were it not for the restrictions of gender in the spheres of education and vocation, restrictions that channelled a woman's life in late-nineteenth-century Canada, Hattie Pierce might well have been *in* the pulpit in a Methodist church that spring day. If Delta had something of the torpor of Washington Irving's fictional Sleepy Hollow, as Lorne Pierce came to believe, there was certainly nothing sleepy about Harriet Singleton Pierce or the home that she created.

By the time Hattie Pierce's three-month-old son was christened Lorne Albert Pierce by the Reverend William Rilance in Delta Methodist Church in 1890,[23] the force of his mother's personality and principles had touched not only her home but also her church and village. She played the organ for services, led the choir, and was prominent in the Sunday School where she and her husband taught. She was also a leading figure in other activities: the Epworth League (a Methodist youth group) and the Temperance Society. In the village, she was known to Methodists, Baptists, a Catholic or two, and the odd non-believer alike for charitable works. She was a friendly and capable presence behind the counter in the Pierce store when her other duties permitted. By the time Lorne's sister was born in February 1892, Mrs Pierce was widely respected (and a little feared) as one of Delta's most active Methodist matrons.

Mind you, certain Delta residents also remarked that there was a "highfalutin" side to Mrs Pierce. Lorne and Sara were allowed to play only with certain children, principally those of the minister and the doctor.[24] Some mused that it was a pity that such a dynamic and religious woman as Mrs Pierce, who brooked no gossip in her house during her frequent musical, church, and temperance gatherings, was hard of hearing, in later life having to use an ear trumpet. Her good friends, such as her fellow church worker Stella Cheetham Green,[25] were apt to cluck their tongues sympathetically when Hattie had one of her dreadful migraines. (Her son was to inherit both the migraines and the deafness.)

Mrs Pierce had not just banned gossip. In addition, no dancing or card playing ("the devil's picture book") were allowed in this pious household. The parlour bookshelves, while full, held no plays at all – not even Shakespeare's – and only the most high-minded fiction. Dun-coloured volumes of fiction reviewed in the *Christian Guardian*, the redoubtable magazine of Canadian Methodism, rubbed shoulders with Sunday School staples of the time like *Elsie Dinsmore* and *Pilgrim's Progress*.[26]

Delta children (the select few allowed in the house) knew that the pressed-glass tumblers in the Pierce kitchen never held even ginger ale. Mrs Pierce believed that the name of that ostensibly innocuous beverage was too reminiscent of alcohol to allow it in her house.[27] But visiting children soon forgot to pine for ginger ale when Mrs Pierce, charismatic and a born teacher, declared, "I think you'll like this,"[28] and began to play a song on the keyboard or tell a story with her droll Irish wit. Her volumes of Scripture and Ruskin lay close at hand, as did her sheets of hymn tunes and classical music for the organ (later a piano). Long after, one little girl recalled her influence: "Lorne's mother was an important teacher in my life. My first memory was a group of three very small children in our living room, Lorne, [Sara], and my very little self – We had been seated quietly, about our organ – and she played – 'The Battle of Waterloo' – telling us the parts as advanced in the music – I can still hear her say – 'Lamentation.'"[29]

Needless to say, a cradle rocked by Hattie Pierce had a lot of momentum. Lorne was programmed by his mother to be not simply a good person and a good Methodist but an outstanding Methodist minister. From the moment she proudly placed the infant Lorne in his willow cradle lined with pink cambric, she never lost sight of this goal, although there appears to have been more than one occasion when her son himself wanted to. At his birth, Hattie began to write a journal for him, an inspirational record which she kept up-to-date until she presented it to him on his fifteenth birthday, 3 August 1905. In later life, Lorne Pierce referred to this journal, not without irony, as "mother's love tale of [my] early years."[30] The journal confirms that Hattie was a paradigm of the turn-of-the-century Methodist mother.

BECAUSE LORNE'S childhood was so interwoven with the Methodism his mother embodied and his father embraced, it is necessary to set forth briefly the nature of the religion he experienced as a child through the prism of the journal Hattie kept for her son. That journal is crucial to understanding the boy's evolving values – both those he accepted wholeheartedly and those he subverted and adapted as he matured.

The view of childrearing prevalent in late-nineteenth-century middle-class Methodist homes was rooted in religious values. The cornerstone of Methodism is justification by faith, that is, "conversion as a conscious and responsible act," leading to "a total subjugation of the self to the will and love of God." As for childrearing, the conception of Christian perfection at the heart of Methodism made it but a short step for Methodist mothers to become perfectionists in all spheres. Accordingly, children in Methodist homes in this era were viewed as "buds of piety," who from the age of four or five could be actively encouraged and educated as developing "candidates for the kingdom." They were to be led to resist sin and accept Christ. Religious decision was encouraged by parents, teachers, and the church as early as possible. What has been called "an optimistic view of the moral status of childhood" justified "direct control over the young"[31] in order to swell the ranks of the young in the Methodist Church – from 1850 the largest Protestant denomination in Ontario[32] – and reform society. The great Canadian divine and educational reformer Egerton Ryerson (later to be a kind of patron saint for Lorne Pierce the publisher) taught that education infused with a dedication to "order and discipline as the foundation of good character" was the key to training the developing child.[33]

The Methodism Lorne Pierce experienced at home, church, and Sunday School was typical of the time – dynamic, strongly middle class, outward-looking, and reform-oriented in both individual and social terms. Lorne and his sister were urged to avoid evil companions and unedifying books. Both home and Sunday School (and his parents were central to both) trumpeted the love of God and the need to avoid sinful ways, epitomized by alcohol, that "most perfidious and dangerous device of the devil."[34] On the Pierce bookshelves, as well as the Bible, books of sermons and devotional tomes, and titles by Ruskin, Edmund Burke, Robert Browning, and Sir Walter Scott, there were tracts attacking Darwin, T.H. Huxley, and the "higher criticism." But to Lorne's parents, the most outward and visible enemy was not natural selection or the higher criticism or even dancing, card playing, or tobacco – Enemy No. 1 was alcohol.

Their antipathy was understandable. After all, the problems of liquor in turn-of-the-century Canada were all too evident. One had only to walk by the licensed local hotel most afternoons or evenings, never mind lie awake on raucous late nights during the Delta Fair, to see the inebriation and attendant problems wrought by what was then known as "the liquor traffic." If church and tavern were the two great voluntary institutions of Victorian small-town Canada,[35] Hattie Pierce knew which institution she favoured and which she deplored. Temperance was a religious and social *cause célèbre* of the day, and one of the earliest causes of Methodists, of women, and of maternal feminists, as the career of Nellie McClung, a small-town near-contemporary of Hattie Pierce, suggests.[36] The temperance movement in Canada had in fact begun in Delta in 1828, with a sermon preached by Dr Peter Schofield.[37]

Lorne was early taught by his mother to abhor alcohol, an aversion strengthened in all the Pierces by embarrassing visits from a relative often "under the influence."[38] Lorne's childish printing is found on a pledge of abstinence signed in May 1897 when he was not yet seven, a pledge he was conscious of throughout his life.[39] It was not unusual for a boy's mother to "sign him up" at a tender age. For example, Samuel Dwight Chown, in later life a leading Methodist clergyman and a Lorne Pierce in-law, took the pledge at the age of four. Moreover, Harriet Pierce was the local Women's Christian Temperance Union (WCTU) president. Young Lorne never had a prayer of encountering King Barleycorn in his own home – unless he caught a whiff of his bibulous relative's breath.

Lorne's signed pledge (accompanied by a badge which read "Tremble King Alcohol we will grow up") is still tucked in the small, blue-bound leather journal his mother kept for him. In that crucial document, Lorne emerges as a lively, precocious, largely tractable, and intelligent child. Hattie Pierce comes across as a loving but exacting Methodist mother zealous to inculcate in her offspring the saving concepts of purity, righteousness, and "sacrificial service."[40]

Lorne's first overnight outing (at eleven months) was a family camping expedition to Robertson's Landing on Lower Beverley Lake with the Methodist minister and his family. Several months later, his mother proudly depicted Lorne at eighteen months old: "Lorne began to preach. Auntie McAdam would get him on a stool and there he would lay it down with hands and voice altho' the words were not very distinct, but then a baby of one and a half years could not be expected to speak very plainly."[41]

Even the birth of Lorne's sister did not distract Mrs Pierce from her sense of mission toward her son. While she extended her sense of maternal duty to her daughter, her son's development remained primary in her eyes. For her part, Sara was to grow into a strong woman, with four children of her own.[42] In Delta, she was raised in the tradition of another maxim of the day: "a daughter is a daughter all of her life." She certainly was a devoted daughter, but she was also a loving sister. Sara was to follow Lorne to Queen's, to the west to teach, and to Victoria College to study. The two were to share accommodation at times in all these places. Later, Lorne, in military uniform, officiated at Sara's wedding to the Reverend Eldred Chester during the Great War. Brother and sister both summered on Lower Beverly Lake – the two families sharing a cottage on Whiskey Island for twenty years. In short, Lorne and Sara enjoyed bonds unbroken until Lorne Pierce's death in 1961.

By the time Lorne was six years old and Sara four, his mother clearly felt that her moral nurture was bearing fruit in both children. An evangelist arrived in the village in December 1896 for five weeks of revival services. It was, after all, the heyday of Ira Sankey and Dwight Moody,

Lorne Pierce and his sister, Sara, c. 1896. Courtesy of Beth
Pierce Robinson

professional evangelists who sought to evoke and update, for the emerging middle classes of late-nineteenth-century Ontario, a religious spirit
of repentance and renewal that harked back to the early days of Methodism in Upper Canada. Of the Delta revival, Hattie Pierce jubilantly
recorded in the journal: "Lorne and Sara gave their hearts to Jesus again
as Mamma had often taught them before. They were wonderfully blest
on Jan 5th 1897. Lorne gave his first public testimony. 'I love Jesus.'"[43]
    Did Harriet Pierce regard this incident as a highlight of a crucial con-
version experience in her son? Was it part of an emphasis on such conversions that was at the emotional heart of the evangelical rural Methodism

in which she herself was raised in the eastern Ontario of the 1860s and 1870s? The journal indicates that she did see Lorne as in the grip of childhood conversion, although by 1897 Methodism was moving from an evangelistic emphasis on individual salvation and dramatic childhood conversion to an advocacy of social progressivism of the sort that Mrs Pierce was foreshadowing in her temperance and charitable community work. In the 1890s, the need for, and even the value of, eliciting from young children such dramatic "testimony for Jesus" was increasingly less emphasized within the Methodist faith. The new trend was to produce young Methodists who could, in the words of John Wesley, the founder of Methodism, "serve the present age" in their life and work.[44] And Harriet Pierce was even keener on the notion of service than on the imperative to testify for Jesus.

Her Methodism in fact typified the blend of evangelical emotionalism giving way to social activism that was manifest in the domestic and religious roles of Methodist women of the day. Her tutelage of her son exemplifies a way of believing on the part of late-nineteenth-century Methodist women that probably began with her own more dramatic "conversion" in girlhood. One scholar notes:

> [Conversion for women was] the beginning of a commitment
> to nurturing the Christian life that involved intensive self-
> examination of daily activities and "useful" social involvement.
> … Women's work in Sunday schools, missionary societies,
> reform movements, and charitable organizations gave them
> opportunities to influence life outside the domestic sphere [while
> d]aily life was invested with religious significance as men and
> women aspired to conform their personal behaviour, homes and
> communities to evangelical ideals.[45]

The passage crystallizes Mrs Pierce's values. But, by the time Lorne was born, dramatic conversion experiences in children were less the norm and less sought after by devout parents.[46]

Looking back on his childhood, Lorne himself expressed distaste for dramatic childhood conversions. The emotionalism of revivalism was a traumatic memory: "I remember," he wrote in 1920, "Father holding me up to the 1/2 painted windows of the old Russell Store [in Delta] where a Revival was in progress and seeing a huge poster in red with white letters reading 'Hell or Heaven – which?'"[47] Lorne was brought even closer to the emotion of revivalism and its consequent activism. For example, not long after the six-year-old boy and his sister attended the revival service described above, the two tots were taken to a temperance lecture where they heard the speaker luridly denounce drink. Mrs Pierce recorded Lorne's reaction:

> What impressed Lorne most was an incident [the speaker] related of a drunken husband ordering his wife to go and get him more beer, she refusing to do so he caught her and cut her throat several times[,] her screams bringing the neighbours who carried her bleeding body to a white bed in the corner over which the motto "God bless our home" hung. The son a boy of about fourteen refusing to eat ... clung to her icy hands until the last breath left her body. She entreat[ed] him to the last to forgive his father ... After the lecture, Papa with others joined the "Sons of Temperance" [...] Lorne and Sara standing up ... with their hands on their hearts too.[48]

As a result of such experiences, Lorne harboured a life-long aversion to the extreme emotion of the revival meeting. He wrote in 1924, for example: "Many ... can remember [their] sense of horror at these [Methodist revival] meetings, the horror experienced when emotionalism ran wild, and when confessions, only meant to be whispered in secret in the ear of God, were shouted from the platform."[49] By contrast, for his mother, as for her contemporaries in church temperance work, horrific stories told to tender minds were acceptable for the sake of reinforcing abstinence or embracing Jesus. But it is not surprising that a sensitive little boy would be emotionally marked by such spectacles. Other Methodist children at this period later recalled being traumatized by revival emotionalism (and, like Lorne, chafing at the restricted social circle imposed by devout parents). For example, Edward Kidd, who grew up in nearby rural Beckwith Township, had similar memories.[50]

Lorne was pressured to fit other traumas into the framework of his mother's piety. The Methodist world view of his parents taught that real-life disaster, even personal disaster, constituted a message of self-abnegation from the Almighty. In 1897 the Pierce shop and barn were destroyed in a fire – a sharp business setback for Ed Pierce, especially coming as it did after years of nation-wide economic downturn. Nevertheless, Hattie wrote in her son's childhood journal of her conviction that, despite the blow to household and village, the conflagration was above all a reminder to concentrate on heavenly things. Further, because Delta's only licensed hotel also burned, she rejoiced inasmuch as the village "enjoyed temperance for a time."

Shortly thereafter, as the temperance advocates met in the Pierce parlour, young Lorne saw his mother, the local WCTU president, campaign to prevent the return of licensed premises to Delta. Petitions and other strategies failed. But, when the rebuilt hotel later became a temperance house, Hattie recorded in the journal: "Oh who can doubt the power, the wonderful love and mercy of an all wise Providence?" Not Hattie Pierce – or her children.

Indeed, in any disappointment, spiritual, financial, or emotional, the Pierce children were admonished by Mother that the very word "disappointment" merely required a change in the initial letter to become "His/appointment," a change symbolizing "the thwarting of [one's] purpose [to] God's better choice for Me."[51] Throughout Lorne's childhood, his mother articulated and inculcated her view of "God's better choices" for the children. By Lorne's seventh birthday in August 1897, Lorne and Sara were Delta Methodist Church's star Sunday School pupils. They stood first and second in the class respectively, despite Lorne's increasing troubles with weak and painful eyes such that the next summer he peered at the Scriptures through spectacles.[52] When Lorne was ten and his sister eight, his mother even persuaded the children to stay home from the blandishments of the Delta Fair. She rewarded the children for their decision not to attend by getting each child "a nice book" after supplementing the amount that the fair would have cost.[53]

Hattie's moral vigilance over Lorne was no less strategic and thorough than her plotting of her temperance initiatives. As a result, her maternal influence comes across as being as potent as strong drink. The 1897 section of the journal has a representative sample of her approach to moral tutelage for a seven-year-old boy, an approach typical of her day. She implored in one entry: "May God help my little son to remember that violation of [God's] laws [is] *sin*! How necessary it is in these days to have armour-plated boys. Boys who have given their hands, feet, lips, ears, eyes, mind and pocket into the keeping of Our Heavenly Father to be used ever, only for Him" (emphasis hers).

It was evident by 1898, however, that Lorne, however thick his spiritual armour-plate, was not going to enjoy good health. His mother ascribed his ups and downs in health – childhood illnesses, weak eyes, lack of physical stamina (all recorded in the journal) – to the dictates of Providence. For example, in September 1898, when Lorne recovered from a fever, Mrs Pierce recorded in the childhood journal that she was sure that he had recovered "for a purpose," a feeling no doubt reinforced that October when her son told her that he wanted to be a missionary. Welcome words to a mother who had dedicated him to the ministry from the beginning. Hattie was clearly imparting to her son the sense of mission at any and all costs which would be so striking in Pierce's life and work.

In short, for the first fourteen years of his life, virtually everywhere Lorne Pierce went – be it home, church, school, father's store, or village streets – there Hattie Pierce was, or one of her close friends, allies, or admirers. Her allies included the Methodist minister. Long after, Lorne Pierce told his daughter that he remembered encountering the minister on the stone bridge when he was a boy of seven and, in the face of his own vacillation about a future call to the cloth, being solemnly told in front of his family: "The Lord needs you, Lorne."[54]

Clearly, young Lorne Pierce was systematically programmed toward a vocation by his mother and her circle. After his mother's death in 1940, Lorne summed up the lifelong effect of the childhood indoctrination he had received from her:

> But I have always felt ordained. I can not explain it. But always
> I have felt set apart even as a young lad. I felt I was the servant
> of something more than a Cause, something very intimate and
> yet immortal, call it God or what you will. And in business, as
> an editor, author and all the rest, even in my [philanthropy] to
> Queen's and the multiplying committee work, I have known that
> I was not my own. I fancy it was the emotional milieu at home,
> especially my Mother's thinking and loving that did it, her heard
> prayers for me, her high talk, and so on to the great moment
> of my ordination [as a Methodist minister], a truly stupendous
> moment ... I feel miserable when I am not doing [good or
> patriotic works].[55]

In 1956 Pierce wrote that, despite his serious heart condition, he was working hard, "pounding away with that utter dedication Methodism bestows upon all her sons."[56] Fittingly, he gendered Methodism as female in the phrase – fittingly because his mother above all embodied for him Methodism's tireless zeal and idealism. As he put it: "Her mind, like her feet, moved quickly."[57] Under her tutelage, Lorne Pierce grew into a driven man, convinced that social usefulness rooted in spiritual precepts must be an imperative in his life.

Harriet Pierce's mothering techniques were extraordinary in their intensity if not in their nature, and suggest her unusual degree of conviction, assurance, and charisma. For example, her son and daughter recalled her commanding method of finding and presenting inspirational quotations: "Sometimes she jotted down a quotation with her own peculiar twist to it, permitting herself to underline a word, substitute what she thought a better one ... One never knew when one of these thoughts, neatly written out on a slip of paper, might be encountered, pinned to a curtain, stuck in a mirror, inserted in one's suitcase when returning to high school or college, or in a birthday gift ... We memorized them as we washed the dishes, composing a sort of chant to assist the memory."[58]

LORNE PIERCE'S boyhood, then, was largely defined by his mother, perhaps even more than most children's was in that time and place. But his father, his elementary and high schools, and his fellow Deltans also played a role. Lorne began formal schooling in 1897, the same year he made his first communion. May was in fact a momentous month: on the 19th he started school and exactly a week later "Mama's little darling" gave his first Band of Hope recitation. His mother recorded it:

> I don't drink beer or cider
> Some folks there are who do
> I'd rather drink *cold water*
> I think it's best don't you?[59]

In school, however, Lorne was not always the "good boy" for which his mother prayed. Delta Public School, a two-room structure with a bell tower and separate entrances for boys and girls, had two compendium grades taught by two female teachers and a male principal. Of his first two teachers, he later wrote: "Miss Halliday, (now Mrs. Walter Phelps) ... gave me my first thrashing and Miss Anna Allyn followed with legion [ones]. I thought that she was ill if I did not have at least one administration of justice, once a day!"[60] Lorne's Tom-Sawyer-like teasing of the girls certainly had a pronounced Scriptural flavour: he told one "tattler" that he would "slay her with the jaw bone of an ass." This sally provoked a whipping from Principal Yates, but not before, Lorne claimed, he had untied some of the knots of "the cat-o-nine tails" in a furtive sortie behind the school's big copper boiler.[61]

Doubtless these deeds of daring grew in memory in the years after Lorne left the village school in the spring of 1904. His mother gravely recorded shortly after he began school that "we have also learned that little boys must also work hard to help themselves."[62] Yet he could not have been as unregenerate as all that: he kept in touch with teacher Anna Allyn ever after. One principal, Robert Hanna, took a shine to him and, with Edward Pierce, was his mentor in joining the Masons.[63] In the company of his fellow students, he seems to have been a blend of bookworm and extrovert, studying with his cousin Stewart Singleton and his friend Charlie Davison (another Delta son of good family) for high school entrance exams, yet also tangling with and outwitting a school bully after high jinks in the schoolyard turned sour.[64]

More significantly, Lorne was by puberty hungry for new horizons and different opinions, fodder not always easy to come by in his carefully regulated existence in a homogenous village, made up largely of observant Protestants of different stripes, overwhelmingly of Scots-Irish-English stock. True, his relatives' homes in nearby centres like Newboro and Perth were welcoming: his Aunt Lucinda Pierce's house in Newboro was in particular "full of music and laughter." But they offered no real contrast to the values of his own hearth.[65]

What Lorne saw when he stepped off the porch of the Pierce house into Delta's streets was similarly circumscribed, and not just because of weak eyes. In Delta, thanks to trees and outcrop-like hills, most vistas are not extensive. Years later, he crystallized his boyhood longings: "I looked at the hills surrounding my home village and thought that if only I could mount to the top I should be able to see to the end of the world."[66] He sought broader vistas by means of books, even if his reading list was carefully monitored. No wonder Lorne was eager to spend wages earned from laying sidewalks on a barrowful of books – to his father's bemusement.

The boy also loitered about the shop of the village carriage maker, but not to eye the forge. Years later, Lorne described his influence: "The old carriage-maker … read 'German theology' and the higher criticism, and loaned me his books. It opened a new world for me. I have rarely felt so [exhilarated] as when speaking to him about the Bible and religion, although the people [in Delta] thought he was an agnostic, a ribald old scorner. But he gave me something that I have never lost."[67] Lorne Pierce was thus conscious – mostly acutely in hindsight, it is true – of the limitations of the Methodism of his boyhood and of his surroundings. As an adult, Pierce criticized Delta's conformist religious and social milieu in an interview: "I was brought up in a Methodist environment … goodness and virtue, so much of it as to prove exasperating at times. We lived next door to the minister, a sample of irreproachable rectitude. I grew tired of hearing about the minister and his amiable wife." Yet, despite his unease over the narrowness of his upbringing, Pierce immediately added that there was also merit in it: "There was something about it that was admirable. It produced fine character. It was fine stuff."[68]

Certainly, Lorne's upbringing shaped some of his core values about literature and culture. These values were to be augmented but not fundamentally altered during his studies at Queen's University and elsewhere. Harriet Pierce was in fact very interested in literature and art, two of the fields in which her son was to immerse himself at Ryerson Press. She transmitted cultural interests not common in Delta: for example, she liked art and the history of art and architecture, with Ruskin a favourite author. And, as her son was to do, she saw literature and art and education as of necessity infused with morality and as a means to an end. For her the end was clearly God, a Methodist God. By contrast, Lorne was to alter the emphasis somewhat or at least place its ends in more general terms: literature and other forms of art were to serve high ideals and national feeling.

Growing up as he did in post-Confederation Ontario during the Laurier boom early in the century, Pierce developed an expansive sense of Canada as an emerging nation, one of seemingly unbounded possibility. (Although his father was a staunch Conservative, Lorne was taken to hear Sir Wilfrid Laurier speak when the Liberal statesman made a whistle stop in the village during his boyhood.[69]) As someone of Irish stock, his sense of Canada was not infused with much colonial reverence toward Mother England of the sort we can discern, for example, in figures such as Professor Pelham Edgar, who was prominent in the literary and academic Toronto that Pierce came to know at university and at Ryerson.[70] Moreover, Canadian literature was by no means absent from Pierce's boyhood reading, particularly in the Methodist publications the family received. The Methodist Church in Canada had strong elements of nationalism in its outlook by the beginning of the twentieth century, so much so that "Methodism assumed that no other denomination had a better claim to leadership in moulding the nation in its spiritual, moral and social progress."[71] One has only to recall the educational reforms of Egerton Ryerson in Upper Canada or the cultural nationalism of the Reverend Edward Hartley Dewart, long-time editor of the *Christian Guardian*, who edited the pioneering anthology of verse *Selections from Canadian Poets* (1864), to appreciate the attention of Methodism to influencing Canadian society. Interest in the culture of the developing nation by influential Methodists found its way into the pages of Methodist magazines, "into the air" of Canadian Methodism, and onto the Pierce bookshelves.[72]

Thus, even in little Delta, the cultural nationalism that coloured Canadian Methodism made itself felt in Lorne's life. He joined – and his mother led – activities of the Epworth League youth group. There was a nationalistic flavour to *Onward*, the league magazine launched by the Methodist Book and Publishing House in 1890: under editor William Withrow, this publication, like its sister publications, "served as vehicles for the church's particular brand of nationalist and imperialist propaganda," an emphasis "in keeping with the church's ambition to effect positive changes in Canada's cultural and social life."[73]

While there is no evidence that home or public school put emphasis on Canadian literature and art as such, there is evidence that Harriet Pierce's view of literature and art in general was crucial to her son's vocation. As we have seen, books – the Bible above all – were important to her. An outward and visible sign of the centrality of the word in the household routine was a daily ritual that the children were very conscious of: "Later on [in life] Mother took up painting and divided her devotion between books and pictures, but through the years nothing interfered with her 'morning watch' … First she took up the worn and marked Bible, and then lesser books. No other book was ever allowed to rest on top of a Bible, and in that way she emphasized her idea of values."[74] Next to the Bible, one set of relatively "lesser books" – the works of John Ruskin – ranked highly with her. So struck was her son by her emphasis on Ruskin's ideas that he quoted Ruskin throughout his life. He adapted some of Ruskin's views on the importance of culture to the common man, of a sense of morality and divinity in art, and of beauty to life – all aspects of Ruskin that his mother appears to have stressed to the children. Sara and Lorne long treasured an essay that Harriet Pierce wrote on John Ruskin, "a long and original paper which few in her station could equal."[75]

The Ruskin that Harriet Pierce had her children commit to memory was the Ruskin of *Modern Painters* (1843) as well as the Ruskin who wrote: "Read your Bible. Make it the first morning business of your life" – one of her favourite Ruskin quotations. She urged on her son Ruskin's emphasis on the beautiful and the good. Emblazoned above the Pierce dish pan for a time for Lorne and Sara to memorize were his words: "We ought to acquaint ourselves with the beautiful. We ought to contemplate it with rapture, and attempt to raise ourselves up with its height."[76] Behind Pierce's future philosophy of education, to be so influential on generations of students through his textbooks, lay seeds of ideas about literature and art that were planted by Ruskin and nourished by his mother. Pierce referred to these ideas in his monograph "Education in a Democracy" (1933): "All education has its roots in religion ... As Ruskin showed, expression is not a matter of grammar and syntax, but its roots are moral; style is not a trick, but the flowering of the spirit; reason gets nowhere except faith give it wings."[77]

Politics and medicine also touched Lorne's life through his parents' social circle. As Lorne dryly put it: "I was only allowed to visit a few homes, the parsonage, the member's home and one or two others, but they were enough."[78] The Pierces' close friends included the local member of the Ontario legislature, Walter Beatty, and his wife. Lorne's exposure to the Beatty family included browsing in their extensive library at their spacious home, a house that, he remembered, fascinated him with its "high ceilings, and old walnut and wide balconies and huge bookcases," as well as family outings to the Beatty cottage at nearby Charleston Lake. Mary Mallory, several years younger than Pierce, was the daughter of another family friend, Dr C.N. Mallory, the Pierces' physician. Interviewed eighty years later, she remembered Lorne as an intelligent, talkative, yet frail boy who seemed far less eager than his mother that he enter the ministry.[79]

There was one way to get around Mother, however, at least to a limited extent. Lorne was to give his mother what she wanted – his ordination – but ultimately on his own terms and in his own way. His path involved two elements. The first was leaving Delta (Mrs Pierce herself wanted him to leave for higher education and ultimately grace the pulpit of a leading Methodist church – preferably within a day's train journey of Delta). Second, between the ages of nineteen and twenty-six, he focused on probationary work in the Canadian west aimed at a career in overseas mission activity within the Methodist ministry. A missionary, after all, could travel far – geographically at any rate – from his mother's side. And Lorne was initially resolved to become a missionary in far-off Japan or China.

Indeed, for a promising young man with a mother who tended to be overwhelming at close quarters, the cloth offered many far-flung possibilities in the early years of the century. The Protestant ministry attracted some of the best and the brightest young men of the day to its ranks as an example to the young in this era – for example, social gospel advocate J.S. Woodsworth, evangelist "Bible Bill" Aberhart, social reformer Ernest Thomas, and Methodist general superintendent Samuel Dwight Chown, to name only a few.[80] The ministry had an attraction for bright young men that is perhaps difficult to grasp today. Moreover, from the church pulpit, "Missions!" (both at home and abroad) was the cry. There was a need, Methodists were told, for dynamic young ministers and ministerial probationers to toil in the crazy-quilt mosaic of the "Last, Best West" where the churches were strained to the limit by the flood of new immigrants, or to go overseas to strengthen Christianity in the missions and theological training colleges of Japan and China. The best-selling Canadian author of the day was the muscular Christian clergyman Ralph Connor, whose red-blooded heroes grow up in the woods and farms of eastern Ontario and go off to flex moral muscle for God in the developing Canadian west. True, Ralph Connor, in real life the Reverend Charles Gordon, was a Presbyterian clergyman, not a Methodist one, but his best-seller *The Sky Pilot* (1899), about a missionary on the western plains, thrilled earnest Protestant lads like Lorne Pierce.[81] In any case, Lorne knew from his parents that Methodists and Presbyterians were moving toward union, a journey largely completed with the formation of the United Church of Canada in 1925.

The visiting ministers who frequently stayed at the Pierces spoke not only of denominational union but also about the stirring call for young Methodists to do the Lord's work overseas among the heathen. And it was a given at home that Lorne was slated to be a minister. The call, the call, the call, service, service, service … that was the message Mother telegraphed to Lorne, day after day, Sundays and weekdays, year after year. While there never seems to have been much question of wholesale rebellion or angry defiance of his mother, the question young Lorne increasingly asked himself about his parents, was, as he put it: "How far should I go in accommodating myself to them?"[82]

It is noteworthy that, when Lorne Pierce became a parent himself, he reacted against the coercive emotionalism of his own upbringing in his spiritual tutelage of his own children. He later told his son and daughter that he refused to emulate "the forced feeding [in religion] I got [from my mother]. Some of it made me suffer physically almost. I am by nature a very reticent fellow when it comes to unburdening my innards, and the situation has to be just right for me to open up on the intimate thoughts and feelings which beset me."[83]

Whatever the pressures of the call, fourteen-year-old Lorne had a more immediate challenge before him in the fall of 1904. His first distance from his parents can be calculated in miles: the ten miles east by rail to the high school in Athens. The previous spring, he had crammed for the high school entrance examinations with his cousin Stewart Singleton: winning his entrance certificate was "the proudest day" of his young life.[84] To reach the world that lay beyond the borders of Leeds County, he first had to get through high school in Athens – and out from behind the counter of his father's store. By 1904, he had already been pressed into service in the business, both behind the counter and as a workman. In fact, Ed Pierce wistfully hoped Lorne would choose to spend his life in the business, whatever spiritual visions Hattie held out.[85] Ed Pierce was no extrovert: despite the devoutness and devotion to hard work he and his wife shared, there is some suggestion that he, like his son, found life with a directed dynamo like Mrs Pierce a little wearing at times.

Supporting Hattie Pierce could be an effort. At least one of her favourite ministers made Ed Pierce's life a trial with demands for all sorts of free service and supplies from the hardware store – "all the way from a meat chopper to chimes for the cutter."[86] But Ed Pierce loved his wife, loved her wit, energy, and spirituality. He was not himself well educated – his heartfelt letters are rough-hewn – but he valued education, religion, and culture. Behind the counter in the store, in the secret confines of the local Masonic Lodge, in church work, he came to a shrewd knowledge of human nature, yet he remained charitable and not cynical – as was to be true of his son.[87]

Only in later life did Lorne Pierce emphasize his legacy from his father, as distinct from his mother's. Interestingly, he often attributed incidents and words to his father that were actually the work of his mother, perhaps in an attempt to "balance the books" of parental influence. Such behaviour is natural enough for a brainy boy in need of a strong father

figure, especially in an era when Methodism was advocating the importance of a father's influence.[88] Edward Pierce certainly provided practical
support for his son's ambitions, pouring several thousand dollars into his
son's education – he underwrote five degrees (admittedly two concur-
rently) from five universities for him. In 1929, at the time of his father's
death, Lorne Pierce summed up the influence upon him of his father's
goodness, generosity, and self-control:

> Over again I have [remembered] … his … quiet goodness,
> unfailing kindness, constant thoughtfulness of us all, the great
> sacrifices, the almost audible groan as he passed out his last $5.00
> bill for school, his proud confidence … Men trusted him …
> In home life he always had the soft answer. Fire there was, his
> eye would flash, but he kept control of himself. In business he
> succeeded by hard work and good sense. There were no easy ways
> … He lived modestly, saved a sufficient competence against age,
> gave liberally to church and charity and educated two children as
> few have been schooled. Even when [his children] got far beyond
> what he could understand or follow, he trusted them, believed in
> them, sacrificed for them.[89]

Lorne's high school years – between 1904 and 1907 – as well as the year
he spent at home before going off to Queen's in the fall of 1908, brought
him more contact with his father as well as his first taste of autonomy.
As he boarded the Athens train for the first time at Delta's little wooden
station in the fall of 1904, he was already a boy marked out for greater
possibilities. By no means every rural or village boy in eastern Ontario
passed the entrance exam to the collegiate institute, or was encouraged
to do so.

For four years, until his graduation in June 1907, Lorne Pierce commuted to Athens, a village of about a thousand people. The imposing
limestone high school building, constructed in 1878, was one of the village's proudest boasts, and had helped to inspire the renaming of the
village from the bucolic "Farmersville" to the high-flown "Athens" at in-
corporation in 1888. Lorne commuted daily by train in the good weather,
and boarded during the week in winter. For watchful, ambitious Methodist parents, Athens High School, a collegiate institute of some 150
students, had much to offer, according to a contemporary account: "The
situation is both central and healthy, the society moral and exemplary,

and the village exempt from many of the temptations to be found in large towns and cities."[90]

The Athens and its high school that Lorne Pierce depicts in his own diary are less idyllic, but he worked hard and on the whole used his measure of autonomy from home responsibly. All his life, he remembered his father's injunction as he left to begin high school: "You have the power to either become a man, and an honour to God, yourself and to us, or something that will break your parents' hearts."[91] For her part, Harriet Pierce fretted in the journal that August: "He has been very closely guarded, and to think of him striking out into the world ... I sometimes *cannot* let myself think of it without tears ... [yet] I know Lorne is not going away without Jesus with him." His mother had reason to pray. It is a measure of her ambition for him that she sent him off to Athens despite his doctor's reservations. She wrote on Lorne's first day of high school: "Dr. Mallory said we were making a mistake in sending Lorne [off to Athens] to school, because his constitution was not sufficient for the work, said he should wait for a year. Perhaps it is a mistake. If he finds the studies too heavy he will come home for awhile."[92] Mallory's concerns were well founded. In January 1905, halfway through his first year, Lorne contracted measles and missed two months of school.

In the meantime, however, the high school freshman displayed intelligence, high spirits, exceptional curiosity, and, importantly for his future career, an ability to impress and win over older people he respected – in particular teachers and other authority figures. For example, once winter drew on, he charmed the town's leading boarding-house proprietor, an invalid widow named Amelia Stowes.[93] Mrs Stowe's devotion enabled Lorne to remain in her house even after vile-smelling chemistry experiments in the basement and orchard-robbing sorties with his friend Charlie Davison, whom she had accepted as a boarder at Lorne's request.[94] Lorne must have revelled in her relative permissiveness. Mother and home were never this laissez-faire.

Pierce's own diary, written some ten years later, suggests that the administration of the high school was rather chaotic at this period, and many of the students rambunctious as a result. For his own part, he managed to combine schoolboy boisterousness and academic ability in judicious measure – even composing a school yell in a sort of combination of the two qualities.[95] He could charm his teachers when he made the effort, a charm he would exercise as an adult. Asked by one teacher to compose an oration on money, he told the class, comically foreshadowing his future role as a cultural philanthropist: "[If I had a thousand dollars] I was going to be a returned missionary, buy out Rockefeller, Carnegie, Astor, Vanderbilt, Astor, and Rothschild and the Kimberley diamond mines, and institute a pension fund for weary and defunct teachers! ... Graham relieved me of all oral exercises even to the day of my graduation."[96]

Lorne responded enthusiastically to classes with the vice-principal, W.C. Dowsley, a Queen's University gold medallist and his teacher in English and classics, and with C.P. Bishop, the history teacher.[97] He intensified his love of nature in botanical excursions with the science master, R.R. Graham, whose dedication to his field "unconsciously taught me to look for our highest happiness while engaged in the work we love."[98]

Lorne's marks, if not some of his hi-jinks, were cherished at home. On 6 January 1905, for example, his mother noted in the journal that she had received a letter from the Athens principal about her measles-stricken son. The principal praised a "faithful pupil ... in a way that ought to make any boy pleased." In future years, Pierce was to become involved in publishing projects with several of his elementary and high school teachers, including Dowsley and Yates, his one-time elementary school principal, and he corresponded with many of them.

Athens High School was followed by a year (1907–08) in Delta as Edward Pierce recuperated from an emergency appendectomy and Lorne filled in for him at the store. In the summer before high school, Lorne had sweated on blistering roofs laying tin sheeting. Now, after high school, temporarily overseeing the store, he placed an order for twenty-eight stoves, a brashness that the Laurier boom fortunately justified with an "exceptional year" for sales.[99] But Lorne's heart lay elsewhere than in the pattern books and ledgers of the Pierce family business. Family tradition has it that he heard the news of his good marks in the high school final examinations with mixed emotions: the seventeen-year-old knew that he would now have to tell his convalescent father that he was off to university, never to return to the store.[100]

There were other tensions during Lorne's year at home, this time about where he would go to university. Harriet Pierce had her heart set on Toronto's Victoria College: given its Methodist theological program, it was the orthodox choice. But Lorne himself was set on Queen's University in Kingston, a Presbyterian institution soon to become interdenominational, which, since the principalship of George M. Grant, had enjoyed a reputation for national service. To Harriet, Victoria College was the "safe" choice ("Satan," she fretted, "plant[s] [allurements] in every corner for the innocent ones"[101]) and the logical destination for a Methodist minister in training. But Lorne did not want to meekly follow the path his mother had laid out for him.

He had probably been encouraged to think of Queen's by his revered Athens teacher, W.C. Dowsley, an enthusiastic alumnus. By contrast, Victoria seemed simply Mother's values writ large. Lorne was aware of Victoria College's reputation for conservatism (had it not seen the trial of one of its professors for heresy just a decade before?), probably through his exposure to the stream of Methodist magazines and ministers that made their way to the Pierce household.[102] He disdained Victoria as "a big sausage factory where all kinds [go] in and all [come] out 'in the cloth.'"[103]

Lorne finally convinced his parents that Kingston and Queen's would do. After all, Queen's had a high moral reputation, and he could live under the watchful eye of Barry Pierce, his father's brother, a retired minister with a roomy house close to campus. Kingston was closer to Delta than Toronto was, and it would be less expensive to send Sara (who would place among the top students in the county when she graduated from Athens High School) to Queen's than to any of the alternatives.

Lorne won this crucial battle, and in September 1908 he set off for Queen's to enter the arts program. His ever-vigilant mother, anxious about the blandishments and temptations the wide world presented to her adored son, had ended the childhood journal with a final injunction about life in the world: "It will take courage to say 'No.' Nay [courage to] Act it – [signed] Mother."[104] But rather, it took courage for Lorne Pierce to say "No" to *Mother*, even in a qualified way. His choice of Queen's was in essence a "not yet" to Victoria and the ministry – and to Mother. The next six years, from 1908 to 1914, spent at Queen's and in the Canadian west, were to cement his character and set him on the path to ordination, study in the United States, ministerial work, military service, and, ultimately, his forty-year cultural crusade at Ryerson Press.

2

Visions, Vistas, and Edith

Queen's University, 1908–1912

Religion is the spirit which must subdue all things to itself, informing science and art, and realizing itself in the higher organization of the family, the civic community, the state, and ultimately the world.

Philosopher John Watson, Queen's professor, 1912 (Pierce's senior year)[1]

I guess Queen's has been my big debauch.

Lorne Pierce on his devotion to his alma mater, 1948[2]

One 1908 September day, Lorne Pierce stepped off the train in Kingston, valises in hand. He dutifully headed for his Uncle Barry's home where he was to board. But he was eager to get to the Queen's campus, where he was enrolled in the four-year arts course in honours English and philosophy. By the time he left Queen's for the west in 1912, Queen's had marked him for life.

The slim young undergraduate fell in love with Queen's: with its severely handsome limestone buildings, and with its lively and congenial student life. Above all, he was enchanted by the university's valorization of the spirit of service and of dedication to the nation, particularly evident in the idealist philosophical values of many of the faculty. Little wonder that photographs of Lorne Pierce during his college years show him looking so happy.

Queen's University, with its charismatic teachers, represented greater intellectual freedom to read and to question than Lorne had ever known in the benevolent despotism of his mother's house in Delta. Here he could dance, smoke, and play cards if he wished. Even more important, he could read freely and debate Darwin and Huxley and a host of other progressive thinkers whom the overseers of his conservative Methodist upbringing had viewed with suspicion. Dancing and Darwin had been equally impossible in Delta. In Kingston, Lorne also wanted freedom from the expectation that he must become a minister. He later admitted: "I came to Queen's determined that I would never let myself think about [the ministry]. I dipped in, and tried to forget it, tried to forget my mother's wish."[3]

However, Queen's was no den of indifference to God and the wider good: its cumulative influence would in fact moderate but also extend the values of Pierce's youth. The idealism of Queen's and of Harriet Pierce's Methodist home were to prove complementary when they met and melded in the mind of Lorne Pierce.

Mother and alma mater (which, after all, translates as "nurturing mother"): these two forces ultimately tended to reinforce each other. Unquestionably, each shaped Pierce profoundly, as he well knew. Yet the bond to Queen's – unlike the attachment to his mother – was not touched by ambivalence. Pierce's children remember that throughout his life he never mentioned Queen's without special exhilaration at the very name.[4]

In particular, Pierce was shaped at Queen's by the legacy of George Monro Grant, principal from 1877 until his death in 1902, and by the ideas of three of his teachers. The three were among the most famous Canadian academics of the day: philosopher John Watson, theologian William Jordan, and English professor James Cappon. Watson ("Wattie" to his students) Pierce admired,[5] his mentor Jordan he loved, and Cappon ("Cappie") he both exalted and deplored. In his publishing career, Pierce was to draw on the help, advice, and influence of Watson, Jordan, and Cappon, as well as on contacts with many other influential people with Queen's connections – among them, political economist O.D. Skelton, financier D.I. McLeod, editor B.K. Sandwell, educationist Aletta Marty, social worker and politician Charlotte Whitton, and historian William L. Grant.

Pierce was also to be haunted by the thwarted potential of two promising fellow students – his cousin Clifford Pierce (Science '12) and his classmate and rival Jack North (Arts '12), friends of his undergraduate days. Both were to die in the First World War. Lorne Pierce never forgot that he had survived the war and military service whereas his two contemporaries had not. The memory of their loss stimulated his own efforts to succeed, and shaded his own success with a survivor's sorrow and guilt.

Pierce's Methodist ideals of service and patriotism, already budding when he arrived at Queen's at eighteen, were to be nurtured there, soon to flower in a tireless dedication to the building of Canada's culture – its literature, its history, its art, its educational life. On Queen's itself, Pierce was to lavish philanthropy throughout his life. He himself was never a rich man, but from the 1920s he donated to his alma mater a formidable collection of Canadiana – books and documents, paintings, prints, sculpture, and even furniture – as well as funds for the purchase of material. He was to spearhead the Queen's Art Foundation, which by the end of the 1940s was to endow the university with an important collection of Canadian and British art, including works by J.M.W. Turner and by Canadian painters Tom Thomson, Paul Kane, A.Y. Jackson, and J.E.H. MacDonald.[6]

Looking back on his undergraduate days, Pierce himself pointed out that Queen's had first given *him* generous gifts: an education, a spouse, an ethos – and even, later, an LLD. But it did more than that, freeing his spirit from the oppressive confines of his Delta upbringing. "I guess," Pierce mused to his daughter in later life, "Queen's has been my big debauch."[7]

FOR THE MOMENT, to get to Kingston, Lorne made some compromises of his own to placate his parents. He was starting out at Queen's under his uncle's eye. As a retired Methodist minister, Barry Pierce was well positioned to make sure that his nephew was not tainted by any resident Presbyterianism, or by any intellectual skepticism that might hover over the university, which was to become non-denominational in 1912. Lorne chafed at such monitoring. However, he liked his snub-nosed cousin Clifford, who was his age and a science student at Queen's. And the two had their furtive moments of fun, as a surviving photograph of Lorne mugging in a mortar board beside a simpering Clifford in a ladies' bonnet during some freshman hi-jinks attests.

Moreover, in second year, when his sister joined him at Queen's, Lorne was able to move to the relative freedom of a succession of boarding houses just off campus.[8] He did so with relief. Kingston cabbies called to the Reverend Pierce's to transport Lorne to a dance were incredulous that anyone in that staunchly Methodist household could be ballroom-bound. Uncle Barry glowered in clerical garb in the entrance way one evening while the irrepressible Lorne set off to pick up Miss Fargy, an early "date."[9] However, the young blade dutifully attended church and Bible classes at Sydenham Street Methodist Church: his attendance was soon fuelled by the fact that Edith Chown, the girl he liked so much, also attended Sydenham.

Queen's undergraduate hi-jinks: Lorne and his cousin
Clifford Pierce, c. 1909. Courtesy of Beth Pierce Robinson

In the fall of 1908, Queen's had a handsome but still relatively modest campus – a scattering of limestone structures on the windy shores of Lake Ontario, not far from where the lake narrowed to the St Lawrence River and the scenic Thousand Islands. For the most part, the campus buildings were still rather raw and exposed in the aftermath of the building program that Queen's undertook in the first few years of the new century under Principal Grant. Grant Hall, with its distinctive clock tower, was only a few years old. Biology Hall had just opened a year before, and in the fall of 1908 two imposing stone buildings, Gordon and Nicol halls respectively, were as yet heaps of stone and board, not finished until Lorne Pierce's second year.

Queen's had some 950 students enrolled in arts and in theology in 1908, most of them earnest young men – and a lesser number of women – from eastern Ontario. Like Pierce himself, they were largely the product of the farms, villages, and Protestant churches of Leeds, Frontenac, and Glengarry counties. Some – for example, Lorne Pierce's popular college contemporary Jack North – were mature students who had spent time labouring in rural schools or farm fields to earn the money for university.[10] In his first year, 1908–09, Lorne found the arts curriculum exciting but also disturbing and unsettling. As he put it a few years later: "My first year at Queen's was awful. All my ideas went up out of sight." He found that he had to wrestle with new intellectual and religious doubts, which led him to insist worriedly in the same letter: "But if a fellow will only go down and dig someday he'll strike the light on the other side and find blue heavens and stars and a faith that will last forever."[11]

Lorne hunkered down over the books at Queen's. As he joined the ranks of Queen's men, he listened and pondered, and increasingly questioned and argued. Queen's was no Babylon, no temple of agnosticism or atheism, whatever Harriet Pierce thought; but for a devout, sheltered boy, the experience of examining religious and social truth was disorienting and troubling at first. Analysis, dissection, and scholarship, be it biblical, as in the Reverend Dr Jordan's Hebrew classes, or literary, as in Professor Cappon's, felt like skepticism, like heresy, even like agnosticism compared to the moral certainties of his Methodist boyhood. But, in fact, Lorne was drinking deep of Canadian idealist philosophy as it was manifested at Queen's, an idealism that fostered service to the nation and to its institutions.

Unlike Adam Shortt and O.D. Skelton before him and economist John Deutsch and W.G. MacIntosh after him – all part of that long defile of "Ottawa men" who taught or studied at Queen's and went on to shine in government service[12] – Pierce never became a civil servant. Yet he was to seek to serve the country nevertheless as editor, publisher, and commentator. The drive to "serve the present age" that he imbibed in his Methodist training was broadened and deepened at Queen's, to be focused on the nation-state. Pierce felt less confident after Queen's about individual salvation, the afterlife, or the divine origin of the Bible, but as a Queen's alumnus he was even more committed to the intellectual and social good of the country than he had been on arrival.

Daniel Gordon, principal in Pierce's time, was far less dynamic in his patriotism than his illustrious predecessor, but the university was still redolent of the spirit of public service and national feeling that had infused it during the tenure of the great George Monro Grant.[13] By the eve of the Great War, the university Grant had shaped, more than any other Canadian university, had come to stand for a Christian commitment to the obliteration of secularization and soulless materialism in society. Queen's stressed the need for its graduates to make intellectual and spiritual contributions to the national life, ideals that would animate Pierce's career.[14]

Lorne got his most potent draughts of Queen's spirit from the triumvirate of Watson, Cappon, and Jordan. Each in his own way preached Arnoldian culture infused with morality and the Hegelian idealism of Scottish philosopher Edward Caird that the three professors had each learned in the universities and churches of Scotland and England. Scotsborn James Cappon and John Watson had studied at Glasgow University under John Caird, Edward's brother. Yorkshireman William Jordan, an able biblical scholar and a graduate of London University, was also a philosophical idealist. Influenced by the liberal and secularizing theology of Queen's as personified by the charismatic Watson and Jordan, and impressed (at least initially) by the intellectual hauteur of Cappon,[15] Lorne Pierce, like so many Queen's men and women, became a full-fledged subscriber to what intellectual historian Brian McKillop has termed as "the Anglo-Canadian moral imperative."[16]

In later life, Lorne Pierce described the charged atmosphere in the classrooms of these men. He wrote of the intellectual excitement about Canada's promise that his professors – with the important exception of Cappon – instilled in undergraduates early in the century:

[Queen's faculty sensed] the import of a new day in Canada. Dr.
O.D. Skelton ... followed the great Adam Shortt, his teacher, in
the Chair of Political Science and Economics ... Down the hall
... J.L. Morrison was reporting with excitement on his discoveries
in Canadian History. William Lawson Grant, son of a former
Principal ... newly arrived from Oxford, his alma mater, was
launched on a career as first full-time Professor of Canadian
History [in 1909] ... in the Dominion ... Few could sit under
Morrison or Grant and not become aware of the Spring growth
of independent nationhood that was burgeoning [before the First
World War]. For those who had eyes to see it, this young nation
had begun its April days.[17]

All Pierce's explanations in later life of how Queen's deepened his patriotism and inspired his devotion to Canadian literature were, of course, formulated with hindsight and very prescriptive. In reality, his philosophy of life and his implementation of it, whether as minister or book editor, emerged more slowly. Moreover, any intense interest in Canadian literature on his part flowered only well after his undergraduate days, following his appointment to Ryerson, as we shall see. Yet Queen's was undeniably seminal to his career and values. Pierce had providentially made the ideal choice of university for himself. Queen's provided a different milieu than Methodist Delta, but one by no means utterly alien to him intellectually or socially.

At Queen's, John Watson, the leading Canadian philosopher of the day, excited Pierce's intellect, an effect Watson had on many students in the course of his fifty-two-year teaching career. By the time Lorne Pierce arrived at the Old Ontario Strand, Watson was a teacher and thinker known across Canada. He imparted to his students an evolutionary, organic view of society. The ideal of the university, Watson stressed to students, was to inspire individuals to consecrate their lives to the common weal. At the centre of Watson's ethical idea lay

> the view [that] "the true good of the individual" was inseparable
> from "the consciousness of a social good." "What holds human
> beings together in society," he said, "is this idea of a good higher
> than merely individual good. Every form of social organization
> rests upon this tacit recognition of a higher good that is realized
> in the union of oneself with others" ... In an increasingly
> complex commercial and industrial society, [Watson offered] a
> rearticulation of the idea of a moral community that could help
> combat disintegrative forces.[18]

What Watson taught in his compulsory honours seminar for senior arts and divinity students – and in 1911–12 Lorne Pierce was one of the most avid of those students – was that "the Christian method was best understood and acted upon, not by depending on traditional creeds or doctrines ... but by the application of idealist social thought to life in the secular world" in order to spiritualize it.[19] As one chronicler of the Presbyterian and idealist ethos of Queen's has pointed out, Watson inculcated in his students the idea that the educated should become part of an intellectual elite who would strive to enrich society both pragmatically and intellectually.[20] During the decade 1910–20, Pierce would carry out much of his future community work in Saskatchewan and in eastern Ontario in just such a spirit, a spirit that would later infuse his editorial work and his own publications on the importance of Canadian culture and nationhood.

Under Watson, Jordan, and Cappon in the lecture halls of Queen's, Pierce incubated his dedication to social betterment and his promotion of a catholic intellectual and spiritualism in the nation. He wrote of Cappon and Watson in the 1920s: "You could go from Cappon or Watson and hold your head high. Their standards were standards of taste, beauty betrothed to truth. They created and fostered the Queen's spirit, which is a tangible thing, something unlike anything I have ever encountered, loyalty to the school, esprit de corps; but there was about it something of a religion too, the glory passing on, the spirit of adventure."[21] For Pierce, "the genius of Queen's" was rooted in the school's intimacy and its homogeneity: "It was born as a college, closely knit to the teacher and the parson. It shared few of the stimulations and dissipations of the cosmopolitan city. The heads of Department ... were men alike, same roots, same sense of obligation, to a certain type of student, so much so that there was an astonishing similarity of general point of view in all of the classes ... most of them went to the same sources. I still marvel at the thought of Watson's prayers, and at the naturalness with which Cappon spoke of religion."[22]

Significantly, Pierce in later life felt that it was as much Watson's approachable personality as the principles of his philosophy that influenced generations of students to commit themselves so deeply to a spirit of service.[23] (Pierce developed just such a manner himself.) Certainly, the students were capable of satirizing both the man and his philosophy, but in the end they were deeply influenced by his outlook. Pierce simultaneously laughed at and embraced Watson's world view. The laughter came first; the emulation followed.

In 1916, for example, Lorne and his close friend Bill Topping, another of Watson's students (and a Kingston boarding-house intimate of Pierce's), both now studying in New York City, wiled away an idle hour before the start of a new term at Union Theological Seminary by parodying Watson's brand of idealism in a "Filosopher's Prayer." The mock invocation ended: "We bless Thee [unknowable Absolute] that ... now we rest in the immeasurable, inscrutable depths of Watsonian Hegelian absolute idealism."[24] Student satire, but when his mood was serious, Pierce's thoughts also moved along the lines laid out by his old teacher. For example, after reading Edward Caird during his divinity studies in New York City, Pierce mused to Edith Chown: "I had a veritable feast with ... Caird [who was] ... a good friend of Dr Watson. Caird is a Hegelian and Watty a Kantian but both are Idealists. I love Idealistic Phil[osophy]. It seems to fit into my own dreams somehow ... dreams that conceive in vision and then endeavour to inhabit in reality. It's a happy way to search for truth, isn't it?"[25]

Pierce went on to indicate how much he cherished, after a very pre-scriptive upbringing, the impulse to analyze and question belief that he saw embodied in Watson's syllabus: "[I] ran across the sentence that John Caird took for his motto as a student and as Principal of Glasgow University. I think I'll make it a headline for my thesis on Faith. 'It seems to me to be supreme negligence, if after we have been established in faith, not to study what we have learned to believe.' That's it exactly!"[26]

Lorne Pierce leaped at Watson's assertion that a church could be de-fined as an organization for making men better – an evolving, not a static, organism. When Watson proclaimed that public service came before private good, and that one "could perform one's social duties in ascending higher forms of service to an ever greater good, whether at the level of the church, the civil service, or the empire,"[27] Pierce took this evolutionary credo to heart. To him, as to Watson, service, belief, and intellectual inquiry seemed compatible, and the world of university an advance, but not an annihilation, of his religious upbringing. He attested in later life that his Queen's education had convinced him that faith and reason could be reconciled, and that some form of service to the nation was imperative.

Yet Watson, however influential, was not the professor closest to Lorne Pierce's heart. That palm went to another speculative idealist: the theology professor – and ordained Presbyterian minister – William Jordan. Jordan, a rumpled and hospitable worthy at Queen's since 1899, was that rarest of creatures – a clubbable Calvinist. Professor of Hebrew and Old Testament exegesis at the university, he had come to Canada in 1889, initially to fill a Presbyterian pulpit in southwestern Ontario. He soon gained a wide following among Protestants across Canada as a preacher, thinker, and teacher.[28] For Pierce, Jordan was among the first and most important in a line of mentors. Throughout his career, Pierce valued the friendship of older men, once declaring: "I don't care a cent for young men; old men who had experience and who have mellowed attract me very much."[29] Jordan took the undergraduate under his wing, entertained him at his home, stimulated his interest in art as well as in theology, and gave him advice and encouragement until his own death in 1939.[30]

Jordan was a philosophical idealist interested in the historical study of the Old Testament and in social reform, interests that Lorne, a member of his Hebrew class, found galvanic. The stocky Yorkshireman conveyed to his students (usually through the blue haze of his tobacco smoke, which swirled around his leonine head) that he had "no interest in a theology that did not touch life and touch it in a big way,"[31] a viewpoint Lorne took to heart.

As an undergraduate, Lorne learned about art as well as religion from Jordan, an avid art collector, especially of British paintings and water-colours. His home on Barrie Street, presided over by his witty wife, welcomed students and alumni "who loved good conversation and fine pictures," Lorne among them. But, as an art collector, Pierce was later to diverge from Jordan, who did not care for the "strident colour and grim starkness" of the work of Pierce's beloved Group of Seven and their precursors like C.W. Jefferys and George Reid.[32] Nevertheless, the ap-preciation of art that Lorne Pierce first learned from his mother was broadened and deepened by William Jordan in the gatherings at Barrie Street.

In fact, the values that Lorne Pierce developed and/or had affirmed at Queen's – the view of life as spiritual, as ideal, as rife with social service – he would apply to the development of national culture: Canada's litera-ture, its education, its art, its community institutions. Jordan taught Pierce to appreciate art; Cappon taught him to appreciate literature; Watson taught him to appreciate social service. An appreciation of aesthetics came in some of Cappon's classes and in lectures in the philosophy of aesthetics given by Professor Samuel Dyde, another long-time Queen's man.[33] But it was Canadian art, Canadian literature, and the Canadian nation in particular to which Lorne Pierce was to devote himself. In contrast to Jordan, who had little use for Canadian art, and Cappon, who belittled Canadian literature, Pierce's own achievement would lie in working out the spirit of national service he learned at Queen's in terms of Canadian *culture*. To do so he would have to look more deeply at the Canadian scene than either Jordan or Cappon, both expatriates moulded in the "Old Country." Further, Pierce's Irish heritage tended to make him skeptical of British models and ideals and their value in Canada, an outlook that distinguished him from a professor like James Cappon.

In fact, the influence of Cappon upon Pierce, while marked, was ex-ceedingly oblique. Pierce paid only back-handed tribute to Cappon's Arnoldian standards of judgment – standards Pierce made largely his own – in a 1929 article in the *Queen's Review*: "Dr. Cappon was unbend-ing in his intellectual and aesthetic integrity. Some might call it narrow-ness, and others label it indifference, but one never got the standards of taste and judgment mixed." Cappon, Lorne asserted primly, taught his graduates to "discriminate" among books in favour of "sound reason, healthy spiritual emotions and good manners." Pierce depicted Cappon as "smil[ing] over the confusion in the world that imagines that [Anita Loos's comic novel] *Gentlemen Prefer Blondes* should be taken as food or [Martha Ostenso's naturalistic novel] *Wild Geese* accepted as a challenge to the divinity in man."[34] Yet Pierce knew only too well that Cappon's smiles of intellectual and moral superiority were often unpleasant, supercilious smirks, sometimes at students' expense. Pierce would later tell critic E.K. Brown that he had been "raised in a way" on Arnold at Queen's, but he always professed an ambivalence about Arnold,[35] an ambivalence that more accurately defined his feelings about Cappon. Why?

The answer lay in Cappon's social and intellectual style. At university, Lorne Pierce, for all his ambition, was still an obscure lad from rural eastern Ontario, one photographed, with the other Athens high school graduates at Queen's, standing self-consciously in an ill-fitting suit.[36] By contrast, whether in his study or lecture hall or on a Kingston street, Dean Cappon was remote and snobbish, the kind of stuffy academic grandee who was "pained to meet his grocer in the badminton club," attitudes that undoubtedly exasperated the merchant's son from Delta.[37] Pierce later observed that he doubted that Cappon ever knew the names of half a dozen of his students and probably "relished the report that he … referred to his classes as 'damned peasants.'" Toward Canadian literature, Cappon expressed only "bland contempt," according to Pierce.[38]

Moreover, Cappon's work on the poetry of Charles G.D. Roberts early in the century – *Roberts and the Influences of His Time* (1905) – whatever its merits, had been written as a kind of sop to "Canadianize" himself. Cappon had in 1888 come from his native Scotland to take up the English post at Queen's amid some nationalist controversy because he had been chosen over Roberts, then a professor at King's College, Nova Scotia.[39]

Yet Cappon was a polished and stimulating lecturer, and a power to be reckoned with. As an undergraduate, Lorne hungered "to make the grade" with Cappon. But Cappon was no Pelham Edgar, Cappon's patrician contemporary at Victoria College's English Department, who took up and befriended promising students – even ones from modest backgrounds (as Edgar would Lorne Pierce in 1914). By contrast, Cappon was inclined to indolence. He spent his holidays in Europe or in the fashionable St Lawrence resort of Metis Beach, not in reading the blotted manuscripts of aspiring young Canadian writers and critics, as Edgar –

and later Pierce – did religiously.[40] The stage was set for an encounter between the two at the close of Lorne's final year at Queen's. Cappon's condescension would help prompt Pierce to make the stimulation of Canadian literature his cause.

Pierce described this crucial encounter with Cappon several times. His fullest account of the incident downplays the humiliation he felt, but it does not overlook the slight to Canadian literary ability and promise. At his last English class, in the spring of his senior year on campus, Lorne bravely asked the lofty Cappon about the merits of the native literature, heretofore ignored by his teacher. Cappon's reply was characteristically belittling of both question and questioner. He made most of the class titter with a sardonic quotation from Robert Service's slangy "The Ballad of Blasphemous Bill," telling Lorne witheringly that this doggerel was "his" literature.[41] Pierce, stung, fell silent. But he remained curious about Canadian culture, as he later remembered: "There was little I could say for I knew nothing at all about Canadian writers, Canadian art or what might be called Canadian culture. However, I went down town to the leading bookshop. The only title by a Canadian writer they had in stock was *The Oxford Book of Canadian Verse*, edited by William Wilfred Campbell and bound in red morocco – a fancy, gilt-edged gift book. With it began my collection of Canadiana."[42] The seeds of Pierce's advocacy of Canadian literature were thus sown – in a perverse way, it is true – by Cappon that spring day. Lorne Pierce was determined to make something of himself, and Cappie's despised Canadian literature would prove to be the vehicle.

IN 1912, HOWEVER, that crusade lay in the future. Dominating Lorne Pierce's present were not only his studies but his absorption in campus life – and the sad, sweet smile of the elusive Edith Chown, a fellow member of the class of 1912, enrolled in the modern-languages program. Lorne tried for over three years to incorporate the chestnut-haired, Junoesque young woman, whose glowing hazel eyes were touched with blue, into his social life – with only limited success. Their first meeting came early in freshman year, at a house party on Alfred Street, near the campus. After graduation, in 1913, Lorne, still carrying the torch for Edith, remembered the sequel wistfully: "The first time I asked your company for a Queen's Ball you ... handed me the proverbial lemon! I hope you never felt conscious of a pair of eyes following you whenever you came in view."[43] The young woman's refusal only fuelled his ardour.

Given his upbringing by a domineering mother, the allure of this attractive – yet reticent and elusive – young woman was potent.

The wonder is that Lorne had any time to pursue romance. As well
as his studies, he was caught up in a fever of extracurricular activity at
Queen's. A driven man, he wanted to shine on campus. By his own account, he "began by joining everything, became a member of the Glee
Club, a member of the Executive for his year, of the Arts Society, was on
the College Journal, represented the Year at all the Homes, was University Delegate to other University Conversats, chaired this and that, [and]
was General Convenor of the Arts Dinner Committee which was the
big show of [his final] year." He immediately added that he "winced to
remember" thus "wast[ing] time."[44]

From one angle, Lorne had little need to repent. He paid a price at the
time, but through his outside commitments he was in fact developing the
social and organizational skills, and the network of contacts, that would
serve him well as minister and editor. In the life of campus and boarding
house, he also found autonomy and variety, things he had longed for in
Delta. In old age, he remembered the delicious freedom of university
days, writing wistfully to his sister: "As I near the discipline of learning
the anthems of heaven, I go back often in memory to Grant Hall, and
the gay, sweet rhythms of the old-time waltzes, with Edith smiling up
at me. I was in heaven then, and did not know it. But Mother objected
to that kind of Paradise, and the odour of Sweet Caporals [cigarettes].
'Lorne, how can you think of it, you a minister marrying a dancing girl!'
'Edith does dance, doesn't she?' And I said, 'Yes, Mother, she dances like
an angel.'"[45]

Lorne's last two years of Queen's clearly included courting Edith
Chown, although at the time he was as close-mouthed in Delta about
his interest in Edith as he was in Kingston about entering the ministry.
His three-year attraction to his classmate had a taste of sweet succour
when, at a fourth-year Levana bazaar at the Young Women's Christian
Association (YWCA), he bought all the handicrafts remaining in Edith's
booth. He then whisked her off for a tête-à-tête over cups of cocoa on
a staircase landing, safe from prying eyes behind the proverbial potted
palm.[46] That afternoon, Lorne became convinced that he had found in
Edith "the fulfilment of hopes and ideals which long had been my ideal
of a woman."[47]

What was Lorne's "ideal woman" like in character and background?
Empathetic and intelligent, with a bubbling laugh, Edith Chown was a

native of Kingston, where her paternal grandfather, Roger Chown, had emigrated from England in 1832 to establish a successful market garden and raise a family of ten. The Chowns were by the turn of the century a well-known business and professional family in Kingston, as well as prominent Canadian Methodists. (Lorne was impressed that Edith's second cousin was the eminent clergyman Samuel Dwight Chown.) Edith Georgina Chown herself was born in Kingston on 14 May 1890, the fourth child and only daughter of Charles Douglas Chown and his wife, Elizabeth Pierce Conley.[48] She experienced loss early. Her mother died on 9 June 1896, when her daughter was just six, leaving a gap in Edith's heart never totally filled even by the love of her three older brothers or the Conley grandmother and the maiden aunts who raised her. After his wife's death, Edith's father worked in Montreal for the Maclean newspaper chain and she attended the Montreal High School for Girls for a time. But, in 1910, just as Edith began her second year at Queen's, another blow fell: her father died suddenly in Montreal.

One of her aunts tried to distract the bereaved girl. Alice Chown was by the time of the Great War a controversial social feminist and pacifist who had shocked conservative, middle-class Kingston early in the century by throwing off the yoke of domesticity after years of nursing her mother, following the latter's death in 1906.[49] Aunt Alice took her orphaned niece Edith on a trip to England, Belgium, and France in the summer of 1910. Once in England, the twenty-year-old Edith witnessed such stirring sights as the funeral cortège of King Edward VII, one of the last gatherings of the crowned heads of Europe before the deluge of the Great War. Aunt Alice also made sure that Edith (who tended to be a little skeptical, like all the Chowns, of Alice's radicalism) visited social projects like the Barnardo homes and heard feminist Christabel Pankhurst speak. Edith, now enraptured, recorded in her travel diary that she was now a "confirmed suffragist." She added indignantly: "It makes me mad to think that every man is given a vote except that he be a lunatic or a criminal. To think of ranking women with this class." Shortly thereafter, Edith and her aunt marched in one of the great London suffragist demonstrations, representing Canada in the procession. Edith described the scene for her diary: "We had not intended to take part at all but merely to go and see it but in the morning we got an urgent note asking us to attend. We got to work and made our banner with Canada across it and maple leaves on it ... We had eight in our [contingent] and each carried a bunch of wheat. The people were just crazy over the wheat and all wanted a piece as we passed. We could hear them say as we passed 'Oh Canada, That's the place['] and other such expressions."[50]

Despite Edith's interest in such issues as the vote for women, Alice Chown, often a shrewd judge of character, believed that her niece was quite conventional and domestically inclined. But at Queen's, Edith did well academically in the modern-language program and threw herself into sports and YWCA work. Her classmates praised her "unusual executive ability" and she was a delegate to the Muskoka Conference of the YWCA in June 1911.[51]

For Lorne, one of Edith's many attractions was that she herself was much less rigidly observant in her Methodism than his mother, and not at all dogmatic. (She told Lorne in no uncertain terms that she disliked the role of minister's wife and that she had "no religion whatsoever" in the doctrinal sense.[52]) For her classmates, she had the lustre of foreign travel and was quietly popular, with many friends, both female and – to Lorne's disquiet – male.

More subtly, Edith Chown was, given her parental bereavements, also emotionally vulnerable, as well as somewhat shy and reserved, in contrast to extroverted, resolute, take-charge Harriet Pierce. Her vulnerability had great appeal for Lorne. In fact, he later wrote to Edith that he had first become deeply attracted to her at the time of her father's death, when the two as yet barely knew each other: "I inquired ... and was told of your sad loss and loneliness. I admired you all the more, your bravery, your heart that was so full ... and [how] your own rooms saw the tears denied the world to see ... I wanted to slide quietly around and tell you how much I really did care. But I did not, I could not. My greatest enemy pride would not let me unbend for I thought you had long forgotten even who I was."[53]

THE CLOSE of Lorne's final year at Queen's was marked by impasse both in his courtship of Edith Chown and in his academic life. Lorne had been hyperactive both socially and academically throughout his time at Queen's. In the spring of 1911, at the end of his third year, never robust, he had collapsed from overwork. That year, true to his Hibernian roots, he had won a prize for an essay on the influence of Irish folklore on Ireland's literature and history. Yet, despite his academic load, he had served as vice-president of the Arts Society. He remembered of that time: "Leisure and I had parted company ... Greek [was] my last exam [of third

Jack North, Lorne Pierce's classmate and friendly
rival at Queen's, c. 1912. Courtesy of Queen's
University Archives

year] and I [was] compelled to ride to the depot [to get the train for
Delta] through weakness, followed by nervous breakdown."[54]

In contrast to the previous two summers, which were charged with
tension with his parents because Lorne had forsaken Delta for summer
teaching in the west, he spent the first three months of the summer va-
cation of 1911 as sole "mechanic and clerk" at the Pierce hardware store.
Meanwhile, his father recovered from heart problems – a bout of peri-
carditis. Lorne spent the last four weeks of the summer camping in the
Rideau Lakes. When he left for Queen's in September 1911, he was even
more certain that he did not wish to be a hardware merchant.[55]

Lorne proceeded to set a more frantic pace at Queen's than ever. He
felt a keen if friendly sense of competition with top students like Jack

North. North, from Glengarry County, was Queen's best English student and had narrowly bested Lorne to be elected president of their year.
He was a prospective minister (Presbyterian) to boot, a vocation in
which, his classmates were convinced, North's "ultimate success … is assured."[56] By contrast, Lorne was very vulnerable academically in graduation year. Despite the fact that his courses were demanding (Cappon's
English class and Watson's honours seminar in particular), he had rashly
agreed to be an editor of the Arts '12 Yearbook as well as the convenor
of the keynote spring banquet of senior year.[57] Both assignments constituted major organizational feats. In graduation year, Lorne was also on
the staff of the Queen's *Journal*, librarian of the Young Men's Christian
Association (YMCA) Book Exchange, and a chorister in the Glee Club.[58]
Moreover, because Edith was still keeping her distance, the hawk-eyed
young senior redoubled his efforts to interest her as graduation – with its
prospect of diverging paths – loomed.

   Lorne's work on the class yearbook was his first (and though he did
not know it, far from his last) major editorial project. The volume was
calculated to "bind the future to the present" thanks to the agency of "the
good Queen's spirit that has dwelt among us."[59] Its pages featured just
the right mixture of solemn injunctions from distinguished faculty like
Principal Gordon and Professor W.L. Grant (Cappon did not trouble to
submit a message) and tongue-in-cheek accounts of sports and activities.
Grant solemnly reminded the students that piety and learning are always
compatible, which must have reassured Harriet Pierce.[60] Lorne wrote
most of the suitably arch entries about each graduate.[61]

   Did he compose the entry beside the photograph of Edith Chown?
It is certainly redolent of Lorne's hopes: "A countenance in which did
meet / Sweet records, promises as sweet …"[62] The yearbook entry for
Lorne himself captured his energy and ambition. It noted his strong
sense of duty as well as his "business ability." (That description must
have made bittersweet reading for Ed Pierce.) According to the entry,
Lorne had "more endurance than Hercules in his successive roles of first
Secretary of the Year, Junior Vice-President of the Arts Society, and
General Convenor of the Arts Dinner Committee." His liveliness and
intelligence were gently satirized: "The sun first smiled at Lorne, and
Lorne first smiled at the sun, at Delta, Ont. In his High School days, he
placed himself under the guardianship of Minerva at Athens, Ont, and
has been wise ever since. Every little goddess has a favorite all her own.
And why not?"[63]

Meanwhile, Minerva's favourite spent an exhausting fall and winter overseeing the arrangements for the spring banquet. The April evening was a triumph complete with "Nobleman cigars ... and the Royal Canadian Horse Artillery Orchestra."[64] The gathering of distinguished Queen's men was headed by Principal Gordon and Ottawa bureaucratic grandee O.D. Skelton, as the extensive coverage of the dinner in the Toronto *Globe* and elsewhere attested.[65] Mackenzie King was the featured after-dinner speaker. The choice was current: intelligent, idealistic, pious, and ambitious, King, recently minister of labour under Liberal Prime Minister Wilfrid Laurier, was at the time widely considered an example to earnest and ambitious young Canadian men dominion-wide. King travelled down from Ottawa to address the Queen's graduates on the relationship of the university to the nation.

At the banquet, the gathering heard King speak about the vital contribution of the universities to the development of democracy in Canada in a manner calculated to impress a patriotic student and would-be minister such as Lorne. King reminded the graduates: "The pulpit, weak in its high mission as it may be, our schools, elementary and advanced, what would all these be once the lamp which lights the halls of our colleges and universities were dimmed, and its rays no longer found their way through open door or pictured casement out into the shadows which surround? ... In a university fitting its graduates for the highest duties of citizenship ... is to be found ... what may be spoken of as an educated leadership."[66]

Lorne, a leader in the making, was usually all ears for such wisdom. But, to his chagrin, he was not at the head table, eating chicken and making toasts in Adam's ale with the others. He was frantically coordinating events behind the scenes. Mackenzie King, the guest of honour – and Edith Chown and her Aunt Charlotte, whom the harried Lorne had invited to the banquet – saw little of him that night. With no time even to grab a chicken leg, Lorne's evening proved to be "endless work and no honour."[67]

Worse was to follow. His fellow students had ribbed him in the yearbook about the academic risks he was running, especially in the stickler Cappon's honours English seminar, through all of his "Herculean" commitments.[68] Prophetic words. After the scramble of final exams, and the dismal knowledge that Edith Chown was soon off to teach in the west, Lorne learned to his horror on 20 April, after his return to Delta, that he had failed the final examination in English.

A measure of his shock over this news was that, as is the case with several of the most traumatic events in his long career, he was largely silent in his diary about the matter. One can imagine how his parents, so worried about his over-exertion and anxious about his future direction, reacted to the setback. Lorne recorded in his diary only the stark statement that, at the convocation ceremonies in Kingston on 24 April, he looked on while Edith, Jack North, and all his classmates, capped and gowned, paraded jubilantly to the platform in Convocation Hall. He himself was seated at the back of the gallery – forlornly distant from the triumphant procession he had dreamed of joining.[69] Tight-lipped, he commented of the event: "We never miss the roses till the spring is gone."[70] He would have to redo the English course by correspondence to make up the credit, deferring his formal graduation until the next spring – assuming that Cappon did not "pluck" him yet again.[71]

It was a dark hour for Lorne Pierce, and the maw of the ministry – about which he felt so ambivalent – loomed. Having failed to graduate, he was ill-positioned to deny his mother's wish about his vocation, or to put off any longer a commitment to Victoria College's bachelor of divinity courses. But he clung to some autonomy: if he was to be a Methodist minister, it would be by his own route. Rather than go directly to Toronto for Victoria's theology course, Lorne's dreaded "sausage factory,"[72] he decided that he would first be seasoned as a probationary Methodist minister in the gruelling mission fields of the Canadian west. His first batch of Victoria's BD courses would be taken by correspondence as he toiled in the mission fields.

But, if Lorne left Queen's on a low note, with his diploma deferred, Queen's had in fact given him much to build on. He left Queen's freed of his fear of what reason might do to faith, a fear implicit in much of the small-town Ontario Methodism of his boyhood. He no longer dreaded either questioning or quest in relation to spiritual goals or theological precepts, thanks to the legacy of Principal Grant and the admonitions of John Watson and William Jordan. More eager than ever to serve the nation in some way, he was by now a young man whose literary tastes and ambitions had been set in motion in reaction to the supercilious James Cappon. All in all, Queen's had set her mark upon his head and heart. Next, Lorne Pierce set off to test his faith and mettle on the raw prairie.

3

"These Waste Places of God's Great Vineyard"

Teaching and Preaching in the Canadian West, 1909–1914

If a man lived to be a Methuselah and spent all the rest of his life on Olympus he could not get out of his ears the tales of sadness or the pictures of want and loneliness from his eyes of the men and women living away up here in these waste places of God's great vineyard.

Lorne Pierce, 1913, about his life as a probationary minister in Saskatchewan[1]

It's a place where your courage gets its second wind.
... I am thankful for the [Saskatchewan] experience, it knocked my head down on my shoulders. It made me realize for the first time that I had a soul that demanded a fair show, that humanity is all of one piece, and ... that nothing can separate us from the love of God.

Lorne Pierce, 1915, reflecting upon his prairie experience[2]

In 1912 the Methodist Church of Canada was eager to oblige Lorne Pierce with a post as a Methodist probationary minister in the west. In Saskatchewan and Alberta in these years, the churches were struggling to establish congregations and schools, strained to the limit by a shortage of clergy and a flood of immigrants from all over Europe and the British Isles.[3]

By the spring of 1912, Lorne Pierce in fact was a veteran of two prairie summers in Saskatchewan. In the spring of 1909, he had chosen to take a summer teaching post in the west.[4] His parents worried that pioneer Saskatchewan – with its crude shacks and haphazard diet – would undermine their son's health. But Lorne was determined, whatever the risks, to earn money and gain experience in his own way, far from his mother's apron strings and his father's wallet flap. He was also acting in the light of Queen's spirit. The heritage of Principal Grant that Lorne was soaking up at Queen's had included recognition of a pressing need to "assimilate and Canadianize huge blocks of Slavs," as the Queen's idealist social activism of the day saw it.[5] In that spirit, Queen's offered extramural courses in the west and had a tradition of sending numerous undergraduates there for summer teaching.[6]

Lorne spent the college vacations of 1909 and 1910 as a teacher in rural Moose Jaw, Saskatchewan. A photograph shows him, just off the train from the east, perched awkwardly on a hay wagon. The soberly clad young student looks skinny, solemn, and scared, a spindly innocent in a rude new world. Lorne looked back ironically on the experience in his diary: "I must have looked strange, a homesick youth of eighteen wearing a derby, black milton [jacket] and gloves, perched on a trunk, rumbling up Main Street Moosejaw!" He added: "The only thing I remember was a stubborn nose bleed and the endless prairie."[7]

His apprehension was well founded. On his first night, he slept two to an iron cot with the hired man in the one-room shack which also housed his host family. He eventually switched to more comfortable quarters with one of the more successful settlers in the area. But the underweight college student initially had to employ a very literal muscular Christianity in the ramshackle school to subdue the loutish late-adolescent bullies among his twenty-odd students. There were happier moments that first summer in the west. One fine June day, he bumped into Edith Chown at the railway station as she changed trains to go to Swift Current to teach until September. Moreover, the feisty easterner so impressed his own pupils and their parents that first summer that, he remembered, "my leave taking [in September] was signalled by taking a group picture of the school with everybody weeping, and the presentation [to me] of a china five o'clock tea set!"[8] The second summer, Lorne taught in the same school, returning to Queen's only in late September. During a stop in Toronto, he spent the $345 he had saved to outfit himself for the academic year ahead. Significantly, he did not even take time to travel to Delta before returning to Queen's, a declaration of independence that his parents must have found painful.[9]

The influence of the west on Pierce deepened – and darkened – when he stepped off the train from the east on 19 May 1912 for a two-year stay. He was now a probationer for the Methodist Church on the prairies, prior to going to Victoria College for the bachelor of divinity studies his mother had long championed. Once in the field that spring, in addition to the prodigious labours of a far-flung preaching circuit that lacked adequate church buildings or proper schools, the student preacher had to prepare to rewrite Cappon's English examination the next spring. He was also doing several of the initial BD courses by correspondence from Victoria College.

Like E.J. Pratt and Northrop Frye, two other Canadian literary worthies who also jolted their way on horseback over the western sod as probationers,[10] Lorne found the prairie circuit a grim life indeed – though he was by far the most successful probationer of the three. In fact, he swiftly made a name for himself as a superbly capable (if feisty) minister-in-the-making, an indefatigable worker and an inspired preacher, a man of the cloth who was a tireless fundraiser and community leader. Eloquence, energy, and the ability to overcome hostility, indifference, and apathy – all these traits brought him to prominence as a probationary minister in Saskatchewan and would later serve him well at Ryerson Press.

LORNE SPENT May to October 1912 working in a 300-square-mile pastorate near Colonsay, Saskatchewan, moving that fall to Plunkett, where he had five preaching stations on a 120 square-mile-circuit.[11] He then moved in July 1913 to Fillmore, a town of about 500, where he had to face "debt, depression and disruption" as well as ill-health until his departure for the east at the end of May 1914.[12] His pastorates were sprawling blanks of prairie on the map, without adequate religious, educational, or governmental infrastructure, territory sprinkled with a veritable babel of settlers of all sorts.

Here, Lorne was on the religious front lines and face to face with the changing nature of Canadian society in a way that would shape his view of his religion and of Canada's cultural needs. His experience was representative. Between 1901 and 1911, over one million settlers had poured into the west. For the Methodists, as for all the churches, "[the] problem was that of keeping pace with the progress of settlement, and as a network of railway lines fanned out over the provinces, they found their resources taxed to the limit. A survey conducted just after the First World War indicated that half of the children in rural Alberta were growing up in entire ignorance of the Christian religion. In the towns and villages, the churches became centres of community life, while students and the lay preachers ranged the countryside on horseback to provide energetic if not always experienced leadership."[13]

Saskatchewan is a case in point. In just ten years, between 1901 and 1911, the year before Lorne arrived as probationer, the number of

A time of testing: Lorne Pierce as a Methodist ministerial
probationer, Saskatchewan, c. 1912. Courtesy of Queen's
University Archives

Methodist adherents in Saskatchewan had ballooned over sixfold, from
12,028 to 78,235. Furthermore, the churches were heavily drawn into
community work in the west by the lack of schools and hospitals as
well as churches.[14] In turn, the movement toward church union on the
part of the Methodist and Presbyterian churches was intensified by the
challenge of serving huge new areas of the west. The nationalist orientation of Methodism was also stimulated by the challenge of the inchoate
prairies. The resultant patriotism and zeal for "Canadianization" in the
church that infused both Methodism and its young probationer is central
to any understanding of Lorne Pierce's motivations during his publish-

ing career. The prairie experience made the churches more nationalistic, as one historian has observed: "Increasingly powerful as naturalisation bestowed the franchise on more and more immigrants was a desire [in the Methodist Church of Canada] to implant Canadian ideals of citizenship. 'Canadianism' became a favorite word in [Methodist] circles."[15]

In Saskatchewan, Lorne was plunged into an ethnic mélange, an eye-opening experience for a young man fresh from homogenous, Anglo-Saxon eastern Ontario. In the parlance of the time, he wrote in his diary of, among others, "Chinamen" (whom he taught English), "Galicians" (whom he met while he organized schools), and "Ruthenians" (who called him their "little priest"). A Jewish family helped him with his Hebrew as he did the correspondence courses toward his divinity degree.

Colonsay, Lorne's first posting, where he shared a shack fifteen miles out of town with Charles Woods, a taciturn young settler, was his first experience of the rigours of the western field. From May to October 1912, the novice "sky pilot" struggled to serve an area of 300 square miles, with little help from his area superintendent and no established congregational infrastructure. In a fetid two-room shack so stifling in the summer heat that he nicknamed it "El Inferno," Lorne struggled with food as well as shelter. He had to cook for Woods and himself, and his misadventures were reflected in a cookie the size and consistency of a stove lid he mailed home to Delta. Frequently fighting off vermin, living on less than subsistence wages,[16] struggling with the feeling of emotional isolation so often experienced by clergymen, feeling alienated by the "barren streets and bummish looking people" of the tiny settlements and sweeping acres he tried to serve, the young easterner felt as if he had been plunged "from Fifth Avenue into a coal mine." He spent his first Christmas alone, "blue as indigo and as spiritless as a wet hen."[17]

Lorne had not been comforted by a visit from his father during his first July as a western probationer. Appalled by the squalour in which Lorne was living and upset by his son's categorical refusal to throw the task over, the elder Pierce cut short his visit.[18] Truly, in many ways, the period 1912–14 was one of the most difficult of Lorne's life. Humiliated by his failure at Queen's, in conflict with his parents, unsure of his vocation, still pining for the hand of Edith Chown, dreading Victoria College, and battling extreme climate and primitive living conditions with a constitution that had more grit than resilience, he found himself in an unenviable position, marked by a bleak present and an uncertain future. Even at the beginning of his first posting, however, he began to demonstrate prodigious energy and vision. He also had one ace in the hole as a community organizer.

In the summer of 1911, Lorne Pierce had become a Mason, a member of Delta's Harmony Lodge. Freemasonry was one bond with his father, a staunch Mason like so many small-town Protestant businessmen of the day. Another committed Mason who figured large in Lorne's life was W.C. Dowsley, his former Athens high school teacher, who had steered him to Queen's. For a middle-class Protestant Ontario boy of twenty-one, joining the Masonic Order was a cherished rite of passage into full manhood. Accordingly, soon after his twenty-first birthday, Lorne had been solemnly invited to join Delta's Harmony Lodge No. 370. He was initiated as a Scottish Rite Mason on 20 September 1911.[19]

Freemasonry's fraternal order linked men across North America and western Europe. In an age without credit cards, rapid communication, quick personal and credit references, or easy travel, the brotherhood provided an invaluable means of "networking" for a young Mason in an unfamiliar place. In the west, Lorne's Masonic ties proved invaluable. Many of his key friends, supporters, and congregants were brother Masons, with whom he initially made contact through lodge affiliations. When he was desperate for a place to stay, a Mason came through. His physician and closest friend in Fillmore, his third posting, was a fellow Mason. When he was without cash or credit in Plunkett, the Union Bank manager, noticing his Masonic pin, came through with a small loan out of his own pocket for a Masonic brother. In short, in Saskatchewan – as would be the case in New York City, Ottawa, Kingston, and Toronto – the ideals and the contacts of the order were to serve Lorne Pierce well. He in turn was to accomplish much community good through the philanthropic projects of the Masonic lodges to which he belonged. The handshake, password, and contacts of the Masonic Order were crucial community, national, and philanthropic building blocks for Lorne Pierce.

Given his use of his Masonic ties for church and community work, it is clear that Lorne's commitment to freemasonry was not made out of fondness for elaborate ritual or mere bonhomie. He conceived of freemasonry as an ideal of brotherhood and community service that he took to heart. In his own life and writing, he would later link the community ethos of the order with the spirit of such movements as theosophy and the social gospel.[20] For example, a decade after his service in the west, he offered the Delta Harmony Lodge "a small foundation library of

Masonic works," resolving to send more at regular intervals, because he believed that "the Lodge should devote more time to social, community and intellectual improvement and not stress degree work so much."[21]

As a newly fledged member, Lorne's commitment to Masonry was already firm. When, within a year of initiation, his area superintendent at Elston on his first Saskatchewan circuit gruffly told him to take off his Masonic pin for fear of alienating some potential congregants, Lorne refused.[22] Moreover, he pressed one of his first Masonic insignia pins upon Edith Chown, a gesture seen by both of them as proof of his serious interest in her.[23] Despite his punishing schedule as a probationer in the west, he continued his degree work within the western lodges, making his way through the ranks of the order. Moreover, he confided to Edith in September 1912 that "[the] few 'Masonic brethren' around here, in Colonsay and Elston ... have proved about the only square people in the district."[24]

In Colonsay, his first posting, ten miles north of the Canadian Pacific Railway (CPR) line, Lorne, who had to establish his own preaching stations, worked with Masons and non-Masons, Canadians and immigrants, to build churches and schools. His first sermon – conceived and delivered in trepidation – was based on a Scriptural text: "I have a message from God unto you" (Judges 3:20). Fittingly, it anticipated his ecumenical and moral approach as an editor a decade later. He described his work on his maiden homily in his diary: "I ran across a thought [about sermonizing] ... in a paper I tried hard to put into practice – [i.e.,] to compete with the novelist in human interest, and with the man of science, in absolute honesty." On 25 May 1912 the probationer held his first service, using the Presbyterian hymnbook, with "four bachelors sitting on the beds in a large one-room shack and [the host] occupying a chair."[25] Henceforth, the "little priest" – as some of his eastern European flock called him – trudged and rode from shack to shack, sometimes working in the fields beside a settler to build a bond with the people, be they Galicians, ex-Ontarians, or, in one case, a Boer war veteran and his "Kaffir wife."[26]

Lorne studied late into the night all that summer, inadequately fed and housed on a paltry mission stipend of $50 a month, a stipend that, despite his pleas, was usually in arrears. The summer was his "fire baptism": the middle-class young Ontarian was appalled by the area's miserable living conditions. He was particularly outraged by the brutal domestic and agricultural slavery endured by many a prairie wife, commenting

on it repeatedly in letters and in his diary. (That perception would later
help to commit him to the artistic and documentary insights of Frederick Philip Grove's prairie-settlement novel *Settlers of the Marsh*, a work
that shocked many Canadians.) "How many lives," Lorne lamented to
Edith Chown, "are offered up each year to the gods of the wheat crop in
the West."[27] As a probationer, he repeatedly despaired that he had been
plunged into the "waste places of God's great vineyard," rife with "tales
of sadness" and "pictures of want and loneliness."[28] Even though he had
dedicated both a new church and a new school by the time he left the
Colonsay circuit for Plunkett on the first day of October 1912,[29] Lorne
continued to be dogged by feelings of futility. He wrote Edith forlornly:
"I cannot point to one solitary soul and say I helped it a little upward or
plucked it from ruin. Consequently I am going away ... with an awful
sense of failure and sadness that I cannot describe."[30]

   The settlers around Plunkett, a small town on the CPR line, were mostly
from Ontario, in contrast to the ethnic mix of the Colonsay circuit. But
the change did not mean the posting was easy. Winter lay ahead, with
a large out-of-town area to be served. The living and social conditions
of the little town of about seventy-five people ("a tiny, scrambled, lonely,
forsaken place"[31]) were stressful. The parsonage – which Lorne sardonically nicknamed "The Teepee" – turned out to be barely habitable for
winter, although Lorne and the townspeople installed such touches as
curtains and a bookshelf. He had to construct his own chimney, which
smoked but functioned. Some organizational work had already been
done in Plunkett, but he was expected to adhere more closely to Methodist ritual and practice than in Colonsay, an orthodoxy that irked him
at times.[32]

   Like many probationers in the region, Lorne Pierce was radicalized
by his experiences, coming to reject the rigidity and conservatism of the
eastern Methodist establishment in the face of the enormous social and
organizational problems confronting the church in the west. Life there
led him to lean toward the tenets of the social gospel, and to conceive
of the church as necessarily and urgently a force for nationalism and
social change. He came to reject any stress on sectarian dogma, given
the pressing social needs of all faiths and denominations on the prairies.
He came to question the utility of working to construct large churches
for each of the various Protestant denominations – "halls of Pharoah,"
he scornfully called them, empty six days out of seven – in areas without
proper schools, libraries, or community halls.[33]

In a land of physical and spiritual hardship, Lorne also had no use for the hellfire-and-damnation approach to his ministerial labours. As a result of this "radicalism," he was criticized vehemently in Plunkett by orthodox Methodists. The latter disliked his rejection of a literal hell, and he was even criticized at a district meeting in Saskatoon as the result of a sermon on the subject. Lorne recorded his rejoinder to the district worthies: "I ... assured them that a worse slavery than that of Egyptian or Syrian or Roman was the throttling of the intellect."[34] When he eventually returned to the east, he was for a time mildly disdainful of the well-fed, smug, comfortable Methodist ministers of Ontario.[35]

In Plunkett, Lorne was still dogged by a chronic shortage of personal funds. His appeals for in-arrears stipend money from the Mission Fund brought sanctimonious letters but no cash.[36] After tearing up cheques sent by his parents (who vehemently urged his return) and receiving the $30 loan from a fellow Mason,[37] he did manage to purchase a pair of horses – Joe and Jerry – only to be reproved for such stylish livery by the district superintendent. It was a galling moment for the young probationer when the equine pair later were confiscated by a creditor. The horses were sold to pay his debts, which mounted as high as $400 at one point.[38]

In Plunkett, the full travail of his western mission hit Lorne – literarily with gale force. The winter of 1912–13 was particularly severe. The combination of raging blizzards and human misery marked Lorne Pierce for life as he persevered in his work "like a burr to a mule's ear."[39] He conducted his first funerals in hellish arctic conditions, numbed in soul and frozen in body. His diary, and his letters, refer to two particularly grim experiences. In December 1912 he arrived after a twelve-mile journey through snow drifts at a snow-bound 12' by 18' shack to conduct a child's funeral. The thermometer read -20°F with a piercing west wind as he read the service:

> [I] shall never forget the squalor. In one corner was a table piled high with potato peelings and dirty dishes, by it a stove ... In the fourth corner was a little cot, on it the [corpse of] the little girl was still lying covered by a cloth. The young father and mother were hanging over it sobbing most pitifully ... the rest of the space being jammed, I had to talk directly over [the corpse]. The heat of the place and all made me deathly sick but I stuck it out, and do not think anyone noticed ... as the people are all races and creeds

I took along a dozen books and we sang such pieces as "Nearer My God to Thee" that all knew. All could sing them, at least start them but I had to finish. For even those burly great fellows, unshaven and uncouth, broke down and kept wiping their eyes with their sleeves or great red bandannas all through it.[40]

Worse lay ahead. During a rest stop at a neighbour's en route to the burial, Lorne admired their two little girls, one a three-year-old. He later wrote of her: "Rarely have there been more beautiful children than Laura. Heaven did truly lie about her. I said at the time [that] she is almost too good to live. Angels usually dwell in heaven. Saturday, January 11, 1913 [a few weeks later,] I was again at that home, this time to perform the last rites of the Christian church over the remains of 'the Angel.'"

After Laura's funeral service, the cemetery lay fourteen wind-swept miles distant in -50°F cold. The little procession – just three men – floundered through two feet of drifting snow. Lorne Pierce, Laura Shantz's father, and a family friend reached the cemetery after an agonizing trek, only to discover that the wooden coffin crib had been left behind. Lorne wrote:

They had forgotten the roughbox so [the two] drove [back] into town, a distance of six miles, leaving the casket on a snow bank. I blanketed Don [the horse] with all I had, and ran and jumped and buried myself in the snow to keep from freezing in the wind that beat the face like razor blades. Finally the two returned, only to discover that the grave was four inches too narrow. Phillips chopped until his hands were frozen, then I got into the grave and finished it. I only recited the one collect[,] the Lord's prayer and pronounced the Benediction. When we reached home Mrs. Shantz was rocking her last child in her arms before the crackling wood fire. It was about four o'clock. They begged me to remain, and altho I had to be seven miles north west of Plunkett the next morning by 10:30 [I] yet acceded to their request hoping that I might be in some small way doing the Lord's work. We went to rest late and in good spirits after a very warm prayer around the family fire. I slept alone between cotton sheets. The wood fire went out and the temperature of the house dropt to 20 below. Although I ate hot porridge until I felt stuffed yet I shivered.

The young minister's ordeal was not over:

> Before I reached the crossing on my way home – a mile away, both
> ears had frozen. I felt myself freezing through and through, and
> had a fight to keep from getting out and resting in the shelter of
> straggling bushes from the piercing wind. Nearing home the horse
> took fright and ran but I didn't seem to care, nor [was I] anxious
> to alight when he [whipped] me around into the yard. Roy Hill
> [a parishioner] came running over and helped me out and into
> the hotel! My face was terribly frozen, cracking in the heat and
> bleeding profusely. Both hands and feet and ears were adamant.
> Such pain as I experienced thawing out in snow and slush I hope
> never again to be called upon to bear. It was nothing short of
> awful. I even now smile when I think of the cheery letters I sent
> home in those days. Of course I was confined to my room for days
> unable to even touch the softest things. Yet the people were all
> so good.[41]

When Lorne met Mrs Shantz years later, she began to recall her daughter's funeral and its aftermath. He had to stop her: the memory was too
traumatic.[42]

LORNE PIERCE began to take the measure of the ministerial vocation
and of the challenges of the west. Spending so much time alone in travel
and in study (though he did manage to see Sarah Bernhardt perform
when she toured the west in January 1913),[43] he had time to think and
to mature, as his letters to Edith attest. Usually unable to afford meals at
the local café, he subsisted on a dismal diet of condensed milk and cornflakes for days at a time while he pondered literature and theology. He
wrote that he was still cramming for Cappon's English examination and
for his correspondence courses from Victoria in theology, "studying from
eight o'clock until one and two in the morning and occasionally turning
out my light with the dawn. Life was very lonesome and cheerless, especially in the long days of that terrible winter of 1912."[44]

During the long, icy nights, Lorne fretted about failure in all sorts of
ways: about the possibility of flunking Cappon's English exam yet again
(he in fact passed), about his fear of losing Edith to another suitor, and
about failing in life as a man and as a minister. Was he fated to obscurity

as a "mediocre backwoods preacher"?[45] Whether hunched over his crude desk or tossing in his lumpy bed, he fretted.

After the grim winter in Plunkett, Lorne was moved in July 1913 to Fillmore. He left Plunkett with a reputation as a very capable and independent-minded Methodist probationer. Lorne had made no bones that he loathed the grey, rigid image expected of him. "Why," he asked Edith plaintively, "must a minister have to look straight up and down his nose and live on sawdust and Ladies Aid bread and never have any fun till he dies?"[46] Accordingly, when told by a church district superintendent that his red tie was unsuitable, he and a colleague defiantly arrived at a district meeting sporting flame-red cravats![47]

Lorne's domestic situation improved in Fillmore. His sister had come west to teach and the two shared a flat over the local Chinese restaurant until Sara, plagued by a tyrannical principal at the Fillmore school, changed schools in December 1913, boarding out of town during the week. At the train stop one day, Lorne bumped into a Queen's classmate – handsome, brilliant, older Jack North, the star of their year at Queen's. Jack North was also a probationer in the west – on a Presbyterian charge at Watrous, Saskatchewan.[48] Lorne felt a sense of rivalry with North that day, as always.

Another Queen's classmate dominated his thoughts. Edith Chown was teaching a tantalizing four stops down the rail line at Forget, fifty miles away. Lorne managed two visits to Edith. She boarded with the Johnsons, a warm-hearted American farming couple, and Mrs Johnson played Cupid to the reticent pair. In courting Edith, the young spark again braved the displeasure of his area superintendent, who did not consider the bubbly Edith the kind of Methodist girl suitable for a young man of the cloth. The officious superintendent even managed to "crash" one of Lorne's visits to the Johnson farm.[49]

In fact, from the very week of his arrival in the west, Lorne had corresponded faithfully with Edith. His letters are a fascinating record of their seesaw courtship as well as evidence of how much the western experience affected each of them. Lorne's letters (some playfully signed "Lorenzo" and addressed to "Bubbles") are heartfelt and calculated to keep her interest and win her love.[50] Her letters to Lorne are frank, appealing, and sensitive. For his part, Lorne wrote to Edith of the weight of his vocation, of his distaste at the prospect of Victoria College, and of his hopes and fears about the missionary life. He saw himself as ultimately destined to minister to the pagan in Asian lands, far from the

Courting the elusive "Butterfly": A gaunt Lorne Pierce visiting Edith Chown at her teaching post in Forget, Saskatchewan, 1913. Courtesy of Queen's University Archives

comforts of Canadian life. He also wrote to Edith not only of his love for his parents but also about their attempts to get him to return east. He remarked tartly of the flow of cheques and letters from Delta calculated to get him to abandon the western missions: "Wouldn't [parents] make you spineless doodads if they got you to do all they 'absolutely demanded'?"[51]

For her part, Edith agonized over her inability to commit to Lorne. Fond as she was of him, she was unsure of her feelings about marriage or her suitability to be a missionary's wife. In a typical letter, Edith wrote wistfully: "It was not my idea to win your affection and then turn you down. Even now I cannot see how I can give you up but yet I must. There are so many reasons why we can only be friends. I have so little sympathy with your chosen work. You know I hate the restrictions that the Methodist ministry places upon you. I should be so frightened to promise to go to China for fear I'd be discontented for I do love my brothers and relatives dearly."[52]

Despite her words, Edith was deeply attracted to Lorne. She had come to the west supposedly only for a teaching job but in effect planned her life such that she was nearby. She replied to his letters faithfully. Lorne's courting of Edith was a drama played out in scattered visits and frequent letters. Summing up his travails in Saskatchewan, Lorne assured Edith that she embodied his womanly ideal: "Amid all the loneliness of these long dreary, months on the northern mission fields I still dared to hope [you would be mine]. Yes even [to] pray that someday I would prove worthy of, and in some way measure up to, that ideal I had found in you." In this letter, written in October 1913, Lorne proposed marriage, promising "to love you as my wife, to honour you and be an honour to you ... the union of two hearts, two souls, two lives for ever."[53] But Edith, torn, felt she could neither accept his proposal nor spurn his friendship. For the moment, Lorne accepted the status quo ("just permit me to be ... a true and a very great Friend who will follow your life in the coming days with deepest interest").[54]

The emotional impasse with Edith bedevilled Lorne all through the months in Fillmore. Owing in part to a smallpox epidemic and quarantine that hit the town soon after his arrival, he had christened it "The Black Hole of Calcutta." Living in a flat and taking his meals at the grandiosely named Imperial Hotel, he managed to reduce the local church's debt from $1,900 to $450, an astonishing feat. His closest friends were the Presbyterian minister and his wife, but life was still a struggle against the elements. He wrote of one "brute" of a February morning with the mercury at -48°F: "[I had] a twelve mile drive into the wind. Had a foot warmer, a covered cutter, a heap of robes, and made the trip in one hour but upon my beak there glistened on my return the blue and green glitter of frost[bite], three fingers had [frozen] in spite of ink stains, two ears had congealed to the hardness of can covers."[55]

The combination of overwork, worry, cold, poor diet, and the *coup de grâce* of a spate of BD exams – on which he scored 79 per cent despite illness – laid Lorne low. He was further exhausted by several weeks of caring for a Fillmore friend invalided in the local hotel with advanced tuberculosis. Lorne himself was bedridden for several weeks in the late winter of 1914 with pleurisy. The fierce attack of pleurisy, quickly followed by two relapses, was a harbinger of worse health to come. When he finally recovered, he did twice manage to slip off to Regina briefly to visit Edith, who had gone there in January to study for her Normal School teaching certificate. On return to Fillmore, he had to conceal the trips from his congregation – after all, he and Edith had gone to a dance, scandalous for a Methodist probationer![56]

Among Lorne's small circle of friends in Fillmore was a physician and Mason, another in the long line of intellectual older men who men-

tored him in his early years. High-minded, visionary, polymathic physicians were in fact a favourite role model for Pierce throughout his life.[57]
Dr Cutten of Plunkett foreshadowed the catalytic roles that Toronto
physician and theosophist Dr Albert Durrant Watson and Vancouver
physician and writer Dr Ernest Fewster were to play in Pierce's editorial
career at Ryerson in the 1920s. By Lorne's own account, the Plunkett
physician was a "man of many brilliant parts, a scholar, an artist with
the violin, [a] single taxer, philosopher, and phrenologist."[58] With Dr
Cutten, Lorne was caught up in a plot complication worthy of the western fiction of Frederick Philip Grove or Sinclair Ross. When the doctor
was unjustly accused of the infanticide of his own baby by a malicious
member of a settlement rife with gossip, Lorne braved community censure to help his friend successfully sue for slander.[59]

Intellectually, Lorne matured during the western years. He began to
read literature more thoughtfully. The grim lives of some of his charges
made him ponder questions of suffering, sin, and the afterlife at a different, deeper level than he had before, even in John Watson's thought-
provoking Queen's philosophy classes. He organized a second school in
Fillmore and set up a literary society.[60] Ever a true son of temperance, he
even led a raid on a blind pig one night.

What held him to his task as minister was not the frequently sanctimonious Methodist Church hierarchy or any belief in a conventional
Christian afterlife. Rather, he was stirred by the spiritual hunger of many
of the men and women he met. For example, he described to Edith a
visit from a hard-living drifter who had insulted him on sight a few
months before. The drifter, he wrote, had sheepishly recalled his previous
encounter with the fledgling minister, telling him, "I told ... you and
your G— religion to go to Greenland, and went away and got drunk.
I've felt sorry ever since and I'm gettin' tired of this life so I'm going to
drop in and see you and maybe I'll get right yet." Lorne added: "It was
paralyzingly cold but we talked on the corner for a long time while the
tears rolled down his cheeks and froze on his great lumberman's scarf
around his throat." He mused of the encounter: "The west is full of men
like that. They are waiting on the roadside everywhere for a word & grip
of the hand and dying for want of it."[61]

LORNE EXHAUSTED himself trying to fill this need. When the spring
of 1914 came, he resolved to return to the east, even though his western
circuit overseers wanted him to return to Saskatchewan, offering a better
location and a bigger salary. For two long, lonely years, however, Lorne

had successfully "stuck it out" in the western mission fields. Despite the hardships, he reflected in his diary that his Saskatchewan years convinced him that "humanity is all of one piece."[62] The west fed his ecumenism as, far from congenial spirits, he had to minister to all the settlers, whatever their origin, language, denomination – or reputation. He wrote of those he served that "few were real Methodists but that makes no difference in the West."[63] He became convinced that what mattered about religion was not the nature of the afterlife, or a rigid ministerial persona, or impressive church structures, but rather a real sense of community and social and cultural activism in the church. His sense of cultural and national mission and of the need for Canadians of different faiths and backgrounds to share a love of community and country took root in Saskatchewan. At the same time, a sense of ministerial vocation slowly began to take hold of him, driven by the spiritual and physical privation he experienced first-hand while attempting to alleviate it in others. In the west, Lorne became more zealous, more ecumenical, more nationalistic, more compassionate, and more outspoken. He became a man as well as a minister in the fullest sense of both terms.

Lorne also developed a shrewd instinct for where power and possibility lay, an instinct that would serve him well in later life. He was an idealist, but one with a shrewd sense of realpolitik. Marginalized as he was within the Methodist Church in the western missions, he wrote of church structure: "I have come to the conclusion that a man has to pretend that he is a man at least and stand up for himself or he'll get unmercifully trodden into the dust, even by his own 'brethren' in the ministry. The power of the [Methodist] conference is placed in a few hands and unless you keep your lamps trimmed and burning and cast upon those brethren you might as well expect the premiership of Madagascar."[64]

In Saskatchewan, Lorne Pierce did in fact "grow up with the country." His struggles – first as a greenhorn college student teaching in a primitive one-room school in the summers of 1909 and 1910 and later as a probationary minister organizing congregations and schools on the raw prairie between 1912 and 1914 – were central to the development of his dynamic concept of the nation and its cultural needs. His Saskatchewan years convinced Lorne Pierce of the need to acculturate newcomers to Canada ideologically and socially as well as materially. The experience also convinced him of the need for Canada to incorporate the experiences and aspirations of the provinces of the Canadian west into the fabric of the national culture. The west was the crucible of Pierce's conviction as publisher about the necessity for Canadian publishers and editors to facilitate the presentation of a vision of Canada in the country's arts and letters, and for that vision to incorporate the reality of life in the western provinces. Like J.S. Woodsworth, who expressed his own concerns about Canadian society's accommodation of immigrants in his tract *Strangers within Our Gates* (1909) as a result of his own formative experiences as a Methodist clergyman in the west,[65] Pierce's sense of the country and its social and spiritual needs was transformed by his western experiences.

There were darker consequences of the western years as well – consequences for his health. Lorne Pierce began to lose his hearing in the west, partly as a result of repeated exposure to frostbite, hypothermia-related damage that probably exacerbated a family predisposition to acute hearing loss. His lungs were also damaged by multiple bouts of pleurisy, his body weakened by overwork and poor diet.

Nevertheless, Lorne left Saskatchewan in the last days of May 1914 with a greater sense both of who he was and what the country had to become – intellectually, socially, and spiritually – to be a nation. Such insights were broadly and inclusively conceived, thanks to the mosaic of pioneer Saskatchewan.

He boarded the train to the east alone. Yet his formal engagement to Edith Chown was not far off – that courtship was well on its way, despite doubts on the part of the sensitive young woman to whom the determined young clergyman had written: "I do not want to marry brains but a soul. You possess both."[66] When Lorne's train steamed into Delta on 1 June 1914, a summer in the picturesque village beside the lake beckoned, even as the war clouds gathered in Europe. There was another cloud on his personal horizon. Would Victoria's divinity program be able to address the ferment aroused in him by his western experience? As September drew nearer, he was full of foreboding: "I hope that Victoria is not the horrible dream of past years, yet, somehow I face it with fear and evil forebodings that theological decorum and the Methodist discipline will be strictly maintained. The theological classes I hope will clear the air for me. I have dug into book after book on problems that have defied me and the more I read the more I sink."[67] A winding road – and the intricate paths of true love – lay ahead as Lorne Pierce stepped off the train from the west into his mother's embrace that June day.

4

Wrestling with "the Gods of
the Methodist Discipline"

*Victoria College, Toronto, and Union Theological Seminary,
New York City, 1914–1916*

I am more concerned over building up a rationale of my own faith
than satisfying the expectations of – excuse the term – intolerant
orthodoxy.

Lorne Pierce on his Victoria College studies, 1915[1]

Accept offer [for an Ontario Methodist pulpit]. Stand by Canada
and Methodism. Was about to go down and sign up with [U.S.]
Presbyterians at 11 a.m. – [Canadian] letter came 10 a.m.

Lorne Pierce diary entry, New York City, 29 April 1916

When he returned to Delta from the west in June 1914, Lorne Pierce
was exhausted by two gruelling years as a Methodist probationer.
The 5'10" youth now weighed under 130 pounds. Mentally, Lorne was
full of "fear and evil forebodings" about what lay ahead at Victoria. His
apprehension about its bachelor of divinity program was increased by
the memory of his one visit there. Two years earlier, as a Queen's undergraduate, Lorne had travelled to Victoria College as a member of a university delegation. The "dull and stodgy" Victoria student gathering, he
wrote sardonically, had reminded him of "a prayer meeting on a stormy
night with the leader absent."[2]

In Delta, moreover, Lorne was once more exposed to relentless parental pressure. His mother had a staunch ally in the local Methodist
minister, the Reverend Reuben Calvert, in pushing for Victoria. Lorne
was racked by severe migraines, an indication of the stress he was under.[3]
As his father set him to work collecting some of the Pierce hardware
business's bad debts, Lorne even considered going back to Fillmore for

another year, abandoning the idea only when the doctor told him it would be "suicidal" for his health.[4]

That summer, and for the next year, Lorne revealed little about his hopes and plans to his parents. He still said nothing about his interest in Edith Chown, even when his mother hinted that a wife would be a good thing for a young minister resolved to go out to China as a missionary.[5] Lorne had doubts about his future with Edith, who still felt unable to commit to him. When she left Kingston in August 1914 to teach in Regina, prior to earning her permanent teaching certificate, Lorne did not even make the short journey to Kingston to see her before departure. Edith wrote him tremulously that she had "hoped to the last hour that you would come before I left but I had no right to hope for your coming."[6]

Events in the larger world were even more troubling. Lorne noted that his twenty-fourth birthday – 3 August 1914 – "had been celebrated by the cataclysm of nations" – the outbreak of the Great War.[7] In late August, Edith wrote that her brother, Gordon, a physician, had joined up. With the blithe patriotism so widespread throughout the Allied nations early in the First World War, Lorne assured Edith: "You should be one of the jolliest Canadian girls with a brother going off to the front. Besides his returning with a wonderful experience, he will be of wonderful value to the Empire in his care of the wounded."[8]

Four days later, the war suddenly became more real to Lorne and all of Delta. The whole village was suddenly "in mourning" because three young men had left to join up.[9] Lorne began to struggle with the question of whether to enlist himself. Like most of his Anglo-Canadian middle-class contemporaries, he was still full of naive optimism about the nature of the conflict, telling Edith: "I would give anything to be able to go. It does seem as if we had been hurled back into the dark ages. But I believe there is no such thing as retrogression. Today is the best day the world has ever seen, tomorrow will be better because a divine purpose is working itself out. Democracy will emerge from this stronger than ever."[10]

The uncertainty engendered by the war made Lorne assert that his ambition as a minister was "to reawaken faith in all its forms in some few men." He maintained that "God is love" … [and that] the world about us is not governed by cold impersonal forces or by a malignant personality but that the unseen is capable of love."[11] His meliorist view of the conflict persisted as the time drew near to go to Toronto. Insisting that the newly declared war was "not only the incubus of militarism but a universal turning to the light," he imagined that England would conquer Germany, while "sparing every man, woman, child and defenceless creature and their universities and art collections."[12]

AT THE END of September, Lorne reluctantly boarded the train for Victoria College.[13] Edith had wondered for some time if he was still forcing himself into his parents' mould in studying for the Methodist ministry.[14] As Lorne registered, he was irritated when Victoria refused him permission to take an extramural credit in Romance language and literature from the University of Chicago. Then he learned that, through an administrative error, many of the courses he had toiled over during the long, cold nights in the west had not been the proper courses for credit in the BD program. Protesting to the college authorities, he resolved to take three years of course work in just two.[15]

In Toronto, Lorne, in company with his sister (who was doing a bachelor of pedagogy at the University of Toronto), and a cousin, Mabel Pierce, found room and board in a rather grand, if somewhat down-at-heels, three-storey turreted grey brick house at 64 St Albans Street, not far from campus. Lorne's second-floor room had a row of windows facing the Ontario legislature, as well as a fireplace and an old-fashioned bell pull, which now summoned no one. With characteristic whimsy, Lorne described his landlords: "The owner is a B.A. Graduate of London, England, [who] wears a silk hat, a monocle, a goatee, and carries an Irish thorn stick and an Irish whisk[e]y breath, talks in what Mr. Lawson calls 'Hyberboles' and swears at his wife, who is an ex-matron from N.Y."[16]

From this raffish atmosphere, Lorne set off each day for the dignified quadrangle of Victoria College, just off Queen's Park. Its dark grey and red Gothic-style buildings – built since the college's removal from Cobourg to Toronto as part of the University of Toronto Federation in 1892 – featured an arch near the entrance to the theology building emblazoned with the motto "The truth shall make you free" to greet the some six hundred students enrolled in Victoria's Arts and Theology Faculty.[17]

Lorne, far from feeling free, felt constrained. Given the nature of his studies and what he saw as the orthodox leadership of Canadian Methodism of the day, he found Victoria full of "fogeys" and "flapdoodle." In contrast to Queen's, where he was a freewheeling arts student tasting the dynamic intellectual legacy of Principal Grant, Lorne was now enrolled in a vocational BD program that was by its nature normative.

Methodism as a whole had not been keeping pace in growth with other denominations since the turn of the century, but the response at Victoria had tended to be insistence on the fundamentals rather than exploration of new directions.[18]

Chancellor Nathaniel Burwash, the grand old man of Victoria, who had retired the year before, had seen to it that Victoria's Methodist ministers-in-training were indoctrinated to meet such challenges of the age as scientific criticism, materialism, and socialism. Before retiring, Burwash gave a speech that showed why the values of Victoria were so dear to Harriet Pierce's heart. He declared that, in the face of the threat of Canadian materialism, "hope lay in [Canada's] moral resources, pure homes, motherhood, strong educational system, religion, best old stock and more recent immigrants of 'the best moral type.'"[19] But, in the fall of 1914, Lorne Pierce craved intellectual variety in his diet, not simply larger helpings of the spiritual staples he had been served in Delta.

In the Victoria divinity program of the day, the goal was "moral formation" that was strongly "national in spirit."[20] Burwash, and his successor Chancellor Richard Pinch Bowles, viewed literature and culture primarily as key tools to assist in the task of moral formation. Burwash had defined culture as "high ideals of right, of honour, of beautiful sympathies and affections."[21] Victoria graduates were to "ensure that ... the nation's leaders in a new age of technical and scientific progress were men of culture and high moral standards."[22] For his part, Lorne phrased the concept irreverently in a letter to Edith: his legacy from Victoria as a minister would be "to bring hope and faith ... concealed in parcels of lectures ... on Eng[lish] Lit[erature]."[23] While such preoccupations with literature for moral aims would certainly colour Lorne Pierce's future editorial work at Ryerson Press, he had already absorbed such values at the Queen's of James Cappon and John Watson. Once again, Victoria seemed a stodgy rehash of what he had already digested.

There was also a certain priggishness and rigidity to the atmosphere at Victoria. Because literature was considered above all a moral tool, there was a suspicion that fiction tended to be morally dubious. Some of Victoria's more cosmopolitan English professors, such as Pelham Edgar, were disdainful of Victoria's daily morning prayers and prim moralism. By Pierce's day, some students had reached beyond Victoria to more liberal Toronto colleges for their literature courses.[24] The conservative cast to much of Victoria was also resolutely evangelical, despite the growing importance of the ethic of social service in the Methodist Church and the attraction of younger Methodist clergy like Ernest Thomas and J.S. Woodsworth to the social gospel.[25] Senior Victoria divinity professors like George Jackson fretted about how to keep "traditional piety and the old methods of cultivating it" and about how to forge "a new kind of evangelism."[26] There was a hint of pessimism, coupled with a siege mentality, in the way Burwash and his contemporaries faced the challenges of the relationship between their creed and wider Canadian culture.[27]

Moreover, though Victoria prided itself on not being narrowly denominational, Lorne sensed evangelical tub-thumping in many of his divinity classes. He had always hated emotionally charged evangelism, and, after the shock of his western ministry, he was preoccupied with questions of faith and with the need for religious cooperation and social amelioration. He was haunted by the material hardships, early deaths, and spiritual deprivations he had seen in Saskatchewan. To his mind, Victoria, with its "intolerant orthodoxy" and "intolerable arrogance," was not addressing the meaning of those experiences.[28]

By November, Lorne was writing Edith that he was "terribly disappointed" in Victoria's "uninspiring" BD program, and that he was casting around for an alternative for his second year, be it the army or another university. He declared that he could get more out of a month's private study at home than out of the twenty classes he would have taken by year's end.[29] His description to Edith of his homiletics class made clear how dissatisfied he and many of his contemporaries were with the program: "[The professor] told us the other day that we must be fiery gospellers and red hot evangelists. When he asked me for a sermon criticism on that plane, I told him plainly that I had no use, nor [had] anyone else for such ecclesiastical hysterics as he advocated ... He raved – that's the word[,] Edith – he tore up and down like a Caliban. But everyone he called on gave him the same thing! O it was rich." Lorne vowed that "someday I'll have a message" but, he added, "thank the Lord it will not be hysterical."[30]

Meanwhile, war fever affected Lorne and much of the student body. He wrote to a friend in November: "Every student is solemn as a sphinx, all feel the awfulness of the cloud hanging over our Empire. Yet we're going to win ... The university here is aflame with patriotism and about half the men are drilling in anticipation of a call to arms, about 2000 in all."[31] The Reserve Officers' Training Corps (ROTC) on campus was captained by the young Vincent Massey, whom Lorne irreverently described as "a young millionaire" on "a fat black pony."[32] The student reservists,

Lorne among them, marched to "Tipperary," improvising their own lyrics: "It's a long way to St. Helena where the Kaiser's got to go."[33] Yet, given Lorne's double course load (thirty-five hours of lectures a week) and other activities such as the Glee Club and the debating society, his Reserve exercises were yet another health risk. The corps drilled from 6:45 to 8:00 a.m. and from 4:00 to 6:00 p.m. daily, and all day Saturday. Lorne recorded getting soaked to the skin on manoeuvres in the Don valley one late October afternoon.[34]

Lorne was striving in other ways. Despite his forthrightness in class, he was winning positive notice on campus. In the Browning Club, he gave a paper on "Browning – His Passion" which traced the poet's "passion for life … his passion for humanity and his passion for Christ" in such works as "Andrea del Sarto" and "Fra Lippo Lippi." The Browning Club was presided over by forty-three-year-old Pelham Edgar, a tall and intimidating grandee always on the lookout for literary talent. (He was to be the mentor of such luminaries as poet E.J. Pratt and scholars Douglas Bush and Northrop Frye.[35]) Lorne's precocity and enterprise prompted Edgar to ask for a copy of the Browning paper. After being on the winning team at the debating society and giving another paper to the Union Literary Society (on Tolstoy) as well as one on spiritualism, Lorne was singled out for a coveted invitation to a gathering at Edgar's home in December.[36]

Yet Lorne's greatest goad to thought in Toronto was not at Victoria College. An outside mentor fed his dissatisfaction with the Methodist status quo. Edith had urged him to visit her Aunt Alice, who was living in Toronto. Alice Chown was to become Canada's best-known first-wave social feminist. In 1914 she was well on her way to becoming notorious in Toronto for her outspoken pacifism during the Great War.[37] Edith knew that her brilliant and iconoclastic aunt would stimulate Lorne. With the skepticism with which the Chown family habitually spoke of the unconventional Alice, she told him what to expect: "I can see you coming away from [Aunt Alice] an ardent advocate of woman's suffrage, feminism, pure food, better housing, shorter hours of labor, [and] a new religion (I think Aunt Alice's last was based on the theory that all there is of God is within us)."[38]

Intrigued, Lorne contacted Alice Chown soon after his arrival. Here he found the intellectual challenge he craved, someone with whom to debate the ideas of Nietzsche, Shaw, and Tolstoy. When Lorne telephoned her to give the reason for the delay in his first visit – his military

manoeuvres – the two began to spar immediately. Lorne excitedly reported to Edith: "Well Edith I stuck my foot in it right up to the hock
joint! The company at Bain Avenue are strictly anti-militarist and out
of all sympathy with the whole fracas! In the meantime I shall do pen-
ance for such a break and read all the peace literature I can secure. Miss
Chown was, at the moment I rang up, reading G.B. Shaw's 'Pygmalion'
and it happened that I was reading his 'Unsocial Socialist.' Now there
you have it all, war, feminism, and socialism."[39] Lorne found Alice's table
talk even more bracing. He told Edith: "I got so many shocks from that
delightful aunt of yours that I have been thinking all week, not in one's
and two's but in groups, bunches, as they tell us we must do in advanced
counterpoint … I crossed swords [with her] on militancy but couldn't
get any farther than 'firstly' when I was deluged with an avalanche of
such argument that I retired in confusion!" He added that he was eager
for more: "It was all so very good … I'm going to get at more of these
radical ideas. I may not adopt them but then great truths do not come
organized and groomed out of all reality like an English turf, they're too
alive to be restrained."[40]

Of course, "restrained" was exactly what Lorne Pierce felt at Victoria, and Alice Chown fed his desire to find a more liberal educational
environment. He was still cautious – given his family loyalties and his
nationalism – about repudiating the bonds of Canadian Methodism.
Nevertheless, Alice Chown challenged him to break out of the mould in
a letter: "Your first concern is to gain the best preparation for your life
work possible and you should not allow your loyalty to any institution to
dwarf you … I shall be very sorry if you are not brave enough to choose
your own freedom."[41]

Thus egged on by Alice Chown, whom he was later to credit with giving him the "needed push from Vic,"[42] Lorne began to think of finishing
his degree at the prestigious, cosmopolitan, ecumenically oriented Union
Theological Seminary in New York City. His Queen's classmate, Bill
Topping, another prospective minister, had chosen to go to Union and
was writing him glowing reports about its curriculum and the prospects
of ordination in the American Congregational or Presbyterian churches.
Moreover, Lorne's Victoria College classmate Eldred Chester, who was
courting his sister, was also planning to switch to Union. That fall, Lorne
sent off an application. Union accepted him and his Victoria credits, and
he rhapsodized to Edith: "Just look at the [Union] classes … Honours
Comparative Religions, Phil. of Religion, Psychology of Soul, Hon[ours]
Sociology, and a course in missions, problems, methods, Chinese lan-

guage, lit[erature], art, religion etc[.,] everything to place real tools in
your hands to work with [as a missionary]. These classes are taken partly
at Columbia and N.Y. University and the rest at Seminary."[43]

Lorne had pangs of conscience, however. He had not told Victoria
about his Union application, fearing that, as a probationer, he would be
"fired or frozen out."[44] The head of Victoria's divinity school had been
kind to him, even though he had forbidden Lorne to take any more extra
classes, telling him that he already had "half again as much as the rest."[45]
Another Victoria professor had agreed to help Lorne with a thesis tentatively titled "A Philosophical Interpretation of the Problem of Faith"
as he wrestled with readings of Nietzsche and Shaw. In December, however, when Union offered him a $180 scholarship, Lorne's craving for
wider horizons mounted despite his scruples about "chucking" Victoria
College. Ever-ambitious, he was also aware, as he later told his son, that
a Union degree would give him lustre in any later career.[46] Moreover, he
dreamed of a year's study at Oxford after Union.[47]

But, by the end of 1914, Lorne's health collapsed. In early December,
just before the last debate of the season (which his team won), he was
"so very tired" that he was unable to sleep. After his return home on
21 December, he took to his bed, with persistent pain in his side. The
doctor, diagnosing pleurisy, decreed that he must convalesce at home for
some months. Lorne told Edith that he was eager to recover as soon as
possible, for he was convinced that "there is a great new era opening just
ahead for me and I must be ready to meet it."[48] But the invalid greeted
the New Year of 1915 plagued by "rackish and feverish anxieties."[49]

Lorne's convalescence – spent at home between December 1914 and
September 1915 – consisted of "resting" Pierce-style – that is to say, engaging in a spate of activity that would have broken a less driven man.
In February, Dean Francis Huston Wallace of Victoria gave permission
for Lorne to write some twelve examinations at home. Lorne was grateful, but also guiltily reminded thereby of his continuing obligations to
"Victoria and Canadian Methodism," which his mother and the Reverend Calvert both pointed out.[50] Would going off to Union after such
accommodation be morally "the square thing?"[51] In addition to poring
over textbooks in the Morris chair in the study, Lorne was soon teaching
semaphore to three dozen Scouts, raising money for the Scout troop,
actively working in the local Masonic lodge, and teaching a Bible class.

Through it all, he was increasingly developing a sense of his own destiny and questioning some of the givens of his upbringing. In particular,
he began to view his parents' Methodist lifestyle with some detachment.

He wondered to Edith if dancing and cards were really so awful as his parents claimed, even as he admitted that he could not now endanger the prospect of his ordination by indulging in such forbidden delights. He wrote a rather jaded description of Sundays in Delta. The letter hints that he found it hard to exercise the free play of intellect in his academic work in such surroundings: "Sunday here is most Puritanic. We rise at seven thirty, at least my parents do, and after breakfast 'look over' as they call it – the [Sunday School] lesson. The school starts at 9 a.m. and is dismissed at eleven. The strain in them is then caught by the [Methodist] class leader and then prolonged for another hour. Consequently the midday repast happens nearer the end of the day. It only leaves a couple of hours until time to rake around for tea and church at seven, and as there is usually some one in, or a bunch to sing after it, I feel about as literary as a brass Budd[h]a."[52]

In such a relentlessly pious atmosphere, Lorne increasingly began to brood over the sacredness of his vocation. He wrote earnestly to Edith: "Already I feel the nearness of the time when I shall take the vows and foolish or not I almost stand dumb in the presence of my 'high calling' ... and even now I feel my command 'Go and Preach – to *all* nations' – coming 'warm from the lips of God.'"[53] Out of such ruminating, Lorne declared that his ideal was to "seek to manifest the spirit of my master." In the spirit of church union and the social gospel current at the time, he espoused a ecumenical, muckraking view of society, telling Edith: "There is much to do and yet churches, communities and individuals stand defending worn out credos and defunct formalities while heartless corporations 'get away with the goods' and we call it civilization! ... There's a task set for us all [–] we must face it – to find the common denominator of our spiritual and intellectual lives." Lorne's view of business as "heartless" had perhaps been sharpened by the news that his father had just lost the $500 he had invested in a Calgary real estate company because its Toronto-based officers were found to have embezzled its funds.[54]

It is doubtful that Lorne shared his more radical ideas with his mother. By March, the two had fallen into the habit of a late-afternoon stroll down to the shores of nearby Lower Beverley Lake to smell the evergreens and watch the gulls swooping over the ice. Still, he lamented in letters to Edith, "you're the only one I can talk with in wee Delta." He told her that he had vowed to use the study time in Delta "to seek for some distinct rationale of the faith that I have – not something inertial, unreasoned and unexplained, but using reason to make that most mysterious doctrine luminous."[55] As he read philosophers and theologians, his mind veered over all sorts of views of the divine. To Edith, he confided that the lakeside walks brought out the pantheist in him: "I try hard not to be a pantheist but try as I may I cannot elude the feeling that God is the great world-heart, and that everything created is God – 'whose dwelling is the light of setting suns' – and in the mind of man."[56] When spring brought the beauty of blossoms to Delta, Lorne rhapsodized to Edith about immortality incarnate in the cycle of nature: "The rose-bush shows its faith in thrusting its silken corona out into the sun. Its subtle perfume testifies to this. The daffodil shows its faith in nature, in trusting to her 'the elfin granary' nestled in its bosom."[57]

A reading of the BD thesis Lorne was working on at this time – eventually completed at Union Theological Seminary as "The Contribution of Modern Systems of Philosophy to the Philosophy of Religion" – suggests that he was seeking a sense of a divine and overarching meaning to life in the face of uncertainty over his health, his future, and the war. In a biographical sense, what is important about the thesis is not Pierce's lengthy summaries of Kant, Hegel, and Schleiermacher, but his assertion that "my fundamental reason for believing in God is that it gives the most meaningful interpretation of life, while its alternative – mechanism – empties life of meaning." For Lorne, it was far more "credible" – and crucial – to believe that "life is fraught with significance rather than that it is empty of spiritual value."[58] In other words, his idealism was firmly in place.

In personal terms, Lorne did something else to assert his identity and the meaning of his life. In February, he began to think of keeping a diary. Between June and September 1915, he penned a long memoir of his life up to the age of twenty-five to begin the first volume. Calling the diary his "Father Confessor,"[59] he began making regular entries by September, a habit that he was to continue for almost thirty years. Keeping the diary must also have been a psychological relief, because in Delta he felt he had to hold his tongue about so much.[60] Still brooding about the war, he had decided to defer enlistment. Edith concurred in his decision, assuring him that "your country needs your mental services more than your physical service."[61] But his letters to her included grim war news: a Queen's classmate killed in action, and the parents of a clerical colleague drowned on the *Lusitania*.[62]

In late March and early April, his side still paining him constantly, Lorne sat down and wrote twelve exams for Victoria College with the Reverend Calvert as invigilator. His boast to Edith that he could learn more in private study than at Victoria was borne out. He received six firsts. Lorne's sister reported from Toronto that Dean Wallace had praised him to his classmates for his outstanding performance despite his illness, calling him "one of the most brilliant men in the university."[63] By May, he felt well enough to register to write ten more Victoria exams in the late summer. He became president of the local baseball club and spearheaded an upgrading of the status of his local Masonic lodge within the Masonic hierarchy. In June, he was asked by the local women's institute to address them on how to raise children. The topic prompted an ironic joke to Edith about his mother's dominance: "I myself was 'rared' along a clothes line, rather tied at the end of one."[64]

Lorne had begun to buck a little at the end of his mother's line, however. His struggles with the Victoria authorities continued as he persisted in his desire to go to Union. As soon as he began meeting obstacles from the Methodist bureaucracy at Victoria and in the west, his spine stiffened. He succeeded in getting transferred to the jurisdiction of the Montreal Conference, leaving his western ministry behind him. But Victoria College still did not want to lose such a promising student. Even the mission board – with whom he was still planning to go eventually to the Far East – was brought into play to oppose the switch to Union.[65] "This fall," Lorne mused to Edith apprehensively, "I have an unusual opportunity, but instead of N.Y. I may yet have to propitiate the gods of the Methodist Discipline."[66] Another bureaucratic ploy had him furious:

> Edith can you imagine the latest[?] The [Methodist] conference
> has made some mistake in recording my mission work in the West
> and the last dodge to hold me up on leaving Vic [is] because I
> have a year's more probation! Furious? I told them unless they
> quit their sickening work and entered me with work complete, I'd
> jump the Methodist ministry entirely. And mind you Edith, our
> local man [Calvert] stuck up when I said that and replied, "Lawn
> [i.e., Lorne] we never like, we senior brethren, to be dictated to
> by probationers!" Ye immortal spooks!! I said "Mr. C. I call that
> unqualified arrogance." That was a week ago and I'm more of the
> opinion still.[67]

Finally, at the end of July, Lorne resolved to go to Union at any cost. He could not bring himself to report his mother's reaction to Edith, choosing instead to describe her ally, Calvert, as "bloated with anger."[68]

He asked Victoria to grant him credit for his planned Union work toward a Victoria BD. He was nervous about the decision, not wanting to abandon either Canada or Methodism. Yet he was resolute, he told Edith: "I only hope [the Victoria authorities] treat me more leniently. I want to be a Canadian and a Methodist. It would almost break my heart to have any strife, or any action that would render my ministry to our church severed. But as your Aunt Alice said – Personality then system."[69]

While he awaited Victoria's verdict, Lorne studied, coached baseball, taught Sunday school, and even managed a week-long canoe trip. With a friend, he paddled up the St Lawrence through the Thousand Islands to Kingston and back home via the Rideau Canal system, turning south toward Delta. The two were "brown as Indians, and hard as nails."[70] In August, on an excursion with friends to Ogdensburg, New York, just across the St Lawrence from Prescott, Ontario, he saw Edith Chown, home from the west for the summer via the Great Lakes steamer *Harmonic*.

Shrewdly, Lorne avoided pressing Edith to agree to marry. As a result of this reverse psychology, she edged closer to commitment. After their meeting, she admitted that, little by little, he had won a place in her life, and that, when she had seen him, she had found herself hoping that he would propose. Still, Edith wrote that she wavered about marriage: "In everything I do I wish for you. I think of you the last thing at night and the first thing in the morning. Does this mean nothing, Lorne? If it does, why do I feel so, and if it doesn't, why can't I say yes? ... I can't understand what holds me back? Is it because you haven't told me yourself?"[71] In response, on her twenty-fifth birthday, Lorne wrote Edith just the declaration she craved: "I love you in a thousand ways that I can never tell ... so, on your birthday, I ... offer, in answer to your question, the choicest gift a man may possess – his love."[72]

Arguably, despite her suitor's zeal, Edith's doubts were well founded in some respects. She rightly realized that much of their courtship had been conducted only through letters. In fact, the two had been able to spend very little time with each other since leaving Queen's. Moreover, Lorne soon informed Edith that he would give up anything for her except his "call."[73] He knew that Edith was unhappy about the thought of life as a minister's wife, especially in foreign fields. In later years, did Edith look back on this declaration of career first as prophetic?

In the meantime, on 16 September, just as he was coming down with a bout of "la grippe," Lorne learned that Victoria had at last given him permission to go to Union.[74] Jubilantly, he wrote one last set of nine examinations for Victoria.[75] The Delta Methodist Sunday School presented him with a set of cufflinks.[76] He left Delta on 28 September, his mother clinging to him in tears, praying "Oh, be strong."[77]

LORNE'S VERY rail journey to New York City forced him to continue defining himself. At Morristown, New York, in an incident that henceforth underlay his desire to give substance to Canadian nationalism, the U.S. immigration agent refused to accept "Canadian" as his citizenship. The official insisted: "O no you ain't [Canadian] – there's no Canadians." Without time between trains to debate, an indignant Lorne had to declare himself Irish![78] He arrived bleary-eyed in New York City at 5:30 a.m. on 29 September 1915. He took the subway to Columbia University and Union Theological Seminary.

Lorne was awed and delighted by Union. Affiliated with 20,000-student Columbia University, Union Theological Seminary had been founded in 1836 by a group of liberal Presbyterians. It had soon gained a reputation for excellence and liberality, with a distinguished faculty and a theological library of half a million volumes. Lorne arrived a few years after Union had declared itself non-denominational (1904) and moved (1910) to a campus on scenic Morningside Heights adjacent to Columbia University and the Hudson River.[79] He joined students from all over the world, including some twelve Canadians, his friends Bill Topping and Eldred Chester among them. Topping, an exuberant "go-getter," also planned to become a missionary. The two shared a double room in residence at Union and hoped to go overseas in tandem, as Lorne had irreverently outlined to Edith the year before: "We are planning ... to cross the 'great divide' together. With my lectures in Chinese and Bill a perfect Chinese linguist I hope to be able to read at least slowly and speak the Ping-Pong parlay-boo falteringly before I go."[80] Meanwhile, the two studied together and enjoyed New York outings.

Lorne loved the spirit of ecumenism and of critical inquiry at Union in contrast to what he saw as the "mediocrity" of Victoria where things were run "like a Hornerite camp meeting."[81] At Union "liberality [was] ... the watchword," and there was a strong flavour of the social gospel in the air. Dazzled, he wrote Edith: "Here is something different from any school you can imagine. Men have come from all over the world. All are men of high academic training and all here to work ... You are always hearing yourself addressed with strange accents. There is none of the

Two Canadian theological students at Union Theological Seminary: Lorne Pierce (right) and his friend Bill Topping, New York City, 1916. Courtesy of Beth Pierce Robinson

'grimness' of the lower schools – I can't describe it. All are [here] to prepare themselves for big things and they only talk of big things." Union's religious and social mores were something of a shock to him, however: "At chapel yesterday when Prof [Harry Emerson] Fosdick was inaugurated the service was a strange union of Roman Catholic and Protestant worship. All the professors smoke. The President gives dances and Barnard College [ladies] are invited. It all seems so strange at first."[82]

Indeed, some of Lorne's early reactions to Union and to New York City were narrow enough to suggest that the boy might be out of Victoria College but Victoria was not entirely out of the boy. Never having lived in a multiracial metropolis, he was at first naively racist and uneasy about this aspect of the city. Four days after his arrival, he told Edith about the place where he and Topping took meals: "We eat at the Rox-borough a rather nifty place just across the avenue. The only objection we have to it is that all the servants are Negroes – all polish and politeness, but black. Bill and I think of going further down to the Berncroft Club where the whole outfit is white – even to the dress suit fronts which are not always [white] in cafes!"[83]

Two weeks later, Lorne's racial attitudes were beginning to moderate as he again wrote of porters: "Wherever you turn here there is a negro porter – 'Morning sah!' 'Help you sah!' One chap is from British Guiana and since he saw our tiny Union Jack he almost lives outside our door. However, they are very courteous and obliging and very handy too."[84] In outings to New York parks, however, where they were surrounded by spooning couples, Lorne and a friend reacted with a puritanical smug-ness that suggested his mother's prayer that he "be strong" morally was being answered: "[We saw] sailors and kitchen maids; young bejewelled, be-gaudy bucks, in flashy cravats and imitation diamonds, and giddy girls in imitation furs chewing Tutti-Frutti. We came around a bend in the walk rather quickly to find two 'under a light' in the midst of the longest kiss I ever saw! It's a great feeling … to walk unscathed through Babylon, with a feeling of serene indifference and superior virtue!"[85]

Lorne's mail from home encouraged such virtue. He was deeply grate-ful to his father, who was financing his education. Edward Pierce wrote his son in true paterfamilias style: "I know you are doing your best to make something of yourself. We are proud of you that we have not anx-ious thoughts that you are going wrong as [are] many others. I am thank-ful for the Health that we are having and that we are able to supply the means. I feel that the Lord is a coworker in all our plans."[86] Meanwhile, Harriet Pierce – whose letters to Lorne often began with "My dear wee Bubbie" – wrote to say that she was "unaccountably lonely" when his usual letter did not arrive one afternoon. A week later, an agitated Lorne fretted to Edith that he had not heard from his parents in a week, "the first time in my life it has ever happened."[87]

If Lorne felt compelled to keep in touch with Delta and its values, he also drank deep of high and low culture in New York. Never again in his life would he have sustained access to such riches, and he made the most of it. In December, he was invited to join Acacia, an elite Masonic fraternity, and he faithfully attended its lectures and dinners. In return, his fellow Acacians dubbed him "no old crumb of a high brow, but a jolly good fellow."[88] (The affiliation also had its practical benefits, just as it had in the west: when he mailed an Acacia pin as a gift to Edith, the postal clerk, a fellow Mason, let it through without duty payable.[89])

Lorne's diary is dotted with exuberant accounts of concerts, musicals, operas, lectures, and speeches – among them, a New York Philharmonic concert, speeches by Teddy Roosevelt and the suffragette Mrs Pankhurst, and the revue "The Kat Kabaret." But Lorne also saw the troubling side of New York – the poverty, the squalor, the slum children. He wrote of one of his daily walks: "Such ... poverty. I never go down to the N[ew] Y[ork] U[niversity] but my heart aches for those hundreds of children crowding Washington Square."[90] On another walk, he and a friend witnessed the police taking away the corpse of a man in evening dress who had just committed suicide.[91]

Such experiences made Lorne think hard about the nature of society and of human life. Given Union's strong social gospel orientation, his devotion to religion as a transforming reality in society was further stimulated. His future community work as a minister in Brinston at the end of the war was seeded in his encounter with the ideas of social gospel advocates like American Baptist clergyman and Christian socialist Walter Rauschenbusch, whose own experiences in New York City's Hell's Kitchen slum in the 1880s had led him to apply Christian beliefs to practical social ethics. In another legacy of his time at Union, in the early 1920s, in the columns of the *Christian Guardian*, Pierce frequently recommended *A Theology for the Social Gospel*, describing it as Rauschenbusch's "beautiful interpretation of the 'Social Gospel,' the very best that we possess ... a classic for years to come."[92] Just as the young Mackenzie King's exposure to the University of Chicago and the work of Jane Addams in Chicago two decades earlier had opened his eyes to the realities of modern urban North America, Lorne was influenced for life by what he saw and learned in New York City.

At Union, Lorne also plumbed the work of Friedrich Schleiermacher, the most influential liberal Protestant theologian of the nineteenth century, whom he took to referring to as "dear old Schleiermacher."[93] Schleiermacher's writings, which stressed, among other things, the need to win back the educated classes to religion, were shot through with romanticism. Religion itself he defined as a "sense and taste of the infinite," a declaration that led him to acknowledge the worth of faiths other than Christianity. In his own religious beliefs and literary tastes,

Lorne was influenced by Schleiermacher's downplaying of dogma and his contention that "people understand the world ... more through imaginative and intuitive experience in nature than by studying it through rational analysis and the scientific."[94] In New York City, Lorne's diary entries make it clear that he responded in this spirit to a performance of Beethoven's Ninth Symphony, which for him expressed in music "my idea of Heaven and God and Love."[95] In his later writing, he was to praise Schleiermacher's toleration and declare: "Methodist doctrine for Methodist doctrine's sake, and considered apart from truth for truth's sake, is as dead as the dodo."[96]

Lorne was once again compressing as much into a year's study as he could, writing seven exams at the end of his first semester and taking thirteen classes in his second semester to be able to complete the requirements for his Union degree in only a year. (Not surprisingly, he was ill no less than five times in October and November 1915 alone with what he called "la grippe."[97]) Preparing for a post in foreign missions, he took a course in comparative religions from Dr Beach, a visiting professor from Yale. Once again he was amazed at the breadth and lack of cant at Union, writing of Beach's approach: "You simply can't be a narrow missionary and study under him. He picks the best fruit from the Chinese tree of religion and knowledge and holds it up with a wonderful smile as if he said 'Isn't it amazing!' ... You know the very best [the Chinese] have – accept it or build on it. You bring so much that is good that they have not – incorporate it. Compromi[s]e to any extent so long as you do not destroy the integrity of your own [religion]."[98] Lorne had found the intellectual openness he had so craved.

Given such stimulus, Lorne did well academically. In the first semester, for example, he wrote three of seven exams with distinction, with an average of 87 per cent.[99] He also took two classes at New York University (NYU) on metaphysics and the philosophy of religion with Dr Charles Shaw, possible because NYU offered a master's degree concurrent with the Union BD. He and Bill Topping spunkily debated with Shaw on the nature of God, with the class supporting the two Canadians, as he told Edith:

We held out for a union of the cosmic and [anthropomorphic] conceptions of Deity, he for the cosmic alone. He said – "You are getting too chummy with God." He called it worshipping the golden calf or calfmorphism. God to us meant a world for all and also a Father, the highest type of man we could conceive of. [Shaw countered:] "Would you have the Deity a nice modern poppa, with a fancy vest, patent leather shoes and carrying a cheque book!" The last lecture he turned to me and said – "Well what is the latest style for the Deity on upper Broadway since Easter?" He seems very anxious over it doesn't he![100]

Lorne gained confidence at Union and developed some American-style showmanship worthy of Sam Slick – or of Teddy Roosevelt. He mused to Edith: "Here I am learning the value of bluff. Everyone has it. If one can make a bluff and then stand squarely behind it something's got to go. I prefer to call it confidence however. The difference between the Canadians here and the Yankees is rather marked in that respect."[101]

But, for all Lorne's high spirits, his year at Union Theological Seminary featured three interrelated sources of tension about his future – his plans to be a Far Eastern missionary, his relationship with Edith, and his need to decide whether to take part in the "terrible, brainless" war.[102] Lorne had voiced a desire to be a foreign missionary since adolescence, perhaps to have a clerical vocation that would place him far from his mother's control. Since the turn of the century, moreover, the Methodist Church had been very active in mission work, both in the west and abroad, and it was natural for a bright young man to think of that field. However, by the fall of 1915, several factors – the war, financial constraints, and unrest in China – had caused the flow of Canadian Methodist missionaries abroad slowed to a trickle. Edith mailed Lorne a newspaper clipping with an ominous headline about unrest in China's Yunan province: "Canadian missionaries Are in Danger in China."[103] Lorne was disappointed to hear in September that the Methodist mission board was planning to send only two men abroad that year, although it held out the hope that he could be sent to Japan or China in October 1916.[104]

A certain ambivalence about mission work also began to creep into Pierce's own thinking. One suspects that, for the ambitious young man, the enormity of the sacrifice, the isolation, and the obscurity of the mission fields as far as his home country was concerned had begun to sink in. The tension showed. Uncharacteristically, he had been struck by a fit of temper when he was approached about mission work at Victoria in December 1914. Mission work, he was now acutely aware, meant being "away from everything that makes life sweet ... [and] partings and sadness." Convinced that the recruiters failed to understand the enormity of the sacrifice, he burst out to them: "I'm going, I'm going, I'm getting ready to go some day if the Lord lets me, and I will go – if you will only take that card and go to the devil."[105] He still spoke of a year at Oxford, which would put off missionary work still further.

Meanwhile, Edward Pierce was writing him, pleading that Lorne's parents and country needed him back in Canada, given that "so many changes will have taken place before you return." Lorne told Edith that his father's letter "nearly tore my heart out as I read it through a mist."[106] He was still resolved to go abroad as missionary, but, as the year wore on at Union, missives from Dr Jesse H. Arnup and Dr James Endicott of the Canadian mission board were ever more indefinite. Finally, in April 1916, Endicott wrote that the board had decided that no men could be sent out in 1916 or 1917. Lorne was crushed.[107]

What next? Lorne's patriotism made him reluctant to accept an appointment through the U.S. Presbyterians to the staff of a theological college in Kobe, Japan, but by the spring of 1916 he was considering it.[108] If he was to go back to Canada, he wanted not a parsonage, but an appointment to a Canadian college, scarce as these were with so many Canadian students off to war. Increasingly, his desires seemed to be turning toward educational work, preferably at the university level. He mused to Edith: "If we could only find a place in one of our Canadian colleges where we might stay until the war is over. It would be getting definitely into the work we intend remaining in. Perhaps we should become so snug in it that we would not want to change ... Mother has always felt that my work would be in Education here, but I have no means of knowing upon what bases Mothers make their assumptions."[109]

Lorne's reluctance to do congregational work in Canada was also tied to his courtship of Edith. Their long separation had largely overcome Edith's reticence. By October, she was writing unabashedly: "I love you more and more each day."[110] Lorne exulted to his diary about the change. By November, she admitted that his long siege of her heart had prevailed: "I made up my mind that I was going to stop trying to come to some decision. I know now that 'it must be so' for I love you so dearly that you seem life itself. You are with me wherever I go. You are my last thought at night and the first in the morning. I feel now that when I see you in June I shall know 'beyond a shadow of a doubt' ... I know I shall love you with all my heart."[111]

Lorne joyously informed Edith that he had long ago bought the engagement ring – a band with five diamonds in a Tiffany setting. Ever the determined optimist, he had actually had the ring made when he was in Fillmore, Saskatchewan. In New York City that spring, he ordered a platinum wedding band for his bride-to-be.[112] But even as he rejoiced, he began to make decisions about their future as a couple. His decisions reveal much about his attitudes toward women and feminism, attitudes that would shape both the future course of his marriage and his dealings as a publisher with female writers. Stimulated as he had been by Alice Chown, he was by no means a wholehearted convert to feminism. While he felt that women had a "sane and legitimate" right to the vote,[113] he was wary of what he saw as extreme feminism.

When they were both still living in Saskatchewan, Lorne had asked Edith Chown if she were still an "equal righter," adding somewhat anxiously: "If you must be one be a nice kind one, not the variety that want to draw and quarter every poor unfortunate son of apple eating Adam."[114] In another letter from the west, he had declared himself "glad we have a better brand of women in Canada who are satisfied to use peaceful means [for rights], rather than shake a tomahawk under the nose of 'poor man.'"[115] Lorne's qualified approach to feminism perhaps resulted from his mother's dominance and his desire not to be subject to "petticoat government" once more. Certainly, he instinctively chose for his wife someone far less strong-willed than his mother; Edith was a gentle and vulnerable young woman without living parents, and her emotional needs were professedly great. Lorne was clearly contracting a marriage where he would be the dominant figure. This state of affairs became apparent in New York City, both in his theoretical view of his fiancée and in the decisions he took.

Lorne in fact subscribed to the traditional view of woman as "inspiring angel" to the opposite sex. Before he left for Union, he had told Edith that she and his mother exemplified "the innate purity of two lofty souls who kept me true [to my ideals]."[116] In New York City, with the engagement in view, he urged Edith to forget her fears about their union in a way that bespoke his conviction that women were meant above all to function as "angels of the house," and as such were primarily creatures of emotion and intuition: "A girl's religion is the religion of love and she can never be satisfied with anything else, warm, sweet and quick to discern, a love that goes out because it must, and in loving finds love. I believe this. Just trust that glory of womanhood Edith and I know you will arrive at a certainty and joy that cannot be dimmed. It is woman's one sure and infallible guide. Love cannot err. I trust to you that yea or nay [to me], the result will be the verdict of your whole Love-nature crying out: 'It must be so!'"[117] "Earth's noblest thing," Lorne wrote, was "a woman perfected."[118] For her part, Edith embraced the role of help-mate, declaring that "teaching or business life never appealed to me, I've wanted to make a home – there to love and be loved." She wished their life together to be one of "understanding, forgiveness and love."[119]

Interestingly, once sure of Edith, Lorne began to write to her in terms that suggested mastery. He began using metaphors of imprisonment and captivity relative to her, as in a January 1916 letter: "You must not be away from me again little sweetheart, never, but so near I can smooth your hair and hold you and kiss your cheeks and forehead and lips[,] just smother you and blind you and make you love's prisoner."[120] Lorne also coined a nickname for Edith suggestive both of his need to have the emotional upper hand and of the future dynamic of their relationship. His cultural feast in New York included a performance of Puccini's opera *Madame Butterfly* in late October.[121] After seeing it, he fell into the habit of ad-dressing Edith as "My own Little Butterfly" or "Cho Cho San."[122] On one level, given that Lorne was expecting to be sent to Japan or China as a missionary, the nickname was perhaps understandable. But he seized on the name and the role for Edith with real tenacity. Four months after seeing the opera, he still referred to it: "You have seen *Butterfly* again by now haven't you? Isn't it a sweet thing. At least the one played here by the Land Opera Co. was divine. That very night I named you my Cho Cho San – my own Little Butterfly. I love the name because it fits you and is my ideal for you. The little girl in the story was so happy at first, but my Little Butterfly will always be proud and happy."[123]

Despite his determination to alter in his own marriage the scenario in which Butterfly is emotionally neglected and abandoned by the Amer-ican officer Pinkerton, Lorne even referred to himself as "Capt. Pink-erton Pierce" in another letter.[124] The nickname in fact foreshadowed the difficulty Pierce would have in devoting a great deal of time to his wife because he felt so driven by the demands of his career. Ominously, during these early days of their engagement, both Lorne and Edith re-ferred to this propensity on his part, while each unwisely (if understand-ably) denied the possibility that it could harm their relationship. When Edith learned in the spring of 1916 that Lorne had been out buying art prints for their future household,[125] she wrote wonderingly: "You are so different from the boy I knew two and a half years ago. I had you cata-logued as a book-worm, shut up in a study, with a placard on the door,

'Silence, no admittance.'"[126] Lorne put the finger on the same tendency in himself in a letter written about the same time: "I pity many a wife of a professional man because his office, his study, his fraternity take all his time. It is a terrible temptation I know – books call down upon you with imperative voices, but which is the greater – an extra book read, that article finished, or the sublime partnership of husband and wife. My great sin is asceticism but I think it is done more to the call of the class room than any natural 'bent.' However when I play you must and when I go you may. And 'If' I turn into a bookmark some time when you want to chat or crave a romp on a road just pinch me!"[127]

Lorne was in fact to prove an exceedingly difficult man to "pinch," and his obsessive work habits were to create marital conflict in the years ahead. But, as Edith had pointed out earlier, one of the limitations of their courtship had been that they had lived at a distance since leaving Queen's. They had never spent more than a day or two together at a time, and never alone, as Edith at least was uneasily aware. She asked Lorne: "Don't you think we have missed a lot by writing our thoughts instead of saying them?"[128] Indeed, by 1916, Edith began to learn what it meant to play second fiddle to Lorne's "call." From the beginning of the relationship, she had insisted she had no taste for the role of parsonage wife. She was frank about it in 1916: "As long as there is no parsonage connected with your plans I shall be with you in whatever you do in Japan, China or Canada, next fall or next year or a year from next fall."[129] Lorne had urged her to be forthright on the subject: "You know we are partners now and you must assert your little ego! You know better than anyone else what you would like and I am willing to make any concession that will enhance your life and fill it with happiness."[130] Although he was being deluged with requests to return to ministerial work in Ontario, where the war had left Methodism shorthanded,[131] Lorne hastened to assure Edith that he would not ask her to submit to the "Inquisition cell," the "slow death" of a rural parsonage: "Do not worry 'wee won' I'll not be an evangelist nor force you to become the mistress of a country manse and teach the Sunday School! No chance! As a country pastor I would be a freak, as an evangelist nihil. There is but one work I am suited for and that I must have."[132]

Soothing words, but events proved otherwise. Edith had to give way, the first of many times. It came about in this way. For all the intellectual excitement of his year of study in New York City, the spectre of war dogged Lorne. The very month of his arrival at Union, he wondered if he should enlist instead, asking himself and Edith if he could perform as heroically in Asian mission fields as he could in Flanders.[133] When he began to hear disturbing accounts of what the trenches were really like from friends who had enlisted, he felt like "a bounder [to be] living in safety and ease."[134] During the Christmas break from Union, en route to Delta by train, Lorne surprised his cousin Clifford Pierce with a visit to the officer training camp in Brockville, where Clifford was preparing to be sent to France.[135] Once back at Union in the new year, Lorne often clashed with pro-German colleagues, particularly after the Canadians were sent into a patriotic frenzy when the Canadian Parliament buildings burned down that February. Some classmates taunted Lorne, asking why he did not enlist if he felt so strongly about Canada's part in the war.[136] Two of his Canadian fellow students had already left Union to enlist. March brought news that Clifford was off to the front, "confident that the Huns are going to be whipped."[137] Lorne himself received a letter from a Montreal clergyman urging him to enlist at once.[138] In reality, however, Lorne did not want to join up immediately. He still hoped that he would not be needed, and that he could instead "embark on what is the passion of my life" – missionary work.[139] But he also worried about the ignominy of ultimately being conscripted rather than volunteering.[140]

Lorne also worried that accepting an American overseas appointment would be "running away" when his country needed him. He was also pained by American ignorance of Canada. He described an encounter with one of his Union professors: "People have the strangest notions of Canada. I walked down the steps the other day with Dr. Brown. It was [snowing] slightly outside. He said – 'I suppose you will begin to live when you see the snow coming. How long does your summer last in Canada?' I wonder if they think we are Eskimoes?"[141]

At the same time, Lorne was brooding about the Methodist Church, and his place in it. Even as he railed against its conservatism, he felt that it needed him. Lorne would occasionally mutter that Union was "social crazy,"[142] but on the whole he applauded its social gospel orientation and thought of working in an urban mission house if he had to return to Canada. He was convinced that the New York experience had given him a range of vision that the Canadian church needed. However, when some Victoria graduates were tapped for Montreal ministries ahead of him, Lorne felt he was being discriminated against as a progressive Union man – as he put it, "taboo'd by the orthodox." He burst out to Edith about the narrowness of the Methodist Church of Canada and the need to change it: "I feel Little Butterfly as if I were back in the Middle Ages, when you had to think and act by the rule of the Vatican, or else have your thumbs pulled by an Inquisition! If we could ever get securely into the church, I wonder if there isn't some chance of bringing a broader vision to it. I am very proud of our old church in many ways, and my heart is with it, else I should not have worked so hard to fit myself to serve in it. But the little prejudice that meets you everywhere makes the heart sick."[143]

Overall, church and country were beginning inexorably to draw Lorne home. The "gods of the Methodist Discipline" had a greater hold on him than he had perhaps realized. He softened toward Canadian Methodism at the end of January, when he heard that Victoria College would grant him a BD *ad eundem* after he had finished at Union, with no further course work.[144] Finally, at the end of April, as he put it to his diary, he decided to return to "stand by Canada and Methodism."[145] Despite the fact that any mission appointment was at least two years away and no position was available at a Canadian theological college, he agreed to accept the rural charge of Frankville and Toledo, small eastern Ontario villages near Delta.[146]

Lorne immediately wrote Edith that, while she might think him "fickle" to accept a rural charge, he felt that he had done "the right thing." He argued that he could not "run away" from the church just because he could not get what he wanted, and that while Canadians were "sacrificing," he could not live in safety under American jurisdiction. Interestingly, he saw the decision as also honouring his mother: "Most of all perhaps, even above loyalty to Canada and to Methodism was a desire to reverence my parents. Everything I am I owe to their sacrifice, and to go back on their church, which to them is home and in which they have worked all their lives, would break mother's heart. It has been her proud ambition to see me, not great in name but great in service, in the church."[147]

What of Lorne's promise to Edith never to accept a Canadian parsonage? There is a elaborate, defensive rhetoric in the letter to her about his decision. He juxtaposed his mother and Edith, seeking to convince her that she was nonetheless primary: "And as I sat in the park, with the breeze blowing across the Hudson upon me, I said, 'I guess Edith will not blame me for trying, in this great crisis of choice, to gratify the dreams of a little mother for her boy, for whom she nearly sacrificed her own

life to give him to the world!' I am not sentimental Edith dear. I love my
mother very dearly, but I love you more, more [than] that mother and all
the world, and in the light of these two loves I have chosen to go back to
Canada."[148] Lorne hastily added that he knew Edith was "disappointed"
and that he too disliked the idea of a parsonage. He released her from all
promises to marry him, yet he still spoke soothingly of "only two years
and then for our little home among the cherry blossoms." Edith wrote
back on 4 May, admitting that his decision was a "very great disappointment." Although she postponed a decision on whether she would join
him in parish work until she saw him, she added, in the tradition of the
helpmate: "I love you too dearly to let you undertake a work alone that
you feel you ought to do."[149] The incident was Edith's first major taste of
self-abnegation as part of "the glory of womanhood," but it was to be far
from her last. Lorne was displaying the single-minded devotion to his
sense of mission that would mark his career.

THE REST OF Lorne's time at Union passed in a blur. He got a last
taste of New York culture, wrote a spate of examinations, and on 12 May
1916 learned that he had received his degree with first-class honours. He
bolstered Edith's spirits by crediting her: "From the day you said 'I love
you Lorne' until now I have felt that nothing could stand in my way."[150]
On 16 May, Lorne and Bill Topping (who had decided to serve with the
American Congregational Church) took part in convocation.

Given Lorne's high academic standing, one of his professors arranged
that he travel home via Boston to be interviewed by the Congregational
Board for an appointment at Doshiba University, Japan. But Lorne was
resolved not to serve overseas under American church auspices. He made
the border crossing into Canada on Victoria Day, and he saw the experience as symbolic. He wrote loftily to Edith, who was still teaching in
Regina: "When I crossed the boundary yesterday a great Union Jack was
waving in a strong westerly breeze and I couldn't help saluting Canada
and you."[151] Once home in Delta, the flag was also in evidence. Lorne
felt the tug of war once more. He described the experience to Edith, who
herself had just had two friends widowed by the war:

> This morning our Delta company of some 50 men from here
> marched away. All were old friends, some older and some younger
> than myself. They swung quickly thru the street leading to the
> station, the town following in silence. Men I had never known

to shed a tear broke down, mothers hung [on] to their sons, and wives with babes in their arms to their husbands. I could hardly bear it. One of the fellows came over to me and shook hands. He said – "There are a lot here that haven't gone – you can get them, you know how to drill them – round them up and come along yourself." Argument was impossible[.] I simply had to walk away.[152]

But a few days later, Lorne became a full-fledged recruit in another army. To his mother's joy, the long-awaited day of his ordination finally arrived – 4 June 1916 – as the Montreal Methodist Conference convened in Smiths Falls. His parents and his sister travelled some twenty miles up from Delta for the service, as did many Delta young people. The assemblage watched as Lorne took his vows, with Roy Stafford, one of his fellow ordinands, garbed in khaki. All Lorne's accounts of his ordination – to Edith, in his diary, to his children in later life – emphasized the sense of mission it aroused in him. He wrote solemnly to Edith that day: "By this ordination both you and I have been set apart. Each new morn will witness our rebirth into a great waiting world of things to be done. As for myself my whole passion is Christ – to know more of Him and to show more of Him."[153]

In the text of his ordination sermon, preached in his home church in Delta on 11 June, Lorne paid tribute to his parents, especially his mother, as "my first and best teachers in the things of God." He continued: "My idea of Christ grew I think when I first looked into my mother's face – I lisped first those two wonderful words Jesus. Mother. Before my birth I was dedicated to the priesthood of Christ. I was conceived in that spirit of consecration. I have known nothing else."[154] Ordination sermons at this time often linked the godly mother and the inspiration of home with the conversion experience.[155] In Lorne's case, the tribute was especially apt. His ordination was to become the organizing principle of his life.

Lorne's ordination came to pass, but the Frankville parsonage did not. Right after the ceremony, the Reverend Basil Thompson, the minister of St Paul's, a prosperous congregation in the Glebe area of Ottawa, hurried up to speak to him about a possible appointment as his assistant. He introduced the fledgling minister to several parishioners who had come out to Smiths Falls. By 8 June, the plum Ottawa post was his. As people congratulated him, Lorne fretted about whether he could be "useful and great in service." He had no wish for congratulations until "I know whether I am a success or not."[156]

As Lorne did the "lonesome, tiresome work" of packing for Ottawa, he worried – about his new post, about his future with Edith, and about the "horrible war." His mother – who had taken two months to write a congratulatory letter to Edith after Lorne had written his parents of their engagement in mid-January – added to his stress. Lorne said nothing to Edith at the time, but in fact his mother urged him that June to think carefully about marrying Edith. After all, Edith Chown was a delicate girl who was not a devout Methodist (why she danced!) and who professedly did not care for the role of minister's wife.[157]

Lorne felt beleaguered. Was his mother correct? And what of the future, with the war raging? True, he had defied the powers at Victoria College to get the academic credentials he wanted, and had come out of two years at Victoria and Union fortified in character and intellect. But what lay ahead? In New York City, he had become more aware of his own Canadianness and of a need for Canada's sense of nationality to gain more definition and more recognition, but in what way could he best serve his country to this end – as a man of the cloth or in khaki?

5

Orange Blossoms, the Cloth, and Khaki

Marriage, Ministry in Ottawa,
and Army Service, 1916–1918

[St. Paul's] is a chance in a thousand and if I make good it simply means I have stepped out of college into first place.

Lorne Pierce on his appointment to St Paul's Methodist Church, Ottawa, June 1916[1]

The man who does not join in the storm and stress of life by the action of inward and spiritual force, clear convictions and strong character is lost.

Lorne Pierce diary entry on his enlistment, 6 March 1917

On 23 June 1916 Lorne Pierce took the train to Ottawa to take up his new duties as assistant minister at St Paul's Methodist Church. Unpacking his carpetbag, he found that his mother had pinned Scriptural quotations to his belongings. "Let not your heart be troubled," he read as he stared at his socks and shirts, "Neither let it be afraid (John 14:1)."[2]

Lorne preached his first sermon at the Sunday evening service on 25 June. The wife of his senior minister, Basil Thompson, greeted him with the news that her husband had been promoted to major in the Canadian Army and was off to serve as a senior chaplain at Petawawa and Valcartier military camps. Lorne would now in effect be in charge in his first posting, a plum pulpit. The congregation of some two hundred families had been organized in 1911 to serve the prosperous middle- to upper-middle-class suburb of the Glebe, which had developed in Ottawa west of the Rideau Canal and south of Parliament Hill and Centretown since the turn of the century.

However, in 1914, war had forced a halt to construction of the Glebe's imposing new Methodist church at the corner of Second Avenue and Lyon Street. When Lorne arrived in 1916, the congregation was still trying to raise $130,000 towards the structure's completion; the church, with its grand dome, would not in fact be finished and dedicated until 1924. Meanwhile, services were held in the finished basement of the structure.[3]

Mrs Thompson generously gave Lorne the use of two rooms in the parsonage, but with his September wedding approaching, he needed to find a flat.[4] In the meantime, he was a little overawed by his new congregation. He wrote to Edith: "The personnel of the congregation is above the average. I don't know how many doctors, teachers, principals, graduates, and heads of departments in the Civil Service there are. All seem to have cars and summer homes."[5] Lorne even found some of his flock a bit "fast." On one pastoral visit to a prominent matron, he drank grape juice while she drank claret and announced that she was off to Bermuda because she was "a nervous wreck."[6]

As he sipped juice in the hot, humid Ottawa summer, Lorne worried about how best to be "great in service." Before him lay a daunting round of services, sermons, Sunday Schools, youth groups from Epworth League to Scouts, pastoral calls, teas, bazaars, baptisms, weddings, and funerals. He had always fretted over his sermons, finding it hard to be both inspirational and "close to the people."[7] One Sunday morning, he even experimented, with the advice of one businessman in his congregation, with adapting the rhetoric of business salesmanship ("Attention, Interest, Decision, Action") to his divine message. "I think," he noted hopefully, "maybe I'll be able to preach yet."[8]

Lorne knew that the Methodism of his day put great stress on the power of the word. By this time, the early emotionalism, revivalism, and experientialism of Canadian Methodism had evolved into a new outlook that infused its sermon literature: "Experience was now clothed in the rhetoric of inspiration and heroic individualism. The religion of experience had become a romantic evangelism."[9] What Lorne gave the congregation of St Paul's was an eloquence updated at Union Theological Seminary, one mindful (despite his one foray into commercial rhetoric) of the pitfalls of capitalism, bigotry, and Scriptural literalism.

The young minister did raise a few eyebrows. Lorne reported to Edith that a vestryman had warned him that two or three congregants "had it in" for him because his last sermon had been interpreted as "socialist."[10]

Later in the year, his sermons on the Virgin Birth and the Holy Spirit, with non-literal views of both, caused "warm discussion."[11] However, in the Glebe, Lorne encountered a Jewish storekeeper who complimented the friendly young minister on his "liberality." In a letter to Edith, Lorne attributed his liberalism to the influence of Union, saying he was thankful that he and Topping had taken courses with Rabbi John Beekman, which had often prompted the duo to walk "up and down Washington Square till dark reconciling the two creeds." In Ottawa, he added, his encounter with the Jewish merchant made him think further about the close-mindedness of much Christianity: "Unfortunately I was the only one – [the] only Christian who talked with him in a sympathetic manner. He wondered at what he called my 'liberalism.' I corrected him and called it Christianity ... I think it is the saddest thing. For 2000 years we have been praying 'That all may be one,' and we Christians have been making an answer to our prayers impossible by our narrowness."[12]

As 4 July, the date of Edith's arrival in Ottawa, drew near, it was harder for Lorne to concentrate on pastoral work. The teaching year over, Edith had left Regina for the Montreal home of her brother Clarence and his wife, Lilian. On the appointed day, Lorne hurried down to Ottawa's Union Station to meet the fiancée he had not seen for a year. As soon as he caught sight of Edith, any doubts his mother may have sown about his choice of bride vanished ("a year of expectation gloriously come true"). Even so, he did not kiss Edith, self-conscious about embracing her in public.[13] The two decorously shook hands, then boarded the Montreal train.

That night, at Clarence Chown's Westmount house, as a table of four played bridge in the other room, Lorne slipped the engagement ring on Edith's finger ("The proudest hour I have lived through"). The two exchanged "love's first kiss" – their first-ever embrace after years of courtship largely conducted by mail.[14] Then Lorne "prayed a little silent prayer with her in my arms that God would keep me true and make me all she deserved."[15] After two chaperoned days, which included an hour in the listening booth of a Victrola store and walks in Mount Royal Park, he had to return to Ottawa. But Edith's anxieties about the engagement, like Lorne's, were allayed. She wrote him on 6 July: "You are everything I could wish."[16]

In Ottawa, Lorne finally found an apartment at 75 Second Avenue in the Glebe. The flat was in a solid three-story red brick house – its bay windows surmounted with gray keystone motifs. He wrote Edith that the two would "play house" while they worked toward a missionary career in Japan.[17]

At this time, Lorne visited patients at the Lady Grey tuberculosis sanitorium on Carling Avenue, a couple of miles from the Glebe. The fear he expressed after his sanitorium visits was not unusual in an age when the "white plague" was a major killer, but his revulsion was ironic in view of the diagnosis he himself would soon receive. He wrote Edith: "The patients were gasping and choking. Isn't that the most horrible disease? ... Everybody seemed to be dying, and walking around like ghosts. I ... wanted to wash, and sterilize myself! I fear the thing like the plague. There is no reason for it, as none of our 'ancestors' have toppled off that way, but it is so loathsome."[18]

Another spectre hung over Lorne. In Ottawa, far more than in still-neutral New York City, the war was omnipresent. One of his first outings was to a war benefit fair, with former prime minister Sir Wilfrid Laurier in attendance. Shortly thereafter, he accompanied a soldiers' day excursion to Britannia Bay and made another trip to Union Station to wave a contingent off to the front. Lorne's clerical garb did not prevent the white feather being waved at him. By the autumn of 1914, the Methodist Church unqualifiedly supported the "righteousness" of the Allied cause, and the enlistment rate among Methodist clergy was high.[19] Within a couple of years, accusing eyes were apt to turn on an apparently healthy young man not in khaki, even a minister. Lorne fumed to Edith about one exchange at a St Paul's prayer meeting, when he was reproached for not joining up by the wife of a Kingston minister who had enlisted. She asked him peremptorily: "When are you going to drop the civilian [status]? Don't you think you should be in it?"[20] Lorne flinched.

For the moment, however, life on the home front was full of promise. After a short visit from Edith at the end of July, Lorne looked forward to a joint trip to Delta in August before their wedding. On 1 August, however, he consulted a doctor "about my ears," the first hint of the major difficulties with his hearing that were to affect his career so profoundly.[21] Meanwhile, on 3 August, his twenty-sixth birthday, he wrote in his diary: "I love my work, and I have been conscious of a big deep love [for Edith] going and coming all day."[22]

In late August, Lorne and his sister picked up Edith at her grandmother's home in Kingston. Back in Delta, the engaged couple set off by automobile one day for a picnic, and were not the least unhappy when car trouble delayed their return to the Pierce home. And then good night – "by the front door, with a bright moon flooding the silent hamlet and the trees about it."[23]

What of Mother Pierce during this visit? Did she welcome her future daughter-in-law warmly during their first-ever meeting? The diary is significantly silent on that point, although Lorne wrote cryptically of a "little sermon" given one morning for his exclusive benefit.[24] Whatever Harriet Pierce said, she was too shrewd not to have recognized that her son's mind was made up about his bride – he was as strong-willed as his mother – and she was also wise enough not to interfere between the couple once they were wed.

For her part, Edith, her wedding only weeks away, was doubtless think-ing of her new life. Like most women of her generation, she had trouble seeing herself as a fully equal partner. Even though she was a Queen's graduate and a qualified teacher, she lacked intellectual self-confidence. She had written Lorne in 1915 expressing her feelings of insecurity and inadequacy: "I am not what you think I am, at the best I am miserably stupid and deficient ... You have climbed up and up, while I seem to have slipped down further and further."[25] Such a reaction to Lorne's extreme idealization of womanhood – an idealization typical of his time – was understandable. But Edith was emotionally vulnerable, having lost her parents early in life.

Aware of her niece's vulnerabilities, Alice Chown had given her prag-matic advice about marriage. In 1913 Alice had written to her niece: "Nearly all the old conventions which you have been taught about womanliness and love are false. The one true thing is that love is the only justification for marriage. Because of your loving nature you will probably come out all right. Do not repress that. Give love."[26] But Alice was also concerned that Edith would not sufficiently value and develop herself independently of Lorne.[27] "I would like to give you such a consciousness of power that you would go out to front life knowing that your fate lay in your own hands. All that I have learnt by experience I want to pass over to you."[28] Around the time of the marriage, she stressed to Edith, not for the first time, the need to develop her own identity: "You must be encouraged to believe in your own potentialities, to have more faith in yourself and to develop them."[29]

Alice was equally forthright when she wrote to congratulate Lorne on the engagement, reminding him how different her niece's nature was from his: "She will never worry you as [I] may, by her radical opinions, she will be thoroughly nice but then she will never have the wild joy

Edith Chown Pierce on her wedding day, Kingston, 19
September 1916. Courtesy of Beth Pierce Robinson

of living the leaping from mental rock to mental rock, and never being
quite sure where she will land." But Lorne tended to resist such insights,
shortly thereafter describing Alice to Edith as too "anxious" for women's
"individuality" and "entire sanctification from matrimonial bondage."[30]
As for Edith, her view of her aunt as eccentric and "too advanced for
me"[31] probably led her to discount Alice Chown's advice about autonomy. Given the differing needs of husband and wife, the stage was set for
major tension in the Pierce marriage.

Alice Chown did announce that she would attend the wedding in
Kingston, assuring her relatives that only a wedding or a funeral could
bring her back to the city where she had been so constrained by domestic
duties as a young woman.[32] Lorne Pierce and Edith Chown were mar-

ried on 19 September 1916, at 11:30 a.m. on a clear and beautiful day, in the parlour of 30 Aberdeen Street, the home of Edith's maternal grandmother, Mrs Thomas Conley. A quarter-century later, Edith remembered the ceremony as "the sweetest thing," with all her "precious aunts" helping to prepare the wedding breakfast and Grandmother Elizabeth Conley "being mother to me and carrying out my mother's last wish" to look after her daughter.[33] Edith's uncle, the Reverend Edwin Chown, officiated. Lorne watched Edith in the fireplace mirror as she entered the parlour, blushing but composed in her white tulle-and-lace gown with a satin bow at the bosom, veil and flower wreath on her pinned-up hair. Lorne's sister and her fiancé, Lorne's college friend the Reverend Eldred Chester, were witnesses.[34]

If Alice could not alter the bride's self-image, she did influence the choice of honeymoon destination. She had written advising "something far away from big cities where you could gaze on the stars and the flowers and be glad that you were alive."[35] Accordingly, the newlyweds set off for Lake Placid in the Adirondacks, where Alice herself had made several visits long before.[36] They spent their wedding night at the Iroquois House on Tupper Lake en route to Stevens House, Lake Placid. There Lorne snapped a honeymoon photograph of Edith in a canoe, an apt metaphor for the balancing act of marriage. Lorne commented in his diary after the return to Ottawa: "I'm happier every hour!"[37] Then he carefully glued in a bit of verse he had clipped from the New York *Times* months before:

> Into my life she came,
> One golden day,
> Softly as blooms come
> Into the May ...[38]

Edith was given a welcoming reception by her new congregation on 11 October. She was anxious to do well in the church and at home: family lore has it that the new bride fainted in the production of her first apple pie. But, despite her fears, Edith plunged into a round of visiting, teaching Sunday School, and working with the young people of St Paul's Methodist Church. She joined the Order of the Eastern Star, the female auxiliary to the Masonic Order. Her new husband was a little discomfited when she even hinted that one of his sermons could be improved.[39] His diary records such cosy domestic scenes as the couple sitting "toasting their shins" by the kitchen range. He wrote of "wonderful vistas of love and happiness,"[40] while Edith in turn praised his "love, kindness thoughtfulness and understanding."[41]

THE NEW COUPLE were popular at St Paul's, but Lorne Pierce was also restless and troubled as the names of friends and classmates dotted the casualty lists from the Western front. Clippings of war news, troop departures, and the obituary of a Victoria College classmate are pasted into this portion of Pierce's diary.[42] Moreover, the Methodist Church was so pro-war at this period that it was criticized for its strong support of the government.[43] In February 1917 the Reverend Basil Thompson was criticized by the labour movement for an openly pro-conscription speech from the St Paul's pulpit during a leave from his chaplaincy at Camp Borden.[44]

The national debate over conscription certainly raised some uncomfortable personal issues for Thompson's assistant. Lorne, who would be eligible for such a draft, must have squirmed in his chancel pew as he listened to Thompson's pro-conscription homily. Did duty and conscience dictate that he enlist now? While he debated, the St Paul's Christmas card for 1916 unabashedly asked for "speedy and righteous victory for the Allies."[45]

Certainly, given that Lorne noted things like paying utility bills in his diary at this time, one suspects that the middle-class comfort of St Paul's did not challenge him sufficiently. The description of his life as assistant pastor that he sent to a Union Seminary newsletter betrays a sense that he had a greater destiny to discover; he wrote that he still hoped to go to Japan as a teacher.[46] He reacted bitterly early in 1917 when yet another round of interviews for a posting in the Far East with the Canadian mission board came to nothing, despite all the board's assurances. Lorne at last gave up his idea of foreign mission fields.[47] Just before that, he received a graphic letter from his cousin Clifford, written behind the lines in France, describing "the cauldron of strife and danger" at the front. His cousin told him that he had been "within sound of the guns" for over four months. Clifford went on to touch on the bond between them: "Someday I hope to be settled down close enough that we shall be able to see much of each other for as you say Lorne we are indeed more like brothers than cousins."[48]

Lorne began brooding over the how and when of enlistment. His parents were opposed,[49] and Edith trembled at the prospect. Certainly,

Lorne's health was not good. He had a long, nasty bout of flu in November 1916 which kept him invalided for several weeks, complicated by a painful nasal operation that month.[50] There were other obstacles as well. To die in battle would be the supreme patriotic sacrifice, but Lorne wanted long years on earth to contribute to church and country. He was candid in his diary entries about his ambivalence about enlisting. A man with a sense of mission, he knew enough about the battlefield to realize that he could well die ignominiously in the mud, all his dreams unrealized. One March day, he asked himself: "What more can a man do than die for his country?" He supplied the answer: "Live for it. It is a longer work and a more difficult and a harder one."[51]

However, Lorne knew there would be a price to be paid if he refused to enlist now. For him, the prospect of being seen as a shirker in the hour of his country's need, and then to be ignominiously conscripted in a few months, never to have the kudos of having voluntarily fought for Canada, was intolerable.[52] On 6 March, escorted by the Reverend Thompson, he went down the Ottawa recruitment office of the Royal Flying Corps, where he was accepted as medically sound and told to await call-up.

Edith broke down at the news, but then stoutly declared that she would rather have him go as "a combatant and a man, than [as] a chaplain and a chair warmer."[53] Some of his congregation, citing his gifts as a preacher, wondered why he wanted to go off to war, but they were not privy to his inner turmoil. The Ottawa newspapers enthusiastically wrote him up as a sky pilot turned combat pilot.[54] On 21 March the new recruit gave what he thought was his last sermon – only to learn that the Royal Flying Corps command had rejected him as over-age at twenty-six.[55] Nothing daunted, by 6 April, he had enlisted as a sergeant in the Army Medical Corps in the No. 15 Queen's Field Ambulance. He made a quick trip to Kingston, where the unit was based, to pick up his acting sergeant's uniform.[56] This time he was accepted: the army was hungry for men and the medicals not exacting.

A few days later, grim news. Before dawn on Sunday, 15 April, Lorne and Edith were jolted awake by a telephone call. Clifford Pierce had been killed at Vimy Ridge. The snub-faced cousin who had played college pranks with Lorne at Queen's was gone forever. Lorne's disjointed diary entry evokes his distress: "Clifford was killed at Vimy Ridge. Poor old chum. He's not dead, assist at morning service. Major [Rev.] Campbell preaches. 'All the angels are not dead.'"[57]

One of the two Great War soldiers whose loss haunted
Pierce: Lieutenant Clifford Pierce, killed at Vimy Ridge,
April 1915. Courtesy of Beth Pierce Robinson

Then the military authorities assigned the new soldier to do recruiting speeches in eastern Ontario. Although the Methodist Church had
openly supported recruiting efforts by the government,[58] Lorne was uncomfortable with the thought of encouraging men to go to the front,
where he himself had not yet served. But he resolved to do his best if
he could not go to France.[59] Acting Sergeant Pierce (he was not officially raised to the rank until October, after he had completed training[60])
began work on 9 April at the recruiting office on Ottawa's Sparks Street,
interesting two prospects the first evening. That spring and fall, he gave

recruiting speeches in such centres as Peterborough and Renfrew, and at the Ottawa Agricultural Exhibition, speaking between reels of the patriotic propaganda film *Canada in Khaki*. That he felt like a shill at times is hinted at in a letter to Edith from a Havelock hotel in May: "Before tea I sat in the parlour working out my oration, while a salesman tried to work a milking machine off on a farmer."[61]

At the end of April 1917, the Pierces left St Paul's and "all its dear good people" forever.[62] Edith found herself back at her grandmother's house in Kingston. The note Lorne had left for her when he enlisted had called her "Sio Sio San," and, like the protagonist of Puccini's opera *Madame Butterfly*, she was tasting the loneliness of a woman left behind by a man in uniform.[63] Lorne was posted to Barriefield Camp, near Kingston, where, after weeks of uncertainty, he was enrolled in the infantry instructor's training course. He had to live under canvas in the muddy, windswept camp on the shores of Lake Ontario, shivering through a wet spring and summer. On watch late one night, he wrote despondently in his diary: "How the wind sweeps old Barriefield these nights, damp and cold from the river. The tents flap their folds like the wings of a great vulture, and the tent ropes snap like scourges in the grasp of an angry Pharaoh. Soon I must march that long lonely wet half mile to Headquarters to hand in my Tattoo report."[64] In a photograph taken at this time, Sergeant Pierce, a wispy pencil moustache on his upper lip, looks thin and drawn.

Lorne still debated about whether to ask to be sent to France. His parents were apprehensive about the possibility, so much so that Edith told her husband to send his parents only "sunshiny letters."[65] Lorne's agonizing over whether to "go across" immediately was made grimmer by visits to his dead cousin's home in Kingston. After one visit, he wrote shakily in the diary that, when his aunt showed him Clifford's mud-spattered trench uniform and gas helmet, returned from the front to his devastated parents, "it was pathetic to see her hug it to her heart."[66]

For the moment, Lorne decided not to ask to be sent overseas. He would serve in Kingston, where he had been posted. He reminded himself that he had a responsibility to Edith to remain in Canada. Feeling that he was not "a born warrior," and unsure that he could stand the "severe physical strain" of the trenches, he was also increasingly driven by a sense of a wider destiny. His mother's Methodist regime and the years at Queen's had left him hungry to serve God and country. Thus spurred, he reasoned that asking to be sent overseas might be contradicting his ordination into God's service: "What about the call to serve [in the ministry]? Do I not owe it to My Maker to preserve what he has set apart? Am I not frustrating his plans for me and for the world?"[67] Using a military metaphor, he concluded that "my *country*, my *wife*, my *God*, my *self*" had "formed fours" to prompt him to remain at Barriefield for the time being.[68]

Even the joyful intervals of Lorne's life were now darkened by the war. In mid-June, he had leave in Delta. There, on 12 June, under an arch of lilacs on a sunny day, Lorne officiated at the marriage of his sister to his friend the Reverend Eldred Chester. Lorne, in uniform for the occasion, broke down at one point during the service. After seeing off Sara and Gus (as his intimates called him) on the long rail journey to their new home – the mining town of Rossland, British Columbia, with its huge new smelter – Lorne was melancholy. He wrote in his diary: "It was a hard thing to do to give the dear girl away. We have been chums so long and when will we see her again? Besides my enlisting seemed to leave the old home deserted. How I pitied poor father and mother – now just where they began, and in that big empty home. How they have toiled, and planned and scrimped for us."[69] He vowed to repay his parents by living the dedicated life they had envisioned for him.

Lorne's diary and letters for this period made it clear that his sense of service was increasingly yoked to a sense of nationalism. The spirit of public service at Queen's, the patriotism of the Great War, his perception of the lack of appreciation of Canada as a nation during his time in New York – all had worked to stimulate his thirst for patriotic service in wartime and beyond. On 1 July 1917, the fiftieth anniversary of Confederation, his diary entry paid tribute to "Miss Canada," the "Princess of Peace," who had been "baptized" by George Brown and Louis-Joseph Papineau with Sir John A. Macdonald as "godfather," and who was now "confirmed" by war. Lorne solemnly dedicated himself to Canada: "How nobl[y] she has developed and what a heritage of moral worth she is garnering for her sons! Canada! ... I wonder what humble part I shall play in the development of our land. O God make it worthy if not great and lasting if not spectacular. Create in me a new heart impelled by duty and devotion. Lift me up that I may draw some after Thee."[70]

In June 1917 Lorne had hoped to be posted as head orderly sergeant to Ongwanada Military Hospital, on the westerly outskirts of Kingston, but a sergeant whose work he did not respect was given the posting instead. Through the summer and early fall, he was held back to do the infantry sergeant instructor's course and serve as an orderly sergeant at Barriefield Camp. He chafed at the disappointment, and at being a "college man" who was not an officer.[71] A commission to lieutenant sought for him by his superiors never seemed to materialize. By September, he was disgusted by what he saw as the organizational mismanagement of the army, its "damnable ignorance and resistance."[72]

Alone in his drafty tent in the long nights, Lorne turned to intellectual pursuits, sitting "on an improvised Morris chair, my spine for a prop and a crude box[-]like affair for a desk."[73] By August, he was planning a flurry of articles, including one on H.G. Wells and Christianity for the Victoria College magazine.[74] But the article that brought him a wide audience was one he wrote for the popular mass-circulation *Canadian Magazine* on "The Gods of This New Era." With the article, he became part of a nation-wide debate on the wider spiritual and social significance of the war. The article, accepted in November 1917, appeared in the February 1918 issue. Pierce, identified as writing "on active service," sought to reassure Canadians about the state of Christianity in the midst of war: "There is much evil in the world, and yet there is so much real and wonderful goodness, love, heroism, and sacrifice that God must be somehow coming to His own in the hearts of men."[75] His Christian idealism was resolute: "The tempest and the earthquake are limited and there is bound to be a progressive accomplishment of a plan and a culmination in the enthronement of righteousness."[76] Pierce, in company with many leading Methodist clergyman, thus strove to interpret the war as "redemptive" in its suffering.[77] He ended by asserting to a war-weary nation that the sacrifice of the war dead of Flanders was not in vain because the fallen's "little homely wooden crosses [are] emblems, not of death and defeat, but of victorious life and a 'love that sought not its own' ... their faith has redeemed the world."[78]

Lorne wrote when the article appeared that his "greatest enjoyment" was Edith's "delight" at its publication.[79] But in a more worldly sense, the young minister-sergeant had managed to win publication in a national periodical, reaching out beyond the Methodist Church – and beyond the pigeonholes of the military bureaucracy – to the country as a whole. The article was a straw in the wind of his future orientation as editor and publisher.

Lorne soon began to tackle a more challenging project in that tent – a manuscript on Russian literature entitled "Suffering in Russian Literature," a project that he was to work on intermittently for the next three years. It was never published, but he did present a paper on the topic to the Montreal Methodist Conference in June 1920. The impact of this paper would change his career path.[80] Not only that: his approach to Russian literature foreshadowed the way he would look at Canadian literature during his editorial career.

In the fall of 1917, Edith had given him a copy of Dostoevsky's *The Idiot*. Lorne, spellbound, pronounced it "amazing" and "exhausting." Russian literature was something of an avant-garde intellectual interest at this time: in England, Lytton Strachey was also absorbed in Russian literature, as was Katherine Mansfield. Two mentors seem to have stimulated Lorne's interest in Russian literature. Alice Chown had long been interested in Russia and in Russian writers like Tolstoy,[81] and she probably prompted Lorne to give his paper on Tolstoy in the fall of 1914.[82] Charles Shaw, Lorne's former professor at New York University, sent him a letter in April 1917 with some information about his own work on Dostoevsky, apparently at Lorne's request.[83] Russia was also very much in the news. In 1917, as the Russian war effort fell apart, and the Bolsheviks came to power, Lorne's diary is dotted with references to Russia.[84]

What Lorne Pierce discerned in Russian literature – in his readings of such writers as Tolstoy, Pushkin, Dostoevsky, and Gogol – was a reflection of Russian religious values. In both the religion and the literature, he believed, the image and the ethos of the suffering Christ – the Christ of the cross – was of overwhelming significance for Russia, a country plagued by a history of suffering and injustice.[85] According to Pierce, at the heart of Russian "national consciousness" lay "the deep-seated Russian instincts of humility, repentance, self-abnegation, self-sacrifice and suffering forever making for liberation, reform and enlightenment ... it is a prayer of aspiration ... a voice that calls thru all Russia's history, art, religion and literature."[86] In his view, "the passion for suffering" lay at "the very heart of all Russian literature." For Pierce, Russian literature was ultimately concerned with spiritual issues that were relevant to all Christians, because it articulated "the mute soul of the suffering multitudes of bleeding Russia."[87] The work of Russia's major writers, Pierce believed, was an evolving record of a quest for spiritual insights, a "treasure house of Beauty, Truth and Love."[88]

In light of Pierce's later career, the importance of the manuscript on Russian literature lies first of all in the evidence it provides that his interests were turning toward literature as early as 1917. Furthermore, he was looking at literature as an evolving national entity, as a force expressive of the development and ethos of a country, precisely the template through which he would view Canadian literature in his work at Ryerson Press. Years before his arrival at Ryerson, therefore, Pierce's concept of a country's literature was nationalistic, evolutionary, and idealistic. As he put it, "a national literature is a national fact, playing its part, both in the spiritual development of the race, and in its moral, mental and material advancement." Literature, he asserted, could be "a vital, evolving force" in the life of a nation.[89] Similarly, at Ryerson, he would view Canadian literature as a force for national cohesion and moral idealism in Canada.

IN HIS military work, Lorne was to learn more about human suffering. By mid-October 1917, he was acting sergeant-major at Ongwanada Military Hospital, in charge of twenty-three orderlies. Ongwanada's patients were military men requiring long-term care for a variety of medical problems – some invalided home from the front with long-term physical or shell-shock injuries. The work was challenging, with disciplinary and dietary abuses to be remedied. One afternoon alone, he wrote, an evening's leave was delayed by "one epileptic fit, one spinal meningitis man in hysteria, two enemas and an appendectomy case."[90] A patient attempted suicide in mid-October, and Pierce recorded grimly a few months later that the man had been sent to the front.[91]

At Ongwanada, Lorne set to work with a will, effecting reforms in the schedule and routines of the kitchen and ward orderlies, changing the inventory system for stores to stop rampant pilfering, and getting a new cook in an effort to improve the hospital food.[92] He arranged such morale-builders for the patients as jars of home-made preserves and concerts by schoolchildren. He worked with the medical staff, sometimes in frustration ("the bland ineptitude of the healing profession is amazing"[93]), to better the lot of the patients. On the wards, the price of war came home to Lorne in a visceral way. One of his patients, for example, was an airman with a head injury who could no longer recognize his wife and children.[94] Lorne frequently had to write to families whose sons were terribly injured or ill; the father of one patient wrote back asking him for reassurance that his son would not be crippled for life.[95]

In the fall of 1917 and the winter of 1918, Lorne managed the occasional day or night's leave with Edith, still living at her grandmother's. He recorded of their first wedding anniversary in September that it had been "so like heaven."[96] Their outings to the park, to an armoury show, and to the theatre were almost like the courtship they had never been

Sergeant-Major Lorne Pierce on duty at Ongwanada
Military Hospital, Kingston, 1917. Courtesy of Queen's
University Archives

geographically close enough to have before marriage. Ironically, Lorne
had to miss a performance of *Madame Butterfly* at the Grand Theatre in
November, but urged that Edith ("my little Cio Cio San") go.[97]

Meanwhile, Lorne's mother wrote him from Delta in November
seeking his advice about the upcoming federal election. As the mother
of a soldier, she was able to vote for the first time in her life. In her fear
of Catholicism, she showed less ecumenism than her Union-educated
son: "Do you suppose we should fear the Catholics as much as the Germans? I find I need educating in political matters since I am entrusted

with such a responsibility."[98] Lorne, for his part, was dismayed by the agitation against conscription in Quebec.[99] He favoured conscription, and thus the Union government, as a pledge of support for the soldiers in the trenches. Acting as a scrutineer on election day – 17 December 1917 – he recorded that "I don't give a whoop for kings or parties, but I love my Canada."[100]

Back at Ongwanada Hospital, Lorne was increasingly frustrated with army inefficiency. On the positive side, he recorded that Major Charles Mundell, his commanding officer, had such confidence in him that his plans were usually endorsed by his superiors. It is noteworthy that, even thirty years after he served at Ongwanada, a nursing sister who had worked with him wrote that she had "always remembered his ability."[101] But, after a month on the job there – the major organizational challenges met, sharing a room with another soldier – Lorne wrote in his diary: "They can't take me away from here fast enough. I abominate it. The same small round of small jobs, bossing lazy orderlies, trying to get a few necessities to run things … But thank goodness some day I'll be back in my own job and with my own folk and with my dearie."[102]

A return to Edith and civilian life soon came, but under a shadow. After a happy family Christmas in Delta, Lorne began 1918 in a brisk mood, resolving to "face the New Year in marching equipment."[103] On 3 February he learned that he was to be sent overseas in four to six weeks to head a draft of some fifty men, nearly half of whom he himself had recruited. Relieved to be finished with Ongwanada's routine, he downplayed his fears about going overseas.[104] But he was soon downplaying different fears. On 5 February, after a medical, his name was abruptly taken off the list for overseas, and Major Mundell was asking if he "coughed or had T.B. in the family." A few days later, a medical board declared it would be "suicide" to send him overseas. Relieved of all military duties, he was put to bed for three days for observation as a patient in the very hospital whose wards he helped run.[105] The diagnosis was suspected tuberculosis, the disease he had so reviled in Ottawa only months before. The paperwork was put in motion for a medical discharge from active duty.

Lorne had had prolonged exposure to tuberculosis in the past. In the spring of 1914, he had nursed a severely ill tubercular man in a stuffy hotel room in Fillmore for days on end. Certainly, the overwork, damp, poor diet, and stress of military life can have done his health no good. Whatever the cause, in 1918 he was dangerously ill. He penned a macabre ditty into his diary:

> It isn't the cough
> That carries you off
> It's the coff-in
> They carry you off-in![106]

Lorne's deeper feelings were hinted at in a quotation from a medical book he read while bedridden at Ongwanada, which he carefully pasted into his diary: "Many men who were supposed to be doomed to death in childhood have lived to astonish the world with their strength and vitality."[107] Given his own uncertain health since childhood, he must have been praying that the quotation would prove to be true of him.

Edith, for her part, hoped that he was "just over-tired and nervous."[108] Lorne's mother wrote that his discharge from the army was "an answered prayer" and that he would surely get well at home in Delta.[109] Edith's Aunt Alice, with her own progressive brand of optimism, immediately sent Lorne a special deep-breathing, fruit, and handicraft regime to follow to ensure recovery.[110] Edward Pierce wrote of the "glad news" that Lorne would be discharged, but, suffering from heart problems himself, he had fainted at the news of his son's diagnosis.[111] What is striking is how seldom Lorne or his family uttered the word "tuberculosis," once the diagnosis was made – so great was the fear the disease inspired.[112]

Before discharge, Lorne had the difficult experience of watching his comrades leave for overseas without him. Seeing his comrades off on 24 February, he vowed that he must, above all, "equal their sacrifice at home."[113] After formal discharge on 14 March, he was finally back home in Delta, too exhausted even to go to church that first Sunday – St Patrick's Day. Feeling "very strange" in civilian clothes, he solemnly repeated his vow "to be a good soldier in another line and endure equal sacrifices."[114] One of the first things he did was join the War Veterans' Association, wearing its lapel badge to show that he had served. Not only did this prevent possible harassment, it spoke to his conviction that he also needed to serve out of uniform. His determination to spare no effort to better the nation was henceforth spurred by his experience of the Great War. Behind his energy and ambition lay the knowledge that he had been spared while his cousin Clifford, and many of his contemporaries, lay in military graves at the front.

Lorne's military service had had some positive effects. He believed that he left active service "a bigger if not a better man," knowing much more of human nature and of leadership.[115] Also, the lack of intellectual stimulation in the army had prompted him to develop literary interests, a precursor of his future editorial career, which, like his excursions into Russian literature, would focus on the moral and national importance of literature. But all that was in the future. In March 1918 Lorne Pierce's immediate challenge was to overcome the illness that threatened his very life.

6

Shining in the Rural Shade

Spreading the Social Gospel in Brinston,
1918–1920

This place ought to become notorious as a resting place, a nerve
sanatorium. It is Sleepy Hollow moved north and rolled out.

Lorne Pierce on his rural pastorate in Brinston, January 1919[1]

The chances are coming faster than I can decide. The main thing is
… to see my duty so clear and distinct that duty and pleasure and
consecration and ability will not be divorced.

Lorne Pierce on offers to leave Brinston, April 1920[2]

Lorne Pierce's Delta convalescence after his medical discharge in
March 1918 was an anxious limbo. Physician Dr Robert Stevens,
once his childhood playmate, confirmed the diagnosis of tuberculosis,
a diagnosis Lorne was able to admit only years later.[3] Edith and his
mother hovered over the invalid, Edith daily preparing large eggnogs.
Between ministrations, Lorne endeavoured to work on his manuscript
on Russian literature in the hope that it would ultimately fill "a felt want
and [prove] of great use,"[4] but his family insisted that he strictly limit
time at his desk. One March day, he discovered just how traumatized his
father was about his illness. He told his diary: "Father can't get above my
illness. I am sure he worries so. When standing up and talking to me in
the store this a.m. his heart took a bad turn. I was quite alarmed. He said
when he recovered that he would possibly go that way and for me not
to be startled."[5] At Lorne's Kingston medical examination in April, the
military doctor advised a year's rest, and even the normally indefatigable
Lorne spoke of remaining in Delta till October.[6]

Meanwhile, war news made the future seem even more uncertain
as the Germans mounted a major offensive on the Western front that
spring. Lorne was both touched and troubled by postcards from army

comrades overseas.[7] By habit, he still woke up at reveille – 5:30 a.m. He wrote in his diary: "How this horrible war drags on and how I wish I were in it!"[8] Lorne described the conscription riots in Quebec that April as "disgusting."[9] Both the grim war news and the divisiveness of the conscription issue at home were hardening his resolve to excel in civilian life at any cost if he could not fight, and affirming his conviction that Canada needed forces working for unity and a common vision of the nation. He was not alone: the First World War inspired in many English Canadians a militant nationalism permeated with "revived ideals of service," one dedicated to forging some form of "organic unity" in Canadian society.[10]

Lorne's rest cure was soon hard to detect. Active as a Mason in Delta's Harmony Lodge, he was disappointed when a move to elect him its head, or "Worshipful Master," came to naught.[11] He spent time woodworking and in taking driving lessons from the Reverend Calvert. In May, after another army medical, Lorne wrote that the physician was "delighted" because he had gained three and a half pounds. Nevertheless, he weighed a meagre 135 lbs. on a 5'10" frame.[12]

By the end of May, Lorne allowed two fellow Methodists to whisk him off to Ottawa, where the Montreal Conference of the Methodist Church was meeting that year.[13] At Edith's insistence, he turned down an offer of a demanding three-church urban parish in the middle-class Ottawa suburb of Britannia.[14] He also turned down the pulpit of Delta Methodist Church, knowing that he would always be seen as the hometown boy.[15] Despite his hopes for a Montreal pulpit that might open a path to educational work, he decided to accept a country parish – Brinston in rural Dundas County, eight miles north of Iroquois, on the ancient flood plain of the St Lawrence River, half-way between Cornwall and Brockville.

BRINSTON WAS on the old Methodist Matilda circuit. Another ambitious Methodist had briefly occupied the Matilda circuit in the 1850s – Albert Carman, who had risen to be general superintendent of the Methodist Church.[16] Lorne wrote gamely in his diary that Brinston was "providential" and "much too good a field – $1,200 and a fine parsonage with scarcely any driving." He declared that he would like to spend "10–12 years in the country" before going "to one of our colleges for the [educational] work upon which I have set my heart."[17]

Despite his optimism, Brinston was precisely the sort of obscure rural charge that Lorne had promised himself – and Edith – that he would never accept. Nevertheless, on 27 June 1918, he and Edith left Delta, with "Gladys," their newly acquired used Dodge roadster, bought with the aid of a loan from Ed Pierce, loaded to the roof. The couple drove along the flat roads and modest mixed-crop farms of rural Dundas County to Brinston for a welcoming reception by their new parishioners. The charge consisted of four churches with a total of 369 members, with regular services to be held in the hamlets of Brinston, Hulbert, Hainsville, and Glen Stewart.[18] Brinston, the hub of the circuit, consisted of little more than a crossroads general store, a few modest houses, and a medium-sized red brick church with a narrow pointed spire beside a rambling, three-storey white wooden manse.

The couple plunged into the work of a rural parish. Gone was Lorne's disdain for a country parsonage as he prayed that he would be able to give the "compassionate love and intelligent sympathy" needed.[19] In one of his first sermons, he told his new congregation that, although he knew little of farming, he wanted to "lead them to the hilltop and let them catch a vision of the world beyond."[20] The hilltop metaphor suggests that, as in the Delta of his boyhood, Lorne longed for wider vistas.

Lorne wrote sermons, conducted multiple Sunday and mid-week services, and made endless calls on dirt roads which were dusty in summer, snow-clogged in winter, and mudholes in between. The phrase "Matilda mud" became a refrain in his diary, and in winter he had to give up his Dodge for a horse and cutter to be able to get around at all. He helped families cope with tragedy – a young mother of nine and her baby both dead in childbirth, a child killed by accidentally ingesting household poison, a woman addicted to morphine. By his first August, the average attendance at Sunday communion services had tripled.[21]

For her part, Edith performed well in her round of Sunday School and parish work. In late August, she was elected superintendent of Sunday schools for Dundas County after a twenty-minute speech at a convention, a talk that "quite surpassed" Lorne's expectations.[22] A few weeks later, they celebrated their second wedding anniversary with a gift of pumpkin pie from one congregant. Lorne mused that it had been "a little trouble catching the 'butterfly' but the gain was worth the pain!"[23] However, even his anniversary message to Edith revealed his relentless drive, expressing the wish that they "grow old in beautiful usefulness."[24] He rarely felt able to spend an evening at home with Edith listening to their new Victrola. By early October, even Lorne worried if his health could stand his "whirlwind pace."[25]

That month, the twin spectres of war and pestilence fell on Brinston. By 17 October, the world-wide Spanish influenza epidemic had closed even the churches in the area: the new minister had buried three flu victims that week alone. Then, on that autumn night, war news: Jack North, Lorne's classmate and friendly rival at Queen's, president of Arts '12, had been killed in France. Shaken, Lorne wrote that North had been "permitted to die in a truly great way," which was so much better than to be "buried as a mediocre."[26] North had gone to glory as a member of the Canadian Mounted Rifles overseas, having enlisted from his own Presbyterian pulpit in another Ontario small town (Sturgeon Falls). His death drove Lorne to brood: Was he himself doing enough? How could he distinguish himself before God and man?

That very night, Lorne was felled by the flu. After ten days of excruciating headache, delirium, and quenchless thirst, with Edith, his parents, and a trained nurse tending him day and night, he was finally well enough to be able to get up for a few minutes. But Edith too had fallen ill. On the morning of 27 October, her heart began to fail. Lorne was helped from his own sickbed to what the doctor feared was his young wife's deathbed. His diary records the harrowing scene: "She looked just like death. Her pulse seemed to flutter, her breath was like a flutter too. She lay back upon the pillow, her eyes closed, mouth slightly open, scarce[ly] alive. I took her cold hand and broke down. She turned and looked at me with a kind of wild surprise and said 'Oh don't cry.' I felt ashamed but couldn't help telling her that she must fight, that we were doing all we could but that she must be brave and fight. Then I had to come out."[27]

All that day Lorne prayed as Edith struggled. In what he called the "darkest hour," he was comforted when his father came back to Brinston to bring the "blessing of home" – and an inspirational note from Harriet Pierce ("Trust Him when dark doubts assail Thee ..."). When Edith rallied at last, Lorne was jubilant, and nakedly emotional: "My little wife improved. She went right up to the pearly gates of the other New Life, but before she passed through she turned and looked, and saw how lonesome I was, and God, who had heard my prayers and had seen my tears ... sent an angel to bring her back. I have had her in my arms many times! Dear little Butterfly!"[28] When Ed Pierce came down with the flu after the vigil for Edith, Lorne's bond with his parents also intensified.[29]

During Lorne's slow recovery that November, he lamented his lack of strength, describing his life to date as "plagued all along with disappointment, ill health and poverty." His ambition can be seen in the comparisons to great men he made about his own situation: "I would love to be able to buy Edith leisure and luxury and some release from monotonous work too. Mozart was buried in a pauper's grave. Kant suffered every minute. Moses died in sight of the Promised Land. I'll trust and try!"[30]

Early on the morning of 11 November, the Pierces were roused from bed as the local doctor rushed in shouting news of the armistice. Lorne hung out the only flag he had – a tiny Union Jack. Later, one of his parishioners called out to him from her clothesline that the news was "the greatest the world has heard since the birth of Christ." But Lorne noted in his diary that, after four weary years of war, there were "more tears and prayers than [rattling] tin pans."[31]

As 1919 began, Lorne wrote that influenza deaths and sickness were "everywhere." Two pieces of news – one bad and one good – made him redouble his efforts to win recognition by the wider world. That December, he had been "very disappointed" when a publisher returned his manuscript on Russian literature, categorizing the rejection as the end of his "first literary venture and leap at fame."[32] He wrote impatiently in early January that snow-bound Brinston was "Sleepy Hollow moved north and rolled out."[33] Yet he had performed well there: attendance was up markedly on the Matilda circuit before the flu struck, and church finances had improved.[34] In December, he had received a letter from James Endicott of the missions board praising his "exceptional" success in raising money for missions. The Matilda circuit had raised almost five times more than Delta or Brockville.[35]

Lorne resolved "to work for L.A.P. more now."[36] For him, that meant advanced academic studies, obviously aimed at getting him out of rural obscurity. He arranged with United Theological College in Montreal to do reading courses by correspondence toward an external doctorate in systematic theology (STD), a course for which his revised manuscript on Russian literature would ultimately be accepted as the dissertation. By January 1919, what little spare time he had in the evenings was spent studying textual criticism of the New Testament for his first examination.[37] His diary records a typical evening: he sat down immediately after supper to pore over works on the New Testament, noting single-mindedly by late evening: "The house is quiet as a tomb. Guess Edith has gone to rest."[38]

In February, good news: another army medical reported "some progress": Lorne's right lung had healed, he had gained twelve ounces in six months, and only the apex of his right lung still had some tubercular symptoms.[39] Whatever the medical board had to say, he pronounced himself healthy, writing by August that he was "going to be strong and do real things that are worthwhile."[40]

Lorne Pierce once remarked that "very early in life I knew what I wanted, and [I] always had a plan for getting it."[41] He now resolved to so excel in church and organizational work that he would win wider notice even from rural Dundas County. Moreover, he wanted to display his intellectual talents, not only by working toward a higher degree but also by writing articles for the *Christian Guardian* and other periodicals.[42] A flurry of activity ensued on several fronts. For example, shortly after the armistice, he spearheaded the formation of a Soldier's Rehabilitation Association around Brinston, to provide returning allowances and other support to returning veterans.[43]

Then, in the months before the referendum on the prohibition of alcohol held in conjunction with the Ontario provincial election of 20 October 1919, Lorne took a page from his mother's book and campaigned energetically against alcohol. In July and August 1919, he organized a committee to mobilize support for prohibition in Dundas County. His campaign culminated in a large rally at Brinston Church on 21 September, which featured a prominent pro-temperance speaker from Toronto – J.W. Bengough, lecturer and cartoonist of *Grip* fame.[44] When the referendum passed a month later with a 350,000 majority province-wide in favour of prohibition, Lorne noted jubilantly in his diary that "everyone worked very hard for victory."[45] The Methodist Church soon noticed the Brinston minister's exceptional organizational and fundraising talents. In November 1919, Lorne was put in charge of four church circuits in four counties to raise money for the Methodist National Campaign.

Lorne's absorption in work caused marital tension. In April 1919, for example, Edith had travelled to Kingston to the sickbed of her Grandmother Conley. She longed for her husband's presence. Lorne, in the midst of a series of spiritual revival services, begged off. Edith wrote to him from Kingston: "When [Grandmother] thought she was passing away this morning she mentioned your name. I was really sorry that you had not come for she loves you so."[46] Lorne's reply suggests determination to succeed in Brinston at almost any personal cost: "Will you tell [Grandmother Conley,] dear[,] that only under these most difficult circumstances am I compelled to wait here. The decision is greatly justifying itself. Pray for us too dearie. Our year is not going to be a failure."[47]

Lorne's parents, for their part, chided him about overwork in the spring of 1919.[48] Shortly after the big prohibition rally that September, Edith confided her worries about Lorne's overwork to Harriet Pierce.

Harriet was sympathetic but could offer no solution, telling Edith: "I wish we could find some way of persuading him to say 'no' to the various invitations[.] We feel quite annoyed at times, but I suppose it is wicked to do that."[49]

IN THE fall of 1919, Lorne embarked on a new spate of activity, one with a strong social gospel orientation. As historians have pointed out, the social gospel was a particularly powerful force in Canadian Protestantism by the end of the First World War, most strongly within the Methodist Church, where it was fed by Methodism's progressive, evolutionary view of society. The spirit of the social gospel – with its emphasis on social betterment rather than individual salvation – was an extension of the world view implicit in such initiatives as temperance and urban-reform work, causes in which Methodism had been active since before the turn of the century. The social-reform orientation in the church had been further intensified by Methodism's emphasis on national service during the First World War, as well as by the desire of the Protestant churches to combat post-war disillusionment and to counter the threat of Bolshevism by seeking to create a more just Canadian society. By the end of the war, Methodism had moved toward a strongly social gospel orientation under the influence of such men as Salem Bland, J.S. Woodsworth, and Ernest Thomas of the broadly mandated Social Service Council of Canada, formed by the Protestant churches in 1913.[50] By 1918, the Methodist Church of Canada was "the most radical religious denomination in North America."[51]

Lorne himself was an admirer of Ernest Thomas, and his time in the west and at Union had made him sympathetic to the need for social reform and for cooperative efforts to build community infrastructure. While serving in Ottawa in 1917, he had been impressed by a paper on rural sociology presented by a fellow minister.[52] By 1919, Lorne understood that social gospel work was now seen as central to Methodism, and could be a path to personal recognition. After all, S.D. Chown, general superintendent of the Methodist Church (and Edith's cousin), was describing the social gospel as "the voice of prophecy in our time."[53]

Lorne had not been able to attend the Methodist General Conference held in Hamilton in September 1918. Nevertheless, he knew what the widely publicized conference resolution had affirmed: the need for Methodism to become involved in community efforts for social justice, to work toward, in the words of the resolution, "nothing less than a transference of the whole economic life from a basis of competition and profits to one of co-operation and service."[54] Moreover, the *Christian Guardian* was urging that local churches become centres for social reconstruction, and that the rural areas be part of the impetus.[55] Just after the Methodist General Conference resolution, Lorne was reading up on social-service work, with an eye to action.[56]

Brinston and rural Dundas County, given their isolation and underdeveloped infrastructure, were ripe for projects in rural community organization and cooperation. Better roads, improved community recreational and cultural programs and facilities, the establishment of schemes for public outdoor lighting in the villages – the Brinston area needed them all. The minister who succeeded in social gospel projects in such an underdeveloped area by working with people of all denominations could thereby gain an impressive reputation. As Lorne put it, his aim in Brinston would be "to make friends with the 'desert experience' and make myself worthy to be sought after."[57]

By the spring of 1919, Lorne had begun to organize area residents – whatever their religion – to construct a community hall in Brinston, convincing the local branch of the Oddfellows, a fraternal order, to share half the cost with the community as a whole.[58] In May, he spearheaded the formation of a Brinston baseball club, which over the next several months metamorphosed into the Dundas County Athletic Association to organize teams and facilities for hockey and other sports as well.[59] Thanks to his lectures and articles about his work, awareness of what he was doing soon snowballed. When the *Christian Guardian* published Lorne's article "Dumb for Forty Years" – about his techniques for getting the laity more involved in community work for the social gospel in Brinston – he won national attention and exulted that he was helping to make the magazine more "progressive."[60]

The arrival in Brinston in July 1919 of Edith's aunt, Alice Chown, who as a socialist feminist had long supported projects aimed at cooperative community living, further fuelled Lorne's social gospel schemes. Always convinced that Lorne was "going to be a leader," she made every effort to influence his community-development work during her six-week stay.[61] Before his Brinston ministry, Alice Chown had urged Lorne to work for social ideals after war's end, telling him that "this war means reconstruction in faith ... in social relations, in national relations." It was, she urged him, "reconstruction time," adding that he should "not let any old loyalties to past traditions hold you away from giving your best service to the coming day, a day when we shall put our faith in the spirit within man and seek in every relation to recognize his individuality and his communism."[62] At the manse, she spent hours discussing Lorne's community-development plans and sharing her interest in the social reforms underway in the new Russia. By August, she had offered him money to buy more books on community development and was sending him information about possible sources of funding for the community hall.[63]

While there is evidence that Alice Chown influenced her nephew-in-law's thinking, Lorne was also aware of the hostility from fellow Methodists that Alice Chown had incurred by her radical pacifism during the Great War. Both Lorne and Edith remonstrated with Alice that summer about the danger of "throw[ing] every thing overboard" by allying herself with extreme American socialist pacifists, prompting Alice to declare defiantly that they should not "pity" her for being on "the foremost ship blazing the new trail."[64] Lorne himself clearly wanted to be progressive, but not to the extent of marginalizing himself within the Methodist Church or in Canadian public opinion. The fate of one of his articles made that clear to him.

That summer, Lorne, like many Western intellectuals, was fulminating against the terms of the Treaty of Versailles. He wrote in his diary: "We have had enough of war but the peace as it stands means more wars. It is an atrocious, unequal, ungodly thing & must go!"[65] At Alice Chown's urging, he completed a hard-hitting article on the treaty called "The Peace That Passes Understanding."[66] Urging Canadians not to "maim the soul" of the enemy, the article denounced the treaty terms as a "Hun-like crime" backed by "a family compact of capitalists" and observed scathingly: "All the idealism of war has been spun by men who never saw a comrade rotting in the sun and no hope of burying him. These heroes when they return are silent ... But one thing war has done, it has compelled all of us to announce our principles. Christianity and the churches are not coterminous. This we affirm at the expense of being heretical. Patriotism is not equal to jingoism and flag-waving."[67]

The article, however, was rejected both by *Canadian Magazine* and by *Queen's Quarterly*. In a note on the manuscript, Lorne wrote that, of the three Canadians who had "raised their voice against the Treaty," Queen's professor O.D. Skelton had been "censured," while he had been forced into "the silence cure."[68] Lorne did not try to publish the article elsewhere, realizing that there were ideological and rhetorical limits beyond which he could not go if he wished to be influential as a churchman and a Canadian.

At the end of August 1919, Lorne gave a week of summer-school lectures to Brinston area residents and clergymen about organizing for community development. Many of his congregants supported his progressive views and community work, despite the opposition of the local reeve and the more conservative inhabitants of Dundas County to schemes such as the community hall which crossed denominational and political lines.[69] Some of his more traditional parishioners complained that he was neglecting the gospel to do social work.[70] But the Methodist minister was ecumenical in other ways as well. He raised some eyebrows when he wore cassock and surplice to assist at an Anglican funeral, the first time he had ever done so, but he asserted in his diary that "the world is growing away from the non-essentials."[71]

Despite the sniping, Lorne largely carried the day with community opinion. In October, he formally launched the Matilda Community Association, serving as its first president. The association was grassroots in nature – as he rather primly put it, open to everyone who was "clean and decent" – with annual dues of one dollar for adults and fifty cents for children.[72] With 300 members within six months, the association, in a spate of meetings, fundraising events, and work bees, raised $1,500, bringing into being by the summer of 1920 a community hall at Brinston with a surrounding hockey rink, park, and playground (the latter still in use in the new millennium), all served by a new grid of outdoor electric lighting. It also worked to better library, school, and adult education resources in the area.[73]

Beginning in the fall of 1919, having bought his first typewriter, Lorne disseminated his ideas by writing articles for eastern Ontario papers and by lectures in area towns and villages outlining the rationale and structure of the community association.[74] Some area newspapers, the Iroquois *News*, for example, were at first reluctant to publish his radical ideas,[75] but by December 1919 the *News* had been won over: "The Community Hall and Forum established at Brinston should radiate a wholesome influence throughout the whole rural district. Sports, too, are coming in for special attention, under the leadership of Rev. Dr. Pierce, the energetic pastor of the Brinston Methodist Church, who evidently believes in the church exerting a more potent influence in the social life of the community, especially among the young people."[76]

An examination of Pierce's writings on community development, later published in booklet form as *The Beloved Community: Social Studies in Rural Progress* (1925), makes it clear that under the banner of the social gospel he was working to foster specific social and intellectual values in rural Canada, values that anticipated the educational and cultural principles he would put into practice at Ryerson Press. Echoing the resolution of the 1918 Methodist General Conference, Pierce's booklet called for the church to "take a deeper interest in the social salvation of our people."[77] Moreover, Pierce's concept of "the beloved community" was framed in terms of the evolutionary idealism that he had absorbed at Queen's. Pierce wrote that in "the heart of man there burns a passion for perfection, which might be called the evolutionary force in the breast of man, the expulsive power which compels him to go out and discover new ideals of value and new forms of life. This is man's work in the world; it is this which gives him his value and his dignity."[78] He advocated a "new social order," which he described as "the family ideal writ large, a group actuated by mutual sympathy and a sense of mutual responsibility."[79] In calling his vision of a new social order "the beloved community," Pierce was echoing John Watson, among others: the idea of community and the struggle to attain it was a dominant feature of John Watson's thought.[80] (The influence of Harriet Pierce's values was also evident in Pierce's stress on home and the mother as foundations for a new Canadian social order.[81])

Pierce would institute literary and educational publishing policies at Ryerson Press designed to nurture an idealistic Canadian nationalism in Canadians and newcomers alike. But in Brinston, he was already calling for "nobler purposes of citizenship," denouncing widespread materialism, and calling for educational initiatives in a manner that anticipates his creation of patriotic textbook series in the 1920s and 1930s. In the Brinston years, he was convinced that, as he wrote, "the educational factor is … an important one in the country's development … The public school must be wonderfully strengthened."[82] Also, Pierce still believed, as he had in the west, that Canada must have nation-wide cultural counterweights to immigration. Home, like school, had to be a building block for national idealism of a certain cast. Rural Canada needed to be a nexus of national idealism in an era of heavy immigration:

The country home is characteristic of the nation. There are the purest national types, unaffected by foreign influences. It is our

duty to keep strong and pure these centres from which go out
our great national ideals. In the flood of immigration which is
coming to our shores we should be swamped if it were not for
the fact that here in the open country we have a strong, virile
native consciousness, a pure national stock which will be one of
our strongest national assets, our greatest insurance against the
disintegrating forces of unlimited immigration.[83]

Pierce's use of phrases like "purest national types" and "the disintegrating
forces of unlimited immigration" are also evidence that his concept of
nationalism was at root a homogenizing one, which valorized a white,
Christian, middle-class mental outlook for the dominion. In an era of
social anxiety over new waves of immigration from Eastern Europe and
elsewhere, Pierce wished to integrate newcomers into Canada's "strong,
virile native consciousness" – his idealistic nationalism clearly infused
with ethnocentric ideals of race, class, and creed. "Our great national
ideals" were to counteract difference to infuse immigrants with the existing values of Canadians, not vice versa.

In his social gospel work in Brinston, then, Pierce focused on church
and home to disseminate and stimulate particular patriotic ideals to the
community; at Ryerson, he would turn his attention to literature and
education in the same spirit. Furthermore, the reading that Pierce was
doing in Brinston toward a doctorate in theology at Montreal's United
Theological College had much the same orientation. One of his courses,
for example, dealt with the evolution of the modern community; the
topic of another was "The Canadian National Consciousness: A Study
in National Idealism."[84]

The young Brinston minster's combination of theoretical eloquence
and concrete community projects won him wider notice. Lorne, overlooking the role of his own writings in his rise, rhapsodized to his diary
that April that his sudden prominence was "just like a romance."[85]
Amid the Matilda mud, he identified with such famous clergymen as
John Keble and Charles Kingsley "who camped awhile in out of the
way places and God made a path to their door."[86] That spring, he was
invited to apply for the pulpit of Montreal's prestigious Douglas Methodist Church, and, although he was not chosen, he was clearly a young
minister to watch.[87] After hearing him preach there, one prosperous
congregant offered to underwrite summer school at Harvard Divinity School. Moreover, Ernest Thomas, head of the Methodist Church's

social services department, had written to Lorne about his community projects, and had recommended him to a Vancouver church seeking a minister.[88] Well-known Canadian journalist Augustus Bridle, then editor of the *Canadian Courier*, asked Lorne to contribute a series of articles on his community work and to come to Toronto and Hamilton to lecture on it.[89]

By April 1920, Lorne had been made a field secretary of the multidenominational Social Service Council of Canada as well as a member of its Provincial Committee on Community Centres. He was soon travelling to Toronto for meetings where his ideas were "eagerly received."[90] The general secretary of the council offered him the prospect of a salaried appointment, telling him that he knew more about community work than "anybody in Canada."[91]

But Lorne's life was about to take another turn. While he was exhilarated by all the attention, he vowed to make a decision about his future course only when he could "see my duty so clear and distinct that duty and pleasure and consecration and ability will not be divorced."[92] The first intimation of his future course – one that would indeed absorb all his idealism and all his strength – came in that April of "romance."

ON 22 APRIL, Thomas wrote to say that the Book Committee of the Methodist Book and Publishing House was meeting shortly to consider a proposal from its new head, Book Steward Reverend Samuel Fallis, to create a new position for the House. Fallis and Thomas both wanted an official who "would act partially as literary critic and adviser, but especially as one who would serve as an expert eye for the whole ministry [by] keeping pastors punctually informed of the very best literature for their own vocational equipment." Thomas added that he considered Lorne ideal for the post, especially because Fallis wanted someone young enough to "grow up with the institution and very largely create his own job."[93] Was Lorne interested?

Though he had long wanted "education work," Lorne wrote in his diary only that he was "not decided yet." Two days later, his reply asked for more details.[94] In the meantime, the Matilda Sunday School had just raised the largest sum in its history for mission work, there were talks on community work to be given, and the Memorial Park was shortly to open in Brinston.

Lorne's biggest challenge in April 1920, however, was the upcoming annual meeting of the Montreal Methodist Conference, to be held in Kemptville. He had been asked to give the annual lecture before its Theological Union on 2 June, the youngest minister ever so honoured. For this occasion he adapted the paper "The Contribution of Russian Literature to Christian Theology" from his Russian manuscript. Once in Kemptville, he shut himself up in his chairless hotel room, sitting on the bed against the headboard for hours with his notes spread out. Finally, he locked his manuscript in his suitcase, resolving to give the entire lecture extemporaneously.[95]

The lecture was a triumph. Pierce was interrupted some six times by applause. With the events of the Bolshevik Resolution so recent, there was much interest in, and uneasiness about, Russia. As one press report noted, the address created a sensation: "[Pierce] delivered a forceful address ... in the course of which he stood up for the Russian people and endeavoured to justify their 'fight for freedom.' He declared that they had been taught to suffer by their writers, whose literature reflected a passion for suffering, and long years of anguish had made pain more possible to bear. The Russian people today were fighting for freedom ... and their motives were not properly understood."[96] Pierce's lecture challenged his audience without alienating them, and characterized literature as a moral and spiritual force, a view dear to the hearts of Methodists. While declaring that he was no Bolshevist, he told his audience that his long study of Russian literature had "put into my heart a sympathy for poor, struggling, bleeding Russia which makes me a better man."[97] Pierce concluded with a ringing question that turned the attention of his audience from the bogey of Bolshevism in Russia to ask whether in the British Empire, including Canada, the moral idealism of English literature was reflected in its political leadership: "Do you ask whether Lenin or Trotsky are working out the spiritual program of the master writers? ... I ask whether the classic literature of England, its moral idealism[,] is [expressed] in the reactionary leadership of the Empire Kingdom and the Dominions!"[98]

Such a call for moral and social regeneration was topical enough to be acceptable, and sufficiently provocative to be stimulating to his audience without isolating Pierce ideologically. In the heyday of social questioning within the Methodist Church, Pierce's talk confirmed him as a young minister to watch: he was unanimously elected president of the Theological Union of the Montreal Conference in anticipation of the next year's gathering.[99] In fact, the whole occasion was ideally suited to convince Book Steward Samuel Fallis (who, unbeknownst to Pierce, was in the audience that day) that Pierce met the desire of the Methodist Book and Publishing House to employ a literary critic and advisor to ministers across Canada. On the most basic level, Pierce displayed fluent literary knowledge inspiring to his fellow ministers. Several listeners rushed up to him asking for reading lists and advice. One questioner even pronounced Pierce a "connoisseur of things literary."[100]

Moreover, Pierce's concept of literature in his work on Russian writers framed literature as an evolving national entity, a spur to national consciousness which embodied "a concrete sense of morality as a force making for national greatness." For Pierce, literature was important above all as a moral and national force. As he put it in his talk, "a national literature is a national fact, playing its part, both in the spiritual development of the race, and its moral, mental and material advancement."[101] For its part, throughout its long history, the Methodist Book and Publishing House had conceived of literature largely in terms of moral and national imperatives. No wonder Samuel Fallis concluded that Pierce was just the man to revitalize the House's Canadian list.

Ironically, however, Fallis, who had cut short a trip to western Canada just to hear Pierce, had trouble finding him to make an offer. All unknowing, Lorne had gone back to Brinston and his pulpit after giving his paper, not returning to the gathering until Monday, 7 June. As his car drew up to the church in Kemptville that morning, his old minister from Delta hurried out to meet him. Lorne's diary records the scene:

> I stopped the car and in a twinkling up ran Mr. Calvert, his happy face beaming and saying excitedly "Come [Lorne]! We've phoned all over the country for you! You've got the chance of your life and don't turn it down!" He then led me to the room where Mr. Fallis of the Book Room was waiting for me. "Well" said Mr. F. "You are the man I've come across the continent to get!" We sat down and he explained the whole matter to me, what was needed and how to fill the bill. He thought that I should have given an answer at once but I told him I was happy where I was and it would take a lot of thinking. He had to leave for Ottawa so I debated pro [and] con all morning[,] p.m. and up till and after my address in the evening when I represented the Social Service Council.[102]

That evening Lorne finally decided in the affirmative: "At 9:10 I sent the wire that sealed my fate and attached me to the Book Room as Literary

Critic and Advisor. I think I shall be very happy in it. It will give me fatherly oversight over 2300 ministers and their reading and over the whole constituency of the Church in Canada, New Zealand and Bermuda. I ought to have a bald spot or a copious crop of grey hair!"[103]

Lorne was delighted with the prospect of the job, although his diary shows his naivety about the kind of dedication and constant grind required in the world of publishing – and about its low salaries. He airily wrote in his entry about the appointment, blithely picturing a leisurely intellectual life without money worries or undue pressure on either Edith or himself: "I have always desired the student[']s life ... with ... time and means to study and travel and chance to write." He added: "We can remain there as long as we care to. The salary increases and the work grows more important. We will likely have our own house."[104]

The reality was to prove far more arduous. Even before Lorne began work, the terms of the job began to expand, in part at the behest of Lorne's enthusiastic cultural nationalism and his visionary propensities. What happened between early June and early August, when Lorne travelled to Toronto to take up his new post, suggests that he was already thinking of the job in loftier terms than advising ministers and ghosting book columns for the book steward. His mindset provides the first hint that, in hiring Pierce, Fallis – despite his desire to choose someone who, as Ernest Thomas put it, could "very largely create his own job"[105] – did not realize what an ambitious dynamo he had just installed at the Methodist Book and Publishing House, a dynamo whose reputation would overshadow his own in less than a decade.

In June 1920, however, Fallis was unequivocally "delighted" that Lorne had agreed to take on "this important work."[106] In early July, Lorne travelled to Toronto for the day to confer with Fallis. He came back in a mood of visionary nationalism, telling his diary that he felt "more than ever that I have a real he-man's job, that of making our Meth[odist] B[oo]k Room the cultural mecca of Canada. My powers are great, my responsibilities enormous but my faith and grit are about ecumenical!"[107]

In June and July 1920, Lorne wrapped up his rural work. In mid-June, he baptized his first Brinston namesake, Lorne Keiker – an index of his high standing in the community. On 1 July the Matilda Memorial Park officially opened. The crowd who flocked to see the new park and community centre generated some $1,500 for the project in gate receipts and donations. Then came the bittersweet round of farewell church services and receptions in Brinston, Hulbert, Hainsville, and Glen Stewart – what Lorne called "these awful goodbyes." He preached his last sermons on 4 July to packed churches, "one of the hardest things I have ever done."[108]

Lorne had been anxious to leave Brinston, but on leaving he could see positive elements to the experience. He later concluded that it was in Brinston he "learned to preach, found [my] own soul, and got [my] health back."[109] Despite his restlessness in the "desert" of Brinston, he was to look back on his time there as "the two happiest years of my life."[110] Lorne had also made the obscure rural circuit a springboard to prominence. He had left the army in March 1918 a sick man with an uncertain future and no pulpit. Just over two years later, he left Brinston as an up-and-coming young minister with bright prospects ahead.

Momentous as were the Matilda Park opening and his farewell engagements in Brinston, none of them was "*the* event" that Lorne's diary refers to that June and July. At his Kemptville lecture, one of the speakers had paid tribute to Edith Pierce, saying that, given Pierce's achievements, "part of the credit was due to the wife [he] had."[111] But Edith was not in Kemptville. After four years of marriage, she was expecting a baby in late July.

Given the circumspection surrounding pregnancy in this era, the first mention of it in her husband's diary had not come until March when he wrote that he was "very happy" about the approaching "visit from 'Fairyland' of a wee treasure."[112] After leaving Brinston in early July, the couple travelled to Kingston to stay with one of Edith's aunts to await the birth. Edith passed the time by sewing baby clothes; Lorne, feeling at loose ends, wrote articles for the *Canadian Courier* on his social gospel work. The baby came on schedule. Part of Lorne's diary entry for the event is worth quoting as one of the rare instances where he gives a close-up of his marital life. His habitual absorption in work is evident as he describes the night of 21 July: "Edith took her usual hot bath and I got into bed [by 11 p.m.] and read *The Expositor*. The articles were 'The Divine Julino' and 'Neall on the Atonement.' When Edith came in she quickly retired and I said: 'Don't let's talk. If I don't get a good sleep tonight I'll bust!' We nestled down to sleep. All was quiet for about 5 minutes when Edith startled me with a jab in the back … exclaiming 'It's coming!' Half-awake, half asleep I didn't know whether it was Death, the Germans or the plague that was making an appearance!"[113] True to clerical decorum, Lorne shaved and put on clean linen at 12:30 a.m. before leaving the house, while Edith "kept us all buoyed up with her cheer and wit." As the taxi took the couple past Queen's University toward Kingston General Hospital, Lorne later remembered that "as we rolled along, hand in hand, it occurred to both of us that we had often rolled down the same avenue on many a gay occasion when we were students there."

Edith's composure gave way to momentary tears at the hospital, as she realized that she was across the hall from the room in which her mother had died so many years before. For his part, Lorne was soon shaken by Edith's suffering in labour, describing her as "near the gates of death to grasp a sweet young life." He set off for a walk to await the outcome.

Lorne walked the nearby Queen's campus for the next three hours. He showed his sense of mission as he prayed that the baby "would never know the humiliating falls I had known, none of the awful battles just to be decent; that given the custody of a life to preserve and train we might be fitted for that exalted service and hand it on beautiful and clean; that personally I might be shriven and that I might be sanctified for its sake." The campus vigil also strengthened Lorne's attachment to Queen's ("my old Alma Mater ... that had given me a lover, then a wife, and now a mother").

As the first birds sang, Lorne returned to the hospital to find that he now had a daughter, "a tiny dark little mite wrapt in a huge shawl." She was christened Elizabeth Louise Pierce, after Edith's mother and Lorne's respectively – Beth for short. The new father wrote that "our happy married days have now been beautifully crowned with a rare little pearl and all we can do is sing Laudamus Te."[114]

On 2 August, Lorne hurried away to board the train for Toronto. The next day, he reported to work at the Methodist Book and Publishing House. Lorne Pierce's Ryerson years – so momentous for him and for Canadian culture – were underway.

7

A New Career and
Health Challenges

Lorne Pierce and Ryerson Press,
circa 1920

When I came to the publishing business [in 1920], I was totally
inexperienced in editorial work and in publishing.
Lorne Pierce, in an interview[1]

To be hit [by deafness] at the beginning of your career is a cruel blow.
It is not so much the physical disability as the frightful spiritual shock
it is to one, with attendant social and other maladjustments.
Lorne Pierce on his own deafness, 1944[2]

There was a whiff of patriotic and personal destiny about Lorne
Pierce's start at Ryerson Press. His appointment was approved on
Dominion Day, 1 July 1920, and he began work at the Methodist Book
and Publishing House on 3 August – his thirtieth birthday.[3] In the spartan fashion of a young rural minister, he rented a room at the Toronto
YMCA for the first few weeks. Pierce was anxious to succeed but outwardly jaunty even in the August heat. He was mercifully unaware that
his first years at Ryerson Press – as the trade book publishing division
of the House had just been christened – would be a time of testing and
trial, achievement, and disillusionment. From the outset, he was challenged by both his new milieu and two major health problems.

In these apprentice years, Pierce had to learn a new trade – book publishing. As he later admitted, he came to the House "totally inexperienced
in editorial work and in publishing."[4] He had to adjust to an amorphous
and largely secularized role, first with the title of "literary critic and advisor" and after 1922 as editor, situated in Toronto as part of Canada's
biggest printing and publishing concern.[5] By the time of Pierce's arrival

High-minded, talented, and ambitious: the Reverend Lorne
Pierce around the time of his 1920 appointment to Ryerson
Press. Courtesy of Beth Pierce Robinson

at Ryerson, Toronto had been for several decades the production and
distribution centre of English-language publishing in Canada, where
publishing companies sought to prosper amid the challenges of serving
a small population over a vast geographic area, without the economies of
scale of British and American publishers.

The Anglo-American Copyright Agreement of 1891 and the Canadian Copyright Amendment of 1900, among other factors, had fostered
the development of agency publication in Canada – a system whereby
a Canadian publisher contracted with a foreign publisher (usually British or American) to acquire the exclusive Canadian rights to publish

and/or distribute the latter's books and protect the copyright of their authors – or, alternatively, whereby a foreign publisher established a Canadian subsidiary to market the wares of the parent company.[6] Since then, agency publishing had emerged as a staple of Canadian publishing, given that "no ... business could survive on the sales of Canadian books alone."[7] Early in the twentieth century, Canadian subsidiary companies like Macmillan of Canada (1905), Oxford University Press (1904), and Thomas Nelson (1913) had been established in Canada for the purpose of agency publication by their respective British parent companies.

William Briggs, book steward of the House from 1879 to 1919, had been a pioneer in the development of agency publication in Canada in the 1890s, acquiring such lucrative agencies as those for the Cambridge University Press (including its edition of the Bible), G.P. Putnam, Oliphant, and American Pansy Books (best-selling Christian juvenile fiction).[8] By Pierce's arrival, other major publishing houses heavily involved in agency publication (and competition for lucrative agencies was often keen) included McClelland and Stewart, Musson, and Copp, Clark.[9] The oversight of agency matters at the House was never Pierce's responsibility, however: that was the domain of the House's Wholesale Department, managed by Ernest Walker.

The House had also long been a major player in textbook publishing, an area where Pierce would be central. The House's chief Canadian rivals in this field were the Toronto firms of W.J. Gage and Copp, Clark: the three firms had been competing in this area since the 1880s.[10]

By 1920, John McClelland of McClelland and Stewart was one of the publishers interested in the original publication of Canadian authors as part of their book list,[11] and the firms of Cassell, J.M. Dent, Musson, and Macmillan of Canada (the latter despite the misgivings of the parent firm) had begun to show appreciable interest in Canadian writing from the 1910s.[12] John McClelland had declared in 1918, buoyed with the Canadian sales for his firm of writers like Ralph Connor and L.M. Montgomery, that he wanted to specialize "as far as possible on the works of Canadian writers."[13] Hugh Eayrs would take over as head of Macmillan of Canada in 1921 and, like Pierce and McClelland, would show a strong commitment to Canadian literature. Pierce wrote of this period that "John McClelland and Hugh Eayrs believed as I did. We were at the beginnings of things as a nation, and we felt under obligation to assist as many spokesmen of our time as we could."[14] Thus, McClelland and Stewart and Macmillan of Canada would be Ryerson's chief competitors in publishing Canadian literature.

However, original publication of Canadian authors was usually a marginal and economically risky venture for Canadian publishers. At the House, William Briggs and his subordinates had been pioneers in this very dicey area. In the nineteenth and early twentieth centuries, Canadian works had most often been published in Canada by subscription or with the author paying printing costs and the publisher deducting a commission of 40 to 50 per cent off the retail price for distributing the book. Editions were usually 500 to 1,500 copies, and even in the uncommon instance when the House, for example, took on an author at its own risk, the author's royalty was usually "ten percent ... on the retail price based on an edition of 500 to 1,000 copies."[15] Clearly, original publication of Canadian books was not usually very lucrative for publisher or author. Moreover, in the early twentieth century, even agency publications of works acquired from British or American publishers had small print runs: novels and poetry were usually in editions of only 1,000 to 1,500 copies, and average sales for a novel in Canada were "usually well under 2,000 copies."[16] By the 1920s, a Canadian publisher would take on average 2,000 copies of a co-published novel for the Canadian market.[17]

At the House, book publication of any sort was historically not its economic mainstay: in the decade before Pierce's arrival, the House's manufacturing departments doing commercial printing and binding brought in twenty-six times the business of its retail operation.[18] Lorne Pierce would learn just how economically and editorially challenging original publication of Canadian writing continued to be, especially since Ryerson was to publish most of its authors at its own risk, in contrast to the industry's usual practice in the Briggs era.[19]

IN AUGUST 1920, however, Pierce's immediate task was to familiarize himself with his new milieu. The Methodist Book and Publishing House, housed since 1915 in a splendid new five-storey red brick Wesley Building at Queen and John streets, was located in the heart of Ontario's capital. Pierce no longer had the large degree of autonomy that he had enjoyed as a rural minister. Now he reported to a demanding superior in the person of House Book Steward Reverend Samuel Fallis, a man of far different personality some twenty-five years his senior. To complicate matters, Pierce had no real mentors or models from whom to learn in his new career at the House. Both Ryerson Press and his post were newly created, the exact scope of his job uncertain. Fallis could not mentor him: the latter had had no direct experience of the book trade or even of church publications before his own appointment as book steward – in essence general manager – of the House at the Methodist General Conference of October 1918. Fallis had come to the House – where he started work in June 1919[20] – from the pulpit of a large and fashionable Calgary church where his impressive sermons, business ability, magisterial bearing, and conservative views had impressed influential congregants like future prime minister R.B. Bennett.

To adapt to his new role, in the months between his election as book steward and his assumption of the post, Fallis visited the offices of the American Methodist Book Concern, the biggest religious publishing house in the world and "an important and logical place of study for the in-coming Book Steward."[21] His trip had been authorized by the Book Committee of the House – in effect the House's board of directors – made up of appointed clerical and lay members from the Toronto, London, Hamilton, Bay of Quinte, and Montreal conferences of the Methodist Church who were charged with overseeing the Toronto publishing operation.[22]

In 1919 Fallis had spearheaded the creation of "The Ryerson Press" imprint within the House for the publication of trade books, which had previously been published under the imprint of "William Briggs," his predecessor, an expression of his desire to make Ryerson Press "not only the publishing house of The Methodist Church in Canada, but also a publishing house of national significance."[23] From the beginning, Fallis told Pierce that the job of literary critic and adviser was to embrace the publishing of Canadian books. Pierce recalled of his job description:

> I was informed that I was to assist the Book Steward by working
> out for him a live publishing programme, and that I was to aid
> the Church at large by advising the membership on books and
> reading, assist our ministers with their search for reading material,
> put a shoulder behind study groups here and there, organize book
> clubs and be generally useful. Being generally useful included
> keeping a watch on the kind of books reviewed and advertised in
> the Church paper, mak[ing] note of the relative merits of our book
> promotion and that of rival concerns, and conduct[ing] "The Book
> Steward's Corner" in *The Christian Guardian*.[24]

In creating the Ryerson imprint and in hiring Pierce, an ordained minister, to promulgate it, Fallis was giving original book publication a new status within the House, given that, previously, "book editorial work had existed as a secondary concern of first the editor of the [*Christian*]

Guardian, then the editor of the [church] periodicals before finally being designated the task of a non-clerical employee."[25]

But, while Fallis gave Pierce this mission, the book steward himself did not have the expertise to show Pierce the way – or the time. Fallis was the top administrator of a huge operation, which included a large printing plant and bindery, a wholesale book department, numerous Sunday School periodicals, and the *Christian Guardian*. The *Guardian* was losing money, and Fallis was also coping with the lingering debt from the construction of the Wesley Building a half-decade earlier.[26]

In retrospect, it seems clear that Fallis fondly imagined in 1920 that, in the young Reverend Pierce, he had hired a dynamic but deferential subordinate, one who would be happy to edit and publish books, ghost write "The Book Steward's Corner" book column for him in the influential *Christian Guardian* (in 1920 Canada's largest circulation weekly magazine, with 40,000 subscribers, produced and printed at the House),[27] and generally make himself useful. In other words, Fallis pictured Pierce as his assiduous and eloquent cupbearer. That Fallis so conceived of Pierce's role is suggested by that fact that, on arrival at the House in August 1920, Pierce, to his disappointment, was assigned a desk in a small alcove in Fallis's office anteroom at which to work – not his own office – and also had to share the services of Fallis's secretary.[28] The stage was set for tensions between Fallis and Pierce.

Fallis expected that young Pierce would publish books – original Canadian titles which would make Ryerson, as Pierce put it, the "cultural Mecca of Canada."[29] Pierce was expected to help to rescue the trade-publishing program from the stagnation into which it had fallen in the period 1914–19 after the glory days of the turn of the century.[30] Certainly, Fallis wished to revitalize and reconstitute the House's tradition of publishing Canadian authors, a nearly century-old tradition which had evolved under Fallis's predecessor William Briggs and his subordinates.[31] Fallis's choice of the name "The Ryerson Press" is suggestive.[32] Since Egerton Ryerson had been not only the founder of the House and the father of Canadian Methodism but also the architect of Ontario's education system, Fallis was clearly declaring ambitious cultural ideals for Ryerson Press that were secular and national as well as religious.

Pierce took his role as literary critic and advisor to heart. Always an overachiever, driven by the demons of his Methodist boyhood, he wanted in all sincerity to function as both editor and writer, both publisher and author, both general editor and copy editor – and to excel at all of these roles. One of the remarkable things about Pierce in these first years –

and indeed throughout his forty-year career at Ryerson Press – was that, given his education and his eloquent pen, he was never content simply to be a leading publisher. He also strove to be an influential critic of Canadian literature and leading spokesman for Canadian nationalism, especially Canadian cultural nationalism. While other publishers who shared his nationalism – Hugh Eayrs, president of Macmillan of Canada from 1921 to 1940, for example – did some writing about Canadian literature and/or Canadian cultural nationalism, they never aspired to the triple tiara of editor, critic, and nationalist sage that Lorne Pierce sought during his forty years at Ryerson Press.

By education and temperament, moreover, Lorne Pierce was more of an intellectual than the bluff, shrewd, self-made Yorkshireman Hugh Eayrs of Macmillan of Canada or the hard-working, intense, abstemious John McClelland of McClelland and Stewart. Pierce had far more education (but, admittedly, far less experience in publishing and at the outset none of the trade's "street smarts") than his two chief competitors, neither of whom were university men. Indeed, few Toronto publishers of the day were university graduates: Pierce, by contrast, boasted no less than four degrees and, in the spring of 1922, was about to complete the doctorate in systematic theology at Montreal's United Theological College he had begun by correspondence in Brinston.

Furthermore, although McClelland and Eayrs were the two publishers who would rival Pierce for promotion of Canadian literature by the late 1920s, both were personally content to function as publishers, rather than strive also to be prolific authors themselves, as Pierce would do. Moreover, as administrative heads of their respective firms, McClelland and Eayrs, unlike Pierce at the House, had time-consuming responsibilities like labour relations and agency publication.

Lorne Pierce's sought-after triple crown of publisher, editor, and author was also inevitably a three-ply crown of thorns. Pierce, despite immense energy and drive, despite formidable innate abilities nurtured by his Methodist mother in Delta so long ago, was taking on a mission at Ryerson Press – a cultural and moral mission – that was bound to exact great personal and professional costs.

IN FACT, any examination of Pierce's career in publishing must explore two physical limitations he was forced to overcome to succeed. Two grave – and little-known – challenges in his life and career became clear during his first five years at Ryerson Press. First, by his early years at Ryerson, Pierce suffered from near-total deafness – profound "deaf-enedness," to use the correct medical term for the condition. Second, his long-time health problems – periodic bouts of bronchitis, pleurisy, pneumonia, fatigue, influenza, and other ailments – were diagnosed at this time as severe systemic lupus.

Either condition, particularly at this era in medical history, would have severely limited most human beings. Pierce, it is true, faced the challenges of both deafness and lupus and to a great extent overcame both chronic conditions to excel in his career. Nevertheless, both conditions greatly affected the way his life and work unfolded.

Pierce himself rightly insisted that it would be "almost criminal" to write his biography without considering the loss of his hearing, "which changed my whole life."[33] Of its effects, he confided to his daughter that "to be hit that way at the beginning of your career is a cruel blow. It is not so much the physical disability as the frightful spiritual shock ... with attendant social and other maladjustments."[34] Remarkably, despite the handicap, he succeeded in publishing, a profession where schmoozing and networking – much of it both oral and aural – is crucial. It is astonishing, for instance, to discover that, throughout his career, Lorne Pierce could not effectively use the telephone, from the 1920s an increasingly vital tool of the trade.

Problems with Pierce's hearing began to appear in the west before the First World War and then in Ottawa in 1916. It continued to deteriorate inexorably throughout the Great War and its aftermath.[35] By 1920, Pierce began to recognize that his hearing loss was both permanent and largely irremediable, given the primitive hearing aids of the period. He also knew the problem could hurt his career. In the spring of 1920, for example, giving the crucial candidate's sermon at Montreal's Douglas Methodist Church, Pierce had realized to his horror that his hearing loss undermined his ability to give the eloquent homily essential to winning a prominent pulpit.[36] Ominously, he did not win the call. During his first years at Ryerson, moreover, Pierce found public speaking increasingly difficult. (After all, for effective public speaking, it is vital to be able to hear one's own voice to modulate for maximum effect.) He also found it difficult to follow speeches or conversations, especially in crowded or noisy settings.

How, then, to cope in the publisher's world of book launchings, literary gatherings, and meetings? How could an increasingly stone-deaf publishing executive function effectively there? Even one-on-one con-

versations were difficult, and Pierce admitted to his close friends that
he found the handicap limiting. For example, he confided in a letter to
poet Annie Charlotte Dalton, herself deaf, that although "many distinguished men of letters" passed through Toronto, "but for this d— deafness I would get hold of some of them. One never gets used entirely to
the blamed thing."[37]

One side effect of Pierce's hearing loss – now well documented by
psychologists who have studied the effects of hearing loss on personality[38] – is that, as a result, he became even more relentlessly focused on
his inner goals. At the most basic level, for example, Pierce wrote and
read manuscripts undistracted by the ringing of telephones in the office
or the voices of his family at home. He could not hear them. In addition, the hearing-impaired often tend to dominate conversations – it is
so much easier for them to speak and be heard rather than try to hear
others. Furthermore, the deaf, especially if they are as talented and charismatic as Pierce, are apt to be the object of the solicitude and accommodation of their family, close friends, and colleagues to an exceptional
degree. Pierce's deafness thus made him more determined, and more
apt to receive the approbation of others. But deafness also fuelled his
relentless drive and single-mindedness, traits whose effects, especially on
his family and close co-workers, could be synonymous with ruthlessness.

There were other dark consequences of Pierce's hearing loss. For the
rest of his life, he had to battle the powerful feelings of depression and
isolation that the deaf suffer as they sense the rich world of sound inexorably slipping away. For example, Pierce lamented that he had never
really properly heard his children's voices. He had always loved music
but after the early 1920s he could never hear it properly. By the 1940s, he
could not hear a church service if seated in the congregation, even with
a hearing aid. At work, even as early as 1920 to 1925, he had to cope with
the frustration of arrangements misunderstood and cues missed because
he could not hear or, worse yet, because he had misheard a crucial conversation, failed to notice a vital nuance in someone's voice, or mistaken
a figure in a discussion of financial matters. At home, his hearing loss
could at times render him oblivious to his wife, his daughter, Beth, and
his son, Bruce, born in January 1923. They agonized about how to relate
to a man who could not hear them as he bent over the desk where he
spent so much of his time at home, and with whom conversation was
difficult even when he finally emerged.[39]

In short, in his first years at Ryerson Press, Pierce was learning the frustrations of deafness – and during an era when handicaps carried a much greater stigma than they do today. In estimating Pierce's life, it is vital to remember – as Pierce knew every moment of his life in publishing – that he accomplished what he did at Ryerson in the face of a handicap that drastically limited him every hour of every day. Furthermore, Pierce's deafness was a limitation that, true to his Methodist stoicism and the social and gender conventions of the time, he rarely discussed openly. Undeniably, however, deafness was one of the major challenges of his adult life.

Pierce's lupus was another formidable obstacle to success. His type of lupus – properly, Systemic Lupus Erythematosus (SLE) – is a cruel, chronic, and capricious auto-immune disease of no certain viral or genetic origin.[40] Also known as disseminated lupus, it is a "chronic inflammatory disease of unknown origin," for which a definitive diagnostic test, the LE cell test, was developed only in 1948. The disease, which attacks many organs of the body, owes its name, lupus – the Latin word for wolf – to its hungry, vulpine depredations on the bodies of sufferers as antibodies assault the body's own connective tissue.[41]

When the records of Pierce's early life are examined, it seems clear that some of the varied effects of lupus (which flares up and remits in an unpredictable pattern) – severe sinus problems, pleurisy, other respiratory as well as cardiac problems, fever, flu-like illnesses, anemia, arthritic symptoms, extreme fatigue – had begun to plague Pierce by early adolescence. For example, Pierce's return home to Delta from Victoria College in December 1914 with exhaustion and the months of illness that followed, his severe respiratory infections in the west between 1912 and 1914, his medical discharge from the army in 1917 – all these episodes are in fact consistent with (especially given the crude diagnostic techniques of the time) the presence of lupus. Was Pierce's supposed tuberculosis, diagnosed by army doctors in March 1917, additional to his lupus or really misdiagnosed lupus?

We cannot be sure, but one thing *is* clear. By the period 1920 to 1925, Pierce was experiencing serious chronic fatigue in tandem with skin, respiratory, arthritic, and cardiac problems. Pierce came to know at first hand why lupus is nicknamed "the disease of 1,000 faces" for the unpredictable ways it attacks the bodies of sufferers. In the early 1920s, his painful skin rashes and sensitivity to the sun finally manifested as a distinctive, periodic, disfiguring red "butterfly rash" over his nose and face. The rash at last enabled doctors of the day to diagnose his lupus.[42]

In the 1920s, the treatments for lupus were primitive (as they are even today, despite the development of steroids like prednisone, because no cure for the disease has been found). The palliatives prescribed could at best only relieve some symptoms. Starting early in that decade, Pierce sat under ultraviolet light to treat his skin rashes (a regimen now known to be highly carcinogenic). He used aspirin, liniment, and other nostrums to ease what he called his "lumbago," the acute arthritic and rheumatic symptoms of disseminated lupus. Pierce usually grudgingly and belatedly treated his frequent bouts of exhaustion with bed rest. Given his work-aholism, such rest time was invariably inadequate but probably the only treatment that brought him some benefit. But inevitably, the cycle of overwork and collapse began again. By the 1950s, moreover, Pierce also had to cope with having to take ACTH, a corticosteroid specifically de-veloped for lupus (the first ever), whose side effects include disruptions of mood and sleep patterns, tissue swelling, and softening of the skeletal structure.[43] Some of the eye problems associated with systemic lupus appear also to have affected Pierce's vision at various times. Moreover, from the early 1940s, "writer's cramp," probably the result of lupus, would disable his right hand, making him resort to laboured penmanship with his left hand or to the typewriter.

One of the most important imperatives for lupus sufferers is to avoid stress and anxiety, a crucial preventative measure at which Lorne Pierce failed dismally throughout his life. After all, Pierce was hard-driving and determined to succeed. In the early years, his secretary nicknamed him "The Whirling Dervish" for the pace he set, while other House employ-ees – in the office and in the printing plant alike – often referred to him, for the most part affectionately, as "OTH." The letters stood for "On The Hop" – a notation he often penned on work orders and memos.[44]

Such notations reflected that Pierce was now caught up in the de-manding world of publishing, as part of a highly bureaucratic, church-run publishing house. The House, with its publishing, agency, printing, sales, advertising, shipping, and magazine divisions, had more than its share of rivalries and inept management, a Byzantine world where church politics complicated publishing politics, as Pierce would discover to his chagrin soon after his arrival. Years later, trying to recover in a few weeks of holiday from an exhausting year, Pierce summed up the ever-present travails of the intensively competitive Canadian publishing world in a letter: "By jing I needed [a rest]. It has been an old hoss of a year, and I am tired of beauty, weary of truth and satiated with goodness, let alone the business of making a go of publishing in this fair dear land, where a fellow deacon in the church or a brother warden in the [Masonic] lodge will [in the publishing trade] snitch one of your agencies sooner than he'd swat a fly!"[45]

No estimate of Pierce's career, then, can ignore the fact that he achieved what he did in spite of two major physical challenges. His achievements in publishing would have been remarkable for a healthy man. But Lorne Pierce was *never* healthy.

WHILE THIS book constitutes a biography of Lorne Pierce, not an organizational history of the Ryerson Press, or of its parent organization the Methodist Book and Publishing House, it is important to set Pierce's career in the context of this venerable, church-owned, and somewhat curious and hybrid publishing enterprise. While Pierce played virtually no role in the business or financial affairs of his publishing house (that was the domain of Fallis and his business subordinates, like accountant Fred Ellins), he headed and enlarged a significant department of the Methodist Book and Publishing House, a fact formally acknowledged in 1922 when Fallis named him general editor of Ryerson Press.

Scholars have done important research on the House, one of the oldest and in 1920 undoubtedly the largest publisher in the dominion.[46] And, as Pierce became more successful, he himself compiled two histories of the firm. At Fallis's request, he compiled, near the end of his own first decade of service, *The Chronicle of A Century, 1829–1929* (1929), marking the 100th anniversary of the House. Much later, six years before his retirement, he produced the monograph *The House of Ryerson* (1954), a volume to honour the firm's 125th anniversary. In these histories, Pierce gave valuable accounts of the evolution of the Methodist Book and Publishing House. One must be mindful, however, that, to some extent, he made of the House's history a personal construct, a happy hunting ground for a mythology of his own editorship – rooting the sources and the values of his editorship in the careers of earlier book stewards and of some of the House's book and magazine editors prominent before 1920.

Pierce was justified in seeing his editorship as part of an intellectual continuum, though perhaps not in as tidily whiggish a fashion as presented in his accounts. For example, he wrote in *An Editor's Creed* that "the Publishing House [has] a sense of history, of tradition, of destiny and ... this ... shapes and colours and motivates everything that the House does."[47] There is no doubt that his editorship did draw on a tradition of moral idealism and cultural nationalism present in the House hierarchy and publication lists since the early nineteenth century.[48] Moreover, as we have seen, the values of Pierce's Methodist upbringing and his education in idealism at both Queen's and the Methodist Victoria College steeped him (despite his dislike of the latter institution) in the moralism, the bookishness, and the cultural nationalism of Canadian Methodism long before he arrived at the House, itself redolent of idealism, nationalism, and moral uplift. Yet, in the nineteenth and early twentieth centuries, the House's base function was to produce the hymn books, magazines, tracts, pamphlets, and Sunday School publications of Canadian Methodism. Its mission and history were utterly alien to any concept of art for art's sake or a disinterested pan-national aestheticism. Furthermore, there was a strain of earnestness in the House's moralism and nationalism, with results for Lorne Pierce that were sometimes comic and sometimes painful.

Pierce consistently enhanced and utilized a construct of Ryerson Press to nurture genuine and persistent cultural ideals. For example, as early as 1921, he created advertisements for the firm which presented Ryerson as a "grand old house" that "really made the beginning of Canadian literature in book form and has, through nine decades, stood in the forefront of encouraging Canadian writers."[49] Certainly, Pierce was not alone among officials of the House in looking back to Egerton Ryerson and his early editors for both inspiration and validation. For example, a bronze bust of Egerton Ryerson long dominated the executive office of Book Steward Samuel Fallis and his successors, a reminder to visitor and incumbent alike of the tradition and example of the first illustrious book steward. For his part, in 1919, Fallis sought to symbolize a link to Egerton Ryerson in his own initiatives by officially adopting the name "The Ryerson Press" for trade imprints whereas William Briggs had simply used his own name.[50] As Lorne Pierce once observed: "How legends grow in this rich gumbo of our fair dear land."[51]

That being said, in 1920, the House genuinely looked back to a record of substantial cultural and religious achievement, as one scholar of the House for the period 1829 to 1926 has concluded:

> Fundamentally, the Methodist Book and Publishing House was an important Canadian cultural institution. Evidence of its influence

appears not only in the number and variety of its publications that survive, but also in the endeavours of a generation of important, early twentieth-century Canadian publishers – John McClelland [Sr.], S.B. Gundy, George Stewart, Frederick Goodchild, Thomas Allen – that it nurtured ... To study the House is to cross the boundaries of Canada's, and more specifically, Ontario's literary, publishing, and religious history. Its exploration confirms ... Louis Rousseau's and William Westfall's assessment that a close relationship has existed "between religion, society and culture in English Canada." Indeed that [Samuel] Fallis and [Lorne] Pierce could so readily envision the church publishing house as [in Pierce's phrase] a Canadian "cultural mecca" only emphasizes the interconnectedness of religion and culture that has prevailed.[52]

In short, the House printing presses, over the century that preceded Lorne Pierce's arrival at its imposing new Wesley Building, had produced not only a flood of religious magazine, newspapers, tracts, and Sunday School publications but a flood of secular material. The latter publications, under Briggs's tenure, ranged from Catherine Parr Traill's *Pearls and Pebbles* (1894) to Robert Service's *Songs of a Sourdough* (1907) as well as lucrative job-printing contracts like the Simpson's and Eaton's mail-order catalogues (both companies were headed by good Methodists, after all) and more prosaic forms, pamphlets, catalogues, and company reports produced for a wide variety of Toronto businesses.

The genesis of what became the Methodist Book and Publishing House began in 1829, when the Reverend Egerton Ryerson, then a newly fledged Methodist minister, bought a printing press at the behest of the 1829 Conference of the Methodist Episcopal Church so that the church could print a magazine, the *Christian Guardian*. As the Methodist Church in Canada evolved in the nineteenth and early twentieth centuries, and as various church unions took place, the House fell under the aegis of the Wesleyan Methodist Church in Canada until 1874, then under the Methodist Church of Canada until 1884, and then the Methodist Church from 1884 until the creation of the United Church of Canada out of the majority Methodist, Presbyterian, and Congregational churches in 1925. As historian Christina Burr points out: "Throughout the entire period between 1883 and 1925 the management of the firm was required to report at the annual conference or, after 1874, the General Conference of the Methodist Church."[53]

When any organization, much less a zealous and outreaching faith like early Canadian Methodism,[54] buys a printing press, the chances are that a flood of publications will soon result. In this case, the dynamic Ryerson and his enterprising fellow Canadian Methodists were building on their heritage. Early Methodism consistently emphasized the importance not only of the Good Book but of good books and publications in general. From John Wesley's time, printing presses were an important tool of revivalism and of education, especially given the Methodist penchant for interdenominational cooperation on social issues.[55] In the Canadian context, considering the volatile and controversial religious and political questions fermenting in Upper Canada between 1829 and Confederation, it is not surprising that the subscription lists of the *Christian Guardian* flourished in these early decades.[56] By 1861 in Ontario – a province where Methodism had the most adherents of any religious group – the *Christian Guardian* had a great deal of influence with many Methodists and non-Methodists alike. By 1890, it enjoyed a paid circulation of 13,094, a figure that rose to 22,029 by 1914. In the latter year, *Onward*, one of the Sunday school publications, had the impressive circulation figure of 101,416, whereas another such periodical for young adults, *Berean Leaf Intermediate*, boasted a circulation of 62,394.[57] Meanwhile, from the mid-nineteenth century, the series of church unions within Methodism noted above produced a larger, continent-wide – and more nationalistic – Methodist church in Canada, which in turn stimulated interest in the church's periodicals.

As for books, in the early days of Upper Canada, what became popularly known as the "Methodist Book Room" had no formal book-publication policy. From the 1830s, the book-publication list "just grew'd" as Ryerson and his church associates saw fit and as funds were available, often by subscription. The first book published by the Press was *The Doctrines and Disciplines of the Methodist Church in Canada* in 1829. Early Methodist itinerant preachers in British North America eked out their livelihood by selling books from the publishing house in New York that they carried in saddlebags. From the 1840s, circuit riders acted as agents for the Upper Canadian Book Room, and were forbidden to buy their own books from other sources. Meanwhile, with book profits directed to the pension needs of retired Methodist clergy, there were many instances of slipshod accounting, overloaded saddle horses, or recalcitrant ministers hounded by the Book Room for unpaid accounts.[58] Even as late as 1914, a weary Lorne Pierce fretted to his diary about accounts past due to the Book Room, an added worry as he jolted by horse and buggy over the mission fields of Saskatchewan trying to organize schools and congregations.[59]

The House grew progressively more complex in its operations, evolving "from an establishment engaged in producing a single denominational newspaper [the *Christian Guardian*] to a business engrossed in wholesale and retail bookselling, commercial printing, periodical publication, book manufacture, and original book publishing."[60] From the pre-Confederation era, however, the policies and publications of the House were influenced by the political and cultural nationalism found in the Canadas generally and among the dedicated and patriotic clerical intellectuals involved with the press and its publications. Egerton Ryerson was the first such figure – and, as Ontario's pioneering superintendent of education from 1844 to 1876, the most influential – but in the pre-1920 period numerous other House officials, cultural nationalists all, left their mark on book and magazine publication projects. These worthies included William Withrow and Edward Hartley Dewart, as well as William Briggs and his employees between 1879 and 1919, including Edward S. Caswell, John McClelland, and Samuel B. Gundy.

The Reverend E.H. Dewart edited the first anthology of Canadian literature, *Selections from Canadian Poets*, published by Montreal's John Lovell in 1864, the very year of the Charlottetown Conference which laid the groundwork for Confederation. At the House, Dewart espoused a policy of encouraging local literature during his long editorship from 1869 of the *Christian Guardian*. In thinking that anticipated Pierce's own, he emphasized the importance of the "subtle but powerful cement of a patriotic literature" in developing a nation.[61]

Dewart's House colleague William Withrow founded the *Canadian Methodist Magazine* (1874–1906), a literary and general-interest publication which featured work by such Canadian writers as Charles G.D. Roberts, Catharine Parr Traill, and Archibald Lampman. In his first editorial for the magazine, Withrow declared that the publication aimed to encourage "the growth of a sound native literature in our young Dominion," one that conformed to "high moral principles."[62] (Pierce emulated Withrow even to the degree of adopting Withrow's characteristic phrase "both hands" as a signature close to many of his letters to bookmen.)

But it was under William Briggs, book steward from 1879 to 1919, and his subordinates that the House knew its first "glory years" as a publisher of Canadiana – although, as was the widespread practice of the day in the inchoate Canadian book trade, the publications of the Canadian writers concerned were usually underwritten by the author either personally or through advance subscriptions. Both church and secular publishing companies (for example, John Lovell of Montreal) rarely published books original to Canada without authorial or other subsidy. The country's small and scattered population, its fragmented book market, and the shifting – but consistently nightmarish – state of copyright jurisdiction and protection in the British North American market in the period 1840 to 1920 made publishers understandably reluctant, and usually financially unable, to assume all the risk of publication.[63]

As Lorne Pierce later reminded Canadians, practically every major nineteenth-century work of Canadian literature was either first published abroad or paid for by private subsidy or subscription – or both. For example, Charles G.D. Roberts's first book of verse, *Orion and Other Poems* (1880), a seminal work of the day, was first brought out by a Philadelphia publisher at Roberts's own expense.[64] Indeed, in the period up to 1920, Canadian writers often despaired of finding a Canadian publisher at all. If they did locate one, their royalties were usually pitifully small, and copyright protection based on first publication in Canada was invariably less advantageous than from first publication in the United States or Great Britain. Furthermore, the work of making publication financially possible was usually either costly or onerous for the authors concerned – given the usual frustrations of scraping together funds, or subscribers, or both. Even authors who had lucrative professions, like senior civil servant Duncan Campbell Scott or Montreal lawyer William D. Lighthall, were nonetheless indignant at having to underwrite their own literary productions. Poet Scott once acidly observed that his Canadian publisher "should be whipped for his indifference."[65] But publishers were largely captive to the economic vicissitudes of the scattered, largely philistine nature of the Canadian market, a market where they usually had to compete with the books offered by far more prosperous United States publishers who enjoyed much greater economies of scale in book production.[66]

Briggs, an able business manager, greatly increased the House's agency-publication activities, sometimes inserting new title pages for Canadian offerings. By the early twentieth century, his Wholesale Department manager, Ernest Walker, hired in 1892, was overseeing the acquisition, marketing, and distribution of the House's agency arrangements with American and British publishers like Thomas Nelson, Blackie, and

G.P. Putnam.[67] A big seller like Marie Corelli's *God's Good Man* meant a printing of 10,000 copies for the Canadian market by the House, an exceptional sales figure for the day.[68] Such arrangements could be profitable, especially when the House had exclusive Canadian rights to popular best-sellers by foreign authors like Arthur Conan Doyle, Marie Corelli, and John Galsworthy,[69] but did little for cultural nationalism in Canada except insomuch as agency profits potentially made it feasible to consider forays into original publication of Canadian authors. Moreover, Walker's characteristic caution was to be a thorn in Lorne Pierce's flesh from the 1920s to Walker's retirement in 1946; an earlier House colleague had also been exasperated by Walker's attitude that "new & untried authors" had to "prove their innocence of being frosts & failures before he will give his faith to them."[70]

During Briggs's tenure, too, the House printing plant won large, lucrative contracts to produce the Eaton's and Simpson's mail-order catalogues, and, at Briggs's instigation, the House also successfully competed on a wide variety of fronts against commercial printers for job printing of Ontario government publications and textbooks for Ontario schools. The House's profitable contracts under Briggs and others foreshadowed Lorne Pierce's steering of Ryerson Press into lucrative original textbook publication.

Perhaps the closest House counterpart to Lorne Pierce at the turn of the century was bookman Edward S. Caswell, who consistently published Canadian writers.[71] An employee of the House from 1881 to 1909, the Goderich-born Caswell encouraged such writers as Nellie McClung, Catharine Parr Traill, Susan Frances Harrison ("Seranus"), and Robert Service. Although restrained by Book Steward Briggs's careful business acumen and shrewd number-crunching, Caswell did much to provide strong Canadian literary content to the House's Canadian book list (under the imprint "William A. Briggs"). In addition, as Pierce did in the early 1920s with his anthology *Our Canadian Literature* (1922), Caswell himself edited and published a Canadian literary anthology, in his case *Canadian Singers and Their Songs* (1902).[72] A strong supporter of the work of Catharine Parr Traill,[73] he also had the prescience to be a prime mover in Briggs's publication of two works by then-unknown authors which became best-sellers – Robert Service's *Songs of a Sourdough* and feminist and fiction writer Nellie McClung's *Sowing Seeds in Danny* (1908).

Caswell, like Pierce after him, tasted the frustrations of working for a church-owned publishing house – the bureaucracy, the sanctimonious-

ness, the narrow moralism, the inefficiency, the infighting, and the low
salaries. And, as with Pierce too, Caswell's involvement with some publications brought accusations of self-interest upon his head. (Scholars
debate Caswell's financial involvement with the publication of *Sowing
Seeds in Danny*.[74]) These accusations were similar to the difficulties
Pierce would have with Fallis and the House stemming from his role as
author or volume editor as well as publisher of several Ryerson publications, including lucrative textbooks.

Unlike Pierce, Caswell ultimately left the House for greener pastures;
he was probably prompted to leave for a senior post at the Toronto Public
Library in 1909 by the House's low salaries and by the controlling if canny
management of William Briggs. Moreover, Caswell, as a non-minister
(unlike Pierce), could advance only to a certain level in the House. Like
other non-clerical House colleagues of the day, he could never hope, for
example, to succeed Briggs as book steward or to edit in-house church
publications like the *Christian Guardian*, positions reserved for ordained
ministers. Another of Caswell's one-time lay colleagues at the House,
John McClelland, head of the publishing firm McClelland and Goodchild – which eventually became McClelland and Stewart – founded
that company in 1911 with another Briggs alumnus after leaving the
House.[75] Other prominent Toronto publishers and bookmen cut their
teeth at the House as lay employees under Briggs. For example, Samuel
B. Gundy left the House in 1904 to become Toronto branch manager for
Oxford University Press.[76]

Unquestionably, Briggs and his gifted subordinates established an impressive record of original publication of Canadian literature in the early
twentieth century. But, by the eve of the First World War, the House's
trade-publication program was in the doldrums. The rate of profit flat-
tened in the decade after 1906, ending a long period of increasing profits
that been evident for more than three decades.[77] The reasons were various: Briggs was aging, public taste was changing, and many of Briggs's
talented underlings had left, leaving less gifted men like Ernest Walker
and E.J. Moore in middle management at the House. As well, in the
1910s, the resources of the House were for several years caught up in the
huge task of compiling and printing a new Methodist hymn book.[78]
On top of all this, as the printing plant needed more room, Briggs was
preoccupied by the construction of a handsome but extremely expensive new home for the House, at the corner of John Street and Queen
Street West in Toronto. Completed in 1914, the block-long Art Deco

Wesley building, with its inscribed main entrance and plaster detailing, was impressive – but it was also plagued with scandal over cost overruns and a controversial land acquisition. Tongues wagged about the "Million Dollar Book Room," a derisive reference to the building's huge cost.[79] Then came the war, which brought other worries to the House. Book sales at first soared (patriotic titles like Jean Blewett's short fiction volume *Grey Knitting* [1915] sold well) but many titles languished as the new plant was plagued with manpower and material shortages. Only six original book titles, for example, were published in 1918, versus twenty-five in 1910.[80]

Change was afoot: Samuel Wesley Fallis was chosen as the new book steward in 1918, and eighty-two-year-old William Briggs was created book steward emeritus. The next year, Fallis created "The Ryerson Press" imprint at the House to publish original Canadian titles. When Fallis's hand-picked new employee, Lorne Pierce, arrived at the Wesley Building in August 1920, he came under the shrewd eye of Book Steward Emeritus William Briggs, who still came in regularly to his office beside Fallis's. But all the veteran Briggs offered Pierce, beavering away in his alcove, was a polite handshake. Briggs was undoubtedly waiting to see how the new employee would perform. Unquestionably, Pierce faced a slippery slope in his new post, as the next decade would reveal.

8

"On the Hop"

Lorne Pierce's Uneasy Apprenticeship at Ryerson Press, 1920–1925

I have a real he-man's job, that of making our Methodist Book
Room the cultural Mecca of Canada. My powers are great, my
responsibilities enormous, but my faith and grit are about ecumenical!
Lorne Pierce diary, 11 July 1920

Somehow I feel that my life is ordained to more than ordinary
burdens and possibly to equally great achievements.
Lorne Pierce diary, 1 June 1924

During his first few weeks at Ryerson, Lorne Pierce wrote enthusiastically to his wife: "Have been very busy. Dictated a whole sheaf of letters today and made out six study courses [i.e., directed reading lists] for the 2600 odd ministers etc. It is some job." Pierce added blithely: "There is the joy of knowing that what I am doing counts. Every book I boost sells like hot cakes."[1] By nature optimistic, Pierce also tended to view his new House colleagues through rose-coloured glasses. About Fallis, he observed that the book steward "could not be more kind if he tried his hardest."[2] As for his new colleagues, Pierce was at first in awe of Wholesale Department manager, Ernest Walker, long-time head of agency publications for the House. He was impressed by Walker's plum job, which involved annual business trips abroad to discuss agency arrangements with companies like Knopf in New York City and Oxford in England.

Pierce was also impressed by another House colleague, E.J. Moore, who boasted to him about his own success as an author and of his financial and publishing acumen. Lorne wrote Edith: "Next door to me is Mr. E.J. Moore, head of the publishing end and he is also an author of some repute. Makes anywhere from $25 to $300 a story. His income last year from his stories was about $1500. He is a great help and I am going to learn a lot from him. Anyhow there is a wonderful chance to work up here and I am confident that the future will be well with us."[3] Moore, nine years' Pierce's senior, had condescendingly assured his new colleague that he planned to write "two or 3" articles on Pierce's "work in Matilda when he gets time for the big magazines."[4]

The vulnerability and up-beat tone of these letters of Lorne Pierce are striking, as are the endearments to "my girlies," Edith and infant daughter Beth.[5] His trust in some of his new colleagues would prove over-optimistic, however. It is not difficult to imagine how ambivalent managers like Moore and Walker – especially Moore, who had been involved in the Canadian list – must have been to see the sudden advent of that quick-witted young eager beaver, the Reverend Dr Pierce. Moreover, before the creation of the Ryerson Press division of the House in 1919, employees like E.S. Caswell usually had to get the cooperation of House managers like Walker and Moore in order to have the financial wherewithal to publish original Canadian titles. By contrast, Pierce would not usually have to consult with colleagues like Walker or Moore to publish Canadian authors under the Ryerson imprint.

The novice bookman now had to acquire not just familiarity with the Canadian literary scene but expertise in it. Before 1920, Lorne Pierce made no bones that, while he was curious about Canadian literature, he (like most Canadians of the day) knew little of it. Edith Pierce was in fact more knowledgeable than he about Canadian literature. For example, in 1914, Edith wrote to him about her love for the poetry of Pauline Johnson. Pierce admitted his interest in the poet, but also his "complete ignorance" of any Johnson poem except "The Song My Paddle Sings."[6] At Queen's two years earlier, he had reacted to James Cappon's scorn toward his question about Canadian literature by buying an anthology of Canadian poetry. But he did not then immerse himself in the volume, eventually presenting it to Edith.

Pierce later reminded an interviewer that he had no experience of publishing or of Canadian literature when he arrived at the House: "When I came to the publishing business, I was totally inexperienced in editorial work and in publishing – in addition my own literary interests could scarcely have been less attuned to Canada's own literary needs … All my chief interests were non-Canadian."[7] However, despite his inexperience, Pierce possessed attributes that would fuel his rise in the book trade: a voracious mind, the determination to read mountains of books and manuscripts, a visionary bent, and a relentless drive to make his mark at Ryerson Press.

As for his overall view of literature in 1920, Pierce's letters and diaries to that date display his nationalism and his engagement with the moral idealism and national coherence he perceived in Russian literature. Now he placed Canadian literature within a similar national and moral template. In 1925, for example, Pierce outlined for Canadians the patriotic and moral qualities that should be predominant in Canadian literature: "We need three things [in our emerging literature:] (1) Utter fidelity to truth; (2) a determination to be ourselves; and (3) a sympathetic atmosphere in which the sublimest beauty, the loftiest justice and the divinest truth might be expected to take root and flourish, when at last they do appear as ultimately they must and will."[8] In other words, Pierce was assessing Canadian literature in the light of the values he had absorbed from turn-of-the-century Methodism – in the spirit of what religious historian William Westfall has called "romantic evangelism," a dedication to presenting the ideal in words and art, believing it could inspire the individual and exalt society.[9]

Moreover, in espousing such a view of Canadian literature, Pierce was also in harmony with (and stimulated by) the cultural climate of English Canada, Toronto in particular, in the early 1920s. At one of Pierce's first business lunches in the late summer of 1920, his table companions represented the cultural nationalism "in the air" which would infuse his publishing career. He proudly described his fellow diners to Edith: "Had lunch at the Arts and Letters Club with [Augustus] Bridle and with Mr. [Lawren] Harris the artist and President of the A[rts] and L[etters] Club and the Ontario Art Association – also with Vincent Massey. Some class."[10] Interestingly, Bridle, not Fallis, arranged this lunch – a hint that the employee was to gain much of his prominence in circles where his boss did not shine, or even frequent.

Of the people at this lunch, prominent Toronto journalist Augustus Bridle, Pierce's host, had already praised his community work in Brinston. The two others at the table, the artist and the arts patron, excited Pierce about the possibilities before him in this brave new cultural world. Lawren Harris, a member of the Group of Seven, the pre-eminent artistic group of the day, was also the president of the Arts and Letters Club, an incubator of Toronto artistic and literary nationalism (soon to be Pierce's favourite lunching and networking venue).[11] As artistic visionary, passionate nationalist, and ardent theosophist (like his fellow artists J.E.H. MacDonald, Frederick Varley, and Thoreau MacDonald, whom Pierce also published and befriended), Harris embodied Pierce's ideological directions.[12]

As for wealthy arts patron (and future governor general) Vincent Massey, Pierce had last encountered him when he was a student at Victoria College in 1914 and Massey his reserve commander. At that time, he had received no particular notice from the patrician Massey. By contrast, in 1920, Massey, an ardent Canadian nationalist (albeit of the anglophile, imperial federation sort, which Pierce, loyal to his Irish forebears, was not), had recently been briefed by Ernest Thomas of the Methodist Church's powerful Department of Evangelism and Social Service about Pierce's impressive community work in Brinston.[13] Massey's presence at lunch that day suggests that, in the minds of Toronto's cultural elite, Pierce was a man to watch.

Lorne Pierce was forever conscious that at the heart of his sense of nationalism lay his appreciation of the Canadian experience in the First World War. For example, he always emphasized that the heroic Canadian military performance at Vimy Ridge was a wellspring of Canadian national feeling in the 1920s. Vimy underlay Pierce's own nationalist impulses, just as the whole Great War experience did the cultural nationalism of the Group of Seven and their contemporaries. Pierce himself linked the two in laying out what he called his "editorial creed," writing that "Canada as a nation was born on that fatal ridge. Canada had paid a terrible price for national sovereignty in the winnowing of the nations and never looked back. In 1920, there was born the Group of Seven ... The whole country seemed to be outward bound, conscious of its emerging identity."[14]

PIERCE'S FIRST few months at Ryerson Press were spent meeting authors, buying and settling into a new home, getting to know the Toronto cultural milieu (as well as his new book steward), and writing reviews for the *Christian Guardian*. The reviews provide an important snapshot of Pierce's literary and social values, values that would largely govern his career at Ryerson Press.

First, Pierce and Fallis. Fallis was impressed by Pierce's energy as he began to churn out reviews and columns for "The Book Steward's Corner," a regular feature in the *Christian Guardian*. The content of these columns more or less conformed to Fallis's own values, although tension between Pierce and Fallis over such topics as feminism and the social gospel was not far off. Pierce was now in effect the ghost writer and mouthpiece for the book steward, one of the most conservative officials at the House, the largest business concern of Canadian Methodism. Given his ecumenical, liberal, and social gospel sympathies, Pierce was in a potentially uncomfortable ideological position. He did share some concerns with most Methodists, from Ernest Thomas on the left to Samuel Fallis on the right, however.

Pierce's writings for the *Guardian* and elsewhere in the 1920s show that his critical principles largely conformed to conservative Methodist views of literature. He still distrusted fiction as a genre too often lacking moral resonance, reminding ministers to avoid much of current fiction or else "sin wilfully" because on the whole "there is no philosophy of life there that will bear scrutiny."[15] His deprecation of the novel constitutes an only slightly moderated version of what the Reverend Nathaniel Burwash, long-time chancellor of Victoria, had maintained: the reading of novels was liable to make "an utter moral and spiritual wreck" of the hapless reader.[16] Thus, despite Pierce's stated dislike of a narrow, dogmatic Methodism in general, he was now in fact articulating the literary moralism of his Methodist education.

Also, Pierce, like many of his middle-aged church and academic contemporaries in the Canada of the early 1920s, was troubled by the values of the "Roaring Twenties," given the decade's constellation of flappers, jazz, and looser sexual mores, as well the proliferation of bootleg liquor in defiance of the temperance legislation in Ontario – which Pierce himself campaigned for in 1919 and helped sustain until 1926. He was as disturbed by the moral laxity he saw in the popularity of flappers and jazz as, for example, the flinty, Presbyterian-bred dean of Canadian intellectuals, Sir Andrew Macphail, editor of the respected (and, significantly, recently defunct) *University Magazine*. Pierce himself was no carefree young sheik in a raccoon coat – as he made emphatically clear to readers of the *Guardian* in an early column. There, Pierce denounced what he saw as the materialism and sensationalism of the early 1920s: "One new fashion follows another in rapid succession. And what shall we say is the last cry to-day? Is it the decollete attire, black fox furs in August, and nudity in November? Is it the craze for self-analysis, Freudianism gone mad? Is it the exotic in life and literature?"[17] Pierce's unease with relaxed modern morality is clear.

But, in the early 1920s, modern morality was not Pierce's only concern. As sole breadwinner for a growing family with a modest income, he was worried by the sluggish economic conditions which prevailed in the period 1920 to 1923. An economic downturn is bad for book sales: it was not an easy time for Pierce to begin in publishing, especially in the traditionally hardscrabble Canadian marketplace. After all, the young book-man was a family man in the big city – who, on a salary of $3,000 a year (adequate but far from lavish, as House salaries historically tended to be), was rapidly discovering how expensive his new surroundings were. Toronto's population swelled in the years after the First World War. As a result, housing was costly, often poorly built, and invariably hard to find for growing middle-class families. After weeks of house hunting whenever he could spare the time, Pierce finally settled on a pleasant but cramped six-room, cedar-shingled house at 56 Wineva Avenue, south of Queen Street East in the middle-class Beaches neighbourhood, a long-ish streetcar ride east of the Wesley Building.

Edith and baby Beth arrived in Toronto on 16 September 1920, three days before the couple's fourth wedding anniversary. Alone in Toronto in a spartan YMCA room in his stressful first weeks at Ryerson Press, Lorne had missed his "girlies," a sentiment reflected in his fourth-anniversary message to Edith:

Our fourth anniversary, happier than ever, and in our own house – Nestledown. We have so much to be thankful for, but most of all I have you to be thankful for.

> "Steel-true and blade-straight
> ...
> A love that life could never tire,
> Teacher, tender comrade, wife,
> A fellow-farer true thru life." R.L.S[tevenson].

Your old lover,
Lorne[18]

In the month that he penned this marital tribute, however, Pierce confided to his diary his worries about the couple's financial inability to duplicate the spacious Brinston manse, especially his large and pleasant study there. Moreover, the couple now had a child to raise: another would soon be on the way.

In addition, financial temptations for Lorne Pierce – for example, socializing at the Arts and Letters Club or buying from antiquarian book dealers – loomed in Toronto. Pierce liked the cultural good life, and he genuinely wanted to be a patron of the arts. Such impulses would help make his reputation in a Canadian literary world where he was almost entirely unknown. But they were expensive. Ed Pierce had always felt that his son had a touch of Irish extravagance to him, and the 1920s were to bring financial and marital difficulties resulting from Pierce's relentless ambition and ambitious good works.

For her part, in 1920, thirty-year-old Edith Pierce was also entering a testing phase of life as wife and mother. From a rural parsonage, she was suddenly plunged into a very different life in a city where she knew few people. Her husband's new career did not provide her with the ready-made social role and contacts of a pastor's wife. A second baby, their long-awaited son, Bruce, would be born to the couple on 5 January 1923. In a small house in an unfamiliar neighbourhood, Edith had to learn to mother, without close female family or friends and initially without household help at a time when housework was much more demanding. Household appliances were primitive: Edith was not to have a washing machine, for example, until the late 1920s.

Edith was, moreover, a perfectionist about her role as "angel in the house," with inflexibly high standards of motherhood, wifehood, homemaking, and hospitality – standards that caused her a great deal of stress. True, she had a university education and some strong feminist influence in her aunt Alice Chown, but she also deeply wanted to excel as traditional wife and mother. She also knew that both her mother-in-law, Harriet Pierce, and her sister-in-law, Sara Chester, were women of exceptional strength and competence. They constituted intimidating role models, with a degree of strength and self-sufficiency Lorne unrealistically felt he could expect of his wife. He told her so on occasion, to her distress.[19]

Lorne and Edith's relationship was also strained by the fact that Lorne, like most middle-class husbands of the day, idealized his wife. Edith was to function as a "true woman" ideal of domestic virtue, with angelic traits of piety, purity, submissiveness, and domesticity. These virtues – to use historian Barbara Welter's description of the patriarchal ideal of true womanhood – were to be focused not only on the home but on inspiring him to greater heights of idealism and achievement.[20] Lorne's lofty assumptions about Edith are very clear in the courtship correspondence.[21]

After marriage, Lorne saw Edith's function as to ennoble him, and conceived of her role as innately subordinate. Edith was to be his emotional bulwark as well as homemaker. Such sentiments, expressed in a letter Lorne wrote shortly before their wedding, embodied traditional gender and marital values of the day: "Your greatest service will be, as it has been, in making me see the meanness and the greatness in myself, and in striving imperfectly but persistently to live what I have seen in you. So after all, tomorrow I go up to this new work [as an Ottawa minister] with a triumphant feeling, for I go with a host – I've God and you."[22] Heavy expectations to live up to. Indeed, Lorne did not realize, either in 1916 or in the 1920s, that casting Edith in such a role was to hold her to standards impossible for any woman to satisfy fully. Furthermore, the "meanness" and the "greatness" within himself to which Lorne referred were qualities more intertwined within him than he imagined, and the life stresses on his own idealism, and thus his marriage, were to prove more problematic than either he or Edith envisioned. Challenges lay ahead for Lorne and Edith Pierce in Toronto, challenges closely linked to the ups and downs of Lorne's career.

IF PIERCE experienced the pressures of traditional marriage at home in the early 1920s, he also addressed changing sexual and social mores in the literature he reviewed in "The Book Steward's Corner" in the *Christian Guardian*. Pierce's upbringing made much of the new modernist sexual and social candour in literature distasteful to him. He was not naive: he had seen some shocking sights in the west as a student teacher and ministerial probationer, and he had encountered squalor, misery, and vice both as a young minister and as a military hospital overseer. Further, as is evident in his work on Russian writers like Dostoevsky and Tolstoy, Pierce recognized that literature must deal frankly with the moral and social problems of a society in transition. But Pierce, even at this early period in his editorial career (before his knuckles were rapped for liberal policies and pronouncements by more conservative fellow Methodists, in particular Samuel Fallis), disliked sexual frankness – or indeed any lack of moral seriousness in literature. One of the bestsellers of 1920 was English aristocrat Margot Asquith's diary, a book that "wowed" book buyers of the day with her avant-garde (for a British prime minister's wife) social and sexual views. In one of Pierce's earliest contributions to the *Christian Guardian*, his puritanical disdain for As-quith's candid diary permeated his review of the work. Revealingly, he conflated traditional gender and literary ideals, equating Margot Asquith's textual revelations with female sexual immodesty: "Her whole performance [in the book] has as much justification as dressing in the street. It is a practice which, if made universal, would be disastrous, a letting down the bars that defies every canon of good taste and good breeding ... [The book is] a crowning illustration of the ultimate abomination to which verbal and ethical desolation may descend."[23]

Strong words. They seem the more conservative when one thinks of the liberal and modernist views in the 1920s of another literary man, born in the same decade as Pierce – F.R. Scott. Frank Scott was the son of an Anglican minister, and in 1920 he was twenty-one years old. In the fall of 1920, Scott was a university student abroad (at Oxford), just as Lorne Pierce had been in New York City five years before. By 1923, Scott, now back in Canada, would be one of Canada's most promising young poets, part of a literary clique at McGill University – brash, irreverent, modernist, and a confirmed and controversial social democrat.[24] By contrast, Pierce's early reviews at about the same period indicate just how far his literary and social values differed from those of emerging young Canadian writers like Frank Scott and A.J.M. Smith.

The divergence between Pierce and many of his literary contemporaries or near-contemporaries in the 1920s would be the greater because of institutional pressure around Pierce at the House. To rebuild the Canadian list, Pierce needed to cultivate older, more traditional (and more artistically conservative) literary figures like Bliss Carman, Charles G.D. Roberts, Gilbert Parker, and Andrew Macphail. Pierce, as an unknown in the literary world, had to gain the confidence of its establishment. At the same time, the anomalies of the Canadian literary scene would also tend to reinforce traditional views in Pierce. In literary Canada in the 1920s, both the burgeoning of Canadian nationalism and the difficult publishing and pecuniary situation of many of its "grand old men" (they were usually men) meant that Pierce and other publishers (Hugh Eayrs at Macmillan and John McClelland at McClelland and Stewart, for example) would be focused on marketing and publishing the grandees to an unusual degree. Arguably, the feeling of the younger writers of the McGill Movement that older, more traditional poets were being exalted excessively was in part the result of the circumstances of the time, when, in the post–First World War burst of Canadian nationalism, older writers returned to Canada to garner belated recognition, not least from Canadian publishers. Bliss Carman came back to Canada in the early to mid-1920s for several tours. He was crowned with maple leaves – but he also needed cash and contracts from publishers, as did his cousin and fellow Confederation poet Charles G.D. Roberts, who returned to Canada to live in 1925.[25]

Accordingly, Pierce was to have his hands full in establishing his own career and consolidating his reputation with the literary old guard. Younger, more avant-garde writers were not his immediate preoccupation. At Ryerson, he needed to win acceptance by the cultural elite of the day – mostly older, conservative males of the ilk of Sir Andrew Macphail, poet and civil servant Duncan Campbell Scott, and critic and University of Toronto professor Pelham Edgar. Among that number, Pierce was particularly anxious to impress his old Queen's professor, James Cappon, and bring him to embrace Canadian literature. These men were established and conservative authors, whose attitude to the emerging modernism of T.S. Eliot, Ezra Pound, James Joyce, and D.H. Lawrence was cautious at best (Edgar and D.C. Scott) and hostile at worst (Macphail and Cappon).

The values of international modernism were also not fully replicated in Canada: the Great War tended to stimulate Canadian nationalism in the arts in a way alien to most English and American modernist writers. For example, the corrosive alienation about patriotism and national feeling found in works like Pound's *Hugh Selwyn Mauberley* (1920) or Eliot's *The Waste Land* (1922) or in American expatriate Ernest Hemingway's *The Sun Also Rises* (1926) was not present to the same degree in the work of many of the young Canadian writers and artists who had come of age in the trenches during the Great War, men like poet John McCrae or man of culture Talbot Papineau (who both died during the Great War), artist A.Y. Jackson, or historian Harold Innis.[26] Canadians had tended to emerge from the war with less of the wholesale cynicism of young British, French, and German and American veterans.

In other words, while wartime military service had taught both Pierce (on the home front) and A.Y. Jackson (in the trenches) that generals were often not worth fighting for, the overall effect of the war had not sunk them in the alienation and hatred for nationalism of many emerging post-war writers outside Canada.[27] Canadian nationalism was part of the work of Canadian modernists, albeit in attenuated form at times. Scholars of modernism in Canada have pointed out that, in the 1920s,

young Canadian writers like A.J.M. Smith and F.R. Scott were influenced by the cultural enthusiasm of the Group of Seven for the stark
beauty of the Canadian landscape as well as by the post-war malaise and
modernist techniques of Pound and Eliot.[28]

For example, such key Canadian modernist poems of the 1920s as
A.J.M. Smith's "The Lonely Land" and F.R. Scott's "Laurentian" owe a
great deal to the vision of the Canadian landscape found in the works
of the Group of Seven. Indeed, A.J.M. Smith's "The Lonely Land," his
most memorable poem about the Canadian landscape, is a clear reference to the Group of Seven canvas of that name. Pierce, too, was to
respond enthusiastically to the Group of Seven's work, and to showcase
their talent in numerous publications. In fact, the strong influence of the
Group of Seven is one of the few commonalities between Pierce's critical
ideals for Canadian literature and those of Smith and F.R. Scott at this
period, which is suggestive of the crucial role that the Group played in
post-First World War Canadian culture.

Overall, however, although Pierce was only thirty years old in 1920,
he came into Canadian publishing in a manner and at a level that guaranteed he had to begin his career dealing with conservative, established
authors of the old school and to largely assume their colours to make his
name. His Methodist background, his new "establishment" surroundings in a church publishing house, and the expectations of the House's
traditional constituency – authors and book buyers alike – would make
change very difficult, at least in his early years in the book business. The
publishing crises he would be embroiled in at the House in the early
1920s would demonstrate this unequivocally to him.

Without a doubt, Pierce's book reviews for the "Book Steward's
Corner" in the period 1920 to 1925 reveal his uneasiness at the changing
moral and cultural milieu of the 1920s in Canada and abroad. Like almost
every established Canadian intellectual in the 1920s – Edgar, Macphail,
Cappon, MacMechan, Watson, Jordan, and many others – as well as
many clerics of all religions, Pierce denounced "the crash of modern materialism" as harmful to social and religious ideals of Canadian society.[29]
Jazz (a particular bugbear of conservative intellectuals and clerics in the
1920s), he denounced as a blight on society, a negative influence on the
young as pernicious as alcohol. Interestingly, he disliked the avant-garde
literature of the Twenties influenced by jazz as much as he did Margot
Asquith's sexual candour. In Pierce's view, both American poet Vachel
Lindsay, then the talk of the North American literary world for jazz-

influenced poems like "The Congo," and his emulators lacked "restraint." In criticizing Lindsay's type of poetry, Pierce wrote worriedly in the spring of 1922: "The modern suffers from a lack of restraint and poise … I am dealing now with a particular kind of so-called modern poetry, which, for want of a better name, I call Jazz Poetry … These jazz rhymesters are able to make an infinitesimally small and unimportant idea go farther than a canary can travel on a bird seed. Some do not even require an idea to cause themselves to be lost in a 'dull, purple and poisonous haze' of poetic ecstasy."[30]

Pierce's unease at jazz and Lindsay's poetry was shared by many literary worthies in the Canada of the early 1920s. At Vachel Lindsay's December 1925 Toronto recital, poet Wilson MacDonald remembered the largely "staid and subdued applause," once the novelty of Lindsay's poem "The Congo" had worn off, from an audience that included Pierce, E.J. Pratt, Bliss Carman, and Pelham Edgar.[31] MacDonald, who loathed modernism, sniffed to his diary that day that Lindsay's work was "interesting for ten minutes" but largely "repetitious and blatant."[32]

Clearly, if Pierce was uneasy about the frankness and self-revelation and sexual suggestiveness of forces as diverse as jazz and psychoanalysis, he had a great deal of company in the Canada of the early 1920s. Issues of race, class, and place – the Jewishness and Europeanness of Freud, the black, working-class, American cultural origins of jazz – also underlay the antipathy of many Canadian intellectuals to these elements of modernism. Pierce's wariness about what he called modern psychology's "almost morbid preoccupation with soul surgery" was an antipathy shared by older critics like Pelham Edgar. Edgar called free association a "disease" and pronounced psychoanalytic theory "wholly valueless for poetry."[33]

Pierce wanted a strong element of patriotism, not soul surgery, in Canadian literature. When he wrote about Canadian literature in the 1920s, his agenda for the country and for the role of Canadian culture within it was already apparent. Pierce sounded a clarion call on this note as early as the fall of 1921. In an article for *Canadian Stationer and Book Trade Journal*, the bible of the book trade, he stressed the importance of the Canadian Authors Association's Canadian Book Week with the warning that Canadians were in danger of losing their "national soul." Pierce wrote: "We are inundated with British and European literature … It is something approaching a scandal the way we boom the American 'Best Seller,' and an equal scandal the way we neglect our own." He went on to characterize the work of Canadian writers as a cultural bulwark needed to assimilate Canada's huge influx of immigrants, revealing a sense of mission that would infuse his publishing program for the next forty years. As in his writing on rural community organization, he advocated a nationalism designed to "Canadianize" the country's "foreign" immigrants by assimilating their values to those of Canadian society: "At a time when an influx of foreign citizens again threatens to tax our assimilative powers, we must nurture that greatest of all Canadianizing factors – The Canadian writer … *If they can grip and direct the minds and imaginations of new Canadians they will have performed a great national service.*"[34] Writers had allies in this noble cause: Pierce's work as a young student teacher and minister in the west in the years before the First World War had taught him the importance of churches, schools, and libraries in assimilating immigrants to their new country.

His desire for French-English entente (with French Canadians firmly within a Canadian federation), born at Queen's and strengthened in the west, also emerges in these early reviews. The theme was to be central to his writings and to the Ryerson book list throughout his career. In 1922 Pierce told readers of the *Christian Guardian* that French ought to be taught in all Canadian schools because such language teaching tends to increase social sympathy.[35] In matters of French-English rapport, Pierce was an early advocate of moving Canadian society and school curriculum in this direction.

Other ideas about Canadian culture and its relation to the national life were percolating in Pierce's brain in these years. In praising the "truth and beauty" in the work of nature poet Wilson MacDonald, which he said was meant to "enrich and ennoble life," Pierce spoke of the need to educate Canadians about their culture. His withering encounter at Queen's eight years earlier with James Cappon about the value of Canadian writers was evidently still smarting: "With one or two noteworthy exceptions our schools pass silently over the makers of Canadian literature. And, what is even worse than neglect, our writers have frequently been described by Canadian teachers and critics as unworthy, characterless and much more. Canada is the only country in the civilized world that does not study its own literature!"[36]

The reviews do reveal Pierce's questioning of some intellectual and theological sacred cows. As we have seen in examining his time at Queen's, Victoria, and Union Theological Seminary, Pierce had long been ready to examine some of the shibboleths of his faith. He was all for scrutinizing biblical and theological dogmatism. Writing of recent tendencies in theology in November 1920, Pierce sweepingly concluded that "we have nothing to lose and everything to gain by a new and fearless scientific treatment of a religious experience."[37] In his own scrapbook clipping of the review, however, there is a rueful postscript in Pierce's handwriting: "This [article] got me a flaying by some old time parsons."

Pierce was also pilloried about some of his other initiatives. In 1920 he received a stinging letter from suffragist Nellie McClung after he brashly sent her a work whose feminism was more radical than her own. McClung, a best-selling House author, commented crisply to Pierce about Madeleine Marx's *Woman*, which he had sent at the urging of Alice Chown: "I cannot see any good to be gained from reading such a book, and I must register myself as one of the objectors to such a book being called *Woman* with the inference that the writer is speaking for all women." McClung continued: "In fact the outstanding feature of the whole book to me is the lack of purpose in this woman's life. I cannot see that she brought any understanding or comfort or guidance into the lives of any of the people she met, and certainly her experiment is not what one would care to recommend to the Girl Guides or the Canadian Girls in Training."[38]

McClung's sharp letter underlines the need Pierce felt henceforth to line up his ducks carefully in courting the Canadian literary world. His ties in the 1920s with Alice Chown illustrate the same point. As was the case in Brinston with his abortive article on the Versailles treaty, he discovered that to support her views was no asset to his own career.[39] In October 1920 Pierce wrote in his diary that, at her request, he had written a review of Alice Chown's book *The Stairway* (1921), which was about to be published.[40] The pioneering autobiographical work dealt, in fictionalized form, with Chown's struggles with societal views about women, and her enthusiasm for such values as cooperative living, greater labour rights, especially for women workers, and pacifism. Pierce's review, however, never appeared. We cannot be sure of the reason: the *Guardian* may well have refused to give exposure to work by the controversial Chown. It is hard to imagine that Samuel Fallis, who had no sympathy for wartime pacifists, would have wanted to give publicity to Alice Chown. Whatever the reason, the review's failure to see the light boded trouble for Pierce. His view of literature was moralistic, but he was still more iconoclastic than many at the House – including the book steward.

By early 1921, however, Pierce penned something that pleased his boss. He wrote a pamphlet, privately published at the House, entitled *Everett Boyd Jackson Fallis*. Its subject, Lieutenant Everett Fallis, was the book steward's son, who, like Clifford Pierce, had been killed at Vimy Ridge. Pierce's account of Everett Fallis's life was framed in the spirit of Rupert Brooke's patriotic 1914 poem "The Soldier." In a telling bit of Canadian national feeling, Pierce deliberately altered the poem's last line slightly as he described Everett Fallis's burial place, Vimy's Villiers-au-Bois Cemetery:

> [It] might well be called a little "City of God," for all its citizens died in devotion to a great faith. It is holy ground and in a very real sense it is Canadian soil. The well-known lines may be fittingly amended to read:
>
> > "If I should die, think only this of me;
> > That there's some corner of a foreign field
> > That is forever Canada."[41]

Many at the House thought the son's death had done much to embitter the father, who mourned his son as "really the only chum I ever had."[42]

For his part, Pierce – whether he volunteered or was drafted – was also playing the dutiful surrogate son in writing the pamphlet for Fallis. Another indication that Pierce was initially seen in this light by his boss is found in his first Christmas card from the book steward. The card, with an engraving of the House, is inscribed with Fallis's ponderous but telling wit: "To the Baby of *the Family. Our First Christmas.* It gives me a wish for many. S.W.F."[43] Ironically, within months, Pierce was struggling for equilibrium in his relationship with Fallis as the Methodist Book and Publishing House and its employees suffered through a major strike. Pierce was "on the hop" over a pile of thorns.

9

A Strike, a Spat, and the Spirit World

Lorne Pierce, E.J. Pratt, William Arthur Deacon,
and Albert Durrant Watson, 1921–1924

I think Pierce will do very well with that splendid [printing] plant at his disposal. He is very broad-minded, and there will be no fool Methodist or even christian complexes to resolve.

Columnist and author W.A. Deacon on Lorne Pierce, 1923[1]

I should like to snatch the secret of [Dr Albert Durrant] Watson. I want very much to tell the world about him … What matter if he believes that we may have, under proper conditions, secret communion with the other side?

Lorne Pierce diary entry, 17 October 1923

Lorne Pierce's diary falls silent between December 1921 and September 1923. The gap suggests not only his hectic schedule but also his feelings of uncertainty in his new career. Given his worsening deafness, his anxiety was undoubtedly intensified by the fear that, if he failed at publishing, he could not return to the pulpit.

Another indicator of Pierce's uncertainty is that, before the diary lapsed in December 1921, it records virtually nothing about the major Toronto printers' strike which affected the House presses in June 1921. For the first few weeks, the strike paralyzed both Ryerson's book publishing program and the House's many church publications as well as its lucrative job-printing contracts. Samuel Fallis served as the chief management spokesman for all of the Toronto printing and publishing companies affected by the labour dispute. For a Methodist Church that had loudly proclaimed to the world its social gospel ideals and sympathy with labour in 1918, the strike was an embarrassment, and showed how awkward it was to reconcile theology with commercial ventures.

The strike by the Toronto Typographical Union, an affiliate of the International Typographical Union of America, began on 1 June 1921 and dragged on acrimoniously for many months.[2] The chief issues were the printers' demands for a forty-four-hour work week and higher wages; the union, whose members were adversely affected by post-war rises in the cost of living, claimed that there had been agreement in principle for shorter hours to be instituted by the spring of 1921 when the last contract had been negotiated in 1919, a contention that the House denied. Even before the strike began, Fallis, with the support of the church's Book Committee, declared that such demands were "not warranted by business conditions."[3]

In the early 1920s, the Canadian economy was experiencing a slowdown. The House, affected like other Canadian publishers by the general economic downturn of 1920 to 1923, had reported a profit of only $111,135 in the spring of 1921, compared to $164,582 a year earlier. As a result, Fallis wanted the forbearance of the union until matters had "stabilized."[4] Furthermore, Fallis insisted that meeting union demands would cost the House about $100,000 a year, in his view an untenable burden.[5] The strong-minded Fallis's position at centre stage in the struggle with the union made life awkward for many within the Methodist Church sympathetic to labour, including his new literary adviser. (Fallis would ultimately hire and train inexperienced non-union workers by the end of July 1921 – "scabs" in the union view – with the result that the House did not again become a union-only shop until the early 1940s.) All in all, as one scholar points out:

> The delicacy of Fallis' position [in the strike] was further
> exacerbated by his decision to accept the chairmanship of the
> Employers' Defence Committee, basing his acceptance "upon the
> principle that I never can refuse to do anything I expect someone
> else to do if I am otherwise free to do it." When the Employers'
> Defence Committee began a vicious publicity campaign that
> attacked the union and clearly "cut across Methodist policy" with
> respect to issues of unionism, collective bargaining, and working
> conditions, the church found it an embarrassing position and
> expressed its displeasure to Fallis.[6]

Even more awkwardly for Pierce, one of Fallis's leading critics was Ernest Thomas – the very man who had suggested that Fallis hire Pierce.

By July 1921, Fallis was outraged because Thomas had pleaded in the press for public understanding of the need to allow time for the House's commercial practices to conform to "the social practices envisaged by the Methodist General Conference of 1918."[7] Fallis, now depicted in the press as "one man who is holding up a settlement in Toronto," sent Thomas a blistering letter, accusing him of a "deliberate" offence which "jeopardized" the House's position.[8]

It is not hard to imagine Pierce's misgivings about Fallis's anti-union strategies. The latter included advertisements denouncing the "loafing" strikers and their "entirely unjustifiable" strike.[9] One can also imagine the kind of scathing remarks Alice Chown or Ernest Thomas made to Pierce about Fallis's aggressive, right-wing stance on behalf of the Toronto Typothetae, as the employers collectively called themselves.

Caught in the crossfire – without influence in the negotiations and expected to be absolutely loyal to the book steward – Pierce began to back away from his old social gospel allies. Even before the strike began, he resigned from Thomas's Social Services Committee, rationalizing to his diary that, given the demands on his time, he had "to drop something." Three weeks before the strike, Pierce was interviewed about his Brinston social gospel work, and noted sardonically in his diary: "Feel that I have moved a long distance from it."[10] A few weeks after Thomas criticized Fallis, Pierce referred to Thomas's Social Service Council as "cooling irons" with which "I have ceased to become active."[11]

Pierce had little choice but to distance himself from his superior's detractors, especially situated as he was right in Fallis's offices, sharing his boss's secretary. In his published writings, he started to move away from a strong social gospel stance. Pierce's essays about his community organization work in Brinston finally came out in the Ryerson Essays of 1925, but they were focused on the rural scene, not urban employment issues.[12] In other ways, in the split between Fallis and Thomas, Pierce began to edge toward Fallis, and we can trace the movement in his articles.

The autumn before the printers' strike, one of Pierce's *Christian Guardian* reviews seemed wholeheartedly supportive of the social gospel, maintaining that it was so dominant in Methodism that "what will not permit of a social interpretation must expect black oblivion."[13] But by 1923, his series of articles for the *Guardian* on the ministerial mission, later republished as *In Conference with the Best Minds* (1927), criticized the social gospel. "Pulpit Vulgarity," published in the *Guardian* in July 1923, attacked "secularization" of the church: "The ministry has taken its

preaching function almost too seriously, and the pew has supinely made
way, or else countered with a burst of social or socio-political zeal, both
of which have unwittingly conspired to oust true worship from most of
our churches."[14]

Pierce castigated a church seemingly too devoted to social secularism:
"People demand that the Church shall take notice of unemployment
and intemperance, do odd jobs for the government in the matter of recruiting, raising loans, urging national industry, promoting war gardens,
advertising school affairs and many more. The minister, of course, is the
one whom the people mean shall do this. And so it is that, instead of an
oratory for prayer, you have the church turned into a ragpickers' paradise."[15] Pierce turned cooler still. A subsequent piece, "The Enrichment
of Worship," advocated a "religion more catholic in its sympathies and
affiliations ... more sacramental in its interpretation and expression of
religion and life,"[16] a stance that many interpreted as a call to move away
from the secular focus of the social gospel.

These pieces, which ignited a firestorm within church circles, undoubtedly chagrined Ernest Thomas. When Pierce's diary finally resumed in the fall of 1923, there is no longer mention of friendly contact
with Thomas. In discussing the uproar, Pierce obliquely acknowledged
his shift of position. One senses his discomfort at suddenly being on the
side of the church establishment. He had once scoffed at Victoria College for its conservatism and stuffiness, and at Methodists like Fallis for
their dogmatism and conservative views. Now Fallis was his employer.

The lack of relish in his October 1923 diary account of the controversy
over his articles suggests his unease. Pierce wrote: "Today the Toronto
Methodist Ministerial Association took the day off to discuss my article on 'The Enrichment of Worship.' [Victoria] Chancellor R.P. Bowles
led the performance with a very sympathetic address. Many were vehemently opposed to me but I got out alive. I dislike notoriety and talk tires
me."[17] In fact, Pierce usually flourished on debate, and his uncharacteristic distaste is probably due to his unaccustomed ideological bedfellows.

Not surprisingly, at this stressful time, Pierce also refers to frequent
bouts of fatigue and ill health.[18] He later referred to "an embarrassing
shallowness" in his writing at this period, and to the need to "learn the
art of renunciation and conserve for and concentrate upon the one great
thing."[19] Was he uncomfortable over the reflection in his articles of his
need to be mindful of Fallis's policies and thus to implicitly declare an
allegiance to a more conservative social stance? Whatever he meant,

Pierce's publication in 1925 of *The Beloved Community* was in effect a farewell to his ardent social gospel advocacy of the immediate post–First World War period.

In general, Pierce shifted to a less activist view of Methodism, with less socially charged ideological calls for catholicity, a change of emphasis reflected in his 1923 pamphlet *Methodism and the New Catholicism*. He declared: "I believe that the reunion of Christendom will meet somewhere near the Great Methodist Idea. The new temple of Religion will be established, in the words of Wesley, on those 'doctrines which include all the rest: repentance, faith and holiness.'"[20] The way was open for Pierce to devote himself more exclusively to "the one great thing": a publishing mission that emphasized an idealistic, nationalistic, programmatic view of religion and culture. Pierce was determined to make Ryerson what he had earlier described as "the cultural Mecca of Canada."[21]

FALLIS SUBSEQUENTLY made some positive gestures toward Pierce, doubtless realizing that his new employee had made some painful realignments. Pierce was promoted in 1922, and in the fall of 1923 Fallis hinted that the House, aware of the Pierce family's cramped quarters on Wineva Avenue, particularly since the birth of Bruce the previous January, would build a house for them in North Toronto. Pierce promptly bought an expensive building lot on fashionable upper Avenue Road that he could ill afford. Alas, Fallis's promise was to evaporate in the course of Pierce's fluctuating fortunes with the book steward.

There was at least one more "surrogate son" interval with Fallis. In the first week of October 1923, Pierce "batched" it with Fallis at his Bala cottage. The pair spun around the lake in Fallis's beautiful wooden inboard (built, to the dismay of many, in the House workshops[22]) before storing it for the winter. Dining nightly at a nearby resort, Pierce and Fallis went sightseeing in the latter's "big new McLaughlin [Buick, which] went beautifully."[23] (If the week did not cement Pierce's relations with Fallis, he did bond with the Buick, and he was to own several.)

In the spring of 1922, Pierce was designated "Book Editor and Literary Advisor" at Ryerson Press, responsible for "the literary policy of the house" which included both assessing manuscripts and "initiat[ing] publications of general importance" under the umbrella of a new Educational Department, which also embraced textbook publication,[24] an area where Pierce would soon undertake important initiatives. At the next meeting of the House's overseer, the Book Committee, Pierce, at Fallis's behest, "spoke of the growing policy of the Book Room in connection with new publications, and the desire of the Book Steward that the Book Room might take its place in the production of some of the most artistic and valuable literature."[25]

Pierce at last received his own office and secretary, Della Dingle. To date, the demands of the *Guardian* columns and the publishing slow-down caused by troubled labour conditions had given Pierce little opportunity to show what he could do as a *book* publisher.[26] Nevertheless, one of Pierce's initiatives in these early years was the Ryerson Essay series on theological subjects. The first nine of these short pamphlets – thirty to forty pages in length, selling for five to thirty-five cents – were published in 1921 and 1922, on such topics as the literal interpretations of Scripture and Old Testament prophecy.[27]

The essays were criticized by some within the Methodist and Presbyterian churches as too "modernist" on subjects like the Virgin Birth, but they received favourable attention in other quarters. By 1924, the Montreal *Gazette* was referring to Pierce as the "brilliant editor of the Ryerson Essays."[28] However, the pamphlets, usually published in editions of 1,000, did not sell well.[29] Years later, Pierce glumly recalled of the series: "Religious and theological works we nibbled at, feeling under obligation to publish good books by our own men, but they nearly all left us in the red."[30]

Red was not a popular colour with Fallis – or the House accountants. Pierce's promotion to editor came at a period when House publications – and profits – had decreased as a result of the strike, exacerbated by a downturn in the Canadian economy. In the spring of 1922, the House showed a net profit of only $71,465.71, a drop of $40,000. Since the founding of the House, a portion of profits had been designated for the Ministers' Superannuation Fund, a contribution that totalled only $10,000 in 1922.[31] Moreover, Fallis's aggressive anti-union position toward the strikers and his hiring of scab labour meant that, in the aftermath of 1921, the House lost the lucrative Ontario government printing contract, taken away by the farmer-labour coalition of the United Farmers of Ontario, then in power in the province. The House was thus anxious to develop new sources of profits from both the printing and publishing sides of the House.

In financial terms, the stage was set for conflict between Fallis and Pierce. As we have seen, under Briggs, the House had done most of its Canadian publishing by subscription or with the author underwriting costs. Now, Pierce, who felt he was "building for the future" toward "the strongest list in Canada,"[32] offered authors like Wilson MacDonald and William Arthur Deacon a 10 per cent royalty, and spent large sums on commissioning and promoting the Makers of Canadian Literature series. Issuing books at its own expense became common practice for the House. Janet Friskney points out: "While at this time other Canadian houses were also by then absorbing production costs of some of the books they published, The Ryerson Press – in its publication in the early 1920s of Canadian authors at an 'unprecedented pace' – was clearly taking the most risks."[33] Indeed, by 1923 the Ryerson list swelled to an unprecedented sixty-one titles. (McClelland and Stewart also published some sixty titles that year, but that total, unlike Pierce's, included agency publication of best-selling British and American authors.[34])

At the same time, in his dealings with authors – with essayist William Arthur Deacon and poet E.J. Pratt, on the one hand, and poet and spiritualist Dr Albert Durrant Watson, on the other – Pierce learned how difficult it could be to reconcile personal and institutional values with the need for broad appeal in general publishing. Pierce was to discover that there was more mud flung and more financial woe on his new path than he had ever encountered on the back roads of Matilda Township.

FROM THE BEGINNING, Pierce showed an ability to attract authors and their manuscripts. In the nationalist atmosphere of the era, manifest culturally in groups as disparate as the Group of Seven and the Canadian Authors Association,[35] Pierce's stance struck a chord among the intelligentsia. He spoke widely about the importance of cultural nationalism, as in a September 1921 article: "At ... a time when the world seems to have been thrown into a huge melting pot we need to preserve our national identity ... giving the world that rare and subtle thing, the Canadian character and ideal. To do this we must preserve our national poise, our independence, and spread out our own soul and interpret our own thought and life in our own way. Therefore our authors must be encouraged to perform this function for us."[36] With such a manifesto, Pierce fit perfectly into the mindset of the dominant nationalists of the day, a mindset summarized by one historian as "a conviction that Canada's problems could be solved by the spread of knowledge and the development of Canadian art, literature, history and symbols; and a conception of their duty as national leaders to mould Canadian public opinion to a new national consciousness."[37]

Given that such prescriptive patriotic zeal was "in the air," it was not long before Pierce's siren call to other young literary nationalists was answered. William Arthur Deacon, a handsome, dark-haired former lawyer who came to Toronto from Winnipeg in 1922 to become *Saturday Night*'s dynamic new book columnist, was soon calling on Pierce, as was his friend, Newfoundland-born poet and Victoria College professor E.J. Pratt. Deacon got a great "lift" out of being invited to lunch and asked if he had material for a book.[38]

Deacon's subsequent letter to his Edmonton confidante, best-selling author Emily Murphy ("Janey Canuck"), shows how expansive were the ideas he was giving authors about the publication possibilities at Ryerson Press. In January 1923 Pierce struck Deacon as being "very brilliant," with "a shrewd business head," and as a "dictator" with unlimited power to publish. Deacon, himself raised as a Methodist, assured Murphy blithely:

Pierce will do well with that splendid [printing] plant at his disposal. He is very broad-minded, and there will be no fool Methodist or even christian complexes to resolve. I think I'll be O.K. Anyhow Pierce is the first man to be willing to publish me; everybody else had refused ... He offered 10% royalty which is pretty good for essays by a new writer, I think. Besides they have more money to spend than anybody else and can afford to drop a couple of thousand where some of the other fellows cannot afford to gamble at all.[39]

However, Deacon was mistaken in viewing Pierce as untrammelled by Methodist values (he was obviously not reading Pierce's reviews in the *Guardian*) – as events with his friend Pratt would show. In the meantime, Deacon signed a contract in 1923 with Ryerson to publish *Pens and Pirates*, a lively collection of critical essays redolent with Canadian nationalism. Pierce and Deacon shared a belief in the need for Canadian criticism to counter the mindless boosterism of literary "log-rolling bees and slippery soft-drink criticism," as Pierce put it in a letter to Deacon. He added: "If there is one thing we need more of in this Canada of ours it is a new school of literary criticism. Some of the old twaddle peeled off by our college professors is enough to kill the trade."[40]

Deacon's friend E.J. Pratt produced a major publishing coup for Pierce that year. Ryerson brought out Pratt's landmark *Newfoundland Verse*, his first major collection of lyric poetry. Pratt's poems of Newfoundland life – for example "The Ice-Floes," with its drama and humanistic values – were perfectly calculated to appeal to Pierce. Pierce's writing about Pratt shows that, while he was cool to the values and style of modernist poets abroad, he saw the tall, balding Victoria professor as writing innovatively on a more congenial, traditional basis: "On the continent, after the Great War, poets and artists revolted against what they called the senile canons of taste. Their new art consisted chiefly in a sort of mental toilet on the balcony above the street. In Canada our poets, for the most part, turned from war themes to old preoccupations and traditional forms ... Unlike the daring ... revolutionaries abroad, maddened by Hera, and reeling drunk with the great world-secret, Canadian writers [like Pratt] showed more reticence and urbanity."[41] Taken by Pratt's "noble attitude toward existence" and the "swift spiritual insight" in his poems, and encouraged by such Pratt admirers as Pelham Edgar and Wesley College (Winnipeg) professor A.L. Phelps,[42] Pierce arranged for 1,000 sheets of *Newfoundland Verse* to be printed and for 500 copies to be bound immediately for distribution. Group of Seven artist Frederick Varley, a friend of Pratt's, designed both the Pratt and Deacon books.[43]

Pierce soon had Varley doing several other important book designs for Ryerson,[44] all part of Pierce's Ruskinesque resolve "to insist that each book be beautifully and solidly bound – a good book and a beautiful book ... what is useful and readable ought to be beautiful." Pierce wanted a "strong list," with the Ryerson imprint guaranteeing that the books were "the best in their field."[45]

The Pratt and Deacon titles duly appeared in the fall of 1923 in the large and varied Ryerson publication list of that year, which also included a Canadian cookbook, another Pierce brainchild, henceforth a perennial best-seller for the firm.[46] Pierce was gleeful when Pratt's *Newfoundland Verse* received what he called "salubrious" reviews "both east and west."[47] Pratt's biographer has described the "phenomenal" response to the book, both in the number of reviews and in their "consistent and unstinted enthusiasm." Many of them hailed "a new voice" in Canadian poetry, as the Toronto *Globe* put it.[48] Near the end of his life, Pierce described the Pratt and Deacon books as the "first outstanding books" he published.[49]

But trouble was brewing with both Deacon and Pratt. There were problems with printing errors in both books during production, which entailed extensive proof corrections, particularly for the Deacon book. This state of affairs was probably connected with the upheaval and inexperience in the production staff produced by the strike and its aftermath, as well as the fact that Pierce's rival E.J. Moore, head of the Book Publications and Publicity Department, still oversaw (not well) printing and proofing of Ryerson books. Moore's resentment of Pierce had grown when, in 1922, he had been moved out of his large office so Pierce could occupy it. Moreover, with Pierce's promotion, Moore now ranked below Pierce in the management structure.[50] For his part, Pierce fumed over poor cooperation from Moore's department, telling his diary that "they don't seem ... to know which end of a good book to take hold of."[51] In addition, Pierce himself was not yet experienced in shepherding books through the press, although he was already actively editing copy: he had Deacon make numerous revisions to *Pens and Pirates* before publication.

Over-optimistically, Pierce printed 1,000 copies of *Pens and Pirates*. He later admitted that Ryerson had published the book out of principle, without projecting recovery of even half of the costs to the House.[52] Reviews of Deacon's "innovative, refreshing and lively" essays were largely positive, but only 206 copies of *Pens and Pirates* were sold in the first nine months, and only seventy more copies over the next two years.[53] *Newfoundland Verse* did better, selling about 500 copies in the first six months. The balance of the run was bought by the House's Educational Department to market as a textbook.[54] Many of these went unsold, however, and Pratt received royalties of less than $100.[55]

While Deacon assured friends that he could not have expected his first book of essays to sell well, even with heavy advertising, he was not easy to deal with about editing, production, or marketing matters.[56] For his part, E.J. Pratt, although he had been told that twenty-six review copies of his book had been sent out, felt – like many an author – that more publicity should have been done.[57] So did Pratt and Deacon's friend Beaumont Cornell, a Brockville physician and author whose long novel *Lantern Marsh* Pierce had also published that year after many revisions. (Cornell so little understood Pierce, however, that at one point he sent Pierce a prescription to purchase alcohol in spite of Prohibition![58])

Rather than faulting Pierce for most of their problems, the three authors blamed E.J. Moore for slighting their books out of enmity to Pierce. In October 1923, spearheaded by Deacon, the trio decided to see Samuel Fallis to denounce production and marketing problems with their books – without first telling Pierce. Pratt admitted this error in diplomacy in a rather sheepish letter to Pierce after the fact, one in which he denounced the "fat-head" Moore. Pratt was quick to assure Pierce of his own continuing "confidence" and "admiration" for him.[59]

Pierce was naturally upset when news of the visit reached him – the one moment he must have regretted no longer operating from Fallis's antechamber. He knew that a generous measure of Fallis's displeasure would fall on him, especially since none of the books had exactly been cash cows. Pierce stoutly denied to the three that there had been any problems with advertising, and pointed out that the Press's lengthy publication list that fall meant that not all titles could appear in all advertisements.[60] Privately, he was furious that he had potentially been undermined in his relationship with Fallis, and he complained of Moore's jealousy and backbiting. Moore was wont to proclaim that he, not Pierce, was the House's true literary adviser and editorial star.[61]

Whatever Moore's conduct, Pierce was particularly aggrieved about Deacon's behaviour. The two subsequently fell out over other matters, including a House bill sent to Deacon for the copy changes made to *Pens and Pirates*. However, neither Deacon nor Pierce could risk all-out war: the editor of Canada's largest publishing house and one of the country's leading book reviewers needed a viable working relationship. When Deacon was let go by *Saturday Night* in 1928, Pierce scrupulously did his best to help Deacon before his re-emergence as book editor for the Toronto *Mail and Empire* later that year.[62]

The worst outcome of the 1923 imbroglio was that – with the exception of Deacon's book on Peter McArthur, already contracted for Ryerson's Makers of Canadian Literature series – neither Deacon nor Pratt ever published with Ryerson again. Pierce's long-time assistant, Blanche Hume, believed that the loss of Pratt was one of the greatest disappointments of Pierce's publishing career.[63] To publish *Newfoundland Verse* in particular was a prescient early editorial decision by Pierce. But Pratt was soon following literary paths down which Pierce felt that he and the House could not go. Contrary to what Deacon believed, Pierce and the House did have some "Methodist complexes" which affected what Ryerson could publish.

Certainly, Pierce himself had reservations about the lifestyles of both Deacon and Pratt. Deacon had come to Toronto from Winnipeg with Sally Townsend Syme. Each had been married to someone else when they had met in Winnipeg in 1918,[64] and in Toronto Deacon lived common-law with Sally Syme until his divorce from his first wife was granted in November 1922.[65] When Deacon was fired by *Saturday Night* in the spring of 1928, Pierce wrote disdainfully in his diary that he believed "further [sexual] immoralities" had been involved.[66]

Pierce was no more comfortable with the hospitable Ned Pratt's
famed poker parties, which featured ample quantities of cards, liquor,
and salty stories, none of them congenial to Pierce. His alienation amid
such rowdy conviviality was compounded by his deafness. At one late-
night gathering, Pierce drank ginger ale and ate sandwiches while Pratt,
Charles G.D. Roberts, and others downed martinis, cracked lobster, told
salacious stories, and mocked Pierce's puritan "restraint." In his diary,
Pierce noted the large quantity of drink and the smallness of the talk and
concluded that "big men ought to be better employed."[67] He reached
much the same verdict about Pratt's poetry when Pratt took liquor as a
theme and wanted Ryerson to publish the results.

The poet wrote to Pierce on the heels of the uproar over the Fallis visit,
offering his next manuscript, a long poem of about fifty pages praised
by Pelham Edgar and others. Pratt wrote that he hoped this time to
have an English or American co-publisher for the work. He added that
The Witches' Brew had liquor as a theme: Would Ryerson Press have any
"qualms" about publishing it?[68] The poem, a satire on Prohibition which
features an underwater spree by the denizens of the deep, certainly posed
a problem for an editor and a church press publicly advocating a "dry"
society. Pierce himself was such a strong temperance advocate that, in
the fall of 1924, he cut short a trip to New York City to return home to
vote against any return of liquor to Ontario.[69] Naturally, Pierce found
Pratt's new poem uncongenial, as Pierce's later article on Pratt makes
clear.[70] Meanwhile, Pierce confided to his old Victoria College friend
Arthur Phelps that Pratt appeared, by writing on such topics, to be "selling out to a popular taste for sensationalism."[71]

Pierce dutifully contacted a couple of similarly conservative American
publishers like Doran and Stokes about *The Witches' Brew*, and received
negative replies. He informed a disappointed Pratt, who continued his
search for a foreign publisher. In September 1924 Pratt announced that
English publisher Selwyn and Blount had accepted *The Witches' Brew*,
and pressed Pierce for a decision on Canadian publication.[72] Squirming,
Pierce realized that publication with Ryerson was impossible. Worse still,
he was about to lose the first major poet that he had enlisted for Ryerson.
Pierce tried to soften his letter of rejection to Pratt with humour and
assurances of good will:

Your *Witches' Brew* has been passed around the Book Room and
both Dr. Fallis and the management generally have taken copious

draughts from its sparkling rim. The general feeling is that a
publishing house so closely connected with the Methodist Church
could not very well act as Canadian distributor of it. Personally I
should like very much to be able to do something for you with this
book ... for your own sake. I hope that the timidity of our house
is not prevalent among the other publishers in town and that you
may be more successful with them.[73]

Pratt's reply (he was, ironically, also an ordained Methodist minister)
was jovial but a little exasperated: "Sorry that the vintage proved a little
too stimulating for vulgar consumption. I understand the situation in
which you are placed, as a firm, by virtue of ecclesiastical affiliations."[74]
Pratt turned to Pierce's rival Hugh Eayrs of Macmillan, whose firm was
to publish all of his major works for the next two decades – to Pierce's
chagrin.

To round out this story, Deacon's next collection of literary essays, published by Ottawa's short-lived Graphic Press, featured an alcoholic title –
Poteen.[75] Was Deacon, who had raised many a convivial glass with Pratt,
taking a sly dig at the "Methodist complexes" of their former publisher?

AS PIERCE shifted away from the social gospel and sought to find his
footing in publishing in the early 1920s, he embraced other new enthusiasms and new personalities, first and foremost physician, poet, and
theosophist Albert Durrant Watson. Pierce – who craved a Toronto
mentor to provide the reassurance he had received from, for example,
Professor William Jordan at Queen's – bonded with Watson. He became
Watson's biographer and editorial collaborator as well as his publisher.
Via Watson, Pierce took up the enthusiasm for theosophy prominent
among many Canadian nationalists and intellectuals of the day.

Even more important, the charismatic Watson, three decades older
than Pierce, offered him encouragement as he sought to make his place
in Canadian publishing. Pierce recognized his own predilection for seeking the guidance of older men, commenting at the end of his life: "My
friends have usually been old fellows, much older than I, but that's all
right. I don't care a cent for young men: old men who have had the experience and who have mellowed attract me very much."[76]

Silver-haired and silver-tongued, Watson was one of Toronto's most
colourful cultural figures. Speculation, publicity – and disciples (whom
he dubbed the "Inner Circle")[77] – had swirled around him for decades.

Pierce's mentor in the early 1920s: physician, poet, and
theosophist Dr Albert Durrant Watson at the Muskoka
Assembly, 1925. Courtesy of Queen's University Archives

Born in Dixie, Ontario, in 1859, Watson, a Victoria graduate, had studied medicine at Edinburgh University, becoming a fellow of the latter's
Royal College of Physicians in 1883. A former president of the Royal
Astronomical Society of Canada, he had a successful medical practice
in Toronto for nearly forty years, and had been publishing poetry and
meditations on life and the spirit since the early years of the century,
some of it with the House.[78]

Watson was a controversial figure, however. In the 1910s he began to be widely known for his advocacy of spiritualism – the belief that human beings could make direct contact with the beyond, a realm that Watson called "The Twentieth Plane" in his controversial book of that name. Around the end of the First World War, with so many deaths on the battlefield and in the influenza epidemic that followed, public interest in spiritualism in the Western world, Canada included, was high. Watson's claims of psychic contact with another plane caused an uproar. His book, *The Twentieth Plane*, published in 1918, an account of seances held at his house under the aegis of the Association for Psychical Research of Canada, included communications ostensibly from departed worthies like Plato, Jesus Christ, and Walt Whitman. The book was in fact dedicated to Canada's war dead: the book's messages from beyond via Toronto medium Louis Benjamin were "to be a light and consolation to those left behind."[79] Watson styled himself the "reporter" for departed souls as various as his mother and Samuel Taylor Coleridge. He had supplied only "punctuation, capitals and unquoted matter" in the text: all else came from beyond.

All the messages in Watson's book are reassuring generalities, such as Dorothy Wordsworth's about the denizens of the other side: "We are all normal, happy folk and we know that love is the sum of all." Prominent Toronto professor James Mavor and others attacked Watson's spiritualism, amid much publicity.[80] The novelist L.M. Montgomery, for her part, whose beloved cousin had died of influenza not long before, speculated on Watson's ideas in her March 1919 journal. Montgomery judged the book "utterly unconvincing," despite her desire to believe such contact possible. She found absurd Watson's contentions that the dead lived in a "pink twilight," nourished by absorbing chemicals. She was amused by the fact that all Watson's reports, except those from his late mother, were from celebrities, and noticed that all the messages were written in exactly the same "awful" literary style.[81] Certainly, the spirit messages found in *The Twentieth Plane* and its sequel *Birth through Death* (1920) are attributed to a motley cast of the late and great, including, in the latter, Savonarola, Ralph Waldo Emerson, and the American popular poet Ella Wheeler Wilcox.[82]

For his part, Pierce had long been familiar with Watson's writings: in a 1914 letter to Edith, he praised Watson's ecumenical ideas about world religion, invoking Watson's belief in the "evolutionary process of

the development of religious consciousness."[83] Like many in Toronto
cultural circles of the early 1920s – Lawren Harris, William Arthur
Deacon, Wilson MacDonald, Bliss Carman, Frederick Banting, Arthur
Lismer, Fred Housser, and J.E.H. MacDonald, among others – Watson
was an adherent of theosophy. The movement, which has affinities with
the pantheistic "cosmic consciousness" so strongly advocated in the late
nineteenth century by American poet Walt Whitman and his Canadian
admirer Dr Richard Bucke, promotes a belief in a spiritual evolution in
an "Ever-Becoming Nature" with a "divinity indistinguishable from a
Universe which is living, conscious and endlessly evolving."[84]

A branch of the Theosophical Society had been founded in Toronto in
1891, modelled on the Theosophical Society founded in New York City in
1875 by the Russian noblewoman Madame Helene Blavatsky. Blavatsky
dazzled the poet W.B. Yeats and many others with her beliefs, including "the concept of dharma or destiny, which postulates that not only
individuals but cultures, nations and races play their particular roles in
the process of cosmic evolution."[85] (In Toronto, moreover, many theosophists were members of the Arts and Letters Club – notably Watson,
J.E.H. MacDonald, and Lawren Harris – the very club where Pierce was
now a devoted member.)

Such beliefs, given that they were so broadly conceived in terms of
universal brotherhood and so little dependent on specific dogma in
synthesizing elements of Eastern and Western mysticism in what one
historian has called theosophy's "flexible combination of theism, spiritualism and mysticism,"[86] were very attractive to someone like Pierce.
Pierce had been schooled in the idealism of John Watson, which advocated the idea of a higher good than the individual, a good which must
permeate society and to which the individual must dedicate the self as it
is in the process of realization.[87] For Pierce, moving from John Watson's
brand of idealism to embracing broad theosophical concepts about the
evolution of spirit through the universe was a short and congenial step.

Furthermore, Mary Vipond has pointed out that the theosophical
idea is particularly attractive to artists and other creators: "[Theosophy's]
appeal to artists lies in the concept of nature as a manifestation of the
spirit, directly realizable and recognizable through art. Art is the instrument whereby the material world can be made spiritual: the artist, by
plunging into the recesses of his soul, can portray eternal truth through
his interpretation of nature."[88] Certainly, the idea of an underlying,
evolving manifestation of spirit was attractive to cultural nationalists

like Lorne Pierce, Albert Watson, Lawren Harris, or W.A. Deacon as a means to divine a common and evolving national idealism in the literature and art of Canada. Albert Durrant Watson called for Canadian poets to take "an important share in creating the nation's ideals and in shaping its character and life," exactly the light in which Pierce viewed Canadian literature.[89]

Watson's spirited and spiritual idealism thus appealed to Pierce. By early October 1920, Watson had already called on Pierce, and soon Pierce was invited to Watson's home on Euclid Avenue to meet "a Persian mystic." Pierce's diary is skeptical about the mystic, whom he cross-questioned despite his difficulty in hearing him amid the crush of the "polyglot crowd" at Watson's dark, rambling old house in a down-at-heels neighbourhood on the western fringes of Toronto's Annex area.[90] But his skepticism did not extend to Watson. In December, he wrote a sympathetic review of Watson's *Birth through Death* for the *Christian Guardian*. He was obviously drawn to the man and his overall values, if not to his belief in spirit messages: "Yet while we can not all scale the twentieth plane, and while we doubt very much the evidence and the process, we are compelled to admit that as for the author himself we all confess to his beautiful character, [and] his scientific knowledge ... We marvel at his simplicity and sincerity."[91] The friendship was well underway.

Pierce never formally joined the Theosophical Society, never endorsed belief in the psychic possibilities of the twentieth plane, but in his diary he wrote admiringly of Watson: "He has suffered because of his spiritualistic experiences. He will be admired and reverenced when he is known. He believes absolutely in the spiritual foundation and nature of existence. Most of us are rank materialists in the last analysis and our ideas of God and immortality are gross."[92] Just as crucially, Pierce also *rejected* the same values as Watson. Like Pierce, Watson wanted Canadians to reject materialism – Watson called it "the Kingdom of Thingdom."[93] He called on Canadian poets "to rescue the people from sordid estimates of success, point them to goals of more abundant life, and lead their hearts to trust only in the highest things."[94] His own poetry stressed beauty, inspiration, and idealism in a landscape infused with pantheism, as in these lines, which Pierce praised:

> In the clouds that split with thunder,
> In the soul athrill with wonder,

> Over all and through and under,
> There is Love and Light.[95]

Pierce, despite the hackneyed quality of the verse, clearly rejoiced in such themes – where, as he described it in his diary, "the spirit world descends and assurances are given us" of man's immortality and godliness.[96] After reading such Watson lyrics, Pierce confidently made speeches to service clubs like the Rotary Club of Welland, assuring them that the national literature had "no sex obsession, no morbidity, no psychoanalysis, but rather the purifying and purging effect of our land."[97] Even Pierce had to admit, however, that, as a poet, Watson was more interested in content than in form and was "not a great technician."[98]

All the while, Watson offered Pierce a warm bath of reassurance about his own worth and mission at a time of uncertainty. Pierce's deafness was now so severe that he could no longer effectively communicate on the telephone,[99] and relations were tense with his parents, who were unconvinced about the wisdom of his new career path and some of his theological ideas.[100] In the face of such worries, Watson offered respite. A 1923 Christmas letter from Watson to Pierce rhapsodizes about Pierce's "really great intellectual energy." Watson went on: "I want you to know ... how fully I realize the joy and dignity, the tenderness and beauty of our friendship ... When I think of our relation, I see all the immortal friendships of history epitomized. History repeats itself, and once more Jonathan helps David to the throne."[101] Heady tonic for a young editor still not sure of himself.

Tellingly, a few weeks later, Watson called himself Pierce's "Sancho Panza," again flattering Pierce with the idea that he was being helped to greatness – and in this case by a distinguished older man.[102] Unfortunately, the Sancho Panza analogy also suggests how quixotic were some of Watson's views and schemes, with mixed results for Pierce. In any event, through Watson, Pierce met a host of other literary figures, many of them fellow travellers of theosophy. Watson's circle included Confederation poet Bliss Carman, Vancouver poet and physician Ernest Fewster, expatriate poet and Philadelphia minister Robert Norwood, and medical researcher and amateur artist Frederick Banting – associations that, for Pierce, coloured his conception of the Makers of Canadian Literature series of critical anthologies he began to publish in 1923. Pierce was delighted when Carman and Watson spent an afternoon trying to convince him of the reality of immortality.[103]

Editor and physician grew still closer. After the two travelled to the Muskoka hamlet of Rossmoyne for a few days of rest in September 1923 following one of Pierce's flare-ups of lupus-induced illness, Pierce so treasured the memory that he named his first Delta cottage "Rossmoyne."[104] For his part, Watson wrote a poem of that title dedicated to Pierce:

> But Nature's glowing sheen and iridescence
> That stream and starlight lend
> Bring fullest joy in the soul-thrilling presence
> Of one unfailing friend.[105]

On another occasion the two made an overnight trip to Hamilton to view an eclipse.[106] By 1924, Pierce had been designated Watson's executor.

Although Watson had backed away from advocacy of contact with the spirit world around 1920 in the face of public uproar about his contact with "spooks," his influence on Pierce could be unorthodox. When he arrived in Toronto, Pierce, as was his habit, routinely used his middle initial in his signature and in his *Christian Guardian* byline, viz. "Lorne A. Pierce." Watson convinced Pierce that it was numerologically propitious to drop the "A." Pierce was amused, but by early 1924 he stopped using his middle initial forever.[107]

Pierce's hero worship of Watson meant that a flood of Watson titles entered the Ryerson lists in the early 1920s, including a 342-page collected *Poetical Works* (1924), complete with an impressive photograph of Watson in the frontispiece.[108] Pierce enlisted both Watson and journalist and writer Margaret Lawrence, one of Watson's adoring "inner circle," to contribute jointly to the Ryerson Essay series. The result was *Mediums and Mystics: A Study in Spiritual Laws and Psychic Forces* (1923). The volume gave Watson a chance to distance himself from seances in favour of general intimations of the cosmic, given that "the soul with vision realizes in spirit and in life that a new morning has dawned in the springtime of the world."[109]

Lorne Pierce was clearly committed to making Watson even better known and appreciated, but in a less controversial way than as an advocate of "spooks," the word with which Pierce facetiously titled his article on *Birth through Death*.[110] Watson's public image as spiritualist caused Pierce himself some embarrassment as his closeness to Watson became widely known. Such knowledge was inevitable, given that Pierce even paid personally for printing 200 copies of the booklet he wrote about Watson in 1924 "to tell the world about him," one hint that Samuel Fallis did not share his enthusiasm for Watson.[111]

Whether in print or in private, Pierce was always a little defensive, knowing what a controversial figure Watson was. In his thirty-page booklet on the master, Pierce assured his readers that Watson, who is "coming into his own," "spiritualizes life consistently and constantly." He also presents him as a martyr to his theosophical idealism: "Few men have been more sadly misunderstood. He has lived most of the creative years of his poetic life under the penumbra of indifference or intolerance."[112] The encomium was obviously intended to vindicate and rehabilitate Watson. As one reviewer pointed out, Pierce does not even mention Watson's former advocacy of the twentieth plane in his effort to present him in the best light. Yet the reviewer admitted that Pierce had conquered his own initial hostility to Watson: "Dr. Pierce is very convincing in an engaging way and [I] at least who was prepared to scoff is now not indisposed to admire."[113] Another review said simply that "Watson ... has found his interpreter."[114]

Critic Margery Fee has described Watson as one of Pierce's "failings."[115] Certainly, Pierce overrated Watson as a poet. But his engagement with Watson reflected his own personal needs in the early 1920s. One index of Pierce's blend of personal and intellectual bonding with Watson is that at one point he persuaded his own mother to buy six copies of Watson's book *Sovereignty of Character* to give as Christmas presents.[116] The appeal to him of Watson's poetry was its high-mindedness. He valued it, he wrote, as much for what it left out as what it encompassed: "Nothing of beauty, truth or goodness is alien to him ... You will look through his verse in vain for morals set to jingly rhyme, for street cries, cheap sentiments, marketable ragtime, and the popular journalese tintinnabulum, which has the form, but lacks the substance of poetry."[117] Such a high-minded view of poetry conformed perfectly with the kind of lofty, conservative aesthetic values Pierce had drunk in as an undergraduate at Queen's, standards of "aesthetic and intellectual integrity," which encompassed "sound reason, healthy spiritual emotions and good manners."[118]

In his booklet about Watson, Pierce also stresses the importance of cultural nationalism, particularly the belief shared by Watson and himself that "a great deal of our Canadian poetry has to do with the greatness and the glory of our national inheritance."[119] In fact, Pierce's first major personal book project at Ryerson was a collaboration with Watson, underway by the fall of 1921, on an anthology of Canadian literature calculated to demonstrate "the glory of our national inheritance" in literature.[120] The first edition of the anthology, *Our Canadian Literature: Representative Prose and Verse*, appeared at Christmas 1922.

CO-EDITING THE anthology was in effect a crash course in Canadian literature for Pierce. He hoped that the anthology, only the second since the war (after Edward Caswell's anthology *Canadian Singers and Their Songs* of 1919 for McClelland and Stewart[121]), would also find a market as a textbook. Watson chose and introduced the poetry section of the anthology and Pierce the prose. Watson's section emphasizes cosmically conscious inspirational poetry. Pierce's section also shows some theosophical touches, particularly in its idea of the evolving "soul" of the literature and the Canadian nation. Pierce writes: "With the solidification of the political life of Canada there also went a crystallization of her spiritual life. The soul of a people was being born as its body took shape … A real national literature was in the process of development, a fact which we are but slowly coming to understand, a fact which some do not yet appreciate."[122]

The anthology was clearly designed to advance this thesis, and to stimulate a national feeling based on presentation of a literature that was deemed integrative of different groups within the nation (or, as Pierce put it, "a spiritual amalgam composed of the minted heart-offerings of the races of the world"[123]). Canadian anthologies, from the first one by Edward Hartley Dewart in 1864, had promoted a lofty nationalism in the literature. Pierce saw *Our Canadian Literature* as nation building because it helped "to explain us [Canadians] to ourselves." He added: "We have produced something of real worth [in literature] … of which Canadians may well be proud. Only by gathering together, carefully and critically, the best that we have produced, may the outline of our greatness be imagined."[124]

Pierce was at pains to stress that Canada was ethnically made up of many strains, not just the British. In fact, the anthology set the tone for all his future literary and editorial efforts in its emphasis on French-English entente, with Pierce exhorting that "we have two great shrines at which we speak two languages; yet we have but one passionate loyalty – Canada!" In mentioning that only space prevented him from including French writers, Pierce looked forward to his own bicultural *An*

Outline of Canadian Literature (1927) (which featured major English and French Canadian writers, past and present) and his Makers of Canadian Literature series of the 1920s, which also encompassed both English and French Canadian writers.

Pierce was also a pioneer in that *Our Canadian Literature* was the first anthology of Canadian writing to include prose as well as poetry. In the prose selections, Pierce deftly blended some of the intellectual and social influences in his own life. Many of the selections – from the writings of Nicholas Flood Davin, Joseph Howe, Sir Wilfrid Laurier, and William Lyon Mackenzie, for example – are about patriotic values and/or the evolution of the nation. Pierce's excerpt from Principal Grant's "Ocean to Ocean" and "Canada, a Link in the Empire" made it clear that the kind of idealistic nationalism he had acquired at Queen's was still a shaping influence on him, one he wanted to disseminate to all Canadians as a kind of unifying tonic.

Pierce's moralistic suspicion of fiction made it the more natural for him to include generous selections of non-fiction. Accordingly, his fiction selections for *Our Canadian Literature* tend to be historical, not contemporary, and to give a sense of the breadth of the country. During his time in the west, Pierce had become convinced of the importance of representing its landscape and concerns in the national culture. Fittingly, then, his prose selections began with Roderick MacBeth on the Hudson's Bay Company as well as Agnes Laut's "The Buffalo Hunt." Other selections were equally documentary of the evolution of the nation from Haliburton's Sam Slick to Moodie's description of her arrival at Quebec as an immigrant and a section of Richardson's novel *Wacousta* (1832). Clearly, Pierce had integrated elements of Watson's cosmic consciousness with his own romantic nationalism to produce a didactic anthology centred on art for nation's sake.

Rather than emphasize the new, both writers focused on the past in the anthology. Robert Lecker points out that Watson and Pierce include only eleven writers not found in John Garvin's two earlier anthologies, *Canadian Poets* (1916) and *Canadian Poems of the Great War* (1918).[125] Moreover, when Pierce included a new writer, like Montreal novelist J.G. Sime, he chose material about the nature of Canada, to extend the nationalistic flavour of the volume into work-in-progress by contemporary writers.

Watson's introductions and poetry selections also stress thematic content rather than form. Lecker rightly notices that Watson has no interest in poetic modernism, and does not select, for example, any of Frank Oliver Call's free verse for inclusion. The poems Watson chooses tend to portray the kind of pantheistic overview of nature that Watson himself favoured. For example, D.C. Scott's early Indian and landscape poems are passed over in favour of weaker poems like "Bells" or "Ecstasy." A theosophical poet like Robert Norwood is given more space than Archibald Lampman. Watson's generalized, mystical tastes are indicated by "Scar-Written," one of his selections from his own work:

> If I could write that wonder-book
> So long imprisoned in my soul
> In one bright word that all might look
> And find God's thought upon the scroll … (73)

For Watson, poetry's "vision must be clear, its feeling pure, its inspiration true, its beauty vivid and wholesome."[126] His nationalism is not quite as powerful as Pierce's, but Watson is careful to embrace the idea of different multicultural threads in Canadian literature, for example, Florence Randal Livesay's Ukrainian song translations. Pierce was anxious to stress the importance of Canadian nationhood rather than the country's membership in the British Empire, and it is likely that he persuaded Watson to drop references exalting allegiance to the empire from the latter's introduction.[127]

Pierce's contention in later life that his nationalism in the early 1920s drew on a widespread feeling of the day is supported by the largely favourable response to the anthology. The book went into a second edition in early 1923, with a third and enlarged edition in November 1923 and a deluxe edition that Christmas.[128] The over 100-page enlargement chiefly consisted in revisions to the poetry section, mostly to include more – and more typical – poems of the major poets, pieces like Lampman's "Heat," Roberts's "The Salt Flats," and Carman's "Low Tide on Grand Pre," as well as a selection from Charles Heavysege, who had been omitted from the first edition. Such additions suggested Watson's inexperience and lack of balance as editor in the first edition. Pierce's revision of the prose selection was less radical. He added a little more fiction, notably L.M. Montgomery's "Dog Monday" chapter from *Rilla of Ingleside*,[129] with its evocation of wartime sacrifice. He added some of Mackenzie King's inspirational writing, but provided political balance by also adding Conservative leader Arthur Meighen on "The Glorious Dead."

The somewhat drab appearance and low price ($1.50) of the first edition is explained by the Ryerson catalogue blurb, which described the anthology as designed "for school use and for the private library, a really worthwhile presentation of Canadian writers."[130] The selection was lauded by the Montreal *Gazette* as "an urgent patriotic duty" of "exceptional merit," and similar praise was offered by Austin Bothwell in the Saskatoon *Phoenix* and by Lloyd Roberts.[131] The book trade's magazine called it "a valuable volume" that no public or private library "can afford to be without."[132] Pierce recorded in the spring of 1924 that the University of Manitoba was going to use the work as a textbook, and a clipping in Pierce's scrapbook from the 1925–26 calendar for Wesley College, Winnipeg, lists it as a text for Arthur Phelps and Watson Kirkconnell's course on "Contemporary and Canadian Poets."[133] One can sense that Pierce was gleeful on two counts: as a cultural patriot and as an editor able to provide Fallis with some of the profit he craved.

Some reviewers of the first edition of *Our Canadian Literature*, however, were critical of the editorial work, Watson's in particular, with calls for more breadth and representativeness that undoubtedly prompted the enlarged edition. The review in the *Canadian Magazine* called the poetry selections in the original version often "uninteresting" and felt that more fiction should have been included in Pierce's section.[134] Deacon, initially critical of the anthology in his *Saturday Night* review, was more positive about the latter version, calling it "twice as good as the original" and "at the moment the most representative Canadian anthology."[135] Both Deacon and poet Wilson MacDonald preferred the Ryerson volume to a rival work issued by Macmillan in 1923, E.K. Broadus and Eleanor Hammond's *A Book of Canadian Prose and Verse*.[136] Privately, however, Deacon chided Pierce about Watson's influence over him in the anthology selections, which he shrewdly insisted had meant that "the sweet and innocuous [was] preferred to the virile. You alone, would not have picked what he influenced you to pick."[137] The changes to the first edition suggest that Pierce knew Deacon was right.

By 1924, Pierce's association with the controversial Watson, while it boosted his morale, also meant trouble. Fallis was a jealous taskmaster, one with little sympathy for theosophical enthusiasts. While Fallis must have been somewhat mollified by the commercial success of *Our Canadian Literature*, Pierce in turn was annoyed because he and Watson were charged for changes to the anthology and Fallis accorded him no royalties for his work on it.[138] Pierce resolved to have contracts drawn up for any future works he himself published with Ryerson.

By the mid-1920s, Pierce would have more problems with the book steward. Moreover, Pierce's onerous personal financial commitment to donating a medal to the Royal Society of Canada, and his controversial decision to publish Frederick Philip Grove's novel *Settlers of the Marsh*, would make 1925 one of the most difficult years in his personal and professional life.

"A Patron of ... Optimistic Snorts and Whoops"

Lorne Pierce, Bliss Carman,
Wilson MacDonald, and Launching the Makers of
Canadian Literature Series, 1922–1925

In my 'Anthology' [*Our Canadian Literature*] and the 'Makers [of
Canadian Literature' series] ... I have assumed the role of chronicler
and interpreter and champion.
Lorne Pierce, diary entry, 17 October 1923

I consider you one of the poorest business men and one of the keenest
writers and one of the finest men I know.
Poet Wilson MacDonald to Lorne Pierce, 19 October 1923[1]

P ierce's association with Albert Durrant Watson brought him valuable contacts with other cultural figures, many with ties to theosophy, a movement at its zenith in the 1920s. Pierce was thrilled to meet
Confederation poet Bliss Carman, another theosophy fellow traveller, as
well as poet Charles G.D. Roberts. In fact, Pierce resumed his diary in
the fall of 1923, in part to record impressions of Canadian literary figures
for posterity, since his office was now a "Mecca" for them.[2]
    Although they had corresponded, Pierce first met Carman when he
hosted a lunch for Watson and Carman at Toronto's King Edward Hotel
in November 1923, shortly before a Carman reading.[3] The sixty-two-
year-old Carman, like his cousin Charles G.D. Roberts, both long-time
expatriates, was enjoying a literary revival in Canada. His resurgence had
started in 1919 through a fundraising campaign to underwrite the medical expenses of his tuberculosis cure. Two years later, Carman had been
crowned with a wreath of maple leaves as "Canada's poet laureate" by
the Montreal branch of the Canadian Authors Association.[4] Although
he responded graciously to acclaim, Carman, based in Connecticut near

"Sunshine House," the New Canaan estate of his long-time muse, lover, and patron Mary Perry King (and her markedly less enthusiastic husband, Dr Morris King), privately considered the gruelling cross-Canada touring "a damn bore." But, as Carman joked: "As I am still living in the illusion of hunger and thirst ... I must go out after the silver dollar of the U.S. and the paper dollar of the Great Dominion."[5]

Pierce was soon assisting Carman. In June 1924 Pierce wrote him in New Canaan, offering to act as "impresario" for a Canadian appearance that summer, thanks to a call from a distant cousin of Edith's. The Reverend C.S. Applegath, a Methodist minister and theosophical enthusiast, had since 1921 been running a summer event on Muskoka's Lake Rosseau – called alternately the "Canadian Chautauqua" and the Muskoka Assembly.

The Muskoka Assembly, modelled on the American cultural chautauqua – part educational conference, part festival, and part "happening" (Applegath had attended one in Chautauqua, New York, where the concept originated) – was held each year at the Epworth Inn on Tobin's Island until the Depression ended it in 1932. Each July, the assembly featured literary, musical, philosophical, devotional, and dramatic events as well as swimming, tennis, and canoeing.[6] Charles Applegath's letterhead described the assembly as an "all summer holiday Community Interpreting the Best in Canadian thought and idealism."[7]

Pierce knew many of those involved in the Muskoka Assembly, including his friend Watson, Alice Chown, Charles G.D. Roberts, and E.J. Pratt. Pioneering educationist Aletta Marty, Ontario's first woman school inspector, like Pierce a loyal Queen's graduate (Arts '93 in her case), had organized a summer school of Canadian literature at the Assembly. She also offered winter book groups held in Toronto, at least one of which featured Pierce as speaker. Pierce had published Marty's influential *An Educational Creed* in his landmark Ryerson publication list of 1923. With such a cast, Pierce enthusiastically told Carman, "the Muskoka Assembly does more for Canadian literature than any other institution of its kind in Canada."[8]

Letters flew between Carman and Pierce as the latter tried to negotiate a better fee for Carman. Pierce planned to attend the Muskoka Assembly. The 1924 program for 20–26 July 1924 lists him as scheduled to lead its morning Bible Hour, usually a walk in the woods "concerned with the renewal of the relationship between the spirit of man and the large Spirit manifest in the loveliness of Muskoka."[9] However, work apparently kept

The bohemian Confederation poet whose work Pierce
loved best: Bliss Carman in the 1920s. Courtesy of
Queen's University Archives

Pierce in the city: his diary records seeing Carman only "between trains"
en route to Muskoka.[10] In any case, the charismatic Carman captivated
the assembly and had to decline an offer to build him a summer cottage
there for annual visits. Carman's success added to Pierce's prestige. The
next year Pierce was again approached by the Muskoka Assembly to
negotiate with Carman for a return engagement.[11]

Pierce shone in Carman's eyes as well, the more so as Pierce, Hugh
Eayrs of Macmillan, and Pelham Edgar set about organizing what one
Carman biographer has called his "staggeringly" successful coast-to-
coast lecture tour of Canadian universities in 1925.[12] Carman, tall, hand-

some, and picturesquely shy in broad-brimmed hat and loose cravat, read to an audience of 1,500 at University of Toronto; 600 came to another recital on the tour to hear a poet who enjoyed a burst of "matinee-idol" status.[13]

Pierce's friendship with Carman soon warmed up. Lunching in Toronto with Watson and Carman after the Muskoka Assembly in the summer of 1924, Pierce was "frankly skeptical" about personal immortality (a skepticism that lasted the rest of his life), showing how far he had travelled from his mother's orthodox Methodism. Watson and Carman, with their theosophical faith in spirit, were dismayed. The trio discussed the matter far into the afternoon, Carman assuring Pierce that "one prepares oneself for immortality by the forward looking, expectant frame of mind."[14]

Carman followed up with a long letter. He implied that, as a patron of poets, Pierce ought to embrace optimism and affirmation, not skepticism: "Your pessimistic attitude … won't do at all, my dear man. All very well to pick holes in the conventional *status quo* of theology, but you can't stop there. I can't see the universe being evolved or created out of a mood of pure skepticism. Gladness and confidence seem to me much more profound than sadness or distaste, as these latter are not creative at all, and are always destined to be evanescent." Carman implied that Pierce had to change to be a true lover of poetry: "O man and brother, you must 'come out of it!' You, *you*, even *you*, have paid good honest money for things written by this feeble erring hand … But how can [you] care for the poetry itself and yet remain at variance with the great bulk of poetry and its major trend … And if you have enlisted yourself as a patron of these optimistic snorts and whoops … you must get in step with their celestial strains. On the horns of this dilemma, dear Lorne Pierce, I leave you for the time being, but with a truly gently blessing. Your friend B.C."[15]

Naturally, Pierce was taken aback at such solicitude from a celebrated poet. He thanked Carman for the "beautiful, brotherly reprimand," even preening a little: "That you took the trouble to remonstrate with me, touched me very deeply. It may be that my philosophy of life is faulty because I have no adequate place in it for a satisfactory philosophy of death … I have smiled in its face on more than one occasion and have no fear for it, and yet my highest argument against [immortality] is that it is unnecessary man should persist, for why perpetuate his wretched mediocrity?"[16] He decided to preserve Carman's "wonderful" letter among his "rare treasures."[17]

It was emblematic of the reorientation involved in Pierce's new career in Canadian literature that, when he referred in the letter to opening a book at random for hints in resolving this cosmic question, the book he chose was not the Bible but a volume of Carman! Moreover, such interactions reinforced Pierce's engagement with Carman's type of romantic nature poetry with its intimations of the mystic and the beautiful.

PIERCE WAS at this time promoting other poets whose work idealized man and nature. The younger writer whose poetry Watson, Carman, Robert Norwood, and others most admired was Wilson MacDonald. MacDonald had turned to poetry only in his late twenties, becoming prominent on the Toronto literary scene after the First World War. Born in Cheapside, Ontario, Wilson Pugsley MacDonald, the son of a tailor turned Baptist minister, graduated from McMaster University in 1902. His subsequent occupations in a rolling-stone style of life included seaman, bank clerk, advertising salesman, vaudeville performer, and newspaper reporter. After about 1906, however, MacDonald began writing poetry and giving recitals in Canada and the United States. In 1912, at the same time as Pierce was in Saskatchewan, MacDonald travelled to western Canada, where he gave readings and organized productions of his own musical comedy, *In Sunny France*, in various small centres.[18] MacDonald was also a talented illustrator of his own work, and could wow audiences with magic tricks involving sleight of hand. On one memorable occasion, MacDonald dazzled the Prince of Wales with magic tricks at a Montreal men's club during his 1919 tour of Canada.[19]

In 1918 McClelland and Stewart published MacDonald's *The Song of the Prairie Land*. As one critic suggests, MacDonald's poetry is traditional and romantic, the work of a man who loves Canadian nature but who is bitterly critical of the values of Canadian life, as in his "A Song to Canada":

> My land is a woman who knows
> Not the child at her breast.
> All her quest has been gold.
> … here is my grief that no longer she cares
> For the tumult that crowds in a rune
> When the white curving throat of a cataract bares
> In a song to the high floating moon.[20]

Two gifted yet problematic Ryerson authors: Poets Wilson
MacDonald and Charles G.D. Roberts at the Muskoka
Assembly, 1925. Courtesy of Queen's University Archives

MacDonald was regularly featured at the Muskoka Assembly: Applegath so admired his poetry that he later wrote a study of it.[21] Unlike
Carman, however, Wilson MacDonald was seldom an easy guest. He
was a vegetarian who detested white sugar; decades later, Applegath's
long-suffering wife, Edna, remembered having to prepare special meals
for him at the Applegath cottage. MacDonald also detested smoking
and did not hesitate to say so. A superb tennis player, he liked to be
surrounded by pretty girls but resolutely clung to a vow of celibacy

before marriage. He abhorred the modern "flapper," telling his diary that "bobbed hair and a well-shaped pair of legs are her sole attraction ... She brought Rome to destruction and will destroy utterly our civilization unless checked in her mad vagaries of life."[22] Alongside such bombastic tendencies was utter certainty about his worth as a poet. By 1919, he was convinced that his writing was "healing to the souls of men" and that he had been "sent into this world to be a bulwark against that mighty tide of atheism, materialism and fleshly lust which [is] threatening our civilization."[23]

Despite his prickliness, MacDonald's work had many admirers, especially among Watson and his circle. As Michele Lacombe puts it, he was in effect the "poet laureate of Theosophy in Canada."[24] MacDonald was attending meetings of the Theosophical Society in Toronto as a member in the winter of 1921.[25] Albert Smythe, the branch founder, wrote a foreword to the second edition of *The Song of the Prairie Land* two years later. Smythe's contention that MacDonald was a "genius ... no doubt whatsoever"[26] echoed Bliss Carman, who referred to MacDonald's "unquestionable genius."[27] *Saturday Night* book columnist William Arthur Deacon (who pronounced MacDonald "a new elemental force in poetry"[28]) and Victoria College professor Pelham Edgar also admired his work.

Watson brought Pierce and MacDonald together at a lunch in June 1922.[29] Pierce responded to MacDonald's work as well, asserting in a 1923 article that he was a poet who "has searched the world to find truth and beauty in order that he might enrich and ennoble life."[30] Like Pierce – and Watson – MacDonald disliked materialism, religious dogmatism, and jazz, denouncing the latter in his "The Song of the Jazz Hounds" where flappers dance to a jazz band:

> Breast to breast and knees to knees
> they have given their flesh to a foul disease.
> What unto them is the poet's song
> or the great gaunt trees in a choric throng![31]

Nevertheless, Pierce was wary of MacDonald's penchant for invective, writing elsewhere that in his satire MacDonald "pontificates too much, scolds too often," falling "away below" his usual imaginative and musical standards.[32] Pierce preferred the "chaste spiritual insight" of MacDonald poems like "In a Wood Clearing":

> ... here I wait
> in a delicious confusion, knowing not whether
> 'tis my heart that beats, or her step that falls
> on the wood mosses of gray, green and silver.[33]

Watson and Pierce featured five MacDonald poems in their 1922 anthology *Our Canadian Literature* – as many as for Lampman and D.C. Scott.

When in September 1922 publisher John McClelland declined Wilson MacDonald's latest manuscript in what the poet called an "ass's verdict,"[34] Pierce took over in grand fashion. Not only did Ryerson publish the *Miracle Songs of Jesus* in 1923, Pierce also brought out a new edition of MacDonald's *The Song of the Prairie Land*, a work congruent with Pierce's belief that the west needed to be represented in Canada's literature.[35] Pierce made plans to publish two more poetry manuscripts by MacDonald, "The House of Rebels" and "The Song of the Undertow." Then, even though MacDonald had never written fiction, in April 1923 Pierce offered him a hefty $250 advance to write a novel called "The Castle of Graymoor."[36]

At first, all went well. Pierce saw a great deal of Wilson MacDonald. One dinner at the King Edward Hotel in February 1923 assembled Pierce, Watson, and Robert Norwood for "a feast of wit and a flow of reason."[37] By October, Pierce was telling his Vancouver friend Dr Ernest Fewster that *Miracle Songs* had "cleaned up one thousand copies in two weeks" and that the as-yet-unpublished "The House of Rebels" was "the most remarkable single contribution to Canadian letters yet." Reviews of *Miracle Songs* were good, with the Montreal *Gazette* declaring that "the spirit of [MacDonald's] poetry is a prophecy of the extent and future of Canadianism," precisely the kind of nationalistic response Pierce had hoped for.[38] Moreover, Pierce had interested an English publisher, Hodder and Stoughton, in publishing MacDonald.[39]

The summer of 1923 had some heady moments for Pierce. Pratt's *Newfoundland Verse* was garnering enthusiastic reviews, even if it did not sell as well as MacDonald's *Miracle Songs*. In the summer and fall of 1923, Pierce promoted MacDonald, sending out letters and circulars across Ontario, Quebec, and in particular western Canada to organize reading tours. He stressed that MacDonald's tours constituted "a distinct opportunity for the people of Canada to hear a man of outstanding merit."[40] In addition, whether or not Pierce promised to underwrite all of the costs of the western tour, as MacDonald later claimed, he certainly

offered some support, and promised to ship MacDonald ample supplies
of *The Song of the Prairie Land* to sell.

About this time, Pierce mused to his diary that at Ryerson he was
finding himself playing the role of "a sort of small-sized Maecenas helping poets and other lame dogs over the stile."[41] Lame dogs sometimes
bite, however. Even in his first praise of MacDonald in his diary, Pierce
hinted at potential conflict in dealing with him: "My constant won-
derment's the comparison between the *man*, his terrible egoism, con-
ceit, adulation-hunting, swooning or gnashing under criticism, fawning
under praise – and the *man's work*; something divine in its loveliness."[42]
MacDonald's circle was well aware that he could be difficult. Robert
Norwood humorously warned Pierce before MacDonald's tour began in
the fall of 1923: "A jewel of gold in a swine's snout is our beloved, brilliant,
wilful Wilson."[43]

Meanwhile, in June, MacDonald was "delighted" by the first copies of
the Ryerson edition of *The Song of the Prairie Land*, beautifully illustrated
with his own designs. In July he handed Pierce the novel manuscript
after working hard at it since April. Ominously, however, MacDonald
brooded that fiction was something uncongenial that he was forced to
work at for the sake of money, and that Pierce's deadline had been far
too tight.[44] In August he grumbled to his diary: "Here the man who
publishes my books solemnly promise[d] me money to tide me over
until my western trip mended my finances. Dr. Pierce however is strong
on promises and weak on fulfilment."[45] Two weeks later, MacDonald
dubbed Pierce the "prince of forgetfulness."[46] He was further enraged
on 1 October when Pierce was able to give him only $50 as he left on his
western tour. Ironically, Pierce also handed him a letter which urged him
to regard the tour as "the chance of his life," assuring him that Pierce
was willing to be his patron "indefinitely, so long as you produce poetry
like 'In the Clearing.'"[47] But MacDonald was still seething in Kenora
two days later, even when he learned that Pierce had just obtained a free
CPR pass for him. MacDonald's diary at this time repeatedly denounces
Pierce's "Methodist hypocrisy."[48]

In fact, over the next few months the tour, with readings in such centres as Winnipeg, Regina, Edmonton, Kamloops, Revelstoke, Duncan,
New Westminster, Vancouver, and Victoria, had logistical problems
which precipitated a flood of invective from MacDonald against Pierce.
One Canadian critic, Stan Dragland, has published a chronicle called

Wilson MacDonald's Western Tour, 1923–1924, a collection of documents recording the imbroglios of this sorry tale.[49] MacDonald was enraged when book shipments were late or failed to arrive, while House employees complained that MacDonald's sales records were slipshod.[50] For his part, MacDonald complained of poverty, but he usually refused to stay anywhere but the best hotels, even as his arrogance and ill humour alienated many prospective supporters.

Furthermore, the brochure about MacDonald sent out by Ryerson included blurbs so excessive ("one of the greatest poets of the Anglo-Saxon race") that many were put off. Ernest Fewster wrote Pierce from Vancouver to say that, while he would do his best to organize a successful reading there, the pamphlet's "extravagance of praise" had "flabbergasted" him, criticism echoed by Pierce's friend, academic Arthur Phelps, in Winnipeg.[51] Pierce, still new to the game of literary promotion, had yet to learn how to calibrate his appeals.

In Regina, on 17 October, MacDonald learned of the death of his father, but grief did not soften him toward his Toronto publisher. Book shipments from the House's Toronto warehouse had arrived late in Regina as well as Winnipeg – undeniably frustrating for MacDonald, who needed books to sell at each reading. When a group of Regina women, headed by journalist Irene Moore, presented him with a gift purse of $90, MacDonald used the gift to reproach Pierce, telling him: "When I received it I thought of Mary's gift to Jesus, and I could not help contrasting the action of the Million-Dollar-Methodist Book room who could easily give $100,000 to the poets and know they were spreading God's message."[52] Issuing a backhanded compliment a few days later, MacDonald informed Pierce that he was "one of the poorest business men and one of the keenest writers and one of the finest men I know."[53] Pierce's pained reaction can be imagined. Ironically, in some respects, the tour should have been good news. Two printings of 1,000 copies each of *Prairie Land* were made, and Ryerson did ship over 600 books to MacDonald. MacDonald sometimes had good houses, and generally positive write-ups. But the poet often alienated his listeners. At Calgary's public library, he bluntly informed his audience that the city could never be a centre of culture as long as more people attended the rodeo than came to poetry readings. Albertan Nellie McClung, for one, was furious.[54]

On the West Coast, MacDonald's habit of referring to the Vancouver Poetry Society as the "Vancouver Poultry Society" did not endear him to Ernest Fewster, one of its leading lights.[55] All the while, MacDonald denounced Pierce and Ryerson Press ("for pure materialism the Methodist Book Room [has] it on every pagan institution in the country").[56] He was now incensed because his tour of the west coincided with the even more successful Carman tour that Pierce had helped arrange. In his diary, stung by MacDonald's "scathing and heartless" letters,[57] Pierce wrote that "for months I have literally carried him on my back and burdened both my mind and heart with him."[58]

Pierce's troubles with MacDonald were accompanied by other authorial brushfires that conspired to complicate further his uneasy relations with Book Steward Samuel Fallis. The very week in October 1923 that MacDonald set off on tour, Ryerson authors Pratt, Deacon, and Cornell paid their surprise visit to Fallis to complain about the House's handling of their books.[59] MacDonald's letters from the west to Pierce claimed that it was at Fallis's insistence that Pierce gave MacDonald only $50 in expense money on his departure, despite an earlier promise by Pierce of more.[60] In fact, Pierce gave *his* own money, not the House's, to MacDonald on departure, at a time when he had little to spare.[61] He had obviously been told that Fallis would not approve any more House funds for MacDonald. Over the next few months, Pierce must have realized how it poisoned his own relations with Fallis to have the House badmouthed across the west by one of his authors. In fact, Pierce's stress level was so high that autumn that he suffered several severe angina attacks, including one on the day of Wilson MacDonald's departure from Toronto.[62]

Pierce must have ruefully reflected that, as a publisher, he would have to retain the ministerial virtue of turning the other cheek. He finally wrote to MacDonald in early November, pleading with him to behave: "Over and over I have given you proof of my friendship, and your letters simply dumbfound me ... Somehow you do not see how your hitting the House hits me ... Please be as frank as you care to be with me, but don't go around lambasting the House. You can't disassociate an editor and a House like that. And every time you go on like that you give me an ugly, spiteful gash, which I know you would be the first one to spare."[63]

MacDonald did not recant. He wired – collect – a long, expensive telegram from Medicine Hat, "absolutely disgusted" because another book shipment was late. He told Pierce that he had cancelled a Lethbridge reading and threatened to switch publishers. Losing patience, Pierce replied: "Your communications have been beneath contempt ... It was madness for you to threat[en] selling your books to some unknown publisher in Vancouver, simply killing yourself to spite the House, forgetting all the while that you are under contract with us."[64] Pierce also informed MacDonald that the two printings of *Prairie Land* had been 1,000 copies each, but that the House simply had not anticipated the volume of orders from him. In November, the second printing was rushed through in two weeks, but even that meant further delays in shipping.

If dealing with MacDonald was like being caught in a train wreck, Pierce was also distressed by an actual train wreck. Days before MacDonald's angry telegram in mid-November 1923, Pierce learned that the CPR train on which his parents (who had been in British Columbia visiting his sister) had been travelling back to eastern Canada had been wrecked in the Rockies. Pierce first saw news of the smash-up on the newsstands as he travelled home to Wineva Avenue on the Queen streetcar. Hours of uncertainty – during which Pierce suffered his worst angina attack to date – passed before a wire arrived saying that Ed and Harriet Pierce were safe.[65]

Incredibly, Pierce was still working on an eastern Canada tour for MacDonald after Christmas, but MacDonald cancelled it to stay in Regina in early 1924 to organize a production of *In Sunny France* to make money for himself. At this juncture, Pierce decided not to publish MacDonald's next two poetry manuscripts, "The Song of the Undertow" and "The House of Rebels," announcing that Ryerson had not been able to interest American publishers in MacDonald's work. Pierce also vetoed publication of MacDonald's manuscript novel, "The Castle of Graymoor," in which Pierce had placed high hopes and a big advance: "[Publication] is off until it is wholly revised and that will be indefinite."[66] Pierce's instincts about the novel's lack of viability were sound: a hackneyed romance in the Walter Scott mould, the novel improbably moves from a North Sea English castle to the Canadian prairies.[67] Even MacDonald later described the novel as "unreal" and "synthetic."[68] He created far livelier scenarios in the west than he could achieve in fiction.

Worse yet, the complaints of Fred Ellins, the House accountant, over MacDonald's snarled accounts made Fallis well aware of the problems that fall. MacDonald told the accounting department in late November that he was withholding money from the sale of books to repay money advanced to him by Irene Moore to buy books. He threatened to sever contracts with the House, saying he was "sick and tired" of its mistakes.[69] Pierce, apparently, barely managed to persuade Fallis not to jettison MacDonald altogether. As the House's profits from publishing MacDonald vaporized amid the accounting mess, Fallis's talk of building a house in North Toronto for his editor evaporated as well.

Pierce at last saw MacDonald in Calgary in February 1924, during one of his annual textbook marketing tours of major centres in the west. Pierce finally gave MacDonald, as he put it, a "real treat of hot tongue," for "damn[ing] me all over the west without cause." Feeling "decidedly better" after the encounter, Pierce took MacDonald with him to meet Charles Mair, one of the grand old men of Canadian poetry.[70] Over the next few years, despite another stormy blow-up in July 1924 over the western tour,[71] Pierce behaved magnanimously to MacDonald, urging him to revise his novel and poetry for publication. MacDonald's response was, however, "reticent" – to use Pierce's phrase. (Meanwhile MacDonald was writing in his diary about the prospect of revising the novel, with insight for once into his own psychology: "The task is hateful to me as I am writing to please."[72])

Ironically, Pierce did not benefit from the publication of MacDonald's next book of poetry, the most successful of his career. In 1926 the short-lived Graphic Press, based in Ottawa, printed and distributed *Out of the Wilderness* at MacDonald's expense. MacDonald continued to self-publish for the next decade. He remained bitter about the publication history of *The Song of the Prairie Land* in his memoirs, ignoring his own role in racking up expenses.[73]

Pierce published a generous review of *Out of the Wilderness* in the *New Outlook*, the magazine that succeeded the *Christian Guardian* after church union in 1925. The review made it clear that he still valued MacDonald's "chaste spiritual insight" in collections that expressed "the marrow of Canada."[74] Book buyers agreed: *Out of the Wilderness* sold more than 7,000 copies – the best-selling book of poetry since Robert Service's *Songs of a Sourdough* (1907).[75] With MacDonald's new book out, however, sales of *The Miracle Songs of Jesus* sank to a pitiful five copies for Ryerson during the last half of 1924.[76]

Meanwhile, even in this burst of success, MacDonald was complaining to his diary about the nation's indifference to his work: "My poetry will bring millions of tourists to Canada in the years to be and she will grow fat at my expense, but what is that to her hog soul?"[77] MacDonald lived until 1967, giving recitals and selling self-published books for most of that time,[78] eking out a living on sales, readings, gifts from his admirers, and, after his marriage in 1935, money earned by his loyal wife,

Dorrie. But, by largely placing himself outside the mainstream of the book trade through self-publication for most of his post-1925 career, MacDonald found himself in a position where his career mattered to few but himself.[79] As for Pierce, his dealings with MacDonald had not destroyed his belief in patriotic nature poetry, but they taught him some hard lessons about dealing with authors and undermined his relations with Fallis.

BY 1923, AS HE learned that counting on the loyalty of individual authors was going to be chancy, Pierce was well into one of his most sweeping projects – to designate a whole canon of Canadian literature as a nation-making enterprise. With the ambitious Makers of Canadian Literature critical anthology series, however, he would run far into the financial red.

In the Makers of Canadian Literature volumes, Pierce conceived an ambitious series designed to foster a bicultural awareness of Canadian literature. Moreover, by including French Canadian literature in the series, and taking on an associate editor from Quebec, Pierce was a pioneer. Some forty volumes were projected (with a volume editor for each), eight of them on French Canadian writers, including a compendium volume on French Canadian literary history. However, only twelve volumes actually came out between 1923 and 1925, before Fallis suspended the series on account of poor sales. A thirteenth volume, *Arthur Stringer* by Victor Lauriston, published in 1941, was only nominally part of the series.[80]

Margery Fee has established the order of publication of the series. In 1923 Albert Durrant Watson's *Robert Norwood* appeared first, followed by four more volumes: William Renwick Riddell's *William Kirby* as well as his *John Richardson*, Peter McArthur's *Stephen Leacock*, and William Arthur Deacon's *Peter McArthur*. Only one volume, Katherine Hale's *Isabella Valancy Crawford*, appeared in 1924, but 1925 saw the publication of three English volumes and up to three French volumes. The English volumes were J.D. Logan's *Thomas Chandler Haliburton*, John Ford MacDonald's *William Henry Drummond*, and James Cappon's *Charles G.D. Roberts*. *Louis Honoré Frechette* by Henri Beaude (as "Henri d'Arles") appeared in 1925. Fee dates two more French volumes, *Francois Xavier Garneau* by Gustave Lanctôt and *Antoine Gérin-Lajoie* by Louvigny de Montigny, to "either ... late 1925 or early 1926."[81]

The idea of the "Makers" series was firmly in Pierce's mind by mid-1922. Pierce saw the series as a means to establish himself and the

Ryerson Press as central to Canadian literature both past and present, following his apprenticeship of "watchful waiting" in his first two years at the House. In October 1923 he proudly recorded in his diary that "in my 'Anthology' [*Our Canadian Literature*] and the 'Makers' ... I have assumed the role of chronicler and interpreter and champion."[82] Pierce interpreted the public interest in writers like Carman, Roberts, Pratt, and Wilson MacDonald as indicative of burgeoning demand for Canadian literature. He wanted Ryerson to be at the forefront of the field, the more so to redress the falling off in Canadian publishing by the House during the previous decade. He told his diary: "[By 1922, it] became imperative to begin somewhere, and with energy I had to show by some token or other that we really were into it. I also had to invent some way of enticing the writing fraternity back to us. I concluded that this series would be the best means. The work needed to be done. The interest in Canadian literature was immense: our National soul was taking form and [assuming] a distinct content just as rapid[ly]. Now seemed to be the time and so 'The Makers of Canadian Literature' were launched."[83]

Pierce thus clearly intended the series as a nation-making exercise. Its very title echoed the landmark, nationalistic Makers of Canada series of historical biographies published by George Morang early in the century.[84] Pierce's elaborate prospectus for his series emphasized its nation-building possibilities, especially given the ground-breaking bicultural nature of the project. Although Book Steward Samuel Fallis was a staunch Conservative, and Pierce's own sympathies lay in that direction, the venture was also bipartisan: both Sir Robert Borden, the former Conservative prime minister of Canada, and Sir Lomer Gouin, Liberal premier of Quebec from 1905 to 1920, contributed testimonials to the prospectus – for a handsome fee of $100 each.[85] Gouin assured prospective buyers that the Makers of Canadian Literature series was to be "in some way, like another page of the great book of *bonne entente*, of which a daily study is necessary if we are to insure the future of our country."[86] Pierce, for his part, stressed in speeches about the series that "Canadians must preserve a national literature as the first step toward national self-preservation."[87]

No one who examines the Makers of Canadian Literature series can miss the romantic nationalism of the venture. Pierce composed a ringing dedication, typeset in flowing script within a border of maple and oak leaves at the front of each blue-and-gold volume: "Dedicated to the writers of Canada – past and present – the real Master-Builders and

Interpreters of our great Dominion – in the hope that our People, equal heirs in the rich inheritance, may learn to know them intimately; and knowing them love them; and loving – Follow." His optimism about the appeal of the series is suggested by the fact that three editions were offered – in school, popular, and deluxe formats, with an option to buy either the set or individual volumes at $1.50 each.[88] Each volume was to be about 150 pages. Moreover, Pierce had conceived a unique format for the series: each volume featured a biographical sketch and a critical appreciation, as well as an author bibliography and an anthology "of the Maker's most representative work." He had already learned, in compiling his anthology *Our Canadian Literature*, how difficult it could be to find material by or about Canadian writers. He therefore resolved that the series "should appeal to the student and at the same time be popular enough to interest and instruct the man on the street."[89]

Pierce engaged prominent Canadiana collector Rufus Hathaway to do most of the bibliographies.[90] Also, five "background" synoptic volumes on Canadian literature were planned: one on French Canadian literature, one on "The Indian" by Marius Barbeau, and others on the Great Lakes region, the west, and the Maritime provinces respectively. (Unfortunately, although Barbeau completed his manuscript and Ray Palmer Baker finished one on the Maritimes, none of the synoptic studies was ever published.[91])

At the outset, Pierce had widespread support for his ambitious and expensive venture. The Advisory Board listed on the ·series prospectus included Dominion Archivist Arthur Doughty, prominent British Columbia historian Judge F.W. Howay, and Dalhousie professor W.L. Stewart.[92] Pierce was encouraged by several prominent literary men in planning the series. Professor J.D. Logan of Acadia University (who, ironically, was to prove a dilatory writer for two titles) urged Pierce to get "cracking" because literary man John Garvin was also planning a similar series in association with McClelland and Stewart. A similar idea had also been floated by Hugh Eayrs, recently appointed president of Macmillan of Canada. Pierce's hopes for educational sales for the series were also bolstered by Logan, who advised him that as "the only systematic teacher of Canadian literature in a Canadian university, I may say there is a great need for such a series – and that it would 'go.'"[93]

John Garvin was indeed planning a similar series with an equally lofty name – "Master-Works of Canadian Authors." Garvin was a rather quixotic figure in the Toronto literary world whose fantasy spinning as a sometime stock promoter at times seemed to infuse his ambitious literary schemes.[94] For example, author L.M. Montgomery was always amused by his tales to her about his role in effecting Canadian publication of *Anne of Green Gables* in 1908: in fact, there had been no Canadian edition.[95] Nevertheless, Garvin had edited *The Collected Poems of Isabella Valancy Crawford* (1905) as well as several anthologies, including *Canadian Poets* (1916); his socially well-connected wife, Amelia, née Warnock, was widely known as the writer "Katherine Hale."[96]

Garvin's proposed series of twenty-five volumes did not have as scholarly a template as Pierce's, but it was definitely competition. Many of the same authors were planned for inclusion – including Lampman, Roberts, Kirby, Parker, and Mair. Some projected Garvin volumes were reprints with new introductions, such as, for example, Susanna Moodie's *Roughing It in the Bush* and George Munro Grant's *Ocean to Ocean*.[97] Like Pierce's venture, Garvin's series was also promoted on patriotic grounds as designed to preserve "too long neglected" works "of which Canadian citizens generally should be proud."[98] But the series was plagued by financial difficulties. The volumes that actually appeared were in the event published by the Radisson Society, a company set up by Garvin himself[99] – McClelland and Stewart obviously having becoming wary of such a financially perilous venture by the summer of 1923.[100] Garvin planned to sell exclusively on subscription, at a minimum unit price of $4.00 per volume.[101] But he struggled financially, postponing payments to his contributors and writing from at least three different business addresses between 1925 and 1928. Only four volumes were ever published: editions of Alexander Mackenzie's *Voyages from Montreal on the River St. Lawrence* ... (1927), Paul Kane's *Wanderings of an Artist among the Indians of North America* (1925), and George M. Grant's *Ocean to Ocean* (1926), along with Charles Mair's *Tecumseh, A Drama, and Canadian Poems* ... (1926).[102]

In 1922, however, competition with Garvin spurred Pierce's zeal for his Ryerson series. Overseeing it constituted a masterwork in itself. First of all, which authors should Pierce include? Some authors – Roberts, Lampman, Carman – seemed obvious choices, but, to Pierce's chagrin, publishing them was plagued by copyright difficulties. Many of Carman's and Roberts's works were controlled by Boston publisher L.C. Page and Company, a ferociously proprietary firm whose head, Lewis Page, stymied any attempt to publish a Carman volume in the series by demanding extortionate permission fees.[103] That Pierce was still green in the publishing game became evident in October 1922 when, a year before he met Carman, he wrote him to propose a "Makers" volume on him, assuring the poet that the as-yet-unassigned volume would be published by the New Year! Pierce blithely asked Carman his preference in editors, proposing bibliophile Rufus Hathaway, writer Peter McArthur, or writer Lloyd Roberts, son of Carman's cousin Charles G.D. Roberts.[104] Carman's response was a kind of primer on publishing for Pierce: the poet clearly found the neophyte editor naive in his methods. While stating that Hathaway could edit such a volume, and that he judged Lloyd Roberts "not ... at all competent" to do so, Carman pointed out that Pierce had placed him "in rather an awkward position in asking me to make this choice ... I must leave it to you to make it yourself."[105] He also politely implied that Pierce's deadlines were fanciful and his critical path not well thought out: "I am rather surprised to note that you wish to have the volume about myself published 'around the new year' ... My experience with publishers, not to speak of myself, would lead me to look upon such a performance in the light of the miraculous. However, you know your own business. But I should strongly advise postponing the issue until the spring at least, as I would wish to see the material before it goes to the printer, for the sake of accuracy in statement. The writer, of course, should have absolute freedom for any critical judgment that he may hold and express."[106] Hathaway in fact set to work on a volume, but so refractory was Page that by January 1924 Carman told Pierce to cancel the project.[107]

The Lampman volume, with Duncan Campbell Scott as editor, also failed to appear, partly because of copyright difficulties with Musson. (This disappointment would help to chill relations between Pierce and Scott for two decades.[108]) In 1925 Pierce was able to publish Cappon's volume on Roberts with Page material included.[109] But he got Page's permission only at the eleventh hour, prompting him to describe Page in his diary as "surely the meanest man in Boston"[110] – an opinion shared by several bruised Page authors, including Roberts and L.M. Montgomery.[111]

Pierce's choice of volume editors for the Makers of Canadian Literature series was also shaped by his allegiances and advisers of the early 1920s. Despite the lacklustre reviews of Albert Watson's work as poetry editor in their joint anthology, Pierce chose him to do the "Makers" volume on Watson's friend and fellow theosophist, poet (and Anglican minister) Robert Norwood. Norwood's pedestrian closet dramas like

"The Witch of Endor" and cosmic lyrics like "The Spinner" ("Hobnailed boots and harps are spun / Out of the substance of the sun") scarcely seem deserving of "Maker" status. But not only was Watson enthusiastic about Norwood, so was Norwood's fellow Maritimer, John Logan of Acadia University. Logan called Norwood the leading Maritime poet in the genre of poetic closet drama – admittedly a restricted field.[112] (Logan also advised Pierce to exclude poet Robert Service, "a damned bad poet" whose verse constituted "bootleggers' booze."[113])

Watson's uncritical volume on Norwood lavishly praised him in terms of poetic ideals they both shared, leading one scholar to pronounce the book the only "obviously bad" volume in the series.[114] Certainly, Watson's praise of Norwood's work is overblown and full of mystical hyperbole: "His spirit breathes the higher atmospheres in concourse with great souls in the free altitudes of thought."[115] Not surprisingly, given such glib rhapsodies, Watson speedily completed his volume, making it the first to appear. That was unfortunate, because, given the volume's superlatives and Pierce's well-known friendship with Watson, the inaugural offering made the series seem destined to be cosy and uncritical. Reviewers were not slow to note this. The modernist magazine *Canadian Forum* tartly observed that the series had been "well-nigh drowned in the dreadful molasses of its initial volume."[116] More traditional literary reviewers delivered much the same verdict. In a warning echoed in the Calgary *Herald*, the Toronto *Mail and Empire* review (important for sales) admonished Pierce: "The editor must be vigilant, or the whole thing will degenerate into an orgy of log-rolling, with all our poets and literary men standing in a circle, each one proclaiming the man in front of him, to be a genius, quite positive that he, himself, will in turn be hailed as one ... In *Robert Norwood*, the first in the series ... [there is] more evidence of friendship than of critical discrimination."[117]

Indeed, Pierce had commissioned other volumes that would have reinforced this impression of "log-rolling" had they actually been published. With Norwood egging Pierce on,[118] Albert Watson was designated a "Maker." The volume was commissioned from Watson's disciple Margaret Lawrence (who, in a letter to Bliss Carman, described her fervent devotion to Watson as "exquisitely chaste"[119] and Watson's influence as like "the real Jesus must have been to his friends"[120]). Moreover, despite the grief MacDonald was giving him, Pierce magnanimously planned to personally edit and include a volume on Wilson MacDonald. At the outset of the latter's stormy western tour in October 1923, Pierce assured the poet that, when the volume appeared in "1924 or so," its contents would "make your audiences declare that the Editor knew long before the people of Canada did, that a new constellation was already swimming in the heavens."[121]

Some of the other volumes actually published in the series did suggest some reciprocal "back scratching," even when their quality was appreciably better than Watson on Norwood. Humorist Peter McArthur edited a volume on Stephen Leacock (the manuscript of which was vetted by Leacock), while McArthur himself was the subject of a volume by William Arthur Deacon. Pierce often had a hit-and-miss time getting editors for the volumes, in part because, at least at the outset, he was not always experienced enough to know whom to ask – and whom not to ask. He was also competing for editors with Garvin, which made for some curious trade-offs between the rival series. For example, Katherine Hale, Garvin's wife, produced the volume on Isabella Valancy Crawford for Pierce, and Garvin planned to edit the Mair volume for Pierce, despite the fact that he planned a Mair volume in his own series. Several volume editors – D.C. Scott on Lampman and Pelham Edgar on D.C. Scott – seem to have shifted from Garvin to Pierce as Garvin's financial fortunes fell.[122]

J.D. Logan had promised to do a Joseph Howe volume for Garvin, but he wrote Pierce in February 1923 that he was forsaking Garvin to edit Howe as well as Haliburton for Ryerson – but Pierce had to swear not to tell Garvin.[123] By January 1924, however, Logan had not delivered either manuscript. In June, Pierce had to return the long-delayed Howe volume to Logan for extensive revisions; he had also found problems in Logan's Haliburton volume. The experience with Logan taught Pierce to be more demanding of other authors. Pierce reflected ruefully in June 1924: "Since [Logan] I have turned back manuscripts a half dozen times."[124]

Pierce had so many "Makers" volumes to commission that he sometimes appeared to proceed on a fill-in-the-blanks basis. But it must be remembered that Canadian literary scholarship was so inchoate in the mid-1920s that there were often no obvious authorities, even for well-known writers. Pierce asked William Renwick Riddell, an Ontario Supreme Court judge and littérateur, to do a volume on novelist Gilbert Parker. Riddell replied that he knew little about him, but he took on William Kirby and John Richardson, while admitting that his knowledge of them was also slight. He told Pierce that, if he would send him

Kirby's and Richardson's complete works, he would read them during "an eight week southern cruise" in the winter of 1923, a venue that must have tantalized the overworked Pierce![125]

Happily for Pierce, Riddell submitted acceptable material within months, although he complained – as did reviewers – that the anthology format was not as well suited to showcase prose writers, Richardson in particular, as it was for poets.[126] Riddell was shocked by some of Richardson's more salacious work, particularly *The Monk Knight of St. John*, to his mind pornographic, which he told Pierce in a horrified letter was "fit only for the stews."[127] Riddell included the same estimate in the published volume, although he omitted his assertion to Pierce that Richardson must have had "senile dementia."[128]

Pierce's most disagreeable "Makers" editor proved to be his old Queen's English professor, James Cappon. Sitting in his new editorial chair at Ryerson, Pierce probably imagined that it would be a kind of vindication for himself and Canadian literature to commission the now-retired Cappon to contribute a volume on Charles G.D. Roberts. After all, Cappon had in 1905 written a short study of Roberts, *Roberts and the Influences of His Time*, that was published by the House. Sadly, what Pierce had fondly anticipated as a new relationship of equals turned out to be another experience of being treated as a vulgar inferior by his old professor.

Pierce approached Cappon about the Roberts volume in January 1923. Cappon haughtily replied that, since there was possible conflict with Garvin's series, he had written to Duncan Campbell Scott and Pelham Edgar to ask for whom they planned to edit volumes![129] In March, Cappon at last agreed to write for Pierce, but stipulated that "my knowledge ... is too slight to enable me to do more than write a coldly formal biographical notice."[130] Cappon was indeed correct about the slight state of his knowledge: his next letter asked what the still lively Roberts had died of.[131]

True to form, Cappon was not abashed by his premature burial of Roberts. His letters from fashionable resorts like Quebec's Little Metis Beach (summer) and the French Riviera (winter) soon made it obvious that he had no intention of putting in the slogging required for a biographical sketch of Roberts. Pierce was left to write it, as Cappon informed him in a chilly letter from Kingston in October 1923 that announced his imminent departure for Sicily.[132] Pierce, a glutton for authorial punishment that October, gamely told his diary that it would be "an honour" for Cappon to "permit" him to write the biography.[133]

Cappon subsequently told Pierce on his return from sunnier climes that Pierce's biography of Roberts was "interesting and thorough" but that he was "sensitive" about having it appear above his own signature. The inference was clear: Pierce fell short of Cappon's critical powers. Pierce, finally fed up, refused to differentiate the Roberts biography, integrating it into Cappon's text. However, he still had to endure Cappon's sneers about his philistine immersion in the vulgar commercial anthill of publishing. Cappon soon dared to caution his former pupil about overwork: "I am really very sorry to hear you have been under the weather, I suspect you have been working and hustling too much. After any hard or prolonged spell of work, take a day or two of complete idling."[134] Pierce fared no better with Cappon when he later commissioned him to write a book on Carman that was not part of the "Makers" series – *Bliss Carman and the Literary Currents and Influences of His Time*, published in 1930.[135]

With the Makers of Canadian Literature series, however, Pierce faced a conceptual problem, as well as some difficult editors. To present a group of writers as part of a nationalistic pantheon makes it awkward to discuss shortcomings. When Pierce approached Sir Andrew Macphail to edit a volume on fiction writer Norman Duncan, Macphail bluntly asked: "Do you want a judgement of his work – or mere eulogy as Watson has done for Norwood ... Much of Duncan's writing is mere gibberish."[136] "Makers of Canadian Gibberish" certainly lacks a nation-building ring, but Pierce stoutly assured Macphail that he wanted "critical appraisement," not "ladling out syrup."[137]

Once the Duncan manuscript was submitted, however, problems arose. In February 1924, after reading Macphail's submission, an agitated Pierce wrote to Macphail: "The question comes up in my own mind, have I not made a mistake in giving Norman Duncan a place at all among THE MAKERS OF CANADIAN LITERATURE. A great deal of your criticism, I feel, is quite in order, but it seems to me that the total result of your treatment in both the Biography and Appreciation was too destructive ... there are many virtues in Duncan, which it seems to me you have overlooked." Arguing that Duncan might not be "important" but that he was "important to us [Canadians]," Pierce proposed that Macphail balance his criticism with appreciation:

I hope that you can see the matter as I do. Here we have an
author, granted a MAKER, and yet, upon laying down your
book, the unanimous verdict would be that the man ought to
be consigned to oblivion but some of his books deserve at least
a temporary immortality. Could you not recast part of your
manuscript, – not to mention the criticism – which criticism is
due – but to gather if you can, the salient features of his strength.
You may do so in such a way as to still confirm your seasoned
opinion that on the whole, his virtues are overshadowed by his
faults; but as it stands now, whatever mention you make of his
virtue is so embedded in the fiercest kind of criticism, that the
whole work defeats our purpose.[138]

Macphail did relent. He did not turn to "booming" Duncan by any
means, but an examination of two versions of the Duncan manuscript
establishes that he softened his strictures on Duncan to produce a more
balanced assessment. Macphail was still crisp in the revised treatment,
writing, for example, of Duncan's "mechanical vernacular ... far beyond
the limits of literary taste" and his failure to achieve "a general style of
his own."[139] His Duncan volume, however, was never published. The exchange between him and Pierce made the latter aware that not all of
his "Makers" were at the same level of achievement. He even admitted
that he could see several of his choices – Duncan presumably included –
"foisted from any future series of *Makers*."[140]

As the correspondence with Macphail suggests, Pierce was a hands-on
copy editor for all the volumes. For example, Deacon's volume on Peter
McArthur, which appeared in 1923, was the occasion of a cool thank you
from Deacon for some of Pierce's editorial changes.[141] Pierce also per-
used as best he could the French volumes in the series. But Pierce needed
a francophone associate editor: for one thing, he was far from fluently
bilingual, and the series required some Quebec literary bona fides to
come across as truly bicultural. Pierce found the ideal associate editor in
notary and author Victor Morin, well known as a historian of Montreal
and president of the Société des auteurs canadiens from 1921 to 1925.[142]

Morin had the contacts to enlist distinguished Quebec authors. He
lined up bibliophile Aegidus Fauteux for Philippe Aubert de Gaspé, dean
of Quebec critics Abbé Camille Roy for journalist Etienne Parent, Senate
translator and copyright authority Louvigny de Montigny for Antoine

Gérin-Lajoie, national archivist Gustave Lanctôt for François-Xavier Garneau, diplomat Pierre Dupuy for poet Octave Crémazie, archivist Séraphin Marion for historian Abbé Henri-Raymond Casgrain, and cleric and author Henri Beaude ("Henri d'Arles") for Louis-Honoré Fréchette. It was also Morin who, in the spring of 1924 after seeing Pierce in Toronto, obtained former premier Lomer Gouin's endorsement for the series prospectus. Morin presented the venture to Gouin, then serving as federal minister of justice in Ottawa, as designed to make the literature of the two peoples known to each other.[143]

Morin and Pierce worked smoothly together, with Morin dealing with the French editors on routine matters. The two met in Toronto at least twice more, in May and October 1925. In the late 1920s, they planned to collaborate on a history of Canadian literature for Montreal publisher Louis Carrier, a project that unfortunately did not materialize.[144] With the "Makers" series, Pierce was the final arbiter, however, and final approval of French volumes and ultimate decision-making power rested with him.

For Pierce, the series served the happy function of making him known and admired in francophone literary circles as an apostle of cultural *bonne entente*. Henri Beaude, after corresponding with Pierce over Fréchette, wrote how pleased he was to "come in contact with a man like you … I want to go to Toronto. I am sure now … to find in you a friend."[145] The inevitable problems of producing a bilingual series did crop up, however. In November 1925 Gustave Lanctôt had to send back the proofs of his Fréchette volume, because the House printers had failed to understand that French and English words were split according to different rules at the end of lines![146]

Pierce must have been gratified that reviews of the three French volumes ultimately published (on Fréchette, Garneau, and Gérin-Lajoie) were generally favourable in both languages, although one young historian, Guy Frégault, dismissed Lanctôt's *Garneau* as "warmed over turnip [navet réchauffé]."[147] Far more typical was the reaction of another Quebec reviewer that the Garneau volume "est de premier ordre" and deserved to be in the schools and in the libraries of all who loved Canada.[148] Archibald MacMechan, writing in the Montreal *Gazette* about the Gérin-Lajoie and Fréchette volumes, praised them as "a royal road to learning about our authors," and the series as "a force working quietly towards the … great end" of French-English understanding.[149]

However, no review, French or English, commented on one curious lapse: Pierce's ringing dedication for the series appeared at the front of the French-language volumes – but only in English.

In English Canada, despite the warnings by reviewers of the volume on Norwood in 1923 about the dangers of back scratching, the reception to subsequent "Makers" volumes was generally positive. In July 1924 the *Canadian Stationer and Book Trade Journal* praised the series as "a valuable addition to Canadian literature ... which presents domestic writers in a new light ... as co-builders and interpreters in the history of the Dominion."[150]

But as any publisher knows, it is one thing for publications to be a critical success – but what about sales? Over the next two years, financial issues – precipitated by Pierce's grand ambitions – clouded both his first major editorial project and his marriage.

Up against the Bottom Line

An "Annus Horribilis" at Home and at Work, 1925–1926

> The Educational Department, which was undertaken to get more
> seriously into the field of the best literature, and to enhance the name
> of the Ryerson Press as something more than a jobber of popular
> reading, is still in the experimental stage, and has made its blunders,
> with consequent problems.
>
> *Book Steward S.W. Fallis, report to the House Book Committee,*
> *April 1926*[1]

> I imagine our friends and my brothers (yes your mother, father and
> sister too) must laugh when they think of the way we live and [you]
> giving prizes, a medal and Canadiana. I suppose it is all [what] you
> want to be – something to your family or something to Canada. It is a
> pity you have us.
>
> *Edith Pierce to Lorne Pierce, May 1925*[2]

Pierce had high hopes for the financial success of the Makers of
Canadian Literature series from both the textbook market and the
public. In February 1922, during a business trip to western Canada, he
wrote Edith that its provincial education departments had responded
"wholeheartedly" to the idea of a "Makers" volume on the region, making
him "sure" of a "a very large sale."[3] Echoing his financial optimism, William Arthur Deacon, author of the "Makers" volume on Peter McArthur,
assured readers of his *Saturday Night* column that the series "should
be one of the most profitable ventures ever undertaken by a Canadian
publisher."[4]

As so often in Canadian publishing, tensions between financial profitability and cultural enrichment were in play. Pierce insisted to his editors
that volumes conform to the required length of some 150 pages, to keep

expenses down. He told Sir Andrew Macphail in January 1924 that "the cost of manufacturing ever frowns above my head,"[5] a personification that suggests the vigilance of his boss. Fallis was, as Pierce put it, "desperately interested in writing a new chapter of progress" with Ryerson, but as book steward he had to be concerned with the bottom line.

Pierce assembled a team to help produce and – more important – to market the series. By January 1924, he had hired three extra staff to help "push" the books, a team headed by T.G. Marquis. New Brunswicker Thomas Guthrie Marquis, a well-known journalist and popular historian, particularly of New France, had, like Pierce, been a student of James Cappon at Queen's. More significantly, he had worked on promoting subscription sales of the Makers of Canada series of historical biographies early in the century for publisher George Morang. Marquis met with Pierce as early as November 1923 to make marketing suggestions.[6]

Pierce was determined to develop a "strong" and "better trained" staff.[7] Toward that end, he also hired two clerical assistants for Marquis – Blanche Hume and Carolyn Davie, the latter a contributor to the *Christian Guardian*. Wyoming-born Blanche Hume, who had once edited the magazine *Rod and Gun*, proved one of Pierce's most propitious appointments. She soon became the ideal executive secretary for him – highly intelligent, efficient, loyal, good-humoured, genteel, and shrewd – and was his strong right arm until her retirement in the spring of 1943. Their personalities meshed perfectly, and she came to enjoy the affection and regard of the whole Pierce family.

Yet hiring staff also added costs to the "Makers" project – already burdened by the costs of book manufacture and payments for copyright material. With forty volumes planned, editorial fees alone were substantial. As late as September 1923, Pierce was offering editors a royalty: 5 per cent on the school edition, 10 per cent on the popular edition (called the "Haliburton"), and 15 per cent on the leather-bound deluxe edition (the "Frechette").[8] But by November 1923 – undoubtedly after intervention by Fallis – contracts were altered to a one-time payment: $400 on receipt of a satisfactory manuscript and $100 on publication.[9] However, even this was very generous. Garvin was offering his editors a per-word rate with a maximum possible payment of just $100.[10]

How did Pierce come to offer remuneration that Margery Fee rightly terms "extraordinarily high"?[11] True, he had to compete with Garvin for editors, but he also seems to have been influenced by the fact that Macphail, a powerful literary figure, had initially demanded $500.[12] Pierce was anxious to produce a first-class series using the best editors and, given his own inexperience, he paid too much. Fee has calculated that, given the sum paid to editors, a "Makers" volume would have to sell 733 copies for Ryerson to begin to make money if the series was sold on subscription, and 800 copies if the book was sold through bookstores.[13]

But from the beginning, the series did not sell briskly. The first five titles appeared in 1923 – the *Norwood* volume by April.[14] By December, Pierce was planning to put the series on a subscription basis – with Ryerson marketing directly to customers via circulars and salesmen – and to pay editors the flat fee.[15] He admitted that the decision to go to subscription was due to "the restricted appeal of some of the volumes."[16] Given the unfavourable reviews of Watson's volume on Norwood, and the relative obscurity of novelist John Richardson in the 1920s, these volumes were probably selling poorly. The volume on Peter McArthur did go into a second edition – but only three years after publication.[17]

Clearly, hiring Marquis in early 1924 was an all-out attempt to raise sales, particularly since Pierce was dissatisfied with the House's sales force, overseen by his *bête noire* E.J. Moore. He grumbled in his diary: "Our book list is growing faster than the sales end can handle it. Poor co-operation. They don't seem to know which end of a good book to take hold of. Still are impressed that we should publish little and take no risks. But I am determined to put our name among the great publishers of America – in quality, quantity and beauty of manufacture."[18] Pierce's subsequent correspondence refers glumly to the "general depression of business": clearly sales had not picked up.[19] Meanwhile, completed manuscripts poured in: some fifteen never-published manuscripts are extant.[20] All of these editors had to be paid four hundred dollars on receipt, which put more financial pressure on the project.

Despite Marquis's efforts, sales continued to languish. To compound Pierce's problems, Marquis alienated the book steward.[21] Pierce, however, insisted that Marquis's advice was "sane and solid" and that he knew "more about Canadian literature than any man in Canada ... he is a splendid acquisition to my department."[22] Ryerson Press also published Marquis's juvenile fairy story *The King's Wish* (1924) at this time, a decision that complicated Marquis's relationship with the House. As a Ryerson author, Marquis was scornful about the House's standard promotion strategies (which were E.J. Moore's responsibility), and even advised other authors not to publish with Ryerson on that basis. He told Pierce, who was thinking of personally doing an edition of William Kirby's *The*

Golden Dog, that he should go to S.B. Gundy at the Canadian branch of Oxford University Press for publication, because Gundy, unlike the House, would give him decent promotion and remuneration.[23]

Then, as copyright legislation came before Parliament, Marquis broadcast his contempt for the copyright position of both Fallis and William Cope, head of the House's printing department. In April 1925 legislation before the House of Commons (it ultimately never got past the committee stage) provided for the retaining of licensing clauses contained in the 1921 Copyright Act. Fallis, Cope, and spokesmen for other major Canadian printing concerns were resented by authors as representing, to their detriment, the interests of printers in favour of the retention of such clauses. Marquis, his elegant mustache quivering with fury, did not mince words about what he saw as Fallis's betrayal of authors. He wrote Pierce from Ottawa, where he was promoting subscriptions to the "Makers" series: "You can have no idea how bitterly the Authors and their friends have felt toward the Ryerson Press. One prospect I called on said, when I mentioned the House I represented: 'The Press, a damned hypocritical institution, professing religion and seeking the privilege of stealing the product of my brains.'"[24]

Marquis went on to assure Pierce that his "Makers" canvassing was going well: "With four salesman at work, the Frechette [deluxe] edition will be sold out within two years."[25] Ominously, however, he added that (despite his employment by the House) he had done some lobbying behind the scenes on copyright to counter both Fallis's stance and that of printers like Dan Rose of Hunter, Rose, and Company, another large Toronto printing and publishing company. Marquis added defiantly: "Dr. Fallis may be annoyed at what I have done on the copyright question; but I do not give a hoot. I worked absolutely for the good of the House, & it can now share in the Authors' victory."[26] What Marquis had done was to write to the parliamentary committee stating authors' opposition, enclosing a letter that Pierce had unwisely written to Marquis echoing his views. Marquis's impulsive action rebounded on both men.

Understandably, Fallis was furious at such insubordination, as he informed both Marquis and the committee. By May 1925, Marquis, pressured to resign, left to seek work in New York City.[27] Fallis "raised Cain" with Pierce for criticizing a House policy behind his back. A "furious" Pierce and a "rude" and "very angry" Fallis had a vitriolic blow-up over copyright and the firing of Marquis.[28] Pierce, failing to question his own actions, felt Fallis had been "petty" about the matter. He was upset because Fallis had long ignored his own advice to develop a House-wide policy on copyright, one that balanced the interests of both authors and publishers.[29] Like the printers' strike of 1921, this was another case where the dual nature of the House as both commercial printing and publishing concern caused conflicts.

All this upheaval left the "Makers" series up "in the air."[30] Fallis vetoed Pierce's desire to hire Grant Richards, a son of the well-known English publisher, to promote the series.[31] Pierce tried other strategies to lift sales: in October 1925 he met with Victor Morin, his associate editor, to get Morin's help in promoting French subscription sales.[32] At a November House meeting about the series, Pierce announced his plan to cut the venture to thirty-five projected volumes to save $5,500, but there was still no chief salesman.

Pierce found it humiliating to have to tell the elderly poet Charles Mair, for whom he arranged an honorary Queen's LLD in April 1924, that he could not publish the Mair volume Garvin had edited for the Ryerson series.[33] Things were worse by the spring of 1926. Pierce, vainly agitating with Fallis to rehire Marquis, wearily wrote that Fallis was "letting the 'Makers' rot."[34] Then Pierce learned that Garvin had scraped together the resources to publish a Mair volume in his rival series. Pierce told Garvin in April 1926: "It has been a bitter disappointment to me that my own 'Makers' has struck a snag for the moment."

Fallis had in fact axed the series. The book steward's description of the project to the annual meeting of the Book Committee of the Methodist Church a few weeks earlier (its last before the committee was reorganized and renamed the Board of Publication under the newly formed United Church of Canada) had slammed Pierce. Fallis referred to "blunders" and "problems" in Pierce's Educational Department. He bluntly consigned the "Makers" to limbo: "Undertaken in a spirit of service to our national well-being, but at a time of economic depression, it has fallen on evil times. After investing a considerable sum in producing and promoting it, we have called a halt until times become more propitious." Fallis added that "extraordinary losses in the Book Departments" had meant that he had allocated a "considerable portion of the special reserve" of what was now to be the United Church Publishing House to cover them.[35] For Pierce, Fallis's report was a humiliating official rebuke. He wrote bitterly in his diary just before the meeting: "Hard sledding! I could resign right now. The House is a batch of puny ability and small conceits." Relations with his boss had reached such a low ebb that Fallis now insisted on reading Pierce's incoming and outgoing mail, scribbling "crude" comments.[36]

For the Makers of Canadian Literature series, times never became "more propitious." In 1942 Victor Morin wrote nostalgically to Pierce: "I came across your letter in which you sadly announced the untimely death of 'The Makers of Canadian Literature.' The project was too beautiful for a chance of success in our age of materialism. Alas!"[37] But, from a business point of view, Fallis cannot be faulted for his decision. The series lost a great deal of money – unfortunately, the exact cost, sales, and printing figures for the venture do not survive – and it would have lost a great deal more had it been allowed to go to thirty-five volumes.

From the point of view of Canadian literary history, however, Pierce showed vision in creating the series, vision that included an unprecedented bicultural focus. But the state of Canadian literary studies in the 1920s simply did not provide a market sufficient to make such a series financially viable in an era without subsidy for ventures of this kind. J.D. Logan at Acadia University offered one of the few post-secondary Canadian literature courses: the possibility of large textbook sales of the series just did not exist.[38] Pierce once observed that there were more courses on embalming offered in Canada than there were on Canadian literature.

The Makers of Canadian Literature series constitutes an important landmark in Canadian literary criticism, despite disappointing sales. Admittedly, some volumes – for example, Watson's on Norwood – were weak; others – and like Riddell's on Kirby and Richardson – were wooden. Yet many of the volumes (Deacon's on McArthur, McArthur's on Leacock, and even, despite his undervaluing of the animal stories, and his shirking of the biographical section, Cappon's on Roberts) were creditable. As Margery Fee points out – and Pierce himself recognized – the series uncovered and preserved a great deal of Canada's early literary history,[39] some of which would have been lost by the time interest in Canadian literature blossomed anew in the 1960s. In an era when reference works on Canadian literature were few, Pierce's effort was valuable. The series was undoubtedly a significant expression of the Canadian nationalism of the 1920s which was born of the war, as Pierce himself emphasized.[40] Moreover, the series did fulfill other of Pierce's hopes. The twelve "Makers" volumes established that the House, through the Ryerson imprint, was again a major force in Canadian literary publishing.

Pierce himself thereby became far better known in both the English and the French Canadian literary worlds as a champion of Canadian writing.

There was another enduring, less positive, aspect to the reputation Pierce made with his "Makers" series, however. For the young modernists around the lively new left-leaning magazine *Canadian Forum*, there was now, thanks to Dr Watson's volume on Norwood, a tendency to associate Pierce and Ryerson with "dreadful molasses" and log-rolling, the kind of boosterism of Canadian literature that they also attributed to the Canadian Authors Association.[41] In the 1940s and after, when Pierce wanted to publish modernist writers like F.R. Scott and A.J.M. Smith, this image would haunt him. But, on the whole, the Makers of Canadian Literature series enhanced the prestige of both Ryerson and Pierce, even though it succumbed to financial woes.

FOR PIERCE, the demise of the "Makers" smacked of defeat. What Pierce often experienced in the mid- to late 1920s was frustration, conflict, and overwork. In fact, his struggles with Fallis constituted part of a wider pattern of change and conflict. Pierce was hugely ambitious and intelligent, a dynamo of energy who found it hard to apply the brakes. Given his increasing deafness and his lupus, there was also a sense of desperation to his drive – a conviction that he had to succeed now, or fail forever. As a result, the scale and intensity of his commitments, both personal and professional, reached levels that precipitated crises in both his office and his domestic life, crises especially acute in 1925–26.

On the home front, Pierce's career commitments of time and money put strains on his marriage. Edith was at home with two infants, in a small, six-room house on a limited income, with no household help and primitive appliances.[42] Lorne remarked in his diary in November 1923 that the couple had been invited out to dinner: "Edith did enjoy it as she has been a prisoner for months."[43] When Lorne was home, however, he usually spent at least three hours a night and much of the weekend working on publishing projects.[44] Furthermore, his deafness made it hard for the couple to communicate at any time.

In the spring of 1925, Lorne's parents did their best to induce him to take time with family by buying him and his sister an island cottage on Lower Beverley Lake just off Delta. Lorne relished its subversive address (mail from the House had to be redirected to "Whiskey Island, Bastard Township, Ontario"), but at best he was there only a few weeks each summer. And when he was at the cottage, he usually spent several hours a day working on manuscripts.

Starting in the winter of 1922, Pierce was away from home for weeks at a time on an annual winter business trip to the west, with shorter trips to Montreal, Kingston, or the Maritimes several times a year. In marital terms, his first trip to the west in 1922, an absence of some six weeks, did not begin auspiciously. He forgot to send his wife, who with their eighteen-month-old daughter was staying with Edith's aunt in Kingston, his itinerary. Edith's comment shows how often she felt marginalized by such behaviour, whether Lorne was at the office or on the road: "I thought of sending to the Book Room for a list [of your whereabouts] but it would look too queer." She added: "I used to feel humiliated when Mr. Moore would phone me telling me that you wouldn't be home or some such message."[45]

Did Edith recall Lorne's statement during their courtship that, if he buried himself in work at the expense of his marriage, she should just "pinch" him?[46] Pinching him would have done Edith little good by the early 1920s. In 1924, absent on a long trip, he told her: "I hope some day we shall have more leisure to enjoy each other."[47] By early 1925, there was tension even in Lorne's teasing of Edith: "You are certainly a thousand times nicer [now] than before you married me. You weren't very nice then, a cold, heartless, say-no little monster. Dangling my heart on the end of a dog-chain!"[48] As Lorne spent ever more time on extra commitments, the references to Edith's "self-annihilation" in the diary hint that he knew that he was trying her to the limit. In June 1924, embroiled in the "Makers" series and myriad other ventures, he wrote in his diary: "[Edith] is the dear sweet woman. Her self-annihilation for her family – L.A.P. included – passes understanding. I dearly love her ... I want to make her proud of me. I want to make things easier for her. How can we arrange a week [of holiday] this summer, a complete change for all of us? We must or bust – or bust anyhow!"[49] Little would change, however: by temperament and circumstance, Pierce was a driven man. Two other factors increased the tension in the Pierce marriage: financial problems, and Lorne's determination that he would have a "literary future" (that is, as an author as well as publisher).[50]

Pierce's 1920s diary entries bristle with anxiety about the expense of a growing family from dental costs to "killing" life-insurance premiums. His initial Ryerson salary – $3,000 a year – was modest, and he received no raise until the end of 1926.[51] Money worries increased when Pierce bought a building lot in fashionable North Toronto in the vain hope of a new, House-subsidized house. Pierce admitted in December 1924 that the payments were a "weight."[52] By 1924, substantial debts dogged him, and attempts to supplement his income with time-consuming personal book projects caused further difficulties at home and at work.

Pierce probably undertook to edit a planned "Makers" volume on Sir Gilbert Parker in part to earn the $500 editor's fee, a project to which he devoted many hours but had to abandon when Fallis suspended the series.[53] Also for monetary reasons, he agreed to write a book (biography, anthology, and bibliography) on educationist James L. Hughes, whose ideas he admired.

James Laughlin Hughes, Toronto's chief inspector of schools from 1874 to 1913, was by the 1920s one of the province's grand old men of education. A champion of the ideas of German educational theorist and founder of the kindergarten system Friedrich Froebel, about whom he had published a book, Hughes turned away from the traditional, authoritarian, "spare-the-rod-and-spoil-the-child" philosophy of education (he lobbied for the abolition of corporal punishment in Toronto schools[54]) to advocate instead every child's innate possibilities and the importance of a positive, nurturing environment for education. As he put it: "By making a child conscious of weakness I am making him weaker; by making him conscious of his power I am kindling the elements that will keep him growing toward the Divine."[55] For Hughes, as for Froebel, a child was "full of holy aspirations" which should be encouraged, as should closeness to nature. Hughes published several internationally respected books on his philosophy of education, as well as a number of volumes of technically crude but enthusiastic verse about his view of childhood. For example, his poem "God Made Them Good," concludes thus about children:

> Don't call them "bad";
> Their comrade be;
> Shine God's light
> That they may see.[56]

Hughes lectured internationally on his educational theories, and his volumes of verse made him well known in Toronto literary circles from the early twentieth century. Toronto cultural chronicler Greg Gatenby has observed that Hughes, as educator and local literary figure, enjoyed "a

public profile such as no educator has in our time."[57] Pierce's involvement with such a famous educator would be useful when he began to
edit and market elementary and high school textbooks in a major way.

Hughes had published a book of verse with the House in 1916.[58] By
1921, he was calling on Pierce about his manuscript on Robert Burns,
published by Ryerson the next year.[59] Pierce was never as close to
Hughes as he was to their mutual friend Dr Watson, but he did write
an enthusiastic article about Hughes for *Canadian Magazine* in November.[60] The article praised Hughes as "one of the greatest spiritual forces in
the Dominion" who was a dynamic "patriot, preacher, pedagogue, poet."
Pierce asserted that Hughes deserved "an honourable place among the
'Makers of Canada' as one of the fashioners of its life and literature."[61]
B.K. Sandwell, then editor of the *Canadian Bookman*, wrote to express
his surprise that anyone would consider Hughes underrated for literary
merit.[62] The elderly Hughes, with posterity in mind, offered to underwrite a book on himself by Pierce by paying for publication costs and
passing on the royalties to Pierce.

From the spring of 1923 to September 1924, Pierce worked frantically
in whatever time he could snatch to expand his article into a book, aug-
menting the original article with long quotations from autobiographical
articles by Hughes, commendations by other educational authorities, and
excerpts from Hughes's prose and poetry. The book adds little to Pierce's
article and has a choppy, "cut-and-paste" quality. However, Pierce, perhaps chastened by Sandwell, was now more critical of Hughes as poet
("not consistently good"[63]), a fact the largely favourable reviews of the
volume noted approvingly.[64]

For the moment, however, the book created more tensions in Pierce's
career and marriage. In September 1924 Fallis declined to let Ryerson
publish the book, even though Hughes was underwriting the costs.
Pierce was obviously shaken by Fallis's refusal: he even preserved in
his diary a message slip about an immediate offer from S.B. Gundy at
Oxford University Press to publish it – an offer he accepted.[65] Fallis's
refusal came at the climax of "some warm argument" between the two
about "other matters." Pierce resolved to be more hard-nosed, and to
continue to strive to shine as both publisher and author: "I am sorry to
go outside my own house [to publish a book]. But in big business there is
not much sentiment lost, and it is hard getting used to it. However since
I am an editor as well as an author, I shall have to do my best for my own
interests as well."[66]

True to his resolve to function in two spheres, by December Pierce was pressuring Fallis for extra remuneration for his work as editor of the "Makers" series, arguing that he had conceived the idea and that "the work was done entirely outside office hours and at tremendous cost in energy and denial."[67] Fallis ignored the request. Pierce drafted material to tackle him again on the subject in the winter of 1925, arguing, among other things: "If tomorrow I die my wife ought to participate in that which I created and for which she has made great sacrifices."[68] One can imagine Fallis's rebuttals: the series was already unprofitable and work on it could be considered part of Pierce's duties, no matter when that work was done.

Fallis was also undoubtedly feeling publicly overshadowed by Pierce. However, Pierce could not seem to recognize that his growing profile further alienated his boss, whose own treatment by the press, as during the 1921 printers' strike, had been largely unflattering. For example, in March 1925, Pierce returned from western Canada to be greeted by a "grand slam" of publicity in the Toronto papers about the fact that he had earlier uncovered a valuable and hitherto unknown collection of papers relating to novelist William Kirby. Pierce described the publicity in his diary as "a little disconcerting" but added that "several have said it will be a feather in my cap and that it will do the House a lot of good." The "several" did not include Samuel Fallis, whom Pierce somewhat obtusely described as "not elated" when Pierce reported to him on the achievements and gruelling work of his western trip in the midst of the "grand slam" of press coverage.[69]

Two months later, in May 1925, came Marquis's leak of Pierce's letter criticizing Fallis's copyright stance to the parliamentary committee concerned. In a week of "terrible" conflict, Fallis forced Pierce to cut back on the size of his staff after their May clash. Pierce was outraged: "I had carried on the work of four men – Literary Advisor, Editor, Education Manager and Subscription Department and he wanted my staff cut to one stenographer!"[70] Yet Pierce, about to go off to Ottawa to be lionized by the Royal Society of Canada, again failed to recognize that his prominence was yet another continuing flashpoint with his boss.

As it happened, Fallis's earlier refusal to publish the Hughes book came on Lorne and Edith Pierce's eighth wedding anniversary, most of which Pierce spent as usual at the office. In his diary, Pierce contrasted the "rather trying" atmosphere there with home: "I found peace and goodwill when I came home and that is all that counts. It *was* a romance. It *is* a romance. Thank God."[71] But Edith's goodwill was being tested. Throughout 1924 and 1925, James Hughes repeatedly deferred paying her husband for royalties on the 1,000 copies of his biography, the very book that had swallowed so much precious family time. Struggling with bills, Pierce recorded in his diary in December 1924 that he hoped for an instalment on royalties before Christmas. But he did not receive payment – $308 – from Hughes for another eighteen months, two years after publication.[72]

Yet another book of Pierce's at this time epitomized the strains created in the marriage by his authorial ambitions. In 1923, anxious to undertake more prestigious projects, he agreed to write a biography of poet Marjorie Pickthall. Ironically, whereas once he had described his literary appointment as a real "he-man's job,"[73] in *Marjorie Pickthall: A Book of Remembrance*, he presented an idealizing and patriarchal narrative which cast Pickthall as an ideal of both traditional femininity and traditional poetic ideals in the face of changing values for women and literature in the 1920s.[74] With regard to his marriage, Pierce's biographical construct of Pickthall created a fantasy "other woman," who distracted him from his family.

In terms of Canadian literary history, Pierce's biography was the culmination of a pattern long evident in Pickthall's critical and publication history. Throughout her career, Pickthall was consistently depicted by male critics as a fragile, romantic, idealistic maiden writing verse to which exactly the same adjectives were applied. Born in England in 1883, Pickthall, the only child of Arthur Pickthall and his wife, Lizzie Helen Mary Mallard, had grown up in Toronto, where her engineer father had settled in 1889. She attended Bishop Strachan School. Coming to notice early in the century by winning literary competitions in Toronto newspapers, she had published her first book of poetry, *The Drift of Pinions*, in 1913.[75] After the trauma of her mother's death in 1910 and her father's subsequent remarriage, Pickthall left Canada for England in 1912, relocating to British Columbia in 1920, two years before her sudden death.

During her short career, Pickthall wrote many short stories as well as poems, shrewdly placing them in the leading British and American periodicals of the day. She also produced novels and children's books. Her early career had been overseen by two leading literary men – Pierce's Victoria College professor Pelham Edgar and McGill's Sir Andrew Macphail, editor of *University Magazine*, an outspoken foe of the new woman. With Pickthall in England after 1912, Macphail (who habitually

Canadian poet and fiction writer Marjorie Pickthall, the subject of Pierce's 1925 biography. Courtesy of Queen's University Archives

conceived of women as in need of some form of patriarchal control[76]) and Edgar assumed the dominant role in the choice and production of her first volume of poems in 1913.

During a period as a clerk at Victoria College Library before her departure from Toronto, Pickthall was often acerbic about the literary men who guided her. She once wondered if her first book of poetry would not become a "fine mess" between them.[77] Pickthall herself disliked the "fragile poetess" stereotype of her. She once shocked a doting hostess who assumed she would admire a supposedly kindred spirit like Wordsworth's ethereal Lucy Gray by telling her that she would like to "slap"

Lucy Gray.[78] In later career, after learning that Edgar had lamented that she was publishing little poetry, she wrote to tell him drily that "though I must live up to my reputation for being lamb-like under criticism," her decision was pragmatically market-oriented: poetry paid little in comparison to fiction and her verse manuscript in hand was difficult to publish, unlike fiction.[79]

Despite Pickthall's distaste for the cloying gender stereotypes that distorted her public image, her death only solidified that patriarchal portrayal. Professor Archibald MacMechan's eulogy typified the persistent romantic, ethereal image of her as "in the world but not of it."[80] Pierce's *Marjorie Pickthall: A Book of Remembrance* is a reverential volume penned in this vein, exquisitely bound in violet and gold cloth, enshrining a literary and gender ideal of feminine sweetness and sensitivity.[81] The endpapers, illustrated by Group of Seven artist Frederick Varley, feature a sweet-faced, delicate maiden in Grecian garb, seen amid an idealized landscape of stars, flowers, birds, rabbits, squirrels, and boughs.

Pierce had taken over work on the volume in 1923 from poet Helena Coleman, friend and patron to Marjorie Pickthall. Despite his brutal work schedule, Pierce eagerly sought the task.[82] He saw the Pickthall volume as a vehicle to integrate him with the tradition of romantic lyrical nature poetry in Canada and as proof of the increasing trust of the literary establishment. In October 1923 he exulted to his diary: "Miss Helena Coleman seems to be willing to trust the precious task to me at last! No one must approach her Marjorie Pickthall but those who have clean hands and a warm heart."[83]

Coleman emphasized to Pierce the need for the most painstaking "restraint and delicacy" with "as few words as possible" about the personal.[84] Pierce embarked on the project with a sense that he needed to satisfy an influential readership, including Coleman and Pickthall's father (both readers of the manuscript), by avoiding harsh scrutiny or the revelation of the painful, unpleasant, or incongruous. His own concept of biography at this time was equally circumspect, despite his awareness of the changing view of the genre evident in such works as Lytton Strachey's *Eminent Victorians* (1918). Rejecting psychology's "almost morbid preoccupation with soul surgery" as a biographical approach, he believed that "the true conception of biography is the portrait of a soul in its adventures through life."[85] Moreover, he felt the need to respect a "lady" recently deceased: the narrative was styled "a book of remembrance." He had other restrictions as well, imposed by the possessiveness of at least one male literary grandee about his "protegée." Sir Andrew Macphail refused to let Pierce see any of Pickthall's letters to him on the grounds that they were either "too personal" or "too businesslike."[86] Clearly, Pierce's narrative was shaped and limited by interpenetrating ideals of poetry, womanhood, eulogy, and decorum that he both absorbed and perpetuated in the literary world of the day.

The language of Pierce's foreword to the book showed the appropriations and tensions of his narrative. He justified his text about Pickthall as "in every way a labour of love," asserting at the outset: "The main purpose [herein] ... has been to tell the story of her life simply, and, where possible, to let Marjorie Pickthall speak for herself."[87] But he then switched from the first person singular to the pronoun "we." Though he seems to equate "we" with "myself and Pickthall's friends and admirers," there is a clear sense that, for him, biographer and subject spoke as one. To use literary theorist Ira Nadel's term, there is a significant "shift in the level of telling."[88] Whatever the plural signifies, there is no doubt that Pierce presented the virtues of both the life narrative and the artistic achievement as stereotypically feminine: "I hope we have performed this [text] as Marjorie Pickthall herself might have done, with becoming reticence, with sensitiveness, avoiding dogmatism, and ever cautious for the true, the beautiful and the good."[89]

For Pierce, Pickthall's work supposedly mirrored her alleged nature as a woman, and both life and work embodied literary and gender ideals. That is, to his eyes, both the woman and her work were beautiful, pure and fragile as well as primarily emotional and intuitive, not intellectual, rational, or systematic. As Joanna Russ has pointed out, much of the critical writing about women's work posits that the talent emanates from an emotive "nowhere and it bears no relation to anything." Pierce's analysis conforms to this pattern, with Pierce seeing Pickthall's work as "miraculous," another common way in which female artistic achievement has been discounted.[90] In other words, Pickthall's major poems are deemed unaccountable in terms of who and what she was, mysterious in a manner in which he never characterized the work of male writers such as Albert Durrant Watson or James Hughes: "It is, perhaps, enough to behold here a shy, simple lovable girl busy with paints and poetry, and to recognize yonder [her poems] 'The Immortal' or 'Bega' without trying to elucidate the miracle. How did it happen, and when? For few poets have we so much [biographical] data, and still of none are we less able to explain. It is, perhaps, enough to wonder."[91] Pierce's diary makes it clear that such ideas about women writers were current in his circle. For example, he records an August 1924 dinner with Carman and Watson where the trio discussed Pickthall, agreeing to a man that she epitomized "beauty that is fragile as a flower – little intellectual or ethical substance, but sheer loveliness and melody."[92] Little wonder that in his text Pierce rejected any notion that Pickthall could have written out of "any doctrinal system of ideas" or "by reasoning of any kind."[93]

Pierce thus inevitably portrays Pickthall as an icon of literary delicacy and good taste in Canadian literature, a sort of madonna of traditionalism. He depicts her as an exempla of purity and refinement, "a challenge to bad artists dealing in cheap sentimentality, in muttering compromise and bad taste, and to all those who stress commonplace and subsidiary things." Even the "paganism" that Pierce sees in her nature poetry is defined as a "sanctified sensuousness" that is "typically Canadian."[94] In his concluding chapter, the construct of Pickthall that Pierce has created is clearly intended as a counterpoint to modernism: "Her contact with nature purified her spirit, cleansed it of all morbidity, and thus, while her contemporaries were wearing themselves out in artistic disputes over sex, psycho-analysis, and kindred concerns, she was pursuing essential truth and beauty to their happiest and holiest hiding place."[95] Pierce even muted Pickthall's own voice in the work to make her more conventionally feminine. He quotes her complaint about the frustration of being a woman, of not being able to "stir things up" as a man could because of a suffocating and "superficial femininity."[96] But his narrative never analyzes her assessment of her plight. Moreover, an examination of the typescript of the book shows that even some of Pierce's final excisions to the text tend to make Pickthall seem more conventionally feminine in her interests. For example, two entries from Pickthall's 1899 girlhood diary about her enthusiasm for books on the Royal Navy and on the Franklin expedition were dropped while more stereotypically "girlish" rhapsodies are retained.[97] Also, any discussion of anger, depression, or grief in Pickthall's life is muted or passed over in what Pierce called "reverent or understanding silence."[98] In this idealizing narrative, Pierce refuses to dwell on any anger or deviance or extreme emotion in his female subject as he constructs a literary and gender ideal – just as he shied away from discussing or addressing his own wife's difficulties with their marriage.

Critical reaction to Pierce's Pickthall book after its publication in April 1925 demonstrates how deeply embedded in the established Canadian literary world of the day these values were. Many other literary men were uneasy about the direction of literature in a decade of jazz, flappers, more sexual freedom, and the subversive liberties of best-selling female writers, for example, the literary candour of a Margot Asquith or the flippancy of an Anita Loos in *Gentleman Prefer Blondes*. Reviews applauded Pierce and his valorization of Pickthall as a feminine and literary ideal. The Toronto *Globe* commended Pierce's depiction of a "shy, lonely girl." Another reviewer pronounced Pierce "eminently fitted" to write of Pickthall's life of "passionless purity."[99] The *Canadian Bookman* assured readers that Pierce had respected Pickthall's virtue – metaphorically of course – in terms that were also echoed in an Edmonton newspaper: "Marjorie Pickthall might well have challenged the most prurient of [modern] biographers and stood unscathed, for a purer soul has seldom been garmented in flesh. But Dr. Lorne Pierce has given a revelation of purity in a book that will stand among the classic biographies."[100] Critic W.T. Allison expressed surprise that Pierce had found so much to say: "Those who knew this quiet retiring woman could not dream that much space would be required to chronicle the events in her short and uneventful life."[101] Austin Bothwell, another well-known western literary man, was amazed at the young Marjorie's bookishness, given her gender. In an astonishing assessment, he wrote that "with the single exception of Anne of Green Gables, and she was a girl in a book, this is the only known case in Canada of a fifteen year old girl exclaiming 'It is lovely' of a book."[102]

In the 1940s and the 1950s, when Pickthall's kind of lyrical nature poetry was out of fashion, Pierce was to construct her as even more fragile and marginalized in comparison to "virile talents" like E.J. Pratt.[103] And, although Pierce would be supportive of writers like novelist Laura Goodman Salverson and poet Dorothy Livesay – even subsidizing the latter's childcare in the 1940s so Livesay could write – in the 1920s he often treated women writers and their reputations in a conventional, gender-essentialist way, expecting them to be "true women." Visiting poet Pauline Johnson's grave in 1924, for instance, Pierce marvelled that her poetry, "whatever her private life may have been," still managed to have "a note of clear, resonant purity in our national literature, sweet with the fragrance of wild wood."[104] The indiscretions of male luminaries like Roberts or Carman affected him far less in his assessment of their work, although he also tut-tutted over their moral irregularities.

The very strength of Pierce's idealization of Pickthall as a woman in the period 1923–25, however, also suggests a powerful personal need to idealize her. So does his failure to mention any male love objects or interests for Pickthall or even their absence (in a real transgression of the norms of the era for evaluating a woman's life). In fact, Pickthall became a kind of symbolic "other woman" in the Pierce marriage, a fantasy creation on whom Pierce lavished time and praise. Amid marital stresses, what better "other woman" for a high-minded minister to devote himself to than a dead one – a woman in his eyes dedicated entirely to literature and without taint of earthly desire? As Jean-Paul Sartre so sardonically put it of the biographer's freedom to shape his subject – "a corpse is open to all comers."[105]

Pierce became infatuated with his construct of Pickthall. He wrote of his labours far into the night on his portrait of her: "It is worth it all, even though I get nothing for it in a monetary sense, just to have dwelt so long with radiant beauty, and to have stood so near to the soul of sweet, simple goodness." (Tellingly, despite Pierce's debts, he decided to divert his royalties from the sales – 2,000 copies were printed – to Pickthall's father, who had medical expenses, a decision it is not clear he told Edith about[106]).

In a 1924 letter Pierce sent his family a drawing, made during his weeks-long annual business trip to the west, which suggests Pickthall's role as a symbolic "other woman." In the drawing, captioned "Daddy Lost in a Book," Pierce is depicted hidden behind a large book, open and clutched to his bosom, titled *Marjorie Pickthall by Old Tired Bones*. Below, his one-year-old son awakes in a large empty room, crying "Where's Daddy?"[107] To his beleaguered and exhausted wife, Lorne evoked the traditional muse role for women as consolation in another letter: "Life has been very full for me – so fast & furious ... But you belong to that pantheon of women in my mind, Mary ... Beatrice and Eloise – women who made achievement possible and inspired it."[108]

Even when Pierce was home, his family felt marginalized by Pickthall work. In August 1924, during the two-week holiday the family spent in Delta, Lorne himself recorded that he spent most of it revising *Marjorie Pickthall*.[109] After the family's return to Toronto, Edith felt she had to take the two children on day-long weekend outings so that Lorne could be alone at Wineva Avenue to work at Pickthall.[110] Lorne was uncharacteristically negative in his diary at this time about the difficulty of working at home. In March 1925, lamenting that he lacked "the salary ... to build what we need," he called the small house he had once affectionately dubbed Nestledown "intolerable": "I have a tremendous amount of writing to do, and how can I face it in this shack!"[111] Even

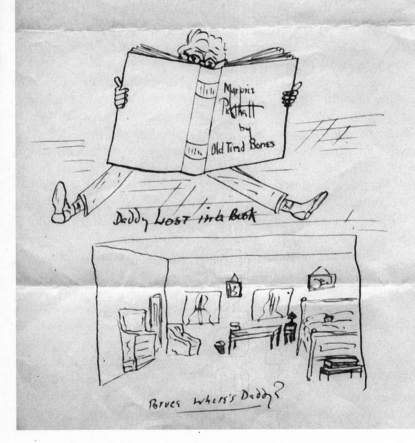

Pierce's drawing in a 1925 letter to his wife: the images suggest that his absorption in the Pickthall biography constructed the latter as symbolic "other woman." Courtesy of Queen's University Archives the Pierce family Christmas card that year featured a Marjorie Pickthall poem (ironically titled "Solitude").[112]

WHAT MADE 1925 an "annus horribilis" in the Pierce marriage was not just the Pickthall book, however. Lorne had written of Edith just the year before: "I hope to be able to keep her respect for ever – it is the basis of all love."[113] Part of Edith's respect for him lay in her faith that he was candid in his dealings with her. As she put it in a letter to her family in 1915, she believed Lorne to be "pure gold ... upright in everything he does."[114] But some of his priorities were to trouble her. Lorne wrote in his diary in 1924 that he had three major "dreams" for Canadian literature: one was the "Makers" series, while the two others were a "library of Canadian literature set apart for research ... and a suitable award conducted by the highest academic society of Canada to foster highest literary achievement."[115]

Starting in the early 1920s, Pierce fulfilled his dream of a library of Canadian literature by collecting rare Canadiana, which by November 1923 he had generously decided to begin donating to Queen's University for scholarly use. He presented the first consignment (some 3,000 volumes) in July 1924 to synchronize with the opening of the university's new Douglas Library.[116] Margery Fee has written that this vast collection of books and manuscripts, still a major resource for Canadian scholars, which Pierce augmented throughout his life and in his will, is one of Pierce's greatest contributions to Canadian culture after his editorial work at Ryerson Press.[117] Pierce henceforth worked with successive Queen's librarians, Nathan Van Patten, E.C. Kyte, and Pearson Gundy, to augment the collection.

In the early 1920s, Pierce was cash-strapped. Yet it is striking in the diary how often he laments household expenses or his mounting debts, only to refer to material acquired for his Canadiana collection.[118] In 1925 Edith presented her husband with a satirical newspaper clipping about the obsessive nature of collecting, a "malignant disease" that made its sufferers "lose ... all warmth of heart."[119] For Edith, this was no light-hearted protest. She later confided to Blanche Hume that, at this period in her marriage, she "used to think that my new winter coat (that should have been) went on the shelves at Queen's."[120]

When Pierce initially donated the collection to Queen's, he included his wife, a fellow Queen's graduate, as one of his reasons for the donation in a phrase that made her sound like another collector's find, citing "the sentimental reason that I found my wife there" as well his "deep pride" in the "glory of [Queen's] traditions." Pierce nevertheless asked that the collection be called "The Lorne Pierce Collection of Canadian Literature at Queen's University."[121] It is a measure of Edith's conviction that they had *both* made material sacrifices to create the collection that she later insisted that it be called "The Edith and Lorne Pierce Collection."[122]

Painful memories of the ruthless side of Pierce's third dream, one that finally spurred her to open protest in 1925, may account for Edith's un-usual assertiveness about renaming the Queen's Collection. In May 1924 Pierce offered the Royal Society of Canada a gold medal, to be awarded annually to honour achievement in Canadian literature, whether in French or English.[123] So keen was Pierce that he was conferring with sculptor Bela Janowsky on designs for the medal months before the Soci-ety formally accepted his proposal in November 1924.[124] Pierce was flat-tered when the Society proposed to call it the "Lorne Pierce Medal,"[125] but assured D.C. Scott that he had asked the designer to make his name "as inconspicuous as possible."[126] He was downplaying his involvement in other ways. Pierce did not tell Edith that he had formally contracted with the Society to pay the cost of striking the medal each year, and that he had undertaken to endow the medal as soon as he was financially able. Furthermore, he promised the Society to make "the same provision incumbent upon my heirs," which meant that he was keeping his wife in ignorance of an obligation potentially binding her in the event of his death.[127] Even when Edith commented that it seemed odd that the So-ciety would name the medal after him, Lorne said nothing.[128]

Days after his copyright wrangle with Fallis in May 1925, Lorne set out for Ottawa, without telling Edith that he was to present the medal at the Society's sessions. On 18 May he wrote Edith boasting about being lionized there ("all stood clapping most heartily ... a grand welcome"), but still mentioned nothing about underwriting the medal.[129] Edith was thunderstruck when Lorne's secretary, Della Dingle, accidentally let the truth slip. Telling Lorne that he had done her "the greatest injustice" of their marriage, she wrote that, while the medal might give him pleasure each year, "to me it will mean nothing but pain – heart-ache." To Edith, the deception seemed "to have knocked the very bottom out of our lives together: You may feel you are justified – perhaps you are. I know I would not have given it my approval in our [financial] circumstances. I imagine our friends and my brothers (yes your mother, father and sister too) must laugh when they think of the way we live and [you] giving prizes, a medal and Canadiana. I suppose it is all [what] you want to be – something to your family or something to Canada. It is a pity you have us."[130]

Lorne did indeed so desperately want "to be something to Canada" that he had compromised his principles. That weekend he cut short a visit to Delta – and his first tour of the new cottage – to "surprise" Edith by returning home early. What then passed between the two is not recorded. What is clear is that, from that date, Pierce did his best to ease household burdens on his wife, and found more money for domestic needs. Edith had hardwood floors, a new set of dishes, and some new furniture by August and a maid by December.[131] Just months after Edith's protest, however, Lorne nevertheless served as guarantor for a $500 note for the perpetually cash-strapped Charles G.D. Roberts – risky indeed. The next year, when he returned to the Royal Society for the first awarding of the medal – to Roberts – and his own unprecedented surprise induction as a fellow, he assured his wife that in "all my conversations with the Fellows I have associated your name as sharing the idealism and sacrifice."[132] Did Lorne wince when the fellows praised him as a "young maecenas" in inducting him?[133] Many times over the next three decades, he emphasized his wife's support, but Edith had suffered a blow. She confessed to her son many years later: "When we were living on Wineva Ave. I saw that your father had much to give to Canada and I had little, so I let him give his much and stood behind him every step."[134]

Pierce's hearing and health problems made him desperate not to fail. In his diary at the end of 1924, he wearily asked: "Where will this work all end? Mount Pleasant [Cemetery]?"[135] He was plagued by bouts of gastric, joint and chest pain, and respiratory troubles which periodically confined him to bed (including a week-long collapse in September 1925). A painful butterfly rash of lupus on his face had to be treated with X-ray by the spring of 1926. Seeing his disfigured face, many Royal Society fellows felt they were inducting a doomed man: one Society physician advised Pierce to go to Chicago to seek medical help.[136]

Pierce's hearing loss brought ever more isolation and frustration. He wrote Edith from British Columbia in March 1925 after an outing to the theatre with his sister that he "of course couldn't hear a word."[137] By 1926, he was giving away his large homiletic library, knowing that sermons were inexorably becoming "a thing of the past," given his hearing problems.[138] His deafness was so severe that even visitors to the office commented upon it: poet Wilson MacDonald was furious when Pierce spurned his suggestion to consult an osteopath in search of a cure.[139] About this time, Edith told Blanche Hume what a "cross" Lorne's handicap was for them both: "The restoration of his hearing would be the most wonderful gift in the world for me. I believe it is the cause of his exhaustion at the end of the day."[140]

Pierce placed great hopes on a medical consultation about his deafness at the Lockwood Clinic in the fall of 1925. Learning there was nothing to be done, he vowed: "Music may leave my world, but beauty never so long as I can see – or feel and think!"[141] Nevertheless, he shared his disappointment with his mother. She admitted her own deafness was "very trying" at times, but, ever the staunch Methodist, admonished him: "The thing for us to do is to be sure that our handicap is consecrated."[142] Brave words from both mother and son, but how much anger, how much apprehension, and how much frustration in reaction to his deafness and his lupus drove Pierce's pursuit of his goals? He once commented that deafness made writer Frederick Philip Grove more "reserved," "depressed," and "self-centred."[143] Pierce knew from experience.

PERHAPS BECAUSE 1925 was so difficult, Pierce wrote little about the formal enactment of church union between the Methodist and Presbyterian churches in June, although he had long advocated it. On the subject, Pierce told readers of the *Christian Guardian* that, while one might take pride in the contributions of various denominations to religious experience, "Methodist doctrine for Methodist's doctrine's sake, and considered apart from truth for truth's sake, is as dead as the dodo."[144] Pierce was stirred by the consummation service on 10 June in Varsity Stadium, which he attended with Dr Watson, calling it "one of the biggest days of my life ... the greatest day since Mecca." He warned in his diary that, if the new United Church "did not demonstrate a great intellectual forward movement, a colossal warming of the hearts of man, [and] a gigantic cleaning of the springs of life, it will fail."[145]

Pierce's rapture about church union was probably tempered by his worries over the direction of things at Ryerson, about to function formally as the United Church Publishing House. Before Pierce's departure for a July holiday at his new island cottage, Rossmoyne, Fallis complimented him on his work. Pierce reflected on how rare that was: "Dr. Fallis today said that in me the House had the best editor of any House in Canada. The compliment was one of two in five years!"[146] Yet he was not sure that the *New Outlook*, the magazine which now replaced the

Christian Guardian, would continue his book column, despite Fallis's recommendation to that effect. Pierce refused to submit articles on an individual basis for acceptance or rejection.

In a brooding letter to Albert Durrant Watson from the cottage, Pierce revealed that four of his articles were languishing with the editors. Calling the handling of things "not candid and not honest," Pierce lamented that it was "rather sadly typical of the whole headquarters." Suggestively, he spent his first cottage holiday building a wall along the edge of a cliff, and he told Watson how greatly he had needed his "belief in me" over the last five years at the House: "My responsibilities are almost too heavy and too important for one of my years, although I have tried not to take myself too seriously; but they make terrible demands upon my mental, physical and spiritual strength."[147] Pierce finally heard in mid-September that *New Outlook* editor William Creighton would continue his column, but he only noted wearily in his diary that it meant "more work."[148]

The travails of 1925 were not done, however. In February 1925, during a stop in Winnipeg on a trip through the west, Professor Arthur Phelps had invited Pierce to a lecture by writer Frederick Philip Grove. Grove had published two volumes of essays with McClelland and Stewart, *Over Prairie Trails* (1922) and *The Turn of the Year* (1923), but at the gathering afterwards Grove pressed the manuscript of a novel on Pierce.

Two nights later, at the Fort Garry Hotel, Pierce began dutifully reading Grove's manuscript at 7:20 p.m. Mesmerized, he read until 2 a.m. The next morning, Grove came to a room-service breakfast, to be told by a bleary-eyed Pierce that his novel, *Settlers of the Marsh*, was a "classic."[149] Pierce exulted to Edith that Grove was "a real genius and it will be a rare privilege to put him across."[150]

Publishing Grove proved stressful. The novel dealt with the dark story of prairie settler Niels Lindstedt, an immigrant who ends up being seduced by, marrying, and murdering a prostitute, Clara Vogel. The novel had already been turned down by Macmillan, ostensibly because it was too long but also because, as was hinted in the rejection letter, its sombre tone and "squalid" subject matter were distasteful if "absolutely truthful."[151] Pierce later wrote that he, too, was apprehensive about one episode in the novel (probably Niels's first sexual encounter with Clara Vogel): "I thought the essence of the matter could be conveyed in some other way. The book would have its difficulties anyhow, and I felt those few pages would cause more trouble than they were worth."[152] In Winnipeg that winter morning, Pierce and Grove had a "long and bitter" talk over the scene – as well as the need to cut the "great length" of the manuscript. Pierce later wrote that Grove "would not change a line, and as usual [he] assumed the toga of a high prophet, full of holy rage. It was all true as described, and he implied that he was there, the real Kilroy! Under the bed!"[153]

To his credit as publisher, Pierce ultimately told Grove that the scene could stay: Ryerson would "go the full distance with him." Pierce later said ruefully: "Neither of us could imagine then what that would mean."[154] Why did Pierce publish the novel? After all, he knew it was bound to provoke controversy for flying in the face of what one historian has called the "puritanical sexual morality" of the Canada of that day.[155] The key to Pierce's intrepid commitment to publish probably lay in the fact that the book spoke to him in a deeply personal way. As a teacher and as a student minister on the prairies, Pierce had experienced the bleak reality of settler life in what he had called "the waste places" of God.[156] Pierce knew that Grove had captured suffering and endurance central to the early immigrant history of the west. Moreover, Pierce felt a commitment throughout his editorial career to publishing material that dealt with the experience of the west, books ranging from Wilson MacDonald's *Song of the Prairie Land* to works by novelists Grove and Laura Goodman Salverson, critic Edward McCourt, poet Anne Marriott, and many others. From the early 1920s, he publicly stressed his belief in the importance of developing "a western literature, national in spirit and expressing what is going on" in the west.[157] Pierce, therefore, courageously told Grove that he would publish, that "an editor was bound at some time or other to fight for his life."[158]

Pierce formally accepted the novel in April and it was published in September 1925.[159] Pierce even found an American co-publisher, George Doran, who printed the work, Ryerson taking 2,272 copies for the Canadian market.[160] But things went badly from the beginning. In August, Grove wrote Pierce that the first advertisement for the book placed by E.J. Moore's department had got his name wrong, calling him Frederick *William* Grove. He was even less pleased when Doran's dust jacket for *Settlers* called it a "North Country Romance," certainly a ludicrous misnomer for what transpires.[161] Grove believed that this howler – not the only dust-jacket blooper by Moore in these years[162] – had "killed" U.S. sales by alienating serious critics and misleading buyers; moreover, the book "swarmed with misprints."[163]

Matters escalated from farce to imbroglio. While the novel received favourable reviews from Arthur Phelps and Montreal *Star* critic Stanley Morgan Powell, what Phelps called its failure to "preserve the usual Anglo-Saxon delicacies" about sex soon caused a ruckus.[164] Winnipeg academic W.T. Allison, a frequent book reviewer for the western press, thought *Settlers* a serious work but objected to its "free circulation ... on grounds of the decencies."[165] One Grove scholar has chronicled the fuss in the Winnipeg and Toronto press over the circulation of "salacious" novels in early 1926, and the rumours (in fact unfounded) that major libraries like Winnipeg's had banned *Settlers of the Marsh*.[166] Grove heard other lurid rumours: Eaton's in Winnipeg was selling the novel only under the counter, and the Toronto Public Library was loaning it only "to mature people of good character."[167] The Groves actually were reviled by some in their home town of Rapid City, Manitoba, because of the "shocking" work. The elementary school teaching post of Grove's wife, Catherine, was challenged, albeit unsuccessfully, by a group of irate parents.[168]

Pierce found his own publishing house no broader-minded than Grove did Rapid City. "Angry mail" and "delegations of various sorts" deluged the House.[169] According to Pierce, the House, particularly Fallis, gave him a "wild ride." Fallis, "furious" about the controversy, refused to read the novel.[170] Pierce, fearing that his "time had come," was bailed out by a fluke: a commendatory letter out of the blue from a distinguished Conservative politician dear to the heart of Samuel Fallis, himself a "deep-dyed Tory." Pierce later described the scene of his deliverance:

> One day [Fallis] walked into my office, and laid a letter before me
> ... It read: "I congratulate you on having the literary insight to
> recognize a work of art when you see it, and having the courage
> to publish it. Your[s] truly, Arthur Meighen, Prime Minister." Dr.
> Fallis smiled: "I have said before, and I say again, that we have
> the best editor in Canada," and he walked out. The war was over.
> The House would stand back of [Grove] and his book, no matter
> what the cost, and, I am thankful to say, back of the beleaguered
> editor also![171]

Pierce's account of the incident shows just how much in jeopardy he felt his job was in the "annus horribilis" of 1925–26, even as his principles and his marriage were undermined by his desperate financial equivocations in the Royal Society medal affair.

Pierce's trials with *Settlers of the Marsh* also extended to sales. It is a truism of Canadian literary history that Canadian moralism about fiction often meant that sales of a scandalous book suffered.[172] So it was with *Settlers*, which sold poorly in both Canada and the United States. Three years after publication, Pierce had sold just over 1,000 copies in Canada, less than half of what he had hoped: total sales for both countries were a disappointing 3,685 copies.[173] Ryerson sold so few copies of the book in 1927 that it did not even make up a royalty statement for Grove.[174]

Given the combination of controversy and poor sales, Pierce ultimately declined to publish *Our Daily Bread* and two other novel manuscripts which Grove submitted to Ryerson in 1926,[175] especially since the House had been unable to interest an American co-publisher. Pierce found Grove's aggrieved letters that spring, which implied that Pierce had not done enough for him with *Settlers*, "painful."[176] Meanwhile, without at first informing Pierce, Grove, at the urging of his friend Phelps and critic William Arthur Deacon,[177] was beginning his ill-fated involvement with Ottawa's short-lived Graphic Press, which published his *Search for America* (1927). Pierce and Grove would have virtually no further contact on publishing matters until the late 1930s. In the interim, however, Grove did do something that "hit hard" when Pierce later learned of it. Awarded the Lorne Pierce Medal in 1934, Grove, financially strapped, pawned it to buy a radio for his family.[178]

Pierce's "annus horribilis" ended in May 1926 with a death that shook him deeply. On 3 May, on arrival at the House, Blanche Hume, weeping, handed him a note.[179] At the age of sixty-seven, Albert Durrant Watson had died suddenly before dawn of heart failure.[180] Pierce wrote that he and Watson had "loved like brothers," and he took comfort in learning that one of his own articles as well as a book he had loaned Watson had been on Watson's bedside table. Moreover, mourned Pierce, "he had spoken of me in his last hour and wished his watch to be given me."[181]

Pierce, as Watson's executor, made the funeral arrangements for his mentor. He was asked to deliver one of the eulogies, which he at first refused to do because his face was so disfigured by lupus rash. In his diary, Pierce brooded over Watson's passing ("Good, loving, cultured, happy, singing spirit adieu!"), even as no sign of Watson's new existence in a twentieth plane seemed to materialize. A distraught Pierce wondered if deafness stilled even voices from beyond: "I have felt today that [Watson] who believed so completely in the other life, would break through and return to me if he could. Perhaps he can if I could only hear. How kind he always was over my scepticism. He knew there was a spirit world because he had seen it. Auras, yes, and voices too."[182]

With Watson's death, Pierce was driven more inward. Margery Fee has described Watson, a mediocre poet and anthology editor, as one of Pierce's "failings."[183] In a broader sense, however, Watson was a crucial source of moral support to Pierce in his first years in publishing. Mourning Watson made Pierce dwell on his own mortality. Ten days after Watson's death, Pierce went to a Toronto cemetery and chose a burial plot for himself.[184] But he also made a more hopeful purchase that week, one designed to improve his relationship with Edith – a new, larger house.

Pierce was again gathering his forces. His editorial program had to find a firmer financial footing if he was to continue publishing an appreciable number of serious Canadian literary works. Paradoxically, success, like failure, would again mean trouble on two fronts: with the book steward and at home.

"Lyrical Wild Man"

Poetry Chapbooks and the Lure of
Textbook Projects, 1925–1950

As you know, I have been a sort of lyrical wild man [for the last sixteen years] insofar as the publication of Canadian poetry has been concerned, and this in spite of the far from musical noises that have been emerging from our accounting department.

Lorne Pierce to Charles G.D. Roberts, 1941[1]

It would be a great mistake and a great loss if you discontinue the Chap Books. They have come to really mean something and a certain standard has been set.

Poet Arthur Bourinot to Lorne Pierce, 1950[2]

By 1926, Lorne Pierce felt beleaguered on many fronts. For some of the House's traditional authors and prospective customers – those who deplored such offerings as Grove's *Settlers of the Marsh* (1925) in fiction or the Ryerson Essay series – his literary taste was too modern and his theology too radical. At the same time, however, modernists in religion deplored Pierce's retreat from the social gospel, which Pierce made evident in articles and speeches in the 1920s, emphasizing his shift by collecting many of them in book form in his *In Conference with the Best Minds*.[3] To further complicate matters, young literary modernists of the day decried the "intolerable molasses" of Albert Watson's *Robert Norwood*, the inaugural volume in Pierce's Makers of Canadian Literature series.[4]

Pierce, in short, was pleasing no one wholly. He teetered in the dangerous position of having moved away from one set of alliances – the conservative religious and literary circles that the booklists of William Briggs and his editors had appealed to earlier in the century – without

Edith and Lorne Pierce's children, Bruce and Beth, about the
time he wrote *Marjorie Pickthall: A Book of Remembrance* (1925).
Courtesy of Queen's University Archives

being securely established either intellectually or financially with a new
readership. To be a successful Canadian publisher is always a financial
and ideological high-wire act. But by the end of the 1920s, Lorne Pierce
was swaying dangerously on the wire. He needed a safety net, but it
would not appear for some time.

In his personal life, Pierce was also unbalanced by all the baggage
of a mid-life crisis, with Edith often depressed and overworked. Their
children, Beth and Bruce, aged six and three respectively in 1926, increasingly needed their father's attention – but Lorne had little time or

energy to spare from mountains of manuscripts. Describing the second-floor study in his new home on moving day in June 1925, Pierce felt "a spirit of work taking hold of me."[5] Moreover, the Pierces' new brick and stucco house – at 233 Glengrove Avenue in North Toronto – constituted an onerous financial outlay even as Pierce finally sold the building lot on Upper Avenue Road.

Furthermore, in 1926, Pierce had not yet won the wholehearted approval of his aging parents for his Ryerson career, an endorsement crucial to his peace of mind. Ed and Harriet Pierce were by no means sure that Ryerson Press was the pre-eminent instrument of power by which Lorne could fulfill their Methodist sense of mission for him. To his mother, who rarely let a novel in the house, the uproar over Pierce's publication of Grove's *Settlers of the Marsh* (1925) – given its plot featuring prostitution and murder – would have been upsetting, whatever her assurances to Lorne.[6] Was he failing his mother and the Lord?

Moreover, when Samuel Fallis pointed out columns of red ink to Pierce, the book steward was questioning more than just the recently axed Makers of Canadian Literature series. The House's overall returns were not rosy. Between 1920 and 1925, the annual amount the House had been able to channel into its ministerial superannuation fund (the traditional repository for its excess profits) had fallen from a high of $30,000 in 1920 to as low as $10,000 in May 1922 and May 1924, at the close of the House's fiscal year.[7] Fallis had to grapple with the ongoing effects of the general economic downturn in the early 1920s and the 1921–22 printers' strike (which had seen overall House profits drop from some $111,135 in 1921 to just $71,465.71 in 1922), as well as the coming-due of debentures issued by William Briggs in the previous decade to finance the construction of the Wesley Building.[8]

Unfortunately, Book Committee minutes for these years do not include summaries of profit and loss for the House's individual departments such as manufacturing and Sunday School publications. Such a practice was typical of the type of persistently woolly financial management and auditing practices of the House, practices that would help to effectively bankrupt the concern by the 1960s. The new United Church Publishing House's Board of Publication did receive somewhat more detailed annual and cumulative audit figures starting in the 1926–27 fiscal year. But there was little sustained good news in these figures. The records reveal some dangerous vulnerabilities in the fiscal state and organization of the firm, an entity that of course – as Janet Friskney's history makes clear – was neither founded on nor driven by capitalist values.[9] By the mid-1920s, some of the House's traditional profit sources were slowing or falling short.

Over the years, gross revenue for retail books had risen from a total of some $223,000 for the four-year period 1915–18 to a total of $325,000 in the period 1919–22, an increase of some $102,000.[10] But it was the House's agency publishing program of foreign best-sellers, overseen by Ernest Walker, that brought in the bulk of revenues, not Pierce's original Canadian publications – though, in fact, the published financial reports for these years do not break down returns for agency versus original publication books, even after the creation of "The Ryerson Press" imprint in 1919.

Disturbing trends were alarmingly explicit, however, in the figures reported to the House's newly reorganized and renamed Board of Publication for the fiscal years 1926 and 1927. Losses in the book departments – figures that again did not differentiate between retail publishing under Pierce and agency publishing under Ernest Walker – increased from some $4,475 in 1926 to $8,350 in 1927.[11] The money-making workhorse of the House continued to be its Manufacturing Department, the custom-printing operation managed by William Cope. But overall profits, eroded by losses in the book departments, were increasing only marginally, from $81,966 in 1926 to $83,851 the next year.[12] This was certainly not an impressive return for an organization with gross revenues of over $5,000,000 a few years earlier.[13] Even more ominously, the *New Outlook*, which replaced the Methodist *Christian Guardian* after church union, was, like its predecessor, losing a great deal of money. The magazine lost $28,978 in 1926, losses cut to $14,234 the next year once the admittedly heavy costs of launching a new magazine moderated somewhat. These worrisome financial trends put more heat on Pierce to succeed financially with his own department.

ON TOP OF everything else, spurred on by House Accountant Fred Ellins, Fallis was questioning another new Pierce venture – the Ryerson Chapbook series of poetry booklets. Pierce launched the series in 1925, part of his campaign to make the Ryerson Press pre-eminent in Canadian literary publishing. Like the "Makers" series, the venture had many praiseworthy cultural attributes but lost money. Nevertheless, the poetry series would feature new titles yearly for the next four decades, finally coming to an end in 1962 under Pierce's successor, John Webster Grant.

Pierce stuck with the Ryerson Chapbook poetry series up to his retirement despite gaining a reputation with the financial men at the House as a "lyrical wild man" who repeatedly lost money on what Ellins deplored as frivolous verse.[14] Certainly, the series was another feather in Pierce's cap, helping to establish Ryerson as a publisher serious about belles lettres. However, the 1925 launch of the chapbooks created yet more pressure for Pierce to come up with some big financial successes in his publishing program to offset unprofitable titles which stimulated Canadian cultural nationalism.

THE RYERSON Chapbook series was created by Pierce in 1925 primarily as the result of two factors. Pierce recognized that publishing Canadian poetry was important to Ryerson's prestige. He also recognized that books of poetry – with rare exceptions like Robert Service's perennial best-seller *Songs of a Sourdough*, which Briggs had published in 1906 – lost money. His imaginative solution was to publish chapbooks: short, softcover booklets of poetry – usually twelve to sixteen pages in length. This relatively inexpensive format satisfied his desire for a handsome publication, given the uniform series design. (Pierce commissioned the original design for the series from J.E.H. MacDonald, a design later updated and simplified on several occasions by his son, artist Thoreau MacDonald.[15]) Further, most poets were asked to publish chapbooks with Ryerson on a non-commercial basis, and most agreed. These authors were asked to contribute some money to the venture and/or to take back half of the modest print run (usually less than 500 copies) to sell and distribute themselves.

The chapbook format thus allowed Pierce to publish poets, especially young and promising ones, without the major financial risk of a hard-cover book with a big print run. For their part, poets did not have to contribute substantially toward publication of a hardcover book, as had usually been the case in Canadian publishing up to the 1920s. Pierce's idea for the format probably came from the chapbooks produced in the early 1920s by the Vancouver Poetry Society under its president Ernest Fewster, a group with whom Pierce began his long association on his first textbook tour to British Columbia in the fall of 1923.[16]

Relatively cheap as the format was, however, the Ryerson Chapbooks still posed some financial liability for the firm, and authors sometimes resented their proposed involvement in the cost and logistics of print-ing and distribution. But, despite the tensions, Pierce published nearly

Good friends and congenial poets: Pierce and members of the Vancouver
Poetry Society, c. 1925. Standing, left to right: Charles G.D. Roberts, Pierce,
Ernest Fewster. Seated: Bliss Carman, Annie Charlotte Dalton, A.M.
Stephen. Courtesy of Queen's University Archives

200 titles between 1925 and 1960.[17] Gifted poets like Anne Marriott,
Al Purdy, and Alfred Bailey enjoyed early publication in book form in
the Ryerson Chapbooks, making the series a significant contribution to
Canadian literary history, as scholars have pointed out.[18] And in later
years many other respected names in Canadian writing – such as Bliss
Carman, Norman Levine, Audrey Alexandra Brown, Ernest Fewster,
W.E. Collin, Doris Ferne, Arthur Bourinot, F.O. Call, and Dorothy
Livesay, for example – were published in the series. The chapbooks
also spawned imitators. McClelland and Stewart's "Indian File" series,
launched in 1948, owed much to the Ryerson Chapbook series, as any
comparison of their respective offerings makes clear,[19] and Fred Cogswell's Fiddlehead books of poetry in the 1950s were similarly influenced
by Pierce's pioneering concept. Moreover, when editor John Sutherland
launched the poetry publications of First Statement Press in 1945 with
Irving Layton's *Here and Now*, he invoked the Ryerson Chapbooks as
a model. Sutherland had written poet Dorothy Livesay in the spring

of 1943 that he envisioned "selections of poetry similar to the Ryerson chap-books, perhaps improved in form and increased in size (and, I have no doubt, in quality)."[20]

Pierce, having conceived of the Ryerson Chapbook series by August 1925, wanted to launch it with a booklet by Charles G.D. Roberts. After some two decades in the literary centres of New York and London "piping for them that pay the piper," Roberts, the Grand Old Man of Confederation poets, was back in Canada. Pierce had been active in arranging readings and publicity for the talented (if libertine) older poet. For example, Pierce – in company with Roberts's son, writer Lloyd Roberts, and others – organized Roberts's successful public reading on 4 February 1925 at Toronto's Massey Hall, his first Canadian appearance in seventeen years.[21] Determined to capture all the literary lions of the day for the Ryerson list, Pierce set to work to publish Roberts, whose nationalistic spirit and "cosmic" poetic vision he revered.[22] The enthusiastic response to Roberts's Massey Hall reading before a full house bolstered Pierce's conviction that any association with Roberts – as with Carman – would add to Ryerson's prestige. At the same time, Pierce was at once repelled and fascinated by the unconventional lifestyle of both Roberts (an inveterate womanizer) and Bliss Carman (long-time lover of his married patron, Mary Perry King).

On the subject of Roberts's trail of kited checks and fondled women, Pierce and Halifax professor and critic Archibald MacMechan privately agreed that they wished they did not know so much about Canada's "native geniuses."[23] Pierce was appalled when Roberts made "risque" references about Carman's love poetry in front of a "disgusted" Edith Pierce at a Royal Society banquet.[24] Indeed, for the rest of Roberts's career, Pierce had Blanche Hume discreetly caution any attractive young Ryerson Press secretaries to keep a desk between themselves and Roberts – a bottom pincher – at all times.[25] Yet, despite such moral hazards, Pierce was quick to realize that the novelty of the poet's return to Canada after decades abroad made Roberts ideal to launch Ryerson's Chapbook series.

Pierce soon published an article on Roberts in the *New Outlook* as well as material on Carman. The Roberts article delighted the poet by emphasizing that his work after the publication of *Orion* (1880) had been infused with the landscape and "spirit of Canada." Pierce was to elaborate this theme in his 1933 Alumni Address at the University of New Brunswick.[26] Accordingly, despite the fact that the notoriously territorial Boston publisher L.C. Page controlled much of Roberts's work, Roberts agreed to inaugurate the Ryerson Chapbook series, and to let Pierce seek Canadian rights to volumes of his published by the British firm of Constable. In his diary, Pierce declared that he wanted "the strongest list in Canada ... [for] I feel I am building for the future." The entry shows his high hopes for the chapbooks: "In launching my Poetry Chapbook idea I have been looking about for someone to commence with, who will give the whole thing standing and distinction. Roberts has consented to give me a few poems for this initial number. I shall have [in the series] Pickthall, W[ilson] MacDonald, [Albert] Watson, [Arthur] Bourinot, [Edward] Sapir, and possibly the Vancouver group [i.e., Bliss Carman, Ernest Fewster, A.M. Stephen, Annie Charlotte Dalton, etc.]."[27]

Pierce did kick off with an eight-page booklet by Roberts, *The Sweet o' the Year* (1925). Two years later, outside the chapbook series, Ryerson published a forty-six-page book of poems by Roberts, *The Vagrant of Time* (1927) – a volume that was, as Pierce proudly noted in his *Outline of Canadian Literature* (1927), "the first book of [Roberts's] poems to be published exclusively in the Dominion since *Orion*."[28] In one way, Pierce's feat was considerable. Unfortunately, however, much of Roberts's best work remained in thrall to Page, who refused to grant permission to reprint it except for outrageously high fees. As a result, the handsome 1927 volume, whose 500-copy print run featured an autographed photograph of Roberts in the onion-skin-covered frontispiece, recycled some of the chapbook poems and some of Roberts's weaker work – all material outside Page's net.[29] For instance, *The Vagrant of Time* included a jingoistic poem titled "To Shakespeare in 1916," written in the wake of the German sinking of the *Lusitania*, as well as some hackneyed love poetry – all of which seemed dated by the late 1920s. There were a few of Roberts's better pieces – such as the clever "Philander's Song" and "The Sweet o' the Year" – but the latter was in fact the title poem of the recent chapbook. As a result, the poetic quality of *The Vagrant of Time* was undermined by Roberts's modest output in the 1920s and the fact that, hard up for funds, he had sold so many of his copyrights to Page. Still, that Pierce had captured the returning grandee did lend lustre to Ryerson's list.

Whatever their literary merit, Samuel Fallis knew that the Chapbook series and other poetry publications like *The Vagrant of Time* were sure money losers. In the fall of 1926, he sent his editor an "impertinent note" to that effect, one that made Pierce want to "wring his neck."[30] Pierce was thus forced to be ingenious in subsidizing the Chapbook series and other poetry titles, to some extent at least. Roberts, given his literary prestige and empty wallet, was not asked to finance the inaugural chapbook. But Pierce had *The Vagrant of Time* underwritten by advance subscription, a reversion to earlier, more fiscally conservative methods of Canadian literary publication.[31]

In the early years of the Chapbook series, Pierce resented what he saw as Fallis's "meddling" with his editorial prerogatives. Fallis ordered Pierce to turn down "The Devil's Device," a long poem by Canon Frederick George Scott, a respected Confederation poet. Fallis saw the poem as "immoral" – presumably because, like Milton's *Paradise Lost*, it gave too much exposure to the Devil's viewpoint even if the outcome was never really in doubt! Pierce, who first received Scott's poem in July 1924, was caught between Scott's imperious impatience over what were (to him) mysterious delays in accepting the manuscript, and Fallis's determination to prove that he was in charge by having Pierce refuse a manuscript unlikely to make money or please the orthodox.[32]

In January 1925 Pierce finally informed Scott that Fallis objected to the poem's publication even as a chapbook on moral grounds. A bewildered Scott – ironically writing in the very year he was elevated to the post of archdeacon of the Anglican cathedral in Quebec City – countered: "The book is not a tract or a Sunday school book but I think it gives, in perhaps a lurid colouring, a true picture of certain elements in our modern life-puzzle, and will make people think."[33] To no avail. Publication was stymied.[34]

Throughout the first years of the chapbooks, Pierce veered and tacked to avoid offending the bottom line too flagrantly, a practice that continuing losses made necessary long after Fallis ceased to be book steward. On average, several chapbooks a year were published, featuring a variety of poets. Pierce in fact consistently strove to vary the range of the series, and to include distinguished older poets as well as emerging young artists, a strategy not without awkward moments. In 1928 he asked Susan Frances Harrison ("Seranus"), the respected Confederation-era writer whose work he wished to publish at the suggestion of his House predecessor, Edward Caswell, to pay publication costs "owing to the difficulty of disposing of even a limited edition of these little books." Harrison refused.[35] She also refused to sell 150 copies of the chapbook.[36]

Nevertheless, Pierce gamely published Harrison's sixteen-page chapbook, *Later Poems and New Vilanelles* in an edition of 250 in 1928. One of the most interesting books in the series, its cover featured the handsome

J.E.H. MacDonald black-and-white Art Nouveau design for the series, a striking scene of a forest pine with a foreground of wildflowers and a mysterious draped figure in the background. (Amusingly, MacDonald's son, Thoreau, later replaced the draped figure in the scene with a Rocky-like mountain.)

Despite largely positive reviews and some success in encouraging promising writers, Pierce found the Ryerson Chapbooks challenging to publish from many points of view. The series initially won some praise, as Pierce recorded happily in his diary.[37] The *Canadian Stationer and Book Trade Journal*, the trade magazine of Canadian publishing, for example, was enthusiastic, writing in 1926 that the aim of the series was "ambitious and worthy of note by book-sellers." The magazine praised the retail price of sixty cents as realistic, confident that "lovers of poetry care more for verse of high quality than for costly bindings."[38] But poets complained about the short length of the booklets and the lack of prestige in being published in softcover; booksellers disliked the format, difficult for display purposes.

Moreover, from the moment he launched the chapbooks, Pierce was inundated by mediocre manuscripts on hackneyed themes, leading him to ban "all religious and patriotic poetry" from the series, rather ironically for a cultural nationalist at a church publishing house.[39] Sales were always modest, and, as the Depression set in, sales fell further and the number of titles was cut back. Pierce published thirteen chapbooks in 1927, but in 1933 he issued just two titles. When poet Ralph Gustafson wrote in December 1933 to inquire about publishing with Ryerson, Pierce suggested that only a chapbook might be possible, "not a commercial affair." Pierce added that even the small chapbook runs needed the cooperation of the author to dispose of, especially given the times.[40] In the end, Gustafson published no Ryerson chapbook.

As editor of the chapbooks, Pierce strove to maintain quality and variety in the series, even as he periodically had to cut back the length and format of the booklets to save money – some were as short as six pages. The poets were sometimes no happier than the Ryerson bean counters. For example, in the late 1940s, Marjorie Freeman Campbell, chagrined that Pierce had cut her manuscript to eight pages, wanted to delay publication of her second Ryerson chapbook until Pierce found more of her poems acceptable.[41] Pierce replied that he had gone through her work "two times at home" in order to select only her "very best." He stressed his mindfulness of quality as well as costs: "I have been rather severely criticized during the last few years for letting Chap-Books go through that were lacking in distinction and we are trying to be more careful."[42] Pierce also refused to be foxed when Campbell asked him to rule on the acceptability of a new poem she had in mind, telling her that she must "write it as you see it" and that would determine the eventual length of the manuscript.[43] In the event, two years later, Ryerson at last published her *High on a Hill* (1949), a sixteen-page chapbook.

One way in which the series was valuable to young poets is that, from the beginning, Pierce himself selected manuscripts, giving poets useful feedback on their work. Even when he declined a manuscript, he often pointed out which poems seemed promising, and suggested that poets submit a further selection later, as was the case with Fred Cogswell in the 1950s.[44] Meanwhile, he continued to publish the series despite continuing pressure from the business office, which, he wrote in 1951, felt that "every dollar spent on poetry is money wasted!"[45]

The Ryerson Chapbooks have not always been viewed positively by Canadian critics. The series encompassed both modernists and traditionalists, eastern Canadians as well as western and central Canadians poets, unknown poets as well as established ones, and even dead poets (Carman, Pickthall).[46] However, a myth has sprung up that Pierce's series overwhelmingly neglected modernist poets in overwhelming favour of traditional and romantic verse in the vein of watered-down Carman or Pickthall. Margery Fee, for example, in discussing Pierce's Ryerson Chapbooks, comments: "It ... seems possible to argue that [Pierce's] Romantic tastes denied some Modernist poets an early book, or chapbook publication, with Ryerson. If the poets represented in the Ryerson chapbook series (1925–1962) are compared with those represented in the *Canadian Poetry Magazine* (1936–1968) it becomes clear that although the "sweet singers" were more than fairly represented in both, *Canadian Poetry Magazine* makes a genuine and earnest effort to include social and modernist poets, while the Ryerson series does not publish any of these poets until long after they have become well-known elsewhere." Fee adds that "no well-known modernist or social poet ever appeared in the Ryerson chapbooks before 1950 and it seems that Pierce's taste in poetry is to blame."[47]

While Fee does note that initiatives like the chapbooks establish Pierce's centrality as critic and publisher, her criticisms of Pierce's selections are not borne out by the publication lists for the series. The complete list of Ryerson Chapbooks, up to 1950 in particular, demonstrates that two of the central works of the modernist canon in the poetry of social concern, Anne Marriott's *The Wind Our Enemy* (1939), about the devastation of the prairies by drought, and Dorothy Livesay's *Call My People Home* (1950), about the internment of Japanese Canadians, were in fact published there, each receiving considerable attention. Moreover, a roll call of modernist writers appeared in the series before 1950: Frank Oliver Call, L.A. Mackay (pseudonym John Smalacombe), Norman Levine, Doris Ferne, and W.E. Collin, as well as three titles by Anne Marriott (whose work Pierce admired greatly). It should be pointed out, too, that the economics of publishing one poem in a monthly periodical like the *Canadian Poetry Magazine* are not really comparable to the cost of publishing a poet in book form – even in chapbook form.

In fact, the range of poetry Pierce selected for the Ryerson Chapbooks during his four decades of editorship shows remarkable breadth, balance, and prescience. Louis Dudek, a leading modernist editor and poet not known for mincing words, praised Pierce in 1952 for his "fine work ... for Canadian poetry," an assessment reinforced by the numerous publication credits to Ryerson in the Dudek and Irving Layton anthology *Canadian Poems 1850–1952* for Contact Press (1952). Dudek later wrote poet Phyllis Webb that Pierce had usually made a "good selection" of poets for his chapbook and other poetry publications, never obviously omitting the "frank or experimental" in verse and giving poets the benefits of Ryerson's good distribution network.[48]

Admittedly, at times Pierce, like any editor, modernist or traditional, was ruled by extraneous motives or made choices that reflected his own agendas. Marjorie Pickthall, for instance, was a curious choice for a chapbook in 1930, eight years after her death, but the more traditionally romantic, lyrical verse of a Pickthall or an Audrey Alexandra Brown was certainly closer to his heart than more modernist fare.[49] One female poet, Elsie Woodley, wrote Pierce in 1930, after he had published her chapbook *Bittersweet*, feeling rather overshadowed by patriarchal power: "In future, I should prefer to communicate directly with you, instead of through my father, as I have done so far. He agrees with me that this will prevent possible confusion and misunderstanding."[50]

But, on the whole, Pierce published a range of verse, modernist and traditional, that reflected the diversity of both geography and poetry in Canada. It is noteworthy that whenever poets, whether traditional (Arthur Bourinot) or modernist (Louis Dudek), heard that Pierce thought of ending the series, they usually wrote to urge him to continue it.[51] In 1954 young poet and professor Fred Cogswell of Fiddlehead Press proved particularly magnanimous in his pleas that the chapbooks continue, given that Pierce had ruled a year earlier that Cogswell did not yet have enough suitable poems to justify a chapbook.[52] Pierce, equally magnanimous, in turn congratulated Cogswell in 1954 on starting the Fiddlehead Poetry series from his base at the University of New Brunswick, a venture clearly influenced by the Ryerson Chapbooks. Pierce later published two chapbooks by Cogswell in his series.[53]

AN EVEN larger challenge than the chapbooks loomed for Pierce in the late 1920s. His time was increasingly consumed, as it would be for much of the next decade, and at regular intervals throughout his career, by textbook projects – the area of book publishing economically crucial to his own welfare as well as that of his department and the House as a whole. Around the time of Pierce's 1922 promotion to editor, Fallis gave him a mammoth task – to make Ryerson Press a leader in original textbook publishing in Canada.[54] The new task required him to make regular trips to both western and eastern Canada in order to lobby provincial governments and departments of education in order to capture the market for high school and elementary textbooks.

Traditionally, given the small and geographically dispersed Canadian book market, publishing firms have eagerly sought a place in the lucrative textbook field, with its large print runs and commensurate profits. Pierce knew that success in the textbook game was essential if he was to be a great and long-lasting head of Ryerson Press. Success would bring the profits the House needed to prosper and generate the financial cushion to enable him to publish prestigious (but largely unprofitable) literary and historical works in an era before government subsidy programs for publishing. He had other motives as well. Most obviously, he wanted to supplement his own modest salary. Pierce joked that he was "a spendthrift from County Wexford," but he was anxious to pay off the debts that he, the head of a growing middle-class Toronto family with a concomitant taste for collecting Canadian art and books and philanthropic causes, had accumulated. Finally, there were ideological considerations. Pierce never viewed textbook publishing simply as a cash cow for himself or the House. Rather, he infused the venture with his own idealism and cultural nationalism. He believed that "made-in-Canada" textbooks, particularly in history and literature, were ideal vehicles for inculcating Canadian children with a national spirit infused with such values as patriotism, love of truth and beauty, and commitment to French-English entente. Pierce also believed firmly that the dictum "as the twig is bent, so is the bough inclined" was true as far as making children good, nationalistic, enlightened, culture-loving adult citizens was concerned. For example, when Edith was teaching in Saskatchewan in 1912, Lorne pointed out that children constituted rich ground in which to implant a nation's intellectual and spiritual values. Given the right approach and the right tools in the classroom, he wrote, "a little culture ... comes to them almost unconsciously."[55]

When he arrived at Union Theological Seminary in the fall of 1915, Pierce was sufficiently intrigued by pedagogy to take a course in educational psychology, a newly emerging field. He found the material "a real delight."[56] At this time, Pierce also expressed frustration with the largely mediocre education he felt he had endured in Delta, at high school in Athens, and in Victoria's divinity program. Teaching in the west in 1909 and 1910, he was critical of the pedestrian textbooks of the one-room schools of Saskatchewan. He lamented to Edith in 1915: "How long oh Lord, how long shall our [Canadian] schools be meat mills where all go in and come out uniform sausages!"[57]

The House was also anxious for success. Fallis saw textbook sales as key to increased profits. The printing of school textbooks had frequently generated a lucrative portion of the House profits from the Manufacturing Department.[58] In the decade before Pierce's arrival, however, the House's presence in the textbook field had ebbed markedly. Moreover, in the past, the House had often simply bid for the (re)printing of textbooks, rather than involving itself in the commissioning, editing, and marketing of them. Not so Pierce. As one article put it: "Lorne Piece decided to go out and build a series of school-books that would appeal to departments of education from the Atlantic to the Pacific ... In time, these came to be adopted in all the provinces of Canada, including Newfoundland, and their publication [is of] ... national significance."[59]

Pierce proclaimed his national cultural mission from the beginning of his involvement in textbook sales. In 1923, for example, he published an article in the *Christian Guardian* which attacked Canada's lack of homegrown textbooks and the tendency to accept barely altered, foreign-content American texts or to cling to a stifling colonialism with British materials. Even Egerton Ryerson, who had involved the House in textbook publishing as early as 1845, came in for some sharp words:

We Canadians have been singularly ignorant of and indifferent to our native writers. Possibly this has been due to the strong imperial tradition, fostered by our ancestry and emphasized by innumerable tokens of that tie to the Mother Land. The old Fourth Reader, adopted by Dr. Egerton Ryerson from Ireland without a change, contained but one lonely quotation from a writer of Canada, and this was scarcely Canadian. Subsequent Ministers of Education have almost entirely ignored our own writers until a very recent date ... Even to-day the selections of longer English poems which will be used this fall in our schools contain not a single Canadian poem.

Pierce claimed that Canadians had too long accepted "without demur" American school texts at the expense of Canadian literature. He labelled Canada "the only country in the civilized world that does not study its own literature!"[60]

For the next decade, Pierce publicly stressed the need to properly educate Canadian youth through Canadian-made textbooks. What brought him success in this venture was not only his own Herculean labours and those of his collaborators, but also the fact that Canadian schools were ripe for change in the 1920s and 1930s. In the aftermath of the First World War, there was a flowering of Canadian nationalism, and a feeling that Canadians should have access to literature and art which reflected such a heightened sense of identity. The artists of the Group of Seven and their allies of pen and palette – many of them Pierce's friends and associates (for example, J.E.H. MacDonald, C.W. Jefferys, B.K. Sandwell, William Arthur Deacon, Frederick Banting, Wilson MacDonald, Thoreau MacDonald, Donald Creighton, Hugh Eayrs, and others) – were in the 1920s active in advocating a better and more autonomous Canadian culture differentiated from that of the United States on the one hand and Britain, headquarters of the empire, on the other. Pierce's former Victoria College professor, Pelham Edgar, the dean of Canadian critics, had long stressed to Canadians that the country needed works that interpreted "us to ourselves."[61]

In fact, for Pierce, and for scores of his like-minded Canadian contemporaries, the development of national consciousness was, in the words of one historian, "an idealistic and spiritual goal, a great ideal" that relied on education to promote mutual understanding and a belief in the inspirational power of literature and art to foster national myths, heroes, and symbols.[62] Through his textbooks, as with the poetry and fiction he published, Pierce plunged into the work of cultural nationalism, rapidly making himself a dynamic figure in what has been termed a web of "popularizers and propagandists who served as the channel whereby the work of Canadian artists and intellectuals was funnelled to the people."[63]

Pierce's speeches and articles in the late 1920s and 1930s hammered home the theme that original textbooks designed to inculcate patriotic feeling were essential to building Canadian national feeling. His nationalism was constructed on the premise that new immigrant groups had to be acculturated, not form "undigested" agglomerations of difference. The "inchoate" state of the nation made such acculturation critical, he declared in a 1930 address at Mount Allison University. Otherwise Canada lacked cohesion: "We have no distinctive flag, no generally accepted national song, no saga, no classic racy of the soil … Small communities, separated by immense distances, work out their destinies as best they can. Undigested groups of foreign peoples cling tenaciously to their speech and customs."[64]

For Pierce, assimilation to the dominant ethos was desirable and the means lay in a "national" education – in the sense not of a uniform structure of grades but rather in the acceptance nationwide of congruent materials to foster cohesion. Young Canadians in particular needed to study their own literature and history to foster and promote "a vivid and intelligent national self-consciousness" as "an act of self-preservation." In education, he stressed that "our teachers of literature would do well to group the best we have accomplished in these fields about their themes … Later our youths will set out as self-conscious Canadians, enriched by their native social inheritance."[65] In other words, Canadian-made textbooks were needed to breathe a romantic idealism about the country and its history into young students to make them upright and enthusiastic Canadians.

As a key factor to advance Canada's "development of an inward life, [and] the evolution of a collective spirit," Pierce saw the curriculum of the "little red school house" as "the cement to bind us [as] a people to one another." Such a goal demanded new textbooks in schools across Canada, he argued, textbooks that answered both the requirements of idealistic nationalism and the imaginative needs of a growing child, the latter concern very much to the forefront in North American educational theory of the 1920s and 1930s. Pierce was emphatic: "Our courses in literature, and history, in both public and high schools, must be radically changed. No longer can the old button-boy, bric-a-brac collection of snippet readings serve our purpose ... there are certain permanent interests and ideals alive in the minds of children. Around these dreams and enthusiasms we must build our texts on literature, history and service ... In this way, the very best of all that we have produced may be related, at the proper time and in the right manner, and find its beautiful flowering in a higher national citizenship."[66]

In a deft blend of salesmanship and nationalist construct, Pierce was able by 1930 to tell his audiences about his new textbook series for elementary and high schools – chief among them, the Canadian Treasury Readers, the Ryerson Books of Prose and Verse, and the Ryerson Canadian History Readers. All were series that, as Pierce pointed out, he had recently formulated in a patriotic spirit: "These problems [of fostering national feeling] I have already attempted to answer in several texts for schools ... The generous encouragement which they have received in departmental authorization, and in the gratifying results which they have received in our schools, will in some way justify these talks."[67]

Pierce was thus the centre of a decade-long effort to produce the first widely used all-Canadian graded series of readers and other textbooks for Canadian elementary and high schools. He did not do it alone. To edit the textbooks, Pierce recruited collaborators for each volume, men and women with varied expertise in school teaching and text editing. His early collaborators in putting together elementary and high school readers included educator Arthur Yates and Professor C.L. Bennet of Dalhousie University. George Wrong, a well-known University of Toronto historian, wrote a history of Canada published by Ryerson in 1921. Pierce would later oversee its expansion and reissuing, marketed by 1929 as *The Story of Canada* by Wrong and two collaborators.[68] Another textbook venture, the Ryerson Canadian History Readers, Pierce's series of over 102 booklets (fifteen to thirty-two pages in length) on Canadian history for Canadian schools, launched in 1925, were produced by dozens of authors – historians, teachers, and professional writers and journalists – including Pierce himself (who wrote five of them[69]). Artist C.W. Jefferys, a gifted illustrator of long experience, did much of the illustration work. Jefferys's romantic visual images from Canada's past (the material details – clothing, fences, farm implements, muskets – painstakingly researched) contributed to the financial and pedagogical success of the series.

Pierce's popular history texts for Canadian schools were even more whiggish and inspirational in content than the Canadian poetry and prose selections in his elementary and high school readers and English literature texts. Historian Carl Berger has defined the perspective of the romantic historians of Canada, from Francis Parkman in the nineteenth century to Donald Creighton in the twentieth. The definition applies perfectly to Pierce, his commissioned writers, and his visual collaborator Charles Jefferys in the Ryerson Canadian History Readers. Berger writes: "The romantic historian ... thought of history as a drama and he sought to tell a story. He searched for a significant theme in which a large number of interesting individuals acted on a wide stage and he tried to communicate the drama of the story through narrative."[70] Indeed, for Pierce, the significance of history was as a "binding necessity" in order that "fervent and intelligent national sentiment should be created in the schools."[71] He defined history as a "series of sublime events," a "highway, well-defined and obvious," a visionary epic of "progressive evolution."[72]

Pierce's Ryerson Canadian History Readers focused, therefore, on "great" events and "great" men (and several women) from the era of early exploration to the story of hydro-electricity. Grouped under such romantic headings as "Stories of Heroes," "Stories of Heroines," and "Fathers of the Dominion," the booklets exemplified the concept of history that Pierce wished to promote. Students would be exposed to a coherent, inspiring, evolutionary narrative of Canada's history. They in turn would allegedly aspire to be dynamic, patriotic Canadians, or as Pierce put it: "History is a *story*, in which dramatic and romantic elements are stressed ... [topics] consist of biographies and romances bearing on a single theme in such a manner as to reveal the streams of history, that is ... narratives of human progress along various lines ... As the pupil sees the main streams of history he arrives at an idea of his own place in the epic of man's progress. He will wish to share intelligently in it, and enrich the narrative as best he can."[73]

Pierce quickly realized that he needed authors for the History Readers who could write inspiring prose. Accordingly, he commissioned many of the booklets in his series of history readers from well-known writers of popular history of the day, such as Lawrence Burpee, Agnes Laut, Thomas Guthrie Marquis, Isabel Skelton, and Mabel Burkholder. Certainly, all the texts exude inspirational and nationalistic sentiments. In *Maisonneuve*, for example, one of the booklets he himself wrote, Pierce ends by exalting what Canada owes to its New France past: "Never shall we cease to remember Sieur de Maisonneuve, that brave and gallant gentleman, who carried the spirit of a worthier crusade into the unfriendly wilds of New France."[74]

Bonne entente was not the only value stressed in this romantic nationalism. Given the valorization of technology at this time, consistent with Pierce's own progressivism (evidenced, for instance, in the rural electricity cooperative he set up in Brinston in 1919), "modern" values are as stirring as those of the founders of New France. For example, journalist Blodwen Davies's booklet *The Story of Hydro* was styled a "hydro-electric romance" because "Canada owes her history and her nationhood to her waterways," which, in being harnessed, will "give homes and employment to thousands who turn to Canada as a new land of hope and glory."[75]

Macmillan of Canada produced a rival series to which Hugh Eayrs gave similarly stirring titles: "Canadian Men of Action" and "Canadian Statesmen." The Ryerson history booklets outpaced their Macmillan counterparts, winning endorsements from provincial departments of education and the Imperial Order Daughters of the Empire (IODE), and praise from both educational magazines and the Toronto *Globe*. In the spring of 1932, Pierce proudly reported to the House's Board of Publication that, even in the midst of the Depression, 15,000 of the Ryerson Canadian History Readers had been sold in the past year to Nova Scotia alone.[76]

Pierce had created the readers, and made the gruelling journeys to market them, all the while editing manuscripts in jolting railcars. In 1922 alone he travelled over 11,000 miles by train in two business trips to western Canada and one to the Maritimes.[77] He thus came to know the people and groups active in education all across Canada – be they ministers of education, their deputies, textbook committees, or teachers' organizations – not to mention rival salesman and authors, especially those of W.J. Gage and Company (headed since 1919 by its masterly editor-in-chief, John Saul[78]) and Macmillan of Canada (where the chief players were the shrewd, patriotic, hard-living Hugh Eayrs and his subordinates, especially the quick-witted, debonair Jack Gray). In the mid-1920s Gage and Macmillan were Ryerson's chief competitors in the field. All three firms knew that the real pot of gold in the textbook arena lay in the development and marketing of general readers for elementary and high schools. This was a prize that Pierce was determined to win.

On the Long Textbook Trail

The Rocky Road to Success with the
Ryerson–Macmillan Readers, 1922–1930

Attention may be called to the large element of Canadiana in [this reader] ... Beginning with the elements of literary appreciation ... the next movement [of the pupil] must be inward to the fundamentals of character-building, and then outward to [Canadian] citizenship.

Lorne Pierce's preface to his first reader, 1927[1]

It doesn't take one long to weary of this [textbook game]. It is full of politics and sharp corners.

Lorne Pierce to his wife, Edith, 1925[2]

Pierce was disturbed to find on his first western tour in 1922 that the Ryerson imprint was virtually "unknown west of the great Lakes" and that the "oldest publishing house in Canada" had made "scarcely any impression at all upon the educational and literary life of the country."[3] Moreover, in an era of strong sectarianism, he realized that the "church publishing house" connotations of the "semi-religious" name "Ryerson Press" were "bound to scare away many"[4] from the company as a general publisher. Pierce resolved to broaden the Press's image and its penetration of the western and Maritime markets. Despite the difficulties posed by his deafness, he gave seventeen speeches on that trip, emphasizing "the necessity for a new national independence and consciousness in order to achieve the highest art and to make the most significant spiritual contribution."[5] Not everyone, however, had faith in Pierce's mission, even at the House. Of the other departmental heads whose operations would benefit from successes in the textbook field, only William Cope, head of the Manufacturing Department, helped to underwrite Pierce's travel expenses of about $500.[6]

Lorne's long western journeys may have been cultural building blocks in publishing for him, but he lamented in February 1924 to his diary that he "dread[ed]" the long trips, invariably preceded by a "mad scramble" at home because it was "a real enterprise to leave a small family alone for so long."[7] It was an even more taxing scramble for the wife left behind. Lorne was not even able to telephone home; telegrams were expensive and infrequent. Edith was on her own. And would Lorne succeed?

Whatever Edith's thoughts, her distress was apparent. For example, she was frequently ill in the fall of 1926, and the doctor prescribed bed rest. Two years later, Lorne rushed home from Winnipeg on 4 March on the return leg of a western trek after learning that "Edith had been ill for weeks ... with a collapse" despite a "good housekeeper, furnace man and [maid] Ada."[8] He had been gone since 24 January.

Such crises clearly strained the marriage, a matter that rarely surfaces in the Pierce diary. About his deepest troubles, the diary is often silent or sketchy. But a "man-to-man" letter from Pierce's Vancouver friend Ernest Fewster establishes that Edith had voiced her unhappiness. Fewster wrote: "I suppose your wife still henpecks you a bit, you didn't say in your last letter how you were getting along now, maybe she's quit hollerin' and bawlin' you out for awhile ... Well anyhow, Lorne, you have my sympathy & I ought to know having been married myself nigh on 30 years."[9]

The House executive suite was not happy either. In the late 1920s, Pierce's relationship with the book steward continued to be strained. As a result, Pierce's lupus flare-ups worsened: his diary for these years is a litany of work, illness, and collapse. However, the aftermath of Pierce's first western trip at least seemed positive in professional terms. According to Pierce, Fallis responded to his urgings to reorganize the House, mandating a comprehensive literary policy – formulated and managed by Pierce. More basic restructuring involved the amalgamation of the House's wholesale, retail, and mail-order departments to eliminate organizational waste in shipping and ordering.[10] By 1927, Pierce's new office boasted the "rogue's gallery" of photographs of distinguished writers – a pantheon that included Carman, Roberts, MacDonald, Lampman, Pickthall, and Pauline Johnson – that visitors would admire for the next three decades. Some visiting writers to the sanctum, such as Wilson MacDonald, complained about the placement of their own photographs!

Pierce returned from the west in 1922 with a few promising textbook authorizations (that is, made an approved choice for use as a school textbook by the department of education concerned) – for example, George Wrong's *History of Canada* (1921) was authorized in Saskatchewan and British Columbia. Knowing that he needed seasoned, well-connected educational consultants to win big in the "textbook game," Pierce engaged George Locke, chief librarian of the Toronto Public Library since 1908, to advise on publishing, "book conditions and [to be] general 'handy man'" and University of Toronto educational psychology professor Peter Sandiford to advise on editing education texts.[11]

Pierce's long sojourns away from Toronto had negative effects as well, however. Book Steward Samuel Fallis and his successor, Donald Solandt, understandably tended to defer Ryerson Press matters until Pierce returned. He usually faced weeks of extra work – a "hopeless mess" – the moment he returned, even though the journey itself had generated even more work.[12] Not until Blanche Hume became his secretary in 1924 did Pierce really begin to feel that there was someone in his office to "hold the fort." Yet, even then, his struggles to keep ahead of the heavy load of correspondence so necessary in the book trade continued: he would sometimes get off over fifty business letters in a morning.[13] Only when he hired Frank Flemington as his editorial assistant in 1940 did he have someone to focus solely on basic editorial problems through letters and, even more important, handle the telephoning he could not.

One reason Pierce sought reliable subordinates to work under him in the textbook trade was that he found some of the work uncongenial and even distasteful. At times, his diary does show gusto about competition with rival publishers, especially John Saul of Gage Publishing. In April 1924, just back from the west, he wrote gleefully in his diary that despite Saul's "hammer lock hold on the West … he can't live forever and we are getting in there." But that entry also recorded the kind of dubious ethics and inside influence inherent in textbook sales. Hoping to make textbook sales in Alberta, Pierce noted: "John Saul had been working with one of the [Alberta] inspectors revising the [civics] manuscript left by a deceased inspector and this is almost certain to be authorized. I didn't make a great deal of headway there … Saul has [the supervisor of schools] mesmerized." But well off moral high ground himself, Pierce immediately referred to his own "henchmen" who were "on the ground" in Alberta, and how J.T.M. Anderson, head of the Saskatchewan Conservatives, had promised sales if his party came to power.[14] Such tactics were the realpolitik of the textbook game and Pierce was in the thick of it.

By the beginning of 1925, as Pierce made yet another round of the western capitals, he lamented: "It doesn't take long for one to weary of this job. It is full of politics and sharp corners. I am playing the game in the open and may lose, but am going to satisfy my own conscience." A worthy resolve, but in the next breath Pierce noted how "canny" and almost "crooked" one official he dealt with was.[15] At first, in the face of temptation to cut corners, his epistolary complaints to Edith grew even stronger: "I loathe, abominate, despise and damn this business."[16] A primrose path – its yellow the colour of gold – promising royalties for him, sales for Ryerson, culture for Canada – beckoned.

Back at the House, the atmosphere was at times ugly: to Blanche Hume, Fallis had become a "dragon." At this time, he assigned Pierce the time-consuming task of putting together *The Chronicle of A Century* (1929), a volume to commemorate the centenary of the House. Pierce, already overworked, was hard-pressed to complete the task,[17] and he felt that Fallis was likely to be very critical of what he did produce in any case. He collected memoirs and solicited recollections by various employees, past and present, of the House, included a series of illustrated profiles of the book stewards, and tried to make time to shape the mass of manuscript into a centenary volume.

Not surprisingly, given the animus between them, Fallis was so enraged by Pierce's original entry on him in *Chronicle* that, after publication, he had the book recalled, and the two pages on himself rewritten and reinserted, an expensive gesture that so annoyed Pierce that he even recorded it in the bibliography of his own work two decades later.[18] Fallis, like Pierce, was not well; overweight and aging, he was operated on for appendicitis at one point. Pierce was sure that he had never gotten over the loss of his favourite son, Lieutenant Everett Fallis, at Vimy Ridge. Moreover, his wife and another son died in the 1920s.

DESPITE FALLIS's displeasure over Pierce's wearing two hats as publisher and author, he continued to turn out articles and books. He agreed to produce for the *New Outlook* a series of profiles on Canadian writers for the United Church's Young People's Societies which were studying Canadian literature,[19] to run in the magazine between October 1926 and April 1927. Pierce stipulated, however, that both French and English Canadian writers had to be included.[20] He also decided that the profiles – which treated writers from New France to the present – should be expanded into a book, which he felt would be marketable as a textbook and work of reference.

In many ways, Pierce's decision was shrewd. Like his anthology with Watson, the project constituted another crash course in Canadian literary history, knowledge that could only enhance his work as Canadian publisher. At the same time, in writing *An Outline of Canadian Literature (French and English)* (1927), he made valuable contacts with such luminaries as Quebec littérateurs Monseigneur Camille Roy, rector of Laval University (to whom Pierce dedicated the book), Dominion Archivist Gustave Lanctôt, and "Makers" French editor Victor Morin, as well as leading English Canadian literary figures. Pierce wanted his work on French Canadian literature to show expertise, "proper perspective," and "critical standards." His hours of labour on *Outline* were greatly extended by the time it took him to read in French. Only his bicultural ideal kept him going: his diary laments how time-consuming his self-appointed task was proving to be.

In his *Outline*, Pierce set out to place "English and French authors side by side, link the constitutional development with the literary development of the Dominion, [and] divide the country's literature into a series of sections which simplifies reference" as well as provide an extensive bibliography.[21] As he irreverently put it to Morin, the book was designed for those who "have time only to lap and not to drink."[22] The volume made clear Pierce's espousal of French-English *bonne entente*, reproducing in the frontispiece both his letter of dedication (in French) to Camille Roy and Roy's generous reply, which commended Pierce's breadth and painstaking method.[23] Pierce's foreword called for a complete end to Canada's "unenviable distinction of being the only civilized country in the world where the study of its own literature was not made compulsory in the schools and colleges." He reminded his readers that his was the first attempt to present Canadian literature with French and English writers "side by side," given that "they must [in future] share equally in any attempt to trace the evolution of our national spirit." Pierce also asserted that more work needed to be done on aboriginal culture to establish the contribution of a non-writing people to Canadian culture, a topic on which he also gave a speech.[24]

Pierce's *Outline* is an ambitious compendium, blending biography, bibliography, and criticism. As one critic noted, Pierce clearly valorized moral, high-minded, romantic idealistic writing over any other, and the work "set the method and plan that were to follow in much Canadian criticism after his time."[25] His taste continued to be for the romantic, the nationalistic, and the pastoral over the realistic, the detached, and the urban. Accordingly, he praises the work of Carman, Roberts, Lampman, and Wilson MacDonald, and prefers the prose of Marjorie Pickthall to that of Mazo de la Roche, Martha Ostenso, or Frederick Philip Grove. He also adroitly avoids any close analysis of the current post–First World War literary scene with the rationale that it is "too close" for "detachment." Grove's 1925 novel *Settlers of the Marsh*, which brought Pierce so much controversy, is touched on briefly as "unmercifully candid and critical," "sombre" and "stark," although he does (rightly) insist that "few more powerful novels [have been] published in Canada."[26]

Certainly, Pierce's pioneering picture of French Canadian literature for anglophone audiences – his most significant achievement in the book – is shot through with stereotypes of French Canadians pervasive in English Canada in the 1920s: francophones are seen as rooted, tenacious, and inward-looking. Yet they are also, in Pierce's view, potentially amenable to a country of two peoples where they constitute a linguistic and cultural minority, since their culture has increasingly flourished in post-Conquest "peace and security": "When the fate of Canada was decided [in 1759] on the Plains of Abraham there was assured in the new *regime* a colony of seventy thousand souls in the province of Quebec, tenacious of their language and laws, loyal to their ancient faith, and proud of their community customs and the high traditions of their national lineage. Upon this, a century later, in the celebrated 'sixties' was founded the golden age of French Canadian literature."[27]

As an enthusiastic English Canadian nationalist, Pierce envisions for both literatures a future of synthesis and rapport, whatever the byways of each. His optimistic conclusion, triumphantly dubbed "The Genius of Canadian Literature," uses the touchstones of Irish and Russian literature (from the standpoint of history, two somewhat ironic choices to present in a vision of a harmonious culture) to foresee the emergence of a cohesive Canadian culture despite linguistic, religious, and geographical diversity and "an ever increasing multitude of new Canadians, each bringing his own intellectual and social inheritance."[28] Pierce asserts in his *Outline* that this destiny will be attained not through "foreign capital" or "foreign magazines" but rather "through the intensive study of our history, its romantic events and inspiring personalities, as well as an increasing devotion to our national literature. Here, for better or for worse, speaks the soul of Canada; here is the highway, broad and beautiful, which shall cross every divide, and create the enduring *entente cordiale.*"[29] Once again, a certain construct of literature and history constitutes a specific brand of national glue.

Although *Outline* had only a modest sale (it was never reprinted nor, interestingly, was it ever translated into French), the volume, like the "Makers" series, broke new ground in its bicultural approach, and was a *succès d'estime* for Pierce, particularly in Quebec. The textbook market for Canadian literary history was still minuscule, but Pierce's book was used as a text in Vernon Rhodenizer's course in Canadian literature at Acadia University in 1928. (Rhodenizer brought out his own handbook two years later).[30] Pierce's own copy of his book boasts a flattering inscription by Louis Carrier of Montreal's Mercury Press, praising Pierce as a leader of a new bicultural generation.[31]

After its launch in January 1928, the reviews of the book in Montreal's *La Presse* and Quebec's *Le Soleil* were warm.[32] While the influential *La Presse* acknowledged that Pierce's grasp of Quebec literature was not exhaustive, the review emphasized that his bicultural approach was invaluable to the development of the mutual familiarity essential for both cultures. For its part, Quebec City's *Le Soleil* somewhat gilded the lily by calling Pierce the most important and influential critic in English Canada ("le critique le plus important et le plus écoute du Canada anglais"), a verdict that would have astonished Pelham Edgar, Andrew Macphail, or Archibald MacMechan. Both the French reviews concluded, however, that the book added greatly to Pierce's prestige in anglophone and francophone cultures alike. MacMechan's largely positive review joked that Pierce "fatigues one by the hugeness of his output. Not being tired himself, he is the cause of tiredness in others."[33]

To read *An Outline of Canadian Literature* today is to admire Pierce's ambition, which, married to unstinting effort and deeply felt idealism, resulted in a pioneering bicultural treatment of Canadian culture. It is clear, too, that Pierce, perhaps looking to the textbook market, pulled his punches somewhat in his critical assessments of individual Canadian writers. If one compares the book to his 1932 paper on "English Canadian Literature, 1882–1932" for the Royal Society of Canada, it is obvious that he was much more critical of worthies like Roberts, Carman, and Mazo de la Roche than he revealed in 1927. In the Royal Society paper, for example, there are strictures about Gilbert Parker's "dull evangelism and trite homiletics"; Wilfrid Campbell's "fanatical imperialism" is criticized, as is Wilson MacDonald's "vindictiveness" and "chaotic" social poetry; Roberts's poetry is said to be often ruined by "the commonplace moral tag"; and even Bliss Carman is faulted for a "narrow" world view despite his "eclectic" mystical poetry. Such comments are absent from Pierce's *Outline* assessment. Nevertheless, in the 1932 paper, Pierce's nationalistic core concept of Canadian literature restates his *Outline* dictum that "the literature of a nation [is] one of its proudest assets, one of the most eloquent symbols of separate existence and conscious destiny."[34]

FRENCH CANADA may have welcomed Pierce's *Outline*, but Sam Fallis spurned it. He refused to let Ryerson publish either *Outline* (in the event published by Louis Carrier) or three manuscripts relating to William Kirby that Pierce had been toiling on with Kirby's grandson and namesake. With regard to his position at the House, Pierce felt even more beleaguered when Ernest Walker, the House's head of agency publishing, agreed with Fallis that it was uneconomic for the firm to take one thousand copies of the American Cokesbury Press edition of Pierce's collection of ministerial essays, *In Conference with the Best Minds*, written for the *Christian Guardian* in the early 1920s. Pierce had been forced to find an American publisher after Fallis vetoed that manuscript.[35] Clearly, the tension between Fallis and Pierce was invading the management ranks as each man wondered who had his colleagues' support. Intrigue and gossip were rife. Urged by Peter Sandiford, Pierce began to think of a sabbatical from Ryerson or of leaving publishing to teach university or for some other career. But where was a plum position to be found? And how could he cope with his deafness in it? How would he be able to support his family? And what would become of his vision for Ryerson Press? Pierce stayed at Ryerson, though he smarted under Fallis's barbs and fretted about money.

Pierce's diary in these years highlights his need to get out of debt, an urgency quickened by the fear of financial ruin "in the air" once the Great Depression began to be felt across the nation in late 1929. Even his New Year's resolution that year had been to get his head "out of the financial noose." Increasingly, he fixated on success in the textbook market for school readers as the only real route to both fame and fortune.

But several personal and professional crossroads lay ahead of Pierce before he could achieve any marked success with the readers. For one thing, the forging of a closer bond with his parents in the late 1920s was followed by loss.

Starting in the summer of 1925, what holidays Pierce could snatch were spent at the Whiskey Island cottage. For his aging parents, the brief summer interludes with Lorne, Edith, and the children were precious.

In the spring of 1926, moreover, Lorne Pierce was honoured in a way that meant much to his father. Pierce was elected to the Masonic office of Worshipful Master, head of Delta's Harmony Lodge No. 370 – his father's lodge and the one into which he himself had been initiated in 1911. Lorne knew that devotion to freemasonry was one of the principal bonds he and his father shared. As he put it, his father loved and liked to feel close to his children even after the education he paid for brought them "far beyond what he could understand or follow."[36] Over the next year, Lorne made several trips to Delta to preside at lodge functions, regretting only that his chronic fatigue blurred the "beautiful ... ritual" of Masonic ceremonies.[37]

Two years later, at the 1928 Queen's University Convocation, Pierce experienced what was – along with his ordination as a Methodist minister – one of the sweetest filial moments of his life as he received an honorary LLD. His parents saw him hooded and congratulated by such worthies as former Prime Minister Sir Robert Borden and Senator Andrew Haydon (the latter not yet tainted by the Beauharnois Scandal) at historic Grant Hall on a stifling May day. Pierce's diary noted boyishly: "Mother was much taken with my top coat and examined it approvingly in front of Senator Haydon." Later, his parents told him that the honour had at last confirmed for them the rightness and importance of his choice of a career in publishing.[38]

But Pierce's joy was soon clouded. A few weeks later, he urged his father, who was "not at all well," to come to Toronto to consult a cardiologist. His sister – whose own home life was made difficult by the severe bouts of depression suffered by her husband, Eldred Chester, now a New Westminster minister since 1926 – hurried east. On 10 June 1928 sixty-four-year-old Ed Pierce saw the Toronto doctor. The diagnosis – irremediable cardiac and arterial deterioration – was in that era a death sentence. In one of his most moving diary entries, Pierce described his father's brave response:

I shall never forget the sweet, brave look on Father's face, as he listened to his sentence. He smiled – a most beautiful smile. He knew only too well.
...
Mother had clasped him in her arms before he went down, and when he returned [home] she sought his face with her loving eyes for a look of hope. Father smiled bravely as I led him to the chesterfield ... [At bed time] I helped him undress and when I

had given him his "night tablet" he flung his arms around me, and gave me a kiss. His lips quivered as I stroked his hair.[39]

At Sunday dinner, Lorne asked his father to lead the family in prayer at his son's table for what would be the last time. Ed Pierce "thanked God for the privilege of meeting again, for the old loves, and asked that when we were all through we might together meet in the heavenly rest."

Later, the ever-generous father tried to get his son to accept $2,000 to lighten his financial load, but Lorne refused. Ed Pierce then reminisced with his son, telling him that the little tin till from Lorne and Sara's childhood "business" in the hardware store was still under its counter all these years later. Lorne recalled their leave-taking in his diary: "Once more I told [Father] of all I owed him ... He said that he should be satisfied but would like to live to see us all a little farther on. He was melting and then gave way to grief. I went over and stroked his hair and told him again that I realized more and more my debt to him and Mother and that all I was or would be was due to them. He said 'I know I have your love.' ... Then they were gone. We were very lonely." At lunch later that day, eight-year-old Beth and five-year-old Bruce each found a two-dollar bill folded in their napkins, a farewell token from their grandfather.[40]

That summer Ed Pierce rallied a little, as his son came to the Whiskey Island "camp" in July. Bittersweet moments culminated with an emotional family dinner on the verandah in Delta before Lorne, Edith, and the children returned to Toronto on 26 July. Lorne's own health took a turn for the worse – culminating on 26 September, when, in Halifax during a business trip to the east, he was hospitalized for "typhoid or appendicitis." He was not well enough to return to the office until 23 October, although he wrote five articles while bedridden.[41] To top it all, the Royal Society medal was again causing trouble: the firm he paid to produce the metal went bankrupt. Lorne wrote in his diary that "surely [this is] the last chapter in the commedia of accidents over the medal."[42]

At Christmas in Delta, Ed Pierce was obviously near his end. On 4 January, after an urgent call that his father had pneumonia, Lorne arrived home after midnight. Too late. The sight of his father's nurse on the platform told Lorne that his father was gone. Ed Pierce, calling gently for Lorne and Sara, had died courageously at about 10 o'clock that evening as his two children hurried home.

More grim news followed. As Lorne oversaw funeral arrangements the next day, a telegram arrived. Six-year-old Bruce was dangerously ill with pneumonia. Lorne returned to Toronto that night to find "all in

Edward and Harriet Pierce on the verandah of their imposing Delta home, bought after the sale of the Pierce hardware store in the early 1920s. Courtesy of Beth Pierce Robinson

tears." The day of his father's funeral was spent far from Delta, in mingled anxiety and grief. Lorne sat in the study with his diary at the hour of his father's funeral, as Edith briefly left their critically ill son's bedside to comfort him. In this difficult time, Lorne mused on his father's "goodness and love" and mentally traced the route of the funeral cortège, starting in the Pierce house and then moving through the streets of Delta toward the cemetery miles away at Forfar, where his father would "rest beside his parents again – their boy home from the long earthly pilgrimage."[43] During Lorne's brief interval in Delta, Harriet Pierce had tried to put her husband's dressing gown ("Father's mantle") on Lorne, but he "could not" bear it. Now he vowed to fulfill his father's legacy of "a good name, a passion for helpfulness, unfailing gentleness, thorough goodness" and to "be a son to mother in all ways, and make her days … happy." He solemnly resolved to be true to the legacy of his Delta home: "If my home gave me anything it was the legacy of character, utter trust in all-encircling and never-failing love, and that there was no greatness but goodness, no honour but service."[44]

A few days after the funeral, Lorne returned to Delta to help his mother with his father's estate. He found it so painful to pass his father's empty room that he used the back stairs to avoid it. But there was no chance to grieve. On 19 January another telegram from Edith recalled him to Toronto. Bruce's pneumonia-clouded lungs needed to be aspirated in hospital. Without a whimper, "poor wee Bruce" underwent the procedure and slowly began to recover, first in hospital and then at home with an (expensive) trained nurse in attendance.

AT THE OFFICE, Pierce's pre-eminent goal of success in the textbook field became more critical as book sales plummeted with the advent of the Depression. As he noted wearily in his diary in 1931, "all energy goes on publishing schemes and the *Readers*."[45] Three years earlier, Lorne Pierce had the idea that Ryerson and Macmillan should become allies in the school textbook trade, collaborating to produce and market a series of readers and English literature textbooks for Canadian elementary and high schools. It was in many ways a clever strategy (the Gage and Nelson publishing companies had a similar alliance). In April 1929 Hugh Eayrs of Macmillan agreed in principle with Pierce about the latter's proposal for a joint venture in this area.[46] As Eayrs quickly grasped, by combining their efforts, the two companies could bring into joint play their different strengths in a drive to win sales away from mutual rivals, chief among them the Gage-Nelson readers spearheaded by Gage's John Saul. Macmillan and Ryerson could thus share the risk, divide costs, and pool their contacts and allies among the various departments of education to win big in the textbook field. Pierce was to spearhead the editing of the texts, since he himself had been working on creating a new series of readers since 1926, a project with which he had already had some success.

Pierce recognized that Eayrs, a born salesman, was a valuable ally. An unparalleled schmoozer, Eayrs was able to dazzle any prospective customer, be it during a game of golf or a hand of bridge or poker, over a cocktail or a glass of Scotch – or by presenting a vision of Canadian culture at a bare-topped boardroom table in a provincial education office. As one colleague put it, Eayrs's "swift rise" in Canadian publishing "was attributable to great personal charm, boldness to the point of effrontery, publishing flair and a somewhat erratic brilliance."[47] Yet the stage was also set in this alliance for tension between Pierce and Eayrs: both had large egos, and their lifestyles were very different. Pierce, for example, did not drink while Eayrs was to grow increasingly bibulous, perhaps in response to the stressful life of a Canadian publisher. Pierce, for his part, was a workaholic who resented Eayrs's habit of spending several weeks in England each summer, far from immediate textbook worries. Pierce (and Edith) also fumed over the time taken up by Eayrs's high-powered Toronto social life in the smart world of golf and cocktail parties. In 1929, for example, Edith wrote sarcastically to Lorne about her difficulty in getting a message to Eayrs because the latter was out for dinner and golf during a business trip: "Some people take it easy."[48] Moreover, Hugh's smart and stylish wife, Dora Whitefield Eayrs, a sometime collaborator with Pierce, could not have been more different from Edith. Harriet Pierce might have called her "fast."[49]

Pierce had first come to know Eayrs soon after his own appointment to Ryerson, spending an hour tête-à-tête with him at a reception for Bliss Carman in November 1923, an encounter that prompted the first mention of Eayrs in Pierce's diary.[50] No wonder: one Eayrs pronouncement on Canadian culture the previous year sounded as if it could have been ghost written by Lorne Pierce: "The war did to Canadian letters what years of academic study might never have done. It taught us our place as a distinct national entity and so awoke national consciousness which found expression through a national literature."[51] By the date of his cocktail confabulation with Pierce, Eayrs was a legend in Toronto publishing circles, having become president of Macmillan of Canada, a branch of the prestigious English publishing firm, two years earlier, at twenty-seven.

Hugh Smithurst Eayrs, a bull-necked, Roman-nosed Yorkshireman, was born in Leeds in 1894, coming to Canada at eighteen to make his way as a freelance journalist. He had worked for Toronto newspapers, joining the magazines of publisher J.S. Maclean in early 1916 after impressing Maclean with some of his biographical sketches in the Toronto dailies. As Eayrs later put it with his characteristic humour, in working for Maclean, the versatile young journalist "bestrode (quite unlike any Colossus ...) three weekly and four monthly publications," including *Maclean's Magazine*, the *Canadian Stationer and Book Trade Journal*, and *Hardware and Metal* (the latter publication undoubtedly read by Ed Pierce).[52] A versatile wordsmith, Eayrs even wrote the serial "The Last Ally" for *Maclean's*, a potboiler later published by George Doran in New York and Hodder and Stoughton in London as *The Amateur Diplomat*. Snagging a job offer from Frank Wise, head of Macmillan of Canada, during a sales call to the Bond Street offices where the Canadian branch had been established since 1905, he joined Macmillan of Canada's educational department (especially important to that firm since its purchase of George Morang's educational publishing firm in 1912).

After a managerial crisis at Macmillan of Canada and the departure of Frank Wise, Eayrs was asked by Macmillan's head office to become Canadian president in February 1921. It was an inspired choice: Eayrs proved a dynamic publisher, and, like Pierce at Ryerson, he speedily established an impressive publication record in Canadian literature. He told the Canadian public in 1925, after four years at the Macmillan helm, that he wished to make his firm "more than an importing house for our [foreign] agencies" because Macmillan of Canada "should be definitely allied with the work of men and women within our borders …. As a result nearly one hundred [Canadian] books other than school books have been published in the last four and a half years [by me]. A very small number had been published [by Macmillan] in the previous sixteen years."[53]

Not being burdened with Methodist unease about the value of fiction, some of Eayrs's early literary publication landmarks included a brilliant English translation of Louis Hemon's novel *Maria Chapdelaine* (1921) by William Blake, Raymond Knister's novel *White Narcissus*, and the latter's landmark anthology *Canadian Short Stories* (1928).[54] Moreover, to Pierce's chagrin, E.J. Pratt had turned to Eayrs to publish *The Witches' Brew* in 1925 after Pierce had been compelled to decline it, and he had stuck with Macmillan thereafter.

Certainly, Pierce felt a sense of rivalry with Eayrs (and vice versa). Eayrs, although he at times liked to downplay the fact, to some extent followed in the ideological footsteps of Frank Wise, his predecessor as president at Macmillan of Canada and a cultural nationalist of the 1920s.[55] Paradoxically, one of the Canadian authors Eayrs encouraged was none other than Lorne Pierce. When Samuel Fallis refused to publish Pierce's edition of William Kirby's *Annals of Niagara* or his later biography of Kirby, Eayrs agreed to publish the works in 1927 and 1929 respectively. His publication of the Kirby biography was probably a testament to his desire to win over Pierce.[56] By the time *William Kirby: Portrait of a Tory Loyalist* appeared in December 1929, Pierce had been working on Kirby projects for five years and was heartily tired of both Kirby and his demanding grandson and namesake.[57]

The book, more of an annotated scrapbook and chronology of Kirby than a true biography, lacks gusto, and is larded with long quotations from Kirby's reminiscences, correspondence, and other material to "give a picture of the time." While Pierce states that Kirby's authorship of the novel *The Golden Dog* and *The Annals of Niagara* makes him a "modest master-builder" of Canada,[58] he paints an unattractive picture of a narrow, unreflective, intolerant, knee-jerk monarchist whose "ideas did not change in half a century." Pierce even offers the opinion that Kirby was not really a true "man of letters" but rather a "Victorian squire" who "happened to write two books that outlived him."[59] Moreover, when the first copy of the book came to Pierce from the Macmillan plant, he noted dismissively in his diary that it would be a "long time" before he read it.[60] Not many others read it either – sales were disappointing, according to Eayrs.[61]

Other publishers, such as Gundy of Oxford University Press and Montreal's Carrier, had also published books by Pierce in his drive to have a career as an author.[62] (In 1930 Carrier, impressed by Pierce's standing among Quebec intellectuals, even offered Pierce the presidency of his publishing firm at $7,500 a year – a position Pierce fortunately turned down, since Mercury Press would go bankrupt two years later.[63]) For his part, Eayrs tried on several occasions to tempt Pierce to leave Ryerson to work for Macmillan of Canada. E.J. Pratt told Pierce in June 1927, during one of Pierce's rare golf outings, that Eayrs "wanted him" for Macmillan.[64] Then, in August 1930, when Eayrs and Pierce formalized the Ryerson-Macmillan agreement for joint readers, Eayrs again offered Pierce a job, at the tempting salary of $5,000 a year, a $1,000 increase over what he was then earning. But Pierce again refused, as he did two years later, in August 1932, when Eayrs offered him a vice-presidency, clearly not wanting to be Eayrs's subordinate.

So the textbook venture in 1929 was cooperative – between Pierce and Eayrs, between Macmillan and Ryerson. But, as Pierce well knew, it was one thing to agree to produce and market a ground-breaking series of all-Canadian readers; it was quite another to put together such a series. Readers had to be designed for successive student reading levels, with selections organized for easy teaching, including introductions to each selection as well as background manuals. Moreover, Pierce wanted to emphasize Canadian material infused with cultural nationalism – but at the same time, the selections could not offend regional sensibilities.

Despite the challenges, Pierce was reflecting the spirit of the times in producing such readers. Historian Mary Vipond has described the groundswell of opinion in the Canada of the 1920s about the need to Canadianize textbooks.[65] In his memoirs, publisher Jack Gray of Macmillan recalled the atmosphere of change in Canadian pedagogical circles when he began to market the Ryerson-Macmillan readers in 1930: "Though many of the people I had to call on were experienced teachers and some were learned men we had one thing in common: curriculum revision, – not fact-changing a few textbooks, – but rethinking the whole purpose and object of the schools – was a new experience for us all, and produced in us a common excitement ... A more perceptive curriculum would release new energies and interests in children, lay the foundations of a new breed of men, [and] the air was full of a new jargon from Teachers' College, Columbia University."[66]

Pierce himself made a couple of hurried trips to New York City to research readers in the city's superb libraries, especially Columbia's. He also needed a collaborator for his primary school readers with the extensive classroom experience that he lacked, and to that end he turned to veteran Edmonton teacher Arthur Yates. His diary entry for November 1926 about his decision to work with Yates shows that money as well as idealism drove him: "Hope we make it go. I need some sideline like that to bring in the money. At present we seem to be living one hop ahead of the sheriff!"[67] The collaboration began during a western trip in early 1927. Pierce recorded in his diary that Yates had given him "splendid cooperation. Think they will go."[68] His letters to Edith conjured up "nice yellow money buds" and a fantasy of "regular hours, fine meals, good company" when the textbook ship came in.[69]

In the summer and early fall of 1927, Pierce and Yates produced an outline of the first reader in the series. Pierce then continued the work alone, putting in many days of frenzied "grind," with an eye to getting the readers accepted in British Columbia, the first target market.[70] In late July, with the family in Delta, he staged a three-day textbook blitz in the empty house, working eighteen hours a day and subsisting on cornflakes and milk, jokingly pronouncing it "the Franciscan life."[71] By August, he wrote that he had been "rushing" Book One of the readers for a week to get it into production by 1 September, juggling it with work on the next two volumes in the hope of capturing the British Columbia market for all three.[72]

However, Pierce was discouraged in November 1927 when Fallis turned down a world history textbook that he, Yates, and another collaborator were also working on. Fortunately, another punishing weeks-long round of the educational authorities in the west from Manitoba to British Columbia that winter renewed Pierce's hopes for the ultimate success of the readers.[73] But all the pressure on the over-stretched Pierce to produce material – by now, he had several readers (Books One to Seven) to revise and needed to create Books Ten and Eleven as well as get Book Eight to press – forced him to bed with heart problems in late March 1928. Furthermore, Edith had collapsed a few weeks earlier, and he had rushed home early. Beth and Bruce, aged eight and five, saw days when both parents were bedridden – not for the last time. A few months later, Beth presented her father with her first "book," a little bound sheaf entitled "Poems for little Children by Beth Pierce." To his diary, Pierce called the gift "my loveliest literary honour." Yet, for Beth Pierce in later life, the moment was bittersweet, embodying as it did a child's recognition that books were the one sure-fire way to capture her father's attention.[74]

During May and June 1928, Pierce snatched every moment possible from the office to work on the readers at Glengrove. He anxiously awaited consignments from Yates, material that he then revised, Canadianized, and supplemented with notes and other editorial material in a white heat. His oscillating relationship with Fallis temporarily took a turn for the better when, in the fall of 1928, the British Columbia government ordered 3,600 copies of Book One of the readers, after ordering only 600 the previous year.[75] Earlier that year, the western governments had urged Pierce to complete Books One to Six as quickly as possible.[76]

The promise of success demanded still greater effort. In late July and August 1928, Pierce met with Yates for a few days, and then worked on Book Two, "a much better book," and "mapped out" Book Three. His diary entries indicate that Yates was tiring of the grind.[77] But Pierce was heartened when New Brunswick placed a number of his texts on its "recommended" list for school books. In late August, he spent a weekend at E.J. Pratt's cottage in Bobcaygeon. Hugh Eayrs and Arthur Phelps each dropped in to visit. During this lakeside weekend, Pierce's idea for a collaboration with Eayrs on the readers was probably hatched. Pratt entertained his two friends with stories of his work-in-progress, the epic poem *The Roosevelt and the Antinoe*: Pierce must have sighed over the fish that got away and into Eayrs's net. But by the next summer, he and Eayrs were linked, at least as far as readers were concerned, in a roller-coaster alliance.

More pressure ("the worst") was not long in coming. In November 1928, as Pierce anxiously awaited a draft of material from Yates to be able to compile Book Three, the latter abruptly pulled out. Meanwhile, the response from educational authorities seemed positive, with one reader soon to be approved for Grade 9 in all British Columbia schools,[78] leading Pierce to chortle to his diary: "If [the whole series] goes we shall buy a city!"[79] At this time, as well as all his other publishing work, several textbook projects were simultaneously competing for Pierce's attention – a history of England approved in Manitoba, the readers, Wrong's history of Canada, and others. Each required adaptation for individual provinces, meetings, discussions, correspondence, production decisions, and the like. Then in April 1929 came the discouraging news that Book Three of the readers had not been approved in British Columbia after all – more work was therefore needed.

By late 1928, another demanding phase – selling the series in tandem with Hugh Eayrs – loomed, even as Ed Pierce lay dying in Delta and Lorne's Glengrove household longed for attention. Edith, however, was supportive of Lorne's textbook initiative to the limits of her strength. She, too, was convinced that at the end of the drudgery lay both financial security and a saner pace of life. That will-o'-the-wisp was to tantalize the couple for the next six years. Meanwhile, Pierce, ill with angina in May 1929, nevertheless corrected textbook proofs in his sickbed.[80]

In the wake of his father's death, Pierce was even more anxious to find a way, as put it to Edith, "to begin to live" by getting "my head out of the noose ... not only in the matter of unsensible loads of writing, but also in the matter of money." He was also conscious that ambition had tarnished his idealism, and undermined his relationship with Edith. He assured Edith that they could "turn over a new leaf":

> I shall try to remember the need for idealism, and I see it ought
> to have a place, if [it is] not in our home, where under heaven
> ought one to look for it? I hope you get your teeth fixed, and your
> wardrobe replenished, whereupon and whereat we will saunter out
> more frequently to amusements and other things. We have [led]
> a silly life in a way, and we must mend. No married life can go on
> as we were going, without hitting the reefs. I do not mean that we
> were unhappy. I loved only one woman in my life, kissed only one
> sweetheart, and I feel the same way still; but we were getting thin
> as a home and that must stop.

Pierce too wistfully dreamed of an idyll of togetherness despite his relentless ambition: "We ought to plan to be alone together more, leave the children an evening or afternoon in good care. They will appreciate you more, and we will find the time to love – moderately! Oh, this business of living is a real one, especially when one has the ambition I have. It is like Ibsen's Brand 'all or nought.' But we are intelligent people, and we must learn to live more wisely. The children must have that legacy, more by far than a mere name."[81] Brave and wise words, perhaps, but well-nigh impossible for Pierce to fulfill, given his personality. Tellingly, moreover, the reference to Ibsen and the "business of living" in fact echoes the phrasing of his analysis of Canadian literature in his conclusion to *An Outline of Canadian Literature* (1927).[82] Even Pierce's love letters now echoed his professional life.

By early 1930, Pierce was in fact at the stage of complete breakdown from overwork after a "hectic and silly pace" that included supplying material for a section on Canada in Hector Bolitho's empire poetry anthology project, as well as producing three books on Kirby and numerous articles – including pieces on Pratt, Bishop John Strachan, and Solomon Jones, a Loyalist physician and settler in the Brockville area. He called his commitments "the hangman's neck-tie" but, paradoxically, the hangman was himself.[83] His father's death, coupled with the sudden death in June 1929 of Bliss Carman (whose biography he had resolved to write), seemingly accelerated his desire to excel.

Pauses for reflection were rare. On 6 January 1930 Pierce and Eayrs formally agreed to their reader collaboration, and the rate of Pierce's royalty for editing the readers was set. Pierce was to discover to his sorrow, however, that signing pacts in the morally perilous textbook game was a Faustian bargain. The old proverb (one undoubtedly heard in the Delta house in Pierce's childhood) runs: "Be careful what you wish for. You might get it." By the mid-1930s, Pierce would, fairly or not, come to cast Eayrs as a sort of Mephistopheles, one who whispered that Pierce had been tempted, and had fallen.

14

Cross-Canada Success for the Ryerson-Macmillan Readers

In the Shadow of Copyright, 1930–1936

[E]ducation must conserve, and somehow perpetuate enhanced, the moral, spiritual, and intellectual achievements of the race as represented by the national community."
Lorne Pierce on education, 1933[1]

Discretion prevented one from asking who had done the offending editorial work [in the readers] and no explanation was ever offered. Lorne Pierce said, almost too often, that no one would ever hear the truth from him.
John Gray of Macmillan on the Canada Books of Prose and Verse 1935 *plagiarism crisis*[2]

Two weeks after Lorne Pierce and Hugh Eayrs signed the Ryerson-Macmillan collaboration agreement, Pierce's health collapsed. On Valentine's Day 1930, his physician prescribed prolonged "forced rest." At the news, Vancouver poet Ernest Fewster, like many in Pierce's circle, questioned his relentless pace: "Why do you do it? What the devil – in a Methodist sense – do you mean by it? ... Are you so tired of us that you want to get away from us?"[3] With a $500 cheque from the House to cover expenses, a cheque accompanied by a sympathetic letter from Samuel Fallis,[4] Pierce, along with his wife, went to Virginia to recuperate.

He did not return to Toronto until the end of March. In the course of his convalescence, he toured Jamestown, Richmond, Williamsburg, and Washington, and called on Bliss Carman's muse, Mary Perry King, in Connecticut en route home to discuss his planned biography of the poet. Edith had earlier returned to Glengrove Avenue and the children. Although she prized the "second honeymoon," she also told her husband: "I am not looking for [your] early complete recovery. You have worked too hard for too long."[5]

Once he was back in harness on 7 April,[6] the settling-in of the Great Depression after the stock-market crash of October 1929 gave greater urgency to textbook initiatives. Trade book sales were falling precipitously with no immediate prospect of recovery. The book steward's annual reports to the Board of Publication of the United Church chronicle the dismal figures for both trade books and textbooks in the early Depression. In the spring of 1929, before its onset, the returns of the book departments of the House were positive, with profits of $10,112.03, up from $5,120.23 the year before (the figure encompasses both Walker's agency department and Pierce's trade division). Moreover, the improvement in profits was partly the result of Pierce's textbook initiatives, particularly the elementary readers (then called the Golden Treasury Readers), Wrong's *History of Canada*, and the Canadian History Readers. His Treasury Readers were beginning to find acceptance, with British Columbia being a case in point, and the History Readers were doing well in Ontario and the Maritimes.

The figures for the House's book departments for 1930, by contrast, were abysmal. The book departments lost $311.50 that year. The figures were worse in 1931: losses were then $1,094.97. Other publishers were doing no better. For example, Ottawa's ambitious, upstart Graphic Press in Ottawa went bankrupt. Macmillan drastically curtailed its domestic publication list, as did McClelland and Stewart, which fought to pay off heavy debts.[7] Other Toronto firms were similarly hard hit.

Clearly, success for the Ryerson-Macmillan textbook initiative was vital for both publishers. The pressure on Pierce was increased by the fact that the House lost some of its traditional agency agreements during the early 1930s – most of the lucrative Harrap line, for example.[8] Furthermore, by the early 1930s, given the proven unprofitability of ventures like the Makers of Canadian Literature series and the Ryerson Chapbooks, Pierce knew he was going to have to cross-subsidize if he wished to continue to publish belles lettres.

Textbook revenues would therefore have to become Ryerson's cash cow.[9] True, education budgets were being slashed as government tax revenues declined, but a certain level of textbook purchases was always necessary because of attrition and obsolescence in textbook supplies. Moreover, if Pierce and Eayrs could win approval in principle for new purchases, to be made as soon as the economy improved, their own business prospects would be brighter.

Nationalism, not just the bottom line, infused the project: the Ryerson-Macmillan readers featured a nationalistic logo on spine and title page with a central maple leaf and stars (the number of the latter indicating the volume number in the series) designed by Thoreau MacDonald. The elementary volumes for grades 1 to 6 were christened the Canadian Treasury Readers while the high school volumes for grades 7 to 12 were called the Canada Books of Prose and Verse.[10] These texts could and would be revised somewhat for the requirements of different provinces, if necessary – an essential if nerve-wracking and time-consuming practice known in the textbook trade as "field editing." For instance, the readers were even sold to pre-Confederation Newfoundland schools, with "Canada" removed from the title to suit the needs of the British colony.[11]

Nevertheless, the prospectus for the Canadian Treasury Readers, written by Pierce in the summer of 1931,[12] beat the nationalist drum. Educators were told that the texts were "edited by outstanding Canadian Educationists, to meet Canadian needs and reflect national ideals" and "designed, printed and bound by Canadian craftsman."[13] Pierce had even contracted with the art printing firm of Rous and Mann to include in each reader "a full-colour reproduction of a significant work of art representative of the spirit of our country," which he pronounced "a new feature in educational books."[14] He knew that interest in such patriotic initiatives was real. Three years earlier, for example, an article in the *Manitoba Teacher* praised his "well-planned and illustrated" readers and declared: "It is satisfactory to note that Canadian authors are well represented."[15]

To succeed, Pierce, Eayrs, and their respective staffs faced extensive sales and lobbying work in the field in the early 1930s. In 1930 Macmillan had hired the intelligent and urbane John Gray, a skilled educational representative who would later become president of Macmillan of Canada. Similarly, Pierce had that year hired Gilbert C. "Pat" Paterson, who held an MA degree and had taught at Regina Collegiate and edited a magazine published by the Saskatchewan Teachers' Alliance, all of which had given him useful contacts in western educational circles.[16] Like Gray, Paterson put in a killing pace in the field. Pierce's March 1931 diary entry about Paterson's reports from western educational centres suggests how venal the textbook game continued to be: "Word from Paterson that Prose and Verse III, recommended by Sask[atchewan] Com[mittee] for authorization, was killed upon overtures from someone to Dr. Huff on the basis that it was Tory in its outlook!"[17]

Pierce further beefed up his educational sales force, taking on Owen Sheffield in the fall of 1931 and Victor (Val) Seary, MA, a well-connected former Nova Scotia Department of Education official from Halifax, and Harry Berry, BA, in April 1934.[18] Seary and Berry would become key Ryerson educational employees. They were later joined by Campbell (Cam) Hughes, from the late 1940s Pierce's stalwart educational sales manager.

In the early 1930s, however, Pierce and Eayrs themselves were very much "hands on" in fighting for authorization of their texts by provincial departments of education. Like their rivals, they appointed advisory committees and made consultants of teachers and other education officials in the various provinces to promote their texts and to help tailor readers to the requirements of particular provinces.[19] As John Gray later commented, these widespread practices "often trembled on the brink of corruption," given that teachers and officials stood to profit in income or prestige from decisions that they influenced directly or indirectly.[20] Pierce and Eayrs made many major sales blitzes of western Canada together – gruelling multi-stop journeys by train to all the region's major centres – for example, in October 1931, March, August, and November 1932, and August 1933. Moreover, Pierce carried the draining double load of both editing and promoting the readers.

In many ways, in committee appearances and in appointments with educational and political officials, the two were a splendid team. However, Pierce and Eayrs also got on each other's nerves. Each secretly believed himself to be the superior bookman who had contributed most to the success of the joint venture without sufficient reward. Another complication was the involvement in the series of Hugh Eayrs's wife, Dora. She was a co-editor of some of the texts (mostly for the selection of illustrations, although there is little evidence that she and Pierce actively collaborated[21]), accompanying Eayrs and Pierce on some of their sales journeys. Dora and Hugh Eayrs had a tumultuous relationship, one that ultimately caused them to split up before Hugh Eayrs's death in 1940. During their troika journeys across Canada, Lorne wrote to Edith that the couple quarrelled and drank to excess – at least to his mind (he remained a committed teetotaller).[22] On the other hand, Hugh Eayrs must have been irritated by Pierce's ministerial scrutiny on these marathons.

By the early 1930s, Pierce had taken to reading murder mysteries for relaxation[23] – a lowly genre of literature that Ryerson Press did not publish – whenever he could snatch the time on the long train journeys. The trio's first trip, in October 1931, was buoyed by promising authorizations and new liaisons with employees in the western fields.[24] However, Pierce needed all his eloquence to make credible his role as textbook creator: his brief classroom experience made educators question his qualifications, as John Gray's memoirs make clear.[25]

Family and economic concerns also weighed on Pierce at this time. During the 1931 trip, he spent time at a Saskatchewan hospital with his sister, whose husband was now the minister of a Saskatoon church, as she received radiation after breast-cancer surgery. Once back in Toronto, Pierce was glad to be able to send her $50 out of his textbook royalties that year, as well as open a $485 savings account ("our first real nest egg") with Edith at the Canada Permanent Trust Company.[26] The Depression even affected Pierce's royalty payments, however. Eayrs postponed Macmillan's share of the royalty payment due in December 1931, since his firm was "hard up." Pierce, though "frightfully pinched," agreed.[27]

FEBRUARY 1932 brought a grim interregnum in Pierce's textbook initiatives. Samuel Fallis had returned in January from a holiday in Calgary "sick to death."[28] As Fallis lay "sinking fast," Pierce declared himself disgusted at the jockeying within the House among potential successors and kingmakers, chief among them being Donald Solandt, the associate book steward. Pierce himself refused the book stewardship, but he did use his simultaneous refusal of an offer from Eayrs to become Macmillan's vice-president at a salary of "$7500 plus extras" ("our house will do the right thing yet if given a chance") to win a graduated raise in salary from Ryerson – from $5,000 annually in 1932 to $6,000 by 1934.[29]

Fallis died at home, aged sixty-six, on 7 February. His funeral took place on a cold and wet Ash Wednesday.[30] From the House, only Pierce, Solandt, chief accountant Fred Ellins, and a few other department heads attended the private funeral at Fallis's home, rubbing shoulders with the likes of Prime Minister R.B. Bennett, who had been a Calgary congregant of Fallis. The public service at Howard Park United Church was almost feudal, as Pierce recorded: "400 employees in file to have last view of the Chief, 50 or 60 ministers carrying out the floral tokens. Dr. Solandt and … I to the cemetery. Bleak and grey."

The weather at Fallis's interment foreshadowed the climate of Pierce's relations with Donald Solandt. Once Pierce refused the post, Solandt was designated book steward by the Board of Publication in March 1932 until the appointment could be confirmed at the next General Council of the United Church. Unfortunately, there was little rapport between Pierce and a man he found cold and Machiavellian, despite their shared alma mater. Solandt had earned three Queen's degrees, including an MA in 1906, before filling Presbyterian pulpits in Kingston and Winnipeg, and at church union in 1925 he had been brought into the United Church Publishing House as assistant book steward from his former post as business manager of Presbyterian publications.[31] After Fallis's death, things initially seemed auspicious when Solandt, a stringent money man (a skill certainly needed at the House), discovered an irregular account of $50,000 with E.J. Moore's name on it.[32] Moore, Pierce's old detractor, speedily left the House under a cloud. But there was little peace for Pierce during Solandt's brief tenure.

Meanwhile, Pierce and Eayrs were overjoyed when they won approval to proceed with the readers during presentations to each of the four western provinces in March 1932.[33] By then, they had sold some 11,000 copies of Books One and Two of the readers in British Columbia, as well as the right to submit the whole series for western authorization in September 1932: a punishing deadline, even if it discomfited their rivals (chiefly Gage-Nelson). Pierce noted ruefully: "From now till Fall I shall have to keep at it every hour." With his now-habitual wishful thinking, he immediately added: "If we win, I shall turn a new leaf, and begin to live."[34]

By April 1932, Pierce had the first nine readers done, the art work chosen, and the volumes almost "ready for the machines," as he usually referred to the printing process.[35] His labours were lightened by news from Monseigneur Roy, rector of Laval, offering him an honorary doctorate, certainly an unusual accolade for an anglophone Protestant intellectual in the 1930s and a tribute to Pierce's devotion to bonne entente.[36] Pierce soon set off on another hurried trip to New York City to ferret out reader material in the city's libraries. By July 1932, he had rented "Cory Cliff," a small cottage on the Scarborough Bluffs, as a weekend place to "hide out" with Edith and do textbook editing. Pierce was now toiling ("the strain has been frightful") on workbooks and teachers' manuals for the readers.[37] But he was increasingly "disgusted" about what he viewed as "no help of any account" from Macmillan. He muttered about Eayrs's golf and his annual summer trips to England, forgetting that Eayrs had to have a solid rapport with his English parent firm.[38]

On 7 September 1932, a few weeks after Pierce's forty-second birthday, he presented the completed set of the Canada Books of Prose and Verse to House and Macmillan officials. Dr S.D. Chown, the grand old man of Methodism and now chairman of the General Council of the United Church, and William Cope, head of the Production Department (who had the nerve-wracking job of getting the set printed on time), presented the first set of texts to Donald Solandt, the new book steward. Edith sent Lorne flowers for the occasion. She, like other family members of House employees, was invited to the Queen Street offices to view the books after the initial presentation. On this red letter day, the ceremony had been, Pierce noted in his diary, a "very fine, friendly 20 minutes." The readers were displayed on a flower-bedecked table. Eayrs pronounced the volumes "beautiful" and "streets ahead in literary content of anything that has been done."[39]

There was a brief honeymoon with Solandt as Pierce dutifully lobbied for Solandt's confirmation at the General Council meetings that September. Pierce cancelled his planned late September holiday as he oversaw work on the readers, especially for approval in Nova Scotia, and he and Eayrs planned another western initiative for November 1932. All the while, Pierce felt continuing financial pressure. Driving E.J. Pratt home one 1932 fall day, Pierce was surprised to find that the poet and Victoria College English professor, like himself an ordained Methodist minister, now had "a fine new home." After six years on Glengrove, Pierce, in concert with Edith, was also planning to trade up. But, he mused to his diary, he wanted to wait "to see the actual funds before I actually take the step."[40] He also fretted that his car had become a "rattle-trap," so much so that he chose to travel to Delta that fall by train.[41]

Fortunately for his prospects, the news was good in the west and in Nova Scotia, with the Ryerson–Macmillan series winning major approvals for several volumes in both places. But when problems cropped up in Nova Scotia, Pierce was so exhausted that he had to take to his bed for a week before Christmas 1932.[42] That December, however, the popular magazine *Saturday Night* did a profile of him ("A Lover of Books") in its well-known "Among Those Present" column of profiles of prominent Canadians. Columnist Jean Graham praised the "slender, dark and graceful" Pierce for his intellect and his solid Delta origins. She also rhapsodized over "his bubbling Hibernian blood" and passion for

French-English entente as well as his "discerning" and "kindly" "book of beauty" about Marjorie Pickthall, which had won "Dominion-wide praise." (Graham's enthusiasm was real: she and Pickthall were friends and fellow cross-dressers, part of a circle of women who liked to wear military garb, a predilection not featured in Pierce's Pickthall book.[43])

Happily for Pierce, Graham's piece plugged the Ryerson-Macmillan series as "better and brighter" than the usual depressing textbook fare. She assured *Saturday Night* readers that Pierce and "his assistant, Miss Dora Whitefield" (Mrs Hugh Eayrs) were emphasizing a "taste for good literature" and "a liberal allowance to Canadian authors" in their "idealistic" poetry and prose selections. The column ended with a rave for the project aimed at a national audience: "Everything is done to stimulate a love for the best literature in the pupil ... The editor has shown the tact and wisdom which must be the attributes of him who could lead the rising generation in paths of peace and progress. Dr. Pierce has proved himself a patriot, indeed ... countless Canadians will thank him for his work."[44]

As 1933 began, Pierce started to score more significant educational publishing successes, which included textbooks published by Ryerson alone. For example, in January he won Ontario approval for fourteen Ryerson vocational textbooks and two spellers, totalling 100,000 copies a year. (Ryerson had earlier published a very successful senior accounting textbook.[45]) His reputation in educational publishing was also growing. In early 1933 both the Manitoba Educational Association and the University of New Brunswick asked Pierce to make major addresses (the latter conferring an honorary LLD).[46]

However, some of the victors were beginning to squabble over the spoils. Pierce noted in February 1933 that Hugh Eayrs and Donald Solandt were "at war."[47] Similarly, during a month-long textbook trip out west the previous November, Pierce and Eayrs had clashed over sales strategy as soon as they set off: Lorne told Edith that an exhausted and demanding Eayrs was "aggravating and petulant."[48] In the early 1920s, when he was still a book trade ingenue, Pierce once observed that in the textbook game Toronto publishers regarded each other "with suspicion and even malice."[49] He was steeped in such venom now.

NEVERTHELESS, Lorne Pierce was publicly setting out his educational policy in a way designed to attract and inspire Canadian educators. His address to the Manitoba Educational Association that May, which he reprinted as a brochure, is the clearest expression of the idealistic, nationalistic tenor of the readers, implicitly highlighting the contrast between the idealism that permeated the texts and the pragmatism needed to successfully market them. The speech makes it clear how much Pierce owed to progressive theorists like Johann Pestalozzi and Cyril Norwood, then headmaster of Harrow (he quotes Norwood extensively), in rejecting a system of education too rigidly conceived and too heedless of the needs of the individual child. Pierce also emphasized the need for spirituality and idealism in education as a bulwark of democracy, citing Ruskin's dictum that all education has its roots in religion to buttress his own contention that the "goal of learning" is "goodness" and "wisdom."[50] Naturally for the era, given the power of fascism in western countries such as Italy and Germany by 1933, Pierce stressed the need to use education to safeguard democracy, which he defined as "the progress of a people working toward social and spiritual ends."[51] Like the American educational theorist John Dewey, who in fact was teaching at Columbia when Pierce was a student in New York City, Pierce believed that the curriculum could be used to shape citizenship and to train students culturally as well as vocationally.[52] He conceived his readers in the spirit of Dewey's belief that schools should concern themselves with the "maintenance of proper social order and the securing of the right social growth."[53]

Many threads in Pierce's intellectual development came together in his intellectual framing of the readers. While Pierce's references to Ruskin and to the primacy of idealism showed the influences of the values of his mother and of Methodism upon his educational thinking, his stress on the essential, progressive unity of all existence showed his debt to theosophical and Masonic ideals. He assured educators of "the solidarity of mankind," given that "the essential unity of all thought and experience is an overwhelming objective fact."[54]

What is striking as well in Pierce's educational philosophy is his insistence on the pre-eminence of literature and the humanities as a curricular lynchpin – in contrast to the early-twentieth-century vogue for the social-sciences approach in education. Pierce was adamant that "history and the social sciences are futile unless ... they appraise the ideals and ideas which have motivated men."[55] Near the end of his career, he assured an education professor that the emphasis in his textbooks, so dominant in the field for thirty years, had never been primarily that of social science: "The ... obstinately-held idea [in the textbooks] was, that this was a literary series, and that prose and verse should have distinction. We have found it difficult to maintain this standard always, but we have definitely avoided the reader in social science. We think we should continue to use the topical divisions, that they should represent fundamental interests and needs, and that there should be prose and verse selections of definite literary merit, graded as precisely as possible, and placed in ascending order of difficulty if possible."[56]

Moreover, in Pierce's view, education, rooted in the spiritual, was essential to the foundation of a national character. Throughout his textbook work, he stressed that the "national character, that vital and ideal grace which distinguishes [a nation] from other countries, is the mind and spirit of its school masters." Pierce identified the components of Canadian nationalist ideology in education as various yet interwoven: he pointed to the "streams of French influence, the Loyalist tradition in the Maritimes and the democratic ideal fostered by Egerton Ryerson."[57] In a similar fashion, he had earlier, in a 1929 essay calling for English-French entente, pointed to Quebec as a commendable bulwark of spiritual conservatism and strong national identity which the nation's educators, among others, should be conscious of:

> We have much to learn from the French [in Canada]. One thing
> we shall come to understand is, that learning and morals must go
> hand in hand. If the history of the last twenty-five years means
> anything, it repudiates and condemns the pride of knowledge
> without good taste, of scientific inquiry without reverence, of
> theories about liberty without inhibitions of religious faith, and
> hungry ambition with[out] public ethical standards and private
> morals ... one thing is certain: if our teachers and preachers,
> artists and authors, our people generally west of the Ottawa
> [River], and south of Gaspe, can sympathetically appreciate the
> amenities of the hearth, the traditions and customs of the people,
> the passionate love of the altar, in short, the urbanity, strength
> and character of the French people, education, literature, art and
> business will take on a new dignity throughout the land.[58]

Pierce stressed that the "inchoate" state of the nation made the use of textbooks as national glue vital: the counterbalance to "undigested" foreign immigration lay in a "national" education and in the materials used for it.[59] In advocating education as a tool of national cohesion, Pierce avoided the lurid nativistic excesses that some of his white, native-born, middle-class peers embraced in the Canada of the 1920s, through, for example, membership in the xenophobic Native Sons of Canada, founded in 1921. But he firmly believed that immigrants needed to be acculturated to the Canada of Egerton Ryerson, Principal Grant, and the Confederation poets, among others. Canadians therefore needed to study Canadian history and literature to foster a "vivid and intelligent national self-consciousness" as "an act of self-preservation."[60] Clearly, Pierce sought to inculcate a nationalism based on traditional values, one that would introduce new groups in society to a construct of the country based on the old Loyalist, French, and British streams, suitably enlightened. (Pierce was no enthusiastic lover of England – his Irish heritage saw to that – but his collaborator, Hugh Eayrs, was Yorkshire-born and, like many English Canadians, more British-oriented.[61])

To play with Pierce's own metaphor, the nationalist ideal presented in his readers was calculated to "digest" difference and acculturate the children of newcomers to a white, middle-class, Christian construct of Canada framed in terms of French-English entente and British forms of government. Ethnic, class, and gender differences are subsumed in an homogenizing project designed to produce "a strong, intelligent and united nation" of a very particular ideological and social type.[62] Accordingly, all through these years, Pierce asserted that the curriculum of the "little red school house" would create "self-conscious Canadians" enriched by their "native social inheritance," which would be the "cement to bind us [as] a people to one another."[63] In 1943, describing the record of the Ryerson Press, Pierce pointed to textbooks as one major achievement, for they were the means by which the "youth of Canada had been provided with the best possible character-forming, cultural and educational material in an attractive way."[64]

An examination of Pierce's textbooks from their inception in the mid-1920s through the early 1960s bears out their didactic role in presenting a vision of Canada that emphasized common values, the beauties of nature as seen by the Group of Seven and their contemporaries, and the sense of community and pioneer spirit among its people as conceptualized by writers from the Confederation poets to Pierce's nationalist friend and contemporary B.K. Sandwell.[65] The Canada Books were unprecedented constructs of literary and social indoctrination specifically designed for young Canadians. For example, Grade 8 students who studied Book Two of the Canada Books of Prose and Verse were exposed not simply to

Shakespeare and Longfellow, long standard high school fare, but to works by fifteen Canadian writers, including Bliss Carman's "Songs of the Sea Children" and Stephen Leacock's "My Financial Career." The final section of the reader was called "The Land We Love." French Canada was presented through selections from Ringuet's novel *Thirty Acres* in translation, and a poem about the glories of Quebec City was followed by a request that students name other spots reminiscent of "glorious deeds in developing Canada."[66] Canadian authors were highlighted in the table of contents or in an index in each text, facilitating special attention to the generous selections of Canadian material in the classroom.

By contrast, in 1930, the approved Gage series of readers, chief rivals to the new Ryerson-Macmillan series (the latter would in many cases supplant them in the west and much of Canada over the next five years), was – as Hugh Eayrs scornfully observed to Pierce – "obviously Canadianized editions of American books. In fact, I imagine they are hardly Canadianized but simply manufactured in this country."[67] Earlier texts in Canadian schools had usually been equally devoid of national sentiment. Historian James Shotwell recalled in his memoirs, for example, that as a late-nineteenth-century schoolboy in the southern Ontario town of Strathroy, his school readers were adapted from the American McGuffey Readers. The only Canadian history text he encountered in either elementary or high school was "a little paper-bound pamphlet of thirty or forty pages" which dealt chiefly with the War of 1812. Even this feeble Canadian content was not introduced until 1887, and then only as the lowly appendix to a manual of English history, the main text.[68]

Shotwell's experience of the school curriculum before the Great War was typical. Canadian historian Arthur Lower, remembering his time as a schoolboy in Barrie, north of Toronto, commented sarcastically that his textbooks were so saturated in British imperialism that "the wonder is that the tender plant of Canadian nationalism survived at all."[69] Pierce's own school experience in eastern Ontario at the turn of the century had been similarly bleak in nationalist terms, from elementary school to university. No wonder Pierce had put a chapter called "The Field of School Texts" in his 1932 essay *Unexplored Fields of Canadian Literature*, calling for well-written texts with strong Canadian content.[70]

Similarly, given the nationalist educational vacuum that Pierce perceived, Book Three of the Canada Books of Prose and Verse, for example, designed for Grade 9 students, radiated a vision of Canadian citizenship. The concluding section of the reader was dubbed "Our Heritage" and included praise of British institutions as they had evolved in Canada. Among the twelve selections was an excerpt from George Monro Grant urging French-English amity and acceptance of new immigrants. The textbook described Grant himself as one who "never wearied of urging the cause of unity in Canada, or of proclaiming the great future awaiting Canada as a nation." Questions appended to this section (formulated by Pierce) called on teachers and students to think about the chief legacy of France to Canada, and about how new Canadians could contribute to Canada. This bias was reinforced by other selections such as W.S. Wallace on "The Canadian National Spirit" and, in the 1948 edition of the reader, by a Second World War essay on Royal Canadian Air Force (RCAF) war graves in England meant to impress on students the idea that "a nationhood bought at such a price will not be little noted or soon forgotten."[71] Clearly, Pierce's Ryerson-Macmillan textbooks embodied a very specific construct of Canada, a myth of nation with definite ideological, class, ethnic, and racial biases.

IN 1933, HOWEVER, the textbooks were by no means all successfully placed in schools Canada-wide. Plagued by health problems, Pierce delivered his University of New Brunswick doctoral address on Fredericton poets Charles G.D. Roberts, Bliss Carman, and Francis Sherman with a severe respiratory infection.[72] Edith and the children spent two months in Delta in July and August, but most of Pierce's summer was taken up in revising the Canadian Treasury Readers and in a trip west with Eayrs in early August.

In December 1933, after yet another joint "hunting trip" to the west,[73] came "great news." The western provinces awarded 75 per cent of their projected allocation for readers to Ryerson-Macmillan. In their moment of triumph, in a gesture that suggested the importance of their alliance (and its potential for strife), Eayrs and Pierce "marked the winning of the race" by exchanging gold rings that Christmas, each "suitably inscribed." The rings were as different as the two men: Pierce chose a lapis lazuli ring, and Eayrs a signet one.[74] Meanwhile, Book Steward Donald Solandt, ringless, fretted that overall House sales were down 12 per cent in the nadir of the Depression.[75] (Probably owing to the costs of promotion and production, Pierce's Educational Department was not showing a profit, having posted a loss of $5,631.07 at the end of February 1933.[76]) Pierce, by contrast, confidently told his diary that "expenses are down, and prospects are away up ... we must reorganize and ... get more brains into the business."[77] Over the next three years, the textbook business brought increasing sales and royalties but also increasing acrimony between Eayrs and Pierce, and bitter clashes between Pierce and Solandt. It also brought a personal crisis for Pierce over the editing of the readers. But at first, all seemed promising. Based on textbook sales, Betsey Jefferys, daughter of Pierce's friend artist C.W. Jefferys, was hired full-time as secretary to assist Blanche Hume in October 1934.[78]

Though the textbook business was on the upswing and the titles numerous, trade books were still doing badly. Retail books had lost over $8,404.19 in the fiscal year ending on 28 February 1933, and the losses were almost as bad – $6,243.68 – at the end of February 1934. Pierce noted wearily in his diary in January 1934 that he was "putting nothing on the General list until our sales force improves."[79] Even then, retail books would lose $6,952.75 over the next fiscal year.[80] But organizational conflict, rather than teamwork focused on solutions, was again the norm at the House. Donald Solandt was becoming increasingly hostile toward Pierce, even promoting Pierce's subordinate Elsinore Haultain, Ryerson's advertising manager since 1933, without Pierce's knowledge. Pierce refused to go to management meetings with Haultain in attendance to protest the move.

Pierce's bitter relations with Solandt culminated in his being called on the carpet by the new book steward in February 1934. Head in hands, Solandt behaved, according to a seething Pierce, "with all the finesse of a pachyderm," chastising Pierce's "high hat" conduct and decisions. Pierce listened indignantly, his eyes closed and his hearing aid set out between them. By his own account, he replied to the denunciation in a voice barely above a whisper, without attacking Solandt, even calling in employees to refute accusations about his own conduct. He concluded by declaring that, with Edith's consent, he was hereby submitting his resignation letter, which he laid down before the startled book steward. Solandt, realizing that Pierce was the last employee the House could afford to lose at this time, became for the moment more conciliatory.[81]

An unpleasant scene, and one that had its effect on morale at the House. Another manager, also unhappy with Solandt's policies, told Pierce to his discomfiture that he had won "a victory for all the managers." Why such conflict between Solandt and Pierce? In their confrontation, Pierce had pointed out to Solandt that he had been a House manager for fourteen years and Solandt for "only eighteen months and that I would run my department in my own way."[82] Certainly, Pierce needed autonomy to perform effectively. But he failed to recognize (as with Fallis) that, with the increasing success of the readers, he increasingly put the book steward in the shade. In 1934 Pierce confided to his diary that he expected to earn over $4,000 in royalty income, a handsome addition to his gross salary of $6,000 that year.[83] Moreover, he had now become a national figure in education, and worked with the president of Macmillan, Hugh Eayrs, on what were in effect equal terms. Donald Solandt would have had to be an exceptional man not to feel threatened by Pierce.

The management offices of the House were thus not a happy place in these years, despite the fact that reader orders were pouring in – for example, for 11,500 copies of Book Four of the Canada Books of Prose and Verse in the spring of 1934 alone and a total of 32,000 Ryerson-Macmillan readers for Alberta. Total reader sales for 1934 amounted to 300,000 copies as Pierce struggled to ready volumes for Cope's printing plant at the House.[84] His secretary, Betsey Jefferys, remembered that as she brought news of another big order for readers to the printing plant at this time, plant manager Cope sarcastically asked whether Pierce needed the order "on the hop" as was his wont – and his nickname.[85]

CHANGES IN Pierce's lifestyle made his increased income apparent. In the spring of 1934 Basil Campbell, a civil engineer, developer and son of the Confederation poet Wilfred Campbell, offered Pierce the purchase of a fine new house on a large lot, as well as half the adjoining vacant lot, in newly fashionable and bucolic York Mills. The house sat on the edge of Hogg's Hollow not far from the Don River, a green enclave only a few blocks from the home of Lorne's artist friend and collaborator C.W. Jefferys.[86] Lorne, Edith, and the children fell in love with the spacious stone and wood house, the more when Campbell offered the services of a friend to landscape the lot professionally at an advantageous rate, a prelude to the splendid garden that the couple both dreamed of. The house cost $14,500, plus the cost of purchasing the half-lot. Campbell in turn offered $7,000 for the Pierce's Glengrove Avenue home.

After hesitating over the expense of the upgrade from a house of brick to a house of stone (after all, they had started out in a house of sticks on Wineva), Lorne and Edith took the plunge, moving into 5 Campbell Crescent on 17 May 1934. Situated as they were in an area seen as practically in the country, they christened the property "La Ferme," the French name signifying Lorne's devotion to *bonne entente*. The name also evoked the property's horticultural potential, realized in Edith's and

Lorne's inspired gardening (with the aid of their indispensable gardener/ handyman George Coppin) over the next two decades. Daughter Beth remembers that "the garden [wove] ... a gentle zephyr through all the sorrows and pressures" that her father experienced at home and at work, particularly with the onset of Second World War.[87]

The handsome dining room at Campbell Crescent was a centrepiece of the splendid home which Edith ran. Both Pierce children remember the nightly formality of dinner, where each child in turn was expected to be an intelligent and cultured conversationalist with their witty father. His hearing aid was set to catch their words as much as possible, a set-piece interlude with a parent so often sequestered in his spacious new study, complete with fireplace. That spring of 1934, Pierce was also realizing that fourteen-year-old Beth and twelve-year-old Bruce were growing up. In February 1934 he marvelled at Beth's talent and self-possession as she acted in a play at Hart House. The matinee prompted a rare vignette of his children's activities in the diary for these years. Bruce, his father noted fondly, was in "his glory as a rough sailor" in the production.[88]

Meanwhile, anyone envious of Pierce's handsome new home was probably discomfited by his summer 1934 holiday plans. Edith and Lorne had always yearned to go to Europe, where he had never been. (Alice Chown had taken her niece to England in 1910.) In the summer of 1934 Edith's close friend Marion Walwyn was leading a guided tour of Europe. As part of Pierce's reward for the readers' success, Eayrs and his firm paid the $1,900 cost of the couple's two-month-long tour of Europe in July and August 1934 while the children went off to summer camp.[89] Eayrs's note about footing the bill for the trip called "Dear old Lorne" his "pal, who, God knows, has been and is and will be the sort of pal a man treasures." Eayrs wanted Pierce to enjoy a "grand rest and change."[90] As it turned out, this breezy promise of ongoing camaraderie was far from prophetic.

Nevertheless, the European trip, which began when the couple sailed on the liner *Duchess of Atholl* in the second week of July, returning in the first week in September, was a dream come true for Pierce. He drank in the delights of France, Switzerland, Italy, Austria, Germany, England, and Scotland: cathedrals, castles, museums, cafés, hotels, and historic landscapes and landmarks. But this was 1934, and the trip was darkened by the grim realities of fascist power, with an atmosphere in Germany, Italy, and elsewhere of "pent up hate and cold malice and will for revenge" that, Pierce later recalled, "made me physically ill."[91] The tour group arrived in Austria in August on the heels of the murder of Austrian Chancellor Engelbert Dolfuss, with fighting still going on in the hills around Graz during their visit there. Pierce, troubled at the threat of fascism so palpably evident all around him, became convinced that "a tornado was thundering out of the East."[92] A few years later, he and Edith were to aid Dr Richard Maresch, their guide in Vienna that August, when the Maresch family came to Toronto as refugees.

As the spectre of a new war loomed, the shadow of the last fell on the journey. Pierce made a painful pilgrimage to a Great War military cemetery near Vimy Ridge for a moment of reflection at the 1917 grave of his cousin and contemporary Clifford Pierce. He wrote sombrely to his children about the battlefield: "We were glad to get away from it – the endless tokens of a murderous frenzy. Rose bushes in places were climbing over concrete gun emplacements. Vimy Ridge, where Clifford fell."[93] On a lighter note, Pierce, out on a Paris stroll, asked a gendarme in painstaking French, "Où est le Champs Elysée?" only to be told flatly in American-accented English by the gendarme: "You're on it, Bud." He and Edith dallied in a Paris sidewalk café and later travelled to the Passion Play at Oberammergau, once Pierce overcame his Methodist scruples about such papist pageantry.[94] He found the splendour of Europe's great cathedrals especially moving, bound up as their architecture was with the symbolism of freemasonry so precious to him. His experience of these cathedrals found their way into eloquent descriptive passages in *Master Builders*, a 1937 booklet on freemasonry.[95]

Pierce's small travel diary is crammed with details and statistics about monuments, paintings, and buildings seen. Despite his workload on return, he set out to compile a scrapbook of "views and folders and booklets" about his first – and last – visit to Europe.[96] Blanche Hume joked that her boss was "not really the same" upon his return: "He has seen Venice!"[97] Indeed, Pierce had finally seen the Venice of Ruskin, which his mother had so often talked of during his Delta boyhood as she pressed upon him the three volumes of Ruskin's *The Stones of Venice*.

Once back at the House, Pierce plunged into the pressure of textbook matters, continued acrimony with Donald Solandt, and growing difficulties with Hugh Eayrs. He would later discover that his educational manager, Gilbert "Pat" Paterson – whom Pierce had chided on several occasions for talking against him to others in and outside the House – was intriguing against him with Solandt, and possibly with Eayrs as well.[98] Eayrs on occasion came to Pierce's defence in his difficulties with

Solandt, but Lorne's increasing prosperity and prominence was also evidently beginning to gall Eayrs. For his part, Solandt, despite the terms of the Ryerson-Macmillan agreement, believed that Pierce was not entitled to extra remuneration for editing the readers, a stance reminiscent of Fallis's refusal to give Pierce extra money for his work on the "Makers" series outside office hours. Pierce's contention that the work on the readers, like that on the "Makers," was done on his own time was seconded by Eayrs and is clearly supported by the documentary record.[99] Of course, such moonlighting is bound to be highly contentious in corporate terms, as Pierce found to his sorrow.

Furthermore, Eayrs was pressuring his collaborator over textbook matters. In October 1934 he complained to Pierce that the House, with the exception of Pierce's labours, had not contributed equally in time and sales effort to the readers compared to Macmillan.[100] But Pierce felt exactly the opposite.[101] The tension was increased by the fact that the two firms were still keen competitors in other areas of the textbook market. Nevertheless, in early 1935, Pierce proudly wrote to his mother that Ryerson-Macmillan reader total sales had reached an impressive 300,000 copies for 1934, with "good sales" expected in 1935.[102] He was then reorganizing his department, hiring a new storekeeper, Clovis Lafleche, and destroying a huge inventory of unsold stock, a major writedown which meant a $6,952.75 loss for his department on the annual reports and a large posted loss in the Educational Department despite reader-fuelled profits of about $25,000.[103] Sensible measures, but trouble loomed nonetheless.

THE STORM broke in the spring of 1935 – only barely and belatedly manifesting itself in Pierce's diary. He referred to the problem in passing on 17 August 1935, his first diary entry since 10 May: "A most annoying copyright feud has broken out between Ryerson-Macmillan and Gage-Nelson. I am revising all readers, Treasury and Canada Books this summer."[104] Revising all the readers was in fact so time-consuming that Lorne Pierce had cancelled his 1935 summer holiday. What precipitated such a mammoth task in such haste? Accusations of plagiarism. This in fact was not simply an "annoying" charge but a serious crisis that threatened to sabotage sales of Book One of the Canada Books of Prose and Verse – the revised volume based on the first reader that Pierce and Arthur Yates had collaborated on beginning in 1927, of which tens of thousands of copies had been sold.[105] The charge, moreover, threatened the credibility of the whole series, not to mention that of Pierce himself.

The crisis began in June 1935. Publishers Gage and Nelson, which had joined forces to field rival readers, protested to both Ryerson-Macmillan and the Alberta educational authorities that Book One of the Canada Books of Prose and Verse – 10,000 copies of which had been printed and shipped for use that fall in Alberta schools – contained material ("sixteen examples of plagiarism in editorial notes and comments"[106]) taken from elsewhere, chiefly an American Rand-McNally reader for which Gage-Nelson held Canadian copyright. By 26 June 1935, John Gray, Macmillan's educational manager, was spearheading thorny meetings to solve the matter with both Gage-Nelson executives and the deputy minister of education for Alberta. Naturally, Gray hoped that this solution would not involve either litigation against Ryerson-Macmillan or withdrawal of the readers from Alberta schools, both of which would be disastrous for the two publishing houses in terms of both expense and credibility. Whatever the solution, it was clear that Book One would have to be revised. Worse yet, there seems also to have been some suspect material in Book Two of the Canada Books of Prose and Verse. Clearly, all the readers would have to be combed for potential problems – and quickly.

The situation was particularly awkward because, for the past few years, Ryerson and Macmillan had taken a very hard position on copyright. Eayrs and Pierce had been denying rival firms the right to use any selections in their readers for which Ryerson and Macmillan held copyright, including selections from important authors like Kipling, Hardy, and Masefield. They did so even if those selections were not included in their own readers. Technically, the two firms had the right to do this, but it was "tough" bargaining, the ethics of which John Gray debated with Hugh Eayrs – who seems to have come up with the strategy – because such stonewalling might deny students the best possible material in some of their textbooks. Gray later wrote that he "thought Lorne Pierce too innocent to understand the full enormity of this plan," but in fact Pierce and Ryerson collaborated in it.[107] As a textbook editor, Pierce knew how important good selections were, and would have understood the ruthlessness of the tactic. He was probably not proud of it, though, since it was never mentioned in any of his many references to textbook matters in his diary. Now, Gage-Nelson had Ryerson-Macmillan in a difficult corner, and could press their advantage.

According to Gage-Nelson – and neither Pierce nor Eayrs nor Gray ever disputed that a copyright violation had occurred, insisting only that it was inadvertent – some of the contextual material in the reader, such as that dealing with selections from Robert Louis Stevenson, had been lifted directly from an American Rand-McNally reader.[108] Pierce had written an introduction to a section of the reader entitled "Home Life," a section that included two pieces by Stevenson.[109] How exactly this duplication occurred is unclear. Pierce never addressed the issue directly, and, at his direction, the papers dealing with his textbook work were culled, along with sensitive material on a variety of subjects, by his trusted assistant, Blanche Hume, before being sent to Queen's in the 1940s.[110] According to documents in the Macmillan of Canada papers, however, Pierce told Eayrs, Gray, and others that material from another source clipped to the Stevenson selection as background for the drafting of his introduction to the "Home Life" section was left there by mistake when the section was sent for typesetting and printing at the House. The error was not detected by Pierce. Thus, Pierce maintained, the material was unwittingly incorporated holus-bolus into the Ryerson-Macmillan reader.[111]

But, for Hugh Eayrs, there was a difficulty with this explanation. The paragraph ordering of the material appropriated, as well as some of its phrasing, had in fact been rearranged in Pierce's reader. Therefore, it could not have been a simple matter of an excerpt from another company's reader slipping through the editing process untouched. Moreover, in the first version of the reader that Yates and Pierce produced in 1927, no Stevenson selections were included at all, meaning that the copyright violation occurred later, under Pierce's watch, not Yates's.[112] In the Ryerson-Macmillan version of the reader, Dora Whitefield, Eayrs's wife, is listed as co-editor, but there is no evidence of her doing any editorial work on it with Pierce, though she received a royalty for the readers, probably for assistance in choosing illustrations. (In fact, Eayrs told Solandt in 1933 that Pierce received reader royalty payments from Macmillan, not the House, for the Macmillan half of the editorial work done on Pierce's own time, while Pierce's work for Ryerson as editor was covered by his House salary.[113])

What Pierce's diaries do record, however, is his several quick trips to New York City in the late 1920s and early 1930s to consult American reader collections at Columbia University and elsewhere at a time when he felt under great pressure to produce readers for the Canadian market for the good of the country, the House, and his own financial security. All the available evidence, then, suggests that Pierce was responsible for the material which posed the problem. Did he take material from other sources and under pressure forget in several instances to revise it sufficiently to avoid violation of copyright? Only Lorne Pierce knew. Hugh Eayrs and his subordinate John Gray had their own private thoughts on the matter. In fact, while to others Eayrs presented the scenario of the undetected clipping, privately he told Pierce that the explanation did not fit the facts, that the violation of copyright could not have been simply a clerical error.[114]

By the end of 1935, Ryerson and Macmillan, after lengthy negotiations, managed to save their bacon. The two firms had settled between themselves on 4 November how the crisis was to be handled in terms of a settlement with Gage-Nelson. Subsequently, an agreement was signed stipulating that Ryerson-Macmillan would pay Gage-Nelson some $300 in compensation for copyright violation. Of course, the matter had been much more expensive than that, involving as it did the revision of the whole series and the need to change plates for the volumes already published.[115] Moreover, Ryerson and Macmillan agreed to end their draconian practice of systematically denying copyright material controlled by them to rival firms.[116] Unquestionably, the whole episode was embarrassing for Ryerson-Macmillan, and especially for Pierce.

To Hugh Eayrs, it might well have seemed that Lorne Pierce was at last revealed to be as morally fallible as any of his peers. John Gray's memoirs emphasize Pierce's marked reticence about the whole episode: "Discretion prevented one from asking who had done the offending editorial work and no explanation was ever offered. Lorne Pierce said, almost too often, that no one would ever hear the truth from him, and so far as I know no one did; but something in his manner – a foxy, almost libellous little smile, suggested the scandal he could unfold. He was after all Lorne Pierce and no one – not anyone – would dream of accusing him of such unprofessional and unethical shortcuts."[117]

The plagiarism crisis was undoubtedly a dark hour for Pierce. On 14 November his diary tersely noted the agreement and his weary labour over long months: "Entire summer gone in on revision [of] *Treasury* and *Canada* readers. Dispute over copyright settled November 4 at joint House meeting. Most friendly. Inter Provincial [Education] Committee of four Western Deputies greatly impressed with revised *Prose and Verse I*. Sending revised proofs to each December first. Now putting final touches on Book II."[118] Only six months after the plagiarism crisis was settled did Pierce allow himself to show real emotion about it, calling it a "nightmare" in a letter to Hugh Eayrs. The subject had come up because Eayrs feared that there might be copyright problems with some other reader material. Pierce replied on 8 June 1936 in a letter marked "confidential": "I have looked through the revised Treasury Readers, and, thank Heaven, the two selections you mentioned are revised. I caught some things in most of the Readers when revising [last year]. After the plagiarism mess I went at it, and combed all the books and [teachers'] manuals. So far as I know, the new edition is clean, but this business has become such a nightmare, that I have the jitters."[119]

Part of the "nightmare" was that, whether or not the plagiarism crisis had caused Eayrs to respect Pierce less, their exchanges after 1935 were certainly sharper. Eayrs told Pierce bluntly weeks after the crisis was settled that he had been "tired [for] some years of the claim on your part for sole credit for the entire series of readers ... and for the auxiliary material. You were assisted by me far more than you have ever cared to recognize."[120] Clearly, whatever the truth of the matter, the copyright crisis had caused Pierce to lose face with Eayrs.

Pierce's relations with Donald Solandt also sank to a new low from the time of the plagiarism controversy in June 1935. From that date, Solandt treated him in a way that Pierce summed up in February 1936 as "exasperating and brutal" after Solandt accused him of bad faith in contract commitments for one of the readers. Pierce told his diary that the accusation was "all rot."[121] In early 1936 Pierce even threatened to resign or to go to the church authorities over Solandt's excoriations.[122] So worried was Blanche Hume about her boss's health at the time of the reader crisis and its aftermath that, in her own diary, she quoted Bliss Carman's poem "To One in Despair" to the effect that Pierce's staff feared that some "irreparable day" they would suddenly "find [him] gone."[123]

But the person who was "suddenly gone" was Donald Solandt. On 7 August 1936, while on holiday in Delta, Pierce was shocked to learn that the sixty-five-year-old Solandt had died in Toronto the day before of heart problems. Back in Toronto to serve as pallbearer, Pierce lamented that the two had not had a "complete reconciliation."[124] A permanent successor would not be appointed until June 1937, but Pierce would never again be treated harshly by senior House personnel, the book steward in particular. Henceforth, Pierce's years of experience, his national reputation as a literary and educational editor, and the successful sales of the readers would make him the Grand Old Man of the House, well-nigh immune to challenge.

In fact, whatever the recriminations and whatever the ethical price, the Ryerson-Macmillan readers had been highly successful in the market and would continue to be so for decades. Once the memory of the copyright controversy faded, and with Solandt gone, the focus rested on the large printing runs of the reader series as Ryerson-Macmillan consolidated sales in the Maritimes and Ontario after impressive success in the west. In March 1936, for example, Pierce proudly announced that Book One of the Canada Books of Prose and Verse was now in use in Nova Scotia, Prince Edward Island, Manitoba, Alberta, British Columbia, Ontario, and Newfoundland.[125] In 1934 Alberta had bought 32,000 copies of four readers in the series, and in 1938 a winning contract for readers in Nova Scotia meant a sale of 60,000 books.[126] These hugely successful readers became widely used, in a variety of titles and revised editions (some forty printings in all), in much of English Canada over the next thirty-five years. By 1961, the textbooks for grades 7 to 12, still in use, had a combined national sale of 200,000 copies per year.[127]

Profit margins, while solid, were never the bonanza that Pierce and Eayrs originally envisioned. Given Depression conditions, the provinces could drive hard bargains on the initial orders. Once a low unit price had been established, it was hard to raise prices substantially in subsequent contracts. Even by 1948, Ryerson calculated that Books Three to Six, for instance, retailed for no more than eighty cents a copy, with the profit per copy fluctuating between thirty-three and forty-three cents.[128] Moreover, profits had be divided between the two firms, and the printing costs and tight price spreads were a constant source of tension between Ryerson and Macmillan.[129] Looking at the annual returns on reader sales in the late 1930s, Eayrs was wont to grumble to his sales manager, John Gray, over the fact that the textbooks had brought "a substantial increase in sales for a few years" but at such "ruinous prices as to make it barely worth while."[130] But of course reader sales had kept both firms busy during the Depression, and had thus given employment to scores of workers.

Pierce continued to receive annual royalties from the readers – "the cream," as the family called it. Relatively speaking, the payments, set in 1930 at a rate varying between 2 per cent and 5 per cent per reader in the series,[131] were most substantial in the early years when large initial quantities of the readers were ordered. In June 1936, for instance, Pierce received a $5,000 royalty check for a seven-year contract with the Ontario government for two of the Canadian Treasury Readers, some of which went in the bank ($500 in an account for Edith), some to pay debts, and some for a new Buick.[132] For the next twenty-five years, royalty payments would roughly double Pierce's modest Ryerson salary. In 1948, for example, Pierce's tax return listed his salary as $5,599.92 and his royalties as $5,855.55.[133] In the last three years of his life, from 1959 to 1961, his royalties hovered around $6,000 a year.[134]

But the money went on far more than Buicks. Whatever his uneasiness over some of his editing practices (and perhaps because of it), the spirit of philanthropy present in Pierce since Delta days was fed by the royalties. In the 1950s, Pierce told Pearson Gundy, librarian of Queen's, and ongoing recipient of his valuable Canadiana collection, that the readers represented "the cause of all my extravagance. They have paid for all those extravagant gestures of collections and trusts and so on."[135] He donated generously to many other organizations, including the Canadian Hearing Society, the Royal Ontario Museum, the Art Gallery of Ontario, the Bibliographical Society of Canada, and the Canadian Writers' Foundation as well as to individual artists and writers such as C.W. Jefferys, Thoreau MacDonald, Audrey Alexandra Brown, and Yves Thériault. Indeed, in just one example of his many benefactions over the next twenty-five years, in the months after the copyright crisis was settled and around the time Pierce received his $5,000 royalty check for Ontario textbook sales, he acquired the Isabella Valancy Crawford Papers and other Canadiana for Queen's and bought the painting *The Westward Passage* from artist C.W. Jefferys.[136] If there was a whiff of expiation in all this, perhaps it was in the spirit of a quote from William Kirby that Pierce used in the conclusion to his biography of Kirby: "Well, it is *not* a good world – nobody can say that it is save those who wilfully blind themselves to facts. How can a world be good in which money is the moving power, and self interest the guiding star? The wonder is not that it is bad, but that there should be any good left in it."[137]

If royalties and the resulting benefactions would henceforth be a constant in Pierce's life, the pressure caused by periodic revisions and initiatives in the textbook field would also give him no rest. For the rest of his career, the readers had to be revised at roughly four-year intervals to satisfy the need for periodic textbook authorizations or curriculum changes in various parts of Canada. Pierce had his educational sales team, and worked with various editorial collaborators, but the primary responsibility for the readers always fell on his shoulders. John Gray, who became head of Macmillan's a few years after Hugh Eayrs's death in 1940, has described some of the exhausting textbook journeys he and Pierce shared in the 1940s and 1950s.[138] As Pierce toiled away at yet another revision of a reader volume in 1950, Gray even joked to him about the pressure: "Don't worry about the pistol at your head because I know, that in circumstances of this kind, thanks be, you are bullet-proof."[139]

Witticisms were all very well, but sometimes the compromises necessitated by provincial sensitivities about some of the textbook material were uncongenial to Pierce. History texts were a case in point. In 1940 the Alberta government of Premier William Aberhart, with its Social Credit pro-business outlook, demanded revisions to the social-studies textbook *The World of Today*, including to a passage that suggested that the grain grower was "being cheated on every side" by the profiteering of grain traders and elevator and milling companies. After a drawn-out correspondence, the passage, as well as a few others in the text, was altered to read more blandly: "The grain grower felt that he was not receiving value in return for his labour as compared with the rewards derived from many other occupations."[140] Such "field editing" was not a part of the textbook game that Pierce relished. Four years later, he wryly observed to a Maritime publisher that a single Canadian history for schools was "not a likely possibility": "There will have to be a lot more ripeness and wisdom, a lot more sympathy and good manners before we are likely to agree on anything of that sort. It demands a point of view, an attitude toward life, coming and going, that is not yet possible in so young and mixed a nation, and it will only complicate and worsen the matter if we add to these emotional appeals for the Maritimes or the Prairies or the Polar Regions."[141]

Not surprisingly, given such hard-won pragmatism, Pierce became highly regarded in Canadian educational circles for his vision as "begetter and architect" of the series.[142] Madeline Young, who assisted Pierce in revising readers in the late 1950s, called his "guiding hand" unique in that "no other text-book editor … has [Pierce's] distinction in literature."[143] For his part, C.L. Bennet, a Halifax teacher and textbook collaborator with Pierce in the 1940s and 1950s, emphasized Pierce's nationalist and cultural vision as textbook editor in April 1960, a few months after Pierce's retirement. Bennet wrote to one of Pierce's colleagues: "As general editor, [Pierce] fathered the books; and as long as they retain their original character he should be recognized; he had a principle, and kept to it, and it was easy to work with him because we both knew what we were working at and for."[144]

Historian Mary Vipond has described the widespread concern in the 1920s about the need for Canadian textbooks in the schools and the concern of historians like George Wrong and W.S. Wallace that teaching and textbooks should promote "patriotism and intelligent loyalty."[145] Clearly, one of Pierce's greatest influences on Canadian culture, as a key figure in this drive for made-in-Canada textbooks, was his unprecedented creation of widely used textbook series that took account – from a very particular and elite perspective characteristic of the era – of "the political, social, scientific and literary history of the country" to provide what he called in 1941 "an education for citizenship."[146]

Much has been made of the burgeoning of interest in Canadian literature and Canadian history in the 1960s and 1970s, but arguably, starting in the 1930s, school texts like the Canada Books of Prose and Verse did much to lay the groundwork for such a burgeoning by inculcating in students a particular vision of Canada's cultural achievements, albeit from a very unitary point of view which overlooked and/or homogenized ethnic, class, and gender difference. Lorne Pierce's major endeavours in this area, infused as they were with a particular concept of nationhood, are important to an understanding of how the construct of nation was conveyed in twentieth-century Canada. Given the widespread penetration and longevity of the Ryerson-Macmillan readers in public schools across Canada between 1930 and the early 1960s, Pierce's influential brand of textbook nationalism has been too long overlooked by scholars.

15

From Romantic History to Academic History

Publishing C. W. Jefferys and Harold Innis, 1921–1951

[A] teeming horde of boys and girls in thousands of schools across the land ... learned from [C.W. Jefferys's] pictorial histories the principal characters and outstanding events of Canada's past, those things most worthy of devotion and of remembrance in this fair land.

Lorne Pierce on C. W. Jefferys, 1951[1]

It is my belief that only by a deep immersion in ... the political, social, scientific, and literary history of the country can an 'education for citizenship' be achieved.

Lorne Pierce on the importance of Canadian history, 1941[2]

Lorne Pierce's activities as a purveyor of romantic history involved another, powerful dimension – the visual. He thought the role of art in influencing the imagination was so important that, for one of his Canada Books of Prose and Verse, he himself wrote a primer for students on "How to Look at Pictures" in order to discover "the truth and beauty that are in them."[3] In his long alliance with artist C.W. Jefferys, whom he commissioned to illustrate the Ryerson Canadian History Readers from the mid-1920s and whose best-selling three-volume *Picture Gallery of Canadian History* he published between 1942 and 1950, Pierce played a crucial role in establishing Jefferys as the dominant visual mythmaker of Canada's past in the first half of the twentieth century.

As well as fostering this romantic construct of history, Pierce was also, from the 1930s, engaged in promoting the pioneering economic history of Harold Innis. In their work on the landmark Relations of Canada and the United States series, underwritten by the Carnegie Endowment for International Peace, Innis and Pierce displayed a gritty, pragmatic nationalism in their dealings with their collaborators south of the border, notably James Shotwell and J. Bartlet Brebner. As a result, Pierce was an important (and to date largely unacknowledged) force in the establishment of a new academic history.

PIERCE'S PROMOTION of artist C.W. Jefferys was closely tied to his own love of romantic history and his conviction that Jefferys's work embodied its values. In October 1930, when Pierce outlined his view of history, one that lay behind the widely used Ryerson Canadian History Readers, he emphasized the need for "the *story* of our Dominion" to be presented "in simple, vivid and dramatic style, emphasising at all times the romance of incident and character" in order to stimulate "an alert and intelligent national self-consciousness in the young."[4] He immediately mentioned Jefferys's historical drawings for the readers, adding that Jefferys would "shortly make them available with his own interesting comments for our home and school libraries."[5]

In fact, in the case of the Ryerson Canadian History Readers, Pierce used Jefferys's illustrations as a centrepiece for these books' romantic vision of nationhood. He thus played a crucial role in the establishment of Jefferys as Canada's most popular twentieth-century illustrator of our history. The two men shared a proselytizing vision of Canada's past which Jefferys drew and Pierce successfully marketed. Jefferys's textbook illustrations – as well as the Ryerson volumes devoted exclusively to his historical depictions – offered tens of thousands of Canadian readers, particularly schoolchildren, a romantic, epic, and whiggish vision of Canadian history, the incarnation of a nationalist ideology shared by author and publisher.

Pierce and Jefferys first met in 1921, at a time when Pierce, seeking to establish himself at the House, was particularly keen to publish work that reflected his own impassioned nationalism. Jefferys was chosen by the Ontario Department of Education to illustrate George Wrong's history of Canada, published by Ryerson.[6] The artist intrigued Pierce by telling him about meeting the "very shy" Marjorie Pickthall when he had illustrated three of her children's books for the publisher Musson early in the century.[7] Pierce and the tall, silver-haired Jefferys speedily discovered that they shared a desire to excite Canadians about their history and to bring together French and English in Canada.

Twenty-one years Pierce's senior, English-born Charles William Jefferys had settled in Toronto with his parents in 1881 at the age of twelve.

After classes at the Ontario College of Art and training at the Toronto Lithographing Company between 1885 and 1890, Jefferys became an illustrator for Toronto newspapers. He had joined the Toronto Art Students' League in October 1888, spearheading the publication of the league's annual art calendars between 1895 and 1904, a landmark in Canadian art. These drew their inspiration from Canadian landscape and poetry, a spirit exemplified in Jefferys's contributions, including his well-known "Rebels of 1837 Drilling in North York." Jefferys spent the period 1892 to 1900 as an illustrator for the New York *Herald*, but his real loyalties lay with Canada.

Between his return to Canada in 1900 and the beginning of his association with Pierce in the early 1920s, Jefferys painted two rural landscapes Pierce also loved: the Ontario countryside and the prairies. Jefferys first encountered the prairies in 1910 – at the same time that Pierce was a summer teacher in Saskatchewan – becoming one of the earliest artists to depict the landscape successfully on canvas.[8] From 1912, Jefferys's interest in historical illustration grew through his work on the university edition of the Makers of Canada series of historical biographies for publisher George Morang and on T.C. Haliburton's *Sam Slick Sketches*. The latter publication was frustrated by the death of his American publisher until, forty years later, Pierce convinced Imperial Oil to purchase and repatriate the illustrations and personally edited them for publication by Ryerson in 1956.[9]

Pierce's devotion to enhancing Jefferys's reputation was rooted in their mutual desire to bring Canada's history alive in a vivid narrative fashion for Canadians. Jefferys told Pierce, soon after they met in 1921, that he wanted to produce a new kind of historical illustration "to get away from the dull vignettes of historical events, and drab busts of historical worthies, and, as he put it, 'make them step down from off their plinths and live.'"[10] Jefferys wanted to make sure that "even small girls and boys at school could ... be proud of their heritage." To a vision so congruent with his own, Pierce responded with enthusiasm, promising him that "as editor, I would do all I could to help him realize his dream."[11]

The two men began thirty years of tête-à-têtes about Canadian history, often over a meal at the Arts and Letters Club or at Jefferys's York Mills studio. Unfortunately, because they met regularly, relatively little revealing correspondence has survived, though in notes Jefferys often stressed how eager he was to get together with Pierce for a "real confab" not about mere business details.[12] At Christmas 1925, Jefferys presented

Pierce with a pen-and-ink sketch of Marie Hébert, a gift that emphasized their closeness and shared vision of Canadian history.[13] Then, in
a 1929 letter, Jefferys wrote Pierce of his gratitude for "the respect and
sympathy of ... discriminating people like yourself" in his attempts to
deal with "inspiring themes."[14]

Between 1925 and 1931, Pierce gave Jefferys a major assignment – to
make a certain construct of history "live" for schoolchildren. He commissioned Jefferys to create over two hundred illustrations, maps, and charts
for the Ryerson Canadian History Readers.[15] Surveying Jefferys's work
for the series, he publicly commended him for producing not "wretched
fillers" but for bringing alive "the great scenes of our history." In that 1931
commendation, Pierce spoke of his hopes that Jefferys would produce
(and Ryerson would publish) "a complete pictorial history of Canada."[16]
He obviously saw Jefferys as a kindred patriot whom he was determined
to publish despite the dismal book market of the Depression. In 1930
Ryerson had done the printing for a book put out by the Toronto *Star*,
using the plates of a series of historical drawings of Canada done by
Jefferys for the newspaper.[17] Within four years, Ryerson had begun publishing volumes exclusively devoted to Jefferys's work – *Canada's Past in
Pictures* (1934), a revised and expanded version for Ryerson of the *Star*
series, was followed by the best-selling *Picture Gallery of Canadian History*, issued in three volumes in 1942, 1945, and 1950.

Pierce went to great effort to reinforce Jefferys's artistic reputation.
In the 1940s he commissioned William Colgate to write a booklet on
Jefferys for Ryerson's pioneering Canadian Art series,[18] and he was a
prime mover in a major exhibition, sponsored by Ryerson Press, of Jefferys's historical work at the Art Gallery of Toronto in 1942, a show that
then toured western Ontario. Pierce spearheaded another Ontario tour
of Jefferys's historical drawings in 1945, and published articles and introductions to Jefferys's work.[19] In 1952, following Jefferys's death, Pierce
negotiated with Imperial Oil to buy the artist's immense collection of
historical drawings and notes as a national treasure and resource.[20] In
short, Pierce spared no effort throughout his editorial career to ensure
Jefferys's canonical status.

From the first, Pierce recognized and identified with the mythmaking
power of Jefferys's images. He commissioned Jefferys's art not just for
his painstaking research into the material history of the scenes depicted,
but above all for the epic and dramatic power which gave visual – and
visionary – unity to a variety of Ryerson publications, many of them

aimed at children. As his funeral oration for Jefferys makes clear, Pierce saw him as a visionary artist who shared and disseminated Pierce's own ideals for the nation:

> [A] teeming horde of boys and girls in thousands of schools across the land ... learned from his pictorial histories the principal characters and outstanding events of Canada's past, those things most worthy of devotion and remembrance in this fair land ...
>
> His greatest pictures, his most successful murals, are concerned with the heroic and the courageous, and what a company they are. They are all cast in a heroic mould. There is nothing petty about any of them ...
>
> No other artist, no other Canadian, has done so much to knit together into one community of fellowship and purpose all parts of Canada. No one has done so much to build a covered bridge between the English and the French speaking peoples of Canada.[21]

Scholar Brian Osborne has pointed out that the powerful legacy of Jefferys's illustrations of historical materials has been that "his work has constituted the dominant source for the development of a consensual image of Canada's history."[22] This image and its dominance is exactly what Pierce worked toward from the early years of his association with the artist. For example, his introduction to George Wrong's *The Story of Canada* (1929) culminated with an emphasis on such Jefferys's illustrations as "The First [Prairie] Furrow" and "Cartier Erects a Cross at Gaspe" as not simply art but "a contribution ... to the cause of Canadian history."[23]

Pierce became Jefferys's tireless patron. He bought "The Windward Passage," a major Jefferys canvas, for his own home in 1936, giving it a place of honour over the fireplace and hosting a gala evening there with the artist discussing his painting for the guests, including Sir Charles G.D. Roberts.[24] He commissioned Jefferys to illustrate many Ryerson Press titles over the years, including Isabel Skelton's *The Backwoodswoman* (1924) and Morden Long's *A History of the Canadian People* (1942).[25] As Jefferys's daughter put it: "You gave him his first really broad public and helped him attain his goal more than anyone else."[26]

At the most basic level, Pierce largely made it financially possible for Jefferys to concentrate on historical illustration in the last decades of his career. In 1937, after the death of Jefferys's wife, Pierce wrote in his diary: "For almost 18 years he has done superb things for me, and in cash and royalties I have tried to keep him, giving back the originals that he might derive other sums from them. They were always hard up ... Just a fortnight ago ... I tried to jam through a contract on a new book so that I could pinch an advance, for the [account] was far overdrawn."[27] Even as Pierce wrote this entry, his wife was arranging to host a two-day handicraft sale at the Pierce home that one of the Jefferys daughters had originally planned to give at the Jefferys studio before her mother's death.[28]

Given such support by both Pierces, Jefferys joked to Pierce of his own frequent appeals for funds: "You take a begging letter so admirably that you make the applicant feel he's really a deserving case."[29] Saying that Pierce's commitment was the more valuable because "Canadians beat the world ... in giving empty adulation [to artists] in lieu of fair price and a living wage,"[30] he also told him how inspiring he found his call for an epic history that would foster national sentiment in the Canadian people, and how grateful he was for their shared vision of historical art.[31]

Pierce consistently sought to extend Jefferys's audience. During the Depression, he distributed unsold copies of Jefferys's *Dramatic Episodes in Canada's Story* (1930) free of charge to impoverished school districts in the west.[32] In 1934 he sold 3,000 copies of *Canada's Past in Pictures* at a discount to the Ontario Ministry of Education for school use.[33] In 1942, when Ryerson brought out the first volume of *The Picture Gallery of Canadian History*, Jefferys's sweeping three-volume visual history of Canada from the first native-European contact to the early twentieth century, Pierce lobbied the Carnegie Endowment to donate the work to leading American libraries and archives. He made it clear that the volumes were to be inexpensive, so that "Canadians everywhere might not be prevented from possessing this astonishing record of their country."[34]

Pierce was unquestionably more than a publisher to Jefferys: his commitment to Jefferys was clearly to an artist whom he felt expressed his own feelings about the country's history. He was, in Jefferys's phrase, the "midwife" of Jefferys's historical works, particularly his magnum opus, *The Picture Gallery of Canadian History*.[35] It is striking how Jefferys and Pierce both used the vocabulary of childbirth in describing their collaboration, suggesting how closely involved the two were in bringing forth Jefferys's vision of Canadian history. In 1942, when the first volume of *The Picture Gallery of Canadian History* went into a second printing of 3,000 copies, Pierce described the book as "a 'blessed event' for all here."[36] According to one of Jefferys's daughters, artist and editor had jointly arrived at the idea of Jefferys's *Picture Gallery* long before it was published. Pierce spoke of the concept as early as 1930,[37] and an anguished 1948 letter to Jefferys over delays to the third volume again uses the childbirth metaphor: "If you take on any more jobs ... until our magnum opus is completed, I will spew you, verily I will spew you!! I have goaded you and prodded you, stung and tortured you, rallied and railed, jeered and taunted you for nearly twenty years on this one thing! You started to plan it and in the fullness of time Book I came out. Brother, this baby has been a long time being born ... What more can I do except bring you to live with us? I am very sad."[38] When the third volume finally appeared in 1950, a jubilant Pierce told Jefferys that "the best of it all has been the collaboration which to me has been a very precious experience."[39] For his part, Jefferys inscribed Pierce's copy of Volume 3: "To Lorne Pierce whose faith made the production of these books possible." In discussing the inscription, Pierce added that the two "had kept faith with each other," suggesting the degree to which the two had bonded in presenting Canada's past in a "heroic mould."[40]

Given that by 1950, thanks to Lorne Pierce, a whole generation of Canadian schoolchildren had grown up ingesting Jefferys with their ABCs, the trilogy's best-seller status must have led Pierce to feel that some youngsters had taken their lessons to heart, at least as eventual book buyers. The six printings of *Picture Gallery*, with some 2,000 drawings,[41] which had appeared by 1970 suggest that many Canadians had responded to Pierce's and Jefferys's vision of their native land. When one turns to the pictures themselves, particularly some of the illustrations included in both the history readers and *The Picture Gallery of Canadian History*, one can certainly recognize therein the themes that Pierce valorized. As Pierce noted, "the great scenes of our history" are embodied in characters portrayed in "the proper context of their most significant achievements"[42] – in other words, the images are a powerful mythic construct. The images in Jefferys's oeuvre unfold in epic linear fashion from New France to turn-of-the-century Canada (no linguistic barriers in this medium). Significantly, even when Jefferys depicts the divisive period of the Conquest, comparatively few of his drawings focus on actual combat between French and English, emphasizing instead the calmer moments of battle preparation and aftermath.

Whatever the period, Jefferys's protagonists exude earnestness and purpose and an implicit mastery over the landscape. In "Champlain on

Jefferys's *Champlain on Georgian Bay, 1615* from Volume 1 of *The Picture Gallery of Canadian History*, page 93. Courtesy of Library and Archives Canada

(right, above) Jefferys's *Madame Hebert Watching the Departure of the French from Quebec after Its Capture 1628*, from Volume 1 of *The Picture Gallery of Canadian History*, page 97. Courtesy of Library and Archives Canada

(right, below) Jefferys's *Loyalists Camping on the St. Lawrence*, from Volume 2 of *The Picture Gallery of Canadian History*, page 21. Courtesy of Library and Archives Canada

Georgian Bay,"[43] the explorer looks out from a height of land, his European figure dominating both the landscape and the aboriginals below, who are depicted as assisting him in his efforts to master new frontiers. Native onlookers are clearly acolytes in a symbolic tableau in which an imaginative conquest of the land is suggested by the explorer's encompassing gaze. Moreover, the Georgian Bay scenery is depicted in the manner of the Group of Seven, friends and fellow nationalists of both Jefferys and Pierce. But here, unlike the Group paintings of Georgian Bay, Jefferys's "lonely land" is captured in a canvas which celebrates white European destiny in the New World. Another drawing set in New

Jefferys's *The First Furrow*, from Volume 3 of *The Picture Gallery of Canadian History*, page 149. Courtesy of Library and Archives Canada

France, "Marie Hebert, the Mother of Canada," foregrounds a similarly iconic figure of endurance and heroism in a northern landscape. Jeffreys depicts Hébert as a madonna of New World settlement by Europeans.[44]

When the artist turns his attention to the settlement of Upper Canada, the same quality of sturdy stoicism emanates from "Loyalists Camping on the St. Lawrence," which reveals its subjects bathed in firelight beneath the dark northern pines, a "holy family" whom, the portrayal suggests, suffers but will prevail.[45] Similarly, when Jefferys draws the agricultural settlement of the prairies in "The First Furrow," the result again suggests a defining national moment as the groundbreaking ploughman urges his horses toward the standard placed at the end of the furrow.[46] Like so many of the everymen and everywomen engaged in the work of settlement that Jefferys loved to dramatize, his sturdy pioneer symbolizes the making of a nation. Pierce often joked that his role as nationalistic publisher was that of "Pierce the Ploughman," suggesting his degree of identification with Jefferys's iconic nationalism.

As Dennis Duffy has pointed out, Jefferys's largely heroic, romantic, inspirational and didactic vision of Canada's past highly colours the selection of events portrayed in his drawings. As a result, the drawings lead us to consider the values of the artist and his collaborators.[47] Jefferys's images construct a heroic Canada where the so-called noble savage has given way to a nation founded by intrepid explorers and developed by resilient French, Loyalist, and prairie settlers in stirring succession. Between them, therefore, Jefferys and Pierce put forth what Brian Osborne has called "a veritable barrage of artistic historical propaganda and national consciousness raising."[48] Behind these drawings lies the personal and professional alliance of Lorne Pierce and Charles Jefferys, an alliance that, based as it was on a shared vision of Canadian nationhood, fostered many of the projects that brought Jefferys to fame as Canada's premier historical illustrator. Pierce's publication and promotion of Jefferys was one of the most effective ways he ever found to promulgate his own romantic nationalism.

PART OF WHAT made Pierce an important Canadian publisher, however, was the breadth of his commitment to Canadian historical publishing. In the late 1920s and 1930s, even as he published a plethora of romantic history, Pierce also became involved in publishing a more academic and specialized type of historical writing.

As early as 1925, Pierce came up with the idea of a Canadian Historical Studies series.[49] With the help of such knowledgeable amateur historians as Judge F.W. Howay of British Columbia, Dr Clarence Webster of New Brunswick, and Lawrence Burpee, Ottawa-based secretary of the International Joint Commission (all of whom Pierce had met through the Royal Society), Ryerson published four titles in the Canadian Historical Studies series between 1929 and 1933, each of which dealt with a particular aspect of pre-Confederation history of interest to antiquarians and others. The titles included Webster's edition of *The Journal of Jeffrey Amherst* (1931) and Percy Robinson's *Toronto during the French Regime* (1933).[50] Pierce contrived to do this despite the dismal book sales of the Depression years: he circumvented the problem of costs for such a venture by publishing small print runs (500 copies for three of the four works), for which all but fifty copies were sold by advance subscription.

In the shrunken Ryerson publication lists of the early 1930s – largely made up of textbooks, the Ryerson Canadian History Readers, and the small-run Ryerson Chapbooks – two titles demonstrate that Pierce was also fostering the most groundbreaking of the new academic history produced by professionally trained historians. Ryerson published Harold Innis's seminal *The Fur Trade in Canada* in 1930 and, three years later, his

Problems of Staple Production in Canada. Pierce thereby put Ryerson in the vanguard of the new critical, environmental history.

By the mid-1930s, Pierce and Innis were launched on a landmark joint publication project in Canadian history that, while it offered Ryerson attractive subsidies for the series in a difficult book market, also showed Pierce's intellectual commitment to increasing the range and complexity of Canadian historiography. Moreover, in their work on the Relations of Canada and the United States series between 1936 and 1945, Pierce and Innis displayed a gritty, "hands-on" nationalism that led them to insist on Canadians' fitness to edit and publish books in the series in the face of criticism from the Carnegie Endowment and Yale University Press.

The Pierce-Innis relationship was sparked by *The Fur Trade in Canada,* that seminal work of the Laurentian school which outlined a geographical and economic thesis for the development of the nation. Pierce recognized the importance of Innis as a thinker, and integrated into his own writings on Canadian nationality Innis's insight that staples had shaped the nation.[51] For his part, Innis was steering manuscripts by other historians to Pierce as early as 1930.[52] By 1932, Pierce aided Innis by taking over the distribution of his *Peter Pond* when the original publisher went bankrupt, keeping the title in the Ryerson catalogue for over a decade.[53] That year, when Innis told Pierce that he felt his essays on transportation history should be "published at the earliest possible moment," Pierce concurred, bringing out *Problems of Staple Production in Canada* in 1933.[54]

By background, publisher and historian were well equipped to understand each other: the two men had some important experiences in common. Four years younger than Pierce, the feisty, dark-haired Harold Innis was, like him, a workaholic with roots in rural Ontario (Otterville in the case of Innis) whose nationalism had been shaped by schoolteaching in the west and military service during the First World War. Like Pierce, too, Innis had felt strong family pressure to join the ministry (Baptist, in his case), though he had successfully resisted the call. And, also like Pierce, Innis had completed graduate work in the United States: in his case at the University of Chicago (PhD 1920).

By 1933, having made his name with his book on the fur trade, Innis, now at the University of Toronto, was advising Pierce on manuscripts and editing Ruth Grant's *The Canadian Atlantic Fishery* (1934) for Ryerson.[55] In 1935, when Ryerson brought out *An Economic History of Canada* by Innis's wife, Mary Quayle Innis, Pierce so valued the book that he pressed for regular revisions and reissues because, as he told Harold Innis in 1945: "This is still the only history of its kind in Canada and while we have never been able to make much money out of it we feel it ought to be kept up to date and that we ought to keep on promoting it. It continues to do a little better all the time."[56] By 1946, Pierce had even created a series centred around Innis's Ryerson titles, dubbed "Staple Industries of Canada," with Innis as editor. While it is clear that romantic history warmed Pierce's heart in a way that the new political and economic history – especially in Innis's knotty prose – did not, he recognized that Innis was a new and important historical force who would add weight to the Ryerson list.

For his part, by the mid-1930s, Innis gave Ryerson an entree to one of the major historical publication projects of the era – the landmark, multivolume Relations of Canada and the United States series, underwritten by the Carnegie Endowment for International Peace. The series was to be a delicate cross-border collaboration, one that showed the resolutely autonomous Canadianism and Herculean (if not flawless) editorial labours of both Innis and Pierce – and an instance of Innis's ruthlessness in the promotion of his interests (and those of the University of Toronto) as he saw them to the potential detriment of Pierce and Ryerson Press.

The series was conceived as a groundbreaking examination of Canada in a North American rather than in the traditional imperial context, a project made possible by two Canadian-born historians, both University of Toronto graduates working in the United States. Columbia professor J. Bartlet Brebner gave a paper on "Canadian and North American History" to the Canadian Historical Association in 1931, containing the germ of the idea for a series on Canadian-American relations which he convinced his "friend and mentor" James Shotwell, director of the Division of Economics and History at the wealthy Carnegie Endowment for International Peace, to fund.[57] Shotwell secured Carnegie approval for the series in 1932 and funding in 1933, with himself as general editor and Brebner as "chief advisor and planner of the historical volumes."[58] The series was planned as a cooperative effort of some forty volumes, with contributions by Canadian and American scholars on aspects of the economic, political, and social history of Canada and the United States, and Ryerson's part of the project comprised twenty-five books of varied emphasis and approach published between 1936 and 1945, including such canonical works of Canadian history as Innis's *The Cod Fisheries* (1940),

Donald Creighton's *The Commercial Empire of the St. Lawrence* (1937), Arthur Lower's *The North American Assault on the Canadian Forest* (1938), and Brebner's *North Atlantic Triangle* (1945).

Innis, involved at an early stage, was not long in enlisting Pierce. Brebner had suggested to Shotwell that Innis be invited to supervise the economic volumes in the series and the latter attended the first planning conference in 1932 in New York City. According to Donald Creighton, Innis insisted to Shotwell, upon pain of his withdrawal from the project, that there be "no direction or supervision from the United States" except that of Shotwell as general editor.[59] The Canadian-born Shotwell was reassuring about such matters: "From my knowledge of Canada I agree with you heartily about the misunderstandings that may arise if our work looks like an investigation of Canadian things by an American corporation of any kind, even a scientific one."[60]

Other Canadian historians were more basic in their reactions to such a joint project in the Depression. Arthur Lower gleefully told Innis that, after earlier work for Carnegie, "I was agreeably surprised at the size of the check ... [since I was] not expecting anything like it, so that if this project means about the same thing, I am for it, being quite unashamedly willing to write for money."[61] Issues of both money and autonomy occurred to Pierce. Yale University Press was to be the American publisher, and a Canadian partner was needed. Pierce wanted it to be Ryerson, since the series promised both revenue in lean times and, even more important, intellectual prestige. Proud of his own academic credentials, Pierce had always wanted Ryerson Press to shine as a Canadian scholarly as well as general publisher. Although Ryerson was not an academic press, Innis initially lobbied for the contract to go to Ryerson. One of the few alternatives might have been the struggling University of Toronto Press, but, as a Toronto professor and administrator, Innis's relations with the Press were at the time rather prickly. Moreover, Innis respected Pierce's commitment to publishing in the field.[62] In any case, no Canadian publisher of the day matched the expertise of Yale University Press.

The Carnegie affiliation looked financially promising. Carnegie was to guarantee all manufacturing costs for each volume published by Ryerson, and to purchase 784 copies of the 1,500 to be produced of each title.[63] Pierce's confidential memo to Donald Solandt in April 1935 after New York meetings with Shotwell assured Solandt that the "excellence and general format" of Ryerson's Canadian Historical Studies series had impressed the Carnegie officials. Pierce's ambitions for himself and

Ryerson were evident as he presented what he called "a fine cooperative enterprise for great ends":

> I was … able to show that The Ryerson Press, through its long tradition, its stable position, general dependability, and the excellence of its productions, was competent to act as Canadian publisher.
> … The retail sales value of the series will be about $180,000 and our profits should be considerable. The prestige this project will give us, once it is announced to the world, should likewise be notable.[64]

Perhaps it was the patriot in Pierce that prompted him to add: "It is also pleasant to know that Dr. Shotwell and Dr. Brebner, members of the Committee, are Canadians." Certainly, Pierce (and Innis) insisted that the Canadian-produced volumes conform to Canadian (Oxford) usage rather than American.[65] Cultural historian Maria Tippett has written of the Carnegie Corporation's extensive involvement in funding Canadian cultural projects in the 1920s and 1930s, especially in the area of the fine arts and adult education, and of the tensions that such involvement brought, tensions between Carnegie's philanthropy and the desire of Canadian grantees for both adequate funding and cultural autonomy.[66] The difficulties between Pierce and Innis, on the one hand, and Carnegie's administrators in the United States, on the other, over the nature of the series illustrate how markedly this somewhat strained relationship affected the production of some books, including such seminal works of Canadian history as Creighton's *The Commercial Empire of the St. Lawrence*. As Tippett suggests, the "fairy godmother" of Carnegie funding and administration sometimes seemed, from the perspective of Innis and Pierce, to resemble an autocratic stepmother.[67]

Once Carnegie gave the go-ahead for Ryerson to act as publisher in the spring of 1935, Pierce and Innis worked closely for the next decade on the series and other ventures. One of Pierce's secretaries remembered how often Innis was closeted in Pierce's office. On his morning car trip into downtown Toronto, Pierce would often pick up Innis in North Toronto to confer en route. Innis, with Pierce as his staunch ally, led the way in fine-tuning the series primarily as they and their Canadian authors, rather than New York, saw fit. Donald Creighton described how the series had a continental but not an overriding continentalist orientation,

in part because Innis let the economic volumes in each series be shaped
by the interests of the researchers, not by "specifications ... laid down for
each volume."[68]

Pierce and Innis often displayed a sturdy independence from New
York. For example, in 1936 Innis and Pierce, confronted by Shotwell's
reluctance to publish a manuscript on the dairy industry because it was
"entirely a Canadian project," simply planned "without hesitation" to
bring it out in the Staple Industries of Canada series which Pierce had
created for Innis.[69] Pierce's nationalist stance showed pluck, because
Ryerson would thereby have lost the Carnegie subsidy for the volume.
Fortunately, Innis prevailed, and *The Dairy Industry in Canada* appeared
under Carnegie aegis in 1937.[70]

In 1937 Shotwell and Brebner worried that both George Glazebrook's
A History of Transportation in Canada (1938) and Creighton's *The Commercial Empire of the St. Lawrence* were too narrowly Canadian.[71] Shotwell wrote to Innis urging revisions to Creighton's manuscript: "It is a
splendid volume for anyone familiar with Canadian history, especially
Canadian economic history, but for the American south of the line the
names of the actors are completely without meaning and the study becomes local and to that degree misunderstood."[72] Creighton did make
some revisions, but it is evident that his Canadian editor and publisher
had both inclined to his point of view rather than Shotwell's. After publication, Shotwell still hoped for "a history on a larger plan at a later
date,"[73] but Creighton was adamant: "The book has its focus in Canada
rather than in North America as a whole; and to make it otherwise
would, I am afraid, have involved writing another book. I am, therefore,
all the more grateful that you found it possible to include the volume as
it stands in the series."[74]

The sheer size of the series led to problems, and to indignant assertions by Pierce and Innis that as Canadian publisher and Canadian
editor respectively they were equal to the task. The volumes, with foot-
notes and often with specialized maps and charts, were technically demanding to produce and often required heavy editing. Both Pierce and
Innis were overworked by many other commitments. Innis, for example,
became head of the Department of Political Economy at Toronto in 1937,
while he was still working on his own series volume on the cod fisheries;
he collapsed from overwork early that year.[75] Innis told Pierce that he
would be "at his elbow," editing and shepherding manuscripts through

the press, but inevitably complications and delays arose, especially since New York had to be consulted.[76]

In June 1937 Pierce, so "loaded with work" that he did "not seem able to get caught up," noted wearily in his diary that four Carnegie volumes were in the printing plant.[77] Ryerson often sent galleys out piecemeal to speed production. There were problems with the specialized maps for the volumes by Lower and Creighton, and inconsistencies in the layout of both books about which both authors complained.[78] Pierce and Innis must have winced when the notably irascible Lower complained to Innis of "amateur production" values in Toronto versus what he felt were higher editorial standards in the United States.[79]

Moreover, Shotwell was becoming impatient. He complained to Pierce about the copy editing on Creighton's and Glazebrook's books.[80] Things reached a crisis in November 1937 as it became apparent that Innis would himself need an editor to rework extensively the "difficulties and obscurities" of the manuscript of *The Cod Fisheries*, problems characteristic of his writing. Shotwell announced to Pierce that he was sending an editor, Arthur McFarlane, to Toronto, primarily to work on the Innis draft but also "as an emergency piece of work, in which the Endowment is endeavouring to co-operate with you to correct some of the things that have slipped in these particular volumes." Shotwell diplomatically added that McFarlane was a University of Toronto graduate, but the implication that the Canadians were unsatisfactory junior partners was clear.[81]

Worse was to follow. In the spring of 1939, Pierce received notice from Yale University Press that Shotwell intended to terminate the publishing arrangement with Ryerson for the series, as the contract provided. The letter was blunt: "Dr. Shotwell has reached this decision on the grounds of the editorial assistance he feels he must have on the forthcoming volumes to be printed in Canada, and which in view of his experiences with you on the earlier volumes he does not believe you can give him."[82] Yale's Norman Donaldson also conveyed the upsetting news that secret negotiations had taken place with the University of Toronto Press to replace Ryerson. Pierce (and seemingly Innis, to Pierce at least) reacted to the news as an insult to Canadian scholarship and to them personally. Cross-border conflict erupted. Pierce wrote two long, impassioned letters to Donaldson, justifying Ryerson, Innis, and himself with respect to the volumes Ryerson had published, going into detail about seven of them, and insisting on equal partnership:

Needless to say, in view of the shape of the copy which reached us, the vast amount of work and care we spent upon it, the high quality of the printing done, and our net losses to date, we resent your criticism of the editorial work done here ... As partners in this enterprise it was surely your duty to apprise [us] of any dissatisfaction in your office or that of the Endowment. Your notice of cancellation of the contract without warning is rather high-handed don't you think? ...

We repeat that we resent the summary nature of your letter, and its implications we deny.[83]

Pierce's letter made it clear how much he had committed to the series. He spoke of the many hours and evenings he, as well as Innis, had spent copy editing manuscripts. He pointed out that Ryerson had not yet made money on the series because, among other costs, the Press had engaged a subeditor for some of the manuscripts and had bought expensive new typefaces needed to produce some of the books. Clearly, Pierce's real commitment to the series was nationalistic, not financial. Moreover, Pierce and Innis were determined to retain editorial power in Canada. When, in the fall of 1939, it was suggested that Yale handle all the editing, without any Canadian involvement in publishing further volumes, Innis indignantly told Pierce that the "suggestion is disquieting and should be resisted as a reflection on Canadian scholarship as well as on myself and the Ryerson Press."[84]

There is, however, a darker thread to this story. As Innis biographer Alexander John Watson points out, by the spring of 1938, Innis was in fact playing a double game. Without telling Pierce, Innis was urging James Shotwell to drop Ryerson and turn to the University of Toronto Press as Canadian publisher of the series. He told Shotwell in April 1938 that "we have made more than our contribution to the Ryerson Press ... Such a move could strengthen enormously the position of the University of Toronto Press and the position of the University of Toronto." Innis even described Ryerson to Shotwell as incompetent and thus in effect "sabotaging" the series. Watson attributes Innis's behaviour to the fact that, despite his image as a "naively principled scholar," he was in reality what Watson terms a "practical academic politician" with overriding goals for himself and the University of Toronto.[85] Certainly, Innis could be ruthlessly ambitious as an academic in-fighter, and in this case his tactics seem questionable. His double-dealing would certainly have pained Pierce both personally and professionally had he known (which he seems to have not).[86]

In the event, despite Innis's equivocations, Pierce's aggressive assertions of worth to Shotwell and Yale University Press were largely successful. Shotwell backed down, telling Innis that Yale University Press (probably as a result of Pierce's démarches to Norman Donaldson) was not eager to drop Ryerson after all and that Yale had volunteered to take the task of dealing with Ryerson Press off Shotwell's hands and handle all editorial work with Ryerson themselves.[87] Accordingly, Ryerson kept the contract for the series.

Not all of Pierce's initiatives were so successful. In 1940, citing a lack of funds, Shotwell turned down Pierce's proposal for a series volume on Canadian and American literature to be written by rising young Canadian critic E.K. Brown (soon to be hired by Cornell University), a favourite of Pierce.[88] For his part, Innis – now back on side with Pierce, in this matter at least – later labelled the omission of such a volume "ominous," given the importance of cultural relations to a true understanding between nations.[89] But by 1940, with the major economic volumes in print, Innis's involvement with the series, if not with Pierce, dwindled, although he did – ironically in view of his earlier undermining of Ryerson – advise Shotwell in May 1941 "not to antagonize Ryerson" over another volume, advice Shotwell called "well-taken."[90]

Ryerson brought out its twenty-fifth and last volume for the series in 1945, Brebner's *North Atlantic Triangle*. When one considers the Canadian publishing history of the series, it is clear that Pierce stood for a sturdy "hands-on" Canadian nationalism in both publishing mechanics and intellectual orientation, most notably with Donald Creighton's *Commercial Empire of the St. Lawrence*. Whatever the editing and production difficulties – and it is clear that Ryerson's editorial standards were not always flawless as far as academic format and apparatus were concerned – Pierce, with Innis's support, had unquestionably been a midwife for one of the most important scholarly initiatives in twentieth-century historical publishing in Canada. Arguably, no Canadian publisher, including the University of Toronto Press, had at this juncture the resources or the expertise in academic publishing to accomplish more.[91]

Pierce, in ignorance of Innis's 1938 slamming of Ryerson Press to Shotwell, bonded with Innis in their struggles over manuscripts and with New York. In the pair's correspondence in the 1940s and 1950s, Pierce and Innis made no bones about the importance to each of them of stimulating Canadian nationalism. In 1944 Innis commiserated with Pierce about the state of the nation: "The endless religious and language problems and its division of the English between Canadian Canadians and colonial Canadians make one feel more and more pessimistic. You have had a long and tiring struggle with the same problem as a publisher. And of course the difficulties are not lessened by this inability to discuss them in public – the concealed major pettiness is tremendously important. The result of this frustration can be seen in the endless drain of Canadians to American institutions – a drain which requires tremendous energy to resist."[92]

However, there was a certain irony in Innis's reference to "concealed major pettiness" in Canadian issues, given that Innis had concealed things from Pierce in the matter of the Carnegie contract. Furthermore, Innis's prickliness had caused another imbroglio for Pierce about which he was all too painfully aware. In 1939, as a member of the Royal Society of Canada, Innis was at the centre of what Pierce called a "vicious" dispute over the awarding of the Lorne Pierce Medal.[93]

In April 1939 the nominations committee for the medal had recommended that it be awarded to anglophone Montreal historian Colonel Wilfrid Bovey, author of *The French Canadians Today* (1938), a work very sympathetic to French Canadians.[94] The general feeling in the Society was that the nominating committee was giving Bovey the medal to honour his promotion of French-English entente. But Innis saw things differently. Because the Lorne Pierce Medal was designated as an award for contributions to Canadian literature, Innis told Society officials that, while he was "cognizant" of Bovey's contribution to French-English relations, his work did not "show distinction in Canadian literature." Accordingly, if Bovey were honoured, "the medal will be cheapened for the existing holders."[95] Innis declared he would resign from the Society if Bovey got the medal, but – rather ironically in view of the fracas he was causing – he offered $50 toward a *bonne entente* medal to be awarded to Bovey instead. He also wrote Bovey that there was "nothing personal" about his stand, a sentiment Bovey must have found cold comfort.[96]

Pierce, who usually tried to stay out of the nomination process for the medal he had donated, was now caught up in the controversy as Innis and Royal Society officials lobbied him. Innis wrote to Pierce that he believed the award had been meant to go to a French Canadian but that the nominating committee had substituted Bovey instead. A comment on the letter in Pierce's handwriting beside Innis's account of the committee's alleged machinations reads "not really true of course."[97] In a confidential letter, Pierce emphasized to the Royal Society's Arthur Beauchesne, who had headed the nominating committee, that he was "pained and shocked" by the affair and that he himself "must have nothing whatever to do with the Medal which bears my name." That said, Pierce hoped for a solution because Innis would be a "tragic loss" to the Society.[98]

But, in the event, Bovey was awarded the Lorne Pierce Medal at the insistence of the Royal Society executive. Innis then resigned as secretary of Section II of the Society, attacking Beauchesne's "carelessness in the handling of the award."[99] More painful yet to Pierce, the Quebec press got wind of the matter, and Pierce was sent a clipping from a Trois-Rivières paper which described the fuss.[100] Pierce, who understandably stayed away from the 1939 meetings, pointed out in a letter to Beauchesne (who in turn had written him denouncing Innis's "pique"[101]) that the uproar "brings my name into prominence in a way that makes me very sad indeed. I have dedicated my life to good will, and 'la bonne entente' between our peoples. Nothing must threaten this."[102]

Whatever Innis's transgressions against Pierce in the Royal Society or at the Carnegie Endowment in the late 1930s, within a few years Pierce and Innis once more made common cause. After the end of the Second World War, they were disturbed by what they saw as the increasing role of the social sciences, which, as Innis put it, were "spreading all over the place and assuming a general omniscience."[103] More particularly, both Innis and Pierce were concerned about the tendency they perceived in the United Church to emphasize social action at the expense of ideas, without a sufficient stress on the need for ethics and for training in social service. As Pierce put it wryly to Innis in 1947: "The loss of intellectual interest in the Church, its substitution of social action in the hands of half-trained 'experts' would glumly regulate the lives, spiritual and otherwise, of our people and calls for further development in our thinking."[104] That year, Pierce applauded a draft paper Innis sent him on the subject (both were members of a post-war United Church committee pondering Christianity and culture) with an exuberant "Harold old boy you pack a [nasty] punch!" Pierce supplied some punch of his own by writing a crisp concluding paragraph to the paper – one that Innis adopted wholesale – calling for the church to return to an interest in ideas or at least to put more concern for integrity and respect for the individual into the promulgation of social action.[105]

Pierce's own 1947 companion paper on "Christianity and Culture in Our Time," written along the same lines, was dedicated to Innis "In Friendship and Admiration." (Did Innis blush?) Both papers appeared in *The Time of Healing*, the 1947 annual report of the United Church of Canada's Board of Evangelism and Social Service. In his paper, Pierce called for the contemporary Protestant church to foster an intelligent leadership "elite" which was "liberal and nonconformist," one able with "broad sympathy and ripeness ... to distinguish between values and valuables, between the whole man and the social man, between the Christian idea of man and a blind economic determinism."

In these papers, Pierce and Innis, as leading Canadian intellectuals, were concertedly doing their best to provoke greater intellectual dynamism and self-awareness in the United Church in the face of what Pierce described as the need to preserve the "sacredness of the individual," so that man might "preserve his own soul from the suffocating snares of cosmopolitanism, internationalism and pan-Communism."[106] Privately, Pierce wrote to his son of his admiration for Innis. In wartime letters, Pierce described Innis as "one of the big men of our time," later musing about his "thrilling" but dense prose: "[Innis] mistrusts any group that usurps power, political, religious, banking or any other group ... Innis fought through the last [war], was a private, was severely wounded. He hates heads of state who know it all and settle all matters by a wave of the hand."[107] The two were linked by sturdy Canadian nationalism and a distrust of technocrats.

When Innis approached Ryerson Press to publish his book of essays *Political Economy in the Modern State*, Pierce agreed, issuing the book in 1946 at a time when post-war paper and labour shortages were forcing curtailment of the company's list, a measure of his commitment to putting Innis's ideas before the public. He also promised Innis that he would do his best to keep *The Fur Trade in Canada* (1930) in print, despite the fact that Donaldson of Yale University Press had told Innis that it had taken them fifteen years to sell a thousand copies.[108] Ironically, Innis's preface to *Political Economy in the Modern State* included unflattering references to the deficiencies of Canadian publishing as a cultural force and to the "fly-blown romances" of Canadian literature.[109] Nevertheless, Pierce gamely applauded Innis's "gusto and ping" in a display of his own integrity as a publisher: "Halfway through the Foreword I wanted to creep up on you with a shotgun but when I finished it, in spite of my strong disagreement, I decided to stand up in front of you and defend your right to speak as you have."[110]

Pierce continued to comment on and consider Innis's manuscripts – and Innis continued to act as a Ryerson reader – but the 1946 work was Innis's last Ryerson imprint. Carl Berger has written that Innis's contemporaries greeted his forays into communications theory with admiration for his intellectual daring and bewilderment at his theoretical obscurity.[111] Pierce was no exception. In an age before government subventions for academic publishing, Pierce recognized that Ryerson Press literally could not afford to follow Innis down such a tangled path. However, his exchanges with Innis show the humour and diplomacy with which Pierce could convey to an author that his work was not viable for publication. For example, when Innis delivered his abstruse 1947 Presidential Address to the Royal Society on the influence of methods of communication upon civilizations, Pierce jokingly asked him: "What are you feeding Minerva's Owl? Barbed wire?"[112] He later told Innis: "I think 'Minerva's Owl' perhaps needed amplification, at least for me, as did your Oxford lectures [published in 1950 as *Empire and Communications*], for your ability to condense and tip-toe over the stepping stones at the ford leaves me, for one, puffing and huffing far behind."[113]

Understandably, Pierce must have judged that book sales would also lag in a similar fashion. In the event, Oxford University Press, not Ryerson, published *Empire and Communications*. Pierce had considered a Canadian edition, but again his disarmingly self-deprecating comments to Innis suggest that he found the material too limited in its audience: "The more I read [the manuscript] the more humble I became and the deeper [my] blush. I hate to admit it, and I hope you will guard the secret well, but there is an awful lot that I do not know."[114] Beneath the blarney, Pierce's meaning is evident: Innis had left too many readers behind for Pierce to be able to publish him. Similarly, when Innis submitted the manuscript of *The Bias of Communication* to Pierce in 1950, Pierce wondered about "cutting down the papers on communication" which he found full of obscurities and "back-tracking." Upbeat but clearly reluctant, he cited publication costs which made financial aid to publish it desirable.[115] As a result, the University of Toronto Press, not Ryerson, published the book in 1951. The following year, Pierce was to have one final, poignant involvement in an Innis-related publishing project. Days after Innis's sadly early death, he suggested to Donald Creighton that he write a memoir of his friend and colleague. But the University of Toronto Press was to publish that work.[116]

PIERCE'S COMMITMENT to sustained publication of material by artist C.W. Jefferys (as well as of the whiggish Canadian History Readers he illustrated) and by Harold Innis and his colleagues establish that he fostered very different aspects of Canadian history and historiography, often simultaneously. He thus showed uncommon commitment and breadth as a publisher of Canadian history. His heart was with romantic history, and his textbook editing and patronage of C.W. Jefferys as historical illustrator constituted national mythmaking that reached tens of thousands of Canadians in school and out of it, shaping for better and for worse the popular image of Canadian history in the public mind over several decades. But Pierce also went on to publish Innis's more critical works of environmental history, as well as canonical works by Donald Creighton, Arthur Lower, and others, and, with Innis, he helped to ensure some "made in Canada" content in the editing and publishing of the landmark Relations of Canada and the United States series. If Pierce did not publish Innis's work on communications, he at least gave it thoughtful consideration, in comments and suggestions that Innis found useful.[117] Certainly, he published Innis's own works on economic history without any prospect of large financial returns, because he saw Innis as an important Canadian thinker.

As publisher, Lorne Pierce was therefore a crucial figure in both the popularization and professionalization of Canadian history in the mid-twentieth century, albeit one hitherto in the shadow of his authors and artists such as Innis and Jefferys respectively. Pierce's influence as publisher has too often been thought of primarily in terms of his role in our literary history through initiatives like the Makers of Canadian Literature series or the Ryerson Poetry Chapbooks. Yet, in the light of his relations with Jefferys and Innis, it is clear that, during the middle of the twentieth century, Pierce wove his cultural nationalism into the very fabric of Canada's art, history, and education.

16

Through the Depression to Greater Autonomy

Publishing Frederick Philip Grove and
Laura Goodman Salverson, 1933–1954

[Y]ou have taught me, Dr. Pierce[,] almost all that I have learned
about book publishing. I am to you as the jackpine is to the oak.

Book Steward C.H. Dickinson to Lorne Pierce, 1947, on the tenth
anniversary of Dickinson's appointment to the House[1]

There are too many books ... being turned out today ... [that are]
prurient just for the sake of being that.

Lorne Pierce to novelist Laura Goodman Salverson, 1945[2]

In 1930 some three-quarters of the Ryerson publication list – sixty-two
titles out of the eighty-four published that year – were textbooks or
chapbooks.[3] Lean times indeed. It was no different at other firms: in one
Depression year, Macmillan of Canada published just thirty-six titles
out of over two thousand submissions.[4] At the House, Pierce saw at first
hand the toll the Depression exacted on all stages of the book-publishing
process from editing to manufacturing. As Randall Speller points out,
among major Canadian book publishers, "only Ryerson Press printed
and bound its own books, using its own type specimen book, in-house
binding and staff of long-serving craftsman."[5]

One of the few bright notes of the 1930s was Pierce's greater administrative freedom. The death of Donald Solandt in August 1936 ended
years of acrimonious tension with two successive book stewards. By October 1936, Pierce's diary recorded "less tension and better work" at the
House as a search committee was appointed to find a successor to Solandt. In June 1937 Pierce recorded optimistically in his diary: "Rev. C.H.
Dickinson of Montreal is the new Book Steward – 38 years old and looks
good."[6]

Clarence Heber Dickinson – Heber to his intimates – was short, peppy, and bespectacled, with a shiny bald pate fringed with dark brown hair. Born on a farm near St Mary's, Ontario, on 8 October 1899, Dickinson shared some background with Pierce. He grew up with a devout mother who was ambitious for him, and attended Victoria College, graduating with a general BA in 1921. Unlike Pierce, he was "no scholar" and "graduated very modestly."[7] However, like Pierce, Dickinson underwent the rigours of work as a probationary minister in the Methodist mission fields of Saskatchewan and spent a year at New York's Union Theological Seminary, after his ordination in 1924. Returning to Victoria College for a BD in 1926, Dickinson, after three other pulpits, became minister of Montreal's fashionable American Church on Sherbrooke Street in 1931. There he distinguished himself at fundraising as chair of its relief committee. By his own account, some of his critiques of the business ethic raised hackles in his prosperous congregation. Nevertheless, jeweller Henry Birks put him forward for Ryerson's book stewardship when the congregation amalgamated with another to form Erskine and American Church, rendering one minister redundant. Dickinson initially declined the post because he was reluctant to give up preaching and "knew nothing of organized business, and certainly nothing about book publishing."[8] But, six weeks later, he changed his mind. At the time he joined the House, its staff numbered 250, as well as some 150 factory employees, with an annual sales volume of some $3.5 million annually.[9]

As book steward of the United Church Publishing House, Dickinson essentially gave Pierce *carte blanche* as editor of Ryerson Press. In many ways, this deference was understandable. Dickinson, who did not have strong innate literary interests, later admitted that at the House "I depended heavily on my colleagues."[10] Pierce's national reputation, wit, intellect, and successful textbook series clearly awed Dickinson,[11] who felt that Pierce provided "distinguished editorial leadership" which set "a standard ... by which to judge the writings of Canadian authors and poets, and to preserve the work of artists and historians. Only the best was acceptable."[12] Tellingly, Dickinson later wrote an admiring account of his subordinate, not vice versa.[13] Yet, in the twenty-three years they worked together, Pierce consistently supported his superior. There were a few occasions when Pierce winced a little over Dickinson's actions. For example, Pierce was uncomfortable when Dickinson gave speeches that stressed Ryerson's status as a church publishing house: Pierce confided to his children that he liked to have the two "kept separate."[14]

As was standard House practice, Pierce wrote and submitted authors' contracts to Dickinson for his signature (the standard royalty for authors was 10 per cent). But the decisions about who and what to publish were almost invariably Pierce's; Dickinson rarely met authors, for instance. Under him, the in-house publishing committee, directed by Pierce, and made up of six to ten staff members, chiefly the House's department heads, met once a month or so to review Pierce's planned spring and fall lists. But, in fact, Dickinson would later recall, "very, very seldom were any of Dr. Pierce's recommendations declined."[15]

Dickinson also remembered that, by the late 1930s, members of the United Church's Board of Publication (the committee of some thirty ministers and laymen appointed from across Canada by the United Church, which oversaw the House and to which the book steward reported annually), concurred with the view that Pierce's publication lists were patriotic, good for French-English relations, and/or calculated to raise the level of public or school reading – even when they wondered if some of Pierce's publications were not too highbrow or unlikely to make money.[16] It no doubt helped that these goals were clearly in harmony with the role that the House had established for itself since its nineteenth-century beginnings.[17]

In short, by the Second World War, with Dickinson's support, the Board of Publication regarded Pierce and the publication lists of Ryerson Press as embodying prestige, quality, and patriotism. Moreover, the board, like Dickinson, accepted that some publishing profits from Pierce's textbook publications and from Trade Department head E.W. Walker's wholesaling of American and English best-sellers (books for which the House held agency reprinting and/or distribution rights from foreign publishers) would in effect subsidize Pierce's "highbrow" Ryerson publications.[18] Pierce's formidable efforts to establish successful textbook lines and become known as a distinguished and patriotic figure in publishing had finally assured his position at the House.

Dickinson did regularly remonstrate with Pierce about the dangers of compulsive overwork.[19] At the same time, he saw himself as indebted to Pierce for the latter's "magnificent" sharing of his expertise with him.[20] Their relationship is best summed up by a 1947 tribute from Dickinson to Pierce: "You have taught me, Dr. Pierce, almost all that I have learned about publishing. I am to you as the jackpine is to the oak."[21]

Dickinson's deference to Pierce was probably reinforced by their unusual arrangements over Pierce's own textbook royalties. Pierce adopted an unorthodox strategy that ensured that his royalty income would not foster the resentment in Dickinson that it had in his two predecessors. By the mid-1940s, Pierce had established a practice of presenting Dickinson with a generous cheque drawn on his own royalties twice a year, characterizing the gesture as a gift toward the education of Dickinson's two sons.[22] Although we do not know the amounts involved, they were probably in the hundreds of dollars for each cheque, since Dickinson uses terms like "generous gift" and "magnificent gesture" in his notes of thanks.[23]

Given that House salaries, even for executives, were low and that Pierce's total income probably exceeded his boss's because of royalties, the gifts were certainly generous as well as strategic. But the gifts were also ethically and organizationally questionable. It is noteworthy that one of Dickinson's notes to Pierce stresses confidentiality: "I know it is a private matter. We shall keep it entirely to ourselves."[24] Even three decades after Pierce's death, Dickinson fell silent when asked about the matter.[25] After all, accepting such cheques in effect made Dickinson beholden to Pierce. Certainly, if known, the matter would have caused great resentment within the House on the part of other managers, and the Board of Publication would probably have disapproved as well. Clearly, the book steward was in a conflict-of-interest position with his subordinate, while Pierce was implicitly subverting the administrative chain of command. Although Dickinson was inclined in any case to defer to his distinguished editor's seniority and experience in his department with or without such gifts, in hindsight it is unfortunate that the House's low salaries seemed to have inclined Dickinson to accept such an awkward arrangement – and Pierce to offer it. Dickinson had good reason, then, to describe Pierce as oak to his Jack pine: the oak dropped tasty acorns all around Dickinson season after season.

In the late 1930s, however, with the bottom line in House revenues improving somewhat, Pierce could be a little more expansive with time and money in both his professional and personal life. In February 1938 the United Church Publishing House's overall profits began to inch upward, with a net profit for all operations reported at $40,419.89, compared to profits of $26,283.99 a year earlier. Pierce's own departments were bleeding less red ink: his departments reported only a small operating loss in February 1938, totalling $4,415.61 for both retail and educational books, less than a third of the previous year's combined losses of $14,278.01.[26]

Pierce accordingly took on a number of new commitments. He again became involved with Frederick Philip Grove, whom he had not published since the fracas over Grove's novel *Settlers of the Marsh* (1925). In the late 1930s, although he soon cut down on his commitment to Grove, finding his work lacking in uplift and slow in sales, he remained a staunch supporter of the work of novelist Laura Goodman Salverson, whose themes he found more congenial and whose work also touched on the western immigrant experience so important to Pierce.

However, Pierce strongly criticized manuscripts by both writers that touched on themes of sexual promiscuity. As a result of his conservative attitude to fiction, Ryerson Press by the 1940s was increasingly viewed by young writers (Earle Birney, for example) as prim and "fuddy-duddy." Pierce may have been uncomfortable when his book steward emphasized Ryerson Press's link to the United Church, but his own moral values shaped its publication list in both positive and negative ways, as its lacklustre record on the modern novel would show. More positively, in another area of the Ryerson publishing list, Pierce undertook a major, pioneering, nationalistic initiative in Canadian art history with his Canadian Art series in the late 1930s and early 1940s.

Outside his Ryerson work, Pierce also increased his personal activities. In the late 1930s he briefly took on a prominent role in the magazine industry as publisher of the *Canadian Bookman*. He soon got out of this financially draining personal fling as it became clear he had neither the time nor the money to spend in such a venture. Pierce also increased his commitment to freemasonry, contributing both to its literature and to its philanthropic work at the same time as he ascended within the ranks of the Masonic Order. Moreover, the challenges of his own deafness prompted him to move the Masons into the area of philanthropic work with deaf schoolchildren. He himself became a prime force in the founding of a national society for the deaf in the period 1937 to 1940, now known as the Canadian Hearing Society.

PIERCE'S RENEWED involvement with Grove in the late 1930s proved mutually disappointing. Despite the pile of manuscripts that Grove submitted, Pierce ultimately saw fit to publish only two titles – the novel *Two Generations: A Story of Present Day Ontario* (1939) and a 1939 reprinting of Grove's autobiographical *A Search for America*, originally published by Graphic in 1927. Pierce was now a seasoned publisher who had the wherewithal to change his initial intentions, even toward a well-known author, if he found the sales and the direction of a writer's work less than satisfactory.

Perhaps tellingly, Pierce's involvement with Grove in the late 1930s came at Grove's initiative. Grove had settled in Simcoe, Ontario, after the failure of Ottawa's Graphic Press in 1931, which had cut short his editorial position there. The bankruptcy of Graphic also left sales and distribution of Grove's autobiographical work *A Search for America* (1927) in limbo. More than ever chronically short of money, Grove turned to Pierce. The two men now shared more than an interest in Canadian writing and the prairie experience. They also shared a handicap. Grove's hearing, like Pierce's, had increasingly worsened until he was, in his own phrase, "desperately hard of hearing."[27]

In November 1938 Grove wrote to Pierce that he had gathered enough subscribers to print an "author's edition" of his new novel *Two Generations* to be sold privately. Accordingly, he asked Pierce if Ryerson would be willing to issue a trade edition, using the type from the author's edition. Grove told Pierce that following his epics of the west, *Two Generations* constituted his first "Ontario novel" and "even [had] a 'happy ending.'" He added that the work was "so exclusively Canadian" that he had been unable to secure an American publisher.[28] Pierce and Grove met in Pierce's offices in early December 1938. It is poignant to imagine the two men – the ponderous, silver-haired writer and the spruce, witty publisher – each fumbling with his hearing aid as they negotiated. In the event, Pierce brought out 1,000 copies of a trade edition as well as 500 copies for Grove to sell to his subscribers, with Ryerson paying Grove $600 for the trade printing.[29]

Pierce was clearly upbeat about Grove in late 1938. He also agreed to buy 2,000 unbound copies of *A Search for America* which Grove held after the Graphic collapse, and bring them out through Ryerson, as well as acquire for sale some 450 unsold copies of another Grove novel of the Canadian west, *Fruits of the Earth* (1933), from Dent, its publisher. Pierce agreed, too, to try to procure remaindered copies of two other novels held by Macmillan, although, as it turned out, none were available.[30] Pierce concluded a letter to Grove just after their negotiations on a ringing note of commitment that would later haunt him: "It is our present purpose to advertise your works collectively as 'The Complete Works of Frederick Philip Grove.' We are to have the refusal of any novel which you may write, and we look forward to a long and happy association."[31]

It was not to be. Even before *Two Generations* and *A Search for America* appeared in 1939, Pierce received a reproachful note from Grove just after Christmas 1938. The writer deplored the fact Ryerson had not yet paid him for unbound *Search* sheets sent by Grove in early December, holding the delay "responsible for the blackest Christmas I have ever lived through."[32] Over the next several years, Pierce was to become a sort of failed fairy godmother in Grove's eyes. At first, however, Grove was touchingly optimistic about his future with Ryerson. In early 1939 he even sent Pierce suggestions for a Grove monogram to be featured on the covers of a collected series of his works, adding that he had dreamt of a "definitive edition bound in plum-coloured cloth."[33]

Over the next few years, Grove sent Pierce a cascade of manuscripts, including typescripts of his novel "The Master of the Mill" (which he submitted in August 1939), his autobiographical "In Search of Myself" (submitted in March 1940), and his "Ant-Book" parable of human life (March 1940), later published by Macmillan as *Consider Her Ways* (1947).[34] But, by July 1941, Pierce, despite many cordial letters to Grove, had not accepted any of these manuscripts – nor in fact, would he publish anything more of Grove's except an abridged school edition of *A Search for America* in 1947.[35] Pierce had reluctantly concluded that Grove's work had become increasingly drawn-out, radiating "prodigious drudgery." Moreover, as Pierce told one critic (but not Grove): "In all [Grove's] work there is no sanctuary, no overwhelming belief in anything outside himself, no hymn on his lips, no ineffable name, no self-forgetfulness. He plods patiently like an ox from detail to detail." For Pierce, Grove's works lacked idealism, one of Pierce's literary touchstones – "nothing in them for hungry people looking up."[36]

In this respect, Pierce found Grove's manuscript "Felix Powell's Career" bleak, and its central character morally distasteful. He was also reluctant to get burned again over issues of sexual candour as he had with *Settlers of the Marsh* in 1925. He had admired *Settlers*, and felt committed to its western Canadian setting, and so braved the outrage: but neither factor applied to "Felix Powell's Career." The work of autobiographical fiction, which Grove described as "a college story with a multiple sex theme" and which Mrs Grove apparently later destroyed, was uncongenial to Pierce. His distaste was evident in his comments to Grove after he read the manuscript in May 1940: "It would require a great deal of courage to publish. I suppose it is all necessary to the narrative, but I, personally, doubt the necessity for so much circumstantial evidence [i.e., sexual behaviour]. Your picture of Felix Powell is a champion portrait of a cad. He is a very common type, and might need a book written on him. Before that last chapter ends, the crowded raft enters the rapids, and everyone sinks. It is as good an ending as any."[37] Pierce clearly wanted to discourage this type of sexually frank fiction. He was similarly negative to novelist Laura Goodman Salverson about a sexually candid manuscript of hers at this period, one also never published. Meanwhile, in the face of Pierce's distaste, Grove asked him to return the manuscript.

Pierce later revealed that he was also disappointed with *Two Generations*, the Grove novel he published in 1939. His 1949 obituary of Grove for the Royal Society of Canada declared that the book "brought nothing new to the Canadian novel, while its understanding of Ontario and its people was not impressive." He added that Grove's characterization, there as elsewhere, showed "little subtlety or swift insight." In a most damning verdict on a writer, Pierce began the obituary by suggesting that Grove "failed to understand his own world and his own times, much less understand himself."[38] He admired Grove's dedication to his craft, but clearly he was ultimately disappointed in his vision as a writer.

Pierce's experience with the public's and the book world's response to Grove's work in the late 1930s and 1940s largely reinforced his own strictures. Even though the reviews of *Two Generations* were generally positive, with the *Globe and Mail*'s William Arthur Deacon even calling it Grove's "best book" to date,[39] neither *Two Generations* nor *A Search for America* sold well. Pierce told Grove bluntly in the spring of 1941: "Although we continue to catalogue, advertise and carry your ... books ... the sales are negligible, as they are of all Canadian titles without exception."[40] The reason was not that Pierce had not laboured hard on Grove's behalf. For example, in early 1940, he sent *Two Generations* to two U.S. publishers seeking an American edition, and a copy of the novel to MGM to sell film rights, but the consensus was that the story line moved "rather slowly" and that the book lacked appeal for an American print or cinema audience.[41] About the same time, Pierce sent the manuscript of what would become Grove's *In Search of Myself* to American publishers Little Brown and Appleton-Century, only to have both reject it.[42]

Ryerson's readers' reports on Grove's manuscripts were no more encouraging. In 1942 S. Morgan-Powell, book columnist of the Montreal *Star*, reported to Pierce that he was "very disappointed" with the manuscript of "The Master of the Mill" because the novel seemed "to lack the realistic fighting quality I found so stimulating in his earlier volumes."[43]

Pierce himself was even more damning about the book, later terming it "a failure … melodramatic and unreal."[44]

Moreover, in the early 1940s, the labour and paper shortages in publishing as a result of the Second World War could not have made Pierce eager to publish long works by Grove for which neither he, nor Canadian readers, nor American publishers seemed to have any appetite. His initial enthusiasm for Grove ebbed. Grove, for his part, became disillusioned with Pierce. In July 1941, when Pierce rejected "In Search of Myself" after keeping it for over a year, Grove responded that there was a "certain unfairness" to the decision because of the "time element" but that Pierce should know that he was "constitutionally unable to bear a grudge."[45]

Desmond Pacey has pointed out that, given Pierce's "[virtual] promise" of a collected edition in 1938, Grove's "reiterated disappointment" is "perfectly understandable."[46] Furthermore, given that Pierce's letters to Grove did not fully reflect his largely negative assessment of Grove's later work, Grove's disappointment with Pierce's failure to publish "In Search of Myself" is the more understandable. Yet, although Pierce's letters masked his unhappiness, there is a revealing ambivalence in Pierce's phrasing. For example, shortly before declining "In Search of Myself," promising Grove speedy news on a whole batch of manuscripts, Pierce wrote equivocally: "I feel that we have got to do something and do it now for you, or find a convincing argument why we should do nothing."[47]

When Ryerson published none of these manuscripts, Grove bore a grudge, even though Pierce aided Grove in joining the Royal Society and gave him work as a reader.[48] When Macmillan brought out *The Master of the Mill* (1944) – and subsequently published *In Search of Myself* and *Consider Her Ways* – Grove commented trenchantly to Desmond Pacey: "Ryerson's I no longer trust."[49] He told Macmillan in 1945 that Ryerson would never get to publish his collected works even if Pierce made another offer.[50]

Ironically, at this time, Pierce did publish critic Desmond Pacey's *Frederick Philip Grove* (1945), a scholarly study of Grove's work. Pacey, then a feisty and ambitious young professor at Manitoba's Brandon College, wrote to Pierce in December 1943 suggesting a book on Grove.[51] He later recalled that Pierce agreed "after some hesitation," but in fact Pacey quickly received agreement from Pierce in early January 1944 that he do a book of some 25,000 words.[52] Pierce did take some time to comment on Pacey's manuscript: Pacey wrote in December 1944 that he had still not received Pierce's comments despite submitting it at the end of the summer.[53] Pierce then attempted to get Pacey to concur with some of his own judgments about Grove. He suggested – and Pacey agreed – that Pacey's final chapter be expanded to give more consideration to Grove's place in Canadian fiction, a topic that Pierce had vainly suggested that Grove address in *In Search of Myself*. Pierce also shared with Pacey his disappointment in *The Master of the Mill*, but Pacey told him that he did not have as "low" an opinion of that work. Pierce also debated with Pacey about the pessimism and lack of "uplift" in Grove, which Pierce felt to be a failing. He wondered whether Pacey wished to change his last chapter in this respect. But Pacey refused, telling Pierce in March 1945: "The writer's task, in my opinion, is not to uplift us but to make us more fully alive, and the greatest writer is he who is most fully alive in his own age. Now any man who has been fully alive during the last fifty years could hardly fail to be the victim of profound perplexity and even of despondency … Grove is a kind of Canadian Dreiser, but that is to his credit."[54] The exchange between Pacey and Pierce in fact crystallizes the differing views of literature's role held by Pierce and a younger, modernist generation. Pierce, to his credit, let Pacey have his say: Pacey's book analyzes Grove's work admiringly as an "intensely tragic" oeuvre of "perpetual struggle."[55]

Pacey's book on Grove sold no better for Ryerson than its Grove titles had. A later Pacey letter refers to the "financial debacle" of his royalties on the volume.[56] Moreover, Pierce himself, although he was impressed with Pacey generally, and was to publish, and even initiate, major works of Canadian criticism by Pacey in the 1950s, continued to question the accuracy of Pacey's view of Grove. In 1946 Pierce discussed with Queen's professor G.H. Clarke the latter's proposal to edit an anthology of Grove's work to highlight his strengths. He told Clarke that he was "nearer the core of the matter than Pacey" in believing that Grove had "no appreciable influence" in Canadian letters. Pierce added: "There is no fire in [Grove] … no heat, nothing to warm one."[57] A decade later, in an exchange of letters with journalist Wilfrid Eggleston about their mutual suspicions about the accuracy of Grove's account of his early life (the facts of which were not exposed until the 1970s by critic Douglas Spettigue), Pierce commented that "Pacey could not be curbed in his book on Grove."[58] He clearly thought that Pacey had ranked Grove too highly.

Pierce's relations with both Grove the writer and Pacey the critic show that, by the late 1930s and into the 1940s, he operated with more authority as editor of Ryerson Press. He felt free to decide to take Grove on, but also to revise his opinions of Grove's work and to decline to continue publishing him despite his 1938 declaration of intent to do so. Moreover, Pierce now – after over two decades at Ryerson – was not shy to debate the critics he published about their judgments of Canadian writers.

PIERCE AT THIS TIME was also very "hands on" in his dealings with another writer who, like Grove, took the immigrant experience in western Canada as a major theme in novels and memoirs. Laura Goodman Salverson had begun her writing career with McClelland and Stewart in 1923 with the successful novel *The Viking Heart*, an account of Icelandic settlers in Manitoba. Salverson, the Winnipeg-born daughter of struggling Icelandic immigrants, had grown up in the Canadian and American west with a love of Icelandic history and literature, particularly its sagas. She also developed a fascination with the intellectual and spiritual effects of the meeting of the Old World and the New implicit in the immigrant experience. Given his interest in western Canadian themes, Pierce was an important force in the extent to which Salverson, as Kristjana Gunnars points out, was in her day able to bring the ethnic and immigrant experience before mainstream Canadians and win "acceptance" with her "readable and entertaining" novels.[59]

Born in the same year, 1890, Pierce and Salverson also shared some views of fiction and of nationality. The dark-haired, determined Salverson, like Pierce, was more drawn to romance than to realism in fiction, and some of her statements on art were congenial to Pierce. In her writings, Salverson asserted that novels should deal with "great truths," and she exalted the romanticist who – as opposed to the "limited … three-dimensional" realist – "took his characters into a four-dimensional realm, the realm of the mind and the imagination where were found enduring and universal truths."[60] For his part, Pierce wrote admiringly of *The Viking Heart* in 1927, noting that Salverson had "married the spirit of the romantic past to the romantic present."[61] Moreover, Salverson's views on Canadian nationality were close to Pierce's in some respects. Like him, she believed that Canadians of all backgrounds must be inspired to love their country, as one newspaper account of a speech by her makes clear: "Mrs. Salverson found great pride in Canada as a country. She would do away as soon as possible with the term 'foreign' and make all things contribute to one united citizenship … Canada she described as a 'young country,' in which wonderful possibilities lie for citizenship to develop in their right and true course, and in all this will be found the making of life and character."[62]

Critic Daisy Neijmann has pointed out that Salverson was a "convinced socialist" who was "appalled by Canada's lack of [social] support systems."[63] But Salverson (perhaps deliberately) never emphasized these views to Pierce in their correspondence. Further, despite her own socialism, she shared Pierce's coolness toward left-wing fiction of the era. Like Pierce, she stressed the need for idealism, not anything that smacked of socialist realism or of modernist "fragmentation, alienation, and scepticism."[64] She told him in late 1939 that she agreed that "when we have read books such as [John Steinbeck's] *The Grapes of Wrath* we put the book down and there our interest ends. The poet is wiser when he stirs the dreamer in us – strikes a little pain in our hearts."[65]

Neijmann maintains that Pierce did not emphasize what she calls his "imperial Ontario Wasp" nationalism to Salverson,[66] but both Neijmann's characterization of Pierce's nationalism and his alleged silence about it to Salverson are not borne out by the Pierce-Salverson correspondence. In fact, as Neijmann herself notes in her article on Salverson, Pierce was always committed to encouraging western literary expression (and Atlantic Canadian as well, championing as he did Carman, Roberts, and others), even at considerable risk to his own career in the case of Grove's *Settlers of the Marsh*. Pierce was indeed a nationalist, but not an Ontario-centric one. Also, his views on Canadian nationalism were well known to Salverson. Pierce even sent Salverson a copy of his booklet *The Armoury in Our Halls* (1941), which outlined his ideals for Canadian nationalism in wartime. In it, Pierce advocated some ideas about the mission of literature in the face of materialism and of fascism which Salverson in fact found congenial. Pierce wrote: "The literature of a country is the chief Alma Mater of the national spirit, and it should be fostered by every intelligent means. If our literature interprets accurately the Canadian social enterprise to Canadians, and if it explains Canada honestly to others, then that literature has value."[67] He stressed that arts and literature should explore the "native soil" and the "racial inheritance"; he also applauded the fact that many Canadian historians had "ceased to patronize racial and religious groups within our borders."[68] In response, Salverson congratulated Pierce on the booklet in March 1941, saying that she shared his view that Canadian society had lost its sense of direction and was too intolerant.[69] As Neijmann points out, in the Canadian literary world, Salverson was marginalized by gender, class, and ethnicity.

Nevertheless, she and Pierce had similar ideas about Canadian culture and society.

Ryerson Press published four of Salverson's books during the 1930s. First to appear was *The Dove* (1933), a historical novel set in Algiers, based on a tale of Icelandic captives found in fourteenth-century Icelandic sagas.[70] *Black Lace*, another historical novel, centred around the court of King Louis XIV of France, was published in 1938.[71] All of Salverson's books were also brought out by British publishers, which made it financially easier for Pierce to publish her work during the Depression. But, with these Salverson titles, he was also promoting a writer whose approach to fiction at that time matched his own.

What appealed to Pierce in these Salverson novels is best summed up in the introduction to *The Dove* he commissioned from another of her admirers, who praised Salverson for not finding it "necessary to distort a good story into a treatise on psychology" in an age of "modern fiction ... surfeited with realism, behaviourism and analysis of character and motive, to an extent painful to contemplate."[72] Salverson's two other Ryerson titles in the 1930s were even more congenial to Pierce, given their western Canadian settings – the novel *The Dark Weaver* (1937), a tale of Scandinavian immigration to western Canada, and her memoir of growing up in the west, *Confessions of an Immigrant's Daughter* (1939).[73]

By this time, Pierce was well into a warm correspondence with Salverson, whose personal life was not easy but whose letters leavened her travails with her characteristic humour and grit. Married to a rather feckless Canadian National Railways dispatcher whose transfers were frequent – Salverson moved house over sixty-five times during her marriage – she was never secure financially.[74] She often lacked the money to have manuscripts typed, and, at one point her house burnt down with the loss of manuscripts and possessions.[75] Salverson repeatedly thanked Pierce for his "kindness" and "sympathetic humour" in their exchange of letters about her writing.[76] Helen Buss has pointed out that Salverson, who did not learn English until she was ten, overcame disadvantages of gender and ethnicity "to become that most rare of types, a successful Canadian writer in the 1930s."[77] Pierce deserves credit for recognizing and largely supporting her work. But his own values both influenced some Salverson manuscripts and left others unpublished in a way that shows how greatly a publisher can shape an author's oeuvre.

Pierce, given his nationalistic literary credo, must have been delighted when Salverson wrote him in 1935 that *The Dark Weaver* "should be a real Canadian product."[78] Set largely in the fictional pioneer settlement of Maple Bluffs, Manitoba, the novel, which won a Governor General's Award for fiction in 1937, stresses the role of fate ("the Dark Weaver") in the lives of a group of Nordic immigrants and their children in the New World up to the First World War. Pierce's correspondence with Salverson suggests that he may have urged her to soften her picture of the indifference of fate to individuals in *The Dark Weaver*. One Ryerson reader of the manuscript had complained that its tone was "morbid,"[79] but the novel's conclusion lightens it somewhat, possibly as a result of Pierce's editorial suggestions. At the end of the novel, despite the carnage of the war, one key character still hopes that "something eternal, some quality of excellence very splendid in its ultimate aims and final end will come of our cruel blunders, our furious strife, and intermittent search after new forms of beauty."[80] Pierce himself had expressed much the same sentiments at the close of the war, in a 1918 article in *Canadian Magazine*: "The tempest and the earthquake are limited and there is a bound to be a progressive accomplishment of a plan."[81]

In 1939 Pierce had high hopes that Salverson's memoir *Confessions of an Immigrant's Daughter*, a work now recognized as an important text about gender and ethnicity in women's autobiography in Canada,[82] would be successful. The book garnered some good reviews and a Governor General's Award, but its sales were disappointing. Salverson was understandably devastated when her first royalty payment amounted to just over three dollars.[83] Her sad comment to Pierce implied that his interest in her immigrant experience was not shared by most Canadians: "I realized very well when my autobiography bit the dust that no one gives a hoot about any Canadian who has not had the sense to be born of French or English stock."[84]

The dismal sales figures for *Confessions* ushered in a period of disappointment for both Pierce and Salverson over her submissions to Ryerson. In the early 1940s Salverson submitted two manuscripts (neither of which has survived) to the House: the first a novel about anti-Semitism in Canada, and the second a satire of modern sexual mores. "Salute to Life" dealt with the experience of anti-Semitism in British Columbia. Salverson, who was active in Ukrainian and Jewish relief work in Winnipeg in the early 1940s, told Pierce that the novel had been written in the spirit of his own nationalistic denunciation of materialism and intolerance in Canada in *The Armoury in Our Halls*. In December 1941 she wrote of her work on "Salute to Life" that she "had been trying to find a medium for a novel dedicated to the concepts you put so well in your [book]. In addition I wanted to stress the importance of racial unity – this is my pet bug of course and I am not the least ashamed of it."[85]

Unfortunately, the novel found no favour with Ryerson Press's manuscript readers. One, novelist Leslie Gordon Barnard, told Pierce after Salverson submitted the book in the spring of 1944 that he did not feel it would add to her reputation. Reluctant to address the reality of bigotry, readers reported that the novel lacked structure and was full of "social tirades."[86] Salverson certainly felt that the Ryerson readers were unwilling to face the true nature of Canadian society. This may well have been true of the rather conservative Barnard, but Pierce himself bluntly denounced racial and social tensions in Canadian society in his own wartime publications.[87] His hard-hitting prose in those writings makes it doubtful that he would have rejected "Salute to Life" out of a desire for wartime "morale and national unity," as Neijmann hypothesizes.[88] In any case, although Salverson agreed to revise the novel, it was never published. Ironically, a novel by Gwethalyn Graham, *Earth and High Heaven*, also dealing with the theme of anti-Semitism in Canada, published in 1944, became a best-seller.[89]

Pierce's subsequent interaction with Salverson indicates that his own prudery about fiction dealing with sexual subjects did shape the Ryerson list by omission. His active attempts to discourage writers from treating sex starkly or extensively came into play with Salverson in the 1940s, just as they did with Grove in the same period over "Felix Powell's Career." Clearly, Pierce put pressure on his authors – even well-established ones – to avoid candid discussion of sexual themes. Another Salverson manuscript, which she first dubbed "Pleasant Vices" and then "The Gods Are Just," was, she told Pierce, "a satire on sex obsessions." She submitted it after "Salute to Life" failed to please. Pierce was initially very negative about the work, telling her in January 1945: "There are too many books like that being turned out today – prurient just for the fun of being that."[90] On re-reading it, Pierce was emphatic about his dislike: "It pictures a mad world, full of neurotics, and the men and women as well as the youths, need to be spanked, given a dose of castor oil, and put to bed. It is not that anyone is shocked by the story. No one is shocked any longer or blushes about anything. The point that struck me was that so many needless things happen to so many useless people and that nobody gets anywhere." Pierce attacked her characters ("the cockroaches of mankind") with uncharacteristic vehemence: "These people, running around with hysterics, living for nothing, unrobing on balconies, don't seem to get anywhere … Life may be like that among neurotic society women and in homes where the father never whaled the devil out of his son just for luck, and slapped the face of his neurasthenic daughter to a peak just for practice. So many of your characters seem to need a darn good beating up."[91] Pierce told Salverson that he wanted "desperately" to do something for her with the book, but the fact that he refers twice to the need to "salvage" the manuscript makes that possibility seem remote. The book clearly could not have satisfied Pierce unless it had been completely reconceived and rewritten.

After Pierce's first negative letter, Salverson protested that such objections were "musty" in the light of the "striptease abominations" of popular best-sellers of the day like *Forever Amber*. She pointed out that she had already "toned down" the manuscript and cut a "naughty chapter." She stoutly maintained that the work was "amusing and a darn good representation of the post war antics." Her letter, however, also reported that her house had just burned down. Not surprisingly, Salverson indicated that, in the face of disaster and Pierce's negative response, she was not likely to go to all the work and expense (which she could ill afford) of revising.[92] She never again submitted "The Gods Are Just," or anything like it in tone or subject matter, to Pierce. Pierce's literary conservatism about the risqué or the daring in fiction clearly did inhibit his authors. One critic has written that Salverson's work is incomplete in that she avoided recording the "sexual details of life" but Pierce's slamming of this manuscript makes her published record misleading on that score.[93]

All in all, in fact, given Pierce's lingering Methodist distrust of fiction, it was overall the weakest component of the Ryerson list. Early in his career, in the 1920s, he had urged ministers in his *Christian Guardian* column to avoid "wast[ing] time" on most current fiction because "there is no philosophy of life there that will bear scrutiny."[94] As twentieth-century fiction became starker, franker, and less idealistic, Pierce continued to find much that was distasteful in it, as his dealings with Grove and Salverson show. In the 1930s he disliked Morley Callaghan's novels with their "brutal lumber bosses and calloused rum runners."[95] The following decade, he and Canadian poet Tom McInnes corresponded over the "vogue for muck" they found in the work of American novelist John Steinbeck.[96] Such views left little room for modernist fiction on the Ryerson list.

Pierce did attempt to remedy the lack of a strong Ryerson fiction list. In 1942 he created an annual Ryerson Fiction Award, which offered publication and $500 in cash (later doubled) for the prizewinning novel manuscript submitted for publication. But since Pierce was the ultimate arbiter of the award, and tended to have judges who shared his conservative tastes – for example, Montreal *Star* book editor S. Morgan-Powell – the award did not really change the nature of Ryerson's fiction list. Furthermore, even the fiction that Ryerson did publish was blue-pencilled. The first Ryerson Fiction Award prizewinner, journalist G. Herbert Sallans's *Little Man* (1942), the story of a western Canadian-born Great War veteran who lives his life "caught in the web of circumstances," was sanitized at Pierce's request.[97] Sallans reported of his revisions to the manuscript in July 1942: "It's cleaned up. Vulgarisms, profanity, copulation, trimmed to a minimum."[98] The novel certainly was cleaned up – to the point where a foul-mouthed First World War soldier in the trenches mouths such limp dialogue such as: "How the blank-blank long you been ...?"[99] Similarly, the co-winner of the 1945 Ryerson Fiction Award (which was not even awarded in 1943 and 1944), Will R. Bird's *Here Stays Good Yorkshire*, had also been revised at Pierce's suggestion, partly "to reduce the sex."[100] Not surprisingly, by the late 1940s, Ryerson had a buttoned-up reputation for fiction. Earle Birney, who published several books of poetry with Pierce in the 1940s, did not even submit his Second World War novel about the profane and picaresque soldier Turvey to Pierce, although Pierce had written to Birney hoping for a novel from him.[101] Undoubtedly wanting more robust profanity on Turvey's lips than "blank-blank," Birney had McClelland and Stewart publish the best-selling *Turvey* (1949).[102]

It is important to recognize, however, that Pierce was only the most conservative publisher among a very conservative publishing world in the Canada of the 1940s – and not an aberration. At McClelland and Stewart, after quite a tussle with the author, even the young Jack McClelland (who had been a somewhat profane wartime naval officer before joining his father's firm in 1946) had Earle Birney soften such expletives in *Turvey* as "Christ" and "Jesus" and also remove other numerous vulgarities, at one point even sending Birney a list of unacceptable "anatomical references" in the text.[103] In the Canadian book market of the late 1940s and 1950s, McClelland, too, believed that "profanity and vulgarity" could hurt novel sales.[104] He and Pierce were in reality not far apart in their policies on such matters in those years. McClelland, however, went on to enjoy his greatest success as a publisher in the more liberal 1960s and beyond, earning a raffish image (one he cultivated).[105] By contrast, the older Pierce, with the prim image of a church publishing house dogging him and a publishing career that ended in 1960, is forever cast as a prude. Critic Robert Fulford, at the end of the 1990s, still fulminated about Ryerson in the 1950s as "Canadian literature's chief producer of hardcover boredom, proud that it published novels without sexual prurience."[106] Jack McClelland's early moral caution, and his list of banned vocabulary, have been largely forgotten, but the Mrs Grundy label has stuck to Pierce. In any case, in the late 1940s and 1950s, young novelists tended to go elsewhere. John Webster Grant, Pierce's successor, confirmed that when he arrived in 1960 Ryerson's "fuddy-duddy" reputation made it very difficult to attract fiction.[107]

Meanwhile, Pierce published Salverson once more as she returned to a view of life he found more congenial. In 1954 Ryerson brought out Salverson's historical novel *Immortal Rock: The Saga of the Kensington Stone*, winner of the Ryerson Fiction Award that year.[108] The novel is based on a reputed journey to North America in the fourteenth century by a band of Nordic nobles and soldiers originally sent by the king of Norway to Christianize Greenland. The expedition finally perishes, displaying faith and courage, at the hands of Indians in what is now Minnesota. Pierce's view of the book is clear in his dust jacket copy: "With great imaginative power and fine vigour of expression, [Salverson] has made her heroes live again, to enthral the reader and bring inspiration to a world which needs it."[109]

The world may have needed inspiration, but not many readers sought it from *Immortal Rock*. Although reviews praised the novel's "richness" and "sense of the nobility of mankind" and an Australian publisher, Angus and Robertson, took British Empire rights for the book, bringing out an edition in London in 1955, sales were poor.[110] Only 643 copies were sold in Canada the first year, and later sales were even more dismal.[111] The Canadian best-sellers of the immediate post-war era – whether slyly comic novels like Paul Hiebert's *Sarah Binks* (1947) or Robertson Davies's *Leaven of Malice* (1954) or darker works like Mordecai Richler's *Son of a Smaller Hero* (1955) or Adele Wiseman's *The Sacrifice* (1956) – indicate that public taste had moved away from Pierce and Salverson's brand of idealistic, inspirational fiction. In discouraging his writers from work he saw as too bleak, too cynical, or too sexually candid, Pierce arguably did not benefit either his authors or the reputation and returns of Ryerson Press.

Salverson subsequently tried to rewrite *Lord of the Silver Dragon: A Romance of Leif the Lucky*, her 1927 historical novel about Leif Ericson, as a juvenile novel. But, after much agonizing over the manuscript, Pierce found the style too "heavy and involved, judged by present-day interests and tastes" and the genre too commercially chancy to risk it.[112] In another letter, Pierce, while sympathetic, declared that "the fact remains that this publishing house or others that we know of are not especially interested at this time in a reconstruction of the live[s] and times of the Norsemen."[113] And so *Immortal Rock* was to be Salverson's last published work, although Pierce was central in securing her a small pension from the Canadian Writers' Foundation in October 1957 and gave her occasional work as a reader for Ryerson.[114] Salverson eked out life in a small house in Toronto. After personally contributing to the funds for Salverson, Pierce wrote sadly to a Foundation official in 1957: "Boy O boy, what an embarrassing end for one so proud. And you and I know how valiantly she tried."[115]

Pierce, for his part, had given some crucial support to Salverson by publishing her in the commercially lean Depression years and only reluctantly ceasing to do so in the 1950s. Moreover, in the early 1950s, Pierce attempted, albeit unsuccessfully, to help Salverson obtain a Guggenheim Fellowship to do literary research, probably on Norse literature, for a book.[116] Certainly, the importance of her memoir *Confessions of an Immigrant's Daughter*, which Pierce had the vision to publish (and lost money on) in 1939, is today widely recognized for its complex treatment of gender and ethnicity. While Pierce may be faulted for not encouraging writers like Salverson and Grove to extend their range in their fictional treatment of sexuality, because of his own moralistic vision of what literature should be, his interest was crucial in providing publication for Salverson and Grove in the 1930s. The Ryerson list may have shrunk in the Depression, but Pierce still managed to be a significant literary publisher, albeit on a reduced scale, as his involvement with Grove and Salverson shows.

Publishing Art History in the Shadow of the Second World War

Ryerson's Landmark Canadian Art Series, 1937–1948

> [The] work [of the Group of Seven and their predecessors] was the very core and marrow of Canada, and grew out of an informed consciousness of Canada, a great pride in its past, and an utter devotion to the beauty and bewitchment of its changing seasons. These are the real makers of Canada.
>
> *Lorne Pierce, in a talk on Canadian artist Thoreau MacDonald, 1942*[1]

In the late 1930s Pierce initiated a major new publishing initiative, one now recognized as "a vital force in promoting Canadian art."[2] His groundbreaking Canadian Art series focused scholarly attention on the visual arts, an important and neglected area of Canadian culture. As with his earlier Makers of Canadian Literature series, Pierce's pioneering art series embraced both English and French Canadian culture.

The sixteen booklets in the Canadian Art series, published between 1937 and 1948, encompassed landmark studies of major nineteenth- and early-twentieth-century Canadian art and artists. The series included titles on painters Cornelius Krieghoff, Paul Kane, Tom Thomson, and Henri Julien as well as movements like the Group of Seven and its precursor, the turn-of-the-century Toronto Art Students' League.[3] Authors included some of the best-known Canadian artists and art historians of the era: Albert Robson, Marius Barbeau, Thoreau MacDonald, Donald Buchanan, and William Colgate.

Nevertheless, the Canadian Art series, like the Makers of Canadian Literature series, would encounter financial and marketing difficulties. It was also criticized by artists and art historians who had a more avant-garde and/or less nationalistic view of Canadian art. The debate over modernism in art that had been raging in Canada and internationally since early in the twentieth century was to be reflected in the tone and reception of the Canadian Art series, with Pierce embracing a conservative position in the face of "les jeunes" in the art world.

Moreover, sales of the Canadian Art series would be hampered by the lack of Canadian university and college courses in the field in the 1930s and 1940s. In these decades, books about Canadian art had a pitifully small market, whether in individual or textbook sales, and no sustained source of subsidy funding was available. Pierce counted – not always successfully – on profits to the House from textbook revenues to, in effect, subsidize projects like the Canadian Art series. But Ryerson's textbook profits were undermined by the Depression.

Pierce was also to have persistent production problems with the series. Art books, given their complex black-and-white and colour reproductions, are both technically difficult and expensive to produce at the best of times. This is true even of relatively short art booklets which feature a modest number of black-and-white illustrations and only a few colour images, as was the case – of necessity – for Pierce's Canadian Art series. Canada's entry into the Second World War in September 1939 further complicated the venture. Production difficulties – in the form of labour and paper shortages – followed the outbreak of war and continued well beyond war's end. Indeed, the economic circumstances of the war years and of the immediate post-war period made book publishing of any sort a nightmarish business.

One factor remained constant with both the Makers of Canadian Literature series and the Canadian Art series a decade later: Pierce was driven in the inception of both series by his cultural nationalism. His construct of Canadian art had an ideological agenda: through the art series, he sought above all to exalt and unite the nation and its two main peoples, the English and the French, by conceiving of Canadian culture – in this case its nineteenth- and early-twentieth-century art – as essentially national and inspirational in its vision.

Pierce summed up his nationalistic vision of Canadian art most succinctly in his posthumous 1940 tribute to his friend J.E.H. MacDonald of the Group of Seven. Looking back at such nineteenth-century painters as Cornelius Krieghoff and Paul Kane and the artists of the Toronto Art Students' League as precursors of the Group of Seven, Pierce voiced his own credo for Canadian art: "No country is fully a nation until it arrives at self-conscious maturity through its poets and artists ... the world moves ahead because of its seers. Something happened in Canada when the foreign lithographs on the walls of pioneer homes were challenged by the paintings of Kane and Krieghoff ... What we owe to our writers and artists, from Haliburton and Krieghoff down to this day, is beyond compute. They are the real discoverers and master-builders of this nation."[4]

Pierce's arrival at the House in 1920 had coincided with a burst of public interest in the Group of Seven and their contemporaries. At Toronto's Arts and Letters Club, Pierce was exposed to the heady nationalism permeating the art scene. In fact, Group of Seven artist – and long-time club member – J.E.H. MacDonald designed its logo,[5] once describing it as "a Church, a home and a Studio for me."[6] Numerous entries in Pierce's diary corroborate his exposure to the pervasive nationalism of the "music, literature and art" ambience of the Arts and Letters Club. For example, in March 1925, when Pierce lunched at its Elm Street clubhouse, painter Arthur Lismer, seated nearby, dashed off a caricature of Pierce.[7]

Whether in artistic, club, or theosophical circles, as Alison Gillmor has so pungently put it, the Group succeeded in projecting itself as "a united force. The high-flown talk about country and culture, the punchy style of their big paintings, the photographs of the men in sober suits at the Arts and Letters Club, or out fishing on Smoke Lake, all helped to jump-start a much needed national consciousness in the visual arts."[8] At Ryerson, Pierce was soon bent at stimulating just such a national consciousness in art publications, many of which exalted the Group of Seven.

Pierce also heard the siren call of the Group of Seven through his wife. In 1924, having attended an "excellent talk on Canadian art" by Arthur Lismer, Edith urged that the couple become more involved in the contemporary Canadian art scene, not least for the sake of their two children's cultural development. She wrote Lorne: "The Ontario School of Art is trying to foster a real Canadian art – not copying English Art or any other art. [Lismer] said that Canadian scenes lacked the soft lines of the English ones on account of our clear atmosphere ... I wish that we would go over sometime and get acquainted with the paintings, especially of the Toronto men [like Wyly Grier and Arthur Lismer]."[9] Her urgings soon bore fruit, reinforced as they were by Pierce's contacts at the Arts and Letters Club, in theosophical and other intellectual circles, and in his Ryerson Press work with artist/illustrators like C.W. Jefferys and Frederick Varley. Over the next four decades, Pierce forged a significant place for himself in the development of Canadian art history as a nationalistic exponent and publisher of works about Canadian art, art as exemplified by the work of Group of Seven and their contemporaries and successors. According to Pierce, the painters of the Group of Seven, J.E.H. MacDonald chief among them, epitomized a view of the nation and the meaning of life and art he found compelling. He wrote of MacDonald: "Men should contain multitudes, said Whitman, and it was true of this tall, silent, gentl[e] philosopher ... his work will increase in interest and importance to succeeding generations."[10]

In his booklet *A Postscript on J.E.H. MacDonald* (1940), Pierce summed up his concept of the Group of Seven as a whole, a vision that exalted MacDonald as *primus inter pares*. The intellectual influences on Pierce's overview of MacDonald's significance as an artist are eclectic. His analysis draws heavily on elements of theosophy (a major interest of both Pierce and Group members like MacDonald and Lawren Harris in the 1920s). It also blends the ideas and images of John Bunyan's *Pilgrim's Progress* (a staple of his Delta upbringing) with a dash of Masonic idealism and John Watson's cultural nationalism for good measure. All these currents are evident when Pierce characterizes MacDonald's art in ringingly nationalistic and idealistic terms: "Our artists, who still remain the chief glory of our country ... [are] the best spokesmen and interpreters of this Dominion ... Any representative collection of MacDonald's paintings offers proof of the progressive development and enrichment of his experience of order and design, but much more of his increasing awareness of truth and the reason for living at all ... most of his canvases are allegories on the pilgrimage of mankind towards the Ineffable Mountains."[11]

Pierce was keen to promote the vision of Canadian art and Canadian life that he discerned in the work of the Group of Seven and their precursors. Through numerous Ryerson Press publications, of which the sixteen booklets in the Canadian Art series are the most important, he became in the mid-twentieth century an important agent in the dissemination of the ideas of the Group and their admirers about Canadian art, nationality, and culture. At the same time, he himself gradually assembled a small but impressive private collection of Canadian art.

By 1940, the crown jewel of Pierce's personal art collection was J.E.H. MacDonald's masterpiece *The Elements*, which, in company with the equally important MacDonald canvas *The Tangled Garden*, had famously been at the centre of an uproar over the Group of Seven's work at an exhibit at the Art Gallery of Toronto in 1916.[12] *The Elements* is a large painting of northern skies in swirling greens, blacks, and ochres, a canvas whose sweeping wilderness skies overwhelm two tiny human figures crouched over a campfire.[13]

Over the years, *The Elements* acquired considerable company on the walls of Pierce's Campbell Crescent home. At its zenith in the early 1950s, Pierce's personal art collection encompassed works by C.W. Jefferys, Tom Thomson, A.Y. Jackson, Wyly Grier, and Thoreau MacDonald. When the Art Gallery of Ontario was given the magnificent MacDonald canvas as one of Pierce's donations to that institution in 1958, Pierce termed the painting "my most precious possession," above all for MacDonald's "vision of life, its mystery and its meaning."[14] Pierce's art philanthropy reflected his commitment to actualizing the importance of a certain construct of Canadian art to all Canadians.

IN HIS Ryerson career, Pierce's commitment to Canadian art started in the 1920s and intensified in the late 1930s. He began by hiring leading Canadian artists to work on Ryerson publications. On his arrival at Ryerson, Pierce noticed that McClelland and Stewart, whom he considered his chief competitor in publishing Canadian literature, not only employed editor Donald French but also "had the services of J.E.H. MacDonald as artist" and designer for some of its publications.[15] Pierce was therefore quick to start handing out commissions for book design and illustration to the likes of C.W. Jefferys, J.E.H. MacDonald, Frederick Varley, and other gifted Canadian designers. For example, after engaging Varley to design William Arthur Deacon's book of essays *Pens and Pirates* in 1923, Pierce proudly wrote Deacon: "I am taking a very special interest in bookmaking from the mechanical end ... and think that we may get somewhere."[16] Books that Pierce regarded as key works of Canadian literature received special design attention. The titles Frederick Varley designed and illustrated for Ryerson starting in the early 1920s included E.J. Pratt's *Newfoundland Verse* (1923), Charles G.D. Roberts's *The Iceberg and Other Poems* (1934), Earle Birney's *David and Other Poems* (1942), and Pierce's own *Marjorie Pickthall: A Book of Remembrance*. The latter Varley design, like some of Thoreau MacDonald's later designs for Ryerson, is among the finest examples of bookmaking ever produced by Ryerson Press.

Pierce and artist Thoreau MacDonald enjoyed a long and successful collaboration in the design and illustration of Ryerson publications.

MacDonald illustrated many of Ryerson's best-produced titles, starting in 1931 with Blodwen Davies's *Storied York: Toronto Old and New*.[17] He did layout, book jacket, and/or title page design for many more Ryerson publications over the next four decades. Randall Speller has written of MacDonald's prowess in this field, expressed in his "great care to craft text to image, balance page layouts, and select appropriate paper," in the light of his nature-inspired, modernist aesthetic.[18] MacDonald's illustration and design masterpieces for Ryerson Press include the second edition of poet A.M. Klein's landmark collection of poetry about Quebec, *The Rocking Chair* (1953), Duncan Campbell Scott's first Canadian edition of stories of French Canada, *In the Village of Viger* (1945), and a posthumous collection of poems by Thoreau's painter-father, J.E.H. MacDonald, *West to East* (1933).[19]

Pierce also commissioned MacDonald to design various colophons (publishing house logos and emblems) for Ryerson Press publications – usually incorporating nationalistic symbolism – for use on book covers, book spines, frontispieces, and dust jackets. Most designs featured Canadian trees and animals and handsome typefaces, Roman being MacDonald's favourite.[20] Among the best known of these elegant designs is the trademark wind-blown black spruce set against a sunset-lettered "Ryerson Press" found on the spines and title pages of dozens of publications from the 1930s to the 1960s. The beauty and distinctiveness of the MacDonald colophons have stood the test of time, a tribute to both editor and designer. Furthermore, their imagery evokes the cultural nationalism of Pierce's editorial policies.

However, Pierce – as well as MacDonald and design-conscious authors like poet (and art collector) Duncan Campbell Scott – was at times exasperated by manufacturing errors perpetrated by the House printing plant.[21] Ryerson Press was in fact the only major Canadian publisher to do all its printing and binding in-house.[22] This captive operation was a mixed blessing in terms of cost and control. The House plant, while the largest in Canada, did not always have the sophisticated grasp – or the range of specialized presses for art printing – found in smaller, specialized operations, for example, Rous and Mann. Pierce's correspondence throughout his career regularly bemoans production delays and barbarisms by the House typesetting, printing, and binding facilities. For his part, MacDonald once jotted in the margin of one badly manufactured Ryerson book in which he was named as designer: "Shows no evidence of design."[23]

As well as seeking to better the design of Ryerson publications, Pierce also felt a need to publish works about Canadian artists and art history, whatever the daunting production and marketing challenges involved. As art historians have pointed out, it was not until the 1920s that Canadian art-historical publications were produced in any significant number, and what little was published was largely memoir or biography and largely descriptive rather than evaluative.[24] From that decade on, Pierce was among the pioneers in publishing works of Canadian art history. But he was not alone, being joined by fellow nationalistic Toronto publishers Hugh Eayrs of Macmillan of Canada and John McClelland of McClelland and Stewart. For example, journalist and art critic Frederick Housser's popular *A Canadian Art Movement: The Story of the Group of Seven* (1926) was published by Macmillan, a work now seen by scholars as central to the propagation of the myth of the Group of Seven as seminal painters of the spirit of the Canadian landscape.[25] One young Toronto art educator, Helen Kemp, wrote that Housser's book convinced her that "Canada has a definite art tradition, and has established herself as an artistic nation."[26] A major Group of Seven exhibition at the National Gallery of Canada in 1936 further cemented the "canonization" of the Group in these years.[27]

Amid the groundswell of cultural nationalism in art, Pierce was key to the canonizing of the Group of Seven. By the late 1930s, he was publishing far more in the field of Canadian art history than any other Canadian publisher. In 1943 he proudly reminded Lawren Harris: "As you know, this House has become more or less the centre for books on Canadian art in recent years."[28] Pierce was not only pleasing Canadian artists. In fact, at this period, in his textbook projects, he was endeavouring to evoke in the young a taste for Canadian art.

So strongly did Pierce feel about the importance of fostering art appreciation among young people that, in the 1940s, he himself wrote an essay on the subject for one of his hugely successful school textbooks. "How to Look at Pictures" reflects his commitment to educating Canadians about art from a certain perspective. According to Pierce, art is above all representational, idealistic, and culturally cohesive in its effects. In the essay, Pierce's aesthetics are presentist, as he traces a line for high school students from the "flat and rather crude" art of caveman and Egyptians through the "lifelike" light, shade, and perspective of Renaissance and contemporary art. He uses as one example of great art Heinrich Hoffman's famous picture of the boy Jesus in the Temple, a work emblematic of meaning, composition, and design calculated to "kindle our minds and stir our emotions." For Pierce, the artist is one who "selects a scene which pictures for him an idea. From a mass of detail, he chooses what will best explain, in the simplest way, this thought."[29] Accordingly, in any work of art, Pierce assured students, "there is also centre, by which everything is firmly knit into a perfect pattern and held there ... The entire meaning and purpose are as clear as day. Stand further back and look again. It is all alive ... It opens for us a magic doorway into a new and thrilling experience." The artist, wrote Pierce, "endeavours to teach something" but "above all he trie[s], with all his might, to kindle pure enjoyment of the beautiful."[30]

However, Pierce's view of art did not really acknowledge the full range of intention in the work of artists like Pablo Picasso or Diego Rivera – or in Canada in the work of painters like Charles Comfort, Alfred Pellan, Paul-Émile Borduas, Pegi Nicol McLeod, or Paraskeva Clarke, for example, all artists of the day known to him. What of the ugly? What of social criticism? What of abstraction as an aesthetic? Notwithstanding such questions, for Pierce, a work of art was conceptualized as "one single moment of time, a mood, an act, and with the light and shade exactly right – just as if the camera took a snapshot of it."[31] He ignored abstract art altogether. Clearly, Pierce's aesthetic for Canadian art was ambitious and pioneering; it was also conservative, representational, and shot through with cultural nationalism. These biases are also found in many of his art publications.

Pierce's early Ryerson art-related publications tended to be short and/ or visually spartan books, handicapped as he was by the high cost of four-colour reproduction of paintings. Nevertheless, in 1930 he brought out *Painting and Sculpture in Canada*, a short history of Canadian painting by prominent Toronto *Globe* journalist and art critic M.O. Hammond. The next year, Ryerson published a booklet by William Ritchie Watson on Newfoundland-born Montreal landscape painter and Great War artist Maurice Cullen. He also published Blodwen Davies's thirty-five-page *Paddle and Palette: The Story of Tom Thomson* (1930). This hagiographic work constitutes part of the Canadian mythologizing of Thomson in the years following the painter's drowning in Algonquin Park's Canoe Lake in 1917, a fact underlined in the 2002 Tom Thomson Exhibit at the National Gallery of Canada.

It is clear that, in the triage of the Depression publication lists, Pierce singled out works about Canadian art as one publishing priority in hard times. Thus, in 1932, Ryerson's catalogue highlighted Albert Robson's seminal 227-page *Canadian Landscape Painters*, which today is a rare, landmark volume, highly prized by collectors.[32] An important force in Canadian art and literature in mid-century, Robson, stocky, mustachioed, and convivial, was educated at the College of Art. First as art director at *Grip* and after 1915 as the dynamic art director of leading Toronto advertising firm Rous and Mann, he had employed, befriended, and inspired many of the Group of Seven and their contemporaries.[33] In the late 1930s Robson was a major fundraiser for the Art Gallery of Toronto (now the Art Gallery of Ontario) as its vice-president from 1927 until his death in 1939.[34]

At Ryerson Press, meanwhile, 1936 saw the publication of rising young art historian Donald Buchanan's book on turn-of-the-century Canadian impressionist James Wilson Morrice,[35] the research subsidized by his Carnegie Endowment grant (Buchanan's father also appears to have helped with illustration costs).[36] By then, Pierce and Robson were puzzling out how Ryerson could produce a series on Canadian artists, given the considerable financial and technical demands of illustrating art books. Santa Claus came to the rescue: the series was finally made possible by Christmas cards. In the mid-1930s Robson's firm Rous and Mann, which did art printing as well as design, advertising copywriting, and sales promotion,[37] acquired a sophisticated colour press to produce annual collections of four-colour art plates for a line of Christmas cards featuring Canadian paintings. The popularity of the cards paid for the colour plates. In April 1937 Robson wrote to his friend Pierce, urging him to bring out the first few booklets on Canadian artists using illustrations taken from the Christmas card plates: "The thought I had in mind was to produce small booklets ... standardized in size, and carrying ten or twelve colour reproductions of an individual artist, together with a short appreciation of the work of the artist, including enough of his background and point of view to explain his work." Robson had put together a couple of rough dummies of such booklets, which he suggested be marketed primarily in paper cover at fifty cents each. He added optimistically: "There would be a wide sale ... amongst the artists, would-be artists, art teachers, school teachers, educationalists, and in fact, I think there would be a very good sale over the counter in the stores."[38]

Robson suggested that the series be launched with booklets on Tom Thomson (for whose works Rous and Mann had a series of colour plates made for private collectors) and on nineteenth-century artist Cornelius

Krieghoff, whose habitant scenes had made ideal Christmas cards. If the two initial Ryerson booklets were successful, Robson urged Pierce, "they could be followed by [booklets on] a dozen artists" to make "an extremely interesting little library."[39] Robson offered to write as well as produce the inaugural booklets.

PIERCE AND ROBSON initially envisioned a twelve-booklet series.[40] By August 1937, the Tom Thomson booklet was typeset and Robson started putting together the Krieghoff and (their third selection) J.E.H. Mac-Donald booklets. Thanks to Robson, Rous and Mann manufactured the booklets. However, as it turned out, both the Krieghoff and MacDonald booklets featured original illustrations of some works. Production problems and delays with the initial three volumes resulted. Some private collectors, for example, balked – in part for security reasons – at having their treasures reproduced for a wider audience.

At last, by November 1937, the three booklets, each thirty-two pages long, simply entitled *Cornelius Krieghoff*, *J.E.H. MacDonald, R.C.A.*, and *Tom Thomson* respectively, appeared. The covers featured a handsome little pine bough-and-palette colophon specially designed for the Canadian Art series by Thoreau MacDonald, another indication of the importance Pierce accorded to the project. The next year saw the publication of three more booklets by Robson: *A.Y. Jackson, Clarence A. Gagnon, R.C.A. LL.D* (the first series booklet on a francophone artist), and *Paul Kane*. Meanwhile, Robson called upon Duncan McArthur, Ontario's deputy minister of education, hoping to drum up some educational sales.[41]

In the late 1930s, scholarly and/or popular biographical and descriptive books on individual Canadian artists were practically non-existent. Pierce, reminiscing in 1949 about his commitment to Canadian art publications, observed that while artists' works constitute their best record, he had been appalled that, in Canada, "artists have come and gone, and details about them, how they lived, worked and thought, let alone survived, are often scant, vague and useless."[42] To remedy this gap, the short works in Pierce's Canadian Art series provided unprecedented overviews of the life and work of major Canadian artists.

For Pierce, Canada's artists – like its writers – were above all cultural "makers" of great national importance, makers whose works he considered bonding and visionary agents for all Canadians, regardless of language, origin, or region. He was emphatic about the cultural significance to Canada of the Group and their forerunners and inherit-

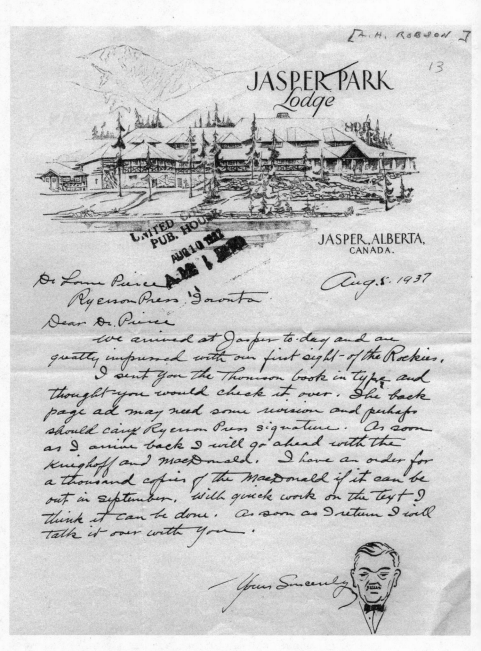

JASPER PARK
Lodge

JASPER, ALBERTA,
CANADA.

Dr Lorne Pierce
Ryerson Press, Toronto.

Aug. 5. 1937

Dear Dr. Pierce

We arrived at Jasper to-day and are greatly impressed with our first sight of the Rockies. I sent you the Thomson book in type and thought you would check it over. The back page ad may need some revision and perhaps should carry Ryerson Press signature. As soon as I arrive back I will go ahead with the Krieghoff and MacDonald. I have an order for a thousand copies of the MacDonald if it can be out in September. With quick work on the text I think it can be done. As soon as I return I will talk it over with you.

Yours Sincerely

A letter with self-caricature sent to Pierce by his Canadian Art series collaborator Albert Robson, 5 August 1937. Courtesy of Queen's University Archives ors – artists like Cornelius Krieghoff, Paul Kane, James Wilson Morrice, Maurice Cullen, C.W. Jefferys, and, in the wake of the Group, Thoreau MacDonald and others. In a 1942 talk at Hart House on Thoreau Mac-Donald, Pierce summed up his convictions about Canadian art and artists: "Their work [is] the very core and marrow of Canada, and grew out of an informed consciousness of Canada, a great pride in its past, and an utter devotion to the beauty and bewitchment of its changing seasons. These [artists] are the real makers of Canada."[43] No wonder Arthur Lismer could joke that the Group of Seven had outlived its usefulness by the mid-1930s because "people were beginning to like [us]!"[44]

In an average length of some thirty-five pages, the sixteen booklets of the Canadian Art series undeniably filled a real (if small) market for inexpensive, concise, chronologies/overviews of the careers of Canada's major artists, past and present. Pierce's cultural nationalism is reflected in the texts – and the choice of artists. The six Robson booklets that launched the series in 1937–38 emphasize the Canadian nationality of the painters discussed, whether the post-Confederation J.E.H. MacDonald or the largely pre-Confederation, and foreign-born, Paul Kane and Cornelius Krieghoff, as Northrop Frye pointed out in his reviews of the Gagnon and Kane volumes in the *Canadian Forum*.[45] There is a militant gospel fervour to this nationalistic view of art. For example, Pierce wrote elsewhere that the canvasses of artists like Krieghoff and English-born Amherst Island watercolourist Daniel Fowler embody "hints of the truth" of the fully "self-conscious Canadian art" achieved, in his view, in the Toronto Art Students' League calendars and in the work of Tom Thomson and the Group of Seven.[46]

Pierce's authors for the Canadian Art series were no less celebratory of the Group and their ilk. In Robson's 1937 booklet *J.E.H. MacDonald, R.C.A.*, for instance, the Group of Seven member is lauded for his talent and "radiant poetical spirit." But what Robson stresses above all is Mac-Donald's nationalism as embodied in his life and work: "Canada shaped his mind, kindled his spirit, and dictated his avocation."[47] Not surprisingly, painters whose ideas and works are more difficult to integrate into such a view of Canada or its art – modernists like Charles Comfort, Pegi Nicol McLeod, Alfred Pellan, left-wing Maritime painter Miller Brittain, and the Quebec members of the Refus Global movement – are largely ignored or downplayed in the series. For Pierce and his authors, the importance of the artists featured in the series lay primarily in their putative national and cultural significance as reflected in their art.

By the 1940s, authors of art books were well aware that Pierce wanted "hands-on" input into the significance of their subjects. For example, in 1948, before William Colgate began work on his monograph *The Toronto Art Students' League*, he requested a meeting to discuss Pierce's views of the league, adding, "I can do little about planning the book, of course, until I learn something of what your own views are."[48] For Pierce and his series collaborators such as Albert Robson, art historian Donald Buchanan, and artist Thoreau MacDonald, art is most valued when it lends itself to analysis as something closely linked to Canadian landscape and society. Thus, Robson's booklet on J.E.H. MacDonald praises MacDonald for being an accessible artist who, as Robson puts it, "widened the sphere of aesthetic appreciation ... He had little sympathy with arid abstractions or any of the 'isms' of modern art and definitely believed that the artist was an interpreter of the beauty of nature as seen through the eyes of an individual personality."[49] Even artists who painted long before the Group of Seven's heyday are whiggishly portrayed primarily as precursors of the patriotic aesthetic apotheosized by the Group. The artist Paul Kane is therefore presented by Robson as "a romantic figure" and "a truly great pioneer" in his pictorial recording of the native peoples and the opening west in the period 1845 to 1871. Robson describes Kane's treks on foot, on horseback, and by canoe through the wild Northwest as pre-Confederation previews of the Group's canoe, snowshoe, and railway-siding painting expeditions in northern Ontario and elsewhere. From Kane's horse to Thomson's canoe – and the resulting canvases in both cases – art constitutes a continuum redolent of Canadian nationalism.

Allegedly more effete modernist painters of 1930s Canada (who of course tend to be anonymous in the text) receive a sideswipe from Robson as he exalts the physically intrepid Paul Kane: "Our parlour-car artists of to-day may well doff their hats to this sturdy pioneer." Robson concludes by ranking Kane's cultural significance as a painter of Canada's Indians and wilderness higher than his technical proficiency: "[Although] Kane's paintings have greater historical and ethnological value than intrinsic artistic merit ... his work is unquestionably of great importance, and his name is an honoured one among our pioneer painters."[50] Clearly, for Pierce, Robson, and the Canadian Art series, nineteenth-century artists working in Canada are assessed above all as cultural nation builders. As a result, for instance, Albert Robson's booklet on Krieghoff concludes that the pre-Confederation scenes interpreted by the Dutch-born Krieghoff in his paintings of Quebec, his habitant scenes in particular, position him as "a skilful and inspired interpreter of its people, the moods of its contrasting seasons, and its grand panorama." Robson quotes A.Y. Jackson to defend Krieghoff against the charge of depicting habitants "as revellers or topers," although he does acknowledge some "pot-boilers" in the Krieghoff oeuvre.[51]

Later volumes in the Canadian Art series tend to cram the artist discussed into the Cinderella slipper of Group of Seven-style nationalism, even when the fit is uncomfortable. The direction of the text of Donald Buchanan's *James Wilson Morrice* (1947), his second study about a painter who spent most of his career in France, betrays this force fit. Buchanan writes of Morrice: "Yet, while that strict creed of nationalism, as stated by the Group of Seven, was foreign to Morrice, he nevertheless always insisted upon an honest understanding of the colours and atmosphere of his native land ... [Morrice is the] forerunner of much that is most vital and independent in contemporary Canadian painting."[52]

Admittedly, some authors of booklets in the Canadian Art series, while nationalistic in their judgments, were more sympathetic to changes in the Canadian art scene and to foreign-oriented Canadian avant-garde painters such as Quebec's Alfred Pellan or Paul-Émile Borduas of the iconoclastic Refus Global movement. For example, Marius Barbeau, in his *Painters of Quebec* (1946), discusses artists whom he finds easy to categorize in terms of Quebec and/or Canadian nationalism, but he also touches on the work of more abstract and resolutely iconoclastic artists. In the former category, he praises the work of Quebec painters Marc-Aurèle de Foy Suzor-Coté and Clarence Gagnon as well as that of artists trained elsewhere, like Swiss-born André Bieler and Belgian-born Henri Masson. For Barbeau, these painters evince the power of "northern woodlands and rivers" in "fostering [Quebec] national consciousness by inspiring in [Quebecers] song, tale, legend, idiom, embroidery, wood carving, painting and romance." Barbeau mentions the Group of Seven's influence on painters like Bieler, Gagnon, and Masson; however, he also stresses the vision and legitimacy of Canadian abstract painters like Pellan and Borduas. Barbeau writes of Pellan's work: "It is up to the spectator to learn and understand [Pellan's] language. His only wish is to provoke an instantaneous visual impression which is aesthetic, and fills a need, without being bothered with preliminaries, explanations or putting in a label to justify his effect."[53]

But other contributors to the series were more censorious of abstract art in Canada, depicting abstractionists as hostile or indifferent to the beauties of Canadian nature and landscape. Thoreau MacDonald (whose colour-blindness arguably made it more difficult for him to appreciate artists like Borduas), in his *The Group of Seven* (1944), called the work of the Group an "unequalled tribute to our country." Appropriately, given such an orientation by Pierce and his collaborators, MacDonald's booklet on the Group was the most popular in the series and went into eight printings by 1969. By the 1952 printing, MacDonald's analysis of the direction of the contemporary Canadian art scene had become increasingly trenchant; his comments on non-representational art showed his own alienation in the 1940s and 1950s from that trend in Canadian (and international) art. With his characteristic blend of environmentalism and forthrightness, MacDonald wrote: "Only a few sturdy spirits have resisted the temptations of abstraction and carry on the traditions of Canadian landscape art opened up for us by the old Group. The landscape itself has had some heavy blows in the postwar boom but a lot of it is still there, still awaiting those able to see and record it. They may have a lonesome time among the moderns, but let them stick it out for the Country needs them."[54] Clearly, Pierce and his closest collaborators in the art series knew what they liked in Canadian art – and it was not abstraction or internationalism. It was nationalism.

DEATH SHADOWED the last eight volumes of the Canadian Art series, published between 1941 and 1948. On 6 March 1939 Albert Robson died unexpectedly of a thrombosis at the age of fifty-seven.[55] It added to Pierce's sorrow that he could find no replacement for the arrangement with Rous and Mann regarding colour plates, although in 1945 Harry McCurry, director of the National Gallery of Canada, did agree to split the cost of the colour plates for Duncan Campbell Scott's *Walter J. Phillips* (1945). After Robson's death, booklets in the series henceforth usually featured just one colour plate, a sad handicap for an art series in aesthetic, marketing, and educational terms.[56]

When Pierce himself wrote about art in the 1940s – for example, when he lectured on Thoreau MacDonald or wrote a booklet on Ontario artist Grace Coombs – his standards remained conservative, representational, and nationalistic. He preferred artists who painted the Canadian landscape (or portraits of Canadians – at least three portraits and two busts were made of Pierce and he commissioned a posthumous pastel portrait of Edith by Alan Barr[57]). Pierce also remained a bicultural nationalist, in art as well as literature. At one point he hoped that the Canadian Art series booklets could be translated into French to give them a bilingual as well as bicultural dimension similar to that of his Makers of Canadian Literature series.[58]

Traditional gender values also emerge in Pierce's Canadian art criticism, most clearly in a short monograph he wrote on painter Grace Coombs, whom he had first met when she was commissioned to illustrate a Ryerson children's book. Coombs, an Ontario artist who had graduated from the Ontario College of Art in 1918 and was a long-time teacher there, produced work that Pierce himself purchased.[59] She had been influenced not only by Canadian poets Agnes Maule Machar and Helena Coleman but also by painter J.E.H. MacDonald, all figures congenial to Pierce. Pierce himself undertook to write on Coombs at the behest of (and with a publication subsidy from) Coombs's husband, James Sharp Lawson, librarian of Emmanuel College, University of Toronto.

Interestingly, the 1949 monograph was not included in the canonical Canadian Art series (Emily Carr was the only woman artist planned for inclusion but the series lapsed before anything on her was written). One wonders why, since Pierce clearly admired Coombs. In any case, running through his analysis of her work is the conviction that true artistic genius is inherently "male." He therefore offers some intricate rationalizations about how Coombs manages to paint well despite her gender. At the beginning of her career, she is described as "a very lovely and shy young woman" amid the Group of Seven's "strenuous climate of [renascent] nationalism."[60] Pierce's analysis of Coombs is thus similar in its patriarchal assumptions to those of his 1925 biography of poet Marjorie Pickthall. Coombs's upbringing with her six brothers (and, seemingly incidentally, two sisters) in pre–First World War Hamilton and Gananoque, Ontario, is depicted as – fortunately for the future potency of her art – of a tomboyish cast: "Playing with six sturdy boys and their hordes of friends gave to young Grace, self-reliance, a certain ruggedness, and a healthy masculine disregard for tears and wasteful emotion. In later life she has shown sympathetic understanding of the masculine point of view, and, while remaining charming and feminine, has revealed small tolerance for superficial femininities." Similarly, Pierce discriminates between Coombs's "polished jewel-like" paintings of flowers and other still life subjects (i.e., traditionally "feminine" subject matter) and the "masculine strength and turbulence" of her wilderness landscapes with their "dominating rugged masses and plunging waterfalls" which have "to be seen to be understood."[61] (Pierce himself owned examples of both Coombs's "masculine" and "feminine" art.)[62]

If Pierce's gender ideas remained conservative, his view of modernism was even more conservative in the 1940s than in the 1920s, not surprisingly given the polarized debates in both the literary and art world in this decade. Pierce thought of abstract art as embodying some of the same forces and values he rejected in modernist literature; he found much of modern art alienating, tending to the amoral or even immoral, and politically, socially, and sexually extreme (usually too far to the left), and morbidly introspective. Such art seemed hostile to his sense of idealism, his nationalism, and his gender and social values. In the Canadian Art series and other art publications, he valorized a certain kind of art to help build a certain kind of nation.

Especially given the dearth of works on Canadian art and artists, initial response to the Canadian Art series was often positive, particularly from those who shared Pierce's and Robson's view of Canadian art. A.Y. Jackson, for example, told Pierce a few months after Robson's death in March 1939 that the first six booklets of the series were very helpful in stimulating interest in Canadian painting; he felt, however, that Robson tended to underestimate the importance of the work of their mutual friend Tom Thomson in the period after Thomson left Robson's employ at *Grip*.[63] Other responses to the series were harder for Pierce to accept. Given the financial vicissitudes of producing the series at all, Pierce was stung by a 1938 review in the *University of Toronto Quarterly* which criticized the colour plates used as old and worn out. With grim realism, Pierce told literary critic E.K. Brown, who was involved with the *Quarterly*, that the assessment was "absurd and entirely unjustified" for this "educational series."[64]

Elsewhere, journalist Donald MacKay reviewed Donald Buchanan's *James Wilson Morrice* and Duncan Campbell Scott's *Walter J. Phillips* (1947) for the *Dalhousie Review*, praising the deeper understanding of Morrice that Buchanan now displayed compared to his earlier (1936) study of the same artist, and calling the Phillips booklet "valuable to a collector." MacKay's review did lament the lack of colour plates in the Phillips monograph after the "generous" number of colour plates in the first six series booklets.[65] His innocent observation must have made Pierce wince. Evidently, in the 1940s, even reviewers of art books did not grasp the grim economics of art publishing in Canada.

In terms of the average book buyer, the series did provoke some nationalistic engagement with Canadian art. In Vancouver in the summer of 1943, a young shipyard war worker, David Farr, later a distinguished

Canadian historian, bought six of the booklets, despite his limited budget, because he knew little of Canadian art outside the work of Emily Carr. He bought several more booklets as a graduate student at the University of Toronto in the fall of 1945. Sixty-five years later, Farr credited the Canadian Art series with making him see art in Canada as a national force.[66]

Unfortunately for Pierce, one tribute the series seldom achieved was decent sales. With the exception of Thoreau MacDonald's *The Group of Seven* (1944), sales were generally small. However, the series was not a financial debacle on the scale of Pierce's large, lavish Makers of Canadian Literature series in the 1920s. Having learned a painful lesson, Pierce did not put his neck so tightly into the noose with the Canadian Art series, limiting both length and colour illustrations.[67] Such decisions were uncongenial but wise in the light of poor returns on art publications for Ryerson. More ambitious books on Canadian art published by Ryerson sold no better – Muriel Miller Miner's 230-page *G.A. Reid, Canadian Artist* (1946) sold only 300 copies in the year of publication.[68]

Despite his long experience of the grim realities of Canadian cultural publishing, Pierce nevertheless found the mostly meagre sales for the Canadian Art series disheartening. As early as 1939, Toronto's Mellors Gallery (where Pierce was a good customer) was returning unsold copies of Robson's *J.E.H. MacDonald, R.C.A.* (1937). Robson's 1938 booklet on A.Y. Jackson sold poorly,[69] and Pierce ended up giving away copies of E.R. Hunter's *Thoreau MacDonald* (1942). In 1942, when Pierce wondered about the feasibility of selling 500 copies of a projected Arthur Lismer booklet about A.Y. Jackson at $1.00 per copy (double the usual price) "for the elite," Lismer replied crisply: "There are no elite."[70] The booklet on Jackson never appeared.

Moreover, Pierce's plan in the 1940s that Ryerson publish a high school textbook on Canadian art, written by Donald Buchanan (from 1947 with the National Gallery of Canada) and *Saturday Night* art critic Graham McInnes, came to nothing after fruitless lobbying of the Ontario Department of Education.[71] Several projected booklets in the Canadian Art series foundered on the shoals of finance – booklets planned on artists Lawren Harris, Emily Carr, David Milne, Frederick Brigden, and Maurice Cullen, Haida stone carvers, and Canadian silversmiths, among others.[72]

The severe labour and material shortages of wartime and its aftermath further disrupted Pierce's publication plans for the series and for the Ryerson list in general. By 1949, these problems were succeeded by serious inflationary and labour relations issues at the House and in the Canadian book trade generally. In 1949, seeing the Canadian Art series peter out thanks to such woes, Pierce fretted to Marius Barbeau as editor and author tried unsuccessfully to come up with "ways and means for the maintenance of the arts series." His letter was uncharacteristically pessimistic: "At present the [Canadian book] market is slow and desolate. Practically every book we publish that deals with the cultural life of the country has a hard time of it."[73]

In fact, financial constraints snuffed out *two* Ryerson art series. Once the Second World War ended, Pierce thought of launching a second series, one devoted to Canadian contemporary art. But rising costs and dismal sales projections killed the plan. One can imagine Pierce's frustration in the late 1940s and 1950s as he had to turn down numerous book proposals from art historians like Robert Hubbard, William Colgate, and Donald Buchanan. By this era, moreover, the National Gallery of Canada, the Art Gallery of Toronto (later Ontario), and other publishers were publishing Canadian art titles. While Pierce undoubtedly rejoiced in greater interest in Canadian art publishing, competition in the market sliced the potential audience of art book buyers even finer.

By the mid-1950s, the Canadian Art series had slipped into the past. True, in 1956, Pierce again considered bringing out a high school-level textbook, tentatively entitled *Leading Canadian Painters*, to match the successful Ryerson textbook *Leading Canadian Poets* (1948), a book of essays edited by Quebec educationist W.P. Percival (the latter had sold some 1,000 copies in Quebec alone). But, in the 1950s, Canadian art history received little attention in the Canadian school system, and costs made the project unfeasible.[74]

Despite the bathos, Pierce had established himself as the most influential editor and publisher of Canadian art, particularly in the late 1930s and 1940s. Bruce Whiteman, biographer of J.E.H. MacDonald, has analyzed the roles of Thoreau MacDonald and Lorne Pierce in making a canonical figure of MacDonald (even over and above the reputation of the Group of Seven as whole) through several Ryerson Press titles by and about this cohort. The publications include MacDonald's poems *West by East* (1933) and E.R. Hunter's *J.E.H. MacDonald: A Biography and Catalogue of His Work* (1940), a "standard work on MacDonald" for four decades with its seminal catalogue raisonné. Whiteman has rightly pointed out that, as editor and publisher, Pierce served as the "powerful ally" of Thoreau MacDonald, himself a "tireless proselytizer" of his father's work.[75]

Pierce, moreover, was the publisher – and hands-on editor – of a key work of Canadian art history, *Canadian Art, Its Origin and Development* (1943) by William Colgate. Published in the same year as E.K. Brown's landmark *On Canadian Poetry* (1943) – another canonical work published and influenced by Pierce – Colgate's 278-page opus was shaped significantly by Pierce's ideas as cultural nationalist. Ironically, the extent of Pierce's influence on its content emerges most clearly in a letter Colgate wrote to Ryerson complaining about charges for galley changes. Colgate pointed out that many of the changes had been made at Pierce's suggestion, not his. For example, Pierce had asked him to add material on "Emily Carr, Jacobine Jones, the amateur artist, James Blomfield and one or two others."

Colgate's acknowledgments in the book itself also highlight Pierce's "hands-on" role: "Dr. Lorne Pierce read the entire manuscript with a care and vigilance for which I cannot thank him sufficiently. Insofar as it is free from errors and ambiguities I owe it largely to his precise knowledge and patient toil."[76] Tellingly, Colgate's book bore all the signs of being one of Pierce's pet titles. It was designed by Thoreau MacDonald and featured a handsome pine bough colophon gracing the title page. Pierce's – and Colgate's – iconic Group of Seven was foregrounded in the book design: the frontispiece illustration was Frederick Varley's iconic *Stormy Weather, Georgian Bay*. The foreword, penned by C.W. Jefferys, set Colgate's text squarely in a cultural/national context, linking as it did "Canadian art development with its environment, its physical background, its social life, its racial traditions and its present and future needs ... as an integral part of Canadian life."[77] Many of the ideas characteristic of the Canadian Art series (and of Pierce's values) are also found in Colgate's analysis. For example, the Group of Seven is described as "the culmination of all the progressive and converging influence of painting in Canada for the last hundred years." Colgate's conclusion, written in wartime, is militantly nationalistic in the Pierce mode: "But with every year, the presence of our natural environment becomes stronger, the foreign element is more quickly assimilated, and the deciding factor that is evolving a national art seems to be the spell of Canada itself."[78]

Reviewers were often critical of Colgate's book. The 1940s proved to be a time of change and controversy in art in the Western world generally – with fierce debates over the merits and meaning of abstract art and

over ideology in art – and the art scene in Canada was no exception. Art
historian Colgate, publisher Pierce, and artist Jefferys were all well over
fifty years old. A new generation of younger, more iconoclastic Canadian
artists and art historians was emerging, a generation less reverential and
sometimes less overtly nationalistic in their concept of Canadian art. For
example, the young Helen Kemp, training as an art educator in the late
1930s at the Art Gallery of Toronto, quoted a reference to Krieghoff as
"Kriegh-offal" in a letter to her fiancé Northrop Frye.[79] As for Colgate's
book, rising young National Gallery art educator Robert Hubbard, in a
1945 review, criticized the text – as had Arthur Lismer, Donald Buchanan, and others – for, as Pierce wryly summarized it, being "too much
of a scrap-book, [with] no integrating theories of art, [and as] ... too
regional and uninformed." Annoyed, Pierce himself penned a letter to
Hubbard challenging the young art historian and his contemporaries
to do better. He wittily eulogized his own experience of Canadian art
publishing – "Any publisher who sponsors Canadian art is thought by
some to be a fool and by others a wastrel, and there is some truth in
both indictments"[80] – and then went on to express his own coolness to
abstraction. Calling some art histories "propagandist" in favour of new
trends in art (without acknowledging how propagandist Colgate's and
his views were vis-à-vis the Group of Seven), Pierce added that "we [as
publishers] are bound, I think, to say that if special emphasis is given to
Pellan he shall not necessarily be recorded as the last word." In defending
Colgate's approach, therefore, Pierce also defended his own literary and
artistic ideology.

Pierce's *cri de cœur* made it clear how beleaguered he felt by the mid-
1940s in his nationalistic approach to Canadian culture. As one scholar
has written, the Second World War was for Canadian art and literature,
as for so much else in the world, a time of "profound dislocation and
relocation of values."[81] In response, Pierce, like many of his contemporaries in the art and literary establishment, was anxious and defensive. He
told Hubbard:

> In the long run I am even prepared to say – and I have written a
> good deal of literary criticism that must sound pretty bad – that
> very often a well-chosen illustration or even an anecdote can
> outweigh a whole hay-wagon load of the puffed rice we pass off
> in this country for art criticism. The comment on Canadian art
> by our young illuminati is totally divorced from any enlightened

comparison with masterpieces in the great galleries abroad. Propaganda has taken the place of information among us, substituting prejudice for principles, and dully repeated formulae and catchwords for insight.

To his credit, however, Pierce told Hubbard of his continued interest in assembling "a group of writers who can undertake a comprehensive history of Canadian art, and place it in the right setting in the cultural development of Canada."[82] He ended his letter by challenging the young iconoclast and his contemporaries to write a better history of Canadian art, which he assured him that Ryerson would publish.

Clearly, Pierce had made himself a major force in art publishing. As a power on the art scene, he was an unabashed proponent of the work of the Group of Seven and their admirers, and consulted closely with such figures as Group members Arthur Lismer, A.Y. Jackson, and Lawren Harris,[83] Group friend and patron Albert Robson, and such distinguished and established older artists as C.W. Jefferys, Wyly Grier (a fierce enemy of modern art), and others. Pierce's correspondence from the 1930s and 1940s also makes it clear that he had the ear of such influential art administrators as Art Gallery of Toronto's Martin Baldwin and National Gallery of Canada Director Harry McCurry. For example, Pierce was key in convincing Baldwin to sponsor a major exhibition on Jefferys in 1942. He also convinced McCurry to host the exhibition on Jefferys despite the National Gallery's policy at the time of not showcasing the work of living artists.[84]

Pierce's personal patronage of art and artists also went far beyond commissioning or buying works of art. Most remarkably, in May 1938 he bought land in suburban Thornhill next to Thoreau MacDonald's home and studio to keep MacDonald's refuge unaffected by industrial development – in the form of a factory planned by a local businessman.[85] In gratitude, the artist, who could not afford to purchase the land himself, presented Pierce with J.E.H. MacDonald's masterpiece *The Elements* – which he had in any case planned to will to his friend and patron – as an expression of gratitude.

Pierce, who also insisted on paying the taxes on the Thornhill lot, kept it for a decade to safeguard the creative environment of his favourite artist, designer, and close friend. When he sold it, Pierce stipulated that only a church or rectory could be erected on the site. Moreover, the legal arrangements for the lot guaranteed the artist a twenty-foot right-of-way on one end of it. Few publishers – and few friends – have gone so far for an artist.[86]

Pierce also got caught up in art philanthropy vis-à-vis his alma mater, Queen's University, an effort that proved bittersweet. In the 1930s he and several other prominent Queen's alumni established the Queen's Art Foundation to finance and purchase works of art for the university. The prime movers in this off-again, on-again venture included prominent Toronto stockbroker D.I. McLeod, Pierce's friend and physician Dennis Jordan (son of Queen's professor William Jordan, an art collector and Pierce mentor), Rosedale philanthropist and art collector Mabel Dalton Segsworth, and scientist and amateur artist Sir Frederick Banting as well as artists C.W. Jefferys and A.Y. Jackson and others. While Professor Jordan's art-laden parlour walls had been a mecca in Pierce's undergraduate days at Queen's, Pierce and the other alumni among his Queen's Art Foundation collaborators had found the austere Presbyterian limestone walls of the university an artistic desert in most other respects. They resolved to act.

As a result, the Queen's Art Foundation, in fits and starts from 1932 to 1944, donated to that university a collection of Canadian and British art, including works by J.M.W. Turner and by major Canadian painters such as Tom Thomson (four works), Paul Kane, A.Y. Jackson, and J.E.H. MacDonald (*The Wild Ducks*).[87] Interestingly, amid all the academic politics involved, the donors experienced tensions with artist André Bieler, a faculty member at Queen's, over what Bieler saw as their too-conventional taste in art.[88] Whether in the Canadian Art series or in the Queen's Art Foundation, Pierce was committed to educating Canadians about art from a conservative and nationalistic perspective which foregrounded the Group of Seven and their ilk as "real makers of Canada."

Whether one considers Pierce's initiatives on behalf of Canadian art in publishing or at Queen's, it is clear that Canadian art of a certain cast had by the 1940s become as important to him as Canadian literature as a tool for the cultural making of a nation. In 1939 he wrote Principal Wallace of Queen's urging the acquisition of more Canadian art at the university: "I do not see how we can have a nation at all, let alone native art and literature – still the best index of our social energy – without a rediscovery of the imponderables … we might repair a fault with an intelligent and planned purchase of good pictures, Canadian and others."[89]

Even as he penned this letter, Pierce was holding on to this ideal of Canadian artistic nationalism in the face of war. The German invasion of

Poland and the subsequent declaration of war by Canada had occurred a month before, in September 1939. Pierce's publishing and personal initiatives in Canadian art were, to his mind, threads of hope for Canada in the midst of the darkness then engulfing the world. But in the 1940s, amid the challenges of the Second World War and its aftermath, he would experience his own personal darkness – both at home and at work.

18

Wearing the Heart Out
in Wartime

Lorne Pierce, Ryerson Press, and the Second World War, 1939–1945

Once more … [I am] glad to see the year [1941] go. Life is so full of pain and stupidity and gross manners … The days are too full, and I am too tired. We try to make good books and sell them but we keep going behind.

Lorne Pierce diary entry, New Year's Eve, 1941[1]

Damn this war. It is destroying the young and wearing the hearts out of those who remain at home and wait.

Lorne Pierce to his daughter, after the combat death of a friend's son, 1943[2]

On 3 September 1939, the day England declared war on Germany, Lorne Pierce, at home in York Mills, wrote sombrely in his diary that it was all an "unbelievable nightmare": "We of 1914–18 thought it would never be again, and now another German madman rises to power. But he is doomed." The family hung over the radio for news.[3] The day before, when Pierce arrived at the Ryerson offices for his usual Saturday morning stint, he learned that Harry Berry, one of his key House salesmen, would shortly be called up. The personnel shortages of the war years at the House were already underway.

Like every Canadian publisher, Pierce worried about what war meant for the book trade as well as for the country. A few weeks later, he confided to novelist Laura Goodman Salverson: "I have been squeezing my head trying to think of some plan of publishing which might assist the House during the war, but I cannot guess what sort of works might be popular … Any book, I imagine, which helps [soldiers and people on the home front] to face life would be popular."[4] Meanwhile, against the backdrop of what Pierce called the "strange delay" of the so-called Phony War – the period before the German invasion of the Low Countries in the spring of 1940 – he and the other House managers frantically reorganized and amalgamated departments as more employees left for military service.[5] But it was not War but another horseman of the Apocalypse that bore down on the Pierce family in these days. Death.

Its imminence became apparent when Pierce and his family arrived in Delta for Christmas 1939. The previous Christmas had been jubilant, with Harriet Pierce rapturous over a new Ryerson publication – Lorne and Sara's collection of her favourite sayings and quotations, a slim booklet that they called *From an Eastern Window* (1938). The title evoked their mother's favourite spot in the Delta parlour, the corner where she loved to read and watch the world as well as instruct her family. This first Christmas of the war, Lorne found his seventy-five-year-old mother suddenly "frail." Her doctor gave him the distressing news that the pain in his mother's side and back was caused by a "growth." As was the medical practice of the day, Mrs Pierce was not told of her cancer. Lorne winced as his mother vainly sought relief with hot-water bottles. In the well-worn Pierce pew at Delta United Church, he found "the crowding memories ... too painful ... I had a hard time."[6] Once back in Toronto, the new year of 1940 began bleakly, given, he confided to his diary, "Mother, the dreadful war and all." He invoked the 23rd Psalm as his New Year's mantra: "I will lift mine eyes unto the hills."[7]

Lorne and his sister resolved to return to Delta as soon as possible, with a specialist in tow. On Wednesday, 3 January, Sara left for Delta. Lorne, despite an acute attack of his lupus-induced "lumbago," suddenly decided on Thursday to join her. When he hurried into the Delta house, his mother awoke to find him at her bedside. His diary entries poignantly tell the tale: "I sat on her left side holding her hand and Sara on her right, also holding a hand. Mother devoured me with her eyes, and beamed seraphically. 'Well! Well! Well!' and [she] turned to Sara all smiles ... while we smiled and kept back the tears, so changed was she, her face flushed and her left cheek red and swollen to the eye." Mrs Pierce soon sank into semi-coma. The death watch began, with Sara and Lorne "scarcely leaving" their mother's side for the next four days. The deafness that mother and son shared came poignantly into play. On Saturday of the long vigil: "We placed her speaking tube at her ear and called 'Mother, Sara, Lorne,' but she was already well across the river into the great world beyond. Her heart by some miracle grew stronger and what we expected would be a sudden collapse [after a stroke] turned into a grim fight against death." Finally, at 6:20 a.m. on Tuesday, Harriet Pierce "grew very quiet, shuddered slightly, and was gone. Sara and I sat on either side of her holding hands across mother's failing life, and vowed that 'Through life till death we will hold fast to each other.'"[8]

Pierce's account of his mother's funeral service, held two days later, on the afternoon of 11 January, in the parlour of the Pierce home and of her burial in the former Methodist cemetery in Crosby on a cold, snowy day evokes the strong bond between them and her vision for his life. Lorne described his mother, laid out in death in her favourite "eastern corner" of the parlour, as still "strong, joyful, splendid, commanding the place, still ruling it from her favourite corner, the one she chose, where for years she would rest upon the chesterfield and look through the large window into the sky and trees."

Lorne and Sara then spent the next few days sadly emptying the Delta house prior to its sale. To see the house mostly bare was, Lorne remembered, "the hardest of all. The heart had gone out of it. As we sorted out all the little simple things during those days we often wept together at their trivial nature. We had so much more. What magic our mother's love had worked all those years to make out of those simple things, books and pictures, a magic world of love."[9] Indeed. For better and for worse, Harriet Pierce had shaped a vision for her son's life, the magic of her love both black and white. He would ponder her influence in the coming years as the immediacy of her presence receded. Four years later, he confided to his son his continuing conviction that, although he did not "roar about it in public," he believed that he had been "dedicated while in my Mother's womb" to a spiritual mission and then "ordained before the world, and [thus] I know myself set apart for a real ministry."[10]

Before he left his mother's house for the last time, Pierce made a solitary vow, described in his diary: "I am more determined than ever to hold high the tradition, and alone in mother's room, with her wedding Bible in my hand I vowed to go with her God and mine, hand in hand to the end, to live more perfectly in the spirit of her house, more fully fulfil her ideals, so help me God."[11] A solemn vow, surely, and a lofty one. But was it wise? The practical implications of this vow were to make Lorne Pierce more than ever a driven man. He sometimes liked to describe his dead mother in the old-fashioned evangelical phrase as "safely over." But was he safely over her?[12]

Her memory haunted him. A service was held in late July to dedicate the pulpit and communion table in Delta United Church given by Lorne and Sara in memory of their parents. Pierce recorded that the service was "very impressive" but "very hard to attend ... Visited the cemetery twice. The headstone is now cut, it looks so final." He added that he found it a "terrible moment" to pass his parents' old house, now in other hands.[13] Not surprisingly, he made no diary entry at all to mark his fiftieth birthday on 3 August, a day he spent trapped at the office in Toronto, called back by various publishing imbroglios, despite his promise to quickly rejoin Edith at the cottage.

Pierce continued to mull over the spiritual and psychological effects of his mother's sense of mission for him. In one letter, written around Mother's Day 1945, he mused to his daughter about the fact that, though the family had regularly attended North Toronto's St George's United Church, he and Edith had not given their two children an intensely religious upbringing. He explained: "I guess I went too far over in trying to save you from the forced feeding I got [from Mother]. Some of it made me suffer physically almost." Pierce admitted that, as a result of his mother's religious emotionalism, he himself had become "a very reticent fellow" about his deepest thoughts and feelings. He observed: "But I see now where I could have done better [in sharing my spiritual beliefs]. Religion has been so real to me, the great Over Soul so very present, prayer so definitely a reality, the plan and purpose and wisdom and love in and behind life so vital and alive, that I take it as naturally as the weather." He added (with an interestingly ambivalent choice of verb): "I have never *escaped* the wonderful sense of dedication I had as a young chap and a student volunteer for foreign missions, let alone my ordination, the realest moment in my life."[14]

Other letters to Beth struck a similar note. Pierce attributed the sense of always having "felt ordained" that had infused his work as minister and publisher to "the emotional milieu at home, especially my Mother's thinking and loving." He noted: "I would rather have that feeling of dedication to the good life, to the highly useful life, dedication as the minister of a people, my Canadian people, [than] be rich. I could be happy in a hut and do that.[15] In another letter, he conceded that there was an element of compulsion to his sense of mission: "I feel miserable when I am not ... [being socially useful], and [yet I] am loaded with fiddling concerns that keep me from it."[16]

As he weighed in the balance the obsessive striving his mother had instilled in him, Pierce came to believe he had been too absorbed in his career at the expense of both his family and his own overall well-being.[17] He felt, as he put it, "burned out before my time" even as he forged on.[18]

THERE WAS much at the office to "burn out" Pierce. Sales in the 1930s had ranged from abysmal in the depths of the Depression to lacklustre late in the decade; they dropped back to abysmal with the onset of war. Even the January before the war, Pierce confided to his diary that "business was slow" and that he was still hoping for "a break out of the red" for Ryerson's Canadian list.[19] By the end of 1940, however, poetry sales, never good, were appalling. With "the bottom fallen out of the publishing business," Pierce wrote sardonically that new poetry submissions seemed about as essential as "lingerie in the Arctic." His resolve to keep publishing persisted, however: "We have not forgotten [poetry], and are working our way toward it, with the swift smooth competence of a crab."[20] The fiscal year 1940 ended with a small overall profit of $3,000 in Pierce's department.[21] But Pierce had also been tasked with the Film Department and that was haemorrhaging money for Ryerson (a $5,214 loss), just like the Film Department at Macmillan of Canada.[22]

The year 1941 saw overall House profits quadruple (thanks to printing contracts in wartime for the commercial division) but there was a loss of $4,804.98 in books – although the Film Department made a profit ($1,393.88).[23] To bolster his returns, Pierce was negotiating with L.M. Montgomery to print Canadian editions of her popular Anne series. Ryerson came out with no less than three Anne titles in 1942, including the first-ever Canadian edition of *Anne of Green Gables*, a landmark.[24] The fact that Pierce was willing to risk tangling with the litigious L.C. Page of Boston, who controlled many of Montgomery's titles, showed how keenly he wanted to improve his own bottom line.

Troubles multiplied in 1942: some titles, such as poet Anne Marriot's chapbook *Salt Marsh*, were delayed by paper shortages.[25] Textbook sales, crucial to the viability of Pierce's endeavours, were disappointing in the first years of the war. Moreover, 1942–43 saw overall losses in Pierce's trade books of $3,059.62.[26] The war, in fact, hobbled the book trade. The Canadian branch of publisher William Collins experienced severe paper and labour shortages as well as problems with equipment maintenance as Canadian labour and resources were diverted into the war effort. There were similar problems at Macmillan of Canada.[27] It was just as grim at Ryerson. In the spring of 1943, Pierce wrote Charles G.D. Roberts that the plant bindery had "completely broken down" because it was "so handicapped for want of extra help."[28] In the fall of 1943, he recorded that in one week he had lost both the sales manager and his assistant to the armed services, while his head stock-keeper had given notice. He added "the walls cave in and I am no Stoic."[29] There was some comic relief. Pierce wryly described for his children the flood of mediocre war fiction he received from young writers in khaki: "When a [soldier] writer mentions a blonde ... it lands him in a heap of trash."[30]

The late war years were even more problematic. The Wartime Prices and Trade Board, the federal body that oversaw the Canadian economy, by 1944 required publishers to "submit comprehensive statements of the books they intended to publish during the year, both by title and by weight," urging that publishers cut back on both paper and print runs, among other economy measures. That same year, the board asked printing companies to give priority to textbook titles at the expense of trade books.[31] Given that the House was Canada's largest publisher, Pierce was caught in a frantic juggling act. By 1944, he was forced to postpone publication of some trade titles to satisfy the guidelines. In August, he warned Walter McRaye that his book on Pauline Johnson, scheduled for that fall, would have to be postponed "because of the collapse of our Printing Department."[32]

Two weeks later, in early September 1944, Pierce described for another impatient author, Duncan Campbell Scott, just how grim the publishing crisis was: "On the 28th of June, I had a progress report on all the books already in the factory, practically our entire Fall list. Two days ago we went over the list again and there has been no change – nothing set, nothing printed, nothing bound, – in all these weeks. This means we ... have to transfer many of our autumn titles to the Spring of 1945 and shuffle our prospective publications for next Spring on [to] the Fall of 1946. We are in such a hopeless morass that there is really no use of even planning."[33]

Pierce was right. In the spring of 1945, he had to defer McRaye's book yet again to "whenever we have men to make it and paper to print it."[34] With many such delays, Pierce faced a chorus of unhappy authors, including best-selling novelist Will R. Bird, who ultimately left Ryerson. In May, Pierce told critic Desmond Pacey that his hands were "still high" over his head after a meeting about the crisis because "every book manufacturing plant in Canada is a fantastic mess. The Government will not

allow us to bind any book outside school books until after June 15. We
are having difficulty getting paper, greater difficulty getting board for the
covers."[35]

Thus, although Pierce's department showed a small profit in trade
books in the 1943–44 and 1944–45 fiscal years, and through the end of
November 1945, those figures masked the reality of publications deferred
or delayed.[36] Peacetime brought no immediate relief. In May 1946 Pierce
reported that two booklets in the Canadian Art series had to be sent
out to commercial printers, causing delay and expense, because Ryerson
Press had already "used up our entire paper quota for 1946."[37] Moreover,
the booklist that spring was largely a carry-over from the previous fall,
meaning lost sales because those titles had missed the lucrative Christmas book market and still others had been in turn delayed or dropped.[38]

The war brought other crises as well. For example, by mid-war, anti-
Nazi feeling in Canada prompted an attack on the presence of German
myths of Siegfred in the Ryerson-Macmillan school readers. A September 1944 editorial in the Toronto *Telegram* denounced the inclusion of
myths about "Hitler's Hero" in the Grade 6 Treasury readers, huffing,
"Is there any good reason why the heroes … of German mythology on
whom the Nazi[s] have built their own brutal brand of 'kultur' should
have a place in the selected reading of Canadian children?"[39] A flurry in
the press ensued, with one school official suggesting the use of Victoria
Cross citations instead.[40] Pierce wrote a letter to the editor-in-chief of
the *Telegram* on behalf of the two publishing firms, emphasizing his patriotism, denying any "attempt to glorify war or even the Germans," and
calling the editorial "false and grotesque."[41] Nevertheless, such negative
publicity was worrisome for two firms that counted on strong textbook
sales. No wonder Pierce told one correspondent late in the war that
everyone at Ryerson was "overworked and very tired."[42] He did not add
what his colleagues knew: that he was exhausted and his heart compromised.

All of these demands fed Pierce's impatience and fatigue. By 1944, he
was even pondering retirement, but questions of money and duty held
him back. He wrote to his daughter: "I don't know about holding on here
[at Campbell Crescent]. It is a lot of work for Mother. I am getting very
tired, and I find that I can't stand up to punishment as I used to. There
are times when I would love to quit, take what I could squeeze out of
things [financially], and complete my plans. There are things I must do
before I am done. They need more rest, more leisure than this kind of life

will ever give." Like many Canadians faced with wartime inflation and increases in income tax, Pierce concluded he could not afford to retire.[43]

On the positive side, at the House, the war years would bring Ryerson two Governor General's Awards in 1943 – one for poet Earle Birney's first collection, the modernist *David and Other Poems* (1942), and the other for novelist G. Herbert Sallans's *Little Man* (1942), a Ryerson Fiction Award winner. The novel sold well for Ryerson in wartime Canada and Birney's poems had larger-than-usual sales for the genre.[44]

PIERCE'S WAR WORK made his life more difficult. Early in the war, he took on volunteer work with the Canadian War Services Library Committee, set up by the Department of National Defence. Working with the military to help supply reading material for the troops proved to be a bureaucratic nightmare for Pierce as he fumed over the "brass hats" and their inefficiency – just as he had fumed two decades before as a sergeant in the Great War.[45] Rivalry among publishers and among civilian organizations like the Red Cross and the Imperial Order Daughters of the Empire over supply of books and films to the troops frustrated Pierce further. The squabbling among the "little squirts of colonels and big squirts of IODES" eventually prompted his resignation: he felt he had accomplished all he could in setting up base libraries across Canada.[46]

Nevertheless, Pierce's creativity sometimes bore fruit for the war effort. In February 1942 the chairman of Canada's largely subscribed Second Victory Loan Campaign wrote to congratulate Pierce for inspiring the campaign slogan "Come On Canada," taken from Pierce's title for a Ryerson booklet on the war effort.[47] Moreover, as well as work for the deaf, Pierce became involved in another initiative in the early 1940s, one that was clearly an affirmation of Canadian culture in the face of grim war news. He became the prime mover in founding the Bibliographical Society of Canada (BSC) which would be formally established at a May 1946 meeting at the University Club hosted by Pierce and attended by other key organizers such as Queen's University librarian E.C. Kyte, Toronto librarian Marie Tremaine, and eleven other bibliophiles, French and English. Pierce served as honorary president until his death.[48]

Even here, however, he would face obstacles. One reason that Pierce chose to become honorary president of the BSC was that his hearing problems made active executive roles very difficult. His deafness became even more problematic in the 1940s. He had always been greatly helped by a few individuals adept at being his "ears" – at the office his assistant,

Blanche Hume, and at home his wife and daughter. However, in 1943 Beth left home and Blanche Hume, whom her boss treasured as "my faithful friend and my ears" at Ryerson,[49] retired. "What I owe to you," he later wrote her, "I can never repay."[50] Following Hume's departure, Pierce's disabilities worsened. His secretaries of the 1940s and 1950s remember that his voice would repeatedly trail off into inaudibility when he was dictating letters.[51]

Blanche Hume's successor, Frank Flemington, first hired as his editorial secretary in September 1940, would make telephone calls on his boss's behalf, summarizing the results for him in memo form.[52] The red-haired Flemington, a Mount Allison University graduate who had been a high school teacher before joining Ryerson, became Pierce's right-hand man for the next two decades, handling routine correspondence with authors and shepherding manuscripts through the manufacturing process. Quiet and efficient, utterly trustworthy, and known for his understated sense of humour, Flemington was promoted by 1954 to associate editor of trade publications.

Poet Duncan Campbell Scott and critic E.K. Brown – both involved in several major publishing projects with Pierce in the mid-1940s – made it clear how deafness hampered Pierce's work. In June 1944 Brown told Scott that he had not raised all his concerns in a recent visit to Pierce at his Ryerson offices because "it is so hard to communicate with [Pierce] that I limit myself to one or two topics, and go in for a lot of repetition." Scott, ordinarily no admirer of Pierce, replied: "I feel pity for Pierce in trying to do business with the fearful disability of deafness ... it often gives rise to incidents which seem dubious but which are subject to reasonable explanation."[53] Pierce himself continued to be outwardly stoic about his hearing loss. But, tellingly, he told an intimate in these years that "the tragedy of deafness" had been one of the three shaping forces in his life, along with the influence of his mother and the dedicating power of his ordination.[54] By that time, he was already deep into major organizational work for the deaf.[55]

Pierce's overall health deteriorated under wartime pressures. After a heart attack in the winter of 1942, he spent four months in bed, and two more as a semi-invalid, a fact he and Hume concealed from Ryerson authors as much as possible.[56] Indeed, Pierce never identified his constellation of severe illnesses as lupus to staff or authors, probably a shrewd decision given the stigma of chronic illness at this period. He usually deflected all inquiries about his health by saying that he was "first rate."[57]

In fact, Pierce was for the first time compelled to acknowledge that he might well not live long enough accomplish all that he hoped to achieve professionally. His cardiologist bluntly told him so in the winter of 1942 after his heart attack. Pierce's health was not helped by the fact that, during the war, both he and Edith were prescribed barbiturates and/or chloral hydrate for their respective insomnia. Although such drugs were favourite prescriptions of the day, their harmful long-term side effects were not well understood in the 1940s. The vertigo, fuzzy-headedness, prolonged heavy sleep, and physical weakness from which both he and Edith regularly suffered in these years were probably side effects of these powerful opiates.[58] Such a situation was not uncommon in this period. For example, the editors of L.M. Montgomery's journals point out that, during this decade, Montgomery and her husband suffered similar, undiagnosed side effects from taking barbiturates like Luminol and Numinal, prescribed for sleeplessness and depression.[59]

Soon after his mother's death, Pierce generously deeded to his sister his half-share in the Whiskey Island cottage their parents had given them in 1925. By early 1944, he had purchased the more accessible McGhie cottage on Delta's lakeshore. He and Edith were snatching brief annual holidays at "Windrush" (which he initially dubbed "Casa Beverley") by the summer of 1944. One motive for the purchase of the McGhie cottage was Pierce's desire to hold on to generational continuity in eastern Ontario. He hoped that his own children might in future summer at Delta as "the fifth generation to travel" the roads of Leeds County.[60] (However, the cottage also brought some comic complications worthy of a Leacock sketch. For example, Pierce learned one year that his Delta caretaker was clandestinely renting his boat out to tourists.)

Pierce was emphasizing continuity as war precipitated another kind of absence. In the spring of 1943, he and Edith were plunged into the loneliness of an "empty nest" as twenty-two-year-old Beth and twenty-year-old Bruce – their respective jobs and studies deferred – left home within weeks of each other to join the war effort. "The bottom of my world," wrote Pierce wistfully just after seeing Bruce off to an army training camp in Quebec, "in a way [just] fell out."[61] As one friend put it, there was suddenly "a very lonely household at York Mills: the original pair dreaming of the absent ones."[62]

But if Lorne missed his son and daughter, Edith – who had for over two decades devoted herself to home and children – was, at the age of fifty-three, desolated. Volunteer war work with the Red Cross at

Sunnybrook Hospital and other charitable projects, as well as periodically caring devotedly for a procession of visiting relatives, particularly
her fragile elderly aunts, including Alice Chown, by now in her eighties,
occupied Edith but failed to lift her despondency. Lorne summed up
the situation in a letter to Bruce late in the war: "The long days here
get [Mother] down badly. I am on the canter and have little time to be
lonely."[63] For her part, Edith reminded her husband in frustration that,
if he drove himself to an early death through overwork, he could be replaced at work but not at home.[64] Lorne toiled on.

There were other anxieties for the two. While Lorne and Edith were
proud that their two children were part of the war effort, they worried
about their well-being, especially with Bruce in khaki. Bruce, who had
been president of his class in the second year of the commerce program at Toronto, had enlisted in the Canadian Army in 1943 after service with the Reserve Officer Training Corps (ROTC) on campus, soon
becoming a commissioned lieutenant in the Signal Corps. After years
of working on ham radios in the basement of the Pierce home, while
his father fiddled upstairs with various hearing devices, Bruce gravitated
to communications equipment once more. His postings during the war
included Trois-Rivières, Kingston, and Brockville, evoking for his father
memories of his own military service in Kingston during the First World
War. The ever-present prospect of an overseas assignment for their only
son haunted his parents' nights.

Beth also experienced war service similar to her father's in the Great
War. Slender, dark-haired, and graceful, a graduate in occupational therapy from the University of Toronto, Beth worked at the prestigious Johns
Hopkins University medical facility in Baltimore. She then became an
occupational therapist at the big Canadian military hospital in Sainte-
Anne-de-Bellevue, Quebec. There Beth experienced the physical and
mental suffering of severely wounded men repatriated home for treatment and rehabilitation – just as her father had as sergeant major in
charge of the orderly staff at Ongwanada Military Hospital in Kingston.
The bond between father and daughter deepened.

Indeed, Pierce's wartime letters to both his son and daughter suggest that the events of the war aroused traumatic memories of 1914–18
for him.[65] The link between the two wars was made concrete one day
at Campbell Crescent when Edith dug out Lorne's sergeant's tunic to
donate to a wartime clothing drive.[66] Lorne's memories of his cousin
Clifford's death at Vimy in 1917 converged with the fate of Edith's young

nephew, RCAF Flight Lieutenant Douglas Chown. Douglas, a favourite nephew (Pierce had christened him), was a frequent visitor at Campbell Crescent during his military training. In September 1940 his parents – Edith's brother, Winnipeg physician Gordon Chown, and his wife, Bunty – visited for the ceremony at which Douglas received his pilot's wings. Lorne commented to his diary: "May they carry him through to safety."[67] It was not to be. On active service in Labrador a few weeks before Christmas 1942, Douglas Chown's plane crashed on takeoff during a snowstorm. Sometime during the next twenty-four hours, before rescuers arrived, Douglas died of his injuries in the cold, snowy bush. Only the plane's navigator survived.

There were disillusioning revelations to come. As Pierce later confided to his son, the family learned that soon after the young lieutenant's body was recovered, a $100 bill – emergency funds zippered inside his flight suit – was apparently taken from the body.[68] Thus, to the tragedy of loss was added a sickening sense of human venality that one could not blame on the enemy.

With the aching knowledge both of a young man's death and of remorseless theft, Pierce composed the epitaph for his nephew's tombstone in far-off Gander: "Proudly he gave his happy life away / For Canada, for freedom and his God." He phrased his own feelings more trenchantly to his daughter: "Damn this war. It is destroying the young and wearing the hearts out of those who remain at home and wait."[69] When Douglas Frye, another family friend – the Pierces had once driven him to Trenton military base en route to Delta – was killed only a few weeks later, Lorne grieved to his children with uncharacteristic bitterness: "Mother gave me the news about Doug Frye. It was a terrific blow. I was very fond of him. Damn this beastly war. All the best go. The streets are jammed with half-caste swine running away from danger, foreigners, natives, French. That Doug should be lost seems utterly futile and wasteful and wicked."[70]

In one grim week in March 1944, Pierce had to write sympathy letters to three contemporaries who each had sons in combat – two of whom had been killed, while another had been critically injured.[71] (As an occupational therapist, Beth was soon to treat the latter when John Matheson, later a judge, federal member of Parliament, and father of the Canadian Maple Leaf flag, was repatriated to the Sainte-Anne's military hospital to learn to walk after a leg amputation.[72]) For his part, a few months after the shock of Douglas Chown's fatal crash and its aftermath, Pierce did begin to recover some spiritual equilibrium. That March he wrote his children a declaration of faith unusual for him as a parent, in the course of describing a service at the family church, St George's United. Portraying the congregation in his most scathing satiric mode as "full of bacon and beans and burp, a snotty and shallow crew, that paid taxes, but had no profound moral sense," he suddenly observed about the meaning of Jesus' life and teachings: "But the strange thing was [that] ... the principal truth this young man brought ... was, that love was the key to life, that it conquered all, that it was the key to race and religion, to all living and all success. Men were not ready for the idea, and are not yet, but after 1900 years [that belief] still stands, stands in spite of war and greed and bad manners, and someday it must win." Pierce added that the idea that "love [is] the beginning and the meaning and the end of life, in heaven and on earth" grew more "compelling" as he grew older.[73] Both his scathing Irish wit and his spirituality were intensified by the war, sometimes simultaneously.

Regrettably for posterity, by 1943, Pierce's diary had petered out after three decades, a casualty of his acute writer's cramp and lack of time. By the end of the war, he was in fact unable to write with his right hand. Although he slowly taught himself to write in a laboured script with his left hand, he henceforth had to type all his letters and notes.[74]

There were points of light. One stemmed, ironically, from Pierce's heart attack. The night of the heart attack in February 1942, Pierce composed his "A Prayer for One Day Only," which enjoyed popularity in wartime Canada after it was published anonymously in the *Observer*, the United Church magazine. The prayer caught the mood of the times with its appeal for "calm to our tired spirits and rest to our faltering feet."[75] But the happiest day of the war years was undoubtedly Lorne and Edith's twenty-fifth wedding anniversary on 19 September 1941, marked by one of Edith's renowned garden parties, held the next day with tea, ribbon, sandwiches, and other dainties consumed by fifty-five guests amid the flowers ("the day was glorious and everyone reluctant to go"). Lorne rejoiced over the milestone in the Campbell Crescent guest book: "Edith had everything lovely, gladioli and roses. She looked beautiful as any bride in a new gown, wearing a corsage and her Mother's locket and chain. 'She is always beautiful to me!' I wore my usual face." The most "overwhelming moment" for Lorne came when, after the party, Edith presented him with a special gift – Harriet Pierce's silver spoon holder, replated in silver and gold. Lorne recorded that he was "quite overcome. Nothing could have touched me more deeply."[76]

Lorne and Edith, hostess extraordinaire, at an afternoon tea in their beloved Campbell Crescent garden, 1940s. Courtesy of Beth Pierce Robinson

Edith Pierce also recorded *her* impressions of the event in the guest book in an entry that bespeaks both her supportiveness as wife and the high-minded spirit of patriotic service in the Pierce ménage:

> Twenty five years of testing – happiness – great happiness and thankfully proud of my Lorne, my Beth and my Bruce. I loved our guests – our old neighbours, our old friends, and our loyal relatives. Men, who like Lorne, have done their own work to the best of their ability but also have put their hearts into helping somebody else or some cause to make a better, happier Canada, and their wives standing staunchly beside them in their good works.
> A day can never be happier. "Joy rises in me, like a summer's morn."[77]

Edith carefully directed the entry to both Lorne and the children, signing it "Edith" and "Mother."

PIERCE'S CONCERN over the wartime social and political mood of the nation, including the conscription crisis, resulted in two eloquent long essays: one, *The Armoury in Our Halls* – which he wryly nicknamed *The Holes in Our Armour* – was published in 1941; the other, *A Canadian People*, a trenchant *cri de cœur* about Canadian nationhood and French-English relations, appeared in 1945.[78] Pierce wrote *The Armoury in Our Halls* in the spring of 1940 after the fall of France. It was a time of gloom and anxiety, as is evident in the writings of other prominent Canadians, such as Northrop Frye and E.K. Brown. Pierce was in an apocalyptic mood over the fall of Paris to the Nazis, as he confided to his sister: "Everything seems futile after the tragedy ... Our way of life has been too soft. We have demanded luxuries, mistaking them for life, prattled about democracy without trying it or realizing that it had to be defended every day. Now an era has ended, and hard years are ahead, and the sooner we realize this the better." Pierce was critical of modernity in this dark historical moment, when it seemed that the Nazis might win the war. He added grimly: "The old days will never return, but I think better days will come, new values, certainly a clearer idea of life as a brave adventure, and wealth in terms of work and striving instead of this slack silliness we call 'our way of life.' The Trojan Horse has mated with the Canadian Jackass, and its whinny was jazz, its coat a dinner jacket, and its manger a club and road house, a youth driving a car with a radio, and now we pay for it. I think we shall live under a dictatorship for a long time, and that is good."[79] A few weeks later, Pierce penned a similar letter to novelist Frederick Philip Grove.[80]

As a romantic nationalist who emphasized French-English entente ("It is imperative that we know and respect each other's traditions and ideals"[81]), Pierce was troubled by the tensions between Quebecers and English Canadians as another conscription crisis loomed. On the day of the plebiscite on conscription in April 1942, he described Quebec's mood as "ominous."[82] Like many of his contemporaries in the Canadian anglophone intelligentsia, of all ages, Pierce worried that a country sapped by depression and war might not have the will either to survive or to embrace the bicultural national ideals he saw as essential for Canada, ideals he had long declaimed in publications like his booklets *The Beloved Community, Toward the Bonne Entente* (1929), *New History for Old* (1931), and *Education in a Democracy* (1933), as well as in his editorial career.[83] Sharing this pessimism, thirty-nine-year-old E.K. Brown wrote morosely to the elderly Duncan Campbell Scott in late 1944: "I begin to grow doubtful that we shall ever see real peace again, but that is foolish.

Still I began to teach in 1929 and from then to now there hasn't been a single year not overclouded in the world by depression, spectres of war or war itself. I envy you who knew the world before 1914."[84]

For his part, to combat the threat of such "spiritual atrophy,"[85] Pierce brooded in what his friend, art historian Russell Harper, wittily called the "dark Spenglerian bog" of the "theology of crisis."[86] Indeed, in *Armoury*, quotations from Spengler and the need to resist societal decay pepper Pierce's text.[87] As he sent the booklet off to the House print shop in February 1941, he noted to his diary that he sounded "a trifle like a drill sergeant."[88] He irreverently described for his sister why he was sending out 250 copies of *Armoury* to the "usual friends": "I tap Democracy on the bean with a crow bar and come out for the elite, the leadership of the elect, the chosen few! Always believed it, but then I found Spengler and he gave me courage to expectorate in the eye of old man [Democracy]."[89]

By the time he wrote *Armoury*, Pierce had realized that post–Second World War society in Canada, as in the West generally, would be irrevocably changed. He shared the disdain of many Canadian intellectuals – intellectuals as different from him in outlook and age as F.R. Scott – for what was seen as Prime Minister Mackenzie King's lack of political decisiveness, a disdain most famously expressed in Scott's satiric poem "WLMK." In the same vein, Stephen Leacock lamented in a 1942 letter that King's policies on conscription had alienated French Canadians, and that King had thus "brought out in lurid colours the division of the country."[90] Like many Canadians, Pierce failed to see King's predilection for compromise and delay as a tactic necessary to hold together a linguistically and culturally fractious nation. Instead, he wrote impatiently in the opening salvo of *Armoury* that Canada's foreign policy was "nebulous, tentative and timid" while national policy was "vague, divisive and anemic," with the nation's writers and journalists largely "confused or dumb" in response.[91]

Pierce's antipathy to King persisted. In 1944, at the peak of the conscription crisis, he wrote scathingly to his children of King: "The more I see that little damp poultice, the more I loathe him."[92] A year later, he told a correspondent that King should have showed more candour and moral courage on issues like conscription, instead of "maintain[ing] his party in the House by manipulation very largely of the French vote."[93] Like his father, Pierce was a Conservative, but he had long avoided partisan political activity. But so disillusioned was he with King that, late in the war, he even helped another Conservative supporter, his childhood friend Norman MacRostie, write speeches denouncing King's politics.[94]

Pierce made it clear as early as 1941 that he felt Canada was on dangerous moral and social ground. The nation, he opined in *Armoury*, was in thrall to materialism, hedonism, and technocracy at the expense of decisive action, moral awareness, and a sense of tradition. With regard to Quebec, Pierce believed that national unity was threatened by divisive, partisan debates over conscription. In short, democracy and freedom were under threat from national weakness as well as from the Axis assault. Invoking earlier intellectual icons such as Edward Blake and Thomas D'Arcy McGee, Pierce called anew for national idealism: "Political parties for campaign purposes have usurped the idea of national unity, and the *bonne entente*, with the result that both are greatly threatened. That is … highly dangerous. Our educators and writers begin to boast of their cosmopolitanism, forgetting that it is easier to be anything in the world except oneself. French and English we belong to great traditions."[95] In a nod to his friend Harold Innis's communications theorizing, Pierce noted that the "radio and motor car have brought us together," only to add that Canadians "still await the fusing flame of an imperative ideal which will make of us one self-conscious people."[96] He professed his belief that an elite, composed of idealists, must guide Canadians. The nineteen-page peroration concluded ringingly: "Among the armoury in our halls are our invincible leaders and legislators – our historians, our creative writers, our poets and our artists. We depend upon them to awaken our nation, to quicken all our life. They are the responsible minority, clearest of eye, strongest of heart, and with them stand a few teachers and interpreters, who have 'the power to hold the other spellbound by a power derived from what they have experienced.' The days ahead will be dark indeed for all of us unless we have the leadership of our true elite."[97]

As historian Brian McKillop and others have pointed out, ideas like Pierce's about the nation posit a unifying and evolving national ideal that is at base homogenous and homogenizing of difference.[98] Moreover, as was typical of the era, Pierce's vision of the elite is in effect restricted in gender (male), class (educated and thus usually middle and upper class), and ethnicity, with non-WASP Canadians on the margins and francophones seen as problematic in their views of nationhood. Although Pierce still espoused French-English *bonne entente*, one passage betrays his growing consciousness that Quebec nationalism was a hardy and – to his mind – refractory phenomenon indeed: "We [anglophone Canadians] pathetically defer to foreign [i.e., American] opinion, parrot foreign slogans, and ape foreign fashions [in our cultural life]. The strength of our French fellow citizens is due to their determination to be themselves. Tourists call them quaint. Those who know them better call them granite."[99]

The war years made Canadians in all walks of life ponder the nature and future of Canada, especially with the concomitant scientific developments of the era, represented most dramatically by the atomic bomb. In such a climate, Pierce felt that *Armoury* got a "fine reception":[100] certainly, his papers include a spate of letters echoing his concerns. But four years later, Pierce's *A Canadian People* would repeat his worries even more urgently.

The publication of *Armoury* in 1941 did bring Pierce a new author – Wyndham Lewis, the British avant-garde painter, novelist, critic, and gadfly. Lewis, his reputation tainted with accusations of fascist sympathies, had left England with his wife, Anne, on the outbreak of war in September 1939, arriving in Toronto in November 1940 after a sojourn in the United States.[101] The bespectacled, balding, acid-tongued Lewis had tenuous links with Canada: he was born on his father's yacht off Nova Scotia and briefly worked as a war artist for Lord Beaverbrook's Canadian War Memorials project at Vimy in 1917. But, during the Second World War, cut off from his English funds by currency regulations and an outsider to Canadian life, Lewis had a difficult time in Canada before his return to England in August 1945, despite the help of Canadian intellectuals like artist A.Y. Jackson and the young Marshall McLuhan, then on faculty at Windsor's Assumption College.[102]

In May 1941, strapped for money, Lewis showed up at Ryerson Press (probably referred there by Thoreau MacDonald), offering to sketch an initially reluctant Pierce. Later that year, in October, he made several visits to Pierce's office, sketching him at his desk because he was too busy to pose.[103] The result (which Lewis, charmed by the Ryerson editor, made a present of to Pierce, who promptly sent him a check for $30[104]) was a broad-browed, head-and-shoulders study, executed in black and coloured crayon, now considered one of Lewis's best Canadian works.[105] Lewis himself liked it, commenting that Pierce "had a fine head, and beautiful hair, [and he was] an unusual type which I have tried to portray. He reminds me of Bertrand Russell."[106] The pastel brilliantly captures both Pierce's aquiline frame and his air of determination, shrewdness, and idealism. Pierce himself rightly pronounced it "a striking study, vigorous, probing."[107]

The Lewis and Pierce foray into print was less successful. During Lewis's first visit to Pierce in May 1941, the two had seen eye-to-eye about the importance of Canadian art.[108] Lewis then announced that he shared Pierce's views about the need for entente between French and English Canadians, and among the parts of the Commonwealth.[109] Praising *Armoury*, he told Pierce in a follow-up letter that he too had been "wondering a lot about the whole issue you raised there – of nationhood for a small English-speaking state, isolated in a New World, in close proximity to a state so great as the U.S.A."[110] Lewis soon submitted a manuscript, which Ryerson published as a booklet, *Anglosaxony: A League That Works*, in June 1941. In keeping with Lewis's talent for the provocative, the work, as his biographer points out, defends the democratic ideal against those on both the left and the right with the grandiloquent assertion that "democracy is merely a name for the Anglo-Saxon peoples and their traditional way of behaving." On the basis of such lofty constructs, Lewis called for Canadian support of Britain.[111]

Unfortunately, the booklet sank without a trace, selling only 300 copies in three years.[112] Pierce, to placate Lewis's fears of a conspiracy of silence after the book received no reviews at all, met with *Saturday Night* editor B.K. Sandwell in August about Lewis. All in all, *Anglosaxony* was not an auspicious undertaking, although Sandwell subsequently published several articles by Lewis.[113]

Lewis's subsequent scathing fictional satirizing of his Canadian sojourn in his autobiographical novel *Self Condemned* (1954), in which he denounced Toronto as a "sanctimonious icebox," part of "the most parochial nationette on earth," seems not to have targeted Pierce.[114] Nonetheless, Pierce found it "sad to read this bitter book." He later assured a Lewis scholar that Lewis "never spoke like this in my presence."[115] It is telling, however, that after his 1941 interview with Sandwell, Pierce cautioned Lewis that "patient, courteous persistence" was required "to win through to friends and collaborators."[116] This was not advice to which Lewis was by nature suited, and he whirled out of Pierce's orbit for the rest of his Canadian stay.

Pierce once again forcefully expressed his own challenge to Canadian nationhood and democracy at the end of the war. *A Canadian People* (1945) was even more provocative than *Armoury*, designed he wrote, not to exude pessimism but rather to pose a "blazing challenge" to Canadians.[117] Response to it in some quarters was much more marked than to *The Armoury in Our Halls*. Most of the text of *Armoury* was in fact incorporated into the new, much longer (eighty-four pages as opposed to nineteen) publication. The reiteration suggests how persistently troubled Pierce was by the state of the nation and the alleged failure of Canadian politicians and intellectuals to provide real leadership.

In *People*, Pierce stressed that much of his career had been devoted to building "a covered bridge between East and West, Roman Catholic and Protestant, between French and English."[118] But Pierce, renewing his critique of modernity, repeated the obstacles – mass marketing, vulgarity, consumerism, literary cosmopolitanism – threatening Canada's future. He remained pessimistic, telling his readers that as an editor and writer he had always implored all "Canadians to grow up, to have the courage to be themselves. Looking back it all seems quite futile."[119]

A Canadian People went into a second printing within two months (for a total run of 1,000 copies).[120] Pierce received several requests to reprint or excerpt it. Excerpts from *People* were reprinted in 1946 in both *Canadian Book Digest* and the *Ontario Public School Argus*, just as the *Observer* had asked him to repeat some of the arguments in *Armoury* on the need for national idealism in a 1944 article for a series on the future of Canada.[121]

CHANGE WAS in the air in the Canadian book world during the war as well as in the nation itself. The death in April 1940 of forty-six-year-old Hugh Eayrs – who for the past year had appeared ill and aged beyond his years[122] – president of Macmillan of Canada and Pierce's collaborator in the Ryerson-Macmillan textbook series, coupled with the departure of Eayrs's lieutenant John Gray into the armed services for the duration of the war, emphasized how senior and dominant (and lonely) a figure Pierce had become in Canadian publishing.

Eayrs's death left Pierce and the sixty-three-year-old John McClelland at rival firm McClelland and Stewart as the two grand old men of Canadian publishing, but by war's end McClelland had a prospective heir. McClelland's son Jack would join his father's company in 1946 after discharge from the Royal Canadian Navy. That same year, John Gray would return from service to take over as general manager of Macmillan of Canada in 1946, ending a lacklustre wartime holding operation under Robert Huckvale.[123]

By contrast, at Ryerson there was no obvious successor in the wings, even as in May 1945 the House hosted a dinner for Pierce at the Royal York Hotel to celebrate his silver anniversary at the Ryerson Press. With unpublished manuscripts piling up in the plant in the face of a "fantastic mess" of shortages,[124] Pierce mused that night on the price of his achievements as well as their value. Privately, in his worst moments of frustration, he fumed that many of the House staff were "offensively and needlessly dull and inept."[125] Nevertheless, at the banquet, Lorne, his wife and daughter, colleagues, and friends paused to affirm his publishing achievements. Warm toasts made in ice water, several congratulatory speeches, and a beautifully bound scrapbook of tributes celebrated Pierce's accomplishments to date. After dinner, Pierce gracefully responded. The hard, high-pitched voice of the deaf, sometimes uncertain in its modulations, coloured his lively wit, reminding the guests of his courage and resolve.[126]

Pierce's relations with his book steward, while generally good, did bring some difficult moments. Pierce was frustrated when, at the start of the 1946 Christmas season, Dickinson withheld one of Ryerson's popular agency publications because the book – an H.L. Mencken Christmas story published by New York's Alfred Knopf and distributed in Canada by the House – featured a drunken hobo as its protagonist. Dickinson's wife, Isabelle, a keen temperance advocate, had been horrified that the agency department of the House, headed by Ernest Walker, would carry a bibulous Christmas fable. The book steward concurred and, by his own account, sent the books "to the furnace." (Knopf, the U.S. publisher, was furious over this foolish act of prudery, ultimately withdrawing the lucrative Knopf agency, and Toronto book reviewers like William Arthur Deacon were not slow to mock such stuffiness.[127])

When this act of censorship hit the papers in hard-drinking post-war Canada, Pierce, although he had nothing to do with agency publications, was tarred by association. He and Ryerson Press looked old-fashioned and ridiculous in the eyes of many young Canadian book buyers and authors. (After all, about this time, poet F.R. Scott was writing lyrical invocations to martinis – "Martinigram" – and such emerging young writers as Al Purdy had been known to take a drink.) In fact, Pierce himself had long ceased to advocate temperance. Indeed, his mother's death allowed him to move away from the rigid temperance vow she had imposed upon him at the tender age of six. From the late 1940s, Pierce himself took an occasional drink, although he and Edith never served it or had it in the house. Quite rightly, he seemed to regard the temperance pledge his mother had exacted to be a pledge made to her, not God, one that was dissolved upon her death in 1940.

In the 1950s Pierce even elliptically "outed" his post-1940 acquaintance with liquor in a witty letter to his sister: "At the wedding reception in the Granite Club I drank liquor! There were two glasses, one ginger ale with grape juice, the other orange. The orange I found was spiked with gin or something. I took a sip, discovered my sin, held the sip [while] looking for a [potted] palm into which I could expectorate, and failing at an outlet swallowed it. That's sin. That's one thing settled."[128] Macmillan publisher John Gray remembered Pierce's "rare indulgence" in a "very small Scotch" in the late 1940s as the two made their way across the west on gruelling textbook selling trips.[129]

In any case, Pierce privately fumed at Dickinson's action over the Mencken text. He confided to his son that Dickinson publicly often hit "on all eight [cylinders] about the [United] Church and The Ryerson Press, which I like to have kept separate."[130] But Dickinson remained puritanical and proud of it, as he made clear to Pierce in another letter denouncing Ryerson author Earle Birney for vulgar prose in his military novel *Turvey*, which McClelland and Stewart had recently published. Denying that "Puritanism necessarily inhibits art," and seeing "no logical connection between the two," Dickinson insisted to Pierce that writers like Earle Birney "wish ... a type of libertinism which they themselves seem to enjoy and which they glorify as being a part of 'life.'" Implacably, the book steward added that "sewage systems are a part of life but we seldom ever require them for the sake of art."[131] That the House's administrative head took such priggish views tainted the Ryerson imprint in the eyes of the second wave of modernist writers (and book buyers) emerging in the 1940s and 1950s.

Back at home on Campbell Crescent, the garden continued to function as Lorne and Edith's "sanctuary, a blessed healing island of peace," as Pierce put it.[132] At his physician's insistence, he worked more and more from home. In a letter to his daughter, he jokingly evoked his ritual manner of "clearing off" the piles of manuscripts on his desk, appropriately enough in front of a large photograph of Harriet Pierce: "First a pile of debris on the left near the waste basket and then the slow procession of books and papers across the blue blotter, in front of Grandfather's watch and Grandmother's picture, and so into the waiting [brief]case big as a trunk and hungry as a bear."[133] Pierce's study, furnished with

walnut antiques and Oriental rugs, boasted a Jefferys watercolour. Bliss
Carman's Buddha, willed to Pierce by Mary Perry King, graced the fireplace mantel. The windows on each side of the fireplace had splendid
views of the garden, but it is doubtful that he took much time to look
out of them.[134]

PIERCE, like other Canadian publishers, brought out a spate of books
related in different ways to the war, despite shrinking lists (for example,
Sir Charles G.D. Roberts's poetry collection *Canada Speaks of Britain*
[1941] and his anthology of war poetry *Flying Colours* [1942] as well as
poet Arthur Bourinot's *Canada at Dieppe* [1942] and Vincent Massey's
The Sword of Lionheart, and Other Wartime Speeches [1942]).[135] He also
managed to publish works of social and political analysis aimed at the
interests of the wartime market, notably W.E. Harrison's *Canada, The
War and After* (1942) and Harry Cassidy's *Public Health and Welfare Re-
organization: The Post-War Problem in the Canadian Provinces* (1945). In
addition, Ryerson published a wartime series (under the title "Live and
Learn") for the Canadian Youth Commission, consisting of twelve reports on youth attitudes, spearheaded by Dr R.E.G. Davis of the Canadian YMCA, on such topics as health, recreation, citizenship, and family
life.[136]

Finally, Pierce inaugurated two booklet series during the war to
stimulate debate about current events and future possibilities. Ryerson's
Contemporary Affairs series took aim at political, economic, and social
issues of the day. He described the intent of the series to his son as the
war drew to a close: " I am planning a new short series of about six booklets on a now or never line for Canada's post-war reconstruction period
… It is a rip-snorting series by the best brains we can command."[137] The
wide-ranging series comprised some fourteen titles published between
1940 and 1946, beginning with Frank Herbert Brown, A.W.F. Plumptre,
and J. Douglas Gibson's *War Finance in Canada* (1940) and ending with
Samuel Eastman's *Canada at Geneva: A Historical Survey and Its Lessons*
(1946), part of the debate over the new United Nations in the light of the
failure of the League of Nations.[138]

The second wartime series, Canada Must Choose, featured short
works by Canadian intellectuals on a variety of pressing topics, which
the Ryerson catalogue featured with the declaration that "the time has
now come for Canada to make up her mind about her destiny" and about

national unity.[139] The young George Grant, just then on the threshold of a brilliant and controversial career as a Canadian thinker, contributed *The Empire: Yes or No?* (1945). Toronto intellectual C.E. Silcox asked *Must Canada Split?* (1945) while pioneering social worker Charlotte Whitton squared off about *Baby Bonuses, Dollars or Sense?* (1945). Pierce felt the series would not please many Quebecers, but, as he planned it in the fall of 1944, he told his son: "I have hesitated knowing it will cost me my French friends – but we have but one life, so here goes."[140]

Privately, Pierce was complaining to Quebec friends like cleric and historian Abbé Arthur Maheux about the influence in the province of the nationalist Abbé Lionel Groulx and of the Bloc Populaire, which, in Pierce's view, was "determined to drive Quebec into a congeries of parties and feudal political tribes, that will destroy her."[141] It was an opinion that Pierce repeated in *A Canadian People*, where, while accepting that English Canada had often treated the province unfairly, he deplored the inward-looking tendency of some elements of Quebec society. He criticized the nationalist "revenge of the cradle" he saw advocated in the writings of Groulx and others, denouncing it as a "new kind of racial and religious imperialism."[142] Pierce believed such advocacy created "fanatical loyalty to a false ideal or to an untrue legend – anti-conscription, anti-imperialism, pacifism, isolation, Quebec for the French, Canada for the English, anything will do providing it is mad enough, stupid, vulgar and wicked enough." As always, he concluded that the only real solution to the divisions between French and English Canadians was good will and "a generation or two of peace-time education."[143] His belief in discussion and education as a road to cultural *bonne entente* lay behind wartime Ryerson series like "Canada Must Choose" and Pierce's own passionate essay *A Canadian People*.

But the response from Quebec, especially to *People*, was definitely not what Pierce hoped for. For example, with regard to the concerns about Quebec that Pierce summarized in *A Canadian People*, acquaintances and allies like Quebec legislative librarian G.E. Marquis and historian Arthur Maheux merely politely assured him of their own good will.[144] There was little comment on the book in the francophone press, with an editorial in *Le Droit* dismissing Pierce as "utopiste" (utopian) and as too prone to believe that greater fusion of French and English would automatically bring tolerance and unity in its wake. The editorial ended by asserting that true Canadianism ("le veritable canadianisme") consisted in the parallel development of francophone and anglophone culture with no opposition from either culture to the other – hardly Pierce's dream for the nation.[145]

Most francophone commentators were content to note Pierce's high-mindedness and eloquence, as was the case with *Le Jour* and *Le Canada Français*.[146] (One wonders if Pierce would have roused more debate in Quebec if *People* also appeared in a French edition.) In any event, the muted Quebec reaction was not the dynamic assent to his call for rapprochement between the two founding cultures that Pierce sought. Quebec, with its Quiet Revolution ahead, was evolving in ways that Pierce, as a traditional anglophone *bonne entente* intellectual, could not control. Little wonder that, for the first time, notes of bitterness and/or frustration crept into his wartime writings on the nation, whether it was the description in *Armoury* of French Canadians as "granite" or the denunciation in a letter, after a neighbour was killed in combat, of "foreigners," "French," and the Canadian-born who would not join up.

Meanwhile, in these watershed war years, Pierce was also struggling to juggle modernist and traditional streams in Canadian literature in his Ryerson offerings. He thereby sought to maintain his primacy as a Canadian publisher and to demonstrate, as he put it in his diary in 1942, how, in literary terms, "the world is being shaken with this war."[147] In these last two decades of his career, social and cultural change would also unsettle Pierce.

"Tempting Satan and the Bailiff"

Juggling Modernist and Traditional Poetry
in the 1940s and 1950s[1]

I am very anxious that the most adventurous of our younger poets
should be given a hearing.

*Modernist poet and critic A.J.M. Smith to Lorne Pierce about Ryerson's
future poetry publications, 1943*[2]

I think that I can perhaps serve as sort of a middle 'stander' between
[A.J.M.] Smith and the usual Canadian critical attitudes.

Critic E.K. Brown to Lorne Pierce, 1943[3]

We were not impressed with the greatness of the book [*Unit of Five*]
but we felt that this was what the world or the war had done to this
generation of poets. Something rather dreadful has happened to our
young writers and we submitted this not because we believed in it
or thought it great art but as a document – a social document, if you
will – of the time.

Lorne Pierce to poet Dorothy Livesay about the modernist anthology Unit
of Five, *1945*[4]

By the end of the Second World War, Pierce had begun to publish
modernist poets in quantity. His heart still lay with the romantic
traditionalists, but a pragmatic drive to stay at the centre of literary publishing in the 1940s and 1950s – coupled with a recognition that a newer,
starker poetry had undeniably emerged in the crucible of economic depression and war – spurred him to publish writers like A.J.M. Smith,
F.R. Scott, Louis Dudek, Patrick Anderson, A.M. Klein, and P.K. Page.
Ironically, given Pierce's shift in orientation, his important contribution to the careers of the modernists by giving most of them their first

publication in book form has been little recognized by Canadian literary historians.

Modernist writers of the McGill movement generation and their younger confrères were not prompted to publish with Ryerson in the 1940s because of affinities with Pierce's literary views. Pierce seemed to many of the moderns, whether young (Irving Layton, P.K. Page) or middle-aged (A.J.M. Smith, F.R. Scott), to be inescapably a linchpin of the literary old guard. In 1925, at the same time as McGill students A.J.M. Smith and F.R. Scott were emerging as modernist poets anxious to shock the bourgeoisie, Pierce was voicing a far more traditional literary credo in the *Canadian Bookman*, advocating a "national ideal" for Canadian literature. He emphasized the idealistic, romantic, and moralistic: "We need three things [in our emerging literature] (1) Utter fidelity to truth (2) a determination to be ourselves; and (3) a sympathetic atmosphere in which the sublimest beauty, the sweetest music, the loftiest justice and the divinest truth might be expected to take root and flourish, when at last they do appear as ultimately they must."[5] This was not the sort of credo for Canadian writing that A.J.M. Smith espoused that very year in the iconoclastic *McGill Fortnightly Review* or the *Canadian Forum*: Smith denounced Puritanism and defiantly called for a work of art "at once successful and obscene."[6] Furthermore, at the time Pierce highlighted romantic nationalism in the epigraph to his Makers of Canadian Literature series, urging Canadians to "know, love and follow" Canadian writers as "the real Master-builders and Interpreters of our Great Dominion," A.J.M. Smith was by contrast calling for a "cosmopolitan" intellectualism in Canadian writing.[7]

Pierce's long-standing uneasiness about the orientation of Smith and his admirers was unequivocal in *A Canadian People*, where he criticized the valorization of cosmopolitanism in Canadian modernist circles. Pierce countered that the only "constructive way" to view the world of letters was "through Canadian eyes and with the Canadian scene in mind." He indignantly asserted that an "infinite amount of rubbish has been written about the cosmopolitan outlook, the international mind and so on."[8] A.J.M. Smith, for one, undoubtedly recognized that Pierce was criticizing his ideas and those of many of the McGill and *Preview* group of poets, clustered around that little Montreal magazine in the 1940s. *First Statement*, the rival Montreal modernist magazine to *Preview*, was no hotbed of Ryerson admirers either, although Pierce and its editor, John Sutherland, were to find common cause at the end of the

1940s. Overall, then, the pairing of Pierce and the Canadian moderns, in particular the Montreal-based ones, in Ryerson publication projects was no matter of kindred spirits.

However, Pierce wanted to continue to be at the forefront of Canadian literary publishing. As the mid-twentieth-century mark approached, the two surviving "Big Four" Confederation poets, Roberts and D.C. Scott, were elderly: both would be dead by 1947. Thus, however uncongenial he found elements of the work of a new generation, Pierce needed them for his list. Moreover, his contacts with E.K. Brown, a critic respected by A.J.M. Smith and his modernist circle, helped soften Pierce toward them. Brown was to become *primus inter pares* in a stable of critics – Carl Klinck, A.J.M Smith, Desmond Pacey, and others – whose work and opinions Pierce sought out in the 1940s and early 1950s.

For their part, the modernist poets knew that they needed publication in book form to grow as artists. As the 1940s began, in part because of the Depression, very few of them (even though F.R. Scott, Leo Kennedy, A.M. Klein, and A.J.M. Smith, for example, had been writing since the 1920s) had books to their name.[9] Ryerson, as the pre-eminent national trade publisher, offered a wider stage. Besides, the alternatives to Ryerson publication were few. As *Preview* poet P.K. Page recalled of this period: "There was very little market for Canadian poetry in the forties. If Ryerson didn't publish [you,] you had nowhere else to go."[10]

On Pierce's side, one of his motives for publishing writers like A.J.M. Smith and F.R. Scott lay in the dominance and comprehensiveness it gave Ryerson's list. He told Smith in 1944: "We [have published] nearly all the old masters here, worth knowing, and we are certainly going to have all the new masters as well, if I have anything to do with it."[11] Another factor also prompted Pierce to publish the moderns. The suffering of the Depression and of the Second World War brought Pierce to acknowledge a new Zeitgeist, which his publication lists had to reflect. As early as 1939, with the outbreak of war, Pierce was, as he put it in a letter, "squeezing my head trying to think of some plan of publishing which might assist the House during the war." He speculated that "extremes in width and depth" of offerings would be necessary and added: "Whatever happens in this way, I rather think that the boundaries of the world will be drastically changed before we are through, and not least of these will be the social and economic ones ... we still live on the edge of the jungle and all have a little of the blood of the ape and the tiger in our veins."[12] This bleak insight went deep with Pierce: he used the same jungle metaphor four years later to begin his state-of-the-nation essay *A Canadian People*.[13] As he saw it, the modernists were both expressive of and ravaged by the grim forces of the contemporary world. As a result, before the war was out, he felt the need to publish them.

Pierce made his motivation plain when, in 1945, he brought out the modernist anthology *Unit of Five*, showcasing the poetry of P.K. Page, Louis Dudek, Raymond Souster, and others. Pierce told Dorothy Livesay that he had not been "impressed with the greatness of the book." Rather, he asserted, such poetry reflected "what the world or the war [has] done to this generation of poets. Something rather dreadful has happened to our young writers and we submitted this not because we believed in it or thought it great art but as a document – a social document, if you will – of the time."[14]

But, even as he responded to the *force majeure* of a new era, Pierce's old loyalties ebbed slowly. Accordingly, he began the decade by publishing new offerings from an earlier generation. With critic E.K. Brown, Duncan Campbell Scott produced for Ryerson an edition of previously unpublished poetry by Archibald Lampman. Pierce then published several volumes of Scott's work, including his short-story cycle *In the Village of Viger*, in a Thoreau MacDonald–illustrated edition (its first-ever Canadian edition) in 1945, plus Scott's *Selected Poems of Archibald Lampman* two years later. Finally, in a publishing coup four years after Scott's death, Pierce published *The Selected Poems of Duncan Campbell Scott* (1951), edited by E.K. Brown.

Meanwhile, starting with Brown's exchanges with Pierce in the course of publishing both Lampman's *At the Long Sault and Other New Poems* (1943) and Brown's own groundbreaking work of Canadian criticism, *On Canadian Poetry* (1943), Pierce was influenced by the views of a new generation of Canadian critics on Canadian literature past and present. Brown was to function as Pierce's 'middle stander' until his death in 1951 – the critic who, above all others, advised, linked, and helped him to understand and to publish the new generation of writers in Canada.

By contrast, Pierce's dealings with Confederation poet Sir Charles G.D. Roberts in the years before his death in November 1943, aged eighty-three, were infused with the sense that a literary era, not just the life of an individual poet, was ending. That ambiance further impressed on Pierce the need to publish new young poets as the older generation faded.

BETWEEN 1934 and 1943, Ryerson published three books of poetry and an anthology of war poetry by Roberts, in addition to a long biography of him. However, Pierce derived little comfort from the level of either Roberts's sales or his morals.[15] Supportive of the senior Confederation poet since his return to Canada in the 1920s after decades abroad, Pierce had helped organize in 1925 some of Roberts's first Canadian readings in decades. He had subsequently braved the threats of Roberts's American publisher, L.C. Page, to publish two poetry titles by Roberts in that decade and brought out Cappon's volume on Roberts in the Makers of Canadian Literature series.[16] In 1931, moreover, Pierce had, in company with Pelham Edgar and others, convinced Prime Minister R.B. Bennett to create a federal pension for the perennially hard-up Roberts. Pierce, who had personally loaned Roberts money in the past and would do so again,[17] told Bennett: "It is tragic that such a man, three score and ten, the founder of the Canada School of writers, Dean of his Craft, should have to come to want. Outrun in the economic struggle, he is also bewildered with the new cries, and, at his age, unable as he is unwilling to write that sort of [pablum] which the public desire."[18] Roberts got not only a pension (channelled through what became the Canadian Writers' Foundation, a pet project of Pelham Edgar's and later of Pierce's) but also, in 1935, a knighthood. Sir Charles certainly looked the part of the ultra-proper senior Canadian poet, with his silver hair, beribboned pince-nez, courtly manner, and gentlemanly – if at times threadbare – wardrobe, complete with spats.

Looks were deceptive, however: Pierce still judged Roberts's morals to be deplorable in important respects. Roberts's lifelong predilection for propositioning young women (including during his recital tours) and fondness for risqué talk and lewd limericks revolted Pierce.[19] Pierce's diary is scattered with references to the poet's "moral turpitude" and Pierce's conviction that he had "no moral sense whatsoever" in sexual matters.[20]

As an octogenarian knight, Roberts's behaviour did not change. Invited to lunch at Campbell Crescent in January 1941, the day after his eighty-first birthday, Roberts fascinated eighteen-year-old Bruce and twenty-year-old Beth when he laughingly insisted that only an "old and thin ... postage stamp" should separate the foreheads of partners engaged in what Pierce referred to as "the vile dances of these days."[21] Pierce himself was less charmed by such sallies. Roberts's poetry sales were also thin: in the dance of publisher and poet, it was increasingly Roberts who pressed for attention, not Pierce.

Given that Roberts was Canada's senior poet, sales of his *Selected Poems* (1936) had been unusually poor, even when one considers the effect of the Depression on book sales. Of the thousand copies printed, only 131 copies of the trade edition and 26 of the deluxe edition were sold in the first year. Sales sank to 37 copies for 1939. The sales report that year for Roberts's *The Iceberg and Other Poems* (1934) was even more dismal: no copies at all had been sold. By February 1940, Ryerson decided to re-mainder both titles, prompting a letter of protest from Roberts to Dickinson. Roberts plaintively pointed out that no other publishing house had ever remaindered his work, adding: "It remained for a Canadian house to do this!"[22] Because Roberts had not been given the chance to purchase remaindered copies as set out in his contract, he was promised full retail royalties on the remainders – but the titles were remaindered nonetheless.[23]

Pierce was also aware that, by the early 1940s, Roberts's poetic output, compromised by age, angina, and financial anxieties, had dwindled to a poem or two a year, his rare offerings mostly inspired by the war. Even Roberts himself described such poems to Pierce as "[n]ot poetry perhaps, but 'polemics.'"[24] As a result, Ryerson publications by Roberts during the war added little to the poet's reputation (or Ryerson's). *Canada Speaks of Britain* (1941), a mere fifteen pages long, featured Roberts's war poems since the Great War (plus three recent miscellaneous poems) – but most of the handful of recent poems had already appeared in magazines, including the title sonnet.[25] Tellingly, Roberts had pressed Pierce to publish the booklet, not vice versa.[26] *Flying Colours* (1942), the Ryerson anthology of war poetry which Roberts edited, included only two short Roberts poems, one of them, "Resurgant," being the last poem he wrote.[27] Pierce realized that he would have to look elsewhere for major new poetry collections.

Other Roberts publishing projects in which Pierce was involved in the years prior to the poet's death also exuded an end-of-an-era feeling. Since at least 1936, Roberts's long-standing admirer, schoolteacher, poet, and Canadian Authors Association stalwart Elsie Pomeroy of Toronto, had been labouring on a biography of Roberts.[28] Roberts, in part to fore-stall the possibility of a more incisive memoir by his son Lloyd, had been collaborating with Pomeroy so closely that he described the book to Pierce as "camouflaged autobiography," underlining the phrase.[29] John

Coldwell Adams, author of *Sir Charles God Damn* (1986) (a radically less hagiographic biography of Roberts), best sums up Pomeroy's approach as "dedicated to the task of preserving the image by which Roberts wanted to be remembered."[30] Indeed, as his correspondence makes clear, Roberts did in effect "ghost" his own biography as he oversaw what Elsie Pomeroy wrote, week by week – and, from Pierce's perspective, year after weary year.

The biography by Pomeroy (a full-time teacher whose time to work on it was limited)[31] turned out to be a whopper ("far too long" Pierce told Roberts, who had to cut it at least three times) and mediocre to boot ("lack[ing] distinction"). At one point, Roberts, contending with Pierce's demand for extensive revisions, spluttered into the telephone to Frank Flemington: "I would like you to make [Pierce] understand how strongly I resent the presumption that what I consider sandpapered enough is not sufficiently sandpapered."[32]

Significantly, the photograph of Pierce and Sir Charles that the latter had wanted in the biography was omitted. Furthermore, Pierce uncharacteristically dragged his heels in writing an introduction to *Sir Charles G.D. Roberts: A Biography* (1943) for nearly two years. When that introduction finally appeared, it positioned Roberts as the first Canadian poet to forge a uniquely Canadian voice ("first ... to give to the new nation ... songs that made his compatriots jump with joy and pride") – but its tone was lukewarm and somewhat defensive: "We do not make the mistake [of] saying that we [in the person of Roberts] have written the greatest poetry in the world, but we do say that it is among the most important verse in the world for us, because it is about us, has grown out of our own background and experience, and is meant to point the way for us above all other people."[33]

Most reviewers, while respectful of Roberts as a literary icon, were unenthusiastic about the biography.[34] Sales were sluggish: of 1,500 copies printed, only 800 had been sold by mid-1945.[35] Such a response was not surprising. As Adams has pointed out, the book, while a valuable record of some biographical facts, fails to put Roberts in poetic context. One reviewer, Pelham Edgar, himself a long-time supporter of Roberts, sardonically asked the old poet in private: "The truth, but not the whole truth?"[36]

The biography had other liabilities. Publishing it hurt Pierce's reputation, especially with the new generation of writers and critics who denigrated Pierce as "booming" Roberts. E.K. Brown confided to Duncan

Campbell Scott (who himself labelled Pierce one of the "chief offenders" in overblown critical praise) that he was not even planning to buy a copy ("our national criticism at its worst"[37]). Clearly, Pierce's loyalties were being judged, often harshly, by the up and comers, a critique that would persist.

In the years after Roberts's death, Pierce did feel somewhat protective of the poet's reputation, given his status as literary pioneer. At the time of his funeral, Pierce asserted tartly that Roberts had become a national "symbol" despite the "minor honours" accorded him as a poet by "smart young critics who spoke patronisingly about him," although they themselves came across as "rickety jerks and puling squirts" by comparison. He was to repeat these emphatic sentiments to several correspondents, E.K. Brown and Desmond Pacey among them. Furthermore, disapproving as he had been of Roberts's remarriage weeks before his death to his long-time companion, Joan Montgomery, fifty years his junior ("It made me a trifle ill"), Pierce now retrospectively pardoned Roberts's alleged moral failings as "very human" and "pagan in the Greek sense," a characterization he further rationalized by asserting that for Roberts there had been "no sacred or profane in the puritan sense, for all was life and all was good."[38] Pierce devoted considerable time and money to organizing Roberts's funeral ("an era closes"[39]) and his subsequent memorial service in Fredericton as well as commissioning a memorial stone. He also became Roberts's literary executor, bringing out some of the animal stories and Pacey's *The Selected Poems of Charles G.D. Roberts* (1955).[40]

IN THE EARLY 1940s one major Confederation poet remained for Pierce to bag – Ottawa poet and retired senior Indian Department bureaucrat Duncan Campbell Scott, aged eighty-one in 1943. The tall, aloof, and at times acerbic Scott was in the war years still ensconced in his rambling brick house on Ottawa's Lisgar Street. He continued to write as well as to act as poet Archibald Lampman's literary executor, duties he had loyally carried out since his friend's death in 1899.

Pierce regularly thought of the haughty old eagle in his Ottawa aerie, even though the two were not mutual admirers. In the 1940s he still wanted the prestige of a Ryerson imprint on major works by all four leading Confederation poets, ruing that the rights once held by the House to Lampman's poetry had been sold before his own arrival there. In his dealings with Scott, Pierce achieved two things in the 1940s, albeit not without travail: he was finally able to publish significant new titles

by both Lampman and Scott, and, in the course of Scott's collaboration
with E.K. Brown in the editing of Lampman's *At the Long Sault* for Ryerson, he was to cement an alliance with Brown. More than anyone else,
Brown came to embody for Pierce (and for the Canadian literary world
at large, including such powerful men of letters as critics Pelham Edgar
and A.J.M. Smith, book reviewer William Author Deacon, and poets
E.J. Pratt and Earle Birney, for example) a middle-ground perspective on
the Confederation and modernist eras in Canadian literature. In other
words, if the literary guard was changing in this decade in Canada (and
it inexorably was), Brown ("Edward" to his intimates), who had edited
the influential annual "Letters in Canada" supplement of the *University
of Toronto Quarterly* since its inception in 1936,[41] arguably emerged as its
leading critic, one respected by the forces arrayed on each side.

However, the path to the Pierce-Brown alliance had first to pass
by the dragon Scott, intermittently breathing sparks at Pierce. D.C.
Scott had long been disdainful of Pierce. Their dealings over the Scott-
authored and edited volumes Pierce published in the 1940s were uneasy.
As with so many author-publisher tensions (one thinks of Earle Birney
and Jack McClelland in the 1950s and 1960s, for instance), the difficulties
between Pierce and Scott were rooted in publishing and/or textual problems and aggravated by uncongenial temperaments. The relationship had
started off well enough in the 1920s. Scott had been one of the Royal
Society of Canada grandees who had overseen Pierce's admission to that
body after he donated the Lorne Pierce Medal. But relations between
the two cooled rapidly in that decade, initially because the Makers of
Canadian Literature series was killed by Samuel Fallis before Pelham
Edgar's volume on Scott was published. A planned Lampman volume,
edited by Scott, was also scuttled. Scott tended to blame Pierce, especially
since the poet had long felt badly treated by publishers in general. For
example, in 1921, he grumbled to Pelham Edgar about McClelland and
Stewart, observing that "my two-headed beast of a publisher sh[oul]d be
whipped for ... indifference" to his work.[42]

To compound Scott's spleen, he and Pierce soon became involved in
another contretemps, which was partly the result of Pierce's inexperience during his first decade at Ryerson at balancing shrewd critical insights with the realpolitik of dealing with living authors. In 1927 Pierce
planned to present a paper on Scott's work before the Royal Society.
When he blithely sent it to Scott for his comments before delivery, expecting bouquets, Scott reacted with icy fury. Little matter that, to the

twenty-first-century reader, it now seems that the problem with Pierce's paper was not that its judgments were wrong. On the contrary, they were accurate – and for that very reason distasteful to Scott. As a result, Scott's comments on Pierce's paper are curt, ungracious, and at times wilfully perverse – especially when one considers that Scott saw himself throughout his career as a "neglected" by most critics.[43] For example, Scott wrote "wrong" in the margins of Pierce's comment that his poem "Spring on Mattagami" shows the influence of Swinburne and Meredith, an influence Scott himself later confirmed to E.K. Brown.[44]

The real cause of Scott's displeasure is found elsewhere in Pierce's 1927 paper. Latter-day criticism has argued that Scott's poetry was haunted by his feeling that he had failed to take chances or been sufficiently idealistic in his life.[45] Pierce was the first to make this point. He maintained that Scott, "guarded on the one hand by critical detachment and urbanity and on the other hand by the long training of a shrewd [civil service] executive[,] ... holds on to the golden mean .... never for a moment does he become an 'unemployed idealist.'" He then concluded: "Much of Scott's serious work speaks of sadness and disillusionment. One gathers that he has felt and understood life, while he may not have enjoyed it."[46] These are genuine insights, but painful personal ones to a writer already touchy about publishers. Not surprisingly, they aroused considerable annoyance at Lisgar Street.

In turn, in the face of such frost from a senior literary figure at a time when his own position at Ryerson was far from secure, Pierce decided not to give the paper.[47] Too late: damage had been done to the Pierce-Scott relationship, with antipathy aroused in both men. For example, decades later, after Scott's death, Pierce, in a letter to a friend, described Scott as a "chilly and remote" figure who could not touch people's hearts and whose books "sold hardly at all."[48]

As for Scott, his displeasure with Pierce in the 1920s segued into crankiness and grudging compliments to him two decades later. E.K. Brown and Scott worked together between 1941 and 1943, mostly by mail, to put together *At the Long Sault*. As it took shape, Scott grumbled repeatedly to Brown about Pierce and his ways ("we are congenial but not friendly"; "a great dilly dallyer"; "the usual dilatoriness of [Pierce's] firm") or damned him with faint praise ("[Pierce is] a charitable soul, without him Pelham and his [fundraising] schemes w[ou]ld be lost in Toronto"[49]).

Pierce was well aware of Scott's continuing ambivalence toward him. When he unexpectedly received a "delightful" note from Scott at Christmas 1943 after *At The Long Sault* appeared, Pierce quipped: "My faith in Santa Claus has been restored."[50] Indeed, in the end, Scott was sufficiently satisfied with Ryerson and its general editor – and keen enough for a last spate of publications in his old age – that, during the mid-1940s (in each case at Pierce's request), he brought out three more titles with Ryerson: his edition of Lampman's selected poems (1947), the first Canadian edition (1945) of his own book of French Canadian short stories *In the Village of Viger*, and a new booklet on artist Walter J. Phillips (1947) in Ryerson's landmark Canadian Art series.[51] By the time of Scott's death in 1947, Pierce may not have won Scott's admiration, but he had bagged new titles by Scott and Lampman, rounding out Ryerson's "Big Four" list of imprints. He chortled to Brown that the coup would enable him to "die happy."[52]

In 1951 Pierce capped the achievement by bringing out E.K. Brown's posthumous edition of *The Selected Poems of Duncan Campbell Scott*, selected by Brown and Scott's widow, Elise Aylen Scott (with some editorial tinkering by Pierce), a book that included a superb (and still unsurpassed) memoir by Brown as his own memorial to Scott. To make the matter even sweeter for Pierce, McClelland and Stewart had, after some initial resistance, let Ryerson have its rights to publication of the book once young Jack McClelland abruptly declared himself unwilling to work with Mrs Scott.[53] (Unfortunately, the Ryerson title sold poorly – about 300 copies in two years out of a book run of 1,000, a run not exhausted until 1962[54] – although it was well reviewed.)

Brown was also a prize for Pierce. Until Scott's death in December 1947, the urbane and highly intelligent E.K. Brown – ever the consummate academic diplomat[55] – usually saw eye to eye with the poet on literary matters. At the same time, however, Brown developed a rapport with Pierce. His biographer establishes that Brown, whose own father died when he was three, forged mentor-follower relationships throughout his career with a series of older male intellectuals. In this connection, his friendship with Pierce "was enriched by his willingness to accord Pierce the homage he felt due the remnants of a dying age."[56] Moreover, in the early 1940s, Brown's academic ambitions embraced the Canadian literary scene, and Pierce was its leading publisher. Collegiality and ambition alike characterized both sides of the emerging Pierce-Brown alliance.

The reputation of the brilliant Brown – usually found at his desk, the light glinting off his rimless glasses as he lit one cigarette from another, ash drifting onto his invariable dark suit and tie – was growing. For example, in this era, Brown's formidable contemporary Northrop Frye was jealously confiding to his diary that Brown, once his colleague at University of Toronto, had a reputation as "a man on the make."[57] Brown certainly topped Pierce's pantheon quickly. By 1944, Pierce was relying on Brown as his premier adviser on which modernist poets to publish. Significantly, Pierce did not feel he could fully trust his own judgment on modernist work in the way he did about more traditional poetry. The world – and the flavour of literature – was changing too much. Pierce told Brown at one point that manuscripts by P.K. Page and *Preview* poet Patrick Anderson lay on his desk, making him wish that he had "someone like you near me to consult."[58]

Pierce and the younger Brown (aged thirty-eight in 1943) were also having stimulating intellectual debates over what constituted the Canadian literary canon as they pored over the manuscript of Brown's book of literary criticism *On Canadian Poetry*.[59] The groundbreaking study, published in 1943 and revised the following year, sprang onto the Canadian cultural scene as a best-selling (for a book of criticism) and authoritative work. As Brown's biographer has pointed out, the impact of *On Canadian Poetry* was to lower the reputation of Roberts and Carman while increasing the relative stature of Lampman and D.C. Scott as well as that of the later work of E.J. Pratt.[60] The book gave sustained and respectful treatment to the major poets of the McGill movement (A.J.M. Smith, F.R. Scott, and A.M. Klein) and other modernist contemporaries (Earle Birney, Dorothy Livesay). Broadly speaking, early-twentieth-century poets like Marjorie Pickthall, W.H. Drummond, and Wilson MacDonald fared less well in Brown's text – not always easy judgments for Pierce to accept. Pierce and Brown in fact did some serious horse trading during Pierce's editing of the manuscripts of the two editions of *On Canadian Poetry*, although it is clear from an examination of the correspondence that Brown conceded far less than Pierce.[61] The generational shift in the balance of power in Canadian criticism was beginning. But with E.K. Brown, a seasoned negotiator in these matters, Pierce also had the delicious sensation, for almost the first time in his career, of being able to grapple with theoretical issues about the evolution of Canadian literature with a first-rate thinker on the subject.

Pierce's initial contacts with Brown were largely by mail. From 1940, Brown taught in the English Department of Cornell University (broken by an unhappy summer in Ottawa that year writing speeches for Prime Minister Mackenzie King), and from September 1945 at the University of Chicago. Whatever his locale, Brown and his views, in print and out of it, soon became crucial to Pierce. The latter wrote nostalgically after Brown's early death of his "great creative talent," which made working with him "an exciting adventure." Pierce hinted that he had pictured Brown as a possible successor, eulogizing him as a man who would have been "a great editor of a book publishing house."[62] Brown's acute literary judgments impressed Pierce, though he also found some of them unsettling. To take one example: in reading over the manuscript of *On Canadian Poetry* in early 1943, Pierce was startled that Brown accorded Roberts only a few pages, whereas Lampman and D.C. Scott were given an entire section of the book. Brown maintained that Canadian literary history must be "rewritten" and that Carman and Roberts had been overestimated, as he had bluntly told D.C. Scott in a letter.[63] Roberts was still alive at this time, and although Pierce well knew Roberts's shortcomings (he even assured Brown at one point: "I am closer to your position than you might think"), he was also convinced that Roberts deserved credit as the crucial pioneer among the Confederation poets.[64] Both Pierce's sense of justice and his own friendships affected him here. He reminded Brown after the latter had snipped the word "figurehead" from the galleys in reference to Roberts that any downgrading by Brown was "bound to strain a number of my own personal friendships."[65] Brown himself had admitted earlier that criticism of Canadian literature, given the smallness of the pond, was a "dangerous trade" which had made him glad he was a "non-joiner" with "fewer friendships and associations to lose than most who ply the trade in Canada."[66]

BROWN WAS also key to convincing some of the disdainful young moderns to publish with Ryerson Press. In part through Brown, Pierce came into contact with A.J.M. Smith, the latter a link to the *Preview* group of poets in Montreal. In the early 1940s, Smith, thanks to a Guggenheim Fellowship, was on leave from the University of Michigan working on a comprehensive historical anthology of Canadian poetry, which became the landmark *Book of Canadian Poetry* (1943), published by University of Chicago Press. He spent research time in Toronto, getting acquainted with both the corpus of Canadian poetry before the 1920s and with the grandees who knew it best, for example, Pelham Edgar – and Lorne Pierce.

Yet Pierce's relations with Smith were never as warm or as close as with Brown. He quipped to Earle Birney of the success of Smith's 1943 anthology: "I am afraid Smith will get a lot of glory out of this business, but as for gold it will most likely be in his bridgework."[67] Although Smith helped to bring to Ryerson authors from the *Preview* circle, it was more a case of publishing priorities on both sides making for strange bedfellows than of genuine rapport. As well, Smith planned projects with Pierce that never materialized for various reasons, including the submission to Ryerson of a manuscript by poet Margaret Avison. In any case, in the late 1930s and 1940s, Smith was ambitious but less sure of himself than the crispness of some of his early articles suggests. For example, as he set out to edit *The Book of Canadian Poetry*, Smith wanted E.K. Brown to be his collaborator, telling him that "your knowledge and insight into the subject [is] much greater than mine."[68]

Many pragmatic considerations moved Smith to befriend Pierce, and vice versa. Pierce controlled numerous important copyright permissions for Smith's anthology.[69] Both Pierce and Smith realized that, in a changing cultural climate, Smith could serve as the pipeline into the Montreal modernists that Pierce knew he needed to keep Ryerson abreast of the latest Canadian poetry, however uncongenial some of it might be. Pierce promptly brought out Smith's own first book of poetry, *News of the Phoenix*, in 1943. In turn, Smith strongly urged Scott, Klein, Page, Patrick Anderson, and others to submit manuscripts to Ryerson, even as he lobbied Pierce strongly on behalf of these writers: "I am very anxious that the most adventurous of our younger poets should be given a hearing."[70]

By the mid-1940s, then, thanks to links with Smith and Brown, Pierce had become a patron of modernism to a far greater degree than has been recognized. Through Pierce's heedfulness of Smith's counsel, F.R. Scott had two important books of poetry, *Overture* (1945) and *Events and Signals* (1954), published by Ryerson. However, Scott's letters to Pierce were rather cool. Not only was Pierce identified in Scott's mind with the misguided traditionalism and national boosterism satirized in his 1920s poem "The Canadian Authors Meet," but Pierce also made a tactical blunder. In one of his first letters to F.R. Scott, Pierce, unaware of the competitiveness between Scott and his father, clergyman and poet Frederick George Scott, wrote to the son that Ryerson was pleased to publish him, having liked and published the poetry of his father.[71] In any case, F.R. Scott – like most Ryerson authors blithely heedless of wartime paper shortages – did thaw sufficiently to urge Pierce to print more than 750 copies of *Overture*. Scott was confident that there would be a "wide group of readers in Canada on account of my other writings."[72] Clearly, he was hungry for his poetry to have broader exposure than what little magazines like *Preview* could offer.

Pierce and Smith had other fish to fry. In 1942 the two discussed the idea of Smith editing a series of volumes of selected poets for Ryerson, a plan that involved the rather droll spectacle of Smith the modernist suddenly "hot gospelling" what F.R. Scott had scornfully dubbed "native maple" poets. Smith wrote Pierce: "The poets most needed, I think, are [George Frederick] Cameron, Sangster, Crawford (a new selection), Duvar, McLachlan, Howe and Mair."[73] The scheme came to naught, in part because of wartime conditions. In fact, Pierce was negotiating with E.K. Brown, rather than Smith, about editing a selection of the poetry of George Frederick Cameron.[74] On another front, Smith praised Dorothy Livesay to Pierce, who had known the Livesay family well for two decades. Thanks in part to Smith and to a developing friendship with Pierce – one fed by the latter soliciting contributions from Livesay for *Canadian Bookman* in the late 1930s – Livesay became a Ryerson author. When her landmark volume of poetry, *Day and Night*, with its left-wing poems of social concern, some of which dated from the Depression, appeared under the Ryerson imprint in 1944, Smith lauded Pierce for publishing it, adding: "I hope Ryerson's will be able to keep in the forefront of the present very genuine [poetic] revival."[75]

By the late 1940s, Pierce had won a wary measure of respect (or at least forbearance) from many in the new poetic generation, and vice versa. He pronounced Smith "a very decent egg" who showed some "genius" to others in his own circle.[76] Other modernist poets soon praised the new contingent on the Ryerson list. In 1946 Earle Birney, whose own successful *David and Other Poems* had kicked off the modernist list for Ryerson in 1942 (thanks to the good offices of Pelham Edgar), praised Ryerson Press in *Canadian Poetry Magazine* for publishing three of "the most important younger poets in Canada" that year. The three were P.K. Page (*As Ten as Twenty*), Louis Dudek (*East of the City*), and Patrick

Anderson (*The White Centre*). In 1952 poet, critic, and McGill professor Louis Dudek warmly commended Pierce for all his "fine work ... for Canadian poetry."[77]

It is useful to recall here that A.J.M. Smith – seen by many of his contemporaries as the de facto doyen of modernism – had issued a clarion call in the 1920s for new Canadian works to be both "successful" and "obscene."[78] In the 1940s and 1950s, by contrast, Pierce, while he certainly wanted the modernists he published to be successful, was far from comfortable with what he thought readers might find obscene. Ryerson Press was, after all, owned by the United Church, and Pierce's Board of Publication regularly frowned at the Ryerson balance sheet for poetry. Accordingly, he wanted anything too outrageous cut, or he might be forced to drop poetry entirely: as he once joked, he did not want to be accused of tempting Satan as well as the bailiff.[79]

Interestingly, despite Smith's earlier clarion call, when his and Pierce's viewpoint conflicted, Smith and his contemporaries largely acceded to Pierce's editorial cuts, in effect choosing book publication over avant-garde daring. For example, with only mild protests, Smith himself agreed to let Pierce cut two poems deemed offensive from the manuscript of *News of the Phoenix*: "Ballade Un Peu Banale," with its comic blasphemy about Christ intervening to save a heifer from ravishment, and "Between Two Wars," in which "soldiers' crutches had sexual intercourse."[80] Other prominent modernists also proved cooperative when it came to placating Mrs Grundy. Louis Dudek made concessions for publication, as did Patrick Anderson. The sexual imagery of Dudek's poem "Sublimation" – "all unshirted my poppy wishes fall out" – prompted Pierce to ask him to drop it from *East of the City* (1946), while Anderson adjusted lines in his poem "Dancer" for his 1946 opus.[81]

It was a *First Statement* alumnus, however, who proved Pierce's Waterloo vis-à-vis religious and sexual boundary crossing and Ryerson publication. Dealings with Irving Layton between 1954 and 1958 established the point of impasse for Pierce in accommodating the second generation of modernist poets – and vice versa. In the early 1950s Layton wrote Pierce a series of characteristically provocative letters, telling him that he hoped that his latest collection, *The Long Pea Shooter* (1954), published by Montreal's fledgling modernist Laocoon Press, had not "put you on your back" in shock.[82] Layton subsequently harangued Pierce on the need for the "revolutionary effect" of erotica in Canadian poetry, condescendingly informing him that "sex is here to stay,"[83] as he revelled in his self-appointed role as Jewish literary prophet, bard of the senses, and *enfant terrible*. His conviction about the need for sexual candour in poetry was accompanied by an equally impassioned belief that the poet was exempt from censure for what many in the Canada of the day saw as blasphemous references. In turn, Layton would soon position Pierce as "the last great representative of Victorianism in Canada."[84] In short, poet and publisher were on a collision course.

At the beginning of their correspondence, however, Pierce generously praised less libidinous Layton poems like "The Cold Green Element." He wrote a letter of reference to the Royal Society in 1955 on Layton's behalf and even sent Layton some of his own money to support his work.[85] Meanwhile, critic Malcolm Ross was telling Pierce that Layton, while talented, was still artistically "adolescent," with as yet little of substance to say. Layton was, wrote Ross, really at base a puritan himself ("his defiant use of the four-letter word gives him away"). Meanwhile, Fredericton poet Fred Cogswell was cautioning his friend Layton over Pierce's interest in publishing "The Bull Calf": "You can never be sure of Pierce till you've got him in the net."[86] Changing literary times evidently posed a quandary for many Canadian literary figures of the day. Clearly, it was going to be tricky for Pierce to make Layton a Ryerson author.

Indeed, it proved impossible. The next year, Pierce, after some hesitation, decided that the manuscript of what became *The Improved Binoculars* (1956), a collection of poems that incorporated such images as "the blood and balls of Christ," was too indecorous for Ryerson either to publish or to distribute on behalf of its American publisher. Layton was outraged. In early 1957 he denounced Pierce in the press as a relic of literary Victorianism, a sentiment he repeated in a vehement letter to Pierce.[87] Ironically, Ryerson had printed the book at the House for Layton, with Pierce offering him some of the copies free of charge, an offer he did not rescind even after Layton's public denunciation of him.[88] If Pierce concluded that no good deed goes unpunished, he could not have been consoled by a letter from Louis Dudek. Layton's fellow Montreal poet (and periodic enemy) denounced Layton's newspaper "nonsense" to Pierce, but only "privately." Dudek complimented Pierce (but for his eyes only): "You have done more for the poets – and for the poets [we modernists] most approve – than anyone else."[89] Given such a bashful ally, who studiously failed to publicly support him, Pierce must have concluded that the future lay with the modernists. Furthermore, given their style and subject matter, Ryerson could never be their chief publishing outlet, despite the fact that Pierce had in fact now published (Dudek, Smith, Scott, Page, Livesay, Page, Birney) or underwritten (Layton) the cream of the modernist contingent.

Layton came to see Pierce some nine months after he had denounced him as the prime representative of "the Puritan mores and the religiosity of Canadian publishers."[90] In one of the symbolic vignettes of Canadian literary history, the senior publisher and the outspoken young poet met in Pierce's office. According to Layton, Pierce was at his most magnanimous in their October 1957 meeting. Layton saw it as an occasion when two literary generations – the world of the Confederation poets and that of the modernists – touched each other, with Pierce as the bridge between them, as he later told Pierce himself:

> It was a great privilege and an extraordinary pleasure ... to be ushered into your office where the photographs of Carman, Roberts, Lampman et al. stared down at me, I thought, in amused fellowship; anyway circled about our heads like white halos. Though I had asked mutual friends to describe you to me, I was nonetheless surprised when I shook hands with you. Not at the warmth and wonderful friendliness in face and hand, or the intelligent interest in the quizzical eye; these I had been led to expect. No, what flashed through my mind was: "Gosh, this is the 'suavest puritan' that ever breathed outside of Milton and his circle of friends." I could have listened to you for hours and hours talking about Carman – he too must have been a fascinating personality.[91]

But beguiled as Layton might be by Pierce's personality and reverence for Canadian literature, the sad reality was that Pierce and Layton were too far apart in literary values for Ryerson to publish him. The limits of Pierce's considerable – and undervalued – support of modernism had been reached with the work of Irving Layton.

One must conclude that while, for some of the modernists, Pierce was too prudish, too religiously decorous, and too old-fashioned to be congenial, he and the Ryerson imprint also functioned as an essential way station in the literary rise of two generations of modernists from Smith and Scott to Page, Souster, Anderson, and many others. But Layton, the star of the second generation of Canadian modernists, proved too distant from Pierce's values and Ryerson's United Church context for the combination to be possible. By contrast, five years later, a racier, more secular publisher (starting in the Swinging 1960s, at any rate), Jack McClelland, by then effectively at the helm of McClelland and Stewart, his days of finger-wagging at Birney's profanity in *Turvey* well behind him, was urging Layton to add more sexy poems to the manuscript of his anthology of love poetry, *Love Where the Nights Are Long* (1962).[92]

Changing tastes and changing times. It is important to recognize, however, that Pierce and many of the modernist poets of the 1940s and 1950s in fact found middle ground to publish key volumes with Ryerson. In 1960, the year he retired, Pierce reminded Canadians that he had skirted both Satan and the bailiff, so to speak, out of principle to publish new work he knew was significant. He also made clear what one senses in his correspondence. In his mind, the work of the modernists was important but also raw and uncongenial, the bitter fruit of a generation younger than his own which had been deeply affected by economic depression and war. In *A Canadian Nation*, his farewell essay on Canadian culture, Pierce wrote of their work: "We do not have to approve of it all, but we grant their freedom to speak out. Oftentimes they are, like some of our contemporary artists, so thin and meaningless as to embarrass one. They will, having thought and suffered enough, grow up. Meanwhile, it is all very exciting, their candour, their ribaldry and their prevailing disrespect."[93]

Despite Pierce's importance in publishing their first books, in their later careers, poets and critics like F.R. Scott, A.J.M. Smith, and Louis Dudek did no public wreath laying in Pierce's memory. The subsequent critical record has thus scanted Pierce's crucial publication role in the 1940s and 1950s vis-à-vis Canadian modernist poets, a contribution for which Pierce unquestionably deserves recognition.[94] Indeed, by the early 1960s, so stereotyped had Ryerson Press become that Layton's publisher, Jack McClelland, drafted a letter to Layton about the danger to his image of even editing an anthology for Ryerson. According to McClelland, Layton's virile poetic persona would in effect be neutered by association with a church publishing house. McClelland warned Layton that "at this stage in your career – I would prefer to have you arrested for relieving yourself at the corner of [Peel] and St[e-]Catherine than being exposed as the editor of an anthology of new poetry published by the United Church Publishing House … it ain't kosher."[95] He then added that Ryerson "had done more for Canadian literature than any other single publishing house through the years." Nevertheless the implication was clear: Ryerson was now outmoded.

EVEN BEFORE his contacts with Layton made clear the limits to which Ryerson could go to publish the moderns, another event limited Pierce's access to modernist circles. The modernist critic closest to Pierce – the one to whom, in the words of Brown's biographer, he had symbolically passed the torch – was silenced.[96] E.K. Brown had volunteered to edit the *Selected Poems of Duncan Campbell Scott* for Pierce after the old poet's death. Around that time, Brown discovered that he had malignant melanoma. Before the Scott volume arrived in the bookstores in the summer of 1951, featuring Brown's fine introductory memoir, Brown had died on 23 April in a Chicago hospital, aged forty-five.

Brown's widow, Peggy Deaver Brown, confided to Pierce: "Edward always thought very highly of you and *always* enjoyed conversations with you." Even years after Brown's death, Pierce still mourned him, assuring his widow: "Very often I visit his grave [in Toronto's Mount Pleasant Cemetery] and offer a special word of gratitude for his friendship as well as for his splendid contribution to the thought and taste of his times."[97] Professionally, he had good reason to mourn Brown, his "middle 'stander' between [A.J.M.] Smith and the usual Canadian critical attitudes."[98] During the last decade of Pierce's life, his dealings with a new generation of Canadian critics, Desmond Pacey in particular, were to be uneasy in an era of changing tastes and values, and he would struggle to balance innovation and loyalty in his editorial endeavours.

Impresario and Aging Lion

Fielding a New Generation of Critics and Writers, 1940–1960

We [have published] all the old masters here, worth knowing, and we are certainly going to have all the new masters as well, if I have anything to do with it.

Lorne Pierce on the Ryerson list to modernist poet and critic A.J.M. Smith, 1944[1]

Won't you mention what sort of things in [Roberts's] work you think I might talk about [in *On Canadian Poetry*]? I should be quite ready to add a page … [Roberts] does not have a chapter among the masters, but I just can't see him as a master.

Critic E.K. Brown to Lorne Pierce, 1943[2]

I do hope you will not delay publication of the new edition [of *A Book of Canadian Stories*] by further bickering.

Critic Desmond Pacey to Lorne Pierce, 1949[3]

For Pierce, sixty years old in 1950, juggling a stable of emerging critics brought challenges. Nevertheless, in the 1940s and 1950s, he gamely published – and in some cases played off against one another – a stable of key critics of Canadian literature, E.K. Brown, A.J.M. Smith, Carl Klinck, Desmond Pacey, and John Sutherland. Pierce thus fostered the careers of the very critics who eclipsed him as authorities on Canadian literature.

In the early 1950s, however, the death of John Sutherland, following that of E.K. Brown, further isolated Pierce at a time when Canadian literature moved in second-stage modernist directions that often troubled him. Modernist writers, he joked, saw him as "Old Man Pierce," an anachronism standing in the way of literary progress.[4] In the period 1940 to 1960, his last decades at Ryerson Press, Pierce was at times defensive or pejorative when he spoke of, wrote about, edited, or published the work of earlier writers like Carman, Pickthall, or Audrey Brown – even as he sought to ensure that their achievements were not utterly forgotten. By the late 1940s, he felt that he was fighting a losing battle.

Nonetheless, the scale on which Pierce published modernist writers, whatever his misgivings, means that his importance to the modernist publication record of the period badly needs to be re-evaluated. His contribution as executor and editor of Bliss Carman's work is equally important to an appreciation of how concerted the denigration of earlier writers and the exaltation of modernist ones was at this period. Pierce took an editorial knife to Carman's work, but younger critics of the eminence of Malcolm Ross, Desmond Pacey, and Northrop Frye were accessories before and/or after the fact.

PIERCE'S DOWNGRADING of Marjorie Pickthall's literary reputation in the 1940s and 1950s in favour of E.J. Pratt shows his reluctant backpedalling. Gender values had of course an impact on Pickthall and Pratt during their careers, and Pierce's (and society's) changing perceptions of such roles in turn moulded his portrayal of each poet. Pelham Edgar's differing patronage of his female and male poet protégés respectively is illustrative here. Just before the First World War, Pickthall, who, despite the recognition of eastern Canadian intellectuals of her talent, had never been encouraged to attend university after private school, had been given a job as a library clerk at Victoria after her mother's death, thanks to Professor Edgar. By contrast, E.J. Pratt, a brilliant graduate student in psychology, had been given an academic appointment in Victoria's English Department by Edgar, its chair.

To Edgar and his circle, moreover, Pickthall was forever constructed (and marginalized) as, in the words of one of her patrons, Dalhousie professor Archibald MacMechan, "the real song bird singing in the shade."[5] But the delicate feminine image of the poet was to come up against changing societal values about women and their alleged gender attributes. Two decades after Pickthall's death in 1922, during the Second World War and its aftermath, propaganda campaigns exalting Rosie the Riveter gave way to the valorization in consumer advertising of the suburban housewife/mother. In the literary world, the war also saw the publication of such robust Pratt poems of patriotism and masculine martial spirit as *Dunkirk* (1941) and *They Are Returning* (1945).[6] In the era of such masculinist literary and societal themes, Pickthall and her work were put even farther in the shade.

Given such shifting social context, Pierce's depiction of Pickthall's work in his 1943 Victoria College address and in his introduction to the *Selected Poems* (1957) intensified a construct of her as a "poetess" even more delicate, more dreamy, more "imperfect [in] understanding,"[7] and more marginalized than she had seemed in his 1925 biography. He no longer presents Pickthall as an ideal of literary and gender values to be emulated; instead, she is portrayed as the "foreordained end" of the "old poetic tradition" and as a female too frail ever to have been suited for the modern age.[8] Pierce symbolically describes Pickthall as a fragile young library assistant meekly waiting to check out books for rising young academic poet E.J. Pratt. This vignette (which Pierce also included in his 1957 introduction to Pickthall's *Selected Poems*) is told as if it constituted Pickthall's farewell to the world (though in reality she lived another decade, becoming an internationally successful writer of magazine stories). Pierce comments: "Thus the old should ever give way to the new, in a manner suggestive of a ritual. At any rate, [Marjorie] ... a little wistful and not a little lost amid it all, was shortly to see the chaos of the World War, and would scarcely survive it. The new day would demand other gifts than hers." Employing heavily gendered imagery, Pierce then declares that Pickthall's feminine "cloister" and eclipsed "old tradition" had of necessity given way to the (distinctly phallic) "soaring power and robust certitude" of Pratt.[9] This shift is further emphasized in his 1957 edition of Pickthall's poems by Pierce's dedication of the book to E.J. Pratt.

In the 1940s and 1950s, clearly, Pierce was ever more emphatically constructing Pickthall's literary essence as a fragile feminine one. He delivered a dismissive verdict on her achievement in his 1943 talk: "She wrote of men who could take the world in their strong hands and rebuild it alone and according to their will, but she was no consort for these, only in her dreams."[10] In contrast to his 1925 injunction that Pickthall ought to function for modernists as an icon of literary idealism and moral restraint, her importance had by the 1940s become in his view "difficult to estimate." Pierce now granted Pickthall merely "first place among the women writers of Canada in her time."[11] But that woman's realm is depicted as a subordinate and narrow one, long on fragility and short on intellect, producing poetry "where the tendency is toward emotional interpretations of life, and rapture and intuition are substituted for the discipline of reason."[12] As Dean Irvine, Collett Tracey, and others have suggested in relation to female modernist poets of the period, gender stereotypes were strongly (and often detrimentally) at work in the careers of Canadian women poets – dead or alive, modernist or traditional.[13]

By 1957, Pierce's assessment of Pickthall and her work had unquestionably changed for the worse. Arguably, this resulted from the pressure on him to accommodate changes in literary taste (and the devaluation in the social currency of the female gender role of the sequestered maiden) during the Second World War and its aftermath. So much for deceased female poets writing in the Romantic mode. Living ones fared little better, even as Pierce and his allies (Pelham Edgar, *Saturday Night* editor B.K. Sandwell, and others) made last-ditch attempts to publish and popularize their work. There is no more vivid (and depressing) example of this process than Pierce's well-intentioned involvement in the career of Nanaimo poet Audrey Alexandra Brown in the 1940s and 1950s.

AUDREY (as her family and friends called her) was marginalized by four factors: poverty (she came from a working-class family who had fallen on hard times in the Depression); severe, life-long physical challenges (she was handicapped by acute rheumatoid arthritis and in the 1930s spent several months in a body cast after surgery); her female gender; and her distance from eastern Canada's publishing centres. She had been "discovered" by Edgar and others in the late 1920s as a poet of twenty-four – at a time when she had been bedridden for three years at her parents' Nanaimo home by illness. Her Keatsian-flavoured work was soon taken up by Edgar, Sir Andrew Macphail, B.K. Sandwell, and others – the very grandees who had overseen Pickthall's career. Brown's first volume, edited by Edgar and Macphail, was published by Macmillan as *A Dryad in Nanaimo* (1931). The volume sold well for a book of poetry – 1,605 copies in the year of its publication (versus, for example, a sale of less than 100 copies for the 1936 modernist anthology *New Provinces*).[14]

Again, as with Pickthall, an ideal of femininity and of anti-modernism was operative in the initial promotion of a young Canadian female poet(ess). As Carole Gerson has put it in a discussion of the formation of the Canadian literary canon, in an era of waning Romanticism and encroaching modernism, the most crucial factor in career formation were "the backstage decisions of publishers, editors and English professors. These men formed a loose 'invisible college' distinctly masculine in gender and taste that determined who and what got into print."[15] Certainly, Brown was edited and stage-managed differently, and far more high-handedly, than a male poet would have been. She was routinely subjected to the denial of agency so commonly the fate of female writers, and which had earlier so troubled Pickthall. For example, Edgar, with some advice from Macphail, picked all the poems for her first book largely without consulting Brown, isolated in Nanaimo.

Always a notoriously dilatory correspondent, Edgar rarely informed Brown of developments in his handling of her work in a timely or consistent fashion, despite her repeated enquiries. Brown told Lorne Pierce in 1946: "In all these years that my work has been in the hands of Dr. Edgar alone, I never have known exactly where I was: it was always months, sometimes years, before I heard what he was or wasn't doing, if indeed I ever did." Brown added self-effacingly that she was "long past" being "hurt" by this since it was "[Edgar's] nature."[16] Her public image – engineered by Edgar, Sandwell, and others – was that of a fragile, virginal, invalid girl-poet – a sort of dreamy, girlish but misshapen literary curiosity miraculously extant in the harsh modern world.

This representation of Brown as an iconic, reassuringly old-fashioned "poetess" and frail, virtuous, old-fashioned girl is best summed up by a scornful remark about her modernist contemporaries by Duncan Campbell Scott to Edgar in 1938. Scott wrote that Brown deserved some government funding, given that the small sum she desired "would not [even] keep one of the 'up-to-date' poetesses in cigarettes."[17] In short, both Brown's poetry and her person were seen as embodying maidenly virtues of refinement, delicacy, and purity – qualities exalted as antithetical to the perceived sexual frankness, licence, and cynicism of both poetic modernism and the modern woman, as Scott's remark suggests. The expression of this position took some curious forms. In his introduction to *Dryad*, for example, Edgar stated that any modernist scorn of Brown's work was tantamount to assault: "But even the ultra-modernist must refrain from laying violent hands on *Laodamia* [Brown's chief poem in the volume]."[18]

Brown herself, in a maudlin *Saturday Night* profile, was quoted as saying that, given the pain of her severe arthritis and the resultant fatigue, she sometimes felt she would like to crawl into a coffin. She added that such a coffin would have to be "old rose" with "silver handles."[19] But had she already been embalmed in stereotype by her admirers? Certainly in her letters, she deplored the "fulsome overpraise and revolting sentimental publicity" she so often received.[20]

Pierce was to take over the editing and publishing of her work at the end of the Second World War. By then, Edgar and others, including Brown's publisher, Macmillan, realized that her poetry was not going to develop into a challenge to modernism, as they had hoped. Brown's letters to Edgar (described in the press as her "fairy godfather"[21]) show frustration over her isolation and dependency as her sales slumped and the interest of her eastern patrons waned.[22] Another British Columbia poet, a long-time correspondent of Pierce's, described Brown after a chance meeting as "peculiar" and "always alone, limping along."[23] Little wonder.

Meanwhile, poets Earle Birney and A.J.M. Smith had each written negatively about Brown's work, Smith referring dismissively to her poetry and Wilson MacDonald's as the provincial "trills" of "indigenous throstles" deplorably unaffected by the work of Pound and Eliot. The similarly dismissive tone of Birney's *Canadian Forum* review (for which he later privately apologized to Brown, but the damage was done) is suggested by its scornful title: "Moon-wist in Canadian Poesie."[24] Given such polarization between modernists and more traditional poets at this period, literary scholar Brian Trehearne has rightly concluded in his study of Canadian modernism that there is now a need to "value the more traditional strain of Canadian modern poetry equally with the more experimental."[25]

In 1946 Pierce helped Brown financially via the Canadian Writers' Foundation, a struggling philanthropic organization to aid elderly or indigent writers started by Pelham Edgar in the 1930s,[26] and at times he paid her tiny allowance out of his own pocket. Concomitantly, Pierce took over the editing from Edgar, and subsequently became Brown's publisher.[27] He had earlier archly asked another Brown admirer if the young lady was "attached, and, if not, would she entertain a proposition" – for publication.[28]

Pierce sought to stimulate Brown's flagging sales. Although he deplored the marketing of Brown as the invalid poet (his own deafness made him particularly sensitive to such stereotyping), he too assumed a "take-charge" stance as he attempted to "pump up" Brown's image as an accomplished latter-day traditionalist in art and in lifestyle. Pierce and Edgar had earlier made the choice of poems for Brown's *The Tree of*

Resurrection and Other Poems, published by Macmillan in 1937 – without obtaining Brown's final approval. When Brown moved to Ryerson at Pierce's behest after poor sales for her 1944 Macmillan volume *Challenge to Time and Death*, Pierce assured her: "I ... shall be taking the lead [in managing your career] and not Dr. Edgar or anyone else."[29] That Brown should be in charge of her own career never occurred to him any more than it did to others.

Certainly, the literary powers-that-be increasingly saw Brown as peripheral or outmoded. For example, critic E.K. Brown, in the course of his 1943 tinkering with the manuscript of his seminal *In Canadian Poetry* to placate Pierce's literary loyalties, thought it sufficient to add "a phrase" about Audrey Brown's work to acknowledge her. Pierce demanded no more.[30] No wonder that, when tasked about the tone of her poetry, Audrey Brown replied that "all my life, ever since I can remember, I have been terribly conscious of *impermanence*."[31] Pierce himself, like Edgar and Macmillan editor John Gray earlier, started enjoining Brown to stop writing so "repetitively" and "sadly" and so much of "death and loss."[32] But, when Pierce's daughter called on Brown during a 1948 visit to the West Coast, her overwhelming impression of the poet's existence in her "shabby genteel" rooming house was that of "sickness and poverty." So it is hard to see how Brown's tone could have been any different and remain authentic.[33]

Given all these literary taskmasters, it is suggestive that, in one letter to Pierce, Brown's signature is uncharacteristically cramped into a tiny corner of the page.[34] With few available options in her life or work, she dutifully (but unhappily) played the role of a compliant poetess whose publishers and patrons knew best. She later assured Pierce: "You have my completest confidence always, and that you may count beforehand on my approval of whatever you may think best."[35]

Both reviews and sales for Brown's Pierce-edited Ryerson volume *All Fool's Day* (1948) proved dismal. Brown, who, to use her own phrase, subsisted "on the edge of nothing" in a tiny flat above a seedy Esquimalt grocery store on small Foundation and provincial pensions of about $70 monthly (an income that another poet described as at "root-hog-or-die" levels),[36] secretly took a typing and shorthand course. She then took a part-time job (all her health would allow) as "Girl Friday" at a radio-repair shop.[37] Her subsequent letters to Pierce show the limitations of gender in women's occupational roles. She wrote from the repair shop: "Dear Lorne, being employed is such fun! ... If any of my [creative] work was truly good, it will survive: if not, it is only right it should perish. My ego is bolstered by the thought that though I've failed as a poet I've succeeded as a secretary!"[38] Pierce never published another book by Audrey Alexandra Brown – nor did anyone else. He wrote sadly but dismissively to the Foundation's secretary in 1955 about Brown's oeuvre: "She soared up into the blue [as a protégée of Pelham Edgar's], and we all thought she was headed for immortal things. But her style of lyric, like Carman's is dated, while her preoccupation with death and such is tiresome."[39]

PIERCE HAD joined younger confrères in the Canadian literary world in the belief that writers like Carman, Pickthall, and Brown had diminished in importance. It was but a small step to another conviction: that the work of such poets had to be edited and otherwise re-evaluated to suit changing tastes if any of the three were to have a shred of contemporary significance. This conviction, fed by a modernist climate of disdain for most of its literary predecessors, led Pierce to make some unfortunate editorial decisions in the 1950s about, for example, an edition of Bliss Carman's poetry, even if these editorial prunings were widely commended at the time.

By the late 1940s, Pierce himself was bringing to the fore the new generation of men of letters whose reputations as critics of Canadian literature would overshadow his own. Nonetheless, he was generous and indefatigable in his mentorship of young critics, editors, and academics, thereby realizing a life-long dream: to stimulate the English departments of Canadian universities to become more engaged with Canadian literature. Pierce regularly complained to E.K. Brown about, as he put it, "the vast indifference of the universities [to Canadian culture], their unbelievable languor, and often intellectual sabotage." Given the rarity of college and university courses in Canadian literature and art in the 1940s, it is hard to take issue with what Pierce labelled "the ennui and stupor of the universities and the patronizing elegance of the Oxonian heads of English Depts."[40] Certainly, E.K. Brown (one of the exceptions to the general academic torpor) had the same view. Pierce told Brown jubilantly in 1944: "I am looking forward to the day when the Departments of English in Canada, all across the country will pop and [coruscate] with life." That year, the appointment of Desmond Pacey to the English Department of the University of New Brunswick and Edward McCourt to University of Saskatchewan constituted evidence of a long-delayed flowering of cultural nationalism in the academy. Both Pacey and

McCourt were involved in publication projects with Pierce,[41] as was Carl Klinck (who taught at Waterloo and then Western), Malcolm Ross (Queen's and then Dalhousie), and American-based academics E.K. Brown (Cornell and then Chicago) and A.J.M. Smith (Michigan). All published books and read manuscripts for Ryerson Press from the 1940s.

E.K. Brown, as we have seen, was paramount among Pierce's academic protégés from the early 1940s until his death in 1951. More or less second – by several lengths – in the race for Pierce's regard was the feisty, New Zealand–born critic and academic Desmond Pacey, who, like Pierce and Brown, was a former student of Pelham Edgar's. The dark-haired, beetle-browed Pacey had as a young boy emigrated from New Zealand to an Ontario farm with his war-widowed mother. After earning a Victoria College degree in 1938, where he edited *Acta Victoriana*, the college magazine, Pacey had gone to England on a Massey Fellowship, earning a Cambridge doctorate in 1941.[42] He first came to Pierce's notice at the time he made the move from Manitoba's Brandon College to head the English Department of the University of New Brunswick (UNB), a transition bracketed by a year with Ottawa's Wartime Information Board in 1943–44. During this period, Pierce edited and published Pacey's 1945 monograph on Frederick Philip Grove. The headstrong Pacey, however, was never the suave academic diplomat that Brown was. As Pierce put it, Pacey was "not an easy man to handle."[43] Despite Pierce's charm and the passion for Canadian literature the two shared, Pacey's convictions often brought him head-to-head with Pierce over manuscripts. As Pacey's long-time UNB colleague Fred Cogswell put it, Pacey was "biased on the side of realism in fiction and modernism in poetry."[44] Moreover, by the early 1940s and beyond, the critical currents were running with Pacey. As Pierce put it, most Canadian modernists thought that "Old Man Pierce and his Chapbooks belong to the crystal age of the Victorian drawing room."[45]

Unquestionably, Pierce's dealings with Pacey laid bare the inexorable process through which Pierce's influence and ideas about Canadian literature were giving way to the revisionist views of a new generation of critics – manuscript by manuscript, reader's report by reader's report. Pierce was wise enough ultimately to accept the prominence of a new generation, and passionate enough to debate literary questions with many of them.

Pacey, after publishing his study of Grove with Ryerson in 1945 (an account that unwittingly reproduced the false account of Grove's early life that Grove fed to the Canadian literary world), expressed his chagrin to Pierce about the "financial debacle" to himself of its poor sales.[46] But, money matters aside, Pierce and Pacey had already discovered that their views of literature differed significantly. The long-suffering Pierce liked the young critic but found him intransigent in his insistence that fiction had no duty to "uplift" us but only "to make us more fully alive." With more candour than tact, Pacey had admonished Pierce on this score, telling him: "To have been happy and hopeful through the two Wars and the Great Depression would have been either stupid or insincere."[47]

Whatever the respective financial and ideological shocks of the Grove volume, neither publisher nor critic was done with the other. In late 1949 Pierce, after vainly suggesting to the overworked E.K. Brown that he write a book on Canadian literature modelled on *Creative Writing in Australia*, a synthetic work Pierce admired, approached Pacey.[48] Ryerson had earlier published Pacey's anthology *A Book of Canadian Stories* (1947).[49] Pierce and Pacey tussled even over that work. First of all, Pacey attempted to exact a 15 per cent editorial royalty for the anthology instead of the usual 10 per cent. But Pierce was more troubled by some of Pacey's editorial choices. Knowing that Pacey had consulted with A.J.M. Smith about the anthology on the latter's February 1946 visit to University of New Brunswick, as well as corresponding about it with rising young academic colleagues such as Northrop Frye and Roy Daniells,[50] Pierce found some of the stories too "modern" for possible school use (the market where the profits lay in such an anthology), one example being P.K. Page's "Neighbour." He also thought that some popular authors (such as Ryerson money-makers Will Bird and Arthur Stringer) had been ignored in favour of young modernists – and that Pacey had overlooked too many women writers (Sara Jeannette Duncan and Laura Goodman Salverson, for instance).[51]

Pacey countered that space constraints dictated that he "leave out" several women writers, and complained that the anthology was "light already on the more recent young experimental writers." He reluctantly agreed to drop Page's story in the school edition, if not the trade version, all the while defending it vigorously as "highly amusing" with "nothing objectionable."[52] The anthology sold slowly but did go into a second edition. Reviews were generally favourable, with the *New York Times Book Review* praising its "excellence of selection" and "vivid picture of the development of Canadian history."[53] With that modest success under his belt, Pacey displayed more ginger. He protested when Pierce asked Malcolm Ross to edit a book of Canadian essays instead of himself, and was volubly chagrined when Pierce rejected his novel ("Harper's rejected the manuscript at almost exactly the same time, but they were more encouraging than you were"[54]).

Then, in the fall of 1949, Pacey was again vexed – first, because Pierce (who faced rapidly rising production costs) wanted to raise the price of the new, larger edition of the fiction anthology; and second, because Pierce questioned his choice of additional stories. Pacey was blunt: "I am surprised and hurt that you still apparently have little confidence in my taste and judgement ... I do hope you will not delay publication of the new edition by further bickering."[55] Pierce in turn intimated to Pacey that he came across as a little "sharp." Unabashed, Pacey shot back: "Your cordiality to me has declined in the last three years ... I do not think I am being merely captious and temperamental, though I am open to persuasion if you care to attempt it."[56] Long schooled in turning the other cheek, Pierce attempted persuasion. But what is most significant here is that Pierce was not being treated deferentially by a junior critic. There is a sense not only of Pacey's bluntness but also of his different view of the literary landscape – one that he had formed in consultation with Smith, Frye, and others. It was a view that stood in sharp contrast to that of Pierce.

As for the genesis of the canonical Pacey 1952 text *Creative Writing in Canada* – from the 1950s to the 1980s a key work of Canadian criticism for generations of undergraduates and their professors – Pierce told Pacey in December 1949 that he wanted him to write in effect a new version of Pierce's own *An Outline of Canadian Literature*, to "draw a circle around the best [creative writing] we have done."[57] Pacey leapt at the idea, assuring Pierce that "it will be a stimulating book with some new things to say."[58] Conflict was not far off. A 1951 reader's report by Earle Birney pronounced Pacey's book too Maritime in orientation, and too middle-of-the-road in analysis, as well as humourless and dull. Pierce evidently concurred. On 26 February he sent Pacey a long, frank letter about his "grudging and captious" text (calling it by turns "petulant," "cocky," bathetic, and poorly planned in several sections). One of its failings, he said, was that he "always tended to make the author he disliked look silly," for example, Parker, Carman, Crawford, and Sangster. Moreover, wrote Pierce, the book was too long and "not the book we asked for" – it came across as a too-inclusive history, rather than a short summary of the best of creative writing in Canada.[59]

All in all, Pierce's letter constitutes an impressive, hard-hitting critique. It also confirms that Pierce was still a cultural nationalist who saw Canadian literature as a needed "fusing fire" for the country,[60] the more so given the post-war wave of immigration to Canada. Lambasting Pacey for not fully acknowledging French-English tensions and asking if he had read historians like Mason Wade, Pierce opined worriedly: "[In Canada], there is the constant attrition of the older and stronger cultures, Great Britain and the U.S.A. For a young country to stand up against them and survive, let alone develop an individuality, is something very important. But we have a polyglot people, islands of culture almost without number, that in the West care not a hoot for British tradition, the French or any other, but live from day to day."[61] Shrewdly, Pierce's letter to Pacey concluded on a conciliatory note: "We would like to have your book, and we would like to have it as good as we can make it, for it will stand alone perhaps for a long time."[62]

Pacey finally replied when, as he put it, "time ha[d] somewhat healed the scars." He promised to revise and cut his text, admitting: "The book really shifts purpose in the middle: it begins as a quick selective survey and develops into a comprehensive history ... [becoming] neither one thing or the other."[63] In the event, numerous echoes of Pierce's opinions about Canadian literature, many of them expressed in his letter to Pacey, are evident in the published version. For instance, Pacey incorporates Pierce's point that Roberts was important for his influence as pioneer even if he was not the most accomplished Confederation poet, and that Duncan Campbell Scott's work moved toward a philosophical transcendence, one, as Pierce put it in his letter, "above passion and strife[,] desire and reason itself."[64]

But the Pierce-Pacey tug-of-war persisted. Later, when Pierce read Pacey's revised manuscript, which Pierce felt had still needed work, he showed Pacey some teeth. In June 1951 he wrote Pacey that his proposal to edit an anthology of 1940s literature was "dropped" because Ryerson was "inundated" with such material. Further, for the forthcoming school edition of the short-story anthology, "the stories that offend" must unquestionably be omitted. It was "useless our debating the point" if Pacey wanted it accepted as a school text. Turning to the "Creative Writing" manuscript, Pierce objected to the harsh verdict on poets Audrey Alexandra Brown and Wilson MacDonald as mediocre traditionalists: "The trouble is, that I am alive and in the way! One cannot be editor for thirty-one years and not make friends, even if one fails to influence people [to change direction]. To omit certain names altogether would be a lethal blow; and while I do not ask for encomium, I think we can be reasonable, and sporting." Pierce insisted that the book still needed some "blue pencilling." Pacey had told Pierce's assistant Frank Flemington that he would make no more changes but Pierce met that challenge head-on. He told Pacey that he hoped such was "not the case, else we are going to lose a book."[65]

Pierce then followed with more detailed commentary, alternating sticks and carrots. Tellingly for us, most of his detailed commentary on the last section of the book – which featured Pacey's assessment of contemporary writers like Ethel Wilson, Malcolm Lowry, and others – drew very heavily on Earle Birney's reader's report. It is revealing that Pierce felt that he could not completely trust his own judgment on contemporary writing. Pacey would make the changes, and the book was probably the better for it – but Pacey, Birney, and their contemporaries were now the shapers on the critical scene, not Pierce.

Ironically, the concept of critical succession was in fact on Pierce's mind on the day he wrote Pacey. His letter featured an elegy for E.K. Brown, who had died two months earlier. Pierce told Pacey of Brown's last visit to the Ryerson offices that spring, to discuss the effect of Puritanism on Canadian literature. He added sadly: "You would never know that when he said good bye that he knew it was farewell."[66] Pierce undoubtedly wanted Pacey to know that, at the last, Brown had agreed with Pierce's rejection of the grab-bag theory of A.J.M. Smith and others that Puritanism was to blame for the retarded development of Canadian literature. He reiterated for Pacey the same position he had made even more eloquently to Brown during the latter's revisions to *On Canadian Poetry*. Then, he had written Brown:

> We all overdo this colonial and puritan bogey. In our poetry and art there is scarcely a blob of either big enough to weigh in any work that rises above the level *as art*. Our writers in English never mention religion and rarely cant about morals ...
>
> Our poets had little influence outside Canada not because of any defect of colonialism or puritanism, but because of a fatal lack of ideas.

Pierce had added a swipe at A.J.M. Smith's brand of cosmopolitanism: "The contribution of those who have studied abroad and returned with a shallow cosmopolitanism and a too-tidy cynicism has [not] helped us. All our academic writers speak that way, and I am inclined to think that it is humbug."[67] In doing so, he wanted to confirm for Pacey that he himself was right in rejecting cosmopolitanism, and that Brown, Pacey's contemporary, had come to the same view.

As Pierce well knew, Pacey was forging a reputation as a major critic of Canadian literature via his Ryerson publications. Indeed, when one reads the final text of Pacey's *Creative Writing in Canada* – which became the success Pierce promised Pacey it would be, dominating the market until the publication of the more ambitious *Literary History of Canada* in the mid-1960s – one element is striking. Pacey has made many of the changes Pierce wanted, but he is still unsparing of many writers dear to Pierce and his contemporaries. Carman's work, for example, is described as "unworthy of serious critical attention." Pickthall's work is character-ized as "slight in extent and shallow in thought and emotion,"[68] an even more extreme diminution of Pickthall than Pierce himself had arrived at.

Pacey increasingly hewed to his own course. In his introduction to *The Selected Poems of Charles G.D. Roberts*, which he edited for Ryerson in 1955, he included a slap at Carman's early "Vagabondia" poems, a stricture to which Pierce had strongly objected. Pacey sneered at Carman's poems of the period as "the embarrassing spectacle of an effeminate man flexing his flabby muscles and pounding his skinny chest in public."[69] It was hardly surprising, then, that Pierce felt in the 1950s that he could trust no one but himself to edit Carman.

After their power struggles over *Creative Writing in Canada*, Pierce mostly deferred to Pacey. In 1951, in discussing with Pierce their differ-ing opinions of Canadian writers, Pacey described his own critical role as that of "a moderator between the old exaltation and the new vilifi-cation" of Canadian writers like Roberts and Carman.[70] He was being characteristically forthright: Pierce knew that Pacey considered him part of the uncritical "old exaltation." That same year, when Pierce proposed that Pacey update the Carman anthology of Canadian poetry that Pierce himself had already augmented once, Pacey refused, pointedly remarking that instead he was "willing to start from scratch and do a new anthol-ogy of my own."[71] When Pierce convinced a less gifted editor, Vernon Rhodenizer of Acadia University, to "update" the anthology, the result, *Canadian Poetry in English* (1954) – advertised as edited by Carman, Pierce, and Rhodenizer – was savaged by modernist critics. The scornful review in Montreal's little modernist magazine *CIV/n*, entitled "Don't Blame This on Bliss," mocked Pierce and Rhodenizer as "prime examples of the evil companions an unsuspecting poet can pick up through the years."[72]

Pierce, meanwhile, continued to publish Pacey, although privately he recommended Malcolm Ross, not Pacey, to write entries on Pratt and D.C. Scott for a new Canadian encyclopedia.[73] Nevertheless, when Pacey was working on *Ten Canadian Poets* for Ryerson, a work that would be published in 1958, Pierce read the chapters one by one of what he saw as "a very important document."[74] He still tried to stress a few cherished beliefs to Pacey – for example, that Pratt's ordination as a minister needed consideration in any assessment of his poetic vision, and that Roberts, for all his lack of development as a poet, "came first in so many ways that it would be stupid as well as improper not to give him credit."[75] Mostly, however, he resignedly accepted Pacey's judgments, including the decision to have only male poets as subjects of the ten chapters, although, as he reminded Pacey, the influence and importance of women poets like Dorothy Livesay and Isabella Valancy Crawford had been substantial.[76] Significantly, in 1955 Pierce ended one letter about a Pacey manuscript by asking the author to "excuse this long twitter" – self-deprecation that suggested his feeling that critical *gravitas* now resided with Pacey and his contemporaries.[77]

That shift in power was emphasized when Pierce wanted Pacey – who, as one scholar has commented, was "developing into one of the most eminent Canadian literary critics of his generation"[78] – to work on a sequel to *Ten Canadian Poets*, to be called *Ten Canadian Novelists*. Pacey turned Pierce down, telling him that he had agreed to do a chapter on fiction for the *Literary History of Canada* which would occupy him for the next couple of years.[79] Pierce was left to ask who would be publishing the work. Pacey's reply was noncommittal,[80] but in the event the University of Toronto Press would, not Ryerson. A telling moment: although Pierce himself was asked to write the chapter on publishing history for the *Literary History of Canada*,[81] the days when Ryerson was almost invariably the groundbreaking publisher of Canadian criticism were clearly passing. Ironically, the general editor of the *Literary History of Canada* to whom Pacey was giving his "full support" was Carl Klinck of the University of Western Ontario, whose early career Pierce had played a key role in fostering. Klinck himself gives a blow-by-blow account of his contacts with Pierce throughout his career in his memoir, *Giving Canada a Literary History*, beginning with his early work on Wildred Campbell.[82]

BY THE LATE 1950s, Ryerson Press was no longer far out in front as a publisher of Canadian literature, as had been the case in the early 1940s. John Gray, a gifted publisher with a keen literary sense, had taken over as general manager at Macmillan of Canada in 1946 and by the late 1950s was publishing the likes of Robertson Davies, Hugh MacLennan, and W.O. Mitchell. McClelland and Stewart now had dynamic young Jack McClelland, who was essentially running the firm by 1952. Its New Canadian Library series under general editor Malcolm Ross became a pioneering Canadian literary initiative in the field of paperbacks, a format that Ryerson had barely touched, save in the softcover chapbook poetry series born decades before.[83] By the 1950s, in fact, established academics like Ross, Pacey, and Klinck were devoting their energies to publishing projects in which Pierce played no dominant role. So, while Pierce had helped launch the careers of all three – Malcolm Ross published *Our Sense of Identity: A Book of Canadian Essays* (1954) with Ryerson – many of their later endeavours were published elsewhere.

Furthermore, death had cut short Pierce's relationship in the 1940s and 1950s with John Sutherland, another dynamic young editor and critic. There were ironies in Pierce's relationship with Sutherland. In John Sutherland, Pierce became close to a key modernist editor of the 1940s – but only as Sutherland grew more conservative, religious, and nationalistic. And even as the two became friendly, Sutherland's relationship with modernist peers and collaborators like Louis Dudek and Irving Layton – his key colleagues in the era of *First Statement* magazine, launched in 1942 – cooled. In fact, Layton and Dudek launched the small Contact Press in 1952 partly out of unhappiness at the direction both Sutherland's magazine *Northern Review* and First Statement Press were taking.[84]

Sutherland's first brushes with Ryerson were not auspicious. In the early days of *First Statement*, he was a literary leftist, favouring writing in a modernist, social-realist vein. Ryerson Press was not regarded with reverence in such circles. According to Bruce Whiteman, Sutherland had been included in a proposed anthology of McGill student poetry which Ryerson had declined in 1945. Two years earlier, Sutherland had told Dorothy Livesay that he hoped to bring out selections of poetry "similar to the Ryerson chap-books" on the new First Statement printing press. But Sutherland had added scornfully that such booklets would "no doubt" be better "in quality" than Pierce's product.[85]

However, Sutherland's attitude toward Pierce would be transformed over the next few years. Sutherland had long been uneasy with *Preview* editorial board member A.J.M. Smith's division of Canadian poetry into "native" and "cosmopolitan" strains (with the latter definitely preferred by Smith) in the anthology *The Book of Canadian Poetry* (1943). Such tensions culminated in a fracas over Sutherland's withering review of a cosmopolitan book of poetry by Robert Finch in the August-September 1947 issue of *Northern Review*,[86] prompting the resignation of Smith, F.R. Scott, A.M. Klein, and P.K. Page from the magazine's editorial board. At this time, Sutherland "gradually turned his interest toward the more traditional Canadian writers, and away from the larger experimental and militant themes of modern poetry."[87] The literary direction in which Sutherland was moving encompassed Pierce's favourite territory.

Pierce had been quick to support the shift in Sutherland's thinking. *Northern Review* always struggled financially. By January 1946, Pierce had offered Ryerson advertising to the magazine, ads that became a regular feature. In addition, by February 1946, he had sent Sutherland the first of what would be some nine personal cash donations to the magazine over the next eight years.[88] Sutherland welcomed Pierce's money ("very encouraging to feel that someone understands what one is trying to do"[89]), but, more significantly, he also welcomed some of Pierce's ideas. In fact, by the October-November 1949 issue, Sutherland was regularly running a nationalistic quotation from Pierce's *A Canadian People* on the back cover: "No nation can achieve its true destiny that adopts without profound and courageous reasoning and selection the thoughts and styles of another."[90] About the same time, Sutherland was defiantly telling Louis Dudek, his old *First Statement* confrère, that he didn't "believe in your idea that the national spirit is something in the past or that we should assume it can be dispensed with now."[91]

Dudek and Layton became increasingly alienated from Sutherland. Moreover, Dudek shared the unhappiness of Toronto poet Raymond Souster that *Northern Review* now allegedly lacked "the old biff-bam of the war years," because "looking for 'native quality' just shuts the eyes to what is new and different and alive."[92] A year later, in 1952, Dudek and Souster founded the little magazine *Contact* and then Contact Press, whose first book, *Cerebrus* (1952), featured the poetry of Dudek, Souster, and Layton. As Sutherland moved away from the trio personally and intellectually, he moved closer to Pierce. In a 1950 article, Sutherland posed a question that Pierce might have framed: whether the poet "can rediscover the basic religious and moral values of our society."[93]

By this point, Pierce was giving subscriptions to *Northern Review* as Christmas gifts. He and Sutherland met at least twice to discuss the magazine's prospects, and he lobbied Toronto publishers for support after Sutherland attempted to launch and sustain an annual fund to support the magazine in 1950.[94] When the *Canadian Review of Music and Art* folded in 1951, Pierce bought its subscription list to give to Sutherland. He supplied plates of illustrations by Thoreau MacDonald and others gratis for the use of Sutherland's magazine.[95] Unsurprisingly, therefore, Sutherland asked Pierce if he would take "part in the editorship of *Northern Review*? It is an idea which appeals to me very much, and I think we would really make things move."[96] Pierce declined, but his support continued. Two years later, Sutherland confided to Pierce that "we would have gone down the drain long ago without your constant help."[97]

As Pierce and Sutherland made contact, book projects were discussed, including a collection of Sutherland's essays. In February 1947 Sutherland told poet Ralph Gustafson that he had "about 2/3 of the book done" for projected fall publication.[98] However, Pierce, worried about sales prospects,[99] was still sitting on the manuscript in July 1949 when Sutherland wrote him that he wanted to add an article on Pratt and update the one on Klein. Sutherland praised Ryerson's publication of Klein's *The Rocking Chair* (1948), calling it "an important event in Canadian poetry."[100] Pierce returned the articles for revision in August, but the book of essays never appeared, probably a casualty both of Pierce's worries over sales and Sutherland's changing critical perspective on Canadian writing, which was coupled with a distancing of himself from his early work.[101] Yet, as late as 1953, Pierce was still urging Sutherland to publish such a book.[102]

In January 1950 Sutherland also submitted to Ryerson an edition of poems by Imagist-influenced Toronto poet W.W.E. Ross. Pierce probably relished Sutherland telling Ross enthusiastically that he "would very much like to edit" such a Ryerson publication, given Sutherland's sneers about Ryerson poetry titles in the early 1940s.[103] Pierce would certainly have liked to publish Ross. But, as Sutherland wrote Ross,[104] Ryerson was cutting back on its publication list, hard hit by dramatically rising production costs.

Publication of poetry was precisely the area where Pierce got the most flak for financial losses from the House accountant. And losses overall at the Press were still heavy. In 1950 Pierce's annual report to the Board of Publication lamented the "disastrous" costs that had prompted him to make a "drastic reduction" of nearly half in the number of books Ryerson had published compared to five years earlier.[105] Three years later, Pierce was so desperate to cut printing costs that he even proposed that Sutherland himself publish the Ross book – only to discover that Sutherland had sold his First Statement printing press, and that his printing bills were higher than Pierce's.[106] The Ross project fizzled out.

In the meantime, Sutherland sent Pierce a long list of suggestions for a Ryerson poetry anthology. Pierce then asked Sutherland to suggest some contemporary stories from *Northern Review* for possible inclusion in a new edition of Pacey's short-story anthology – another instance of Pierce juggling the younger generation of critics, especially in the light of his struggles with Pacey over that anthology.[107] Ironically, Pacey had earlier written to Pierce commenting on Sutherland's dramatic change in critical direction.[108]

For his part, Pierce tried to convince Sutherland of the merits of writers like Pauline Johnson, Audrey Alexandra Brown, and Charles G.D. Roberts. Sutherland (like Pacey) resisted praise of Roberts, telling Pierce that he found him "pretentious" and "colonial."[109] Furthermore, Sutherland dismissed Brown and her ilk for "fail[ing] to escape in an important sense the parasitic dependence on English poetry with which they begin."[110] (Pierce himself was edging away from promoting her about this time.) As with E.K. Brown and Desmond Pacey, therefore, Pierce discovered that members of the new generation of critics, however much they feuded with each other, usually had some views that discomfited him, leading him sometimes to feel that he was "in the way!"[111]

Pierce did get some comfort from what proved to be Sutherland's last project: a study of E.J. Pratt's poetry, the final fruits of which Ryerson published in 1956.[112] Sutherland had become interested in Pratt as early as 1949,[113] and he published a special Pratt issue of *Northern Review* in 1952 which included his own article on the Newfoundland poet.[114] Pierce would live long enough to see how influential Sutherland's Ryerson book on Pratt would prove to be, but the comfort of knowing that he had published a seminal work was some time in coming. When Sutherland began to focus on Pratt's work in the early 1950s, his unorthodox approach isolated him from most of his critical contemporaries. Yet, as

Pratt's biographer points out, Sutherland's analysis, set forth in his 1952 article and expanded in *The Poetry of E.J. Pratt: A New Interpretation* (1956), which foregrounded elements of Christian allegory and symbolism as key in Pratt's work, ultimately "set Pratt criticism on the course it thereafter adopted." Admittedly, Sutherland's view of Pratt, so different from the standard "rollicking Newfoundland Ned-of-the-cruel-sea" approach to Pratt's work, initially aroused "surprise, [and] even scepticism in some quarters."[115] Pratt himself was intrigued if not wholly convinced by Sutherland's analysis. In reacting to Sutherland's exegesis, Pratt was heard to mutter: "Christ! Did I really mean *that*?"[116] Pierce and Sutherland were thus alone for a time in the desert, so to speak. And even Pierce at first felt that Sutherland needed to refine his Pratt manuscript. But fate forced Pierce's hand in the matter of publishing it – unrevised.

The Pierce-Sutherland entente came about when Pierce, unlike most of Sutherland's former little magazine collaborators, responded positively to his conversion to Roman Catholicism in the fall of 1954.[117] Sutherland was heartened by Pierce's support because, as he wryly put it: "Not all my friends and acquaintances feel it *is* an improvement." He informed Pierce that his work on Pratt had helped to move him toward religious commitment[118] and that, in his critical thinking, he had been influenced by Pierce's belief "that Pratt's religious feelings and ideas are vital to an understanding of his poetry." Sutherland added that he ought to have placed even more emphasis on this idea in his Pratt article. Later, he decided to devote a book to Pratt which centred on this theme.[119]

Pierce stressed much the same view of Pratt to Desmond Pacey as he worked on the manuscript that became *Ten Canadian Poets*: "You know what the Methodist parsonage in Newfoundland meant to [Pratt], the theological training, and the high emotional moment of his ordination. No one ever forgets that."[120] But Pacey was more skeptical than Sutherland, asserting in his analysis that many of Pratt's passages were "difficult if not impossible to reconcile with an orthodox Christian position."[121] Decades later, Pratt's biographer also described as "doubtful" Pierce's view of Pratt's ordination.[122] Thus, it is easy to see why Pierce valued John Sutherland's responsiveness to his ideas, given that, by the mid-1950s, he could no longer count on approbation from the rest of the younger generation of Canadian literary critics.

Sutherland initially submitted his Pratt manuscript to Macmillan, Pratt's long-time publisher, which, not unexpectedly, rejected it (possibly because the conventional interpretation of Pratt that Sutherland disdained was then the most widely marketable view of the poet). The manuscript soon landed with a thud on Pierce's desk.[123] Pierce had long disliked the stag party and sea-shanty view of Pratt but Sutherland's manuscript needed revision. In a long, thoughtful letter, Pierce told Sutherland in February 1955 that the book was "long and not always clear," that the conclusion was weak, and that discussion of its thesis about the centrality of Pratt's Christian spirituality came much too late in the text. Pierce counselled "a little more time on this manuscript."[124]

But Sutherland had no more time: he had only eighteen months to live. Now attending the University of Toronto in order to complete his long-deferred BA, Sutherland fell ill in the summer of 1955. That fall, he was treated at Weston Sanatorium for a recurrence of tuberculosis – only to receive a belated diagnosis of spinal cancer. After surgery that December, his cancer recurred in the spring of 1956. He died on 1 September.

In the end, production of Sutherland's (unrevised) book was rushed through for delivery to his deathbed. As Sutherland lay paralyzed in August, Pierce heeded the plea of Sutherland's friend Father Lawrence Shook, rector of St Michael's College, that he bring out the book. The first copy of *The Poetry of E.J. Pratt: A New Interpretation* (1956), rushed through the press in two weeks, was placed in Sutherland's hands "a day or so before he entered the final coma."[125] Sutherland's magazine *Northern Review* died with him. At the time, the significance of his book on Pratt was not yet evident; in fact, its publication seemed primarily to be another of Pierce's many works of mercy (an "oblation to one we all loved," as Pierce put it[126]). For Pierce, Sutherland's death brought an increased sense of isolation. Whatever their differences, the loss of Sutherland, following upon E.K. Brown's passing five years earlier, deprived Pierce of a critical ally among the younger literary generation of the 1950s.

THE EMERGENCE of small presses and little magazines also affected Ryerson's status and that of its general editor. In the field of contemporary literary publishing at least, Ryerson Press was by the 1950s increasingly seen as a reactionary dinosaur by young Turks and even by younger publishing rivals at the established firms. With the formation of small enterprises like First Statement Press in the 1940s and Contact Press in the 1950s, and the revival of more established Canadian publishing companies under younger editors, Ryerson no longer enjoyed the pre-eminence in Canadian publishing that it had in the 1930s and early 1940s. Furthermore, as Paul Litt, Maria Tippett, and other scholars have discussed, the establishment of the Canada Council in 1957, given its various (and unprecedented) government granting programs in support of the writing and publishing of Canadian literature, also meant that academic presses like that of the University of Toronto would also become more involved in some kinds of Canadian literary publication, a case in point being the University of Toronto Press's publication of the *Literary History of Canada* (1965).[127]

Nevertheless, Pierce did play a crucial and largely unsung role in nurturing a new generation of critics in the 1940s and 1950s whose reputation would soon eclipse his own. He was also saddened that the literary standing of poets he admired, Bliss Carman chief among them, was going into even greater decline in a modernist era marked by polarization of critical approaches. The best way to demonstrate the urgency of Pierce's desire in his last years to see Confederation-era poetry valued, and the unambiguous role of the new generation of critics in that process, is to examine the editing and critical reception of *The Selected Poems of Bliss Carman*, which Pierce himself edited for McClelland and Stewart in 1954. Here we find the ironic spectacle of both the older literary generation, in the person of Pierce, and the new generation of critics, notably Malcolm Ross and Desmond Pacey, effecting, aiding, and/or applauding (before and after publication) the abridgment and evisceration of some of Carman's best-known poems, ostensibly to make his work more "acceptable" to a new literary generation. To add to the irony, the next generation of critics would subsequently condemn Pierce for his abridgments of Carman in the *Selected Poems* – but without examining the degree to which Pierce's editorial practices were seconded by their own immediate critical predecessors. In some cases, the latter had even vetted Pierce's manuscript of the Carman poems.

Pierce had been enraptured with Bliss Carman and his verse since first meeting the poet in 1923.[128] He compiled two collections of Carman's prose: *Talks on Literature and Life* (1926) and *Bliss Carman's Scrap Book* (1931), the latter a posthumously published index to the poet's scrapbook of his uncollected writings. All along, Pierce was frustrated by the copyright difficulties that prevented him from including Carman in his Makers of Canadian Literature series or from publishing much of Carman's poetry.[129] Nevertheless, as we have seen, he was able to cajole critic James Cappon into writing *Bliss Carman and the Literary Currents and Influences of His Time*, though he would be disappointed in Cappon's "dehydrated criticism," describing it to Carman's patron, Mary Perry King, as "about as satisfying as chewing a blotter."[130] Indefatigably, Pierce also published Muriel Miller's biographical *Bliss Carman: A Portrait* (1935).

For four decades, Pierce himself amassed Carman material – books and manuscripts – so avidly that he once joked to Carman that he suffered from "Carmania ... a rare mixture of an incurable disease and ecstasy," where only the wallet "wastes away."[131] In 1945, when Pierce felt he ought to send some of his Carman treasures to the Edith and Lorne Pierce Canadiana Collection at Queen's, he wrote that parting with Carman material "really hurts; in one way I should like to live and die with it under my elbow."[132] Included in the trove was Carman's favourite hat and the Buddha given to him by Mary Perry King.

Perhaps, as Pierce's daughter speculates, a case of opposites attracting explains his fascination with the footloose, libidinous, bohemian Carman. Both men did have a history of tuberculosis and of theosophical leanings, but there the resemblance in their lifestyles stops. Nonetheless, the charisma of the tall, gentle, fair-haired poet ("a striking masculine beauty"[133]) captivated Pierce. After attending a Carman reading in November 1923, he rhapsodized to his diary about the poet: "A man's man, full of faith, optimistic, [with] a simple, homely creed, neither profound nor daring, just a citizen, a lover of the beautiful and the true, a constant friend."[134]

As for Carman's poetry, Pierce – in his *Outline of Canadian Literature* and other writings[135] – saw in it an eclectic, unsystematic, intuitive mysticism, the product of a "melodist supreme" in whose work "simplicity is the keynote." In *Outline*, Pierce crystallized what he saw as Carman's appeal: "His songs of love and the sea are equal to the best in our language, while his interpretation of nature, its mother-love, his belief in one all-including spirit, and his triumphant faith in the immortality of love, truth and beauty, have given his work lasting significance."[136]

Ominously for his later editing of Carman, Pierce, like many commentators, consistently stressed Carman's intuitive, non-rational poetic. "Whatever thought he had," Pierce wrote in *Three Fredericton Poets*, "cannot be called a system." Carman's mind was, in Pierce's view, "unfettered." He was a "seer, not a profound or systematic thinker," with a soul that was "a sort of ante-chamber to the universe of spiritual experience. It refused to be cramped, even at the risk of becoming vague and diffuse."[137] Since Carman's poems were thought of as highly eclectic and non-rational, albeit captivating, commodities, they came to be seen by Pierce and many others as works that could be disassembled or abridged without violating their essence. Furthermore, as Carman's reputation ebbed in the 1940s and 1950s, Pierce, as executor of the Carman literary estate and designated Carman biographer, was positioned to do such tinkering. He felt compelled to do so to try to revive Carman's reputation.

By 1927, Pierce had decided, at the urging of mutual friends like Vancouver poet and physician Ernest Fewster and Carman's confidante and one-time lover Kate Eastman, that he would write Carman's biography.[138] The project would weigh on his conscience for the rest of his life. In many ways, however, he had set himself an impossible task. Carman's peripatetic life and many erotic attachments made writing about him problematic, especially in the conservative Canadian literary world. Even more problematic was the fact that Carman seems to have had at least one homosexual liaison in the 1890s – with a man whom he called "the beautiful Fullerton": bisexual American journalist Morton Fullerton, most famously the Paris lover of novelist Edith Wharton a decade later.[139] Carman himself was conscious of the awkwardness of his life to a biographer, although he seems to have kept mum about his bisexuality, in Canadian circles at least.

Although initially cooperative, Carman soon became what Pierce called "biographer shy" as he peppered Carman with queries, interviewed his intimates, and collected correspondence – or tried to. The poet cautioned a woman friend in 1928: "Good old L.P. But for God Almighty's sake don't let him have any of my letters! He is like all biographers and collectors, consumed with an unholy lust of acquisitiveness ... He would gobble us up hide and hair. Lord, it's too much this peeking and key-holing and gumshoeing. Damned if I like it. I propose to *live* my biography first.[140] Carman's cousin Charles G.D. Roberts once joked that any Carman biography would have to be called "Smothered in Petticoats."[141] Carman's contemporary, novelist Arthur Stringer, put Pierce's biographical dilemma in blunt (if sexist) fashion: "You can't say in cold type that [Carman's] career was really a series of illicit relationships, that in his later years he was practically a 'kept' man, and that his disdain for everything financial actually converted him into a sort of intellectualized gigolo for a florid and affluent lady protector [Mary Perry King]."[142]

Pierce, too, gradually concluded that there was much that he could not say in a Carman biography. He had wanted the biography to be, as he himself informed Carman, "warm-toned [photogravure]," a work that would constitute "a creditable actual full-length likeness." He told Mary Perry King, whose confidant he became, that he wished the book to be "full of 'sweetness and light.'"[143] But, for Pierce, Carman's amours made the prospective biography anything but a sweet prospect – even if, as is probable, he remained ignorant of Carman's bisexuality. He finally admitted near the end of his own life, after four decades of impasse on writing the Carman biography – an impasse he called "a major anxiety and grief" – that to use the letters of Carman's "fabulously long list" of women friends would be "embarrassing." (Carman's letters to his male lover Fullerton would have been even more awkward, had Pierce uncovered them.[144]) Thus, for Pierce, given his desire to exalt Carman, the biography was in effect unwritable. A book that Pierce had once dreamed would be "his greatest work" inexorably slipped away.[145]

By the early 1950s, Pierce was anxious to salvage the poet's reputation. His desire was sharpened by the fact that, in 1940, after the death of both Mary Perry King and her husband, he became the executor of the Carman Estate, administering it in trust, ultimately for deposition to the University of New Brunswick, Carman's alma mater.[146] But how to fulfill the trust? Pierce well knew from his dealings with critics like E.K. Brown, Desmond Pacey, and A.J.M. Smith that they had little flattering to say about Carman in private or in print. Smith, for example, had confided to E.K. Brown in 1942 that he wanted his anthology *The Book of Canadian Poetry* to reflect "a reduction of Roberts and Carman ... to a proper perspective as essentially minor poets." He added that he and Northrop Frye had each found Carman's poetry to be "the world of the arty-poet who uses language as a kind of flower-screen to conceal his emotions," with "little to interest an adult mind."[147] Such views of Carman validate Mary McGillivray's thesis that, for about forty years after Carman's death, "it was fashionable ... to use Carman as a kind of straw man" for all that the modernists deplored in the previous poetic generation.[148]

In a subsequent letter to Brown, Smith was equally scathing, calling Carman's writing "a world of sensibility and intuition (and what a tawdry, roistering, blustering world of sham spirituality it is!")".[149] Pierce was discomfited when Brown's *On Canadian Poetry* similarly (if more politely) devalued Carman. He wistfully suggested in 1946 that Brown "write at greater length" about Carman, adding: "The way in which his name is bandied about is hardly fair to the critics or the criticized."[150] Brown did not take the bait.

At this time, Carman was being treated even more sharply by Desmond Pacey. In *Creative Writing in Canada*, Pacey noted the "predominantly hostile" tone of the writings on Carman by recent critics, observing witheringly: "Carman wrote far too much and ... large masses of his work are unworthy of serious critical attention." He also maintained that it was "time" for a "more judicious estimate of [Carman's] work."[151] One can see how Pierce became convinced that he himself would have to spearhead any rescue of Carman's reputation. His chosen vehicle was a new selected edition of Carman's poetry, one tailored to revive interest in him.

Publishing a selected Carman was no easy task. Pierce, with Mary Perry King, American academic Odell Shepard, and others, had planned such a volume after Carman's death in 1929.[152] However, Lewis Page of Boston, who held publication rights to crucial chunks of Carman's work (Dodd, Mead of New York, in conjunction with Toronto's McClelland and Stewart, held rights to most of the rest), refused to cooperate. Dodd, Mead and McClelland and Stewart had brought out a doorstopper (546 pages) collected Carman in 1931, but that volume, lacking Page-controlled material, had done little for Carman's reputation. Pierce wrote that there was "a lot of wood" in it.[153]

As early as 1948, Pierce began to write to Page, asserting that Page's rights to key Carman volumes like *Pipes of Pan* and *Sappho* had lapsed through long-time non-publication. He voiced his determination to print – at his own personal expense – a "proper *selected* edition" of Carman's poetry.[154] Five years passed before Page finally granted "full and free permission without compensation to include any selections you wish from Carman's poetry published by us."[155] All the while, Pierce made it clear that he was conducting a salvage operation on Carman, telling Page: "You kno[w], as well as I do, that Bliss Carman's verse belongs to another age, and is out of fashion. All I can hope to do for him, and his memory, is the publication of a small selection of his poems from all sources, approximately 100 pages from the hundreds of pages of his collections."[156] Pierce was even blunter in another letter: "[Carman's] prose is dead. Only a small sheaf of [Carman's] verse is worth reclaiming."[157] He expressed much the same opinion to John McClelland, whose firm was to publish the book, given its copyright prerogatives. Pierce emphasized that, although he would not be ready to bring out the volume until 1954, "I am determined to make this the definitive selected edition in my own way."[158]

Given Carman's devaluation by the early 1950s, and Pierce's belief – impressed on him by the critical attitudes of the day – that Carman's "style of lyric" was "dated,"[159] he felt that what was needed was "a small book" of not more than 150 pages. Such a volume was to incorporate "the best of Carman's poems, from all [the] previous books, including *Pipes of Pan* and *Sappho*," which Page had long held to copyright ransom.[160] Such a volume, as we have seen, had been planned immediately after the poet's death in 1929. What is also clear is that, even then, the intention had been to abridge some poems. Pierce's introduction to the 1954 volume mentions that, when a selected Carman was first envisaged, a tentative list of poems was drawn up. He adds, "Suggestions were also made regarding the abridgment of certain poems," because, as he remembered elsewhere, "there were several good stopping points in many of Carman's long poems, those endless trailing quatrains, which we felt might be indicated." Consequently, Pierce claimed, his edited selection constituted "the essential Carman, his best work that could be offered without apology or debate."[161]

The result is a book of just 122 pages, offering seventy-seven Carman poems culled and pruned out of Carman's "vast output." Pierce's introduction indicates that some poems have been cut: "The abridgments have been, in some instances, rather severe. I have not indicated [in the poems themselves] where the cuts have been made, believing that the poems, as they are printed here, would be their own best defence."[162] Severe indeed. It is a shock to examine the manuscript for the volume and see whole stanzas crossed out of such key Carman poems as, for example, "Pulvis et Umbra" (twenty-five stanzas dropped), "A Northern Vigil" (seven stanzas cut), "Spring Song" (ten stanzas out), and "Resurgam" (eight stanzas deleted, including the final one). Inevitably the artistry and impact of the poems are altered, sometimes dramatically. For instance, in "The Sceptics," the elimination of the refrain in which the "naughty little leaves" groan, smile, and laugh at humankind's solemn religiosity entirely alters the tone of the poem, making it less mischievous and mocking.[163] Whatever Carman's defects as a poet, such abridgments, however well intentioned, violated the integrity of his work.

In his understandable zeal to revive Carman's reputation, Pierce made an editorial misjudgment here – but he emphatically did not make it alone. What is fascinating about this volume is that in effect Pierce's 1954 Carman collection embodies a collective willingness on the part of both key traditionalists and modernists to "hack and hew" (to use another Carman phrase) the work of a leading poet of the previous generation to make it more acceptable to latter-day tastes. This is "canon formation" with a vengeance. Not only did Pierce initially plan abridgments in company with Carman loyalists Mary Perry King, academic Odell Shepard, publisher Frank Dodd, and others when the volume was first conceived after Carman's death in 1929, he also sent the poems before publication in 1954 to two critics for their advice and approval, critics named and thanked in his introduction to the selection. One was his contemporary and friend Professor A.L. Phelps of McGill University; the other was Malcolm Ross of Queen's University, one of the rising new critics whom Pierce was publishing in the 1940s and 1950s. When one considers Ross's subsequent endorsement of Pierce's editorial scissoring, and the positive reviews of the volume from key critics like Desmond Pacey, Northrop Frye, and William Arthur Deacon, including praise for the abridging of poems, it is clear that the critical climate of the early 1950s was such that traditional poets were seen to be most acceptable (and arguably *only* acceptable) when their work was altered to suit the tastes of the day. It is also clear that, of all the earlier generation of Canadian poets, Carman was most at risk of having his work tampered with.

There were two reasons for this attitude. By the early 1950s, to many Canadian literary modernists, Bliss Carman was the Confederation poster boy for a now-unfashionable romantic lyricism. His work was characterized as prone to emphasize qualities like magic, intuition, atmosphere, and emotion and to lack intellectuality and systematic thought. Thus, his poems seemed to lend themselves to abridgments. After all (the rationale for cutting went), don't clouds wax and wane, form and reform, shrink in size, and yet retain their beauty nevertheless? Could Carman's poems be any different? As Pacey pointedly declared in his essay on Carman in his *Ten Canadian Poets*: "The first task of a critic of Carman is to perform a surgical operation, to cut away the mass of inferior work."[164]

The consequences of a death of ten thousand editorial cuts to Carman's work did not end in 1954. Malcolm Ross's informed decision to include Pierce's abridged versions of Carman poems in his influential anthology *Poets of the Confederation* (1960) further compounded the distortion of Carman's work. That distortion went unchallenged until John Robert Sorfleet published an article in 1972 attacking Ross's use of abridged versions of Carman (and Roberts) poems in the anthology.[165]

However, as we have seen, in 1954, when *The Selected Poems* appeared, Pierce thought the cuts would help restore Carman's lustre. It is important to note that, for years afterwards, leading modernist critics assured Pierce that he had been right to abridge Carman's work. When he sent his Carman volume to Malcolm Ross before publication, Pierce described the "chief business" under consideration to be "what poems should be deleted or abridged."[166] Ross replied: "It is a good volume as it stands and I was delighted to get a look at it. Everyone has favorites – and principles of selection. There are changes I would make if I were editing the material but I make these suggestions without dogmatizing them." Ross did not object at all to the abridgments. To the contrary, he suggested several poems to omit and some to include. With very few exceptions, Pierce followed Ross's advice to the letter, failing only to include Carman's long poem "Behind the Arras," which Ross favoured.[167]

Twenty years later, Ross still supported Pierce's cuts. He told McClelland and Stewart editor John Newlove that "Pierce abridged rather freely – and on the whole, with reason."[168] Shortly thereafter, he explained why he had chosen to use Pierce's abridged Carman poems in *Poets of the Confederation*, a decision about which he had now become "increasingly uneasy": "I had fully agreed to the use of the shortened versions. In most of the larger poems, Carman lacks structural control and verses are often strung together like beads on a string. Pierce, one of Carman's warmest apostles, felt, as I did, that cutting was desirable in many cases. And I also felt that the shortened versions allowed us a greater range of tone than would otherwise be possible."[169]

The network of critical approval for cutting Carman was far wider, however, at the time *The Selected Poems of Bliss Carman* appeared. Influential reviewers of the Carman volume, whatever their allegiances, enthusiastically endorsed the cuts. In a December 1954 *Globe and Mail* review, headlined "Rare Critical Achievement," William Arthur Deacon stated that the poems were "unquestionably" Carman's best, "often abbreviated to avoid the ancient, friendly charge that 'Carman sings on and on.'" He praised the "newer and finer Carman [that] has been made to appear in these pages," one tailored for "this generation of readers," and added that Pierce now had "the satisfaction of knowing that he has created the poet who will live long into the times of readers yet unborn."[170] In a letter to Pierce, he assured him: "My real admiration could not be greater."[171]

Desmond Pacey's 1954 review was just as positive, assuring readers that Pierce had "done much to enhance our appreciation of Carman by judiciously reducing the bulk of his work to the dimensions of this small book, and by abridging some of the longer poems." According to Pacey, Pierce's skill at omitting lines like "the jaunty and slightly vulgar refrain" of "Spring Song" in fact "made us see it afresh and a very fine poem it becomes."[172] Pierce had even more impressive support. Northrop Frye's review of *The Selected Poems* also praised Pierce's editorial work, raising no objections to the abridgments. Frye declared himself "grateful to Dr. Pierce for confining himself to the memorable work, ignoring the pseudo-Carman, with his stentorian hymns to the Great Beyond like 'Lord of my heart's elation.'"[173]

With such applause from leading members of both the old and new generation of critics for his editor's knife, Pierce saw no need to restore Carman's full texts in the *Selected Poems* when McClelland and Stewart gave him an opportunity to do so in 1960 before a planned reprinting,[174] the same year Ross reprinted the abridged poems in his canonical *Poets of the Confederation*, a widely used student anthology for decades. Even poet Dorothy Livesay, in "Carman and His Editors," her sonnet on the controversy, acknowledged the temptation to cut Carman:

> I think my ghost would rise up in a rage
> If they scissored *me* – or cut away a word!
> And yet, I'm one of them! Have said, behind my breath,
> "Come off it, Bliss, how could you write that line?
> It spoils the whole."

But, she added in an apostrophe to Carman: "Yet why must We desire / you suited to our times? – pre-dated man? ... we have no right / to rip away a word, shatter a phrase."[175]

Livesay's conclusion was closer to that of a new critical generation. In 1972 John Robert Sorfleet attacked Ross's decision to present students with "mutilated poetry."[176] Ross himself, now "uneasy" about his decision, in March 1975 magnanimously asked Sorfleet to "restor[e] the broken bits and pieces of the Pierce."[177] In 1976 Sorfleet's edition of *The Poems of Bliss Carman* was published in McClelland and Stewart's New Canadian Library series (whose general editor was Malcolm Ross), thereby putting back in print the full text of what Laurel Boone has called Pierce's "gutted" Carman poems.[178]

Poet Wilson MacDonald once shrewdly observed that neither Carman's admirers nor his detractors served his reputation well: "The greatest friend of Bliss Carman is the critic who approach[es] his work sanely without either the bias of friendship or of enmity. That young group of radicals ... who disdain Carman almost to the point of contempt, and those narrow-gauge critics who say he is the only Canadian poet to rank with the masters are in one and the same class."[179] MacDonald was right. In the 1950s Pierce and key younger critics were in one and the same camp regarding editing Carman, and the entente was unfortunate indeed.

PIERCE'S drastic abridgment of the Carman poems, done with the approbation of younger critics, is a vivid example of the distortion of a poet's work that can result when an admiring senior editor and critic sets out to "save" a literary reputation while the editor's critical contemporaries, in company with iconoclastic younger critics, are all confident that generational changes in literary taste justify the trimming. As we have seen, Pierce fostered a new generation of Canadian critics, a fact hitherto largely unacknowledged. However, it must also be recognized that this changing of the guard was at times painful for Pierce and dislocating for the Canadian literary canon. And overall, as a senior Canadian publisher and editor, Pierce felt his own power waning.

In the years after the publication of *The Selected Poems of Bliss Carman*, Pierce, after nearly three and a half decades on the Canadian literary scene, increasingly felt that he was, as he put it, "near the exit."[180] By 1954, his long career at Ryerson had just six more years to run, and his life little longer. In the meantime, he faced other painful new challenges. His dedication for the volume of Carman poems was: "For Edith." No one who knew the Pierces wondered why.

"Near the Exit"

Lorne Pierce's Final Decade,
1950–1961

We [at Ryerson] dedicate ourselves to the proposition ... that ... there
is some valid answer, some clue ... to the political, social, economic
and religious problems of our time. We dedicate ourselves to publish
as many of that sort of book as we are shrewd or lucky enough to
find. We are confident that they will sell ... because there will be a
profound need for them."

Lorne Pierce, The House of Ryerson, *1954*[1]

My reason for haste is that I am near the exit. I must take it much
easier, for my angina at times cripples body and will.

Lorne Pierce to Carl Klinck, December 1959[2]

By March 1950, when she finally had surgery, Edith Pierce had long
suspected that something was seriously wrong. A year earlier, however, her physician assured her that the lump in her breast was simply
something to monitor.[3] Edith, never strong, had battled arthritis, cellu-
litis, depression, and other health problems during the 1940s. But, like
most women of her generation, she had been raised to put the needs
of others first. Unquestionably, she did so to the limits of her strength
and beyond. For her family and friends, she was a wonderful cook and
homemaker, an empathetic hostess, and above all a caring and loyal wife
and mother.

During the Second World War, Lorne had confided to his two children how much he depended on Edith's "boundless capacity for affection and forgiveness and good cheer."[4] For him, Edith was "brilliant in
the swift insight of her love and understanding ... her indomitable trust
in all that matters to the soul makes life livable."[5] Male friends teased

Pierce at his Queen Street editorial desk, with his Canadian literary pantheon arrayed behind him and one of Edith's pottery bowls in front of him, late 1940s. Courtesy of Beth Pierce Robinson

him about the extent of Edith's devotion, one of them whimsically envisioning him at the cottage "waited on hand and foot by your charming wife."[6]

At war's end, with her Red Cross volunteer work winding down, her children grown, and her husband as busy as ever, Edith cultivated new interests. She took pottery lessons in the fall and winter of 1945–46,[7] teaching her husband some things in the process. For example, the phrase "the hand of the potter bobbled" suddenly appeared in his correspondence as he tactfully pointed out weaknesses in manuscripts.[8] A 1948 photograph of Lorne at his Ryerson desk shows Edith's first signed piece, a bowl that she had presented to him in April 1946, in pride of place on his desk.[9]

Pierce continued to benefit from his wife's domestic talents. One of her many tea and garden parties at Campbell Crescent welcomed one hundred and fifty Queen's alumni. Then, one summer day in June 1949, a smiling Edith, in lilac-coloured lace and pearls, stood beside her morning-suited husband as she oversaw the ceremony and reception in the Pierce garden for Beth's wedding to University of Toronto Commerce graduate John D. ("Jack") Robinson. Beth became the first of the two Pierce children to wed within a year.[10]

But even with all her interests, Edith found the large empty house, coupled with Lorne's obsession with work, hard to bear. Her despondency was complicated by bereavement. In March 1949 her brother, Gordon Chown, and her aunt, Alice Chown, died within weeks of each other. (Edith's brother Edwin had died not long before.[11]) Edith's Aunt Alice had been over eighty but her passing was difficult nonetheless. Alice Chown had always taken a warm interest in Edith, whose mother had died when she was only five years old. These losses hit Edith hard, and she was frequently ill in 1948–49. As a result, from the late 1940s, Lorne tried to work at home on Wednesdays, dubbing the resulting spate of manuscript reading and letter writing in his study "Hash Wednesdays."

Then came Edith's operation on 17 March 1950 – St Patrick's Day. Edith was wheeled into the operating room with a sprig of shamrocks tucked between her toes for luck.[12] A radical mastectomy was followed by periods of drug and radiation therapy over the next four years. Immediately after surgery, Edith's arm was affected and she was very depressed, though Lorne assured friends and family that she was "brave as a lion."[13] Brave Edith Pierce surely was. At the time of the operation, she was comforted by the fact that she, usually the nurturer, was now the focus of her family's attention. Edith confided to Blanche Hume: "I am sorry to be putting my family through all this but I am lapping up their love and attention like a … pussy-cat."[14]

It is difficult today to comprehend the stigma, shame, secrecy, and fear that usually followed a cancer diagnosis in the mid-twentieth century. Only a very few Pierce intimates knew the nature of Edith's illness. Even in her last days, Lorne and Edith never discussed the fact that she was dying, a silence that added to the anguish. At least Edith, unlike many cancer patients of the day (including Harriet Pierce ten years earlier), knew her diagnosis, and discussed treatments with her specialist, Dr Valentine Stock.[15]

For his part, Lorne, deeply distressed by Edith's illness, confided to a former secretary that he kept "hoping that everything will be all right." He added: "It must have been the gods who planted hope in the human heart, otherwise we would never have survived."[16] Edith found some of the challenges and losses exacted by her illness painful. There were "bitter tears" in December 1950 when she was not well enough to give the Pierce's annual holiday party. For Lorne, too, the cancellation felt like "the end of an era."[17]

During Edith's long illness, the Pierces struggled to find satisfactory domestic and nursing help. They were thankful for the assistance of George Coppin, their long-time gardener and handyman. For the first time, Lorne made more effort to take the holidays that both had needed for so long. In the winters of 1952 and 1953, the Pierces travelled to Florida for month-long stays. The couple also snatched the occasional long weekend away, for example, at Niagara Falls one Easter.[18] Their last weekend respite was at the Guild Inn on the Scarborough Bluffs in the early fall of 1953, a few weeks before Edith became bedridden.

Meanwhile, Pierce himself found the writer's cramp that had plagued him since the early 1940s worsening. He tried to teach himself to write with his left hand, ultimately producing the crabbed script he was forced to resort to for the rest of his life when no typewriter was handy.

On top of everything else, life at the Ryerson offices was highly stressful for Pierce in the years around Edith's cancer diagnosis in 1950. In the post-war period, the effects of rapid inflation, especially rising production costs, adversely affected the book trade, which was not to enjoy sustained good times until after 1955.[19] So it went at Ryerson.

A PRINTERS' STRIKE in late 1947 played havoc with Pierce's book lists, and the eventual settlement contributed to sharply higher manufacturing costs.[20] That fall, Pierce estimated that book publication costs would rise by a "shocking" 25 per cent. He added: "I don't see how we are going to charge $4.00 for novels and $1.50 for school readers and even at that the profit is practically nil."[21] Worse yet, book sales slumped in the late 1940s and early 1950s. Ryerson, like other Canadian publishers, was caught in a nasty squeeze between rising costs and falling sales.

The House's 1947/48 year-end report was not rosy. Pierce's Retail Department turned a small profit of about $4,000, but at the cost of a "drastic" cutback in his planned publication list.[22] Profits in the Educational Department were almost nil ($155.83), a drop of over $5,000. The Film Department lost over $2,600, after showing profits of over $3,000 the year before.[23] These troubles would persist into the 1950s. Ironically, after 1948, precise profit-and-loss figures for the House departments, including Pierce's, were not included in the published annual reports by the book steward to the Board of Publication – in part a strategy (of which Pierce disapproved) to keep such information from the unions.[24]

Whatever the reasons, the foggy financial reporting bespoke the poor administrative state of the House, a feature of the way it was run for much of its history. In the late 1940s, the printing plant employed some

200 people and the various House departments some 150 people – only a score of them in Pierce's area, all part of a structure that was not being efficiently managed at the top.[25] Moreover, decisions about new printing-equipment expenditures were being made by the book steward and his plant managers. In the mid-1950s, the House purchased a hugely expensive letterpress printing press just at the time the industry was shifting to the more economical offset machines.[26] In the early 1960s, management auditors would pinpoint this major capital commitment as a prime factor in fatally undermining the finances of the House. Pierce's textbook sales were helping to prop up an increasingly shaky edifice. But ominously, even the major textbook lines, especially the Ryerson-Macmillan reader series, were ceasing to be such a cash cow.

The elementary and high school readers ("the mainstay of our publishing programme" Pierce called them in his 1954 report to the Board of Publication[27]) were an ongoing concern because of changing times and an aging, chronically ill editor-in-chief. Pierce was increasingly drained by the gruelling travel and revision deadlines required to update the readers in the late 1940s and the late 1950s. Worse yet, textbook sales, while still substantial (over $400,000 in the 1951–52 fiscal year, for example, ranking Ryerson fifth of fifteen educational publishers in Canada[28]), were falling. The reasons for the decline were several: provinces and boards were increasingly demanding customized material in their texts – a stance that meant fewer economies of scale at the printing plant. The province of Alberta, for instance, demanded (and got) revisions to material in one reader text which touched upon the province's developing oil and gas industry. A member of Alberta's social studies committee had complained in 1947 that one of the readers was "too socialistic" and lacked "a chapter on Christian Democracy."[29]

Even more seriously for sales volume, departments and boards of education across Canada increasingly favoured a list of recommended texts in subject areas like literature, thus offering teachers choices rather than one single approved text. This trend meant that a publisher's list of offerings had to be broader; sales and marketing initiatives were even more challenging – and profits lower. Furthermore, with the post-war boom in immigration, the population of Canada was becoming more multicultural. Overall, then, the concept of one single dominant elementary or high school reader series – series that under Pierce's editing had been infused with nationalist ideology – was falling out of favour.

Such changes worried Pierce on two counts – the first economic and the second cultural. First, textbook profits declined, with serious consequences for the House's overall financial position. More important, given such educational and societal changes, a troubling question arose in the mind of a cultural nationalist like Pierce. What would inculcate Canadian nationalism in the minds of the young after the disappearance of a best-selling, unitary set of readers for elementary and high school children? In *A Canadian Nation*, his last meditation on Canadian nationhood and culture, Pierce pointed to the rapidly increasing ethnic diversity of Canadian society and the influence of new media like radio and television. What (and who), he asked pointedly, would henceforth "offer leadership to our fast-growing polyglot population – this living mosaic with colours from the ends of the earth"?[30]

Pierce remained convinced that "the arts and letters of a country are the chief Alma Mater of the national spirit, and they should be fostered by every intelligent means."[31] But, in company with many other intellectuals of the post-war period, such as philosopher George Grant and historians Harold Innis, Arthur Lower, and Hilda Neatby, whose critique of the Canadian educational system, *So Little for the Mind* (1953), was a national best-seller,[32] Pierce was troubled by what he saw as a popular indifference to ideas as well as by uncertainty about just exactly what would now replace religious forces as ethical and cultural glue in an increasingly secular nation.

Beginning in the late 1940s, another shadow fell across Pierce's book list. Ryerson was not immune to the anti-communist hysteria precipitated by a Canadian variant of McCarthyism. In October 1947 Pierce published *Men in Sheepskin Coats: A Study in Assimilation*, a history of Ukrainian immigration to Canada by Vera Lysenko. Lysenko, an University of Manitoba MA graduate who had worked as a high school teacher and journalist, had in many ways written the type of book that Pierce, as a Canadian nationalist, loved to publish. The book told the story of Ukrainian Canadian settlement and its roots in the motherland. It emphasized such topics as culture (including literature, folklore, and religion), national heroes, patterns of settlement, and the struggle for ethnic acceptance by Ukrainian Canadians as they integrated into and contributed to, as Lysenko put it, "the life of the entire Canadian nation."[33] The epigraph to Lysenko's book, drawn from another Ryerson author, Laura Goodman Salverson, expressed an idea dear to Pierce's heart – that "spiritual values ... are the true measure of national greatness."[34] He was undoubtedly delighted with Lysenko's thesis – so close to his own ideals in publications like *A Canadian People* – that Ukrainians and other immigrant groups had become, as Lysenko put it, not "neat little Anglo-Saxons with white collars and blue serge suits ... [but] rather, [part of] the gradual blending of varied ethnic groups into a new, totally different synthesis of all [Canadians]."[35]

Others, however, were outraged by *Men in Sheepskin Coats*, with ugly consequences. By 1947, the Cold War had taken hold. In North America, chill winds were blowing against those who were construed as in any way sympathetic to communism. The defection of Russian embassy employee Igor Gouzenko in Ottawa in the fall of 1945 precipitated the creation of the federal Kellock–Taschereau Royal Commission, active in 1946–47, whose hearings led to criminal charges against a score of individuals, charges centred around alleged Soviet espionage activity in Canada and elsewhere. The net was cast wide, and some innocent people's lives were ruined, despite acquittals in the courts. It became clear that Canada was not immune to the sort of anti-communist witch-hunting soon to surround the Senator Joseph McCarthy hearings in the United States Senate.

One leader of the anti-communist crusade in Canada was McMaster English professor (and from 1948 Acadia University president) Watson Kirkconnell.[36] In 1944 Kirkconnell had published *Seven Pillars of Freedom*, a vehement exposé of communism in Canada, which he presented as a greater threat than Nazism. Kirkconnell was associated with a stridently anti-communist organization, the Freedom Association of Canada (at one point, he even condemned fluoridation of water as a communist plot).[37] In the late 1940s, he was denouncing universities like Queen's and McGill as "hotbeds of Communism."[38]

The multilingual Kirkconnell, active in the Canadian Authors Association, was also known for his literary translations, including his translations of non-English and non-French poets, some of them Ukrainian Canadians. During the Second World War, he had actively promoted Ukrainian Canadian patriotism vis-à-vis the war effort in two booklets on the topic.[39] Not surprisingly, by the time Ryerson published *Men in Sheepskin Coats* in the fall of 1947, Kirkconnell had become closely allied with prominent Ukrainian Canadian anti-communists. Communism was a divisive topic in that ethnic community, given that the Ukraine had been forcibly absorbed into the Soviet Union in 1922.

In the highly charged Cold War climate, Lysenko's book was vulnerable to attack from anti-communists, given that she did not roundly condemn Soviet control of the Ukraine. Neither did she detail the left-wing affiliations, past and present, of some of the Ukrainian Canadian community organizations she discussed. She did acknowledge in passing a marked "division of thought" about the Soviet Ukraine among different Ukrainian Canadian groups.[40] In an apparent attempt to be even-handed (especially since much of her book was actually written while Russia was a wartime ally of Canada), Lysenko, while she conceded that many Ukrainian nationalists condemned Soviet hegemony, also referred to improvement in rates of education and industry in the Soviet Ukraine.

However, Lysenko failed to mention the sufferings attendant on collectivization and famine that accompanied such advances, an unforgivable omission for cold warriors like Kirkconnell. Instead, she emphasized that young Ukrainian Canadians were more interested in Canada than in politics in the ancestral homeland: "It would be difficult to persuade a young farmer whose chief interests are the purchase of a new tractor and the establishment of an agricultural club that he should don baggy red velvet trousers and hasten to the Ukraine to save it from something or other."[41] Lysenko also pointedly assured her Canadian readers that in Canada *the politic interests of the Ukrainian are not different from those of any other ethnic group.*"[42] Such statements made Kirkconnell and his allies in the Ukrainian Canadian community "see Red."

In January 1948 Kirkconnell wrote Pierce a letter which made it clear that he judged Lysenko's book deplorably "soft on Communism." Threatening to publish a damning review of the book, he informed Pierce that the Ukrainian Labour-Farmer Temple Association (ULFTA), one of the organizations whose community activities Lysenko had praised, was in reality "the solid core of the Communist Party of Canada." Insultingly, Kirkconnell added that the Ryerson reader who had approved Lysenko's manuscript must be either "a dupe" ignorant of Ukrainian affairs or "you had better ask him for his Party card." (Pierce himself was probably the chief reader for Lysenko's manuscript.) He also charged that Lysenko had taught at a "Communist" labour college and had at one time boarded with the editor of an "Italian Communist paper." In short, insisted Kirkconnell, "the Ryerson Press is carrying on propaganda ... for the Communist Party of Canada."[43]

Kirkconnell's accusations were echoed in three other letters to Pierce from members of the Ukrainian Canadian community: a Toronto lawyer (who mentioned an unfavourable newspaper review), Winnipeg notary M.I. Mandryka, and a leader of the Ukrainian Canadian Veterans' Association. Mandryka told Pierce that the book's audience could only be "Communists, fellow travellers and deceived people," while the other two correspondents complained of the book's "bias" and "communist propaganda" respectively.[44] After consulting Lysenko, Pierce stoutly defended his author, reminding Kirkconnell that there had been a number of "cordial" reviews of the book "by people whose judgements we value." Pierce added: "We are convinced of [Lysenko's] honesty in all this. She is not a Communist, she says, and we believe her. We are also convinced that she has done her best to be objective and as her publishers we are bound to protect her name as well as our own."[45] Kirkconnell then bombarded Pierce with a sheaf of supposedly incriminating photostats and a revised draft of his review, all designed to show that Lysenko had "throw[n] dust in the eyes of the Ryerson Press." He later suggested that Pierce consult the Mounties about the "Red Ukrainians" with whom he claimed that Lysenko was allied.[46]

Pierce turned to *Globe and Mail* book columnist William Arthur Deacon, in 1948 national president of the Canadian Authors Association. To his credit, Deacon, having earlier told Frank Flemington that Kirkconnell was a "crackpot" on the subject of the alleged communist menace, agreed that Lysenko should be defended. He wrote Pierce stoutly:

> We are apparently quite rapidly reaching the point where people will be condemned on suspicion and I think it highly desirable that people like you and I should not lend ourselves in any way to such practices.
>   ... [Lysenko] is exactly the type to have progressive ideas of a general nature, but I believe her statement that she is not a member of the communist party, and for the sake of sanity in Canada, I refuse to treat her as guilty because a fanatic has accused her on the basis of trivialities in her book.[47]

Deacon had earlier told Pierce that, in talking to Lysenko before the book's publication, he had found her sentiments toward Cold War politics to be a "plague on both your houses" and that there was "nothing ... dangerous" in her book.[48]

Accordingly, Pierce held firm (although he annoyed Lysenko by sending Kirkconnell a copy of her rebuttal of his accusations). In Lysenko's defence, he enlisted John Murray Gibbon, prominent Canadian littérateur and senior Montreal railway executive. Gibbon promptly reviewed the book in the *Canadian Historical Review*, praising it as "a real contribution to our understanding of Ukrainian Canadians."[49] Pierce also told

Kirkconnell that, if the latter published his own review, he wanted the opportunity to include Lysenko's rebuttal. By mid-March, in response to the flood of photostats from Kirkconnell, Pierce threatened him with legal action if he accused Lysenko or Ryerson Press of communist sympathies in print.

Outraged, Kirkconnell informed Pierce (paradoxically, given his own bellicose attitude) that he was "shocked at your use of threats to try to prevent the exposure of traitors pledged to the destruction of our national life."[50] A few months later, he did denounce the book publicly – in a review published in *Opinion*, the English-language monthly magazine of the Ukrainian Canadian Veterans' Association.[51] But Pierce did not withdraw the book, or forsake Lysenko. (It must have been a wry moment for him when the Ryerson Fiction Award winner for 1950 was the popular *Blaze of Noon*, a novel dealing with anti-communist controversy.[52])

Pierce showed real courage in his support of Lysenko. Other Canadians who were similarly accused – in the press and/or in the courts – of communist sympathies were shunned by their associates. For example, federal government economist Agatha Chapman lost her job, her return to work barred even after espionage charges against her were thrown out of court in 1946.[53] By contrast, Pierce went on to publish two novels by Lysenko: *Yellow Boots* (1954), the coming-of-age story of a young Ukrainian Canadian girl, and *Westerly Wild* (1956), an account of a young Manitoba teacher and her immigrant pupils in the Saskatchewan dust bowl during the Depression. Moreover, Pierce courageously published *Yellow Boots* in the face of continuing attacks on Lysenko's history of Ukrainian Canadians. In 1953, the year before the novel was published, a book on the history of the Ukrainians in Manitoba attacked *Men in Sheepskin Coats*, labelling Lysenko one of a "Ukrainian pro-Communist group."[54] Its author claimed that Kirkconnell's review in *Opinion* had "exposed the subtle communist propaganda of Vera Lysenko," falsely adding that the accusation "was never denied by her."[55] These charges dogged Lysenko for decades, gaining credibility by their very longevity. In 1968 M.I. Mandryka, who had written Pierce so long ago to denounce *Men in Sheepskin Coats*, published a history of Ukrainian literature in Canada which renewed the smear: "The obvious pro-communist tendencies deprive this book of objectivity. This was exposed, as a subtle communist propaganda, by Watson Kirkconnell in his lengthy review of Lysenko's book in *Opinion* ... and by Paul Yuzyk in his book *The Ukrainians in Manitoba*."[56] Thanks to this chain of accusation, an article on the prairie immigrant novel published in an academic journal in the 1980s recorded that Kirkconnell had "somewhat harshly" charged Lysenko with "subtle communist propaganda," citing Mandryka as one supporting source.[57] As far as Lysenko was concerned, Pierce may have fended off the "Red-smear" snake but he could not kill it in an era of anti-communist hysteria.

In the late 1950s Dorothy Livesay, when Desmond Pacey was compiling her *Selected Poems* (1957) for Ryerson, did not want him to mention that she had been a Communist Party member for a time in the 1930s. When Pierce was queried by Pacey in late 1956 on the matter, however, he replied that to "evade the matter seriously cripples your interpretation of much of [Livesay's] early work. Certainly you are bound to imply that she took for a long time an extreme left social position."[58] Thus, while resistant to "Red smears," Pierce did not favour cover-up of an author's actual affiliations. Yet he did not shirk from including left-of-centre writers on the Ryerson list, as his publication of the Livesay title, and other books by her during the 1950s, demonstrates.[59] His values were continuing to shape the Ryerson list in both positive and negative ways, a type of publisher's influence that book historian Daniel O'Leary has analyzed in respect to Pierce. In writing of some of his editorial decisions, O'Leary has rightly observed that it is often difficult to distinguish between simple editorial preferences and "covert editorial suppression" of "uncongenial works" in assessing Pierce's decisions.[60] But, in any case, Pierce's editorial power is indisputable, as his stable of authors knew first-hand.

Issues of gender as well as political issues continued to be in play in Pierce's editorship. For example, Livesay also asked that Pacey not analyze her as a "woman poet," an understandable request in view of the habitually gender-biased discussion of female poets like Pickthall and Audrey Alexandra Brown in Canadian literary criticism of the time, a bias of which Livesay was well aware. (Another leading Canadian woman writer, Margaret Laurence, recalled impatiently that at the beginning of her career: "Writing by women ... was generally regarded by critics and reviewers in this country with at best an amused tolerance, at worst a dismissive shrug."[61]) Pierce was less progressive on matters of gender than of political affiliation. He rejected Livesay's wish to be treated without gender stereotyping as "fantastic," commenting to Pacey that "some of her best poems give her away as a woman." His choice of verb ("give her away") shows that a hierarchical concept of gender difference continued to pervade his thinking.[62]

This editorial perspective was evident in the published edition of Livesay's poetry. Pacey's introduction discussed Livesay's "revolutionary dogmatism" in the 1930s and its manifestation in poems like "Day and Night." But he also judged her career in terms of gender stereotypes. The regaining of her "interest in personal emotions and in natural description" after the Second World War was attributed to the influence of "her marriage and domestic responsibilities," as well as the fact that she was "too honest and forthright a person to attempt to follow the sinuous twistings of the party line during the forties."[63] Here Pierce had let Pacey have his way in assessing Livesay, once the question of how to treat political affiliation was resolved.

Whatever the outcome, however, Pierce's support for authors of worthwhile manuscripts, irrespective of their political alliances, was not limited to Lysenko or Livesay, or to the 1950s. Undeniably, Pierce was far more liberal politically than sexually in his views of what he considered suitable for the Ryerson lists, a duality of thinking perhaps not surprising in a Methodist scion of the social gospel. In other words, he may have been prudish – insisting, as he once quipped, that Ryerson fiction be "laundered and fumigated"[64] – but he was not politically repressive as editor.

Other publishers grappled with similar ideological issues. Hugh Eayrs was uneasy about the "redness" of Irene Baird's Depression novel *Waste Heritage* (1939), with Macmillan of Canada requiring some manuscript changes in light of the Defence of Canada Act.[65] Pierce was less cautious. In 1943 he had told his daughter that he fully intended to publish books on the economic and national potential of the north by Raymond Davies "in spite of the fact that he belongs to the national council of the Communist Party, the new Labour Progressive Party ... when a man comes along with the facts I try to give him a chance." Pierce was as good as his word. He also published Davies's second Ryerson book in 1947, the same year as Lysenko's *Men in Sheepskin Coats*, despite the chill that had set in against those with communist affiliations.[66]

Earlier, in the 1930s, Pierce had "a whale of a row" with the book steward of the day, Donald Solandt, when the latter vetoed on ideological grounds Pierce's decision to publish the memoirs of radical clergyman and Co-operative Commonwealth Federation (CCF) founder

J.S. Woodsworth.[67] In such championing of Woodsworth, Lysenko, and others, Pierce probably recalled his own early ministerial career, when he was criticized as too "radical" for his social gospel leanings and interest in Russia. Whatever the reason, he was certainly not in sympathy with Cold War censorship, and showed some courage in resisting it. In 1949, when Dorothy Livesay worried about public criticism of her new Ryerson publication concerning the wartime internment of Japanese Canadians, given her 1930s communist affiliations, Pierce replied steadfastly: "You must know by this time that I do not go around taking a poll of opinion and that if there is any degradation of opinion in Canada I have never contributed to it in that way [i.e., by suppressing manuscripts]. We have allowed our authors to say what they think."[68]

WITHOUT DOUBT, as a publisher in the 1950s, Lorne Pierce needed the courage of his convictions – as well as persistence and inventiveness. His annual reports for the decade highlight both Ryerson's sales difficulties and his ingenuity in trying to surmount them. In much of his writing, the aging editor's distaste for the Zeitgeist is clear. In the conclusion to his spring 1952 editor's report, he wrote: "In a time of bewilderment and violence and vulgarity, we shall more than ever dedicate ourselves to integrity, to decency, to justice, to the inner law and the higher freedom, without which life is impossible."[69]

In addition, Pierce chafed more than ever at the House requirement that Ryerson books be manufactured there, a policy that ruled out savings on costs through competitive bidding. No other major publishing house printed its own books, leaving his competitors more leeway. As a result, Pierce was obliged to refuse or to shorten some manuscripts because he had no hope of publishing them at a viable price.

Overall, Pierce was increasingly impatient with what he saw as short-sighted management practices in the printing plant and agency department of the House, both beyond his control. He was convinced that, as far as agency sales were concerned, the House tended to "cherry pick" best-sellers from foreign imprints for which the House had agency rights, neglecting less tempting fruit on the agency lists. He believed that this practice put lucrative agency affiliations at risk through lack of real initiative. As Pierce put it acidly, the House thereby "shot the buffalo for the tongue."[70] He also fumed privately (as he had for decades) about the largely mediocre House sales force, joking bitterly to his children that the House should at least employ salesmen who "know the alphabet." Moreover, while Pierce liked Elsinore Haultain, the House's long-time advertising manager, he found her marketing ideas "thin as a gnat's ankle."

Was Pierce passing the buck for Ryerson's editorial defects in criticizing the sales and marketing elements of the House? Probably not. Persistent evidence of sloppy or unimaginative House practices found in the archival record as well as the conclusions of a business study of the House by management consultants shortly after Pierce's retirement reinforce his criticisms.

After the Second World War, in response to the challenges of the Baby Boom era, Pierce himself sought to address new interests and new markets. He was conscious of the need to adapt to changes in demographics and in mass culture taking place in the 1950s, even though he found many of them regrettable. As Randall Speller has observed, in 1949 Pierce hired a talented in-house art director, Arthur Steven, realizing that every Ryerson book had to look better to do well in such a competitive marketplace in the increasingly visual age of television and the movies.[71] Yet he also held fast to his lofty vision of what Ryerson ought to publish on its Canadian list. He refused to publish sensational novels or light fiction (for example, the murder mysteries he himself enjoyed), works from other publishers which he described as "shockers to keep the bailiff away."[72] Ryerson Press, like other Canadian publishers, largely failed to get into the "quality paperback" trade and emulate the example of England's Penguin paperbacks and other foreign initiatives until the mid-1960s.[73] Pierce's sense of the elite mission of publishing was unfortunately a factor in Ryerson's increasing lack of competitiveness.

However, Pierce sought to satisfy some burgeoning new consumer interests. His response to the post-war growth of mass tourism, especially automobile tourism, is a case in point. He sought out manuscripts in this area, encouraging, for instance, Brockville amateur historian and writer Ted Curry to produce a "lively Baedeker" which would appeal to "countless tourists" by recounting the history of the St Lawrence River. Here he had in mind public interest in the region aroused by the new St Lawrence Seaway project.[74] Curry's long-delayed manuscript ultimately failed to please, but many others filled the bill. As a result, in the 1950s, Ryerson published numerous titles aimed at the emerging market for Canada-wide travel and tourism, such as Evelyn Purvis Earle's *Leeds the Lovely* (1951) about the lore of historic eastern Ontario, including the scenic Thousand Islands, Katherine Hale's *Historic Houses of Canada*

Pierce and Ryerson author Evelyn Richardson at a prize
ceremony for her novel *Desired Haven*, Halifax, 1954. Courtesy
of Beth Pierce Robinson

(1952), and Will Bird's successful *This Is Nova Scotia* (1950). The latter
was part of a Ryerson series profiling the provinces. In another initiative,
spurred by the excitement over Princess Elizabeth's royal tour of Canada
in 1951, Ryerson brought out *The Royal Tour in Canada, 1951*, a book of
photographs. That book sold well (as did a couple of hockey titles), but a
Ryerson book on Queen Elizabeth II's 1959 visit was a flop.

The book lists of the 1950s had other bright spots. Maritime author
Evelyn Richardson – whose memoir about lighthouse keeping on
a remote Nova Scotia island, *We Keep a Light* (1945), had been such a

success for Ryerson that it went into a fifth edition in 1953, and was also sold to a British publisher – wrote another best-seller with her historical novel of the Atlantic Coast, *Desired Haven* (1953), an American Book of the Month Club selection and a Governor General's Award winner. Nevertheless, a photograph of Lorne Pierce with Richardson at the award ceremony in 1954 hints at his increasing anachronism. The beaming Richardson, some two decades Pierce's junior, is dressed in the height of 1950s fashion, her garb bright and geometrical. Beside her, Pierce, despite his smile, looks weary – sombre in his elegant bespoke suit, his chiselled visage swollen by the side-effects of ACTH, a cortisone he now took to treat his lupus.

Furthermore, given Pierce's high-minded intellectual and nationalistic publishing ideals, there was, on one level, an element of bathos. Pierce was now at pains to assure his Board of Publication, as in his 1952 report, that, to beef up sales, he had "added two books of the it-happened-to-me type, three books of humour, a book on Canadian stamps, and a book on games and parties" to the Ryerson list.[75] As Roy MacSkimming has pointed out in his history of twentieth-century Canadian book publishing, such offerings constitute standard fare for Canadian publishers, whose firms always struggle with the exigencies of the size and spread of the Canadian book market.[76] Pierce himself made the point about the need for "bread and butter lines of some kind," without which "a publishing house dedicated solely to the high and dry would soon wither away."[77] But the incongruity remains.

PIERCE'S sombre demeanour in many photographs from this decade is not surprising in another respect. Both love and heartache lay behind the scenes. After Edith Pierce's 1950 mastectomy, her cancer metastasized by fits and starts – even as she and Lorne welcomed grandchildren. But grandchildren, like children, are, in Shakespeare's phrase, "hostages to fortune." Lorne Clark Pierce, one of their first grandsons, born on 21 May 1951, died unexpectedly of Sudden Infant Death Syndrome on 10 September that year.

The baby's parents, Bruce and Anne Pierce, were devastated at the loss, as were Lorne and Edith. Blanche Hume remembered seeing Edith Pierce's face "crumple with emotion" as she left St George's United Church after the "almost unbearably sad and beautiful" memorial service for the infant.[78] Lorne, who had already dreamed that his infant namesake would carry on his tradition of service and idealism, mused after visits to the baby's grave that December: "I have found the loss of my namesake hard to bear. It must be selfish of me. I had hoped that he might be the one who would carry on. It still seems a needless waste. Now and then I go alone to Mount Pleasant. The other week before freeze-up I took a small evergreen to mark his place, a tiny one, for someday there will be a stone. I helped plant it and I felt better. I don't think I am morbid. I have great reverence for life, and I dread seeing it wasted. However, he rests from his little labours, and has his tree too."[79]

In the face of this blow, the surviving Pierce and Robinson grandchildren seemed all the more precious. One family maid remembers how, about this time, Pierce would stand for hours in the garden at Campbell Crescent with the hose, absorbed in watering the walnut trees in order to enable his grandchildren to pick, crack, and eat the nuts, as he had enjoyed doing in his own Delta childhood.[80]

One artwork commissioned by Lorne Pierce softened the sorrow of little Lorne's funeral service. At St George's, the Pierce family was seated near a magnificent stained glass window commissioned in Edith's honour the year before.[81] The design by Frederick Ramsdale featured Canadian wildflowers and foliage – trilliums, roses, fleur-de-lys, oak and maple leaves – plants chosen to echo the Canadian landscape and Canada's national emblems. The imagery also evoked the beauty of Edith and Lorne's garden at Campbell Crescent, itself still a "blessed healing island of peace," to use Pierce's phrase.[82] The face of the Madonna in the window – the theme of which was "Dedicated Motherhood, Consecrated Childhood" – was modelled on that of Edith's mother. The window, dedicated on 10 September 1950 – some six months after Edith's surgery, and just before her birthday and the christening ceremony for their first grandchild, Beth and Jack Robinson's son Brian – concealed a private tribute in Latin from Lorne to Edith, his "dearest wife." It was hidden away in the design, its location known only to them.

Glass was the ideal medium through which to honour Edith Pierce. In her last years, she collected early Canadian glass, a passion intensified by an August 1953 visit the Pierces made to the site of an early Canadian glass factory at Mallorytown.[83] Edith collected antique Canadian glass knowledgeably, latterly with the assistance of Gerald Stevens, whose archeological dig uncovered the nineteenth-century Mallorytown factory. As her health declined, the collection became her "solace and anodyne."[84] Encouraged by eastern Ontario historian Evelyn Purvis Earle,[85] Edith wrote a booklet, *Canadian Glass: A Footnote to History* (1954), 150 copies of which were printed privately just before her death.[86]

Like glass, life is fragile. By October 1953, Edith was confined to bed. That month, when Lorne received a Coronation medal to honour his publishing work, he brought it home and pinned it on his wife. He wrote to one confidante: "[Edith] deserves a medal more than I do."[87] Did either recall the first awarding of the Royal Society's Lorne Pierce Medal so long ago – a medal that had caused Edith such distress over Lorne's clandestine philanthropy?

By Christmas 1953, Edith was dying. Lorne's pocket diary notation on New Year's Day 1954 was stark: "Edith in great distress. All is change."[88] He had for several months employed both a day and a night nurse in order to care for Edith at home. The book steward, to his credit, asked if Pierce would like a raise, knowing how his medical expenses were mounting in the era before government health insurance. Lorne cashed in insurance policies to help pay for Edith's medical care – unhesitatingly done, but also a financial anxiety.[89]

The melancholy holiday weeks of 1953–54 were, for the first time, unmarked at Campbell Crescent by a Christmas tree or by the Pierces's annual greeting cards, commissioned every year from artist Thoreau MacDonald. Instead, the new year heralded what Pierce later remembered as "the long sad Lenten season [of 1954], that [Edith and I] both knew would be our last together, but that neither dared speak about, the thought being too terrible even to hint."[90] Edith, on heavy pain medication during the last five months of her life, increasingly seemed to Lorne sequestered in a "private and terrible ordeal of her own." He described himself as "hover[ing], a waving reed on the perimeter."[91] Marvelling at his wife's courage, he wrote not long before her death: "She has slipped much. She takes no food. Only sips of water and coffee and fruit juice. There has been a great change. It will not be long now. But her mind is unclouded, she is in command of herself. Quietly asks for the [morphine] hypo. In the most self-possessed way told Beth how she wished to be dressed [for burial]."[92]

Lorne himself was not just distressed: he was also distracted by a new project. Just as Edith entered the final months of illness, he felt obliged to take on the writing of *The House of Ryerson* (1954), a history to mark the firm's 125th anniversary. The fifty-two-page book is a rather lifeless chronology of editors and book stewards, drawing heavily on *The Chronicle of a Century*, Pierce's 1929 centenary House history. One scholar has remarked on the disappointing nature of the work.[93] However, its lacklustre nature is not surprising, given its genesis just before the book's publication in September 1954. Pierce recalled: "The history I wrote with my left hand, sitting hunched like a Methody at prayer in a church, in my deep chair in the living-room, and between visits every few minutes to my [dying] one-and-only in the corner room. It was a dreadful ordeal, and I wonder if something of it dripped through. I can't bear to read it again. It was for the Brethren, the commissioners to General Council and others of my masters." He added curtly: "It is not the history of the House that I should like to see done, and that I shall not do, for I am through with that theme."[94]

Pierce did not even like to have the book mentioned. Only the conclusion is memorable, synthesizing as it does not only his cultural and patriotic ideals for the Press but also his own determination to continue at its helm in spite of Edith's impending death. The book concludes by evoking *Pilgrim's Progress*:

[John] Bunyan's hero stands before us in rags. He stands reading a book, and as he reads he strikes his breast and cries: "What must I do?" We [at Ryerson] dedicate ourselves to the proposition that there is some valid answer; that through our multiplying publications, year in and year out, there is some answer, some clue or hint, to the political, social, economic and religious problems of our time. We dedicate ourselves to publish as many of that sort of book as we are shrewd or lucky enough to find ... They will sell because there will be a great sense of urgency about them, and because there will be a profound need for them.[95]

Pierce commented elsewhere of the writing of the history that at the time he felt he was "often failing in the writing, and often failing as watcher and nurse."[96]

People often die as they live and the Pierce household was no exception. As Edith lay in semi-coma, Lorne received news of yet another professional honour, the fruit of his devotion to French-English entente: "On the 13th of April, just before Edith went, the University of Montreal ... offered me the doctorate in letters. I was able to tell Edith, although she was very low, and getting further and further removed. But she understood, drew me down to her, and said: 'This rounds out our lives!' It was the last thing she said to me. I like to think that our lives *were* rounded out in a way."[97]

Ten days later, on 23 April, at 4:04 a.m., Edith Chown Pierce died at home, in her sixty-fourth year, with her family around her and her garden just beginning to welcome spring.[98] At her burial, following the funeral in St George's United Church beneath the radiance of her stained-glass window, Beth gently placed a nosegay of wildflowers from her mother's garden on the casket as it was lowered into the grave.

Edith, characteristically, did not die without offering words of comfort. In her bedside table, she left a farewell. Her letter reminded her family of the words of an anthem: "The souls of the righteous are in the hand of God." She added: "The days, and often the nights, have been long. But I have a wonderful sensation of God bearing us both up – and I have fallen asleep."[99] Sleep and comfort would long evade her bereaved husband. Nevertheless, in widowerhood, Lorne resolutely adopted as his mantra a phrase that Blanche Hume had cited in her letter of condolence – "shaken, but not overcome."[100] Three days after Edith's burial, he reluctantly gave the gist of *The House of Ryerson* in a speech to the annual dinner of the Board of Publication, feeling "there was no way out" of doing it.[101]

Now, after thirty-eight years of marriage, Lorne Pierce was alone. In the words of poet Emily Dickinson, he irrevocably faced in bereavement an "awful leisure / [his] faith to regulate." He never stopped grieving for his wife, often wistfully referring to "the lovely old days when I had a home."[102] The refrain throughout his private papers is "Lonely" or "How I miss my Edith." For comfort, he often invoked a scriptural couplet: "Fear not the night, though the hours be long – / The Day, O Heart, was glad!"[103]

Pierce's family, especially Beth, did what they could amid their busy lives to provide companionship. Like many of the newly bereaved, he was a little taken aback to find that the flood of attention from friends and acquaintances slowed dramatically within weeks of bereavement. He wrote ruefully the June after Edith's death – sitting solitary in his large York Mills property – that, except for family, there had been "not eight people to call in over eight weeks."[104]

Pierce also stopped going to church, not only because he could not hear the service, but also because he did not welcome the marital designs of several women in the congregation! He had vowed not to remarry, his resolve fortified by what he saw as Sir Charles G.D. Roberts's undignified late-life marriage as well as by a hasty, disastrous remarriage contracted by a friend. The summer after Edith's death, he booked solitary passage on a Saguenay River cruise. The trip that comforted him most, however, was a brief visit to Kingston, a city redolent with courtship memories from his Queen's undergraduate days. On 3 August, his sixty-fourth birthday, his first in over forty years without Edith, he wrote to his sister: "On Sunday, [I] walked every haunt I knew in the old [Queen's] days, even Aberdeen Street where we [wed] ... In the evening I went to Sydenham [Street United Church] and enjoyed the memories. The minister was inaudible, but his gown and hood were pretty."[105]

Pierce's physicians continued to urge that he go south for at least a month each winter. Henceforth, he did try to do so, mostly with his friend Alex Wilson, retired editor of the *United Church Observer* – to Jamaica in 1957 and 1959, to Mexico in 1960. These trips were preceded by a disappointing Caribbean cruise in 1956 on board the *Île de France* with stops in Venezuela, Haiti, and the Bahamas. Pierce found the heavy drinking, banal conversation, and raucous revelry on board deeply uncongenial. At any rate, in warm places – racked as he often was in the cold by arthritis – the aging editor was able, as he put it, to temporarily shed winter's "old coon coat, [and] the porcelain pig."[106] But, as ever, the workaholic in him would not allow him to rest. In Jamaica, for example, troubled by its poverty, he soon became involved in a project to supply Jamaican libraries with more books. He continued work on this project once he had returned to Toronto, writing a report on the island at the request of the new Canada Council.[107]

Back in York Mills, Lorne could not long abide the now-empty house. "Windrush," the Pierce cottage in Delta, he also found too poignant with memories, preferring to leave it to the enjoyment of his grandchildren. Selling the Campbell Crescent house, he moved on 23 August 1955 into a pleasant apartment, which he dubbed "South Ridge," located at 309–49 Glen Elm Avenue, pleased that its windows looked out on the lush grounds of Mount Pleasant Cemetery. Nevertheless, the move was difficult, he wrote – "an ordeal for an old man who loves his scuffed slippers and his worn favourite chair and his well-thumbed ear horn."[108]

The apartment was just east of Yonge Street, a few blocks above St Clair Avenue. Pierce joked about its proximity to Mount Pleasant Cemetery, implying that the latter would be his next address. At the Glen Elm apartment, the building superintendents, Mr and Mrs Wallberg, looked after some of his domestic needs – Marguerite Wallberg cleaning and cooking meals for him with efficiency and kindness. Here he found some measure of peace, writing to his sister in the fall of 1958: "This [letter], I think, brings us to the present moment, looking out into golden trees and blue sky, and knowing that I have been rewarded beyond my small merits with many things, most of all with friendships and with such loves as yours."[109]

The walls of Pierce's apartment were hung with Canadian art – a Horatio Walker, "one of the few signed Tom Thomsons," a Krieghoff, a Jefferys: all small works, for his was "a poor man's collection," as Pierce pointed out to callers.[110] In the living room, he kept a rose in front of Edith's photograph. In 1956 he commissioned a posthumous pastel portrait of Edith from painter Alan Barr.[111]

To ease his solitude, Pierce eventually bought a television, a medium he found disappointing ("What a lot of time I shall waste watching the fights," he wrote satirically) and seldom watched.[112] To honour his wife's memory, he underwrote an expensive project for Gerald Stevens to add to Edith's collection prior to donating it to the Royal Ontario Museum. In June 1957 he presented the collection, along with an accompanying acquisition fund, in Edith's memory to the Canadiana wing of the museum, which still houses her superb specimens of early Canadian glass.[113]

Pierce's staggering philanthropic and committee work in other areas continued – for, among others, the National Society for the Deaf and Hard of Hearing (now the Canadian Hearing Society), the Champlain Society, the Archives Committee of the United Church of Canada, the Toronto Historical Board, the William Lyon Mackenzie House, the Masons, the Art Gallery of Ontario, the Bibliographical Society of Canada, the Carman Collection at University of New Brunswick, the Ontario Archives, and Queen's University (which he jokingly told his daughter was his philanthropic "big debauch"), particularly his Canadiana collection there. But age, debility, and deafness were increasingly limiting his range of activity, resist bodily weakness as he might.[114] Though he often felt frustrated that the boards on which he served were not always smoothly run, he did have a moment of pleasure when his son was elected to the board of the National Society for the Deaf in May 1953.[115]

As for the Canadian Writers' Foundation, Pierce, as he had for many years – most actively since the death of its founder, Pelham Edgar, in 1948 – devoted many hours to establishing the Foundation on a firmer financial and administrative footing. In these years, the Foundation offered aid to such distinguished writers as novelists Marshall Saunders and Laura Goodman Salverson. Pelham Edgar had been a philanthropic visionary, but a gifted administrator he was not. His vest and topcoat pocket were often his favourite filing cabinets.[116] After Edgar's death, Pierce spearheaded the raising of more endowment funds in concert with the other board members, among them Ottawa *Journal* editor P.D. Ross and newspaper magnate Harry Southam. The Foundation's secretary, the capable and energetic Theresa Thomson, like Blanche Hume an epistolary confidante of Pierce, helped him in his fundraising efforts.

ABOVE ALL, Pierce remained at the helm of Ryerson Press. He was convinced, as he wrote soon after Edith's death, that "the only medicine [for grief] of any value at all is work – the routine of work, the necessity of meeting deadlines, the merciless drive of business."[117] The leopard could not change his spots. He worked more and more at home now, coming into the office only a day or two a week, loaded down with a huge basket of material for his staff. Frank Flemington, his assistant editor, handled day-to-day correspondence and oversaw the progression of manuscripts through the press, aided at various times over the years by such loyal and capable Pierce secretaries as Joan Trebell Scott and Mary Paterson. Campbell Hughes, since the late 1940s Pierce's associate educational editor, helped in textbook matters, as did Victor Seary, educational manager since his return from military service in 1946. Pierce also relied on widely known Ryerson educational sales representatives Harry Berry and, in the field, Owen Sheffield. But inevitably, his momentum and his marshalling of new publishing initiatives and contacts, like his strength, flagged. He was inexorably losing touch with the emerging cultural scene.

Pierce still enjoyed some fruitful new friendships and offered some interesting new publications. In the 1950s Ryerson published key books of poetry by Dorothy Livesay and Miriam Waddington as well as *Pressed on Sand* (1955), a chapbook from a young writer, Al Purdy, whose poems Pierce had read in *The Fiddlehead* magazine.[118] For Pierce, perhaps the sweetest moment of the 1950s came at the beginning of the decade. After endlessly cajoling C.W. Jefferys to complete his illustrated history of Canada, Pierce published the third and final volume of Jefferys's iconic *The Picture Gallery of Canadian History* in 1950 to great acclaim. In the 1950s as well, a new friendship flourished, mostly by correspondence, with young Quebec writer Yves Thériault, later famous for his *Agaguk*, published in English translation by Ryerson two years after Pierce's death.[119] The correspondence touched Pierce's heart and his bicultural ideals as he offered Thériault both money and moral support.[120]

Pierce was now unquestionably Canada's best-known publisher, with a public profile comparable today to that of Douglas Gibson, formerly of McClelland and Stewart, or Anna Porter, late of Key Porter Books. He enjoyed the respect (and at times the envy) of other publishers. In 1957

John McClelland wrote to Pierce that he had done "a remarkably good job, and Canadian literature has felt to the full the impress of your guiding hand in the development of Canadian books thorough these past years."[121] Pierce cooperated largely amicably with Jack Gray of Macmillan in their mission to flog the Ryerson-Macmillan readers. The two, so different in age and personality, had got along well during gruelling post-war cross-Canada trips to lobby bureaucrats and textbook committees. Pierce even tried to entice Gray to leave Macmillan and succeed him at Ryerson. His blandishments failed. Gray, a self-styled bon vivant with a more piquant taste in fiction than Pierce's (Gray was to publish Robertson Davies and Sinclair Ross, for example), did not, by his own admission, relish the prospect of heading a church-owned press with all the attendant constraints in subject matter.[122] For his part, Pierce resisted Gray's proposals that Macmillan buy out Ryerson on the still-profitable joint textbook series – a goal Gray largely accomplished in 1961, after Pierce's retirement – an unwise decision by the House since the readers were still a valuable (if dwindling) commodity despite changes in the textbook market.

Flattering articles on Pierce periodically appeared in magazines like *Liberty* and *Time* in the late 1940s and 1950s. Such pieces tended (rightly) to point out that Pierce was unique in the front ranks of the Canadian publishing world in being critic and author as well as editor and publisher. As another publisher put it, only half-jokingly: "If all the writers in Canada suddenly dried up ... Ryerson's would be the only house that wouldn't suffer. Why, that fellow Pierce would merely turn out the year's list of books himself."[123] But amid the bouquets, commentators hinted that Pierce's idealism and high-mindedness represented the end of an era. A 1955 *Saturday Night* article, "Persona Grata: The Romantic Puritan," put it best: "In a wider context ... [Pierce] seems a little isolated today. The faces – and the face of Canada – are changing. Industrial society is giving rise to other problems and new styles, even in traditional Quebec. The historic differences are being bridged for impulses less noble than those for which he has called in the past. 'Canada is committed to an American way of life,' he has said. But the consequences find little reflection in the Book Lists of the Ryerson Press."[124]

Pierce was caught in the "generation gap" of the day. Increasingly, and inevitably, he was stereotyped by the younger generation of writers as passé. Certainly, in the 1950s, it did not help Pierce's image with the literary young that he was publicly expressing opinions in the popular press like the following: "Modern fiction and poetry are shot through with the stupidly nasty, modern entertainment is built upon shoddy cleverness, [and] modern conversation is forever skidding along the edge of the banal and the risque."[125]

One straw in the wind pointing to the diminishment of Pierce's reputation in the minds of the literary young came in 1951 when one of the younger writers whom Ryerson had fostered, humorist Eric Nicol, won the Leacock Award for Humour. Pierce himself drove Nicol to the awards ceremony in Orillia in his Buick. Years later, during the furore over the sale of Ryerson Press to McGraw-Hill in 1970, Nicol penned a column recalling the occasion. The column, meant to be humorous, starkly conveys Nicol's feeling, even in the 1950s, that his editor really belonged to another, waning era. Noting that Pierce had published no less than ten of his books of humour, starting in 1948 ("a tremendous act of faith"), Nicol joked about the "constraints" of being published by Ryerson Press: "The one time I thought of putting a [four-letter word] into a manuscript, a large hand appeared in the sky, pointing at me and accompanied by the rumble of 'NO!'" He portrayed the Lorne Pierce of the 1950s as anachronistic:

> The day I met Dr. Pierce he drove me from Toronto to Orillia
> to receive a Leacock medal. Elderly, so diminutive as to be at
> eye level with the speedometer of his big black Caddie [sic], Dr.
> Pierce placed me in the death seat, disconnected the battery of his
> hearing aid, aimed the car at Northern Ontario, and planked his
> foot down hard on the gas pedal.
>
> The disconnected hearing aid spared him the distraction
> of horns blared at his forthright style of driving as well as the
> screams of his passenger.[126]

By contrast, some of the literary young were more empathetic toward Pierce even if they drew much the same conclusions about the increasingly rearguard nature of his editorship. Writer John Robert Colombo, hired to carry out editorial work for John Webster Grant at Ryerson just before Pierce's retirement, was friendly with Pierce but found him "quite out of touch with the Canadian publishing scene," a condition that he recognized was exacerbated by Pierce's deafness and health problems. After Pierce's retirement, Colombo visited him regularly and took him to visit friends and attend funerals. But privately, Colombo thought (as did Pierce himself at his shrewdest) that, on the grounds of both health and cultural currency, Pierce ought to have retired by the early 1950s. Another of Pierce's editorial staff, Enid Thornton, who had been at Ryerson since the 1940s, agreed with Colombo.[127]

But, if it was time for Lorne Pierce to retire, who could succeed him? That was a vexed question, one repeatedly postponed both by Book Steward Dickinson and by the House's inveterately laissez-faire Board of Publication. When Pierce considered retirement in the early 1950s, Dickinson and the twenty-five-member board, chaired by former Victoria College principal R.C. Wallace, had in September 1951 briefly considered the question of a possible successor. Several months earlier, the Scottish-born Reverend Thomas Saunders of Winnipeg (he wrote for the Winnipeg *Free Press* and filled the prestigious pulpit of Chalmers United Church there) seemed an attractive candidate.[128] Dickinson travelled to Winnipeg to meet with him.[129] But Dickinson pronounced him too bumptious (Saunders was understandably reluctant to take a cut in salary for an understudy post as associate editor and wanted a seat on the Board of Publication) and not cultured enough, despite his traditional, patriotic verse. After all, Dickinson emphasized to Pierce, Saunders had confused the spelling of "principal" and "principle" in one letter: that slip sealed his fate.[130] The board meeting that September produced no other candidate.

There was an added challenge in finding a successor. That September, the Board of Publication declared that Pierce's successor should also be a minister[131] – or at least have been ordained. Pierce himself concurred, on the theory that a minister's "training ... his consecration, his sense of values, his pledge on, his wide range of interests, his sensitivity, make [such a qualification] indispensable in such a House as ours."[132] This stricture of course drastically narrowed the field of eligible candidates.

Furthermore, neither Pierce nor the House wholeheartedly wanted his retirement. The book steward, no true bookman himself, clearly found it hard to imagine Ryerson (and himself) without Pierce. When asked in an interview many years later if Pierce had been vital to the success of Ryerson Press, Dickinson replied instantly: "My, my, oh yes, he was *life* to it – oh my, yes."[133]

It is hard for a dynamic publisher to pass the torch: two decades later, Jack McClelland found it difficult to retreat into a less hands-on role.[134] Pierce, for his part, never seemed to groom possible successors.[135] Frank Flemington, his capable associate editor, did not have the kind of charisma and vision necessary for a general editor. Victor Seary, Ryerson's educational manager, lacked the intellectual force and wide range of interests needed for the job, Pierce believed. Moreover, Pierce felt that Seary, an Anglican, was not committed to the values of the United Church, a qualification he deemed essential.[136] Ryerson educational manager Campbell Hughes, red-haired and quick-witted, was brilliant at textbook marketing, but he never seems to have been viewed by Pierce or the House as a successor, in part because he would have had to be promoted over the less versatile Seary. However, Campbell would later return to head the Press briefly before it was sold in 1970.

In the midst of Edith's illness, when Pierce again talked of retirement, the House once again cast around. One candidate was Northrop Frye, Toronto professor, stellar Blake scholar, and, from 1951 to 1960, E.K. Brown's successor as the editor of the *University of Toronto Quarterly*'s annual "Letters in Canada" survey. After all, Frye, a protégé of Edgar's at Victoria, had been ordained as a Methodist minister. When sounded out about the Ryerson post (twice – first in 1950), Frye declined, citing other commitments and telling Pierce politely: "As editor of the Ryerson Press, your example has [none] the less influenced me in a great variety of ways."[137] Privately, however, Frye, never a people person, had confided to his diary: "The very idea makes my toes curl up."[138]

In 1957 Desmond Pacey (though no man of the cloth) was also considered. Pierce had reservations about him as too "interested in showing off his cleverness, [which has] a brightly shining hard edge."[139] In any case, Pacey responded that it would take a great deal to lure him away from the University of New Brunswick.[140] The mostly likely candidate turned out to be an energetic young minister serving in the northwestern Quebec mining boomtown of Noranda, but that too came to naught.[141]

By now, Pierce was reading some five hundred manuscripts a year, and publishing about fifty, a "superhuman" task for a frail old man, as one colleague attested.[142] He still dreamed of writing his long-planned biography of Bliss Carman before the shadows fell. In addition, he now had another retirement project. In 1959 Carl Klinck asked him to write the chapter on Canadian publishing for the forthcoming *Literary History of Canada*. As Pierce well knew, it would be a mammoth undertaking, for there was little in the way of company histories and accessible source material.

Pierce wanted to get the two projects done quickly, as he told Klinck in December 1959. He was "desperate" to close the Ryerson chapter of his life. His reasoning was stark: "I am near the exit. I must take it much easier, for my angina at times cripples body and will."[143] The image on his 1959 Christmas card – a black-and-white drawing created by Thoreau MacDonald – featured a rear silhouette of a quaint figure in horse and cutter, driving into the sunset. Many recipients sensed the harbinger of personal as well as professional farewell.[144]

In fact, Pierce's designated successor had been chosen in February 1959. John Webster Grant, who joined Ryerson that August, had an academic demeanour and impressive credentials. Born in Nova Scotia in 1919, the year before Pierce arrived at Ryerson, Grant was a slender, courteous, low-key, ginger-haired scholar who favoured "tweeds and a box tie."[145] Latterly a church historian at Union College at the University of British Columbia, he was a forty-year-old Dalhousie University graduate and a Rhodes Scholar with a 1948 Oxford DPhil. To the House's delight, he was also an ordained United Church minister, one with an impressive record of war service as director of information for the federal government's Wartime Information Board.

Like Pierce, Grant had no prior experience of publishing. He started work thirty-nine years to the week after Pierce's own arrival at Queen Street. Grant found the prospect of a period of guidance under Pierce, who was scheduled to step down in January 1960, "a source of special comfort."[146] Moreover, he joined in the wake of a good year for the Press. Pierce's April report to the Board of Publication reflected the somewhat better sales conditions for the book trade which had finally arrived by the late 1950s. Sales had increased 5 per cent, with profits a respectable $261,485 on overall sales of over four million books, including Pacey's *Ten Canadian Poets* (1958), which became a canonical critical work, as well as poet Miriam Waddington's *The Season's Lovers* (1958) and R.E. Rashley's *Poetry in Canada: The First Three Steps* (1958).[147] In the summer of 1959, the future seemed promising after years of poor post-war results.

Grant's trust in Pierce as mentor was not misplaced. Pierce praised his successor to all and sundry. Privately, he stood his ground against Dickinson about imminent changes in administration and executive locale at the House which he felt would hobble Grant. For one thing, the entire House executive cadre, including Grant, was slated to move in early 1960 to splendid new executive offices on St Clair Avenue, miles north of the downtown Queen Street plant. Pierce considered such financial outlay and managerial remoteness folly. To Blanche Hume, he did not mince words: "The Management are busy making de luxe cubicles for themselves, and the proper decor for genius. And to think of my office, with the red-red rug stained by somebody's Fido, and the lounge made of Portland cement, and the forty years of talent that streamed through it into immortality. And now the rug is gone to the rag-pickers, and the desk to the wreckers, and the pictures to Queen's [Canadiana collection], and the editorial throne to [accountant] Ernie Scott who now reigns from it. And my Bust, hoarded by Frank Flemington, is possibly *headed* for the Board Room!"[148]

In terms of Ryerson's future, Pierce was concerned that Grant's powers as editor were not to be as sweeping as his had been. One suspects that House accountant Ernie Scott (who had held the position since 1952 and whose bottom-line orientation was rarely friendly to Canadian literary publishing, poetry in particular) had long wanted to trim the power of the Ryerson general editor. Pierce's retirement was his chance. The book steward was not a strong manager able to broker his executive team. Furthermore, Pierce believed (a conclusion Grant soon shared), Scott had no faith in the business acumen of literary editors.[149] Pierce protested to Dickinson about the fact that, as his Ryerson successor, Grant would be handicapped by being given fewer staff, a smaller office far from Queen Street and, all in all, less power. He admonished the book steward: "Somewhere we have not kept faith with [Grant], and it is a bad way for such a man to begin his editorship ... He will [potentially] put Ryerson at the top of the heap, and bring this House great renown. If he stays. There are too many glittering awards available to him to debate status with us, or recognition of any kind."[150]

Prophetic words, but Dickinson and Scott ignored Pierce's advice. In July 1964 Grant would leave to teach at University of Toronto's Emmanuel College – only four years after succeeding Pierce. At Ryerson, he was exhausted by the work load and unhappy with his low salary. As he recalled in an interview, he was also frustrated by the House's administrative and business woes, in particular the lack of imagination and competence at the top.[151] During his tenure, he made some excellent moves. Quickly discerning that Ryerson had a fusty reputation, he hired two young literary editors with wonderful contacts: Earl Toppings and John Robert Colombo. Also, Carleton McNaught became a frequent and able copy editor for Grant, as indeed he had been for Pierce. Grant gained a reputation, according to Pearson Gundy and others, as a rather cool and "tough" editor in contrast to Pierce. Certainly, he ruthlessly pruned some writers and manuscript readers whom he believed (rightly or wrongly) to be essentially charity cases. He also drastically cut the number of books on the annual Ryerson lists, from fifty titles to twenty-three in one year. His was a new broom, after all.[152]

In the early 1960s, Grant and his two literary lieutenants brought some exceptionally talented young writers onto the Ryerson lists, including Alice Munro, James Reaney, Gwendolyn MacEwen, Phyllis Webb, Hugh Garner, and Milton Acorn. But Pierce's were not easy shoes to fill. In November 1961 Pierce observed shrewdly that Grant had already suffered some "keen disappointments." He added: "[Grant] sees now that it is tough work building a list. I think in time he will warm up, and offer writers a little fervent hospitality. The wall-to-wall broadloom, and ... the formality prevailing down there now [in the St Clair Avenue executive suite] chill some."[153]

Pierce well knew that, in contrast to the atmosphere at the Ryerson offices, "fervent hospitality" (sometimes with alcoholic content and raffish dialogue) was being offered to promising writers by other publishers – above all by the likes of Jack McClelland at McClelland and Stewart and John Gray at Macmillan as well as in the world of small-press publishing conducted with bohemian modernist fervour of various stripes in Toronto, Montreal, Vancouver, and elsewhere. Thus, even as one Ryerson editor passed the torch to another, the pecking order and much else in the publishing business, like the Canadian literary scene overall, was changing.

ZERO HOUR for Pierce – his official retirement date – came on 1 February 1960. In the months before, tributes from authors, fellow publishers, employees, and the public accumulated. In January 1960 the House hosted a retirement dinner (a temperance event) in the Library (now the Library Bar) of the Royal York Hotel where Pierce's Ryerson silver anniversary dinner had been held in 1945. The setting meant that the occasion was bittersweet at best, as Pierce remembered all those from the silver anniversary head table now dead and gone, Edith chief among them.[154]

In one press interview, Pierce told *Time* magazine that the House had mostly given him a free hand (certainly true of the last twenty-five years of his editorship under Dickinson). He stressed that his own values had led him in his publishing policies "to respect those decencies that don't pay but are priceless."[155] The press coverage of his retirement was largely positive, situating Pierce as the grand old man of Canadian trade publishing. But the tributes that meant the most came from two long-time employees: editorial assistant Frank Flemington and the long-retired Blanche Hume.[156] Hume, ever the kindred spirit professionally, shrewdly quoted Pierce's own definition of happiness back to him: "[You said:] '[H]appiness [is] the mature stability, harmony and poise of a man in relation to the facts of life, the life about him as well as the life within his own soul.' You are the living exemplification of what you write. *Wonderful* to have known you. B.H."[157]

Pierce's final day in the office came on 29 January 1960 – nearly forty years after his arrival. That morning, Flemington ferried Pierce to the office in the latter's Buick. The general editor bid farewell to the book steward and made the rounds to say goodbye to House staff. He jotted in his daybook: "[L]eave for home 12:15. *Exit*." The next day, there was a farewell tea with Pierce's Ryerson editorial staff at Frank Flemington's house, which the House had helped him purchase at Pierce's behest.[158]

That spring, Dalhousie University awarded Pierce an honorary LLD, not long after he and Alex Wilson returned from a month-long trip to the Yucatan, where they had read in the sun and toured Mayan ruins – "two old men wandering among buried cities," as Pierce wryly put it.[159] Henceforth, Wilson and Pierce usually had dinner once a week at Murray's restaurant – until Wilson's sudden death in the fall of 1961.[160] Back at his "South Ridge" desk, Pierce tried to settle down to projects like the publishing history – he found the publishers as tardy with material as he had feared – and the Carman biography. In addition, he now hoped to write his memoirs for his children, as Edith had wished.[161] However, he resisted the idea of a biography by W.S. Wallace, or anyone else, insisting that "of all the least, I am least."[162] Touching humility, but the voluminous personal and business records that Pierce donated to Queen's – embracing everything from his mother's letters to his Ryerson editorial correspondence – implicitly invited a biography.

In the summer of 1960, Pierce also edited Gerald Stevens's catalogue on Canadian glass for the Royal Ontario Museum, and generously dispensed both money and art donations to a variety of institutions. His Canadiana collection at Queen's received more money and acquisitions, as he corresponded regularly with librarian Pearson Gundy. He arranged to set up the Edith Chown Pierce Trust to underwrite further acquisitions to the Edith and Lorne Pierce Collection of Canadiana after his death.[163]

But if Pierce's philanthropy held fast, his health did not. He lived less than two years after retirement. In that interval, his systemic lupus, which had eaten away at his body for so long, attacked heart, lungs, eyes, and joints with increased ferocity. In March 1961 a coronary put him in the hospital for six weeks, and he had to convalesce at home with a practical nurse in attendance for weeks longer. He sardonically described his state one lonely April day at his "South Ridge" apartment: "An interminable day. No callers. I went for a walk with my crutch, almost to Yonge St and back, but I found it a trifle too much ... I never thought a Methodist's knees would fail one as mine have."[164]

About this time, a phone call Pierce made to the Ryerson executive offices proved yet another intimation that his light was fading: "They asked what my business was and what my name was. When I said that my name was Lorne Pierce they asked me to repeat, and then said, [']Thank you Mr. Pierce, your line is busy.[']"[165] Pierce was more upset when Campbell Hughes, frustrated by conditions at the House after Pierce's departure (and perhaps disappointed that he had not succeeded Pierce), resigned as Ryerson's associate educational manager six months after Pierce's retirement, joining major textbook publisher Bobbs-Merrill in Indianapolis as editor-in-chief. Stung that this protégé was off to the United States, Pierce wrote him a letter of rebuke that made Hughes's heart "heavy."[166] Neither could know that, in a few years, Hughes would briefly return as the House's acting general manager – even as Ryerson was about to effectively disappear as a publisher.

Resignations were not the whole of Pierce's pain. Many of his friends and contemporaries died in these years; besides Alex Wilson, these included his physician Dennis Jordan (son of his beloved Queen's professor W.G. Jordan), and his minister at St George's, Reverend Willard Brewing. Pierce was increasingly compelled to, as he crisply put it, "live upon the amplitudes within – if any."[167] As for the younger generation, he loved his children and grandchildren, rejoicing in their successes and brooding over their sorrows. Nevertheless, his mind more and more reverted to his lost Edith. He wrote wistfully in April 1961: "As I near the discipline of learning the anthems of heaven, I go back often in memory to Grant Hall and the gay, sweet rhythms of the old-time waltzes, with Edith smiling up at me. I was in heaven then, and did not know it."[168]

By the fall of 1961, despite his jaunty disclaimers, Pierce was mortally ill, and his doctors insisted on yet another hospital stay. His heart and lungs were now irrevocably compromised by lupus, and his right eye was bleeding internally. One of his last business letters, to Queen's Librarian Pearson Gundy, written just before he entered hospital in early

November, shows that his judgment was as acute as ever. But the missive ended on a note of farewell. Pierce elegiacally wished for Gundy that "everything upon which you have set your heart blooms and blossoms and is weighed down with fruit." He ended with the phrase "Both hands," for forty years his signature closing in letters to like-minded spirits.[169]

Then, on 24 November 1961, from room 535 of Toronto General Hospital, Pierce penned what was probably his last letter in shaky, left-handed script to the stalwart Blanche Hume, joking that the physicians were now reading the publisher himself: "I am here abiding a few days longer. All my secrets, so bravely guarded, are no longer hidden. More cardiograms and another X-ray, and so on. I am become An Open Book." The laconic John Webster Grant had kindly come to visit, he informed Hume. Eager for news of Ryerson Press, Pierce bemoaned his reticence: "He just calls, and rarely talks. And he, fresh from the Rialto."[170]

But, for Pierce, death was closer than the Rialto. On Monday, 27 November 1961, his valiant spirit surrendering at last, Lorne Pierce died at the age of seventy-one of lupus-related heart and lung complications.[171] On 29 November a private funeral was attended by his daughter, his son, his sister, their families, and a few close friends, including Blanche Hume. Then Lorne Pierce was laid to rest beside Edith in Mount Pleasant Cemetery. Whatever Pierce's self-professed struggle to believe in immortality – and whatever its outcome – Lorne and Edith there lie, side by side in the Pierce family plot beneath the foliage. Some of Pierce's favourite authors – historian Harold Innis, poet Marjorie Pickthall, critics Pelham Edgar and E.K. Brown – rest not far away.

A public memorial service was held the next afternoon at St George's United Church, conducted by the Reverend Dr A.D. Matheson. The minister, an old friend, spoke of Pierce's benevolent and "victorious life," and of his wife's devotion. He praised Pierce's Christian life of service, with his editor's chair as "throne." Pierce's friend Marshall ("Padre") Laverty, Queen's University chaplain, who seven years earlier had taken part in Edith's funeral service, read the final passage from Pilgrim's Progress with its stirring last line: "All the trumpets sounded for him on the other side."

At the close, Matheson quoted one of Pierce's favourite invocations, so fitting for a man of his quenchless energies: "Give us no rest, O Lord, apart from thee, lest we lose our way, and so miss the happy gate."[172] Among the family, friends, associates, and literary mourners sat a retired minister from Gravenhurst, who had come by taxi from Muskoka. As former chaplain at Gravenhurst's now-closed tuberculosis sanatorium, he remembered Lorne Pierce's regular letters, visits, and gifts of books to two tuberculosis patients throughout the 1920s.[173]

The House held its own memorial service on 6 December. In his eulogy, Book Steward Dickinson reminded House employees of Pierce's strength of character and dedication to his vision of Canada's culture. He observed that Pierce was above all "a great character, a great Canadian and a great Christian. He was a *great* character. One had only to meet him, to have only brief conversation with him to recognize that he was an unusual person ... He was a great Canadian. No citizen ever had higher hopes [or] heavier labours for his nation. Especially he wished to see recorded and preserved the best that has ever been spoken or written or performed in any of the arts by Canadians. He felt that we must know our past if we are to feel any greatness in our present or to have worthy ambitions for our future."[174]

The House's pressmen, for one, needed no reminding. Their union newsletter eulogized Pierce: "He wasn't only the greatest Editor in Canada or the great benefactor of those in the literary world, he was a brother of the common [Joes] ... May his kindly spirit be spread to invade the lives of many – God rest his soul."[175] Lorne Pierce's prodigious career of publishing Canadian books, a career driven by his vision of Canadian culture and nationality, was complete. Ryerson Press, created as a division of the House just months before Pierce arrived there in 1920, would not long survive him.

EPILOGUE

What was the fate of Ryerson Press after the loss of its visionary general editor? *Après moi, le deluge*, the saying goes. Certainly, the decade after Pierce's retirement and death brought a hemorrhage of red ink and the sale of Ryerson Press by the United Church. Pierce's publishing career in fact brackets the lifespan of "The Ryerson Press" imprint almost exactly, arriving as he did in August 1920, less than a year after Samuel Fallis had formally given the new name to the trade division of the Methodist Book and Publishing House. For the next forty years, Pierce made the original Canadian publishing division of Ryerson very much his own creation. By the late 1920s, he had begun to bolster its balance sheet via his own best-selling textbook series, and to infuse its publication lists with his potent vision of cultural nationalism in literature, art, religion, and public affairs, a mission he pursued until his retirement in January 1960.

After Pierce's departure, it all ended sadly – in frantic restructuring and desperate floundering to survive. In 1970 the United Church of Canada, troubled by its mounting losses in the publishing sector over the previous decade, and eager to shed a business it saw as no longer central to its mission – a business where it faced increasing secular competition (much more savvy competition, at that) – sold Ryerson Press.

The 1970 sale followed years of financial and organizational crisis and a revolving door of Press and House managers. In 1964 John Webster Grant, Pierce's successor as general editor of Ryerson, resigned to return to academe, tired of mismanagement at the House and the relentless grind of the publishing trade. His immediate successor, British Columbia–born Robin Farr, a rising young Toronto editor, stayed only briefly. By his own account, he too was appalled at the mismanagement at the House, including the mishandling of its important textbook list.[1] In 1968–69 Pierce's able former educational manager, Campbell Hughes, returned from the United States to serve briefly as House general manager – only to experience the firm's further decline before his departure. Gavin Clark was appointed general manager in January 1970. By that date, Ryerson was verging on bankruptcy, a state of affairs that a monster ten-day-long book sale of warehouse stock at the University of Toronto's Varsity Arena in July 1970 did little to stem.

For one thing, as Robin Farr and Campbell Hughes discovered to their chagrin, Ryerson Press had by the late 1960s effectively abandoned creative and sales control of its educational series to Macmillan of Canada. As John Gray had long urged (and Pierce had long resisted), marketing and content control of the Macmillan-Ryerson textbook series was largely ceded to Macmillan in 1961, after Hughes had resigned as educational editor at Ryerson. The House, in effect relinquishing oversight of the textbook list in favour of simply collecting its share of profits from what would prove to be ever-diminishing sales, thereby imprudently sold Ryerson's birthright for a mess of pottage. Pierce, who learned of this decision shortly before his death, was horrified.[2]

Business analysts brought in to dissect the state of Ryerson Press in the mid-1960s were equally unflattering about the overall managerial state of the House. One source summarizes the several assessments of the House made in this decade: "General mismanagement, failure to reinvest money in the business [and] to replace obsolete equipment and too many [employees] for the size of the business brought Ryerson Press to the verge of bankruptcy" by 1970.[3] The reality is that the House had long been mismanaged, as well as hobbled in its Canadian publishing initiatives by an increasingly restrictive moral mission statement. Moreover, Heber Dickinson was an earnest and hard-working chief executive, but he had little talent for business administration – the heart of the book steward's job description. He also lacked a deep grasp of the Canadian literary scene, a handicap that made it hard for him to see why the Press's book lists were becoming increasingly anachronistic vis-à-vis changing literary tastes in the 1940s, 1950s, and 1960s.

However, it would be unfair to blame only Dickinson for managerial shortcomings at the House. After all, the formal overseer of House operations for the United Church of Canada – the church-appointed Board of Publication – never encompassed any real publishing expertise within its ranks. Unfortunately for the House, board appointees were on balance a well-meaning but laissez-faire group, most with other ecclesiastical fish to fry. Business managers like accountant Ernest Scott seem to have had little real feel for the demands of the publishing business, and the marketing and distribution departments of the House (none of them under Pierce's control) were usually mediocre at best.

Yet one thing must be kept in mind. Given the ever-daunting challenges of publishing in Canada, the United Church of Canada, and its predecessor, the Methodist Church of Canada, deserve praise for devoting money and resources to publishing Canadian books for so many years, and for branching out into general publishing in the House's Canadian list by the early twentieth century. The survival of the House for so long was an important achievement, a net blessing to Canadian literary culture for almost a century and a half.

Nevertheless, by 1964, the future of the United Church Publishing House looked bleak. A 1964 review of House operations by respected accounting firm Woods Gordon (a review that excluded Pierce's old department) pointed out that, for the ten-year period ending in 1962, the House, which had roughly 10 per cent of the Canadian book trade, had enjoyed an overall profit of $1,044,000. But steady decline followed, "culminating in a loss of $35,000 in 1962." Rising labour costs and limited growth in retail sales meant projected losses for the next five years, even should drastically needed cost-cutting, stock-control, and restructuring plans be implemented. Sales were projected to be down 8 per cent for 1963, the previous financial year.[4] Furthermore, given lagging textbook sales, Ryerson was in trouble no matter what the retail returns were for Grant's Canadian book list or for agency books, as a 1961 report by a Special Finance Committee of the House had already pointed out.[5]

At the same time, by the 1960s, the House was undeniably saddled with a large and inefficient captive in-house book manufacturing operation, one no longer enjoying large lucrative outside printing contracts such as department-store catalogues, as had been the case in the heyday of William Briggs at the beginning of the twentieth century. Moreover, as Pierce's son (himself a highly successful independent printer) pointed out, in the 1950s and 1960s the House failed to make the correct technological changes in equipment vital to continued profitability of operations.[6] As a result, the manufacturing plant, plagued from the 1940s by poor labour relations between management and its unions, was churning out at a loss both books and the huge-circulation magazine the *United Church Observer*, as well as a plethora of Sunday School magazines and other church publications (many badly in need of expensive redesigns) from an uneconomic facility burdened with outdated or unsuitable equipment and overstaffing.

In short, as a publishing concern, the House by the 1960s had irrevocably become, in the eyes of many book-trade insiders from writers to rival publishers to booksellers,[7] an old-fashioned, unwieldy, badly managed, and ultimately doomed concern. Its situation was unsustainable, vis-à-vis both Ryerson Press and the House as a whole with its agency, church publication, and manufacturing departments. The United Church began to view the House operation as a millstone. No surprise there: by 1970, the accumulated indebtedness of the House totalled a whopping (for the time) $1.5 million to the banks and $950,000 to the parent United Church.

As a result, the executive of the United Church General Council decided to offer the business for sale – initially to Canadian interests only. Then, in November 1970, it was decided that, since no acceptable Canadian offer for Ryerson Press had been forthcoming, foreign bids would be considered. Accordingly, the church accepted the offer of McGraw-Hill Canada, a subsidiary of American publisher McGraw Hill, to purchase Ryerson Press. Although McGraw-Hill promised to retain Ryerson's authors and its trade division and paperback list for at least five years, Ryerson's sale to American interests – coupled with the earlier sale of Canadian textbook publisher Gage – troubled Canadian cultural and economic nationalists alike. (Ryerson's educational collaborator, Macmillan of Canada, would in 1980 be sold by its British parent to the president of Gage, with its imprint eventually disappearing.[8])

Under the terms of the sale of Ryerson to McGraw-Hill, the United Church retained the House manufacturing division. Losses there continued to mount. As a result, the church put the physical plant and the landmark Wesley building up for sale in the spring of 1971. The large, handsome red brick building on Queen Street East, erected with great cost and controversy by Methodist Book and Publishing House Book Steward William Briggs in the 1910s, so long the home of Pierce and his Ryerson editorial team, ultimately became the headquarters of Moses Znaimer's CITY-TV and MuchMusic. It was a McLuhanesque moment, in that the Wesley Building now housed a newer mass medium under a different (but equally energetic) visionary in a new era of Canadian cultural history. Pierce would have recognized (if not relished) the symbolic nature of this torch passing.

In any case, the church's 1970 sale of Ryerson Press to the American publishing conglomerate McGraw-Hill, and the creation of the McGraw-Hill-Ryerson imprint in Canada, spurred impassioned denunciations of the sale by a range of Canadian cultural nationalists – among them Pierce's children, Bruce Pierce and Beth Pierce Robinson.

They, like many opponents of the sale, were shocked and saddened that Ryerson, a press that had above all epitomized Canadian cultural nationalism, was now American-owned. Articles, editorials, and letters to the press from many quarters questioned the consequences for Canadian cultural sovereignty.[9]

In the short term, the outcry over the sale of Ryerson Press and the evident financial vulnerability of Canadian cultural industries helped to prompt the establishment of the Ontario Royal Commission on Book Publishing. The commission's mandate was to examine the state of Canadian publishing. William C. Heine's brief for that commission would detail the financial mismanagement as well as the infrastructure difficulties endemic to the book trade in Canada, factors that had coalesced to effect the financial collapse of the United Church Publishing House and the sale of Ryerson Press.[10]

It is doubtful whether Lorne Pierce, even had he been physically able to remain longer in the editor's chair, could have halted Ryerson's demise. Both Canadian society – and the publishing trade – were in the grip of a paradigm shift in the early 1960s. Pierce's long-successful textbook series could no longer function as the magic bullet to moderate deficits by cross-subsidization. Post-war immigration, the Baby Boom, and the growing prominence of television as a medium, among other factors, meant that the old dominance of the traditional single-choice textbook series was ending. In the post-1960 world, the wolf could no longer be kept from Ryerson's door. Even Pierce's brilliance and hard work were no longer enough.

Moreover, Pierce's powerful vision as editor and publisher – a vision of romantic nationalism, embodied in so many important Ryerson publications, that was essentially white, middle class, male and WASP, albeit with bows to the French fact in Canada and western Canadian ethnic diversity – now had diminished resonance. The country was increasingly debating questions not only of nationality but also of gender, ethnicity, and race in a rapidly changing social context. For example, Pierce's vision of anglophone *bonne entente* (even the term seems anachronistic now) with French Canada held less appeal for a Quebec in the throes of the Quiet Revolution. Pierce's allies – and his vision of French Canada – had been drawn from an earlier generation of moderately nationalist Quebec intellectuals of a certain age and qualified bicultural leanings – clerics and academics such as Camille Roy and Arthur Maheux of Laval. In his own province, Pierce's francophone allies were franco-Ontarian intellectuals such as Father Auguste Morisset and Father Séraphin Marion of the University of Ottawa, as well as Dominion Archivist Gustave Lanctôt. In the era of the Quiet Revolution and increasing sovereignist strength, such individuals no longer carried the weight they did in earlier times.[11]

The world of publishing, in particular that concerned with publishing Canadian literature, was also changing. The creation of the federally funded Canada Council in 1957 and the subsequent creation of other granting agencies and subsidy programs, both federal and provincial, meant increasing subsidies for the publication of Canadian writing. Paradoxically, this development also meant more competition to publish, not only from the usual suspects like McClelland and Stewart and others, but from both academic presses (for example, the University of Toronto Press) and the small presses which were increasingly springing up or, if pre-existing, morphing into more ambitious enterprises. Such visionary small publishers as Contact Press, House of Anansi, Fiddlehead Press, and many others were founded or expanded in the 1960s. In addition, from that decade, regional publishers in the west and in Atlantic Canada were more of a presence in the trade. The old-time dominance of Ryerson and its peers was a thing of the past.

Even areas of literary publishing where Ryerson had traditionally shone had new beacons. Ryerson's Chapbook poetry series, for example, no longer the leading showcase for Canadian poetry it had been from the 1920s, was terminated by John Webster Grant as old-fashioned and a financial drain.[12] Instead, the work of young Canadian poets as well as of older modernists was being featured by adventurous presses like Fred Cogswell's Fiddlehead Press; the House of Anansi, run by writer Dennis Lee and his collaborators; and a pride of other small presses from Prince Edward Island to British Columbia.

Furthermore, literature itself was changing with the times, as were public tastes. Irving Layton had been bumptious but correct when he told Pierce in the early 1950s that the heyday of more sexually and socially frank poetry and fiction was dawning. The poetry of Layton and Leonard Cohen, for example, and the fiction of Mordecai Richler and Robertson Davies – all best-selling authors in the 1970s and 1980s – were not works that church-owned Ryerson Press could have published with gusto. Too sexually candid, and too stark. Nor did such authors in turn relish the prospect of publication by a church press, even with a new individual in the Ryerson editorial chair. As early as the 1950s, Jack

McClelland had disdainfully informed Irving Layton that to publish so much as an anthology under the "churchy" Ryerson imprint would damage Layton's brand – that is, tarnish his libidinous image.

Even writers whom Pierce had earlier published – Dorothy Livesay, Al Purdy, Miriam Waddington, and P.K. Page, for example – were also producing work in the 1970s and beyond that responded to second wave feminism and/or the experiments of the younger 1960s poets, such as those centred around *Tish* magazine on the West Coast. Had Pierce lived longer, he would not have been taken with a little magazine whose very title was an anagram of "shit" or been eager to publish its contents. The generation gap in editorial values between the Ryerson Press which Pierce had shaped and the outlook of young writers of various stripes had become an abyss by the 1960s.

And yet ... an irony underlies all this cultural burgeoning and ferment of the Expo '67 era and after, an era in some ways so alien to Lorne Pierce's vision and influence. It was Pierce's broad and successful promulgation of his vision of Canadian cultural nationalism – through Ryerson publications, through best-selling textbooks so dominant in the study of elementary and high school English, through the promotion of writers and artists like C.W. Jefferys and the Canadian Art series, and through the wider exposure given to poets like F.R. Scott, A.J.M. Smith, Earle Birney, and Dorothy Livesay – that in the 1930s, 1940s, and 1950s laid a crucial part of the groundwork for the explosion of interest in Canadian culture in the 1960s and 1970s. A generation of anglophone school children had ingested the patriotic and literary stimulation of the Ryerson-Macmillan readers, just as their parents had filled the family bookshelves with Jefferys's engravings of Canadian history and books about the Group of Seven. Pierce's Ryerson Press had been a central publishing forum for it all. As Roy MacSkimming puts it in his history of the Canadian book trade: "[Pierce's] labours generated a fertilization process that would produce better writing in years to come."[13]

In other words, Pierce had helped sow the seeds of the post-1960 cultural boom, even if he would not always have savoured the harvest. He was assuredly the most influential publisher and editor of his era, a figure of enduring importance to Canadians who deserves to be better understood in all his complexity. Unquestionably, for better and for worse, Pierce lived his career-long dream of – as he himself put it near the end of his life – helping to shape "the entire cultural life of Canada," a dream of making Ryerson Press "a tremendous forum for [my moral and nationalist] ideas and aspirations … extend[ing] my mission as an ordained man."[14]

Of course, the Canada of Pierce's vision naturally and inevitably evolved beyond his ability to influence it. Accordingly, in the 1960s and afterwards, other presses and other editors fed and shaped Canadian culture – and wrestled with red ink and all the perils of the publishing trade. For example, in the 1960s and 1970s, Jack McClelland of McClelland and Stewart would experience his own impassioned, brilliant, and red-ink-plagued heyday and eclipse. The stellar Dennis Lee and a host of radical, left wing *jeunes* would make their mark at such presses as House of Anansi and Coach House Press.[15]

Ryerson Press did publish a book about Lorne Pierce before its demise. Heber Dickinson's career at the United Church Publishing House ended with a writing assignment – to pen a profile of Lorne Pierce. One recommendation of the 1964 Woods Gordon report was that the administrative side of the House no longer be run by a minister. Shunted sideways to the position of secretary to the Board of Publication by restructuring in May 1964, Dickinson was given an office and directed to write a biography of his late subordinate.[16] Ryerson Press published Dickinson's *Lorne Pierce: A Profile*, a sixty-page work, in 1965.

Dickinson's slender, admiring monograph drew heavily on Pierce's own writings, as well as on one (uncredited) major source – "Lorne Pierce As I Knew Him," Blanche Hume's unpublished study of her long-time boss, written largely in the 1940s. Dickinson also had at his disposal Frank Flemington's typescript bibliography of Pierce's writings, a project Flemington had begun to work on in the mid-1940s – an updated copy of which had been presented to Pierce at the time of his retirement in 1960.[17]

Dickinson's profile provides valuable vignettes of Pierce's childhood and youth – specifically, of the influence of his mother, of Delta, of Methodism, of Queen's University and of his western sojourns as teacher and minister, and of his marriage to Edith Chown. However, the work is at best a sketch, a brief overview of Pierce's editorial career, a chronology of titles, authors, artists, and organizations. Pierce is rightly depicted as an "intense patriot" who believed that a "nation's writers are its best interpreters." But, sadly, despite Dickinson's admiration for Pierce, he had neither the eloquence, nor the expertise, nor the research acumen (nor the necessary objectivity) to capture Pierce on the wing and to dissect his career. Both Pierce's daughter and Queen's Librarian Pearson Gundy privately lamented the lack of probing analysis in Dickinson's tribute. The book provided only, as Gundy put it, "the shadow, not the substance" of Pierce's career.[18]

There was another tribute to Pierce around that time, however. In Delta, on 12 July 1964, as the summer sun glinted on village buildings whose silvery tin roofs had been supplied by Edward Pierce, an Ontario Heritage Foundation historic plaque was unveiled in Lorne Pierce's honour. Pierce's daughter, Beth, and his son, Bruce, proudly stood amid the beaming guests gathered around the blue and gold provincial plaque. The bronze marker, placed in front of Delta United Church – once Lorne's boyhood Methodist church – pays tribute to Pierce's devotion "to the promotion of Canadian literature." For his part, back at Queen's University, Pierce's beloved alma mater, Pearson Gundy was already working on an edition of the letters of Bliss Carman. Gundy's scholarly offering was meant to compensate for the lack of Pierce's biography of Carman, which Pierce, to his sorrow, had not lived to write. But, without Pierce's indefatigable assembling of Canadiana (a trove enjoyed by scores of subsequent literary researchers), Gundy's book would have been well-nigh impossible to produce.

In any case, with the unveiling of the plaque, the threads of Lorne Pierce's life and work all came back to Delta on a sunny July day – to the eastern Ontario village where he had been born to Harriet and Edward Pierce on another summer day seventy-four years earlier.

PIERCE WAS certainly Canada's longest-serving and most remarkable mid-twentieth-century publisher of Canadian books, overcoming formidable handicaps of health and hearing to realize an influential and unprecedented publishing program heavily infused with his brand of cultural nationalism. Scholar Desmond Pacey, for all his own tussles with Pierce, best characterized Pierce's achievement. In 1964 Pacey reviewed Dickinson's book on Pierce for *Canadian Literature*, one of the important new scholarly journals in the field born in the 1960s which Pierce relished. Wisely, Pacey did not elect to focus on the shortcomings of Dickinson's "honest, unpretentious and affectionate" profile of Pierce in his review. Instead, he mused on Pierce's achievement, and on the need for in-depth analysis of the values for which he stood.

Pacey asserted that Lorne Pierce was for decades "the most influential man of letters in Canada," detailing the list of his achievements and the stable of influential authors he had so arduously assembled. Then, Pacey

asked the question about Pierce which this biography has been framed
to answer: "What impelled him, the son of an Ontario village tinsmith
and hardware merchant, to take up so zealously the cause of Canadian
culture in general and of Canadian literature in particular?"

The question as it stands in Pacey's review addresses only part of the
picture. In any overview of Pierce's life, it is crucial to comprehend that
Pierce was not only Ed Pierce the hardware merchant's son, as Pacey
points out, but also, more crucially for Canadian cultural history, the
son of an art-loving, devoutly Methodist, temperance-activist mother –
Harriet Singleton Pierce. Lorne Pierce always felt, as he confided to
his own son, "dedicated in my Mother's womb."[19] Harriet Pierce's influence was even more vital in the shaping of his character and career
than his father's. Nevertheless, whatever the lacunae in his speculative
question, Pacey's summary of Pierce's importance to Canadian culture is
admirably suggestive: "[Pierce] was a romantic of romantics, who always
assumed the best of people and gave them a sense of their unlimited
capacity ... Lorne Pierce was a very complex figure. He was a Canadian
nationalist, but also a Hebrew prophet; a Methodist preacher but also a
deep admirer of Russian literature; a moral idealist but also an Irish wit.
There is no doubt that he was a great editor and a great Canadian."[20]

Indeed, as the twenty-first century unfolds in a Canada where Canadian publishing, in its now-various technological guises, is more important (and more beleaguered) than ever, it is vital to examine Pierce's
career and legacy as a window on Canadian cultural history in the mid-
twentieth century, an era that still helps to mould us today. Unquestionably, Lorne Pierce did much, in the face of formidable professional and
personal challenges, to shape the print, visual, and educational culture of
his country.

APPENDIX

Lorne Pierce's *A Prayer for One Day Only*

Lorne Pierce wrote this prayer at the end of a sleepless night of coronary pain in February 1942 as he sought faith and comfort in the midst of anxiety about the war and his health. It was widely circulated after appearing in the United Church Observer.

A Prayer for One Day Only

Father of all spirits, we bless Thee once again for the miracle of morning, the birth of this new day, for Thy unfailing care of all things that live and need the light.

Quicken our spirits as Thou dost renew the expectant world at dawn, that we may nobly and richly live these few waking hours, and that in all things this day we may be radiant with Thy love.

Keep us, Lord of light, from daybreak to dark with our faces steadfast toward Thee, so that the high goal of all our striving may never be lost to view.

Unto thy hills we look up.

Grant, Thou Great Physician, that this day may be full of love and empty of fear. When the day is done, and the sun goes down, and night folds us in, bring calm to our tired spirits and rest to our faltering feet. Forgive us and lead us and heal us.

Amen.

NOTES

ABBREVIATIONS

BP/BPR   Beth Pierce Robinson (Kingston, ON)
CFP   Chester Family Papers, Queen's University Archives
EC/ECP   Edith Chown Pierce
LAC   Library and Archives Canada
LP   Lorne Pierce
LPP   Lorne Pierce Papers, Queen's University Archives
PFC   Pierce Family Correspondence, Queen's University Archives
QUA   Queen's University Archives

INTRODUCTION

1   *Ontario Royal Commission on Canadian Publishers and Canadian Publishing*, First Interim Report, 23 March 1971 (Toronto: Queen's Printer 1973), 219.
2   Roy Miki, "The Future's Tense: Editing, Canadian Style," 35, qtd. in Jennifer Macquarrie, "CIV/n: Not a One-[Wo]man Job – The Significance of Aileen Collins as Editor" (MA thesis, Carleton University, 2006).
3   LP to Rev. Garth Legg, n.d. [1958], file 4, box 27, LPP.
4   Maria Tippett, *Becoming Myself: A Memoir* (Toronto: Stoddard 1996), 186.
5   Donald Creighton, *The Forked Road: Canada 1939–1957* (Toronto: McClelland and Stewart 1976), 32. Creighton, whose father was a House colleague of LP, spoke from experience: Ryerson had published some of Creighton's most important titles (*The Commercial Empire of the St. Lawrence* [1937], for example).
6   LP to Gerald Stevens, 20 October 1961, file 9, box 29, LPP.
7   Jack McClelland, qtd. in Roy MacSkimming, *The Perilous Trade: Publishing Canada's Writers* (Toronto: McClelland and Stewart 2003), 30.
8   MacSkimming, *The Perilous Trade*, 29, 30.
9   LP, qtd. in ibid., 30. The quote is from LP, *An Editor's Creed* (Toronto: Ryerson 1960), 3.
10   James King, Jack McClelland's biographer, tells us that McClelland disliked the dual role of editor/publisher and avoided it as much as possible. James King, *Jack: A Life with Writers: The Story of Jack McClelland* (Toronto: Knopf 1999), 187.

11 LP Diary, 11 July 1920, LPP [hereafter LP Diary]. LP began keeping this diary in 1915; he opened it with a memoir of the preceding years.

12 Frank Flemington to Walter McRaye, 14 September 1945, file 7, box 12, LPP.

13 Fallis, appointed book steward in 1918, had the Methodist Book and Publishing House's Central Section of the Book and Publishing Committee pass a resolution creating the imprint of Ryerson Press on 7 May 1919, a trade name that formally took effect on 1 July 1919. See LP, *The House of Ryerson* (Toronto: Ryerson 1954), 30. Pierce's appointment began on 1 July 1920 although he did not actually take up the job until 3 August 1920.

14 LP to Rev. Garth Legg, n.d. [1958], file 4, box 27, LPP.

15 LP, transcript of official Ryerson biography, 1956, vol. 8, Canadian Writers' Foundation Papers, LAC.

16 LP to BP, n.d. [c. 1944], in possession of BPR.

17 Pierce told his sister: "I am pleased that my children are not literary to that extent, and [therefore] will not be writing me up. Boy oh boy and man alive what they could do to me when I am safely in the hereafter." LP to Sara and Eldred Chester, 22 July 1961, box 1, CFP. Pierce also insisted to Queen's Librarian Pearson Gundy that no biography should be written: "Of all the least, I am the least." He made similar protestations ("Nothing important can be said about this person") to his former assistant Blanche Hume in a letter of 13 June 1955, box 1, Blanche Hume Papers, QUA.

18 Pierce's daughter lent the pastel portrait to England's National Portrait Gallery for an exhibition of Wyndham Lewis portraits in the summer of 2008.

19 Certainly, some material was removed by Blanche Hume – for example, letters written by a young secretary who was romantically attracted to him in the 1920s and who was treated for psychological problems.

20 Jack Gray, *Fun Tomorrow: Learning to Be a Publisher and Much Else* (Toronto: Macmillan 1978), and Marsh Jenneret, *God and Mammon: Universities As Publishers* (Toronto: Macmillan 1989).

CHAPTER ONE

1 This journal was kindly lent to me by Lorne Pierce's daughter, Beth Pierce Robinson. Hereafter cited as "LP childhood Journal." Hattie Pierce would keep the journal intermittently, sometimes giving specific dates for entries and sometimes not. The narrative is, of course, very deterministic.

2 See Diane Haskins, *"My Own Four Walls"* (Council of Bastard and South Burgess Townships, 1985), 36.

3 According to Dr Paul Fritz, historian of Delta, the lithograph of Queen Victoria was presented to the town hall by the Women's Institute.

4 The church erected a new structure in 1889. For a history of the church, see Paul S. Fritz, *History of the United Church in Delta, Ontario* (Delta, ON: Delta United Church 2003).

5 "Delta," clipping, n.d, in possession of BPR. For information on early Delta, see Paul S. Fritz, "Lands, Surveyors, and Settlers: The Origins of Bastard and South Burgess Townships, Leeds County, Ontario" [Bicentennial Lecture, Delta Town Hall, 14 June 1994].

6 Stephen Leacock's *Sunshine Sketches of a Little Town* (London: John Lane 1912) was in fact written a few years earlier and published in instalments in a Montreal newspaper.

7 [Lorne Pierce], "The Swamp of Telda," in Lorne Pierce and Dora Whitefield, eds., *The Canada Book of Prose and Verse*, Book Two (Toronto: Ryerson-Macmillan 1932), 385–7. Pierce himself wrote this piece specifically for the highly successful reader series he edited.

8 LP, qtd. in Blanche Hume, "Lorne Pierce: Thus He Appeared to Me," 3, ms. in possession of BPR.

9 LP Diary, 11 September 1915. Here Pierce gives a colourful version of his family genealogy, which, if not, according to his descendants, entirely accurate, certainly demonstrates the sense of achievement and personality he believed was his heritage: significantly, he saw his mother's family history as of primary importance to him.

10 John Singleton, qtd. in C.H. Dickinson, *Lorne Pierce: A Profile* (Toronto: Ryerson 1965), 4.

11 LP to James Roy, 20 March 1945, file 1, box 13, LPP.

12 See Jean Graham, "A Lover of Books ... Dr. Lorne Pierce," *Saturday Night*, 31 December 1932, 8.

13 A discussion of Pierce's ancestry is found in Dickinson, *Lorne Pierce: A Profile*, 3–4, and in the LP Diary.

14 See the Pierce Family Papers and Chester Family Papers, QUA. The "unfailing" frequency of her letters is referred to in Sara and Lorne Pierce, "We Try to Explain," in Harriet Singleton Pierce, *An Eastern Window: A Book of Days* (Toronto: United Church Publishing House 1938), 3.

15 The church was called the Methodist New Connection Church, and was located beside the site of the cemetery where Harriet and Edward Pierce are buried. The structure was replaced with a brick church (now gone) in 1888, two years after Harriet's wedding. See "Focus on: Crosby," *North Leeds Lantern*, September 1984, 3.

16 Ibid.

17 [LP], "Delta Residents Treasure Memory [of] Mrs E.A. Pierce" [obituary], *Brockville Recorder*, 19 January 1940.

18 See Haskins, *"My Own Four Walls,"* 36. According to his obituary, Ed Pierce settled in Delta in 1885.

19 See Karen Dubinsky, *The Second Greatest Disappointment: Honeymooners, Heterosexuality, and the Tourist Industry at Niagara Falls* (New Brunswick, NJ: Rutgers University Press 1999).

20 Hume, "Lorne Pierce," 10.

21 "Memories of A.V. Hicock (July 6, 1880–Feb. 2, 1970)," records, Delta United Church, Delta, ON. Thanks to BPR for this material. The instruments of the town band were destroyed in the 1897 fire which also consumed Ed Pierce's hardware store.

22 See Phyllis D. Airhart, *Serving the Present Age: Revivalism, Progressivism and the Methodist Tradition in Canada* (Montreal & Kingston: McGill-Queen's University Press 1992).

23 LP Childhood Journal. Mrs Pierce records that Lorne was baptized at the age of three months.

24 LP to Blanche Hume, 17 April 1946, box 1, Hume Papers, QUA.

25 See LP to Robert Green, 28 December 1942, which evokes the friendship between his mother and the latter's wife, Stella Cheetham Green. My thanks to historian Paul Fritz of Kingston for sharing this letter about his grandmother with me from his Green-Fritz collection.

26 LP Childhood Journal records Harriet giving the latter to Lorne after his first communion in August 1897; Pierce later reminisced about the former.

27 Bruce Pierce and BPR, interview with author, Perth, ON, 3 May 1990.

28 C.H. Dickinson, "Lorne Pierce – Man of Letters," *United Church Observer*, 15 November 1956, 8.

29 Alice Pierce Waddington to Hilda [Pierce?], 14 January 1957, file 8, box 26, LPP.

30 LP Diary, 16 June 1915.

31 Neil Semple, "'The Nurture and Admonition of the Lord': Nineteenth-Century Methodism's Response to Childhood," *Social History/Histoire Sociale* 14 (May 1981): 157–75.

32 In 1901 Canada's 916,866 Methodists constituted 17.1 per cent of the Canadian population. See Airhart, *Serving the Present Age*, 12, and David B. Marshall, *Secularizing the Faith: Canadian Protestant Clergy and the Crisis of Belief, 1850–1940* (Toronto: University of Toronto Press 1992), 13. For an overview of Canadian Methodism, see Neil Semple, *The Lord's Dominion: The History of Canadian Methodism* (Montreal & Kingston: McGill-Queen's University Press 1996).

33 See Semple, "'The Nurture and Admonition of the Lord,'" 157–75.

34 Ibid., 173–4.

35 Marshall, *Secularizing the Faith*, 127.

36 See Charlotte Gray, *Nellie* (Toronto: Penguin 2007).

37 Fritz, *History of the United Church in Delta, Ontario*, 1.

38 BPR, interview with author, Perth, ON, 3 May 1990.

39 Pierce sensibly seems to have come to think of the pledge as made primarily to his mother rather than the Almighty.

40 Airhart, *Serving the Present Age*, 101.

41 LP Childhood Journal.

42 The four children of Sara Pierce and her husband, the Reverend Eldred Chester, were Helen, Lorne, Paul, and John Chester.

43 LP Childhood Journal.
44 Airhart, *Serving the Present Age*, 60–1.
45 Ibid., 24, 26.
46 For such an opinion, see W.B. Creighton, "The Value of Children to the Church," *Christian Guardian*, 5 June 1918, 5–6, qtd. in Airhart, *Serving the Present Age*, 102. For general background and analysis of the evolution of Methodist practice and belief, see ibid. and Neil Semple's *The Lord's Dominion*. Airhart also sheds much light on the changing roles and images of women in the Methodist Church. Two studies of children and Methodism around this era are Patricia Dirks, "'Getting a Grip on Harry': Canada's Methodists Respond to the 'Big Boy' Problem, 1900–1925," *Canadian Methodist Historical Society Papers*, 7 (1990): 69–70, and idem, "Reinventing Christian Masculinity and Fatherhood: The Canadian Protestant Experience, 1900–1920," in Nancy Christie, ed., *Households of Faith: Family, Gender and Community in Canada, 1760–1969* (Montreal & Kingston: McGill-Queen's University Press 2002), 290–316.
47 LP Diary, 3 May 1920.
48 LP Childhood Journal.
49 LP, *Fifty Years of Service: A Life of James L. Hughes* (Toronto: S.P. Gundy 1924), 39.
50 See Glenn J Lockwood's discussion of Kidd's youth in *Beckwith: Irish and Scottish Identities in a Canadian Community 1816–1991* (Township of Beckwith 1991), 398–428.
51 This play on words is part of Harriet Pierce's dedication to her granddaughter Beth in an inscribed copy of *An Eastern Window*, in possession of BPR. She adds: "Change one letter, then I see that the thwarting of my purpose Is God's better choice for Me."
52 LP Childhood Journal, August 1897.
53 Ibid., September 1900.
54 LP to BPR, n.d. [early 1940s], box 16, PFC.
55 LP to BPR, n.d. [early 1940s], box 16, PFC.
56 LP to Rev. Marshall Laverty, 4 August 1956, property of Laverty estate, Ottawa.
57 Sara and Lorne Pierce, "We Try to Explain," 4.
58 Ibid.
59 In LP Childhood Journal, Hattie gives the date of the first communion as August 1897 ("never had a Quarterly Meeting been to me what that one was"). The same source contains the dates of the beginning of school and the Band of Hope recitation. Hattie probably wrote Lorne's recitation.
60 LP Diary, 16 June 1915.
61 Ibid.
62 LP Childhood Journal, 22 March 1898.
63 LP to Blanche Hume, 17 April 1946, box 1, Hume Papers, QUA.
64 LP Diary, 18 June 1915.

65 Ibid., 28 November 1937.

66 LP to Blanche Hume, 17 April 1946, Hume Papers, QUA.

67 Ibid.

68 LP, qtd. in Hume, "Lorne Pierce," 3.

69 Ibid., 78.

70 Edgar's reverence for England as the mother country is evident in his memoir, *Across My Path* (Toronto: Ryerson 1952).

71 Semple, *The Lord's Dominion*, 388.

72 See Janet Friskney, "Towards a Canadian 'Cultural Mecca': The Methodist Book and Publishing House's Pursuit of Book Publishing and Commitment to Canadian Writing 1829–1926" (MA thesis, Trent University, 1994).

73 Ibid., 133–4.

74 Sara Chester and Lorne Pierce, "We Try to Explain," 3.

75 Ibid.

76 The quotations are cited in Harriet Pierce, *An Eastern Window*, 8, 6.

77 LP, "Education in a Democracy," 7. This booklet is a reprint of an article from *Western School Journal* published by the author in 1933.

78 LP to Blanche Hume, 17 April 1946, box 1, Hume Papers, QUA.

79 Mary Mallory, interview with author, Toronto, 12 May 1992.

80 For a discussion of the evolution of Protestantism at this time, and the nature of the transition from religious to secular activities, see Marshall, *Secularizing the Faith*, Marguerite Van Die, *An Evangelical Mind: Nathaniel Burwash and the Methodist Tradition in Canada, 1839–1918* (Montreal & Kingston: McGill-Queen's University Press 1989), and Semple, *The Lord's Dominion*.

81 Ralph Connor, *The Sky Pilot* (Toronto: Westminster 1899).

82 This is the way Lorne Pierce put the question in a 1916 letter to his fiancée Edith Chown (the choice of whom his parents initially opposed). He was about to tell his parents that they had decided to marry. See LP to Edith Chown, 17 January 1916, box 4, PFC.

83 LP to Bruce and Beth Pierce, 16 May 1945, in possession of BPR. Note the ambivalent juxtaposition of "wonderful" and "escaped."

84 LP Diary, 18 June 1915.

85 Dickinson, *Lorne Pierce: A Profile*, 9.

86 LP to Jack Price, 20 December 1949, file 5, box 18, LPP. He added: "Those were wonderful days when you could hear the minister coming through the deep snow drifts and tell him by the music he made – when you could tell the difference between the music of the Methodist parson and the Baptist minister!"

87 For example, by 1914, thanks to the profits for his business generated by the Laurier boom and his own acumen, Ed Pierce owned three or four small houses in Delta. The Pierces would take Christmas boxes to these families, prompting Pierce to tell his future fiancée: "I'd like to be rich and be a philanthropist." LP

in fact became comfortable by the mid-1930s and a philanthropist even before that. See LP to Edith Chown, 27 December 1914, box 2, PFC.

88 See Dirks, "Reinventing Christian Masculinity and Fatherhood," 290–316. An injunction that Pierce recalled receiving from his father as he set off for high school was penned by his mother in the Childhood Journal. See LP Diary, 15 June 1915, and LP Childhood Journal, 19 August 1904.

89 LP Diary, 9 January 1929, written in Toronto near his son Bruce's sickbed as his father's funeral service was being held in Delta.

90 Thaddeus W.H. Leavitt, *History of Leeds and Grenville (1879)* (Belleville, ON: Mika 1972), 80.

91 LP Diary, 15 June 1915.

92 LP Childhood Journal, 6 September 1904.

93 LP, Diary, 18 June 1915.

94 Ibid.

95 "Venus! Neptune! Mercury! Mars! / Can't you see the Athens stars! / Rozzle Gobble! / Hobble Gobble! / Zip! Boom! Bah! / Athens! Athens! Rah! Rah! Rah!" See LP Diary, 2 September 1915.

96 Ibid., 18 June 1915.

97 Hume, "Lorne Pierce," 11–12. She tells us that his botanical excursions with Graham inspired him to write "The Swamp of Telda" for school readers two decades later.

98 LP Diary, 18 June 1915.

99 Ibid., 21 June 1915.

100 Bruce Pierce, interview with author, Perth, ON, 3 May 1990. LP wrote that he "hated business" in LP to EC, 12 July 1912, box 1, PFC.

101 LP Childhood Journal, 12 May 1897. Harriet was fretting about the temptations Lorne would be exposed to in school.

102 See C.B. Sissons, *A History of Victoria University* (Toronto: University of Toronto Press 1952).

103 LP to EC, 12 July 1912, box 1, PFC. Interestingly, LP writes her that his mother had dreamed of being a missionary herself, and hoped he would fulfill her dream.

104 LP Childhood Journal, June 1905.

CHAPTER TWO

1 John Watson, 1912, qtd. in Brian Fraser, "Theology and the Social Gospel among Canadian Presbyterians: A Case Study," *Studies in Religion*, 8 (1979): 41.

2 LP to BPR, 16 March 1948, box 14, PFC. LP spelled it "debauche."

3 LP to EC, 12 July 1912, box 1, PFC.

4 Both Pierce's daughter and Rev. ("Padre") Marshall Laverty, long-time chaplain at Queen's (in whose appointment in 1947 Lorne Pierce was instrumental),

mention the exhilaration with which Pierce habitually spoke of Queen's. Author's interviews with Rev. Laverty, Kingston, 5 January 1991, and BPR, Pike Lake, Ontario, 10 June 1991.

5 For biographical material on Watson, Jordan, and Cappon (copy-edited in fact by Lorne Pierce), see R.C. Wallace, ed., *Some Great Men of Queen's* (Toronto: Ryerson 1941). The portrait of Cappon that emerges there, while balanced, is not flattering.

6 See LP, ed., *Queen's University Art Foundation* (Toronto: Ryerson 1944).

7 LP to BPR, 16 March 1948, box 14, PFC.

8 Rev. Barry Pierce lived at 60 Victoria Street, Kingston. In his second and third years, Lorne boarded at 76 Division Street with Mrs Williams, a Newboro widow, and took his meals with Sara at Mrs Shannan's boarding house at 212 Earl Street. In his fourth year, he boarded with Sara and another student at 198 University Avenue.

9 See LP Diary, 2 September 1915.

10 The best discussion of Queen's in this period is Hilda Neatby, *Queen's University, Volume I, 1841–1917: And Not to Yield* (Montreal & Kingston: McGill-Queen's University Press 1978), especially 226–84. There were 943 students enrolled in Queen's arts and theology in 1910.

11 LP to EC, 28 March 1916, box 5, PFC.

12 For a discussion of the Queen's ethos of these "Ottawa men," see Jack Granatstein, *The Ottawa Men* (Toronto: University of Toronto Press 1998).

13 See also Frederick Gibson, *Queen's University, Volume II, 1917–1961: To Serve and Yet Be Free* (Montreal & Kingston: McGill-Queen's University Press 1983), as well as Neatby's earlier volume, *Queen's University*.

14 A.B. McKillop, *A Disciplined Intelligence: Critical Inquiry and Canadian Thought in the Victorian Era* (Montreal and Kingston: McGill-Queen's University Press 1979), 198.

15 See Neatby, *Queen's University*, 269.

16 Brian McKillop, *Contours of Canadian Thought* (Toronto: University of Toronto Press 1987), 99. McKillop rightly credits John Watson with a leading role in the transformation of nineteenth-century moral philosophy in Canada into "a broadly moral secular outlook which has dominated much of English Canadian thought in the twentieth century." Pierce, Watson's student, typifies such a transition.

17 LP, transcript of "How I Became a Canadiana Collector: Dean Cappon and Nathan van Patten at Queen's," Lorne Pierce Collection, Queen's University Library.

18 McKillop, *A Disciplined Intelligence*, 218.

19 Ibid., 216. Lorne Pierce took John Watson's honour course on "The Philosophy of Kant" and his "Moral Philosophy" course, both full-year courses. He also attested later that at Queen's he had taken two half-courses and one full

course with Professor Samuel Dyde – an "Introduction to Philosophy," "Logic and Philosophy," and "Seminar in Aesthetics" respectively. Presumably, Dyde was less memorable a teacher since Pierce rarely mentions him. See transcript, "Credits," file 6, box 48, LPP.

20 See Fraser, "Theology and the Social Gospel among Canadian Presbyterians." Fraser points out that Presbyterians like John Watson and the young Mackenzie King "articulated a collectivist liberalism in which people reached their true human destiny by self-sacrifice for the good of the whole," an idealistic vision of society framed in organic terms. Pierce fits exactly into this ethos, the result of the influences from both his Methodist home and Presbyterian Queen's.

21 LP, qtd. in Dickinson, *Lorne Pierce: A Profile*, 16.

22 LP to Dr W.E. McNeill, 20 January 1941, file 5, box 8, LPP.

23 This belief of Pierce's is referred to in Principal Wallace (Queen's) to LP, 3 February 1941, file 6, box 8, LPP.

24 The complete prayer is found in LP to EC, 4 January 1916, box 4, PFC. Two decades after "Wattie's" honours seminar, Pierce was still spoofing as well as emulating his idealism. He included in an anthology of humour former Kingstonian Grant Allen's poem "The First Idealist" about the epistemology of a jellyfish whose brain functioned along idealist lines. Asserting the dependence of reality on his perceptions, the jellyfish declares:

> "... So I come at last, in plain conclusion,
> When the subject is fairly set free from confusion,
> That the universe simply centres in Me,
> And if *I* were not, then nothing would be."
> That minute, a shark, who was strolling by,
> Just gulped him down, in the twink of an eye;
> And he died, with a few convulsive twists.
> But, somehow, the universe still exists.

LP included this poem in John Garvin, ed., *Cap and Bells: An Anthology of Light Verse by Canadian Poets* (Toronto: Ryerson 1936), 67, which Pierce completed editing after Garvin's death on 19 August 1935.

25 LP to EC, 1 February 1915, box 3, PFC.

26 LP to EC, 4 January 1916, box 4, PFC.

27 McKillop, *Contours of Canadian Thought*, 99.

28 On his arrival in Canada in 1889, Jordan became the minister at St Andrew's Church in Strathroy, Ontario. He quickly gained a wide reputation as preacher and thinker within the Canadian church, resulting in the Queen's appointment, which he held, publishing widely from 1899, until his retirement in 1929.

29 LP, qtd. in Hume, "Lorne Pierce," 3.

30 The association encompassed Jordan's son Dennis, a contemporary of Lorne's who became Pierce's physician in Toronto in the 1930s and 1940s.

31 See W.T. McCree, "William George Jordan (1852–1939)," in *Some Great Men of Queen's*, 97–114, for an excellent account of Jordan's personality and ideas.

32 Ibid., 98, 106–7. The continuing friendship between Pierce and Jordan meant that, after Professor Jordan's death in the spring of 1939, with Pierce and Dennis Jordan as prime organizers, the old man's art collection was to form a nucleus of a Queen's University collection of paintings, canvasses augmented by the work of many of the best Canadian artists of the present and past.

33 LP to Dr W.E. McNeill, 20 January 1941, file 5, box 8, LPP.

34 LP, "The Makers of Queen's," *Queen's Review*, 3 (August 1929): 189–92. Anita Loos was a popular writer of the light literature of the Jazz Age.

35 LP to E.K. Brown, 26 May 1948, file 3, box 17, LPP.

36 The photograph of Pierce with the other Athens graduate at Queen's is found in the collection of the Brockville Museum. My thanks to historian Glenn J Lockwood for a copy of this photograph.

37 W.E. McNeill, "James Cappon," in *Some Great Men of Queen's*, 86.

38 LP to W.E. McNeill, 20 January 1941, file 5, box 8, LPP. In this long and interesting letter about Cappon, Pierce's understandable ambivalence about the man shines through. Pierce insists: "I loved Cappon. My wife hated him!" but the letter makes the case for Edith's feelings more convincingly than for Lorne's.

39 Pierce uses the phrase "bland contempt" in the transcript "How I Became a Canadiana Collector" and adds: "The Dean could scarcely be regarded as familiar with or friendly to Canadian culture." For an account of Cappon's appointment to the English Department at Queen's, see John Coldwell Adams, *Sir Charles God Damn: The Life of Sir Charles G.D. Roberts* (Toronto: University of Toronto Press 1986), 58–9. Cappon's early book on Roberts was published in Toronto by Briggs in 1905.

40 For an account of Edgar's career, see Pelham Edgar, *Across My Path*, ed. Northrop Frye (Toronto: Ryerson 1952).

41 See LP to Dr W.E. McNeill, 20 January 1941, file 5, box 8, LPP.

42 LP, "Nathan van Patten at Queen's," reprinted in "Memorial to Cappy," *Douglas Library Notes* (Queen's), 13 (summer 1964): 3–4.

43 LP to EC, 27 October 1913, box 1, PFC.

44 Hume, "Lorne Pierce," 15.

45 LP to Sara and Eldred Chester, 8 April 1961, box 1, CFP. This was written nearly seven years after Edith's death, and eight months before his own.

46 LP Diary, 3 September 1915. The occasion was evidently a sweet memory for Edith too: in 1916, when LP was at Union, she presented him with a Queen's cushion as a reminder of their seating at the Levana bazaar. Levana is the Queen's society for college women, famous on the campus for many years for its candle-lighting ceremony, long held in the freshman year to predict the marital future of the women undergraduates. While women had been admitted to Queen's since the late nineteenth century, the emphasis seemed during Edith's time there to be on turning out a superior brand of "angel in the house." The

Queen's Arts 1912 yearbook featured the pince-nez'd "Lady Advisor" to female students, Mrs McNeil, whose message seemed calculated to reassure those readers fearful of bluestocking graduates: "If [women students] … are unfitted, in any degree, for future wifehood and motherhood, the University, in its relations with women, must be regarded as a menace to our country's well-being" (13). Another faculty member, Professor P.G.C. Campbell, shared his conviction that "no woman shall ever have a biography" (23). See *Year Book … Queen's University 1912* (Kingston, ON: British Whig 1912).

47 LP to EC, 24 October 1913, in possession of BPR.

48 Charles Chown and Elizabeth Pierce (no relation to Lorne) were married on 9 June 1881 and Charles died on 25 September 1910. Edith's siblings were Charles Edwin (b. 1882), Thomas Clarence (b. 1884), and Stanley Gordon Chown (b. 1888). The Pierce diary and papers record regular visits to Edith's brother Clarence and his wife, Lillian, who lived in Montreal, as well as to Gordon (a Winnipeg physician) and his wife and to Ed Chown, also in the west.

49 For an account of Alice Chown's life and ideas, see Diana Chown, Introduction to Alice Chown, *The Stairway* (1921) (Toronto: University of Toronto Press 1988), v–lxxii.

50 Edith Chown, travel diary of trip to England, Belgium, and France, May–August 1910, LPP.

51 Edith Pierce was a member of the Queen's Athletic Committee, convenor of the Levana Athletic Committee, and captain of the '12 Year Ladies Basketball team. See Queen's 1912 yearbook, 36.

52 EC to LP, 27 October 1913, box 1, PFC.

53 LP to EC, 27 October 1913, ibid.

54 LP Diary, 2 September 1915.

55 Ibid.

56 Queen's 1912 yearbook, 64. North, as an aspiring Presbyterian minister, had taken the 1911 Dominion Scholarship in Matriculation Theology, and shone in English classes. In his courses generally he refused "to accept anything less than first division."

57 Lorne took on these posts after narrowly failing to win election to the presidency of his year for 1911–12.

58 LP Diary, 3 September 1915.

59 Queen's 1912 yearbook, 7. The book was dedicated to the governor general, the Duke of Connaught.

60 Queen's 1912 yearbook, 25. For a discussion of Presbyterianism and the social gospel, see Fraser, "Theology and the Social Gospel." The idealist professors of Queen's had their ruthless moments. When John Watson was (unsuccessfully) intriguing to succeed George Grant as principal of Queen's in 1902, W.L. Grant commented sardonically that "idealism in practice is a sorry thing." Neatby, *Queen's University*, 247.

61 LP Diary, 3 September 1915.

62 Queen's 1912 yearbook, 36.

63 Ibid., 67.

64 LP Diary, 3 September 1915.

65 For texts of King's remarks, see "Hon. Mackenzie King at Queen's Dinner," Toronto *Globe*, 5 February 1912; "The Debt Due ... [speech by] Hon. Mackenzie King ...," Kingston *Whig*, 5 February 1912; "Very Prominent Speakers There," Kingston *Standard*, 5 February 1912; and King Papers, mfm. D3419, LAC. My thanks to George Henderson, retired archivist at Queen's, an authority on King, for generously sharing this material with me.

66 Mackenzie King, transcript, "There are three institutions ..." [Remarks for Queen's dinner, April 1912], 2, 3, King Papers, mfm D3419, LAC.

67 LP Diary, 3 September 1915.

68 Queen's 1912 yearbook, 67.

69 LP Diary, 3 September 1915 [copied into diary from LP memorandum of 23 April 1912].

70 Ibid.

71 Lorne did his fourth-year English course by correspondence all during the bleak Saskatchewan winter of 1912–13. He was not actually awarded his degree until the spring of 1913, at a time when he was shivering in a drafty prairie shack, far from the glories of Convocation Hall. EC congratulated LP on the completion of his degree in a postcard dated 29 April 1913, box 1, PFC. LP had written her anxiously on 13 March: "I can not get time to study as I should. I do it on the run and I'm afraid that Cappy will run [i.e., fail] me in April. That Fin[al] Eng[lish examination] is a beast. I can do it, love it, even if it is a beast but it takes grinding ... But our greatest glory is not in never failing, but in rising every time we fall." See LP to EC, 13 March 1913, box 1, PFC.

72 LP to EC, 12 July 1912, box 1, PFC.

CHAPTER THREE

1 LP to EC, 24 June 1913, box 1, PFC.

2 LP Diary, 6 September 1915. This assertion is one of eleven summary points about the meaning of his Saskatchewan years.

3 Semple, *The Lord's Dominion*, 285.

4 For a discussion of Queen's students and teaching in the west, see Neatby, *Queen's University*, 272.

5 Ibid., 274.

6 See ibid., 271ff.

7 LP Diary, 1 September 1915.

8 Ibid., 2 September 1915.

9 Ibid.

10 See David G. Pitt, *E.J. Pratt: The Truant Years 1882–1927* (Toronto: University of Toronto Press 1984), for an account of Pratt's experience as a student minister in

Saskatchewan in 1908; Northrop Frye's letters about his experience as a United Church probationer in the west in the 1930s are found in Robert Denham, ed., *The Correspondence of Northrop Frye and Helen Kemp 1932–1939: Volume I, 1932–1935* (Toronto: University of Toronto Press 1996).

11 His five stations were Plunkett, Wiley, Eltham, Easterlie, and Sweetbriar. For an account of his circuit's size, and his consequent feelings of futility, see LP to EC, 12 July 1912, box 1, PFC.

12 LP Diary, 3 September 1915.

13 John Webster Grant, *The Church in the Canadian Era* (Burlington, ON: Welch 1988), 94.

14 See Airhart, *Serving the Present Age*, 147.

15 Grant, *The Church in the Canadian Era*, 96.

16 LP was supposed to be paid $50 a month as a probationer. He concealed the extent of his penury from his parents as much as he could.

17 LP Diary, 6 September 1915.

18 Ibid., 3 September 1915.

19 Ibid., 2 September 1915.

20 See LP's booklet on Masonry, *Master Builders* (Toronto: Ryerson 1937), and LP, "Present Day Problems and the Mission of Masonry" [address], St Aidan's Lodge (Toronto) newsletter, 16 November 1923, loose items, 1923–25 volume of LP Diary. Pierce's speech declared that freemasonry should "build spiritual bridges between [all] peoples." He saw it as stressing brotherhood in much the same way as theosophy: "Your religion is strange. Your tongue is foreign. Your garb is unfamiliar. Your complexion is not mine. But you desire only goodness, you seek only truth. Therefore, hand to hand I greet you as a brother! We [Masons] must show the way to a new confidence and love or we are doomed."

21 LP Diary, 31 December 1924.

22 Ibid., 21 May 1912 [inserted in 3 September 1915 entry].

23 LP to EC, 13 December 1913, box 1, PFC. Lorne wrote of the pin: "I want you to keep it as long as you care to have it by you, as a silent and sacred reminder of one, a master mason, who prizes honour above all the external advantages of rank and fortune."

24 LP to EC, 25 September 1912, box 1, PFC.

25 LP Diary, 21 May 1912 [inserted in entry for 3 September 1915].

26 Ibid.

27 LP to EC, 30 May 1915, box 3, PFC.

28 LP to EC, 24 June 1913, box 1, PFC.

29 LP to EC, 25 August 1912, box 1, PFC.

30 LP to EC, 25 September 1912, box 1, PFC. Lorne found the people of the district "barbarous"; even Woods, his shack-mate, was at times an insulting "demon" and Lorne longed for a "more congenial occupation." See LP to EC, 12 July and 25 August 1912, box 1, PFC.

31 LP Diary, 25 May 1912 [inserted in entry for 3 September 1915].

32 Ibid., 20 December 1912 [inserted in entry for 3 September 1915].

33 LP to EC, 12 October 1913, box 1, PFC.

34 LP Diary, 20 December 1912 [inserted in entry for 3 September 1915].

35 LP to EC, 6 June 1915, box 3, PFC. Pierce comments on how well fed, well kept, and prosperous the assembled clergy at a Gananoque conference were.

36 He recorded in the diary: "Once in agony I wrote ... my chairman, protesting against the remissness of the Mission Fund payments. He replied 'Have courage[,] brother, windy weather makes a good Englishman.' I replied with a warm letter declaring that while Englishmen may live on wind and some others seemed to, I was a Canadian and required more substantial fare to subsist on. He sent a meek and exasperating line in return: 'Dear Bro. – I am preserving your correspondence to show you when you arrive at years of discretion, how inconsiderate you have been.'" Meanwhile Lorne was subsisting on condensed milk and cornflakes in sub-zero weather. See LP Diary, 25 May 1912 [inserted in entry for 3 September 1915].

37 Ibid.

38 Ibid.

39 LP to EC, 12 July 1912, box 1, PFC.

40 LP to EC, 28 December 1912, box 1, PFC. Lorne also included a detailed account in his diary of 3 September 1915, indicative of the profound way in which he was affected by the experience.

41 LP Diary, 3 September 1915.

42 Ibid., 1 April 1924. In 1924 Lorne revisited old friends and old haunts in Saskatchewan during one of his first western business trips for Ryerson.

43 See LP to EC, 13 January 1913, box 1, PFC.

44 LP Diary, 3 September 1915.

45 The phrase is used in a letter from EC to LP, 13 June 1913, box 1, PFC, as she applauds his decision to go on to a BD program rather than stay in the west.

46 LP to EC, 5 March 1913, box 1, PFC.

47 Dickinson, *Lorne Pierce*, 24.

48 Ibid.

49 Ibid.

50 For example, a letter of 21 October 1912 from Plunkett has some tear-jerking prose about the life of a sky pilot redolent of Ralph Connor or Adeline Teskey: "[I am q]uite alone, and after a long saddle tramp, through the snows to visit some sick or sorrowing home, trying to be to them a ministering angel as they pass through their Gethsemane, I'll return and sit down with the poets for a long, silent, solitary lamplight evening by the fire. And I'll stroll occasionally to the window and pull aside the blind and see ... the winter moonlight brighten the white hills that roll away towards the east, and I will think that you are both lucky and happy [in Kingston] on the other side of them." The hill metaphor is similar to that of his descriptions of his longings during his youth in Delta, suggesting Edith's importance to him even at this early stage of their courtship.

51 LP to EC, 6 April 1914, box 2, PFC.
52 EC to LP, 14 November 1913, box 1, PFC.
53 LP to EC, 27 October 1913, box 1, PFC.
54 LP to EC, [7 November 1913], box 1, PFC.
55 LP to EC, 9 February 1914, box 2, PFC.
56 See LP to EC, 2 March 1914, box 2, PFC. Malicious Plunkett gossip did not spare Lorne: rumours circulated there that Lorne had contracted a "foul alliance" when he left Plunkett, and he had to return for a visit to counteract the rumours. See LP Diary, 25 May 1912.
57 Lorne wrote to Edith, whose brother Gordon was a physician: "I do think the greatest men upon this planet are the doctors who are inspired with a great and holy purpose. Above teacher and preacher they stand next to our master who went about doing good." LP to EC, 21 April 1915, box 3, PFC.
58 LP Diary, 3 September 1915.
59 For an account of the episode, see LP to EC, 30 May 1915, box 3, PFC. Writing Edith of his friend's victory in the courts after long litigation, Lorne added: "Our friendship has been a peculiar one. My senior by thirty years he was my closest friend there. Every night when I came in from a drive he would either come over and sit and talk until I drove him out by tumbling into bed, or lug me over to play chess and listen to a new grand opera record on his Victrola … When I was ill [with pleurisy in the winter of 1914] he would often quote Milton until I could see floating around my green lamp shade all the cherubim and seraphim of the regained paradise."
60 Pierce even gave a paper to the fledging society: "The Literary Society is still alive and active and will be after Wed. Jan. 7 if I do not kill it with my paper on 'Christ in English Literature.'" LP to EC, 3 January 1914, box 2, PFC.
61 LP to EC, 13 January 1913, box 1, PFC.
62 LP Diary, 6 September 1915.
63 Ibid., 3 September 1915.
64 LP to EC, 7 November 1913, box 1, PFC.
65 James S. Woodsworth, *Strangers within Our Gates* (Toronto: Methodist Missionary Society 1909).
66 LP to EC, 1 June 1914, box 2, PFC.
67 LP to EC, 6 April 1914, box 2, PFC.

CHAPTER FOUR

1 LP to EC, 9 May 1915, box 3, PFC.
2 LP Diary, 2 September 1915.
3 LP to EC, 4 July 1914, box 2, PFC.
4 LP to EC, 10 August 1914, box 2, PFC.
5 LP to EC, 13 December 1915, box 4, PFC.

6 EC to LP, 14 September 1914, box 2, PFC. She had earlier written of her difficulties with the relationship, although she admitted that there would be a "great emptiness" in her life without their correspondence: "I have never had a truer friend than you. I honor you and I honor your ambitions. I know that some of my letters have been unkind but they were not written with that idea but rather to try and solve what to me has been the greatest problem of my life." EC to LP, 12 August 1914, box 2, PFC. She was teaching Grade 2 at Strathcona School, Regina.

7 LP Diary, 3 September 1915.

8 LP to EC, 24 August 1914, box 2, PFC.

9 LP to EC, 28 August 1914, box 2, PFC.

10 LP to EC, 24 August 1914, box 2, PFC.

11 Ibid.

12 LP to EC, 22 September 1914, box 2, PFC.

13 LP to EC, 15 September 1914, box 2, PFC.

14 See EC to LP, 24 September 1913, box 1, PFC.

15 LP to EC, 15 September 1914, box 2, PFC.

16 LP to "Billy" [Bill Topping?], 24 November 1914, box 2, PFC.

17 C.B. Sissons, *A History of Victoria University* (Toronto: University of Toronto Press 1952), 236, 247.

18 See Airhart, *Serving the Present Age*, chapter 4 in particular, and Semple, *The Lord's Dominion*. In 1901, according to Airhart, Canadian Methodists numbered 17.1 per cent of the population; by 1921 this had fallen to 13 per cent. See also Marshall, *Secularizing the Faith*, 10.

19 Van Die, *An Evangelical Mind*, 178.

20 Ibid., 115, 127.

21 Ibid., 126.

22 Ibid., 127.

23 LP to EC, 22 September 1914, box 2, PFC.

24 Van Die, *An Evangelical Mind*, 131.

25 Pierce greatly admired Ernest Thomas, who in 1919 was to become field secretary for the department of evangelism and social services of the Methodist Church.

26 Airhart, *Serving the Present Age*, 16. Jackson himself had undergone intense controversy in 1909–10 over his interpretation of Genesis.

27 Michael Gauvreau, *The Evangelical Century: College and Creed in English Canada from the Great Revival to the Great Depression* (Montreal & Kingston: McGill-Queen's University Press 1991), 221.

28 LP to EC, 9 and 17 May 1915, box 3, PFC.

29 LP to EC, 8 November 1914, box 2, PFC.

30 LP to EC, 29 November 1914, box 2, PFC.

31 LP to "Billy," 24 November 1914, box 2, PFC.

32 LP to EC, 8 November 1914, box 2, PFC.

33 LP to "Billy," 24 November 1914, box 2, PFC.

34 LP to EC, 26 October 1914, box 2, PFC. In a letter of 3 October, he also tells Edith that he is a tutoring a class of Chinese students two hours a week.

35 See Edgar, *Across My Path*.

36 LP Diary, 6 September 1915.

37 See Diana Chown, Introduction to Alice Chown, *The Stairway*, v–lxii.

38 EC to LP, 18 October 1914, box 2, PFC.

39 LP to EC, 26 October 1914, box 2, PFC.

40 LP to EC, 1 November 1914, box 2, PFC.

41 Alice Chown to LP, 8 July [1915], box 15, PFC.

42 LP to EC, 20 November 1915, box 3, PFC.

43 LP to EC, 8 November 1914, box 2, PFC.

44 Ibid.

45 LP to EC, [late October] 1914, box 2, PFC.

46 LP to Bruce Pierce, n.d. [Second World War], in possession of BPR.

47 LP to EC, 23 November 1914, box 2, PFC.

48 LP to EC, 12, 21, and 27 December 1914, box 2, PFC.

49 LP to EC, 8 January 1915, box 2, PFC.

50 LP to EC, 6 and 16 February 1915, box 3, PFC.

51 LP to EC, 16 February 1915, box 3, PFC.

52 Ibid.

53 LP to EC, 15 March 1915, box 3, PFC.

54 Ibid.

55 LP to EC, 14 March and 18 January 1915, box 3, PFC.

56 LP to EC, 14 March 1915, box 3, PFC.

57 LP to EC, 2 May 1915, box 3, PFC.

58 LP, "The Contribution of Modern Systems of Philosophy to the Philosophy of Religion" (BD thesis, Victoria College/Union Theological Seminary), "Theism" chapter, 15–16, LPP.

59 LP Diary, 6 September 1915. Lorne wrote: "I am going to make of you my Father Confessor and tell you all my dreams, and all my desires, my thoughts and aspirations. I am going to tell you about everything I see and every person I meet like an old housewife and mind – we're Masons … and Masons never tell!"

60 The diary may be largely silent on differences with his parents because Hattie Pierce on at least one occasion read the diary and entered an inspirational quotation in it.

61 EC to LP, 4 April 1915, box 3, PFC. War fever could take some curious forms early in the Great War. In this letter, Edith described a euchre party, where each table represented a combatant country. Edith drew Germany's table, and the table was awarded a mock iron cross each time their table won.

62 LP to EC, 9 and 17 May 1915, box 3, PFC.

63 LP to EC, 19 April 1915, box 3, PFC.

64 LP to EC, 16 June 1915, box 3, PFC.

65 LP to EC, 9 May 1915, box 3, PFC.

66 LP to EC, 17 May 1915, box 3, PFC.

67 LP to EC, 26 May 1915, box 3, PFC.

68 LP to EC, 25 July 1915, box 3, PFC.

69 LP to EC, 30 July 1915, box 3, PFC.

70 LP Diary, 6 September 1915.

71 EC to LP, 14 September 1915, box 3, PFC.

72 LP to EC, 9 September 1915, box 3, PFC.

73 LP to EC, 24 September 1915, box 3, PFC.

74 LP to EC, 16 September 1915, box 3, PFC.

75 When Lorne received his Victoria marks that October he had not done as well as usual, with a high mark of 75 and a low of 55 among the nine examinations. He concluded that Victoria was giving him a hard time for his independence. LP to EC, 5 November 1915, box 3, PFC.

76 LP to EC, 24 September 1915, box 3, PFC.

77 LP Diary, 1 October 1915.

78 Ibid.

79 For histories of Union Theological Seminary, see Henry Sloane Coffin, *A Half Century of Union Theological Seminary, 1896–1945: An Informal History* (New York: Scribner 1954), and R.T. Handy, *A History of Union Theological Seminary in New York* (New York: Columbia University Press 1987).

80 LP to EC, 23 November 1914, box 2, PFC.

81 LP to EC, 18 October 1915, box 3, PFC. Ralph Horner was a well-known late-nineteenth-century evangelist who had been suspended from the Methodist Church of Canada in 1894 for the extreme emotionalism and radical doctrines of his ministry. See Airhart, *Serving the Present Age*, 49–50.

82 LP to EC, 30 September 1915, box 3, PFC.

83 LP to EC, 3 October 1915, box 3, PFC.

84 LP to EC, 17 October 1915, box 3, PFC. Lorne was still sufficiently biased to write of the maid who cleaned his room, "Thank de Lawd she isn't black!" Pierce and Topping roomed at 600 West 122nd St.

85 LP to EC, 26 November 1915, box 4, PFC.

86 Edward Pierce to LP, 2 November 1915, box 4, PFC.

87 Harriet Pierce to LP, 30 and 9 November 1915, box 4, PFC; LP to EC, 20 November 1915, box 4, PFC.

88 Unidentified Acacia clipping, inserted in LP Diary, February 1916.

89 LP to EC, 20 January 1916, box 4, PFC. Only twenty Columbia students were members of Acacia, whose membership was largely professional men. Just twelve students a year were invited to join on the basis of "educational standing" and "popularity and evidence of success in chosen profession." Lorne had been

vetted for a three-month period by Acacia officers, unbeknownst to him. See LP to EC, 3 December 1915, box 4, PFC.

90 LP to EC, [26 October] 1915, box 3, PFC.

91 LP to EC, 8 March 1916, box 5, PFC.

92 LP, "Book Steward's Corner," *Christian Guardian*, 20 October 1920, 25.

93 LP to EC, 26 October 1915, box 3, PFC.

94 "Friedrich Daniel Ernst Schleiermacher," *Evangelical Dictionary of Theology*, ed. Walter Elwell (Grand Rapids, MI: Baker 1984), 981–3.

95 LP Diary, 27 January 1916.

96 LP, "On Religious Toleration," *In Conference with the Best Minds* (Nashville, TN: Cokesbury Press 1927), 120, 117.

97 See LP Diary, 21 November 1915.

98 LP to EC, 26 October 1915, box 3, PFC. He later paid another tribute to Union: "There is a bigness about the whole place – from the three million dollars the place cost up to the world renowned staff … All [students and staff] have been out in the world and know what life means and all is serious, study, honours, specializing, and broad as the plains of the West." See LP to EC, 13 December 1915, box 4, PFC.

99 LP to EC, 1 February 1916, box 4, PFC.

00 LP to EC, 2 May 1916, box 4, PFC. Lorne and Bill Topping had become a little disillusioned with Shaw, who had been petty enough to reproach them for coming to class carrying another book than his. See LP Diary, 5 December 1915.

01 LP to EC, 16 January 1916, box 4, PFC.

02 LP to EC, 28 December 1915, box 4, PFC, also echoed in LP to EC, 19 October 1915, box 4, PFC.

03 Unidentified clipping, enclosed in EC to LP, 11 January 1916, box 4, PFC.

04 LP to EC, 6 September 1915, box 3, PFC.

05 LP to EC, 5 December 1914, box 2, PFC. He was later upset about his outburst, but it bespoke his ambivalence.

06 LP to EC, 29 November 1915, box 4, PFC.

07 LP to EC, 30 April 1916, box 4, PFC.

08 LP to EC, 10 April 1916, box 4, PFC. Lorne did not want to go out with the Americans: "But after all my heart is with my ain folk and ain kirk and the quiet little land of the Maple, that is thrilling the world today with its heroism. I too ought to be serving [Canada] somewhere, and yet I'm thinking of running away!" When Hattie and Lorne Pierce heard that Lorne had applied through the United States, Lorne's father declared: "He's just a boy, he'll soon see better!" See LP to EC, 14 March 1916, box 4, PFC.

09 LP to EC, 28 March 1916, box 4, PFC.

10 EC to LP, 18 October 1915, box 3, PFC.

11 EC to LP, 29 November 1915, box 4, PFC. A measure of Edith's commitment is that she had drafted a letter to her grandmother and aunts saying that Lorne

was "everything" to her and describing him as "pure gold" and "upright in everything he does." See EC draft to Grandmother [Elizabeth], Harriet and Charlotte Conley, 4 January 1915, box 3, PFC.

112   See LP to EC, 9 December 1915 and 23 March 1916, box 4, PFC.

113   LP to EC, 18 February 1913, box 1, PFC.

114   LP to EC, 2 October 1912, box 1, PFC. Unusually for him, LP "had to leave" early during a Mrs Pankhurst lecture. See LP to EC, 5 February 1916, PFC.

115   LP to EC, 18 February 1913, box 1, PFC.

116   LP to EC, 22 March 1915, box 3, PFC.

117   LP to EC, 24 November 1915, box 3, PFC.

118   LP to EC, [December 1915] en route to Delta, box 4, PFC.

119   EC to LP, 5 December 1915, box 4, PFC.

120   LP to EC, 14 January 1916, box 4, PFC.

121   LP Diary, 28 October 1915.

122   LP to EC, 10 February 1916, box 4, PFC, and 5 November 1915, box 3, PFC.

123   LP to EC, 25 February 1916, box 4, PFC.

124   LP to EC, 14 March 1916, box 4, PFC.

125   As an admirer of Ruskin, Lorne wanted their home filled with the uplifting spirit of art. His purchases included prints of *The Blue Boy*, *Whistler's Mother*, and the *Mona Lisa*, and three Rembrandt prints including *The Night Watch* and Corot's *Dance of the Nymphs*, as well as a Madonna. See LP to EC, 5 February and 10 February 1916, box 4, PFC.

126   EC to LP, 6 February 1916, box 4, PFC.

127   LP to EC, 23 January 1916, box 4, PFC.

128   EC to LP, 4 October 1914, box 2, PFC.

129   EC to LP, 17 January 1916, box 4, PFC.

130   Ibid.

131   LP to EC, 18 February 1916, box 4, PFC.

132   LP to EC, 16 January 1916, box 4, PFC. It is noteworthy here that Lorne framed the refusal of a parsonage primarily in terms of his goals and aptitudes, not her desires.

133   LP to EC, 19 October 1915, box 4, PFC.

134   LP to EC, 26 October 1915, box 4, PFC.

135   LP Diary, 29 January 1916.

136   Lorne became increasingly alienated from his friend Homer Dubs over the war. Finally, in April, Dubs ran "Canada and the Empire down, laugh[ed] at our so-called independence, and h[e]ld the loyalty of the Dominion up to ridicule … When I finished an exhibition of Canadian oratory he was standing in the door and as he shut it he hurled back a dirty, cowardly, insinuating question." It appears that conversation at Union was not always as lofty and high-minded as Lorne had at first thought. LP to EC, 16 April 1916, box 5, PFC.

137   See LP to EC, 21 March 1916, box 5, PFC.

138 LP to EC, 27 April 1916, box 5, PFC.

139 LP to EC, 30 October 1915, box 4, PFC.

140 LP to EC, 18 February 1916, box 4, PFC. Lorne felt it would be "a disgrace to be forced."

141 LP to EC, 10 December 1915, box 4, PFC.

142 LP to EC, 25 February 1916, box 4, PFC.

143 LP to EC, 28 March 1916, box 4, PFC.

144 LP to EC, 27 January 1916, box 4, PFC. His response showed how deeply the wrangling with Victoria had troubled him. He exulted: "So after all I'll be a Vic alumnus and a real Canadian Methodist and not a bad heretic man!"

145 LP Diary, 29 April 1916.

146 See LP to EC, 30 April 1916, box 5, PFC.

147 Ibid.

148 Ibid. Lorne's logic is curious here: he has just clearly stated that it was his mother and country that he had followed in making his decision – certainly not Edith's wishes.

149 EC to LP, 4 May 1916, box 5, PFC. Edith was also worried that without the "heart" for the work, she would not be of much "influence or service to a community" as a minister's wife.

150 LP to EC, 12 May 1916, box 5, PFC. Lorne recounted that one of his professors had returned a paper he had written on theism with the comment "A + Fine!" Of his comment to Edith, it is also true that she would not stand in his way and would defer to his wishes.

151 LP to EC, 25 May 1916, box 5, PFC.

152 LP to EC, 30 May 1916, and EC to LP, 21 June 1916, box 5, PFC.

153 LP to EC, 28 May 1916, box 5, PFC. Details of the ceremony are in LP Diary, 4 June 1916. The sermon was taken from 1 Timothy 4:16: "Take heed unto thyself, and unto the doctrine; continue in them: for in doing this thou shalt both save thyself, and them that hear thee."

154 LP, manuscript of ordination sermon, file 8, box 42, LPP.

155 Airhart, *Serving the Present Age*, 97.

156 LP Diary, 22 and 14 June 1916.

157 See LP to EC, 17 and 21 January 1916, box 5, PFC. Mrs Pierce did not write Edith until 17 March. On 21 January, Lorne described his mother's reaction: "The letter from home was very joyous ... Mothers are the strangest things. Everything that I told them Mother had a presentiment of! 'Today a very settled peace stole into my heart.' That's Mother." Lorne, however, wrote "That's" in such a way that it at first appears to read "I hate Mother." Of his plan to take up foreign missionary work with Edith, Mrs Pierce wrote: "We will spell disappointment with a capital H[eaven]." Not until near the end of his own life did Lorne confide his mother's objections to anyone. See LP to Eldred and Sara Chester, 8 April 1961, box 1, CFP.

CHAPTER FIVE

1 LP to EC, 9 June 1916, box 5, PFC.

2 LP Diary, 4 July 1916. LP observed: "No one else but mother." His parents and sister also sent him inspirational letters on 22 and 25 June respectively. Ed Pierce wrote to Lorne of "God's Plan's" for him and that he had talked with the Reverend Thompson about his son: "He did not want you placed in some obscure corner. But wanted you to be a Big shining light in one of our Big Cities and now you are actually there." See box 5, PFC.

3 "St. Paul's Methodist Congregation to Dedicate New Edifice on Sunday," Ottawa *Citizen*, 19 January 1924. Lorne Pierce spoke at the 1924 dedication service, fittingly – given his shift in mission – on "Our Canadian Literature" and the need for its preservation as a part of national self-preservation. Pierce was taken to task by J.D. Logan in the columns of the Ottawa *Citizen* on 29 January for saying he preferred the sentiments of Robert Stead's "Kitchener in Khartoum" to "In Flanders Fields." Pierce had also called Arthur Meighen's commemorative address at Vimy "one of our greatest literary works."

4 LP to EC, 26 June 1916, box 5, PFC. The parsonage was at 122 Fourth Avenue.

5 Ibid.

6 LP to EC, 12 July 1916, box 5, PFC.

7 For his worries over sermons, see LP to EC, 6 May 1916, box 5, PFC, and LP to EC, 8 January 1915, box 2, PFC.

8 Lorne recorded of the sermon that the comments were "Got them" and "Best yet." See LP Diary, 23 July 1916.

9 William Westfall, *Two Worlds: The Protestant Culture of Nineteenth-Century Ontario* (Montreal & Kingston: McGill-Queen's University Press 1989), 79.

10 LP to EC, 9 July 1916, box 5, PFC.

11 See LP Diary, 3 January 1917.

12 LP to EC, 11 August 1916, box 5, PFC.

13 LP Diary, 4 July 1916.

14 Ibid., and LP to EC, 10 July 1916, box 5, PFC.

15 LP Diary, 4 July 1916. Significantly, when Edith pointed out jokingly that it was American Independence Day, Lorne's reaction was "to wonder if that is a good omen!" He still wanted to be in charge. He had written her on 18 June: "You little libertine! I shall see to it that the word 'obey' *is* in the ceremony. You must obey me in so many things, but they're going to be all nice things Edith, things you'll want to do." See box 5, PFC.

16 EC to LP, 6 July 1916, box 5, PFC.

17 LP to EC, 2 August 1916, box 5, PFC.

18 LP to EC, 11 July 1916, box 5, PFC. In a letter written the next day, he still could not get the horror out of his mind. Was it fear? He still weighed less than 140 lbs. and had a history of pleurisy, colds, and pains in his side.

19 Michael Bliss, "The Methodist Church and World War 1," *Conscription 1917,* Canadian Historical Readings, no. 8 (Toronto: University of Toronto Press 1969), 41, 43. A Methodist minister from Montreal in fact headed the military recruiting drive in Quebec.

20 LP to EC, 9 August 1916, box 5, PFC.

21 LP Diary, 1 August 1916.

22 Ibid., 3 August 1916.

23 Ibid., 19 August 1916.

24 Ibid.

25 EC to LP, 4 September 1915, box 3, PFC.

26 Alice Chown to EC, 8 August 1913, box 15, PFC.

27 Alice had earlier written Edith very explicitly of this need: "You are pretty and attractive … you … are a very sweet girl and you have every reason to believe that you can attract the man you desire, but somehow or other you must gain faith in yourself, and you must learn the strength of your own powers … So far a lot of ideas about modesty and self respect have made you think into yourself. You have wanted to be chosen rather than to choose, that was a nice little falsehood that we were taught, one that lingered from a past age, the modern woman today does the choosing in a very subtle way. All the stories in the *Ladies Home Journal* to the contrary." Ibid.

28 Alice Chown to EC, 30 October 1911, box 15, PFC.

29 Alice Chown to ECP, n.d. [c. 1920], box 15, PFC.

30 Alice Chown to LP, 28 June 1916, box 15, PFC; LP to EC, 29 August 1916, box 5, PFC.

31 EC to LP, 12 July 1915, box 5, PFC.

32 See Diana Chown, Introduction to *The Stairway*, xlvii.

33 ECP, entry about the Pierces' silver anniversary in LP Diary, 11 November 1941.

34 See LP Diary, 16 September 1916.

35 Alice Chown to EC, n.d. [summer 1916], box 15, PFC.

36 Alice Chown had made several trips to Lake Placid for domestic science conferences starting in 1900. See Diana Chown, Introduction to *The Stairway*, xxiiiff.

37 LP Diary, 16 October 1916.

38 Ibid., 19 September 1916.

39 LP noted ruefully in his diary on 1 October 1916: "Awful strain and worse sermon. She told me I could do better."

40 LP Diary, 18 December 1916.

41 Edith's Valentine's tribute is pasted in LP Diary, 13 February 1917.

42 For example, the obituary of Lieutenant (Reverend) Hubert Fenten is pasted into the LP diary entry for 20 November 1916.

43 See Bliss, "The Methodist Church and World War 1," 39–59.

44 Clipping in LP Diary, February 1917.

45 St Paul's Church Christmas card, insert in LP Diary, 2 January 1918.

46 Union Theological Seminary newsletter, box 48, LPP.

47 "The Mission Board apparently do not want men and have no need of me … disgusting." LP Diary, 6 March 1917.

48 Clifford Pierce to LP, 10 February 1917, insert in LP Diary for that date. The letter had a graphic account of raiding sorties into German lines on the front.

49 His father wrote: "I don't think they want men of your stren[g]th and ability at the Front. There is men that can do that while you could do what they cannot at Home. I think there is times in our lives when it is a greater Sacrifice to say no to our conscience when our good judgement will say I cannot fill the job." Edward Pierce to LP, 25 March 1917, LP Diary insert. Lorne told his parents to write him no more such letters, and in an undated reply his father conceded: "Enough has been said."

50 The operation seems to have been part of a (futile) effort to improve his hearing. See LP Diary, 20 November 1916.

51 Ibid., 6 March 1917.

52 Lorne gives the latter as a reason for enlisting in the Royal Flying Corps. LP Diary, 6 March 1917.

53 Ibid.

54 Two undated, unidentified clippings from Ottawa papers – "Methodist Pastor Takes up Flying" and "From the Pulpit to an Airplane" – inserted in diary for March 1917 praise the move and speak of his popularity with the congregation. One Catholic man presented him with a rosary to take with him.

55 LP Diary, 21 March 1916.

56 Ibid., 6 April 1917.

57 Ibid., 15 April 1917.

58 Bliss, "The Methodist Church and World War I," 43–4.

59 LP Diary, 4 May 1917.

60 See Certificate of Military Instruction for Lorne Pierce, 31 October 1917, box 24, PFC.

61 LP to ECP, 23 May 1917, box 6, PFC. He was relieved when his speech elicited yells and clapping. When he had finished, "the roof nearly came off with applause."

62 LP Diary, 24 April 1917.

63 LP to ECP, 26 March 1917, box 6, PFC. Lorne assured her about enlistment: "But I am coming back darling, and we will have a grand new honeymoon, and a happier home because we both did our duty."

64 LP Diary, 7 June 1917.

65 ECP to LP, 23 July 1917, box 6, PFC.

66 LP Diary, 20 October 1917.

67 Ibid., 18 May 1917.

68 Ibid.

69 Ibid., 14 June 1917.
70 Ibid., 1 July 1917.
71 LP Diary, 8 July 1917.
72 Ibid., 22 September 1917.
73 Ibid., 7 June 1917.
74 "H.G. Wells," *Acta Victoriana*, 43 (December 1917): 133–8. Pierce saw Wells as essentially Christian in spite of the latter's denials. He put it most succinctly in "The Gods of this New Era": "[Wells] makes his religion justify the soul by giving a real reason for man's existence, his dignity and destiny, and the unity, character and might of his spiritual life" (280). LP, "The Gods of this New Era," *Canadian Magazine*, 1, no. 4 (1918): 279–84.
75 LP, "The Gods of this New Era," 281. Many clergyman were attempting at this time to find "redemptive divine purpose in the struggle." S.D. Chown, general superintendent of the Methodist Church of Canada, proclaimed his conviction in 1916 that the trials of war would usher in a "higher national life." See Gauvreau, *The Evangelical Century*, 259.
76 LP, "The Gods of this New Era," 281.
77 S.D. Chown took just such a position in the pages of the *Christian Guardian* on 12 December 1917. See Bliss, "The Methodist Church and World War 1," 47.
78 LP, "The Gods of this New Era," 284.
79 LP Diary, 2 February 1918.
80 See LP, "Suffering in Russian Literature," file 14, box 39, LPP. LP presented another version of this paper to the meetings of the Montreal Methodist Conference in Kemptville in June 1920, with the title "The Contribution of Russian Literature to Christian Theology." He revised this in 1921 and 1922 as a dissertation for his extramural doctorate in theology (1922) from United Theological College in Montreal, under the title "The Contribution of Russian Literature to Religious Experience." The conference version is in file 4, box 37, LPP.
81 See Diana Chown, Introduction to *The Stairway*, xviiff.
82 LP Diary, 6 September 1915.
83 Charles Shaw to LP, 26 April 1917, box 6, PFC.
84 For example, LP Diary, 19 March 1917, refers to the fall of the Romanovs.
85 LP, "The Contribution of Russian Literature to Christian Theology," 4, file 4, box 37, LPP.
86 Ibid., 5.
87 Ibid., 1, 12.
88 Ibid., 4, 7. Pierce's analysis of Pushkin exemplifies his approach: "Pushkin sealed Russian literature with an idealism born of the travail of realism and humanism. He showed that suffering was not a solution of the problems of life, but a process that led to a fuller realization and a deeper appreciation of life. 'He looked into infinity and knelt,' and with him has knelt a whole nation. He was

the leaven that leavened Russian thought and life … The heart of Pushkin is a
shrine and a holy place worn by the knees of pilgrims, princes and moujik, and
of suffering men everywhere" (7).

89 Ibid., 1.
90 LP Diary, 20 October 1917.
91 Ibid., 23 October 1917 and 7 February 1918.
92 Ibid., 25 October and 1 November 1917.
93 LP to BP, n.d. [1944], box 16, PFC. Beth Pierce was working at Sainte-Anne-de-
Bellevue Veterans' Hospital as an occupational therapist, prompting her father
to reminisce about Ongwanada.
94 LP Diary, 13 November 1917.
95 Henry Barnett to LP, 24 February 1918, box 6, PFC. Barnett, a fellow Mason,
thanked "Brother Pierce" for his "kindly and brotherly trouble" in sending "the
first full account of poor Percy's accident."
96 LP Diary, 19 September 1917. He recorded that Edith had written that "every day
was happy because my dearest filled them with love, kindness and thoughtfulness."
97 LP Diary, 16 November 1917.
98 Harriet Pierce to LP, 19 November 1917, box 6, PFC. The reference to Catholics
probably arose from the fact that Ontario Catholics were embroiled in a political and judicial battle to preserve their educational rights in the province.
99 LP Diary, 25 December 1917.
100 Ibid., 18 December 1917.
101 Olive O'Neill to LP, 15 December 1947, file 1, box 15, LPP. She also remembered
that he had worked diligently at his Russian literature paper.
102 LP Diary, 15 November 1917.
103 Ibid., 4 January 1918.
104 Ibid., 4 February 1918.
105 Ibid., 5 and 7 February 1918.
106 Ibid., 7 February 1918.
107 Ibid.
108 ECP to LP, 7 February 1918, box 6, PFC.
109 Harriet Pierce to LP, 14 February 1918, box 6, PFC.
110 Alice Chown to LP, n.d. [spring 1918], box 15, PFC.
111 ECP to LP, 14 February 1918, box 6, PFC.
112 Even ten years later, Lorne avoided uttering the word directly. He wrote to Bliss
Carman, perhaps the most famous Canadian former TB patient: "When you
came to Canada on your triumphal tour, after the Saranac retreat, I was just out
of the army, laid away for the same reason." See LP to Carman, file 9, box 21,
Bliss Carman Correspondence, LPP.
113 LP Diary, 26 February 1918.

114　Ibid., 17 March 1918.
115　Ibid., 13 February 1918.

CHAPTER SIX

1　LP Diary, 18 January 1919.
2　Ibid., 22 April 1920.
3　LP to Beth and Bruce Pierce, postmarked 13 February 1945, in possession of BPR.
4　LP Diary, 30 March 1918.
5　Ibid.
6　Ibid., 7 May 1918.
7　Sergeant H.E. Suthers and two others, postcard to LP, May 1918, box 6, PFC.
8　LP Diary, 15 April 1918.
9　Ibid., 3 April 1918.
10　Bliss, "The Methodist Church and World War I," 59. In English Canada, some voices on the left, especially among socialists, dissented from this militant nationalism, only to be "drowned out in a wave of patriotic sentiment," according to Ian McKay, *Reasoning Otherwise: Leftists and the People's Enlightenment in Canada, 1890–1920* (Toronto: Between the Lines 2008), 421.
11　LP Diary, 19 May and 3 July 1918.
12　Ibid., 19 May 1918.
13　The Montreal Conference was an area of jurisdiction within the Methodist Church of Canada that also included Ottawa and parts of eastern Ontario.
14　LP to ECP, 31 May 1918, box 6, PFC.
15　LP Diary, 7 May 1918.
16　Carman was general superintendent of the Methodist Church of Canada from 1883 until 1915.
17　LP Diary, 9 June 1918.
18　List of members of Matilda churches, file 12, box 48, LPP. Brinston had 141 members, Hulbert 116, Hainsville 99, and Glen Stewart 13. The service schedule for a typical Sunday was a gruelling circuit over mediocre roads, with services in Hainsville at 10:30 a.m., Brinston at 2:30 p.m., and Hulbert at 7 p.m. See LP Diary, 17 November 1918.
19　LP Diary, 3 July 1917.
20　Hume, "Lorne Pierce," 6.
21　LP Diary, 4 August 1918.
22　Ibid., 31 August 1918. Lorne was a little envious of his wife's performance. He wrote that he came away from the convention "anxious to do something that would count" but that Edith was now "a county officer and I only a township!"
23　Ibid., 19 September 1918.

24 LP to ECP, 25 August 1918, box 6, PFC.

25 LP Diary, 1 October 1918.

26 Ibid., 17 October 1918.

27 Ibid., 5 November 1918.

28 Ibid.

29 That bond was intensified further in March 1919 when Harriet Pierce underwent surgery in Brockville for a hysterectomy. Lorne wrote anxiously in his diary: "She must get well. If ever there was a saint she is." The letter his mother wrote before surgery must only have fuelled her son's relentless drive: "If I should not see you again here, we'll all meet at Home beyond life. In the meantime keep the home-altar fire burning brightly. If we haven't the devotional we haven't very much. A great work is yours. With endless love, Mother." See Harriet Pierce to family, 18 March 1919, box 6, PFC.

30 LP Diary, 10 November 1918.

31 Ibid., 11 November 1918.

32 Ibid., 3 December 1918.

33 Ibid., 18 January 1919.

34 See ibid., 4 August 1918 and 11 February 1919.

35 The letter is mentioned in LP Diary, 18 December 1919. The Matilda circuit raised $474.15 versus $100 for Delta and $80 for Brockville. Given that the mission board had failed to send Pierce overseas, Endicott's praise is ironic.

36 LP Diary, 30 December 1918.

37 Ibid., 13 January 1919.

38 Ibid., 14 April 1920.

39 Ibid., 26 February 1919.

40 Ibid., 23 August 1919.

41 Hume, "Lorne Pierce," 9.

42 In March 1919 he sent off an article on German Loyalists in Upper Canada to *Canadian Magazine*, which was accepted. See LP, "The German Loyalist in Upper Canada," *Canadian Magazine*, August 1920, 290–6.

43 LP Diary, 28 November 1918. In the entry for 2 August 1919, Lorne recorded welcoming receptions for two privates on the circuit, one of whom was presented with a check for $25.

44 An advertisement for the rally is inserted in LP Diary, September 1919.

45 Ibid., 25 October 1919.

46 ECP to LP, 13 April 1919, box 6, PFC.

47 LP to ECP, 16 April 1919, box 6, PFC. Lorne concluded: "Now I must close for I have a lot to do at sermons and [S]unday, and [attend a Soldier's Rehabilitation Committee meeting] ... I have to be there ... to see that our big idea is not lost before it really grows."

48 See ECP to LP, 6 March 1919, box 6, PFC.

49 Harriet Pierce to ECP, 2 October 1919, box 6, PFC.

50 For a discussion of the ethos of the social gospel, see Richard Allen, "The Social Gospel and the Reform Tradition in Canada 1890–1928," *Canadian Historical Review*, 49, no. 4 (1968): 381–99, and his *The Social Passion: Religion and Social Reform in Canada 1914–1918* (Toronto: University of Toronto Press 1971).

51 Bliss, "The Methodist Church and World War I," 39.

52 LP Diary, 11 March 1917.

53 Allen, *The Social Passion*, 16.

54 See ibid., 72.

55 Airhart, *Serving the Present Age*, 130.

56 LP Diary, 10 November 1918.

57 Ibid., 13 April 1920.

58 Ibid., 2 April 1919.

59 Unidentified newspaper clipping on formation of Brinston baseball club, insert in LP Diary, May 1919.

60 LP, "Dumb for Forty Years," *Christian Guardian*, 3 March 1920, and LP Diary, 8 March 1920. Ironically, his payment from the *Christian Guardian* was a $4 credit at the Book Room, his future employer. Pierce joked that the sum amounted to only a dime a year. See LP Diary, 12 March 1920.

61 Alice Chown to ECP, n.d. [1920], box 15, PFC.

62 Alice Chown to LP, 7 May [1918], box 15, PFC.

63 Alice Chown to LP, 18 July 1919, box 15, PFC.

64 Diana Chown, Introduction to *The Stairway*, xlix, and Alice Chown to LP, 28 August 1919, box 15, PFC.

65 LP Diary, 10 July 1919. He had been brooding on Versailles for some time, writing in the 5 March entry that year: "The peace conference goes on. If the barons muddle things up much more & the dukes fuddle much more there will be another war. The moral aims are already lost in the avalanche of selfish claims. And so much precious young life gone too! Oh the pity of it all. Shame on us everyone."

66 LP Diary, 10 July 1919.

67 LP, "The Peace That Passes Understanding," file 4, box 39, LPP.

68 Ibid.

69 Some opposition from the local reeve and others is recorded in LP Diary, 9 and 19 May and 2 August 1919.

70 Hume, "Lorne Pierce," 21.

71 LP Diary, 28 February 1920.

72 See LP Diary entries for October 1919 and undated clipping from the Brockville *Recorder and Times*, insert in LP Diary, April 1920.

73 LP Diary, 14 April 1920.

74 In April 1920, for example, Lorne lectured in Brockville on his community work, noting sardonically on his diary that the *St Lawrence News* would probably cover the talk "for the benefit of the real reactionaries." See LP Diary, 26 April 1920.

75 LP Diary, 6 September 1919.

76 Iroquois *News*, undated clipping pasted in LP Diary, 19 December 1919.

77 LP, *The Beloved Community: Social Studies in Rural Progress* (Toronto: Ryerson 1925) (70 pp.). Pierce's own annotated copy, now in the possession of BPR, bears a handwritten note: "This book was originally a full-length study of some 125 pp. of MS. It considered my whole philosophy of Rural Sociology. I not only used Brinston as my laboratory, but later, when my independent research work was done, consulted over 100 works. As Sec'y of the Rural Survey Commission I made elaborate notes … . The whole MS. was lost, and in view of constant demand for this material took my portable typewriter in the summer of 1924 to Marion Walwyn's chicken farm and typed it practically as it stands here. It ran serially in the *Guardian*, the type being 'lifted'" (5).

78 LP, *The Beloved Community*, 11.

79 Ibid., 6.

80 Leslie Armour, "Canada and the History of Philosophy," in Terry Goldie et al., eds., *Canada: Theoretical Discourse/Discours Theoriques* (Montreal: Association for Canadian Studies 1994), 33.

81 Pierce wrote that "in the centre of the home stands the mother, the nation's chief judiciary, the world's greatest educator, queen of the hearts and creator of the lives of men … It is our duty to discover means whereby the mother may have greater opportunities … to realize herself and to realize her dreams for her children and the children of other mothers." LP, *The Beloved Community*, 48–9.

82 Ibid., 54.

83 Ibid., 49.

84 LP, "Credits [list of his doctoral courses]," box 48, LPP.

85 LP Diary, 24 April 1920.

86 Ibid., 13 April 1920.

87 See ibid., 25 March 1920. The minister at Douglas had been a guest speaker on Pierce's circuit in April 1919. Clearly, Pierce's networking was paying off. See LP Diary, 7 April 1919.

88 Ibid., 28 February 1920.

89 Between 5 June and 15 October, Pierce published eight articles on community organization in *The Canadian Courier*, later revised for *The Beloved Community*. The lectures are recalled in LP to Tom MacInnes, 19 May 1948, file 8, box 17, LPP.

90 See LP Diary, 24 April and 3 May 1920.

91 Ibid., 24 April 1920.

92 Ibid.

93 Rev. Ernest Thomas to LP, 22 April 1920, file "Loose Items from Diary 1920–1923," LPP.

94 LP Diary, 24 and 26 April 1919.

95 Ibid., 5 June 1920. He had also done a frantic day of supplementary research at the McGill library during his trip to Montreal to preach at Douglas.

96 "Two Changes in Methodist Church Pastors in Ottawa," unidentified clipping, insert in LP Diary, June 1920.
97 LP, "The Contribution of Russian Literature," 3, file 4, box 37, LPP.
98 Ibid., 16.
99 Unidentified clipping, insert in LP Diary, June 1920.
100 Ibid., 5 June 1920.
101 LP, "The Contribution of Russian Literature," 1.
102 LP Diary, 18 June 1920.
103 Ibid. Interestingly, he seems to have accepted the job without consulting Edith, who was back home in Brinston.
104 Ibid.
105 Ernest Thomas described Fallis's wish in a letter to LP, 22 April 1920, file "Loose Items from Diary 1920–1923," LPP.
106 Samuel Fallis to LP, 10 June 1920, file 1, box 1, LPP.
107 LP Diary, 5 July 1920.
108 Ibid., 3 and 9 July 1920.
109 Hume, "Lorne Pierce," 21.
110 LP, handwritten note in his copy of *The Beloved Community*, 56.
111 LP Diary, 5 June 1920.
112 Ibid., 30 March 1920.
113 Ibid., 27 July 1920.
114 Ibid.

CHAPTER SEVEN

1 LP, transcript of interview with Ronald Hambleton, n.d. [1955], file 11, box 42, LPP.
2 LP to BP, 13 February 1944, box 13, PFC.
3 LP Diary, 18 June 1920, records a letter from Fallis saying his salary would be paid as of 1 July 1920.
4 Ibid.
5 LP Diary, 18 June 1920.
6 George Parker, "The Agency System and Branch-Plant Publishing," in Carole Gerson and Jacques Michon, eds., *History of the Book in Canada: Volume Three, 1918–1980* (Toronto: University of Toronto Press 2007), 164. As Janet Friskney points out, the 1900 Copyright Amendment prohibited importation into Canada of works for which a Canadian publisher had arranged a Canadian edition, a ban that encouraged agency arrangements. See Janet Friskney, "Beyond the Shadow of William Briggs, Part 1: Setting the Stage and Introducing the Players," *Papers of the Bibliographical Society of Canada*, 33 (1995): 129.
7 George L. Parker, "The Evolution of Publishing in Canada," in Yvan Lamonde et al., eds., *History of the Book in Canada: Volume Two, 1840–1918* (Toronto: University of Toronto Press 2005), 18.

8 George L. Parker, *The Beginnings of the Book Trade in Canada* (Toronto: University of Toronto Press 1985), 236. The keen competition in the agency business is exemplified by the fact that, as Parker points out, the Cambridge agency left the House after George Stewart, who had once worked for Briggs, joined former House employees John McClelland and Fred Goodchild's eponymous seven-year-old firm in 1913, which morphed into McClelland, Goodchild and Stewart a year later (236). Stewart and McClelland captured the Cambridge agency on a 1914 business trip to England, according to Carl Spadoni and Judy Donnelly, "Historical Introduction," *A Bibliography of McClelland and Stewart, 1909–1985: A Publisher's Legacy* (Toronto: ECW Press 1994), 25. Other information on the early history of McClelland and Stewart is found in George L. Parker, "A History of a Canadian Publishing House: A Study of the Relation between Publishing and the Profession of Writing, 1890–1940" (PhD thesis, University of Toronto, 1969).

9 Friskney, "Beyond the Shadow of William Briggs, Part I," 136.

10 Parker, "The Evolution of Publishing in Canada," 30.

11 See Spadoni and Donnelly, "Historical Introduction," 19–53.

12 Janet Friskney, "Beyond the Shadow of William Briggs, Part II: Canadian-Authored Titles and the Commitment to Canadian Writing," *Papers of the Bibliographical Society of Canada*, 35 (1997): 198.

13 John McClelland, qtd. in George L. Parker, "Trade and Regional Publishing in Central Canada," *History of the Book in Canada: Volume Three, 1918–1980*, 169. Admittedly, in the case of Montgomery and Connor, McClelland was publishing works first published in the United States for which the firm had acquired Canadian rights.

14 LP, *An Editor's Creed* (1960), 3.

15 Friskney, "Beyond the Shadow of William Briggs, Part II," 172–3.

16 Friskney, "Beyond the Shadow of William Briggs, Part I," 136–7.

17 Janet Friskney, "Towards a Canadian 'Cultural Mecca': The Methodist Book and Publishing House's Pursuit of Book Publishing and Commitment to Canadian Writing 1829–1926 (MA thesis, Trent University, 1994), 293.

18 Friskney, "Beyond the Shadow of William Briggs, Part I," 136. Clearly, commercial printing was more profitable than book publishing.

19 From the 1920s, this was also to become the common practice at other publishers like Macmillan of Canada and McClelland and Stewart as well. At the House, the book steward continued to be the signatory for publishing contracts, including Ryerson authors.

20 Janet Friskney to the author, 30 December 1992, discussing the beginning of Fallis's career. See also her "Towards a Canadian 'Cultural Mecca,'" 242–317.

21 Friskney, "Towards a Canadian 'Cultural Mecca,'" 249.

22 Ibid., 46–57. The book steward, as well as the editor of the *Christian Guardian* and the Sunday School publications, were members of the Book Committee,

whose executive committee met only semi-annually. Fallis reported to the Book Committee but, as Friskney points out, given the infrequency of its meetings by Fallis's time, more power and greater managerial freedom fell to the book steward.

23 W. Stewart Wallace, Foreword to *The Ryerson Imprint* (Toronto: Ryerson 1954), 4.
24 LP, "A Brief Survey of the Editorial and Educational Departments of the House," 2, file 2, box 14, Board of Publication Papers, United Church Archives, Toronto.
25 Friskney, "Towards a Canadian 'Cultural Mecca,'" 264–5.
26 Ibid., 250–1.
27 The figure given by Lorne Pierce in a letter to Edith Pierce which discusses his review duties, n.d. [August or September 1920], box 6, PFC. Pierce commented ruefully on his duty to assess and recommend "hundreds of books" on religious and clerical subjects on the House's behalf: "A poor sermon in Hainsville didn't count much, but here an error would be awful!"
28 Pierce's disappointment at his office arrangements is evident in LP to ECP, n.d. [August or early September 1920], box 6, PFC.
29 LP Diary, 11 July 1920.
30 Ibid. In the light of other evidence, it seems probable that Pierce thought of his job in grander and more ambitious terms than Fallis did. "Cultural mecca" has the scope and ring of Pierce's prose and thinking, not Fallis's. For a discussion of the "glory days," see Friskney, "Beyond the Shadow of William Briggs, Part I" and "Beyond the Shadow of William Briggs, Part II."
31 See Friskney, "Towards a Canadian 'Cultural Mecca.'"
32 "Methodist Book Room Now The Ryerson Press," *Canadian Bookman*, 1 (July 1919): 79. The article referred to the House as "the senior publishing house of the Dominion." It also pointed out that Briggs would still be "daily at his office in his capacity of Book Steward Emeritus, to which he was elected by General Council last year. His successor, the Rev. S.W. Fallis, has now taken office after an extended trip through Canada in the interests of the Book Room."
33 LP to Myrtle Grace, 10 December 1945, file 2, box 12, LPP.
34 LP to BP, 13 February 1944, box 13, PFC.
35 See LP to EC, 1 August 1916, box 5, PFC, and ECP to LP, 1 October 1919, box 6, PFC.
36 LP Diary, 25 March 1920.
37 LP to A.C. Dalton, 8 July 1936, file 4, box 6, LPP. Pierce's frustration with deafness is evident in his uncharacteristic use of profanity, albeit with dashes.
38 See, for example, Susan Rezen and Carl Hausman, *Coping with Hearing Loss* (New York: Dembner 1985), and Harold Orlens, *Adjustment to Hearing Loss* (San Diego, CA: Singular 1991).
39 BPR, interview with author, 10 June 1991, Pike Lake, Ontario.

40 "Systemic Lupus Erytematosus," *Primer on Rheumatic Diseases: Journal of the American Medical Association*, 30 April 1973, 701–10.

41 Irene Smith, "Lupus: It's Time to Get Acquainted," Kingston *Whig Standard*, 19 October 1992. The effect of lupus on another literary life is analyzed in Brad Gooch, *Flannery: A Life of Flannery O'Connor* (New York: Little Brown 2009), 191ff.

42 Danny Sinopoli, "Life Need Not Be a Struggle for Those with Lupus, Victim Assures," *The Royal Gazette* [Bermuda], 31 October 1995, 21.

43 Gooch, *Flannery*, 193.

44 See, for example, Pierce's "OTH" flag on a letter from M.E. Nichols copied to House employees about distribution problems with Nichols's *The Story of the Canadian Press*, 3 December 1948, file 10, box 17, LPP.

45 LP to Charles Clay, 19 July 1949, file 1, box 15, LPP.

46 See Parker, *The Beginnings of the Book Trade in Canada*; Christina Burr, "The Business Development of the Methodist Book and Publishing House, 1870–1914," *Ontario History*, 85, no. 3 (1993): 251–71; Dana Garrick, "The United Church of Canada Board of Publication Collection: A Major Resource for the History of the Book in Canada," *Papers of the Bibliographical Society of Canada*, 32 (spring 1994): 11–30; and Danielle Hamelin, "The Methodist Book and Publishing House: Publishing and Canadian Nationalism," in "Nurturing Canadian Letters: Four Studies in the Publishing and Promotion of English-Canadian Writing, 1890–1920" (PhD thesis, University of Toronto, 1994).

47 LP, *An Editor's Creed*, 2.

48 See Friskney, "Towards a Canadian 'Cultural Mecca.'"

49 Ibid., 268. The quote is from an ad for Ryerson Press in *Canadian Stationer and Book Trade Journal*, October 1921, 55.

50 See Friskney's discussion of this in "Towards a Canadian 'Cultural Mecca,'" 137. Naturally, there was a need to discontinue the use of the name of the retiring William Briggs. Moreover, to use the imprint of "The Ryerson Press" also distanced some of the house publications from the label of the "Million Dollar Book Room" or "Million Dollar Book House" that had arisen in the controversy over the purchase and cost of the splendid new House headquarters, the Wesley Building, in the 1910s, which Friskney describes. The phrase "Million Dollar Book Room" was to periodically haunt Lorne Pierce in letters of complaint during his first decade at the House, however.

51 LP to Blanche Hume, 25 October 1958, box 1, Hume Papers, QUA.

52 Friskney, "Towards a Canadian 'Cultural Mecca,'" 319–20.

53 Burr, "The Business Development of the Methodist Book and Publishing House," 252.

54 William Westfall speaks of the dynamism of early Canadian Methodism where God was seen as "an active and interventionist power who continually transformed people and the affairs of the world." A perfect faith for the frontier by reason of its itinerant organizational set-up, Methodism had an optimistic and

dynamic relationship to social change, be it through publishing, education, or temperance advocacy. See Westfall, *Two Worlds*, 41ff.

55 Marguerite Van Die, *An Evangelical Mind*, 140.

56 LP, *The House of Ryerson* (Toronto: Ryerson 1954), 7. In 1831 one-quarter to one-third of subscribers were not Methodists.

57 Figures are taken from Burr, "The Business Development of the Methodist Book and Publishing House," Table 1, 254.

58 John Webster Grant, *A Profusion of Spires: Religion in Nineteenth Century Ontario* (Toronto: University of Toronto Press 1988), 66ff.

59 LP Diary, 3 September 1915.

60 Friskney, "Towards a Canadian 'Cultural Mecca,'" 1.

61 E.H. Dewart, "Introductory Essay," in E.H. Dewart, ed., *Selections from Canadian Poets* (1864) (Toronto: University of Toronto Press 1973), ix.

62 "A Native Methodist Literature [editorial]," *Canadian Methodist Magazine*, 1 (January 1875): 76–7.

63 See Parker, *The Beginnings of the Book Trade*.

64 Charles G.D. Roberts, *Orion and Other Poems* (Philadelphia: Lipincott 1880).

65 D.C. Scott to Pelham Edgar, 16 March 1921, Pelham Edgar Papers, Pratt Library, Victoria College, Toronto. Scott pulled no punches, writing of his "two-headed beast of a publisher," McClelland and Stewart: "If I was Service or Ralph Connor how fawning and considerate & compliant they would be."

66 Duncan Campbell Scott to Pelham Edgar, 16 March 1921, Pelham Edgar Papers, Victoria College Archives, University of Toronto.

67 Parker, *The Beginnings of the Book Trade*, 236.

68 Friskney, "Towards a Canadian 'Cultural Mecca,'" 136–7.

69 W.S. Wallace, *The Ryerson Imprint* (Toronto: Ryerson 1954), 3.

70 E.S. Caswell to Nellie McClung, 16 May 1908, quoted in Friskney, "Beyond the Shadow of William Briggs, Part II," 191.

71 Michael Peterman and Janet Friskney, "'Booming' the Canuck Book: Edward Caswell and the Promotion of Canadian Writing," *Journal of Canadian Studies*, 30 (autumn 1995): 60–90.

72 E.S. Caswell, ed., *Canadian Singers and Their Songs* (Toronto: Briggs 1902). This selection of holograph poems and photographs of Canadian poets, a book of some forty pages produced with the help of the Ladies' Aid Society of Toronto's Broadway Methodist Tabernacle, was expanded by Caswell and issued in two subsequent editions (1919 and 1925) by McClelland and Stewart.

73 See Friskney and Peterman, "'Booming' the Canuck Book," as well as Charlotte Gray's *Sisters in the Wilderness* (Toronto: Harper Collins 1999), a biography of Traill and Moodie.

74 See Peterman and Friskney, "'Booming' the Canuck Book," and Mary Hallett and Marilyn Davis, *Firing the Heather: The Life and Times of Nellie McClung* (Saskatoon: Fifth House 1994), 232–4.

75 See Parker, "The Evolution of Publishing in Canada," 31.

76 Parker, *The Beginnings of the Book Trade*, 249.
77 Burr, "The Business Development of the Methodist Book and Publishing House," Figure 1, 259.
78 Friskney, "Beyond the Shadow of William Briggs, Part II," 197.
79 Friskney, "Towards a Canadian 'Cultural Mecca,'" 138.
80 Wallace, *The Ryerson Imprint*, 56–7 and 64–5.

CHAPTER EIGHT

1 LP to ECP, n.d. [August 1920], box 6, PFC.
2 LP to ECP, n.d. [August or early September 1920], box 6, PFC.
3 LP to ECP, n.d. [August or September 1920], box 6, PFC. This is a different letter from above.
4 LP to ECP, n.d. [August or early September 1920], same as Arts and Letters club letter.
5 LP Diary, 23 August 1920.
6 LP to EC, 10 March 1914, box 2, PFC.
7 LP, transcript of interview with Ronald Hambleton, n.d. [1955], file 11, box 42, LPP.
8 LP, "Canadian Literature and the National Ideal," *Canadian Bookman*, 7 (September 1925): 143–4.
9 Westfall, *Two Worlds*, 195.
10 LP to ECP, n.d. [August or early September 1920], box 6, PFC. This is the letter that also refers to books he praises selling "like hot cakes."
11 See Augustus Bridle, *The Story of the Club* (Toronto: Ryerson 1945), for an account of the Arts and Letters Club and its role in Canadian culture.
12 For a discussion of the Group of Seven and their nationalism, see Ross King, *Defiant Spirits: The Modernist Revolution of the Group of Seven* (Vancouver: Douglas and McIntyre 2010), and Peter Larisey, *Light for a Cold Land: Lawren Harris's Work and Life – An Interpretation* (Toronto: Dundurn 1993).
13 LP Diary, 28 February 1920. Both Harris and Massey were heirs to the Massey-Harris farm-implement fortune.
14 LP, *An Editor's Creed*, 2–3.
15 Lorne Pierce, *In Conference with the Best Minds*, 232. LP reprinted some of his early *Christian Guardian* writings in this book.
16 Nathaniel Burwash, qtd. in Gauvreau, *The Evangelical Century*, 130.
17 LP, *In Conference with the Best Minds*, 51–2.
18 LP to ECP, 19 September 1920, box 6, PFC.
19 ECP to LP, 3 September 1920, box 6, PFC. One of the difficulties in discussing the relationship – one whose course was vital to Lorne Pierce's career – is that most of the archival record that has survived was generated by Lorne. Edith,

moreover, as was the norm for a woman of her generation, was slow to criticize her husband publicly or privately. Finally, when something really stressful happened to Pierce, he often fails to mention it in his otherwise voluble diary. Pierce had Blanche Hume, his devoted assistant, read and selectively "cull" his papers before donating them to Queen's. Pierce's marital tensions are present in the documentary record, but with far less amplitude than other aspects of his life.

20 See Barbara Welter, "The Cult of True Womanhood, 1820–1860," *Signs*, I, no. I (1974): 151–74.

21 See, for example, LP to EC, 22 March 1915, box 3, PFC. Here Pierce talks about how his mother and Edith, with "the innate purity of two lofty souls," had shaped and inspired him.

22 LP to EC, 22 June 1916, box 5, PFC. His "new work" is the ministry at St Paul's in Ottawa.

23 LP, review of *An Intimate Diary* by Margot Asquith, *Christian Guardian*, 20 October 1920, 25.

24 F.R. Scott, a Rhodes scholar, was at Oxford from 1919 to 1923. See Sandra Djwa, Introduction, in Sandra Djwa and R. St J. Macdonald, eds., *On F.R. Scott* (Montreal & Kingston: McGill-Queen's University Press 1983), ix–xxii. Scott's literary career is traced in Sandra Djwa, *The Politics of the Imagination: A Life of F.R. Scott* (Toronto: McClelland and Stewart 1987).

25 For a discussion of expatriate writers and the Canadian literary world, see Nicholas Mount, *When Canadian Literature Moved to New York* (Toronto: University of Toronto Press 2005).

26 Pierce observed of Harold Innis in a letter written during the Second World War: "[Innis] mistrusts any group that usurps power, political, religious, banking or any other group ... Harold Innis fought through the last [war], was a private, was severely wounded. He hates heads of state who know it all and settle all matters by a wave of the hand." LP, letter to Bruce Pierce, postmarked 14 August 1945, in possession of BPR.

27 For his part, Group of Seven member A.Y. Jackson, who became a war artist, wrote in a letter about military service before his own enlistment: "The hero's job is a pretty thankless one. There are lots of institutions and big fatheads in this country not worth laying down one's life to preserve." Jackson is quoted in Heather Robertson's Introduction to *A Terrible Beauty: The Art of Canada at War* (Toronto: Lorimer 1977), 10–11.

28 Brian Trehearne, *Aestheticism and the Canadian Modernists: Aspects of a Poetic Influence* (Montreal & Kingston: McGill-Queen's University Press 1989), 235ff.

29 See, for example, LP, "The New Jerusalem," *Christian Guardian*, 21 September 1921, scrapbook, box 52, LPP. Here Pierce praises G.K. Chesterton as an "indefatigable and joyous protagonist for the things of the spirit" in opposition to "modern materialism."

30 LP, "Jazz Poetry," *Christian Guardian*, 29 March 1922, scrapbook, box 52, LPP.

31 Wilson MacDonald, "Moonlight and the Common Day" (autobiography), 918–19, box 11, MacDonald Papers, LAC.

32 Wilson MacDonald Diary, 8 December 1925, box 10, MacDonald Papers, LAC.

33 LP, *An Outline of Canadian Literature* (Toronto: Ryerson 1927), 191. Pelham Edgar, qtd. in "Young Writers Killing Poetry due to Disdain of Principles of Communication: Dr. Pelham Edgar's View," London *Free Press*, 13 April 1938, and Edgar, "The Changing Aspects of Poetry," *Queen's Quarterly*, 44 (autumn 1937): 335–43.

34 LP, "Why a Canadian Authors' Week?" *Canadian Stationer and Book Trade Journal*, September 1921, 26. Emphasis added.

35 LP, "In Honour Preferring One Another," *Christian Guardian*, 10 May 1922, scrapbook, box 52, LPP.

36 LP, "Wilson MacDonald – Poet," *Christian Guardian*, 4 July 1923, scrapbook, box 52, LPP.

37 LP, "Some Recent Tendencies in Theology," *Christian Guardian*, 3 November 1920, scrapbook, box 52, LPP.

38 Nellie McClung to LP, 10 November 1920, file 1, box 1, LPP.

39 See Diana Chown, Introduction to Alice Chown, *The Stairway*.

40 LP Diary, 19 October 1920. The review has not survived among Pierce's papers.

41 See [LP], *Everett Boyd Jackson Fallis* [pamphlet], n.d. [1921], n.p., copy in the Lorne Pierce Collection, Douglas Library, Queen's University. Pierce's authorship of the pamphlet is indicated not only by the prose style but by a small addendum at the front: "Appreciative acknowledgement is made of the work of Dr. Lorne Pierce, who edited this brochure, preparing the copy from correspondence, photographs and other material gathered from various sources."

42 Samuel Fallis, qtd. in LP, *Everett Boyd Jackson Fallis*, n.p.

43 Samuel Fallis to LP ["The Book Room" 1920 Christmas card], insert in LP Diary, December 1920. Emphasis in original.

CHAPTER NINE

1 W.A. Deacon to Emily Murphy, 14 January 1923, Deacon Papers, Fisher Rare Book Library, University of Toronto.

2 For an account of the strike, see Friskney, "Towards a Canadian 'Cultural Mecca,'" as well as Allen, *Religion and Social Reform in Canada*, and Sally F. Zerker, *The Rise and Fall of the Toronto Typographical Union 1832–1972: A Case Study of Foreign Domination* (Toronto: University of Toronto Press 1982). The strike did not in fact peter out until 1925 and, according to Zerker, was "disastrous" for the union: "Important printing establishments in Toronto were lost to the union during the 1921–1925 strike, never again to be regained" (196).

3 Book Committee Minutes, 5 May 1921, Board of Publication Papers, United Church Archives, Toronto, qtd. in Friskney, "Towards a Canadian 'Cultural Mecca,'" 253.

4 "Resume of Address of Dr. Fallis," 30 April 1921, scrapbook of 1921 printers' strike, box 13, Board of Publication Papers, United Church Archives.

5 Fallis to A.E. Humphries, 23 December 1921, box 13, Board of Publication Papers, United Church Archives.

6 Friskney, "Towards a Canadian 'Cultural Mecca,'" 254.

7 Allen, *Religion and Social Reform in Canada*, 186.

8 Fallis to Ernest Thomas, 23 July 1921, box 13, Board of Publication Papers, United Church Archives.

9 "The Picket" [advertisement], box 13, Board of Publication Papers, United Church Archives.

10 LP Diary, 6 May and 13 June 1921.

11 Ibid., 12 August 1921.

12 LP, *The Beloved Community*. Wallace's bibliography of Ryerson publications lists the publication date as 1924, but the LP Diary clearly indicates 1925.

13 LP, "The Book Steward's Corner," *Christian Guardian*, 20 October 1920, 25. In a review of 27 October 1920, Pierce also backed away from the Russia he had been so enthusiastic about before coming to the House: "It will be shown that the dictatorship [of the proletariat] was merely that of two very clever, cunning, unscrupulous idealists, trying to both pull on the late Czar's crown at the same time" (25).

14 LP, "Pulpit Vulgarity" (1923), *In Conference with the Best Minds*, 159–60.

15 Ibid., 161–2.

16 LP, "The Enrichment of Worship," *In Conference with the Best Minds*, 193–4. This piece appeared in the *Guardian* in the fall of 1923.

17 LP Diary, 11 October 1923.

18 Ibid., 16 September 1923.

19 Ibid., 17 October 1923.

20 LP, *Primitive Methodism and the New Catholicism* (Toronto: Ryerson 1923), G14, author's proof copy, file 12, box 39, LPP.

21 LP Diary, 11 July 1920.

22 LP to W.L. Cope, 22 January 1954, file 3, box 13, Board of Publication Papers, United Church Archives. Pierce is reminiscing with Cope, head of the printing plant at the House and his frequent ally, about life under Fallis.

23 LP Diary, 11 October 1923.

24 LP, ed., *The Chronicle of a Century 1829–1939* (Toronto: Ryerson 1929), 247. There was an in-house publication committee made up of the book steward and his managers, which met monthly, to whom Pierce had to report on his policies, but in practice the only real veto power lay with the book steward himself. In

an interview with C.H. Dickinson, one of the later book stewards, Dickinson described Pierce as only "lightly supervised," with the committee essentially rubber stamping his publication decisions. C.H. Dickinson, interview with author, Woodstock, ON, 21 September 1993.

25 Book Committee Minutes, 8 May 1923, Board of Publication Papers, United Church Archives.

26 According to Wallace's *The Ryerson Imprint*, Ryerson published only six titles in 1921, compared to sixteen the following year.

27 First in the series was the 1921 booklet *Was John Wesley a Premillenialist?* by Franklin Harris Ball. See also Samuel Peter Rose's *Old Testament Prophecy* and Albert Morris Sanford's *Literalistic Interpretations of the Scriptures*, both published in 1921.

28 "An Open Letter to ... Kew Beach Presbyterian Church" [pamphlet], 24 October 1924, 22, scrapbook, box 52, LPP, and review of *Primitive Methodism and the New Catholicism*, 2 February 1924, scrapbook, box 52, LPP. LP pasted in a page of newspaper letters about the series with the notation: "These letters are but a few of the scores lambasting my Ryerson Essays for their 'modernism.'" The scrapbook also includes the undated clipping from the Montreal *Gazette*.

29 Friskney, "Towards a Canadian 'Cultural Mecca,'" 271.

30 LP, "A Brief Survey of the Editorial and Educational Departments of the Publishing House," 4, box 14, Board of Publication Papers, United Church Archives.

31 Friskney, "Towards a Canadian 'Cultural Mecca,'" 257–8. According to Book Committee Minutes, superannuation contributions rose to $15,000 in 1923, dropped by $5,000 in 1924, and rose again to the 1923 level in 1925.

32 LP Diary, 20 August 1925.

33 Friskney, "Towards a Canadian 'Cultural Mecca,'" 323.

34 See Carl Spadoni and Judy Donnelly, *A Bibliography of McClelland and Stewart Imprints, 1909–1985: A Publisher's Legacy* (Toronto: ECW Press 1994), 221–33.

35 See Mary Vipond, "National Consciousness in English-Speaking Canada in the 1920s: Seven Studies" (PhD thesis, University of Toronto, 1974).

36 LP, "Why a Canadian Author's [sic] Week?" *Canadian Stationer and Book Trade Journal*, September 1921, 26.

37 Vipond, "National Consciousness in English-Speaking Canada in the 1920s," 1.

38 Deacon to LP, 15 April 1952, file 2, box 21, LPP; see also his letter of 15 February 1961, file 7, box 29, LPP.

39 Deacon to Emily Murphy, 14 January 1923, Deacon Papers.

40 LP to Deacon, 16 October 1922, in John Lennox and Michele Lacombe, eds., *Dear Bill: The Correspondence of William Arthur Deacon* (Toronto: University of Toronto Press 1988), 26.

41 LP, "Dr. E.J. Pratt and His Poetry," *Ontario Library Review*, 13 (February 1929): 92.

42 See Phelps to LP, 5 June 1923, file 6, box 1, LPP. Phelps, a Victoria College class-mate of Pierce, owned a cottage at Bobcaygeon near both Pratt and Deacon, from where this letter was written.

43 Printing and binding estimate for *Newfoundland Verse*, file 3, box 1, LPP, and LP to Pratt, 23 January 1923, file 6, box 1, LPP.

44 The books included Pierce's own *Marjorie Pickthall: A Book of Remembrance* (1925) and Tom MacInnes's *Complete Poems* (1923). See Maria Tippett, *Stormy Weather: F.H. Varley: A Biography* (Toronto: McClelland and Stewart 1998), 138–9.

45 LP Diary, 17 October 1923.

46 Nellie Lyle Pattinson, *A Canadian Cook Book* (Toronto: Ryerson 1923), 416 pp., which went through several subsequent editions.

47 LP to Pratt, 21 May 1923, file 6, box 1, LPP.

48 David G. Pitt, *E.J. Pratt: The Truant Years 1882–1927* (Toronto: University of Toronto Press 1984), 232.

49 LP, transcript of interview with Ronald Hambleton [1955], file 11, box 42, LPP.

50 Friskney, "Towards a Canadian 'Cultural Mecca,'" 274. LP Diary for 16 September 1923 records that Moore was "very cut [up] at having to leave his office" to relocate Pierce in the spring of 1922.

51 LP Diary, 12 November 1923.

52 See LP to Pratt, 29 November 1923, file 6, box 1, LPP.

53 See Clara Thomas and John Lennox, *William Arthur Deacon: A Canadian Literary Life* (Toronto: University of Toronto Press 1982), 96.

54 See invoice, Educational Department, 29 February 1924, file 4, box 1, LPP.

55 Pitt, *E.J. Pratt: The Truant Years*, 301.

56 For example, Deacon accused Pierce of a lack of candour about the publishing schedule, and in another instance he apologized to Pierce for what Deacon insisted was a "slight remark." See Deacon to LP, 1 February 1923 and 19 September 1923, file 4, box 1, LPP.

57 See, for example, Pratt to LP, 7 August 1924, file 10, box 1, LPP.

58 See Beaumont Cornell to LP, 25 April 1923, file 3, box 1, LPP. The prescription is still attached.

59 Pratt to LP, "Friday" [mid-November 1923], file 6, box 1, LPP.

60 LP to Pratt, 29 November 1923, file 6, box 1, LPP.

61 LP Diary, 17 October 1923.

62 See ibid., 21 April 1928.

63 Blanche Hume to LP, 19 May 1947, file 2, box 15, LPP.

64 See Lennox and Lacombe, *Dear Bill*.

65 See Thomas and Lennox, *William Arthur Deacon*, 62.

66 LP Diary, 21 April 1928.

67 Ibid., 13 May 1928.

68 Pratt to LP, 1 December 1923, file 1, box 6, LPP.

69 See LP Diary, 28 November 1924. Pierce was disgusted when Toronto voted to go "wet" by some 50,000 votes, although the Ontario Temperance Act was upheld province-wide.

70 LP, "Dr. E.J. Pratt and His Poetry," *Ontario Library Review*, 13 (February 1929), 92–4.

71 Phelps later told this to David Pitt, Pratt's biographer. See Pitt, *E.J. Pratt: The Truant Years*, 287.

72 Pratt to LP, 24 September 1924, file 10, box 1, LPP. The English firm had also agreed to act as representative there for *Newfoundland Verse*.

73 LP to Pratt, 16 December 1924, file 10, box 1, LPP.

74 Pratt to LP, 18 Dec. 1924, file 10, box 1, LPP.

75 W.A. Deacon, *Poteen* (Ottawa: Graphic 1926).

76 LP, qtd. in Hume, "Lorne Pierce."

77 The phrase that Watson used to describe the circle around him in his Preface to *Birth through Death: The Ethics of the Twentieth Plane: A Revelation Received through the Psychic Consciousness of Louis Benjamin* (Toronto: McClelland and Stewart 1920), 11.

78 The House, for example, published Watson's *The Sovereignty of Character: Lessons from the Life of Jesus of Nazareth* (1906) and *Three Comrades of Jesus* (1919).

79 Watson, *The Twentieth Plane: A Psychic Revelation* (Toronto: McClelland and Stewart 1918), 3.

80 See Michele Lacombe, "Theosophy and the Canadian Idealist Tradition: A Preliminary Exploration," *Journal of Canadian Studies*, 17 (summer 1982): 104–5.

81 See L.M. Montgomery, 29 March 1919, in Mary Rubio and Elizabeth Waterston, eds., *The Selected Journals of L.M. Montgomery, Volume II: 1910–1921* (Toronto: Oxford University Press 1987), 312.

82 See Watson, *Birth through Death*.

83 LP to Edith Chown, n.d. [May 1914], box 2, PFC.

84 See Lacombe, "Theosophy," 100–1.

85 Ibid., 101.

86 Michael Bliss, *Banting: A Biography* (Toronto: University of Toronto Press 1984), 192–3.

87 McKillop, *A Disciplined Intelligence*, 198–9.

88 Mary Vipond, "National Consciousness in English-Speaking Canada in the 1920s," 490–1.

89 Albert Durrant Watson, *Robert Norwood* (Toronto: Ryerson 1923), 77.

90 LP Diary, 26 October 1920. Watson's house and the immigrant neighbours around it whom he treated – sometimes for free – are described in Lawrence Dare [Margaret Lawrence], "Sancta Simplicitas," *Willison's Monthly*, May 1927, 468–9.

91 LP, "Spooks," *Christian Guardian*, 22 December 1920, scrapbook, box 52, LPP.

92 LP Diary, 17 September 1923.

93 Watson to LP, 26 July 1925, file 4, box 2, LPP.
94 Watson, Introduction to his *Poetical Works* (Toronto: Ryerson 1924), vi, proof copy, file 10, box 83, LPP.
95 Watson, qtd. in LP, *Albert Durrant Watson* (Toronto: Ryerson 1924), 27.
96 LP Diary, 17 September 1923.
97 "Rotarians Hear Pierce," St Catharines *Standard*, 5 November 1924, scrapbook, box 52, LPP.
98 LP, *Outline of Canadian Literature* (Toronto: Ryerson 1927).
99 In a letter to educationist Aletta Marty, LP apologizes for not being able to follow their conversation on the telephone, and adds: "Telephoning is one of my painful experiences." See LP to Marty, 15 November 1923, file 5, box 1, LPP.
100 The tension with his parents is recorded in LP Diary, 7 April 1921.
101 Watson to LP, 20 December 1923, file 6, box 1, LPP.
102 Watson to Pierce, 28 January 1924, file 11, box 1, LPP.
103 LP Diary, 9 August 1924.
104 Ibid., 16 September 1923.
105 Watson, "Rossmoyne," *The Poetical Works of Albert Durrant Watson* (Toronto: Ryerson 1924), 43. The poem is dedicated "To Lorne A. Pierce," showing that Watson had not yet taken a dislike to Pierce's middle initial.
106 LP Diary, 25 January 1925.
107 LP to Blanche Hume, 17 February 1959, box 1, Blanche Hume Papers, QUA. For example, in letters written to Sir Andrew Macphail, Pierce's signature changes between January and February 1924.
108 While sales figures for this volume are not available, it is doubtful that it sold well. The volume's length as well as the quality of the paper and frontispiece photograph hint at subsidy by Watson or his "Inner Circle" – or in effect by Ryerson.
109 Watson and Margaret Lawrence, *Mediums and Mystics: A Study in Spiritual Laws and Psychic Forces* (Toronto: Ryerson Essays 1923), 68 pp. Lawrence, one of Watson's "Inner Circle," became his literary executor, and Pierce commissioned her to write a biography of LaSalle for his Canadian History Readers.
110 LP, "Spooks," *Christian Guardian*, 22 December 1920, scrapbook, box 52, LPP.
111 LP Diary, 17 October 1923.
112 LP, *Albert Durrant Watson*, 27.
113 Unidentified review in the Saskatoon *Phoenix*, 31 January 1925, 36, scrapbook, box 52, LPP.
114 Unidentified review, Winnipeg *Tribune*, 2 February 1925, scrapbook, 36, box 52, LPP.
115 Margery Fee, "English Canadian Literary Criticism 1890–1950: Defining and Establishing a National Literature" (PhD thesis, University of Toronto, 1981).
116 LP Diary, 5 December 1925, records that Dr Watson "inscribed them beautifully."
117 LP, *Albert Durrant Watson*, 12.

118 LP, "The Makers of Queen's," *Queen's Review*, 3 (August 1929): 189–92.

119 LP, *Albert Durrant Watson*, 12.

120 See Watson to LP, 12 September 1921, file 6, box 1, LPP.

121 E.S. Caswell, ed., *Canadian Singers and Their Songs* (Toronto: McClelland and Stewart 1919). A shorter version had appeared in 1902 and a third edition was published in 1925, perhaps to compete with *Our Canadian Literature*.

122 LP, Introduction to *Our Canadian Literature: Representative Prose and Verse* (Toronto: Ryerson 1922), 127.

123 Ibid., 129.

124 Ibid., 129, 128.

125 Robert Lecker, "Watson and Pierce's *Our Canadian Literature* Anthology and the Representation of Nation," unpublished paper, kindly sent to the author, 28.

126 Watson, Introduction to *Our Canadian Literature*, 11.

127 Robert Lecker points out that such a passage was dropped between the manuscript and printed versions of the anthology. "Watson and Pierce's *Our Canadian Literature* Anthology and the Representation of Nation," 13.

128 Friskney, "Towards a Canadian 'Cultural Mecca,'" 271. The month of its first appearance is noted in Pierce's diary.

129 L.M. Montgomery, *Rilla of Ingleside* (Toronto: McClelland 1921).

130 The Ryerson catalogue entry is pasted in the back of the copy of the anthology held at LAC.

131 Reviews of *Our Canadian Literature*: Montreal *Gazette*, 16 February 1924; Lloyd Roberts "Books and People," *The Listening Post* (Montreal), March 1924; and Austin Bothwell, Saskatoon *Phoenix*, 5 April 1924. All found in scrapbook, box 52, LPP. Favourable reviews also appeared in the *Christian Guardian* and *Acta Victoriana*, both n.d., scrapbook, box 52, LPP.

132 "Brief Reviews of the Latest Books," *Canadian Stationer and Book Trade Journal*, February 1923, 55.

133 Unidentified clipping, scrapbook, box 52, LPP.

134 *"Our Canadian Literature," Canadian Magazine*, May 1923, 96.

135 Deacon's original review appeared in *Saturday Night*, 3 March 1923, 8, and the second on 29 March 1924. See scrapbook, box 52, LPP.

136 Wilson MacDonald, "Canadian Viewpoint," unidentified clipping, scrapbook, file 16, box 25, Wilson MacDonald Papers, LAC.

137 Deacon to LP, 5 October 1926, file 5, box 2, LPP.

138 LP Diary, 1 February 1924.

CHAPTER TEN

1 Wilson MacDonald to LP, 19 October 1923, file 4, box 1, LPP.

2 LP Diary, 17 October 1923.

3 Ibid., 16 November 1923.

4 The "shameless maple-wreath photo," as Carman drily dubbed it, was widely reproduced in the press after the tribute by the Montreal Branch of the Canadian Authors Association on 28 October 1921. See H.P. Gundy, ed., *Letters of Bliss Carman* (Montreal & Kingston: McGill-Queen's University Press 1981), 284.

5 Bliss Carman to Ernest Fewster, 7 October 1925, transcript, file 14, box 6, Bliss Carman Correspondence, LPP.

6 See Sylvia DuVernet, *Muskoka Assembly of the Canadian Chautauqua Institution: Points of View and Personalities* (The Author: Muskoka Graphics 1985); and Patrick Byer, "Reviving Chautauqua," *Muskoka Magazine*, August 1983, 82–7. In the early 1920s, for example, the program featured "The Little Theatre in the Woods" run by Margo Gordon of Hart House Theatre.

7 Bliss Carman to LP [on Assembly letterhead], 6 August 1924, file 12, box 1, Bliss Carman Correspondence, LPP.

8 LP to Carman, 4 June 1924, file 9, box 21, Carman Correspondence, LPP.

9 Pierce to Carman, 15 July 1924, file *Muskoka Magazine*, 9, box 21, Carman Correspondence, LPP; and Sylvia DuVernet, "Muskoka Assembly: Once a Widely-Known Lake Rosseau Centre," *Muskoka Sun*, 19 July 1984, 40.

10 LP Diary, 9 August 1924. As Pierce's daughter, Beth Robinson, points out, one photo taken in 1925 at the assembly shows a man resembling Pierce in the background, but the figure also resembles William Arthur Deacon, who had a cottage in nearby Bobcaygeon. For the photo, see Byer, "Reviving Chautauqua," 82–7.

11 LP to Carman, 7 May 1925, file 9, box 21, Carman Correspondence, LPP. See Constance L. Davies, "Poets on Holiday," *Canadian Bookman*, August 1925, 130.

12 Muriel Miller, *Bliss Carman: Quest and Revolt* (St John's, NL: Jesperson 1985), 258. See also LP to E.C. Kyte, 28 February 1945, file 4, box 12, LPP.

13 Mary B. McGillivray, "The Popular and Critical Reputation and Reception of Bliss Carman," in Gerald Lynch, ed., *Bliss Carman: A Reappraisal* (Ottawa: University of Ottawa Press 1990), 13–14.

14 LP Diary, 9 August 1924.

15 Carman to LP, 24 September 1924, file 12, box 1, Carman Correspondence, LPP. Emphasis in original.

16 LP to Carman, 30 October 1924, file 9, box 21, Carman Correspondence, LPP.

17 LP Diary, 29 September 1924.

18 Biographical details are drawn from the finding aid to the Wilson MacDonald Papers, LAC.

19 Wilson MacDonald Diary, 31 October 1919, vol. 10, MacDonald Papers. This was at the St James Club, Montreal.

20 MacDonald, qtd. in Richard Duprey, "Wilson MacDonald," *Dictionary of Literary Biography*, vol. 92, 216–17.

21 Sylvia DuVernet, "Memories of Muskoka Assembly Reassembled," *Muskoka Sun*, 18 August 1983, 39. Applegath wrote "Bugler of the Dawn" in 1949, as part

552 Notes to pages 206–8

of a graduate degree at Ashland College, Ohio. Pierce considered publishing it, but did not.

22 Wilson MacDonald Diary, 8 August 1922, vol. 10, MacDonald Papers.

23 Wilson MacDonald, "Moonlight and the Common Day," autobiographical manuscript, 675, vol. 10, MacDonald Papers.

24 Lacombe, "Theosophy and the Canadian Idealist Tradition," 108.

25 Ibid., 103.

26 Albert Smythe, Introduction to Wilson MacDonald, *The Song of the Prairie Land*, 2nd ed. (Toronto: Ryerson Press 1923), 8.

27 Carman to R.H. Hathaway, 15 April 1922, file 18, box 8, Carman Correspondence, LPP.

28 W.A. Deacon, "Wilson MacDonald's Poetry," *Saturday Night*, 11 March 1922, scrapbook, vol. 25, MacDonald Papers.

29 Wilson MacDonald Diary, 1 June 1922, vol. 10, MacDonald Papers.

30 LP, "Wilson MacDonald – Poet," undated clipping [4 July 1923], scrapbook, vol. 25, MacDonald Papers.

31 Wilson MacDonald, qtd. in "Moonlight and the Common Day," 856, vol. 10, MacDonald Papers.

32 LP, "*Out of the Wilderness*," *New Outlook*, undated clipping [1926], scrapbook, vol. 25, MacDonald Papers.

33 Pierce and Watson included this poem in their anthology *Our Canadian Literature*.

34 Wilson MacDonald Diary, 28 September 1922, vol. 10, MacDonald Papers.

35 Wallace's *The Ryerson Imprint* gives the date 1921 for *The Miracle Songs*, but both Pierce and Wilson MacDonald's diaries make it clear that the 1923 date is correct. MacDonald did, however, publish some copies of the poem himself in 1921. See LP Diary, 17 October 1923, and MacDonald Diary, 30 October 1922, vol. 10, MacDonald Papers.

36 Wilson MacDonald Diary, 21 April 1923, vol. 10, MacDonald Papers.

37 Ibid., 2 February 1923, vol. 10, MacDonald Papers.

38 Review of *The Song of the Prairie Land*, Montreal *Gazette*, 23 June 1923, scrapbook, vol. 26, MacDonald Papers.

39 Pierce to Ernest Fewster, 22 October 1923, file 4, box 1, LPP.

40 LP circular letter, 16 September 1923, repr. in Stan Dragland, *Wilson MacDonald's Western Tour, 1923–24: A Collage ...* (Toronto: Coach House Press 1975), n.p.

41 LP Diary, 3 September 1925.

42 Ibid., 17 October 1923. Emphasis in original.

43 Norwood to LP, 6 June 1923, file 5, box 1, LPP.

44 Wilson MacDonald Diary, 3 June, 3 May, and 18 July 1923, vol. 10, MacDonald Papers.

45 Ibid., 23 August 1923, vol. 10, MacDonald Papers.

46 Ibid., 6 September 1923, vol. 10, MacDonald Papers.

47 Pierce to MacDonald, n.d. [October 1923], vol. 1, MacDonald Papers.

48 For example, Wilson MacDonald Diary, 1 and 4 October and 12 December 1923, vol. 10, MacDonald Papers.

49 See Dragland, *Wilson MacDonald's Western Tour.*

50 LP to MacDonald, 8 November 1923, vol. 1, MacDonald Papers.

51 Ernest Fewster to LP, 10 October 1923, file 4, box 1, LPP; Phelps to LP, 12 November 1923, repr. in Dragland, *Wilson MacDonald's Western Tour*, n.p.

52 MacDonald to LP, 19 October 1923, file 4, box 1, LPP.

53 MacDonald to LP, n.d. [Regina, October 1923], file 4, box 1, LPP.

54 MacDonald, "Moonlight and the Common Day," 798, vol. 10, MacDonald Papers.

55 Ibid., 808–9, vol. 10, MacDonald Papers.

56 The quotation is from MacDonald to LP, n.d. [Regina, November 1923], in Dragland, *Wilson MacDonald's Western Tour*, n.p. Dragland also includes a 8 November 1923 letter from journalist Austin Bothwell in Regina to Arthur Phelps in Winnipeg (which was forwarded to Pierce) mentioning that MacDonald "knocks Ryerson at every opportunity."

57 LP Diary, 28 October 1923. Pierce added: "Still I believe in him and shall go on as if nothing happened. His letters will be found in my papers."

58 LP Diary, 17 October 1923.

59 Ibid., 15 October 1923.

60 MacDonald to LP, n.d. [Regina, late October 1923], repr. in Dragland, *Wilson MacDonald's Western Tour*, n.p. MacDonald says of underwriting his tour: "You made me three distinct promises and … did not keep one of them but I know this was the fault of the higher-ups."

61 LP Diary, 15 October 1923.

62 LP to MacDonald, 23 October 1923, vol. 1, MacDonald Papers. It was at this time that Pierce and Fallis travelled up to Fallis's Bala cottage.

63 LP to MacDonald, 8 November 1923, file 4, box 1, LPP.

64 LP to MacDonald, 15 November 1923, vol. 1, MacDonald Papers.

65 LP Diary, 28 October 1923.

66 LP to MacDonald, 8 November 1923, file 4, box 1, LPP. Another undated letter in the same file, probably written a few days before, mentions the books of verse and the U.S. disinterest.

67 See MacDonald, "The Castle of Graymoor," manuscript, vol. 15, MacDonald Papers. A synopsis is reproduced in Dragland, *Wilson MacDonald's Western Tour*, n.p.

68 MacDonald, "Moonlight and the Common Day," 777, vol. 10, MacDonald Papers.

69 MacDonald to Ryerson Press, n.d. [early December 1923], repr. in Dragland, *Wilson MacDonald's Western Tour*, n.p.

70 LP Diary, 1 April 1924.

71 MacDonald Diary, 11 July 1924, vol. 10, MacDonald Papers.

72 Ibid., 1 June 1925, vol. 10, MacDonald Papers.

73 MacDonald, "Moonlight and the Common Day," 971, vol. 10, MacDonald Papers.

74 LP, review of *Out of the Wilderness* by Wilson MacDonald, *New Outlook*, n.d., file 17, vol. 25, MacDonald Papers.

75 Clipping from *Canadian Stationer and Book Trade Journal*, March 1927, file 17, vol. 25, MacDonald Papers.

76 Ryerson Press royalty statement, 20 February 1925, vol. 5, MacDonald Papers.

77 MacDonald Diary, 24 November 1927, vol. 10, MacDonald Papers.

78 Pierce did aid MacDonald with publishing in the 1950s; Ryerson printed copies of both *The Lyric Year* in 1952 (not 1951, as Wallace's *The Ryerson Imprint* would have it) and *Out of the Wilderness* in 1957, offering to distribute some of both titles under its imprint. But Pierce seems more motivated by empathy for Mac-Donald than publishing advantage. The latter title sold just two copies in 1959. See MacDonald Diary, 14 October and 7 November 1952, vol. 8, MacDonald Papers, and 1959 royalty statement, "Ryerson Press" file, and Frank Flemington to MacDonald, 21 November 1952, both in vol. 5, MacDonald Papers.

79 He had been warned of this danger by one of his western benefactors. See Irene Moore to Wilson MacDonald, n.d. [fall 1923], vol. 1, MacDonald Papers.

80 See Arthur Stringer to LP, 25 April, 5 May, 3 June, 22 August, and 10 September 1939, file 7, box 7, LPP. Stringer commissioned and paid for this volume to re-place an earlier one by Grace Blackburn, considered lacking by both Pierce and Stringer, which was never published. Blackburn, however, had warned Pierce that her knowledge of Stringer was "slight." See Blackburn to LP, 23 February 1922, file 4, box 1, LPP, and LP Diary, 6 November 1928.

81 Margery Fee, "Lorne Pierce, Ryerson Press, and the Makers of Canadian Liter-ature Series," *Papers of the Bibliographical Society of Canada*, 24 (1985): 54.

82 LP Diary, 17 October 1923.

83 Ibid.

84 See Ian E. Wilson, "Creating the Future: Canada and Its Provinces," in La-monde et al., eds., *History of the Book in Canada, Volume Two, 1840–1918*, 175.

85 See Morin to Gouin, 18 July [should be September] 1924, vol. 35, Sir Lomer Gouin Papers, LAC.

86 "Makers of Canadian Literature" prospectus [1924], 4, box 21, PFC.

87 "National Literature [Report of LP speech in Ottawa]," *Canadian Stationer and Book Trade Journal*, July 1924, 60.

88 LP to Sir Andrew Macphail, 23 September 1923, vol. 3, Macphail Papers, LAC.

89 LP to Macphail, 29 September 1923, vol. 3, Macphail Papers.

90 See LP to Wilfred Eggleston, 3 January 1952, file 9, box 26, LPP.

91 According to Fee's "Lorne Pierce, Ryerson Press, and the Makers of Canadian Literature Series," that manuscript can be found in Barbeau's papers in the Can-

adian Centre for Folk Studies Archives at the Museum of Civilization, Ottawa, and Palmer Baker's is in QUA.

92 "Makers of Canadian Literature" prospectus [1924], 1, box 21, PFC.

93 John D. Logan to LP, 18 September 1922, file 2, box 1, LPP.

94 His letters to prospective editors for his series were often written on stationery headed "Federal Finance Corporation Limited – Bond and Stock Brokers." See Garvin to W.D. Lighthall, 27 December 1922, vol. 2, Lighthall Papers, LAC.

95 See entry for 15 February 1931 in Mary Rubio and Elizabeth Waterston, eds., *The Selected Journals of L.M. Montgomery, Volume IV: 1929–1935* (Toronto: Oxford University Press 1998), 107.

96 J.W. Garvin, ed., *The Collected Poems of Isabella Valancy Crawford* (Toronto: Briggs 1905), and J.W. Garvin, ed., *Canadian Poets* (Toronto: McClelland and Stewart 1916).

97 Garvin to W.D. Lighthall, 27 December 1922, vol. 2, Lighthall Papers.

98 "Master-Works of Canadian Authors" prospectus, vol. 3, Macphail Papers.

99 Lawrence Burpee later commented to Pierce: "John Garvin was the President and moving spirit in the Radisson Society, which, as you probably know, was not a society in any proper sense but merely a familiar type of publishing organization ... I believe the Radisson Society died with him [in 1935]." Burpee to Pierce, 18 October 1939, file 4, box 7, LPP.

00 In a January 1923 letter, Garvin names McClelland and Stewart as publishers for the series, but by July he names only the Radisson Society. See Garvin to W.D. Lighthall, 30 January 1923, vol. 2, Lighthall Papers, and Garvin to Sir Andrew Macphail, 9 July 1923, vol. 3, Macphail Papers.

01 Garvin to W.D. Lighthall, 30 January 1923, vol. 2, Lighthall Papers. The unit price depended on which of three bindings the subscriber selected.

02 See Garvin to Macphail, 14 April 1928, vol. 3, Macphail Papers. Garvin was now presenting the price as $4.80 a volume, or $120 for the "unnumbered library edition deluxe."

03 LP to Bliss Carman, 28 December 1923, file 9, box 21, file 9, Carman Correspondence. ("[Page] demands such terrific cash advances, it makes the scheme almost impossible.") L.M. Montgomery's travails with Page are described in Mary Henley Rubio, *Lucy Maud Montgomery: The Gift of Wings* (Toronto: Doubleday 2008).

04 LP to Carman, 26 October 1922, file 12, box 1, Carman correspondence, LPP.

05 Carman to LP, 10 November 1922, file 12, box 1, file 12, Carman Correspondence, LPP.

06 Ibid.

07 Carman to LP, 2 January 1924, file 12, box 1, Carman Correspondence, LPP. Hathaway's manuscript is at QUA.

08 See Duncan Campbell Scott to LP, 8 May 1923, file 13, box 1, LPP.

09 See James Cappon, *Charles G.D. Roberts* (Toronto: Ryerson 1925).

110   LP Diary, 31 December 1924.

111   See Rubio, *Lucy Maud Montgomery*, 140ff. Roberts declared his dislike for Page and his methods in a letter to Ralph Gustafson. See Roberts to Gustafson, 14 January 1941, repr. in Laurel Boone, ed., *The Collected Letters of Charles G.D. Roberts* (Fredericton: Goose Lane 1989), 600.

112   Logan to LP, 8 October 1922, file 2, box 1, LPP.

113   Ibid.

114   Fee, "Lorne Pierce, Ryerson Press, and the Makers of Canadian Literature Series," 55.

115   Albert Watson, *Robert Norwood* (Toronto: Ryerson 1923), 113, 114.

116   "Literary Criticism?" *Canadian Forum*, August 1924, scrapbook, box 52, LPP.

117   "Makers of Literature in New Series of Books," Toronto *Mail and Empire*, 26 May 1923, scrapbook, box 52, LPP. "You Scratch My Back …" Calgary *Herald*, 22 February 1924, is also found there.

118   See Norwood to LP, 6 June 1923, box 1, LPP.

119   Margaret Lawrence to Bliss Carman, 3 October 1927, file 2, box 21, Carman Correspondence, LPP.

120   Margaret Lawrence to Bliss Carman, 4 September 1927, file 1, box 21, Bliss Carman Correspondence, LPP.

121   LP to MacDonald, n.d. [late September 1923], vol. 1, MacDonald Papers. Pierce does not seem to have ever begun work on it.

122   In a list of the "Master Works" enclosed in John Garvin to W.D. Lighthall, 27 December 1922, vol. 2, Lighthall Papers, these two volumes and editors are listed. But by 19 April 1924, letters between Pierce and Scott make it clear that there has been a move by both Edgar and Scott to Pierce's series. See Scott to LP, 29 April, 19 August, and 26 November 1924, file 11, box 1, LPP.

123   J.D. Logan to LP, n.d. [6 February 1923], file 5, box 1, LPP.

124   LP to Logan, 5 June 1924 (registered letter), file 8, box 1, LPP.

125   William Riddell to LP, 23 January 1923, file 6, box 1, LPP. More on Riddell's literary and legal career can be found in Brian McKillop, *The Spinster and the Prophet* (Toronto: Lester, Orpen and Dennys 2000).

126   Riddell to LP, 15 June 1923, file 6, box 1, LPP; and Fee, "Lorne Pierce, Ryerson Press, and the Makers of Canadian Literature Series," 54.

127   Riddell to LP, 27 June 1923, file 6, box 1, LPP.

128   William Renwick Riddell, *John Richardson* (Toronto: Ryerson 1923), 151.

129   LP to Cappon, 10 January 1923, file 3, box 1, LPP.

130   Cappon to LP, 17 March 1923, file 3, box 1, LPP.

131   Cappon to LP, 5 July 1923, file 3, box 1, LPP.

132   Cappon to LP, 27 October 1923, file 3, box 1, LPP. This was the same month that Pierce was having difficulties with Cornell, Pratt, and Deacon over their Ryerson publications.

133   LP Diary, 18 November 1923.

34 Cappon to LP, 7 December 1928, file 1, box 3, LPP.

35 Cappon to LP, 18 October 1930, file 8, box 3, LPP.

36 Macphail to LP, 9 November 1923, file 5, box 1, LPP.

37 LP to Macphail, 8 November 1923 and 24 January 1924, vol. 3, Macphail Papers, LAC.

38 LP to Macphail, 8 February 1924, file 9, box 1, LPP.

39 Both versions of the manuscript are found in the "Norman Duncan" file, vol. 5, Macphail Papers.

40 LP to Macphail, 13 February 1924, vol. 3, Macphail Papers. Pierce does not specify which authors.

41 Deacon to LP, 8 December 1923, file 4, box 1, LPP.

42 "Notice biographique," Fonds Victor Morin, Centre de Recherche en Civilisation canadienne-française, University of Ottawa.

43 See Victor Morin to Sir Lomer Gouin, 5 May 1924, vol. 35, Gouin Papers, LAC.

44 LP Diary, 25 September 1927.

45 Henri Beaude to LP, 11 November 1924, file 6, box 1, LPP.

46 Gustave Lanctôt to LP, 7 November 1925, file 2, box 2, LPP.

47 See David M. Hayne, "Lorne Pierce et la littérature québécoise," *Voix et images*, 8 (winter 1992): 232–47. The Frégault reference is on 235.

48 Robert Roquebrune, "Un livre de M.G. Lanctot," unidentified clipping, scrapbook, box 52, LPP.

49 "The Dean" [Archibald MacMechan], "Makers of Canadian Literature," Montreal *Gazette*, n.d., scrapbook, box 52, LPP.

50 "An Admirable Series," *Canadian Stationer and Book Trade Journal*, July 1924, 57.

CHAPTER ELEVEN

1 S.W. Fallis, "Annual Report of the Book Steward to the Book Committee April 9, 1926," 6, Board of Publication Papers, United Church Archives, Toronto.

2 ECP to LP, 20 May 1925, box 7, PFC.

3 LP to ECP, 20 February 1922, box 7, PFC.

4 W.A. Deacon, "The Bookshelf," *Saturday Night*, 14 July 1923, 8.

5 LP to Macphail, 8 January 1924, vol. 3, Macphail Papers, LAC.

6 Marquis to LP, 9 November 1923, file 5, box 1, LPP.

7 LP Diary, 4 January 1924.

8 LP to Macphail, 29 September 1923, vol. 3, Macphail Papers.

9 See LP to Macphail, 29 September, 8 November 1923, and 8 May 1924 (with copy of agreement), vol. 3, Macphail Papers. The delay in remitting the $100 was to guard against excessive editorial changes at the proof stage.

10 Garvin to Macphail, 3 February 1923, vol. 3, Macphail Papers.

11 Fee, "Lorne Pierce, Ryerson Press, and the Makers of Canadian Literature Series," 57.

12 See LP to Macphail, 8 November 1923, vol. 3, Macphail Papers.

13 Fee, "Lorne Pierce, Ryerson Press, and the Makers of Canadian Literature Series," 57.

14 LP to Bliss Carman, 27 April 1923, box 21, Bliss Carman Correspondence, LPP.

15 LP to Macphail, 12 December 1923, vol. 3, Macphail Papers.

16 Ray Palmer Baker to LP, 19 December 1923, file 3, box 1, LPP.

17 See Thomas and Lennox, *William Arthur Deacon*, 99.

18 LP Diary, 12 November 1923.

19 LP to Charles Mair, 23 May 1924, box 1, file 9, LPP.

20 See Fee, "Lorne Pierce, Ryerson Press, and the Makers of Canadian Literature Series," 62–3.

21 See J.D. Logan to S.W. Fallis, 5 March 1924, file 7, box 1, LPP. Logan complains about Marquis as reader of the former's Howe manuscript.

22 LP Diary, 15 April 1924.

23 Marquis to LP, 18 April and 18 May 1925, file 2, box 2, LPP.

24 Marquis to LP, 18 April 1925, file 2, box 2, LPP.

25 Ibid.

26 Ibid.

27 Marquis to LP, 18 May 1925, file 3, box 2, LPP.

28 LP Diary, 3 May 1925.

29 Ibid.

30 Ibid.

31 Ibid.

32 LP Diary, 6 October 1925.

33 LP to Charles Mair, 16 May 1925, file 2, box 2, LPP.

34 LP Diary, 22 March 1926.

35 S.W. Fallis, "Annual Report of the Book Steward to the Book Committee April 9, 1926," 6, Board of Publication Papers.

36 LP Diary, 30 March 1926.

37 Morin to LP, 12 July 1942, file 4, box 9, LPP.

38 Margery Fee states that, in the 1920s, only seven Canadian universities offered courses focused at least in part on Canadian literature. See Fee, "English Canadian Literary Criticism 1890–1950: Defining and Establishing a National Literature" (PhD thesis, University of Toronto, 1981), 147.

39 Ibid., 51. Pierce himself believed that "in time to come my 'Makers of Canadian Literature' will be increasingly more valuable because of what it has salvaged and preserved." LP Diary, 21 August 1924.

40 LP Diary, 17 October 1923. "The interest in Canadian literature was immense: our National corpus was fast taking shape owing to the war ... Now seemed to be the time and so 'The Makers of Canadian Literature' were launched." Ironically, Pierce's next sentence reads: "Their success is already assured."

41 See "Literary Criticism?" *Canadian Forum*, August 1924, scrapbook, box 52, LPP.
42 LP Diary, 21 August 1927. LP gave the royalties from his book, *In Conference with the Best Minds*, to Edith "insisting that she buy [a washing machine] this week."
43 LP Diary, 9 November 1923.
44 Ibid., 17 October 1923.
45 ECP to LP, 24 February 1922, box 6, PFC.
46 LP to ECP, 23 January 1916, box 3, PFC.
47 LP to ECP, n.d. [spring 1924], box 7, PFC.
48 LP to ECP, 3 March 1925, box 7, PFC.
49 LP Diary, 20 June 1924. Even here, LP also refers to her long refusal to marry him, suggesting the tension between them at this time.
50 LP Diary, 14 October 1926.
51 Pierce's salary was raised to $4,000 in December 1926 after years of lobbying Fallis on the matter.
52 LP Diary, 31 December 1924.
53 Ibid., 29 September 1924.
54 See Greg Gatenby, *Toronto: A Literary Guide* (Toronto: McArthur 1999), 80.
55 James L. Hughes, *Froebel's Educational Laws* (1898), repr. in A.D. Watson and Lorne Pierce, eds., *Our Canadian Literature* (Toronto: Ryerson 1922), 288.
56 This is the first poem in page proofs of Hughes's *God Made Them Good: True Stories of the So-Called Bad*, file 5, box 37, LPP.
57 Gatenby, *Toronto: A Literary Guide*, 58.
58 James L. Hughes, *Songs of Gladness and Growth* (Toronto: Briggs 1916).
59 Ibid., and idem, *The Real Robert Burns* (Toronto: Ryerson 1922).
60 LP, "James Laughlin Hughes, LL.D: Patriot, Preacher, Pedagogue, Poet," *Canadian Magazine*, 58 (November 1921): 57–62.
61 Ibid., 57.
62 Sandwell to LP, 21 June 1921, file 1, box 1, LPP.
63 LP, *Fifty Years of Public Service* (Toronto: Oxford University Press 1924), 199.
64 See "Spelled Down 'Ringer' So Hughes Won Boots," unidentified clipping, 34, scrapbook, box 52, LPP.
65 Telephone message slip from James L. Hughes, file "Loose Items from Diary September 19, 1923 – November 21, 1925," LPP. Gundy agreed to publish within two hours of Fallis's refusal. LP Diary, 19 September 1924.
66 LP Diary, 19 September 1924.
67 Ibid., 20 December 1924.
68 LP, notes on "Makers of Canadian Literature series" [February or March 1925], 1925 Western tour file, box 7, PFC.
69 LP Diary, 22 March 1925.
70 Ibid., 3 May 1925.
71 Ibid., 19 September 1924. Emphasis in original.

72 LP Diary, 20 December 1924 and 4 May 1926. Two rather sheepish letters from Hughes to LP of 29 April and 3 May [1926] refer to the long delay, file 1, box 2, LPP. Gundy had printed 1,000 copies of the book.

73 LP Diary, 11 July 1920.

74 See Sandra Campbell, "'A Girl in a Book': Writing Marjorie Pickthall and Lorne Pierce," *Canadian Poetry*, 39 (fall/winter 1996): 80–95.

75 Marjorie Pickthall, *The Drift of Pinions* (Montreal: University Magazine 1913).

76 For example, Macphail's views on woman's place are made abundantly clear in his *Essays in Fallacy* (New York: Longmans 1910): not surprisingly for a man of his deeply conservative orientation, one of the "fallacies" he seeks to demolish is feminism.

77 Marjorie Pickthall to Helena Coleman, 26 February 1913, Pickthall Papers, Victoria College Library, Toronto.

78 The story is related in Jean Blewett, unidentified clipping, 8 May 1925, scrapbook, box 52, LPP.

79 Pickthall to Pelham Edgar, 21 February 1921, vol. 1, Wilson MacDonald Papers, LAC (MacDonald had been given the letter by Edgar).

80 Archibald MacMechan, qtd. in LP, *Marjorie Pickthall: A Book of Remembrance* (Toronto: Ryerson 1925), 147.

81 LP, *Marjorie Pickthall*.

82 See Helena Coleman to LP, 14 April, 10 June, and 10 September 1923, box 59, Pickthall Collection, LPP.

83 LP Diary, 28 October 1923.

84 Coleman to LP, 24 July 1924, box 1, file 7, LPP. Clearly, some of Pickthall's women friends also perpetuated a cloistered, patriarchal construct of her life. Later in the 1940s, Coleman was to censor and repossess some of the Pickthall letters Pierce had given to Victoria College Library. See Coleman to LP, 12 April and 11 November 1943, file 8, box 9, LPP.

85 LP, *An Outline of Canadian Literature* (Toronto: Ryerson 1927), 191.

86 See Sir Andrew Macphail, undated memoir of Pickthall, box 67, Pickthall Collection, LPP. Macphail supplied this to Pierce in lieu of the original material.

87 LP, *Marjorie Pickthall*, vii.

88 Ira Nadel, "Biography and Theory or Beckett in the Bath," in James Noonan, ed., *Biography and Autobiography* (Ottawa: Carleton University Press 1993), 12.

89 LP, *Marjorie Pickthall*, viii.

90 Joanna Russ, *How to Suppress Women's Writing* (Austin: University of Texas Press 1983), 90–1.

91 LP, *Marjorie Pickthall*, 51.

92 LP Diary, 9 August 1924.

93 LP, *Marjorie Pickthall*, 200.

94 Ibid., 197, 165.

95 Ibid., 166.

96 Pickthall, qtd. in ibid., 104.

97 LP, transcript of *Marjorie Pickthall*, 27, file 5, box 38, LPP.

98 LP, *Marjorie Pickthall*, 62.

99 "True Poet and Canadian," Toronto *Globe*, 23 April 1925, and E.J.R., "Marjorie Pickthall," Hamilton *Spectator*, 25 September 1926, both in scrapbook, box 52, LPP.

100 Albert E. Smythe, "Marjorie Pickthall," *Canadian Bookman*, May 1925, and W. Everard Edmonds, "With Pen and Pencil," Edmonton *Journal*, 29 August 1925, both in scrapbook, box 52, LPP.

101 W.T. Allison, "A Monument to Marjorie Pickthall," Calgary *Herald*, 9 May 1925, file 12, box 67, Pickthall Collection, LPP.

102 Austin Bothwell, "A Canadian Bookshelf," Saskatoon *Phoenix*, 16 May 1925, 149, scrapbook, box 52, LPP.

103 See LP, "Marjorie Pickthall: A Memorial Address ... April 7, 1943, in Commemoration of the Twenty-Fifth Anniversary of the Poet's Death," *Acta Victoriana*, 67, no. 6 (Graduation Issue): 21–30; and LP, "Marjorie Lowry Christie Pickthall," *Canadian Who Was Who*, 2 (1938): 349–52. By the time of LP's edition of *The Selected Poems of Marjorie Pickthall* (Toronto: McClelland and Stewart 1957), Pickthall's IQ seems to have deteriorated markedly: now "rapture and intuition are substituted for reason" in her poetry in his view, while her body "scarcely sustained the demands of a cloistered life in times of peace" (Introduction, 15, 19).

104 LP Diary, 1 April 1924. There is also a hint of racial stereotyping in the reference to a "wild wood" flavour in Johnson, who was of mixed white and Mohawk parentage.

105 Jean-Paul Sartre, *The Family Idiot: Gustave Flaubert*, vol. 1 (Chicago: University of Chicago Press 1981), x.

106 The quantity is mentioned in LP Diary, 20 December 1924.

107 The drawing is found in LP to Edith, Beth, and Bruce Pierce, n.d. [spring 1924], box 7, PFC.

108 LP to ECP, n.d. [spring 1924], box 7, PFC.

109 LP Diary, 19 September 1924.

110 BPR, interview with author, Pike Lake, ON, 26 July 2000.

111 LP Diary, 12 March 1925.

112 The 1925 Pierce Christmas card is found in box 1, Blanche Hume Papers, QUA.

113 LP Diary, 20 June 1924.

114 EC to her Conley grandmother and aunts, 4 January 1915, box 3, PFC.

115 LP Diary, 9 August 1924.

116 Ibid., 9 November 1923 and 9 August 1924. See LP to Principal Taylor, 19 July 1924, in file "Loose Items from Diary September 19, 1923 – November 21, 1925," LPP. The number of volumes is mentioned in LP to D.C. Scott, 8 August 1924, vol. 76, Royal Society of Canada Papers, LAC.

117 Fee, "English Canadian Literary Criticism 1890–1950," 199.

118 See, for example, LP Diary, 31 December 1924, where he complains about household expenses and then discusses the "many" rare volumes he has purchased for the Queen's collection and the kind of material he hopes to acquire.

119 "This Should Bring Grist to the Rummage Sales," unidentified clipping, scrapbook, box 52, LPP. Pierce wrote beside the clipping: "To L.P. with his wife's comp[liment]s Oct. 23 1925."

120 ECP to Blanche Hume, n.d. [c. 1950], box 1, Hume Papers.

121 LP to Principal Taylor, 19 July 1924, file "Loose Items from Diary September 19, 1923 – November 21, 1925," LPP.

122 This was in 1946, at the time a catalogue of the collection was being prepared by Queen's Librarian E.C. Kyte. See Kyte to LP, 11 April 1946, file 8, box 13, LPP: "We are going to call it 'The Lorne and Edith Pierce Collection.' How's that?" Beth Pierce Robinson emphasized her mother's uncharacteristic insistence on recognition in an interview with the author, Perth, ON, 2 August 1991.

123 Pierce told D.C. Scott in proposing the terms of the award: "It is not intended the medal shall necessarily be awarded annually, but only when an outstanding contribution has been made to Canadian literature." LP to D.C. Scott, 8 August 1924, vol. 76, Royal Society of Canada Papers, LAC. In practice, the medal has usually been awarded annually.

124 See LP to D.C. Scott, 3 July 1924 [typed copy], vol. 76, Royal Society of Canada Papers, LAC, and Scott to LP, 17 November 1924, file 11, box 1, LPP.

125 D.C. Scott to LP, 17 and 26 November 1924 (typed excerpt), vol. 76, Royal Society of Canada Papers, LAC.

126 LP to Scott, 20 March 1925, vol. 76, Royal Society of Canada Papers, LAC.

127 LP to D.C. Scott, 23 September 1924, vol. 76, Royal Society of Canada Papers, LAC.

128 ECP to LP, 20 May 1925, box 7, PFC.

129 LP to ECP, 18 May 1925, box 7, PFC.

130 ECP to LP, 20 May 1925, box 7, PFC.

131 LP Diary, 23 August 1925 and 12 December 1925.

132 LP to ECP, 19 May 1926, box 7, PFC.

133 LP Diary, 20 May 1926.

134 ECP to Bruce Pierce, n.d. [1950], box 14, PFC.

135 LP Diary, 28 November 1924.

136 See ibid., 29 April, 2 May, and 20 May 1926.

137 LP to ECP, 3 March 1925, box 7, PFC. He had the same difficulty when he attended a session of Parliament later that spring.

138 LP Diary, 19 June 1926. Pierce recorded the next winter that he had preached two "horrible" sermons and again resolved to stop. LP Diary, 24 February 1927.

139 Ibid., 20 March 1926.

Notes to pages 247–9

140 ECP to Blanche Hume, 13 June 1926, box 1, Hume Papers, QUA.

141 LP Diary, 26 October 1925.

142 Harriet Pierce to LP, 30 October 1925, box 7, PFC.

143 LP, transcript of Grove reminiscences, file 4, box 38, LPP. These were done in the mid-1940s for Desmond Pacey.

144 LP, "On Religious Toleration," repr. in LP, *In Conference with the Best Minds*, 117. LP added that the history of religious intolerance was "humiliating."

145 LP Diary, 10 June 1925.

146 Ibid., 24 June 1925.

147 LP to Watson, 19 July 1925, file 21, box 2, LPP.

148 LP Diary, 16 September 1925.

149 Ibid., 11 February 1925. In the 8 February entry, Pierce refers to the manuscript by its earlier title "The White Range Line House." In a memoir of the incident written decades later, Pierce wrongly dates the episode to 1924, but his diary establishes 1925 as the correct date. See LP, transcript of Grove reminiscences, file 4, box 38, LPP. Pierce's misdating has caused some confusion in later accounts, for example, in Pitt, *E.J. Pratt, The Truant Years*, 286, where LP is depicting as defending the novel's publication in 1924 instead of 1925.

150 LP to ECP, 13 February 1925, box 7, PFC.

151 Hugh Eayrs to Grove, 25 February 1924, vol. 2, John Gray Papers, LAC.

152 LP, transcript of Grove reminiscences, file 4, box 38, LPP.

153 LP, letter to Wilfrid Eggleston, 27 October 1956, vol. 19, Eggleston Papers, LAC.

154 LP, transcript of Grove reminiscences, file 4, box 38, LPP.

155 Vipond, "National Consciousness in English-Speaking Canada in the 1920s," 363.

156 Pierce uses the phrase in LP to EC, 24 June 1913, box 1, PFC. In *Settlers*, the novel's heroine refuses Niels Lindstedt because of the hardship of her mother's life as a farm wife. Similarly, Pierce's prairie diary and letters comment on the "slave" lives of many of the settler women. See for example, LP to EC, 12 October 1913, box 1, PFC.

157 "Commends New Literature in Canadian West," Winnipeg *Free Press Bulletin*, 19 February 1924. A letter from Vancouver poet A.M. Stephen shows Pierce's reputation in this area: "The Western group which you contacted here, in Vancouver, are your friends and you may count upon our loyalty. You have much in common with us – are working along similar lines – discovering and giving form to the inchoate thing called a 'Canadian national spirit.' There is no other work so much worth while – for Canadians." See A.M. Stephen to LP, 19 July 1924, file 11, box 1, LPP.

158 LP, transcript of Grove reminiscences, file 4, box 38, LPP.

159 Margaret Stobie, *Frederick Philip Grove* (New York: Twayne 1973), 139, 111.

160 Friskney, "Towards a Canadian 'Cultural Mecca,'" 293.

161 Grove to LP, 28 August and 12 September 1925, file 1, box 2, LPP.

162 Howard Angus Kennedy, for example, was also furious that year with Moore over the misleading dust-jacket blurbs on his *The Book of the West*. See Kennedy to E.J. Moore, 6 March 1925, file 1, box 2, LPP. Pierce took to writing the jacket material for most books himself. He commented: "The critics and reviewers all lean upon these twitters on the book flap, and for that reason I try to make sure they say the right things! There is a lot of skulduggery in everything!" See LP to Beth Pierce, n.d. [early 1940s], box 16, PFC.

163 Grove to E.J. Moore, 21 December and 17 November 1925, repr. in Desmond Pacey, ed., *The Letters of Frederick Philip Grove* (Toronto: University of Toronto Press 1976), 32, 24. Moore was also responsible for proofing books at this period.

164 Stanley Morgan Powell, review in Montreal *Daily Star*, 31 October 1925, and Arthur L. Phelps, review in *Saturday Night*, 5 December 1925, both repr. in Desmond Pacey, *Frederick Philip Grove* (Toronto: Ryerson 1970), 105–6, 113.

165 Stobie, *Frederick Philip Grove*, 112.

166 Ibid., 111–13.

167 Arthur Phelps, recounted in ibid., 112; J.F.B. Livesay to Grove, 19 March 1926, Grove Collection, University of Manitoba.

168 Stobie, *Frederick Philip Grove*, 113–16. Grove himself did not lose a teaching post over the novel, as LP states in his obituary of the author: Grove had resigned from the high school principalship of Rapid City in June 1924. See LP, "Frederick Philip Grove (1871–1948)," *Transactions and Proceedings of the Royal Society of Canada*, 1949, 113–19.

169 LP, transcript of Grove reminiscences, file 4, box 38, LPP.

170 LP to Wilfrid Eggleston, 8 July 1957, vol. 19, Eggleston Papers, LAC.

171 LP, transcript of Grove reminiscences, file 4, box 38, LPP. The reference to Fallis's politics is from LP to Wilfrid Eggleston, 8 July 1957, vol. 19, Eggleston Papers, LAC. There Pierce also concludes: "Meighen's letter was my D.S.O." The incident is not dated in either source, but, if Meighen was prime minister at the time, it must have occurred between June and September 1926.

172 For a history of such values, see Carole Gerson, *A Purer Taste: The Writing and Reading of Fiction in English in Nineteenth Century Canada* (Toronto: University of Toronto Press 1989), 17ff.

173 Grove gives figures in a letter to Watson Kirkconnell, 24 January 1928, repr. in Pacey, ed., *The Letters of Frederick Philip Grove*, 77. Canadian sales after three years were 1,099 copies.

174 See Stobie, *Frederick Philip Grove*, 140.

175 See Grove to LP, 14 January 1926 and 8 April 1926, repr. in Pacey, ed., *The Letters of Frederick Philip Grove*, 33–5. Macmillan would publish *Our Daily Bread* in 1928.

176 LP to Grove, 28 April 1926, qtd. in Stobie, *Frederick Philip Grove*, 139. Stobie observes that Grove "seemed intent on striking out at someone, to make someone suffer for his disappointment at the reception of his book."

177 See Thomas and Lennox, *William Arthur Deacon*, 70. Phelps told Deacon that Pierce had been "timid" about the censorship storm and thus was hesitating over accepting further works from Grove.

178 See LP to Grove, 29 March [1946], file 9, box 7, LPP.

179 LP Diary, 3 May 1926.

180 "Dr. A.D. Watson Passes," Toronto *Telegram*, 3 May 1926.

181 LP Diary, 3 May 1926.

182 Ibid.

183 Fee, "English Canadian Literary Criticism 1890–1950," 169.

184 LP Diary, 14 May 1926. This plot was in Scarborough Lawn Cemetery, but he eventually acquired one in Mount Pleasant Cemetery, burial place of Marjorie Pickthall, Timothy Eaton, and many Toronto worthies.

CHAPTER TWELVE

1   LP to Charles G.D. Roberts, 20 October 1941, file 5, box 8, LPP.

2   A.S. Bourinot to LP, 22 April 1950, file 1, box 19, LPP.

3   LP, *In Conference with the Best Minds*.

4   The phrase was used in the *Canadian Forum* editorial on the series. See "Literary Criticism?" *Canadian Forum*, August 1924, scrapbook, box 52, LPP.

5   LP Diary, 4 May 1926.

6   The diary is largely silent on Lorne's parents' responses to such issues around this period, usually a sign that Pierce was troubled by something too uncomfortable to address directly and/or at length.

7   See Book Committee Minutes, bound volume, 1913–1926, Board of Publication Papers, United Church Archives.

8   Friskney, "Towards a Canadian 'Cultural Mecca,'" 257–8.

9   Ibid., 244ff.

10 All figures from these records are rounded to the nearest thousand dollars.

11 See "Profit and Loss Summary," Board of Publication Minutes, bound volume, 1927–1948, 18, Board of Publication Papers.

12 Ibid. Cope's Manufacturing Department was responsible for $39,211 of total profits in 1926, and $38,013 in 1927, almost half the total profit for each year.

13 Turnover figures were not stated for 1926 and 1927 in the Board of Publication minutes, a fact that would have concerned any astute accountant. Turnover for 1922 was listed at just under $5,000,000 in the 1918–22 quadrennial report: Book Committee Minutes, bound volume, 1913–1926, 191, Board of Publication Papers, United Church Archives.

14 LP to Charles G.D. Roberts, 20 October 1941, file 5, box 8, LPP.

15 Thoreau MacDonald modified his father's original 1925 design for the series in 1942, as of Mary Elizabeth Colman's *For This Freedom, Too* (1942). According to Frank Flemington, the cover design was made even simpler with Arthur Bourinot's *Treasures of the Snow* (1950). Three years later, the chapbooks began

to be bound in hardcover, with the original design, as of Sherwood Fox's *On Friendship* (1953). That design was further simplified, however, beginning with Thecla Bradshaw's *Mobiles* (1955). By the end of 1960, just before Pierce's retirement from Ryerson Press, he had published 194 chapbooks in the series. See Frank Flemington, "Appendix C: The Ryerson Poetry Chapbooks," in his typescript "Lorne Pierce: A Bibliography," Lorne Pierce Collection, Queen's University Library. Flemington lists the publications to the end of 1960.

16 See Vancouver Poetry Society, *A Book of Days, 1916–1946* (Toronto: Ryerson 1946), 22. This history of the society quotes poet and member A.M. Stephen about the source of Pierce's chapbook idea; since Pierce published the history, the explanation seems credible.

17 See Flemington, "Lorne Pierce: A Bibliography," which lists 194 titles between 1925 and 1960. A chronological listing to 1954 is also found in Wallace, *The Ryerson Imprint.*

18 Lennox and Lacombe, *Dear Bill*, xviii–ix. Alfred Bailey published *Tao* in the series in 1930, while Marriott had three: the landmark *The Wind Our Enemy* (1939), *Calling Adventurers* (1941), and *Salt Marsh* (1942). Purdy contributed *Pressed on Sand* (1955) and *The Crafte So Longe to Lerne* (1959).

19 For the Indian File series, see James King, *Jack: A Life with Writers: The Story of Jack McClelland* (Toronto: Knopf 1999), 35, 49. McClelland, who was urged to create the series by his editor Sybil Hutchinson, also had his share of financial and authorial headaches with it. His series used Indian motifs in its design, hence the name, and garnered prestige and three Governor General's Awards for McClelland and Stewart. The series began in 1948 with Roy Daniells's *Deeper into the Forest* and ended in 1958 with John Glassco's *The Deficit Made Flesh.*

20 John Sutherland to Dorothy Livesay, 9 April 1943, repr. in Bruce Whiteman, ed., *The Letters of John Sutherland 1942–1956* (Toronto: ECW 1992), 7.

21 See LP Diary, 25 January and 5 February 1925.

22 For his estimate of Roberts, Carman, and others of the Group, see LP, *Three Fredericton Poets: Writers of the University of New Brunswick and the New Dominion: Alumni Oration, Encaenia, May 19, 1933* (Toronto: Ryerson 1933). Pierce also spoke of the work of Carman and Roberts as evoking not only the beauty of the Maritimes but also their "robust moral purpose" (16).

23 Archibald MacMechan to LP, 28 May 1927, file 9, box 2, LPP.

24 LP Diary, 24 May 1927.

25 Betsy Jefferys Fee (who worked for Lorne Pierce in the 1930s), interview with Beth Robinson, Toronto, spring 1988, taped interview in possession of BPR.

26 LP, "Charles G.D. Roberts: An Estimate," *New Outlook*, 9 December 1925, scrapbook, box 67A, LPP; LP, *Three Fredericton Poets.*

27 LP Diary, 20 August 1925.

28 LP, *An Outline of Canadian Literature* (Toronto: Ryerson 1927), 71–2.

29 According to the note in the front of *The Vagrant of Time*, 485 of the 500 copies printed were sold by subscription.

30 LP Diary, 9 September 1926.

31 See Ibid., 9 September 1926 and 18 April 1927.

32 See F.G. Scott to LP, 26 July 1924, 21 November 1924, 2 December 1924, and 11 January 1926, in file 11, box 1, LPP, as well as file 7, box 2 (for last letter cited), for some of the manoeuvring surrounding submissions by Scott to Ryerson.

33 F.G. Scott to LP, 9 January 1925, file 4, box 2, LPP.

34 F.G. Scott to LP, 14 February 1925, file 4, box 2, LPP.

35 LP to "Seranus" (Susan Frances Harrison), n.d. [1928], file 7, box 2, LPP. Caswell had urged that Pierce publish her in a letter of 20 June 1924, file 7, box 1, LPP.

36 See LP to Seranus, 9 November 1928, and her reply of 12 November 1928, file 1, box 3, LPP.

37 LP Diary, 5 December 1925.

38 "Boosts Canadian Poetry," *Canadian Stationer and Book Trade Journal*, 26 October 1926, 94.

39 See George Whalley to LP, 12 July 1945, file 4, box 13, LPP, which refers to Pierce's "arbitrary restriction upon religious and patriotic verse for the Ryerson Poetry Chap-Books."

40 LP to Ralph Gustafson, 6 December 1933, file 4, box 5, LPP.

41 Ryerson had published Campbell's *Merry-Go-Round* (1946).

42 LP to Marjorie Freeman Campbell, 25 June 1947, file 7, box 14, LPP.

43 LP to Campbell, 7 August 1947, file 7, box 14, LPP.

44 Fred Cogswell to LP, 2 April 1953, file 3, box 22, LPP.

45 LP to Theresa Thomson, 14 November 1951, vol. 8, Canadian Writers' Foundation Papers, LAC.

46 For example, Pierce published Marjorie Pickthall, *The Naiad and Other Poems* (1930), eight years after her death, as was the case with Agnes Maule Machar's *The Thousand Islands* (1935). Bliss Carman's *Music of Earth* (1939) appeared a decade after his death.

47 Margery Fee, "English Canadian Literary Criticism 1890–1950," 195, 198.

48 Louis Dudek to LP, 17 November 1952, file 2, box 21, LPP, and Dudek to Phyllis Webb, 1 July 1951, Webb Papers, LAC. Thanks to Lorna Knight for a copy of the letter to Webb.

49 Marjorie Pickthall, *The Naiad and Five Other Poems* (Toronto: Ryerson 1930). Pierce had chosen six unpublished poems from a Pickthall manuscript.

50 Elsie Woodley to LP, 30 September 1930, file 4, box 4, LPP. Her chapbook was published that year.

51 See, for example, Bourinot to LP, 22 April 1950, file 1, box 19, LPP.

52 See Fred Cogswell to LP, 2 April 1953, file 3, box 22, LPP. Pierce had told him that only eight of the poems he had submitted were of interest for publica-

tion, and asked him to submit some others in a few months. Pierce rejected his manuscript "The Corn King" a year later, however. See LP to Cogswell, 13 September 1954, file 2, box 24, LPP.

53 See Cogswell to Pierce, 2 April 1953, file 3, box 22, and 13 September 1954, file 2, box 24, LPP. Pierce published Fred Cogswell's *The Haloed Tree* (1956) and *The Testament of Cresseid* (1957).

54 LP's diary entry for 31 December 1921 records: "Dr. Fallis tells me I shall represent the House on a mission to the coast in Feb. to interview Premiers of four Western Provinces re school texts."

55 LP to EC, 12 July 1912, box 1, PFC.

56 See LP to EC, 26 October 1915, box 4, and 12 April 1916, box 5, PFC.

57 LP to EC, 8 October 1915, box 3, PFC.

58 Friskney, "Towards a Canadian 'Cultural Mecca,'" 130–1.

59 *Newsletter* of the Bibliographical Society of Canada, 3, no. 2 (1959): 4.

60 LP, "Wilson MacDonald – Poet," *Christian Guardian*, 4 July 1923, scrapbook, vol. 25, Wilson MacDonald Papers, LAC.

61 Pelham Edgar, "A Confession of Faith and a Protest," *University Magazine*, 8 (April 1909): 314.

62 See Vipond, "National Consciousness in English-Speaking Canada in the 1920s," 533ff.

63 Ibid., 540.

64 LP, *New History for Old: Discussions on Aims and Methods in Writing and Teaching History* (Toronto: Ryerson 1931), 15.

65 Ibid., 15.

66 Ibid., 21, 22, 26.

67 Ibid., 9. The "talks" refer to Pierce's Mount Allison lectures.

68 George Wrong, *Ontario Public School History of Canada* (Toronto: Ryerson 1921), 365pp. Ryerson also published his *Ontario Public School History of England* that year. In 1929 Ryerson published the revised work: George Wrong, Chester Martin, and Walter Sage's *The Story of Canada*.

69 Pierce wrote *Judge Haliburton, Maisonneuve, Rev. James Evans, Rev. John Black,* and *Rev. John McDougall*. A complete list of them is found in Frank Flemington, "Lorne Pierce: A Bibliography," and a year-by-year listing in W.S. Wallace, *The Ryerson Imprint*.

70 Carl Berger, *The Writing of Canadian History* (Toronto: Oxford University Press 1976), 223.

71 LP, *New History for Old*, 26, 31.

72 Ibid., 36.

73 Ibid., 31.

74 LP, *Sieur de Maisonneuve* (Toronto: Ryerson 1926), 24.

75 Blodwen Davies, *The Story of Hydro* (Toronto: Ryerson 1931), 26.

76 United Church Publishing House, 1932 Report to the Board of Publication, box 21, Board of Publication Papers.
77 LP Diary, February–March 1922 memoir.
78 For a sketch of John Saul, see "John Saul Dies," *Canadian Stationer and Book Trade Journal*, 15 June 1939, 12.

CHAPTER THIRTEEN

1   Preface to *The Ryerson Book of Prose and Verse*, Book One, ed. Lorne Pierce and Arthur Yates (Toronto: Ryerson 1927), ix–x. Wallace's *The Ryerson Imprint* lists the publication date as 1928, but the frontispiece of the reader gives 1927.
2   LP to ECP, 18 February 1925, box 7, PFC.
3   LP Diary, February–March 1922 memoir.
4   Ibid., 22 March 1925.
5   Ibid., February–March 1922 memoir.
6   Ibid.
7   Ibid., 1 April 1924.
8   Ibid., 10 March 1928.
9   Ernest Fewster to LP, 5 March 1931, file 7, box 4, LPP.
10 LP Diary, February–March 1922 memoir.
11 Ibid. Ryerson published Locke's text *Builders of the Canadian Commonwealth* in 1923, with a second edition in 1926.
12 LP Diary, 15 April and 9 August 1924.
13 Ibid., 28 November 1928.
14 Ibid., 1 April 1924.
15 LP to ECP, 18 February 1925, box 7, PFC.
16 Ibid.
17 See LP Diary, 4 November 1928.
18 See the entry for *The Chronicle of a Century* in Frank Flemington, "Lorne Pierce: A Bibliography," Lorne Pierce Collection, Queen's University Library.
19 LP Diary, 9 September 1926.
20 LP to Victor Morin, 10 January 1927, reel 4, Victor Morin Papers, Centre for Research in French Canadian Culture, University of Ottawa.
21 See the entry for this title in Flemington, "Lorne Pierce: A Bibliography."
22 LP to Victor Morin, 10 January 1927, reel 4, Morin Papers.
23 Lorne Pierce, *An Outline of Canadian Literature (French and English)* (Montreal: Louis Carrier 1927), dedication and reply.
24 LP, Foreword to ibid., n.p.
25 Donald Stephens, "The Literary History of Canada: Its Modest Successes," *Canadian Literature*, 24 (spring 1965): 11–12.
26 LP, *An Outline of Canadian Literature*, 43, 39–40.

27 Ibid., 3.

28 Ibid., 237.

29 Ibid.

30 Margery Fee, "English Canadian Literary Criticism 1890–1950," 304. Fee sees Pierce's *Outline* as "clearly" an outgrowth of his Makers of Canadian Literature series, overlooking its genesis in the *New Outlook* series (300–1).

31 This copy of LP's *Outline* is in the possession of BPR; the dedication is dated 16 January 1928 at Toronto's Arts and Letters Club. The dynamic Louis Carrier was a bilingual former journalist, son of a French father and an English mother, and an air force veteran of the Great War, whose Mercury Press, with its "remarkably bilingual and bicultural list," was forced into bankruptcy by the Depression in 1931. He was also the publisher of the modernist magazine *Canadian Mercury*. See Bruce Whiteman, *Lasting Impression: A Short History of English Publishing in Quebec* (Montreal: Véhicule 1994), 63–4.

32 "Literature Canadienne," *La Presse* (Montreal), 20 January 1928, and "Chronique Littéraire: *An Outline of Canadian Literature*," *Le Soleil* (Quebec), 8 March 1928, both in scrapbook, box 52, LPP.

33 Archibald MacMechan ("The Dean's Window"), review of *An Outline of Canadian Literature*, unidentified clipping, scrapbook, box 52, LPP.

34 See LP, "English-Canadian Literature, 1882–1932," *Royal Society of Canada Transactions*, 1932, 55–62. The quote is on 55.

35 LP Diary, 14 October 1926.

36 Ibid., 9 January 1929.

37 Ibid., 26 May and 1 August 1926.

38 Ibid., 3 May 1928. The Beauharnois scandal involved a payment given by the Beauharnois Light, Heat and Power Company to the governing Liberals prior to the election of 1930, in exchange for the right to build a new hydroelectric station.

39 Ibid., 11 June 1928.

40 Ibid.

41 See ibid., 22 September to 22 October 1928.

42 Ibid., 15 October 1928.

43 Ibid., 9 January 1929.

44 Ibid.

45 Ibid., 6 February 1931.

46 Ibid., 26 April 1929. The entry reads: "Eayrs has taken up my idea of a year ago" regarding a joint series.

47 John Gray, manuscript history of Macmillan of Canada, vol. 1, John Gray Papers, LAC.

48 ECP to LP, 15 October 1929, box 8, PFC.

49 See ECP to Harriet Pierce, 26 January 1932, box 9, PFC. Edith makes it clear that she is not at ease with the couple, no matter how outwardly welcoming their hospitality.

50 LP Diary, 21 November 1923.
51 Hugh Eayrs, "Publishers Are Getting over the Fear That Putting out a Canadian Book Is Taking [a] Chance," *Canadian Stationer and Book Trade Journal*, October 1922, 27.
52 See "Hugh S. Eayrs Waxes Reminiscent," *Canadian Stationer and Book Trade Journal*, March 1934, 14, 46.
53 Hugh Eayrs, qtd. in George L. Parker, "A History of a Canadian Publishing House: A Study of the Relation between Publishing and the Profession of Writing 1890–1940" (PhD thesis, University of Toronto, 1969), 211.
54 See Bruce Whiteman et al., *A Bibliography of Macmillan of Canada Imprints 1906–1980* (London, ON: Dundurn 1985), and Carl Spadoni, "A Bibliography of Macmillan of Canada Imprints, 1906–1980: First Supplement with Corrigenda," *Papers of the Bibliographical Society of Canada*, 28 (1989): 38–69.
55 Hamelin has traced the debt that Eayrs owed to Wise in this respect. See Danielle Hamelin, "Shaping the Canadian Reading Public: The Macmillan Company of Canada, 1906–1921," unpublished paper for the Canadian Historical Association meetings, Ottawa, 1992.
56 Eayrs also published Pierce's edition of the Kirby-Tennyson letters. See LP, ed., *Alfred, Lord Tennyson and William Kirby* (Toronto: Macmillan 1929), 71pp.
57 LP Diary, 13 December 1929.
58 LP, *William Kirby, Portrait of a Tory Loyalist* (Toronto: Macmillan 1929), 4.
59 Ibid., 4, 461.
60 LP Diary, 13 December 1929.
61 Hugh Eayrs to William Kirby [grandson], 25 February 1930, file 16, box 37, Macmillan of Canada Papers, William Ready Archives, McMaster University.
62 LP, *Fifty Years of Public Service: A Life of James L. Hughes* (Toronto: S.B. Gundy, Oxford, 1924), and LP, *An Outline of Canadian Literature*.
63 LP Diary, 14 February 1930.
64 Ibid., 26 June 1927.
65 Mary Vipond, "National Consciousness in English-Speaking Canada in the 1920s," 79ff.
66 John Gray, draft of chapter 7 of his memoir *Fun Tomorrow*, 16, vol. 17, Gray Papers, LAC.
67 LP Diary, 29 November 1926.
68 Ibid., 12 February 1927.
69 LP to ECP, 12 February and 4 August 1927. LP letters to her with similar sentiments are 22 February and 24 February 1927, all in box 8, PFC.
70 LP Diary, 5 August, 19 August, and 25 September 1927.
71 Ibid., 26 June 1927.
72 Ibid., 19 August 1927.
73 Ibid., 10 March 1928.
74 Ibid., 23 May 1928.

75 Ibid., 20 June 1928; Fallis's "good humour" when LP sees him for "the first time in weeks" is mentioned on 12 June 1928.

76 Ibid., 25 February 1928.

77 Ibid., 30 July and 4 August 1928.

78 Ibid., 29 November 1928; the approval is noted on 9 March 1929.

79 Ibid., 7 December 1928.

80 Ibid., 3 May 1929.

81 LP to ECP, 6 October 1929, box 8, PFC.

82 LP, *An Outline of Canadian Literature*, 241. "The Canadian has not yet acquired the quality of detachment; like Ibsen's Brand, he is all or nought. For one thing he lives too much in the swim of things to see clearly the direction of the current. The chief trouble is that he rather likes to be about what he calls his business." The last line of this piece of literary criticism could also be seen as relevant to Pierce's marital tensions.

83 LP Diary, 1 September 1929.

CHAPTER FOURTEEN

1 LP, *Education in a Democracy: Address to the Manitoba School Association, May 1933* (Toronto: Ryerson 1933), 2.

2 John Gray, *Fun Tomorrow*, 172.

3 Ernest Fewster to LP, 16 March 1930, file 9, box 3, LPP.

4 Samuel Fallis to LP, 8 March 1930, file 9, box 3, LPP. Fallis's compliment about Pierce's indispensability seems ambivalent: "Of course there is no use of sidestepping the fact that no one can do your work."

5 ECP to LP, 8 March 1930, box 9, PFC.

6 LP Diary, 14 February to 7 April 1930.

7 For a discussion of the effects of the Depression on Canadian publishing, see MacSkimming, *The Perilous Trade*, 119ff. McClelland and Stewart's plight is set out in Spadoni and Donnelly, "Historical Introduction," *A Bibliography of McClelland and Stewart Imprints*, 30–2.

8 LP Diary, 22 June 1930.

9 William Heine discusses the tendency for firms to seek profits from the textbook sector in his manuscript "Brief to the Royal Commission on Book Publishing" [1971], 7, LAC.

10 Starting in the 1940s, the readers were also marketed under such titles as *The New World Readers, Beckoning Trails, Our Heritage*, and *Life and Adventure* in some revisions. See, for example, J.C. Bates and Lorne Pierce, eds., *Life and Adventure, Canada Book of Prose and Verse*, Book Two (Toronto: Ryerson-Macmillan 1948).

11 Hugh Eayrs to C.G. Mosher, 23 November 1931, file 6, box 170, Executive Series, Macmillan Papers, William Ready Archives, McMaster University.

12 LP Diary, 22 August 1931.
13 Draft prospectus for Canadian Treasury Readers, 1931, file 6, box 170, Executive Series, Macmillan Papers.
14 LP to Albert Robson, 16 October 1931, file 6, box 170, Executive Series, Macmillan Papers. Robson and Pierce, who were friendly, also collaborated on numerous Canadian art-history projects for Ryerson.
15 Review of *The Ryerson Book of Prose and Verse*, Book One, *Manitoba Teacher* (January 1928), clipping, scrapbook, box 56, LPP.
16 LP, "A Brief Survey of the Editorial and Educational Departments of the Publishing House" [1940s], 6, box 14, Board of Publication Papers, United Church Archives. Paterson is listed as editor of the *Saskatchewan Teacher* on magazine letterhead in 1929 at the time he was lobbying Pierce for a job with Ryerson. See G.C. Paterson to LP, 13 November 1929, file 7, box 3, LPP.
17 LP Diary, 1 March 1931.
18 Ibid., 19 April 1934. The information about Seary is found in LP, "A Brief Survey of the Editorial and Educational Departments of the Publishing House," 6.
19 The intricate machinations that went on in getting allies and advisers is apparent, for example, in Hugh Eayrs to LP, 14 October 1930, file 9, box 3, LPP.
20 Gray, *Fun Tomorrow*, 151.
21 In a letter to Donald Solandt, Eayrs said that Macmillan provided and selected the illustrations, and did copyright searches for selections. See Eayrs to Donald Solandt, 1 March 1933, file 4, box 5, LPP. Dora Eayrs's exact role is shadowy, as John Gray comments: "Dora Whitefield was Mrs. Hugh Eayrs. That she was highly intelligent and widely read I knew, but that was only a partial qualification for school-book editing. What did either editor [Pierce or Dora Eayrs] really know of the abilities and interests of children at these levels?" Gray, *Fun Tomorrow*, 159.
22 LP to ECP, 30 July 1933, box 10, PFC.
23 S.S. Van Dine was one of Pierce's favourite mystery writers. LP Diary, 28 May 1930.
24 LP Diary, 11 October 1931.
25 Gray, *Fun Tomorrow*, 159.
26 LP Diary, 11 October 1931.
27 Ibid., 4 December 1931.
28 Ibid., 25 January 1932.
29 Ibid., 25 January and 12 February 1932. The detail on the Macmillan offer is found in LP to Harriet Pierce, n.d. [March 1932], box 9, PFC. According to his daughter and son, Pierce always said that one reason he had no interest in the post of book steward was that he wanted to be "an editor or nothing," not a "shopkeeper."
30 "Rev. S.W. Fallis Is Taken by Death Following Illness," Toronto *Globe*, 8 February 1932, 1.

31 "Rev. Dr. Solandt Is Dead, Following Heart Seizure," Toronto *Star*, 6 August 1936, 2.

32 LP Diary, 12 February and 12 March 1932.

33 LP to ECP, 25 Feb. 1932, box 9, PFC.

34 LP Diary, 12 March 1932.

35 Ibid., 31 April [*sic*] 1932.

36 Ibid.

37 Ibid., 24 July 1932.

38 Ibid.

39 Eayrs to LP, 6 September 1932, file 1, box 5, LPP.

40 LP Diary, 16 October 1932.

41 Ibid., 24 July and 16 October 1932 .

42 Ibid., 29 December 1932.

43 Jean Graham to LP, 5 Feb. 1926, file 5, box 2, LPP.

44 Jean Graham, "A Lover of Books ... Dr. Lorne Pierce, F.R.S.C.," *Saturday Night*, 31 December 1932, 9.

45 See untitled profile of Lorne Pierce by Victor Seary, enclosed in Victor Seary to BPR, 11 August 1975, in possession of BPR.

46 LP Diary, 23 January 1933.

47 Ibid., 17 February 1933.

48 LP to ECP, 8 November 1932, box 9, PFC.

49 LP to ECP, n.d. [1922] from Calgary, box 16, PFC.

50 LP, *Education in a Democracy*, 7, 5.

51 Ibid., 4.

52 Entry on "John Dewey," *Columbia Encyclopedia*, 535.

53 John Dewey, qtd. in Margaret Wente, "Dumb and Dumber: Schools 'r' Us," *Globe and Mail*, 11 September 2001, A16.

54 LP, *Education in a Democracy*, 7.

55 Ibid.

56 LP to Professor Philip Penner, Faculty of Education, University of British Columbia, n.d. [c. 1959], file 4, box 28, LPP.

57 LP, *Education in a Democracy*, 1, 6.

58 LP, *Towards the Bonne Entente* (Toronto: Ryerson 1929), 23–4.

59 Ibid., 15.

60 Ibid.

61 One example of "field editing" occurred in 1936. Pierce, after a request from a Manitoba education official, inserted an extract from one of King George V's broadcasts at the end of Book Two of the Canada Books in the aftermath of the monarch's death. See Hugh Eayrs, memorandum, 3 March 1936, file 3, box 170, Executive Series, Macmillan Papers.

62 LP, "A Brief Survey of the Editorial and Educational Departments of the Publishing House," 7.

63 LP, *New History for Old* (Toronto: Ryerson 1931), 21, 22, 26, 9.
64 LP, qtd. in "$50,000 to Pensions from Publishing House," *United Church Observer*, 1 May 1943, 21.
65 B.K. Sandwell, "Address of the Common People," in C.T. Fyfe and Lorne Pierce, eds., *Our Heritage, Canada Book of Prose and Verse*, Book Three (Toronto: Ryerson-Macmillan 1948), 528.
66 "The Land We Love," *Life and Adventure, Canada Book of Prose and Verse*, Book Two, ed. J.C. Bates and Lorne Pierce (Toronto: Ryerson-Macmillan 1948), 444.
67 Eayrs to LP, 27 Nov. 1930, file 9, box 3, LPP.
68 James Shotwell, *The Autobiography of James Shotwell* (Indianapolis, IN: Bobbs-Merrill 1961), 26–7. No wonder that Shotwell, as an official of the Carnegie Foundation, was to generously underwrite Ryerson publications in the landmark Relations of Canada to the United States series in the 1940s and 1950s. See Sandra Campbell, "From Romantic History to Communications Theory: Lorne Pierce as Publisher of C.W. Jefferys and Harold Innis," *Journal of Canadian Studies*, 30, no. 3 (1995): 90–116.
69 Arthur Lower, *Canadians in the Making* (Toronto: Longmans 1958), 350.
70 LP, *Unexplored Fields of Canadian Literature* (Toronto: Ryerson 1932), 21–3.
71 George Monro Grant, "Canada – A Link in the Empire," and D.A. MacMillan, "For Ever Canada," *Our Heritage, Canada Book of Prose and Verse*, Book Three, 514–16, 512. This reader was in its thirty-third printing by 1965.
72 LP published his University of New Brunswick Alumni oration as *Three Fredericton Poets* (Toronto: Ryerson 1933), 30pp.
73 LP Diary, 17 September to 9 November 1933.
74 Ibid., 24 December 1933.
75 Ibid.
76 Board of Publication Minutes, February 1933, box 1, Board of Publication Papers, United Church Archives. The educational figures were omitted, probably inadvertently, from the February 1934 minutes, again suggesting the slipshod management practices of the House.
77 LP Diary, 24 December 1933.
78 Ibid., 19 April and 8 October 1934.
79 Ibid., 21 January 1934.
80 Sales figures for these years are drawn from the annual reports in box 1, Board of Publication Papers, United Church Archives.
81 See LP Diary, 18 April 1934. Reminiscences of Ryerson employees like Betsey Jefferys and Blanche Hume, admittedly both loyal Pierce admirers, corroborate Pierce's account of Solandt's animus.
82 LP Diary, 18 April 1934.
83 Ibid., 25 January 1934.
84 Ibid., 19 April 1934; the Alberta figure is found in box 171, Executive Series, Macmillan Papers. The total sales figure for 1934 is found in LP to Harriet Pierce, n.d. [January 1935], box 10, PFC.

85 Betsey Jefferys Fee, taped interview with BPR, n.d., Toronto, in possession of BPR.

86 Pierce also published a children's book by Basil Campbell in 1934 called *Tony, a Truly, Truly Story or Something of That Sort.*

87 BPR, notes for her manuscript of LP Diary selection for 28 February 1933–8 December 1943.

88 According to a flyer in the possession of BPR, the Children Players staged two sets of performances of "Franchette from France" and "Twice Is Too Much" at Hart House Theatre on 18 February 1934.

89 LP Diary, 16 March 1934.

90 Hugh Eayrs to LP, n.d. [June 1934], file 8, box 5, LPP.

91 LP, *A Canadian People* (Toronto: Ryerson 1945), 2.

92 Ibid.

93 LP to Harriet Pierce, 22 July 1934, box 10, PFC.

94 LP to BP, 2 August 1934, box 10, PFC.

95 LP, *Master Builders* (Toronto: Ryerson 1937), 45 pp.

96 LP Diary, 8 October 1934.

97 Blanche Hume to Annie Charlotte Dalton, 9 October 1934, file 8, box 5, LPP.

98 See LP to G.C. Paterson, 17 September 1938, file 2, box 7, LPP.

99 Hugh Eayrs wrote Solandt to this effect on 1 March 1933, file 6, box 170, Executive Series, Macmillan Papers.

100 Hugh Eayrs to LP, 4 October 1934, file 1, box 170, Executive Series, Macmillan Papers.

101 For example, this complaint is made in LP to ECP, 4 October 1929, box 8, PFC.

102 LP to Harriet Pierce, n.d. [January 1935?], box 10, PFC. LP says he has just received the figures on sales for the readers for 1934.

103 LP Diary, 17 February 1935, and Board of Publication Minutes, Bound Volume 1927–1948, Board of Publication Papers, United Church Archives. Perhaps as a result of destroyed stock, a loss for the Educational Department of $20,712.52 was actually posted in the minutes for the fiscal year ending 28 February 1935 as well as a loss of $6,952.75 in the Retail Department.

104 LP Diary, 17 August 1935.

105 According to John Gray's memoir, 10,000 copies of Book One had been sold to Alberta alone by 1933. See Gray, draft of chapter 8 of *Fun Tomorrow*, 1, vol. 7, John Gray Papers, LAC.

106 [John Gray] to Hugh Eayrs [then in England], 20 June 1935, box 171, Executive Series, Macmillan Papers. Gray's memoir *Fun Tomorrow* misdates this crisis as occurring in 1933, but the Macmillan material establishes 1935 as the correct date.

107 John Gray, *Fun Tomorrow*, 158ff.

108 The first printing of the *Canada Book of Prose and Verse*, Book One, in 1927, then entitled *The Ryerson Book of Prose and Verse*, edited by Pierce and Arthur

Yates, had no Stevenson selections at all. The 1932 printing of it, however, had some augmented material, with the editors now listed as Lorne Pierce and Dora Whitefield. It seems clear that Pierce himself was responsible for the changes to the 1932 version. Two selections by Robert Louis Stevenson are included: "A Letter to Alison Cunningham" in a section called "Homes" and Stevenson's requiem in the section of the reader dubbed "Requiem." There is an introduction called "Foreword: Homes" by Lorne Pierce which covers both selections, which is where some of the copyright violation occurred.

109 LP, "Foreword: Homes," in Lorne Pierce and Dora Whitefield, eds., *The Canada Book of Prose and Verse*, Book One (Toronto: Ryerson-Macmillan 1932), 225. There was a "Foreword: Homes" in the 1927 version of the reader, but it was not signed by Pierce and no material by Stevenson was included in it. See Lorne Pierce and Arthur Yates, eds., *The Ryerson Book of Prose and Verse*, Book One (Toronto: Ryerson 1927), 161.

110 Blanche Hume to LP, 1 March 1945, file 3, box 12, LPP.

111 This explanation by Pierce is referred to in Eayrs to LP, 7 November 1935, file 6, box 170, Executive Series, Macmillan Papers.

112 See the "Home Life" section of *The Ryerson Book of Prose and Verse*, Book One (1927), 161ff.

113 Hugh Eayrs to Donald Solandt, 1 March 1933, marked "Private" with b.c.c. to Lorne Pierce, file 4, box 5, LPP. Eayrs points out that Macmillan editorial work consisted of choosing the illustrations and textual selections "under Dr. Pierce's editorial direction." He does not name Dora Eayrs as doing this work but he names no other person at Macmillan. The primary editor was unquestionably Pierce.

114 Hugh Eayrs to B. Clarke, 22 July 1935, file 6, box 171, Executive series, Macmillan Papers; Eayrs to LP, 7 November 1935, file 6, box 170, Executive Series, Macmillan Papers.

115 These costs were probably a major factor in the posting of a loss of $12,184.04 to the House's Educational Department at the end of the 1935–36 year in February 1936. See Book Committee Minutes, Bound Volume 1927–1948, Board of Publication Papers.

116 As well as the discussion in Gray, *Fun Tomorrow*, 165–73, see file 9, box 171, Executive Series, Macmillan Papers.

117 Gray, *Fun Tomorrow*, 172.

118 LP Diary, 14 November 1935.

119 LP to Eayrs, 8 June 1936, file 3, box 171, Executive Series, Macmillan Papers.

120 Eayrs to LP, 14 January 1936, file 3, box 170, Executive Series, Macmillan Papers.

121 LP Diary, 3 February and 20 January 1936.

122 See, for example, LP Diary, 14 November 1935 and 3 February 1936.

123 This is recalled in Blanche Hume to LP, n.d. [1946], file 7, box 13, LPP.

124 LP Diary, 7 August 1936. See also "Rev. Dr. Solandt Is Dead, Following Heart Seizure," Toronto *Star*, 6 August 1936, 2.

125 LP to Dr McKechnie, 16 March 1936, file 1, box 170, Executive Series, Macmillan Papers.

126 The Alberta figure is from file 6, box 171, Executive Series, Macmillan Papers, and the Nova Scotia figure is in file 40, box 170, in that collection.

127 John Webster Grant, Report of the Book Editor to the Board of Publication, April 1961, file 17, box 45, LPP.

128 Report by Harry Berry, Ryerson sales manager, 15 April 1948, file 12, box 38, LPP.

129 See, example, Eayrs to LP, 16 January 1935, file 1, box 170, Executive Series, Macmillan Papers regarding printing charges to Macmillan for the readers, which were printed at the House.

130 Gray, *Fun Tomorrow*, 172.

131 For example, the royalty was 2 per cent for each volume up to Book Six, and 5 per cent for Books Seven and Eight. See LP Diary, 3 May 1930.

132 LP Diary, 6 June and 8 October 1936.

133 Pierce's 1948 tax return is found in box 45, LPP.

134 C.H. Dickinson to John Gray, 3 Jan. 1964, file 12, box 38, LPP.

135 LP to Pearson Gundy, 11 Dec. 1954, file 4, box 23, LPP.

136 LP Diary, 11 February and 22 March 1936.

137 LP, *William Kirby*, 464.

138 Gray, *Fun Tomorrow*, 339–42.

139 John Gray to LP, 25 January 1950, file 6, box 19, LPP.

140 Material dealing with these changes, including an annotated copy of the text, with these changes on page 82, is found in file 11, box 13, Board of Publication Papers, United Church Archives.

141 LP to John W. Regan, 1 August 1944, file 2, box 11, LPP.

142 C.H. Dickinson, qtd. in C.L. Bennet to LP, 2 April 1948, file 2, box 17, LPP.

143 Madeline Young to LP, 11 October 1958, file 1, box 28, LPP. See Madeline Young and Lorne Pierce, eds., *Beckoning Trails, Canada Book of Prose and Verse*, Book One (Toronto: Ryerson-Macmillan 1948).

144 C.L. Bennet to Campbell Hughes, 9 April 1960, file 1, box 29, LPP.

145 Vipond, "National Consciousness in English-Speaking Canada in the 1920s," 81.

146 LP, *The Armoury in Our Halls* (Toronto: Ryerson 1941), 8.

CHAPTER FIFTEEN

1 LP, *In Memoriam Charles W. Jefferys, O.S.A., R.C.A., LL.D. 1869–1951* (Toronto: Ryerson 1951), [2].

2 LP, *The Armoury in Our Halls* (Toronto: Ryerson 1941), 8.

3 LP, "How to Look at Pictures," *Our Heritage, Canada Book of Prose and Verse*, Book Three, 212–15.

4 LP, *New History for Old*, 41. Pierce gave these lectures in October 1930 at Mount Allison University. Emphasis in original.

5 Ibid.

6 George Wrong, *Ontario Public School History of Canada* (Toronto: Ryerson 1921).

7 C.W. Jefferys to LP, 6 December 1923, file 4, box 1, LPP.

8 For details on Jefferys's career, see Robert Stacey, *C.W. Jefferys 1869–1951* (Ottawa: National Gallery 1985), and *Charles William Jefferys 1869–1951* (Kingston, ON: Agnes Etherington Art Centre 1976).

9 See C.W. Jefferys, *Sam Slick in Pictures: The Best of the Humour of Thomas Chandler Haliburton*, ed. Lorne Pierce (Toronto: Ryerson 1956).

10 LP, Introduction to ibid., v.

11 LP, typescript of talk on Jefferys for plaque unveiling, York Mills, 30 August 1960, file 2, box 29, LPP.

12 Jefferys to LP, 5 January 1932, file 2, box 5, LPP.

13 LP Diary, 21 December 1925.

14 Jefferys to LP, 31 December 1929, file 5, box 3, LPP.

15 LP, Preface to C.W. Jefferys, *The Picture Gallery of Canadian History*, vol. 3 (Toronto: Ryerson 1950), xii.

16 LP, *New History for Old*, 59.

17 C.W. Jefferys, *Dramatic Episodes in Canada's Story* (Toronto: Ryerson 1930).

18 William Colgate, *C.W. Jefferys* (Toronto: Ryerson 1945).

19 As well as the material cited here, these included LP, "C.W. Jefferys, O.S.A., R.C.A., LL.D," *Ontario History*, 41, no. 4 (1949): 213–16.

20 This collection is now held by LAC.

21 LP, *In Memoriam Charles W. Jefferys ... Address at Memorial Service, Oct. 11, 1951*, printed brochure, LAC [2–3].

22 Brian Osborne, "'The Kindling Touch of Imagination': Charles William Jefferys and Canadian Identity," in Paul Simpson Housley and Glen Northcliffe, eds., *A Few Acres of Snow: Literary and Artistic Images of Canada* (Toronto: Dundurn 1992), 42.

23 LP, "Publisher's Foreword" to George Wrong, Chester Martin, and Walter Sage, *The Story of Canada* (Toronto: Ryerson 1929), vii.

24 Jefferys to LP, 12 June 1936, file 5, box 6, LPP, and LP Diary, 11 February 1936 [guest book insert].

25 Jefferys to LP, 28 July 1924, file 8, box 1, LPP; a bill from Jefferys for illustrations to Long's book dated 21 February 1942 is in file 2, box 9, LPP. See Isabel Skelton, *The Backwoodswoman* (Toronto: Ryerson 1924), and Morden Long, *A History of the Canadian People*, vol. 1 (Toronto: Ryerson 1942).

26 Katherine Jefferys Helm to LP, 15 July 1952, file 3, box 21, LPP. Helm felt that only Mrs Jefferys, who acted as her husband's business manager and much else, had done more for him.

27 Ibid.

28 LP Diary, 8 December 1937.

29 Jefferys to LP, n.d. [c. 1936], file 5, box 6, LPP.

30 Jefferys to LP, n.d. [c. 1937], file 3, box 9, LPP.

31 Jefferys to LP, 14 April 1932, file 2, box 5, LPP. He was responding to Pierce's praise of him in *New History for Old* (1931) for depicting "the great scenes of our history" with characters like Joseph Howe and explorer Alexander Mackenzie in "the proper context of their most significant achievements."

32 Jefferys to LP, n.d. [1934?], file 2, box 6, LPP.

33 A.H.A. Colquhon, Ontario deputy minister of education, to LP, 9 June 1934, file 3, box 4, LPP.

34 LP to James Shotwell, director, Carnegie Endowment, 10 July 1942, file 6, box 9, LPP. Pierce reminded Shotwell that they had discussed the Endowment buying "a few hundred for distribution in the States," which Shotwell thought feasible.

35 The term is used in a Jefferys letter: "I shall take on no other job till The Picture Gallery triplets are safely delivered. Make your midwifely mind easy. I feel the final labour pangs, and shall concentrate." Jefferys to LP, 13 February 1948, file 7, box 17, LPP.

36 LP to Jefferys, 3 December 1942, file 3, box 9, LPP.

37 LP, *New History for Old*, 59.

38 LP, memo to C.W. Jefferys, attached to Jefferys to LP, 13 February 1948, file 7, box 17, LPP.

39 LP to Jefferys, 2 November 1950, file 3, box 19, LPP.

40 See LP, transcript of talk on Jefferys for plaque unveiling, York Mills, 30 August 1960, file 2, box 29, LPP.

41 LP, Preface to C.W. Jefferys, *The Picture Gallery of Canadian History*, vol. 3, xiii.

42 LP, *New History for Old*, 59.

43 This drawing appears both in C.W. Jefferys, *The Picture Gallery of Canadian History*, vol. 1 (Toronto: Ryerson 1942), 93, and in his *Canada's Past in Pictures* (Toronto: Ryerson 1934).

44 This illustration is well known. As well as appearing in *The Picture Gallery of Canadian History*, vol. 1, 97, it is also found in *Canada's Past in Pictures* (1934) and in *The Canada Book of Prose and Verse*, Book One, 399.

45 This illustration is found in both *Canada's Past in Pictures* (1934) and in *The Picture Gallery of Canadian History*, vol. 2 (Toronto: Ryerson 1945), 24.

46 See Jefferys, *The Picture Gallery of Canadian History*, vol. 3, 149.

47 Dennis Duffy, "Art-History: Charles William Jefferys as Canada's Curator," *Journal of Canadian Studies*, 11, no. 4 (1976): 11–12.

48 Osborne, "'The Kindling Touch of Imagination,'" 44.

49 LP Diary, 8 November 1925.

50 The other titles in Ryerson's Canadian Historical Studies series were Judge F.W. Howay's *The Dixon-Meares Controversy* (1929) and Zimmerman's *Captain Cook*

(1930). Only 250 copies of the Cook volume were published. For an assessment of the importance of Howay's work to British Columbia historiography, see Chad Reimer, *Writing British Columbia, 1784–1958* (Vancouver: UBC Press 2009).

51 See LP, *The Armoury in Our Halls*, 5. Pierce pointed to "climate and basic industries" as factors in Canadian life. The Laurentian school saw Canadian economic development as being based on staple products and as flowing east-west, not north-south, along the axis of the St Lawrence River and the rivers and lakes that connected with it all the way to the Pacific coast.

52 Innis to LP, 24 October 1930, file 1, box 4, LPP.

53 It is still listed on page 93 of a Ryerson catalogue dating from about 1946 found in file 20, box 37, Innis Papers, University of Toronto Archives.

54 Innis to LP, 30 September 1932, file 2, box 5, LPP.

55 Innis to LP, 23 October 1933, file 5, box 5, LPP.

56 LP to Innis, 1 August 1945, box 4, Innis Papers; LP to Mary Quayle Innis, 26 November 1953, file 7, box 22, LPP, discusses another revision.

57 Donald Creighton, Introduction to J. Bartlet Brebner, *The North Atlantic Triangle* (1945; repr. Ottawa: Carleton Library 1966), xvi–xx. See also Berger, *The Writing of Canadian History*, and the discussion in Donald Wright, *The Professionalization of Canadian History* (Toronto: University of Toronto Press 2005).

58 Berger, *The Writing of Canadian History*, 145.

59 Donald Creighton, *Harold Adams Innis: Portrait of a Scholar* (Toronto: University of Toronto Press 1957), 79–80.

60 James Shotwell to Innis, 27 July 1932, box 11, Innis Papers.

61 Arthur Lower to Innis, 19 November 1933, box 11, Innis Papers.

62 See LP, "Memo for Dr. Solandt," 16 April 1935, file 3, box 6, LPP.

63 LP, "Memorandum re the Canadian-American Research Project," 7 May 1935, file 17, box 45, LPP.

64 LP, "Memo for Dr. Solandt," 16 April 1935, file 3, box 6, LPP.

65 LP, "Memorandum re the Canadian-American Research Project," 7 May 1935, file 17, box 45, LPP. Pierce himself inserted this clause, which appears as an emendation in his own hand. As Innis biographer Alexander John Watson points out, Innis was also insistent to Shotwell on this point. See Alexander John Watson, *Marginal Man: The Dark Vision of Harold Innis* (Toronto: University of Toronto Press 2006), 204.

66 Maria Tippett, *Making Culture: English Canadian Institutions and the Arts before the Massey Commission* (Toronto: University of Toronto Press 1990), 141–54.

67 Ibid., 151. This phrase was used in a 1935 letter from painter Arthur Lismer to Harry McCurry, director of the National Gallery.

68 Donald Creighton, Introduction to Brebner, *The North Atlantic Triangle*, xix.

69 Innis to LP, 18 May and 30 July 1936, file 5, box 6, LPP.

70 J.A. Ruddick, W.M. Drummond, R.E. English, and J.E Lattimer, *The Dairy Industry in Canada*, ed. Harold Innis (Toronto: Ryerson 1937).

71 See J. Bartlet Brebner to Donald Creighton, 20 and 26 October 1937, box 14, Creighton Papers, LAC.

72 James Shotwell to Innis, 29 April 1937, box 14, Creighton Papers.

73 James Shotwell to Donald Creighton, 28 October 1937, box 14, Creighton Papers.

74 Donald Creighton to James Shotwell, 3 November 1937, box 14, Creighton Papers.

75 Creighton, *Harold Adams Innis: Portrait of a Scholar*, 100. A later Innis biographer, Alexander John Watson, speculates that both overwork and emotional problems resulting from the married Innis's attraction to a colleague, Irene Biss (later Spry), were involved in this collapse. See Watson, *Marginal Man*, 195, 223.

76 Innis to LP, 30 July 1936, file 5, box 6, LPP.

77 LP Diary, 10 June 1937.

78 Arthur Lower to Innis, 4 and 16 November 1937, box 1, Innis Papers, and Donald Creighton to LP, 8 and 9 November 1937, box 14, Creighton Papers.

79 Arthur Lower to Innis, 16 November 1937, box 1, Innis Papers.

80 James Shotwell to LP, 13 November 1937, file 10, box 6, LPP.

81 Ibid.

82 Norman Donaldson, Yale University Press, to LP, 22 May 1939, file 5, box 7, LPP. It must have been the more galling to Pierce not to receive the news directly from Shotwell.

83 LP to Norman Donaldson, 1 June 1939, file 5, box 7, LPP. In the same file, a draft letter by Pierce to Donaldson, written in late July or early August 1939, speaks of the "unjust" and "summary" transfer, and declares that "collaboration on any other than a cordial basis is impossible."

84 Innis to LP, 9 September 1939, qtd. in Berger, *The Writing of Canadian History*, 109.

85 Innis to James Shotwell, 2 April 1938, qtd. in Watson, *Marginal Man*, 206.

86 Innis was certainly ruthless when critic E.K. Brown was touted for the post of dean of graduate studies at Toronto in the 1940s, a post Innis himself wanted. He seems to have been instrumental in a whisper campaign that Brown, as a "lapsed" Catholic, would not be acceptable to the Catholic St Michael's College. Brown got wind of this and other difficulties and withdrew from the competition, and Innis became dean. See Laura Groening, *E.K. Brown: A Study in Conflict* (Toronto: University of Toronto Press 1993).

87 See Watson, *Marginal Man*, 207.

88 James Shotwell, letter to E.K. Brown (carbon), 20 August 1940, box 1, Innis Papers.

89 Harold Innis, *Changing Concepts of Time* (Toronto: University of Toronto Press 1952), 3.

90 James Shotwell to Innis, 6 May 1941, box 1, Innis Papers. Shotwell did propose to Pierce later that year that University of Toronto Press edit three series volumes and Ryerson publish them, but I can find no evidence that the former ever in fact became involved with the series. See James Shotwell to LP, 28 August 1941, file 6, box 8, LPP.

91 The fact that Yale University Press ultimately pressured to keep Ryerson as Canadian collaborator suggests that Ryerson was doing the best job possible for a Canadian publisher at this date. Whatever the glitches, both the publishing history and a perusal of the volumes themselves suggests a more positive conclusion than the verdict of "unfortunate" for the Carnegie's association with Ryerson Press – the adjective used in a discussion of the series in Wright, *The Professionalization of Canadian History*, 138. Moreover, Wright himself points out (128) the financial and other difficulties that Macmillan of Canada experienced in publishing a similar project in the 1930s, the Frontiers of Settlement series.

92 Innis to LP, 12 April 1944, file 8, box 10, LPP.

93 LP Diary, 7 June 1939.

94 Wilfrid Bovey, *The French Canadians Today* (Toronto: Dent 1938). Carl Berger gives an account of this fracas in *The Writing of Canadian History*, 109.

95 Innis to Arthur Beauchesne, 2 May 1939, vol. 76, Royal Society of Canada Papers, LAC.

96 W.S. Wallace to Arthur Beauchesne, n.d. [April 1939], vol. 76, Royal Society of Canada Papers.

97 Innis to LP, 3 May 1939, file 6, box 7, LPP.

98 LP to Arthur Beauchesne, 3 May 1939, vol. 76, Royal Society of Canada Papers.

99 See Arthur Beauchesne to Wilfrid Bovey, 12 May 1939, and Harold Innis, undated letter of resignation [May 1939], copy for Arthur Beauchesne, vol. 76, Royal Society of Canada Papers.

100 "Ceux de la Chère Entente [clipping]," *Le Bien Public* (Trois-Rivières), 8 June 1939, file 4, box 7, LPP.

101 Arthur Beauchesne to LP, 17 June 1939, file 4, box 7, LPP.

102 LP to Arthur Beauchesne, 22 June 1939, file 4, box 7, LPP. Pierce was later involved in a change of procedure to have medal committee nominations approved by the executive to avoid such fiascos. See LP to Victor Morin, 17 October 1939, file 6, box 7, LPP.

103 Innis to LP, 12 April 1944, file 8, box 10, LPP.

104 LP to Innis, 19 March 1947, box 6, Innis Papers.

105 LP to Innis, n.d. [1947], box 6, Innis Papers. The conclusion Pierce suggests in the letter – and it is a crisp summation of Innis's rather contorted paper – became the last paragraph of Innis, "The Church in Canada," in *The Time of Healing*, 22nd Annual Report of the Board of Evangelism and Social Service (Toronto: United Church 1947), 47–54.

106 LP, *Christianity and Culture in Our Time*, 11, 4, 12.

107 LP to Bruce Pierce, 14 August 1945 [postmark] and n.d. [February 1944 or 1945], in possession of BPR. In August 1945 Pierce had just heard Innis speak to the Arts and Letters Club about his trip to Russia.

108 LP to Innis, 11 November 1946, box 6, Innis Papers. The figure from Donaldson is quoted in Berger, *The Writing of Canadian History*, 97. Similarly, in 1945, Pierce offered to distribute the 134 unsold copies of *Peter Pond* to colleges and universities rather than simply remainder them. See LP to Innis, 7 December 1945, box 4, Innis Papers. .

109 Harold Innis, *Political Economy in the Modern State* (Toronto: Ryerson 1946), xi.

110 LP to Innis, 18 April 1946, file 8, box 13, LPP.

111 Berger, *The Writing of Canadian History*, 194.

112 LP to Innis, 28 April 1947, box 6, Innis Papers.

113 LP to Innis, 6 November 1950, file 6, box 19, LPP.

114 LP to Innis, 6 December 1948, box 8, Innis Papers.

115 LP to Innis, 6 November 1950, file 6, box 19, LPP.

116 Donald Creighton to LP, 4 December 1952, file 1, box 21, LPP.

117 See Innis to LP, 9 November 1950, file 6, box 19, LPP.

CHAPTER SIXTEEN

1 C.H. Dickinson to LP, 7 May 1947, box 13, PFC.

2 LP to Laura Goodman Salverson, 11 January 1945, file 2, box 13, LPP.

3 See Wallace, *The Ryerson Imprint*.

4 Parker, "Trade and Regional Publishing in Central Canada," 171. Parker adds that "not all of them" were Canadian authors.

5 Randall Speller, "Book Design in English Canada," *History of the Book in Canada, Volume Three, 1918–1980*, 378–86.

6 LP Diary, 19 June 1937.

7 C.H. Dickinson, interview with author, Woodstock, ON, 21 September 1993.

8 Details of Dickinson's career are based on my 1993 interview with him and on C.H. Dickinson, "The Story of My Life" [c. 1992], 25 pp., a copy of which is in my possession.

9 Dickinson, "The Story of My Life," 12.

10 Ibid.

11 John Webster Grant, interview with author, Toronto, 22 September 1993.

12 Dickinson, "The Story of My Life," 18.

13 C.H. Dickinson, *Lorne Pierce: A Profile* (Toronto: Ryerson 1965).

14 LP to Bruce Pierce, n.d. [Second World War], in possession of BPR.

15 Dickinson, 1993 interview.

16 Ibid.

17 See Friskney, "Towards a Canadian 'Cultural Mecca.'"

18 Dickinson, 1993 interview. By the 1940s, Pierce had diverted profits from his department into a house fund for publishing Canadiana that would not otherwise be financially feasible. See LP to H.H. Langton, 2 July 1947, file 4, box 15, LPP. Dickinson said in the 1993 interview that the amounts in this fund were always modest.

19 See, for example, Marie McKenzie [Dickinson's secretary] to LP, n.d. [fall 1945], file 5, box 12, LPP.

20 Dickinson, 1993 interview.

21 Dickinson to LP, 7 May 1947, box 13, PFC.

22 Notes of thanks from Dickinson testify to this continuing practice. See, for example, Dickinson to LP, 9 February 1948 ("Your magnificent gesture ... Although you have done it before ... touched me deeply") and 9 May 1948, file 5, box 17, LPP, as well as Dickinson to LP, 22 March [1955], file 2, box 24, LPP.

23 Dickinson to LP, 18 September 1953, file 4, box 22, LPP, and 9 February 1948, file 5, box 17, LPP.

24 Dickinson to LP, 18 September 1953, file 4, box 22, LPP.

25 This was clear in the 1993 interview with Dickinson.

26 Board of Publication Minutes, 1927–1948, figures for fiscal years ending 1937 and 1938, Board of Publication Papers, United Church Archives.

27 Frederick Philip Grove to LP, 19 February 1944, file 7, box 10, LPP.

28 Grove to LP, 21 November 1938, file 1, box 7, LPP.

29 Grove to W.J. Alexander, 1 December 1938, in Desmond Pacey, ed., *The Letters of Frederick Philip Grove* (Toronto: University of Toronto 1976), 339, and LP to Grove, 6 December 1938, file 1, box 7, LPP. The letter to Alexander gives the figure of 400 and the LP letter 500. I have accepted Pierce's figure, since it was not questioned by Grove.

30 See Pacey, ed., *The Letters of Frederick Philip Grove*, 345n.1.

31 LP to Grove, 6 December 1938, file 1, box 7, LPP.

32 Grove to LP, 28 December 1938, in Pacey, ed., *The Letters of Frederick Philip Grove*, 344. In the event, according to a note by Blanche Hume on LP's letter of 6 December 1938 to Grove, Grove had been paid $435 by 13 February 1939 for both the *Search for America* and *Fruits of the Earth* arrangements: file 1, box 7, LPP.

33 Grove to LP, 4 January 1939, in Pacey, ed., *The Letters of Frederick Philip Grove*, 345.

34 Grove to LP, 30 August 1939, 16 March 1940, and 25 March 1940, all in Pacey, ed., *The Letters of Frederick Philip Grove*, 362, 382, and 382–3.

35 Frederick Philip Grove, *A Search for America*, abridged J.F. Swayze (Toronto: Ryerson 1947). The abridgement was 296 pages instead of the original 448.

36 LP to G.H. Clarke, 21 October 1946, file 6, box 13, LPP.

37 LP to Grove, 6 May 1940, file 9, box 7, LPP.

38 LP, "Frederick Philip Grove (1871–1948)," *Proceedings of the Royal Society of Canada* (Ottawa: Queen's Printer 1949), 118, 113.

39 William Arthur Deacon, review of *Two Generations* by Frederick Philip Grove, *Globe and Mail*, 5 August 1939, excerpted in Desmond Pacey, *Frederick Philip Grove: Critical Views on Canadian Writers* (Toronto: Ryerson 1970), 157. Pacey documents several other positive reviews.

40 LP to Grove, n.d. [spring 1941], in Pacey, ed., *The Letters of Frederick Philip Grove*, 408n.2.

41 William James Fadiman, MGM Pictures, to LP, 29 January 1940, file 8, box 7, LPP; C. Morrison Fitch, Greystone Press, to LP, 29 January 1940, file 8, box 7, LPP; and Harper Brothers to LP, 9 January and 6 February 1940, file 9, box 7, LPP.

42 Little Brown to LP, 5 April 1940, file 9, box 7, LPP, and Grove to LP, 30 May 1940, in Pacey, ed., *The Letters of Frederick Philip Grove*, 391.

43 Stanley Morgan-Powell to LP, 2 May 1942, file 2, box 9, LPP.

44 LP, "Frederick Philip Grove (1871–1948)," 118.

45 Grove to LP, 12 July 1941, in Pacey, ed., *The Letters of Frederick Philip Grove*, 411–12.

46 Desmond Pacey in Pacey, ed., *The Letters of Frederick Philip Grove*, 381n.3.

47 LP to Grove, 4 June 1941, file 4, box 8, LPP.

48 See Grove to LP, 23 April 1941 and 10 February 1942, both in Pacey, ed., *The Letters of Frederick Philip Grove*, 406 and 418.

49 Grove to Desmond Pacey, 28 February 1945, in ibid., 465. He made the same observation to Ellen Elliott of Macmillan, 7 December 1945, in ibid., 478.

50 Grove to Ellen Elliott, 14 December 1945, in ibid., 481.

51 Desmond Pacey to LP, 29 December 1943, file 9, box 9, LPP.

52 Desmond Pacey in Pacey, ed., *The Letters of Frederick Philip Grove*, 459n.2, and Pacey to LP, 14 January 1944, file 2, box 11, LPP.

53 Pacey to LP, 9 December 1944, file 2, box 11, LPP.

54 Pacey to LP, 21 March 1945, file 6, box 12, LPP.

55 Desmond Pacey, *Frederick Philip Grove* (Toronto: Ryerson 1945), 123.

56 Pacey to LP, 9 January 1947, file 1, box 15, LPP.

57 LP to G.H. Clarke, 21 October 1946, file 6, box 13, LPP. The proposed Grove anthology project – which had been put forward by Clarke, not Pierce – never materialized.

58 LP to Wilfrid Eggleston, 27 October 1956, as well as Eggleston to LP, 24 October 1956, file 1, box 25, LPP. For Grove's biographical deceptions, see Douglas O. Spettigue, *FPG: The European Years* (Ottawa: Oberon 1973).

59 Kristjana Gunnars, "Ethnicity and Canadian Women Writers," *Room of One's Own*, 14, no. 4 (1991): 40. Gunnars points out, however, how little serious academic interest there has usually been in ethnic writing in Canada, and analyzes

the restrictions of "otherness" for writers marginalized by gender and race/ethnicity.

60 "Mrs. Salverson Gives Novel-Writing Rules [clipping]," Regina *Leader-Post*, 25 May 1943, box 8, Laura Goodman Salverson Papers, LAC.

61 LP, *An Outline of Canadian Literature*, 40.

62 "A large and appreciative audience," typed transcript of unidentified newspaper article, [late 1920s], box 8, Salverson Papers.

63 Daisy Neijmann, "Fighting with Blunt Swords: Laura Goodman Salverson and the Canadian Literary Canon," *Essays on Canadian Writing*, 67 (spring 1999): 145.

64 Ibid., 149.

65 Salverson to LP, 18 November 1939, file 7, box 7, LPP.

66 Neijmann, "Fighting with Blunt Swords," 166n.13. Pierce himself could be scathing about Ontario's Loyalist heritage: "In time, it stood for privilege, for smugness, for callous indifference to the rights of others, for a deadly feudal regime in government, church and education." See LP, *A Canadian People* (Toronto: Ryerson 1945), 74.

67 LP, *The Armoury in Our Halls*, 4.

68 Ibid., 7, 5, 14.

69 Salverson to LP, 12 March 1941, file 6, box 8, LPP.

70 Laura Goodman Salverson, *The Dove* (Toronto: Ryerson 1933, and London: Skeffington 1933).

71 Laura Goodman Salverson, *Black Lace* (Toronto: Ryerson 1938, and London: Hutchinson 1938).

72 J.A. Royce McCuaig, Introduction to Salverson, *The Dove*, 12.

73 Laura Goodman Salverson, *The Dark Weaver* (Toronto: Ryerson 1937, and London: Low 1937) and *Confessions of an Immigrant's Daughter* (Toronto: Ryerson 1939, and London: Faber and Faber 1939).

74 For a discussion of Salverson's career, see Neijmann, "Fighting with Blunt Swords"; the reference to her moves is found at 144. Pierce himself commented sadly of her economic travails and her hapless husband in 1957: "They have rented a small house out Eglinton way [in Toronto], and hope to find a boarder. It all looks pretty pitiful. However, I shall keep in touch with them. Her husband can not be depended upon. He gets a job for a day or a week, and blows. No anguish comes near him. But Laura suffers enough for both." LP to Theresa Thomson, 5 October 1957, box 8, Canadian Writers' Foundation Papers, LAC.

75 Laura Goodman Salverson to LP, n.d. [stamped 21 February 1945], file 2, box 13, LPP.

76 Salverson to LP, n.d. [November 1935], file 3, box 6, LPP.

77 Helen Buss, *Mapping Our Selves: Canadian Women's Autobiography in English* (Montreal & Kingston: McGill-Queen's University Press 1993), 175.

78 Salverson to LP, n.d. [1935], file 3, box 6, LPP.

79 See Salverson to LP, 25 August 1938, file 3, box 7, LPP.

80 Salverson, *The Dark Weaver*, 385.

81 LP, "The Gods of This New Era," *Canadian Magazine*, 1, no. 4 (1918): 281.

82 See, for example, Kristjana Gunnars, "Laura Goodman Salverson's Confessions of a Divided Self," in Shirley Neuman and Smaro Kamboureli, eds., *A Mazing Space: Writing Canadian Women Writing* (Edmonton: Longspoon/NeWest 1986), 148–53, as well as her "Ethnicity and Canadian Women Writers," 40–50.

83 Salverson to LP, 21 July 1955, file 9, box 24, LPP. She later told Pierce that "the shock of that experience almost finished me as a writer." Salverson to LP, n.d., file 7, box 26, LPP.

84 Salverson to LP, n.d. [stamped 6 June 1947], file 2, box 16, LPP. For one favourable review, see E.H.W., *Queen's Quarterly*, March 1940, 128–9.

85 Salverson to LP, 7 December 1941, file 6, box 8, LPP.

86 See Neijmann, "Fighting with Blunt Swords," 155–6.

87 See LP, *The Armoury in Our Halls* and *A Canadian People*. He wrote in the latter: "The fanatical parsons, the crackpot priests, the slimy friends of the people, the mandarins of the proletariat, and all the imbecile demagogues that set home against home and people against people, these will merit the odium of history as at present they merit the disgust of every decent Canadian" (62).

88 Neijmann, "Fighting with Blunt Swords," 156.

89 Gwethalyn Graham, *Earth and High Heaven* (Philadelphia: Lippincot 1944).

90 LP to Salverson, 11 January 1945, file 2, box 13, LPP.

91 LP to Salverson, 23 February 1945, file 2, box 13, LPP.

92 Salverson to LP, n.d. [stamped 21 February 1945], file 2, box 13, LPP.

93 Barbara Powell, "Laura Goodman Salverson: Her Father's 'Own True Son,'" *Canadian Literature*, 133 (summer 1992): 81.

94 LP, "The Minister in His Workshop," in *In Conference with the Best Minds*, 232.

95 LP, "English-Canadian Literature 1882–1932," *Transactions of the Royal Society of Canada* (Ottawa: Queen's Printer 1932), 62.

96 Tom MacInnes to LP, 1 May 1945, file 5, box 12, LPP.

97 See LP to G.H. Sallans, 19 January 1942, and his reply of 21 January 1942, both file 6, box 9, LPP.

98 G. Herbert Sallans to LP, 30 July 1942, file 6, box 9, LPP.

99 G. Herbert Sallans, *Little Man* (Toronto: Ryerson 1942), 3.

100 Will R. Bird to LP, 4 June 1945, file 7, box 11, LPP.

101 LP to Esther Birney (wife of Earle Birney), 3 May 1944, file 5, box 10, LPP.

102 Earle Birney, *Turvey* (Toronto: McClelland and Stewart 1949).

103 For Birney and McClelland's correspondence on the subject in 1949, see Sam Solecki, ed., *Imagining Canadian Literature: The Selected Letters of Jack McClelland* (Toronto: Key Porter 1998), 4–14.

104 Jack McClelland to Earle Birney, 16 June 1949, in ibid., 8.

105 See King, *Jack*, for an account of McClelland's career.

06 Robert Fulford, "Kulture Television," *Toronto Life*, September 1998, 67.

07 John Webster Grant, interview with author, Toronto, 22 September 1993.

08 Laura Goodman Salverson, *Immortal Rock: The Saga of the Kensington Stone* (Toronto: Ryerson 1954, and London: Angus and Robertson 1955). The record is unclear, but Salverson seems to have withdrawn a manuscript entitled "Heritage" in 1947 because too many revisions were requested by Pierce on the basis of readers' reports after she had unsuccessfully entered it in the Ryerson Fiction Award competition that year. See Salverson to LP, two undated letters [1947?], file 2, box 16, LPP.

09 LP, inside jacket text of *Immortal Rock*.

10 William Arthur Deacon, "Kensington Stone Inspires Vikings' Canadian Daughter," *Globe and Mail*, 20 November 1954; Jean Swanson, "Ryerson Fiction Award Book," Saskatoon *Star Phoenix*, 20 November 1954; and LP to Salverson, 8 and 11 March 1955, vol. 1, Salverson Papers.

111 The Ryerson royalty reports list 643 copies sold for the year ending 30 November 1956 (1,510 copies were printed), with a further 268 copies sold by 31 January 1956. Salverson's royalties from this were less than $300. See vol. 8, Salverson Papers.

112 Laura Goodman Salverson, *Lord of the Silver Dragon* (Toronto: McClelland and Stewart 1927), and LP to Salverson, 19 July 1955, vol. 1, Salverson Papers.

113 LP to Salverson, 22 July 1955, vol. 1, Salverson Papers.

114 See LP to Theresa Thomson, 14 September 1957, vol. 9, Canadian Writers' Foundation Papers, LAC, and Mary Daly (Ryerson editorial secretary) to Salverson, 8 November 1957, vol. 1, Salverson Papers. Daly's letter enclosed a cheque for $30 for reviewing manuscripts; a note on the letter says that Salverson reviewed manuscripts occasionally for the next three years, after which she was not called on by Grant, Pierce's successor.

115 LP to Theresa Thomson, 7 December 1957, vol. 9, Canadian Writers' Foundation Papers.

116 Elsinore Haultain, advertising manager, Ryerson Press to Salverson, 4 November 1954, vol. 1, Salverson Papers.

CHAPTER SEVENTEEN

1 LP, *Thoreau MacDonald: Being a Talk on the Artist Given in Hart House ...* (Toronto: Ryerson 1942), 8.

2 Jo Nordley Bergo, "Picturing Canada," *History of the Book in Canada: Volume Three: 1918–1980*, 73.

3 Of the sixteen booklets in the Canadian Art series, six were by Albert Robson: *Cornelius Krieghoff* (1937), *Tom Thomson* (1937), *J.E.H. MacDonald, R.C.A.* (1937), *A.Y. Jackson* (1938), *Clarence Gagnon, R.C.A., LL.D.* (1938), and *Paul Kane* (1938). After Robson's death, the series continued with Marius Barbeau, *Henri Julien* (1941); E.R. Hunter, *Thoreau MacDonald* (1942); Marius Barbeau, *Coté, the Wood-*

Carver (1943); Thoreau MacDonald, *The Group of Seven* (1944 and subsequent editions); William Colgate, *C.W. Jefferys* (1945); Marius Barbeau, *Painters of Quebec* (1946); Donald Buchanan, *J.W. Morrice* (1947); Duncan Campbell Scott, *Walter J. Phillips* (1947); Marius Barbeau, *Cornelius Krieghoff* (1948); and Dorothy Hoover, *J.W. Beatty* (1948).

4 LP, *A Postscript on J.E.H. MacDonald 1873–1932* (Toronto: Ryerson 1940), 10–11.

5 Gatenby, *Literary Toronto*, 153.

6 J.E.H. MacDonald, notes on Arts and Letters Club, vol. 3, MacDonald Papers, LAC.

7 LP Diary, 22 March 1925.

8 Alison Gillmor, "The Group of Seven Grows Up," *Globe and Mail*, 27 July 2002, D9.

9 ECP to LP, 12 March 1924, box 7, PFC.

10 LP, *E. Grace Coombs (Mrs James Sharp Lawson) A.O.C.A., O.S.A.* (Toronto: Ryerson 1949), 11.

11 LP, *A Postscript on J.E.H. MacDonald 1873–1932*, 8–9.

12 Pierce refers to this well-known controversy, which brought the Group of Seven much public notoriety, in his presentation of the painting to the Art Gallery of Toronto. See transcript of LP's remarks, 20 May 1958, file 1, box 27, LPP.

13 For a discussion of *The Elements*, see Bruce Whiteman, *J.E.H. Macdonald* (Kingston, ON: Quarry Press 1995), 33. Thoreau Macdonald's *The Group of Seven* (Toronto: Ryerson 1944), 2, discusses the early controversy over the canvas.

14 LP, transcript of remarks at the Art Gallery of Toronto, 20 May 1958, file 1, box 27, LPP.

15 LP, transcript of interview by Ronald Hambleton, n.d. [1950s], file 11, box 42, LPP.

16 LP to William Arthur Deacon, 19 November 1923, file 4, box 1, LPP.

17 Margaret E. Edison, *Thoreau MacDonald: A Catalogue of Design and Illustration* (Toronto: University of Toronto Press 1973), 73.

18 Randall Speller, "Book Design in English Canada," *History of the Book in Canada: Volume Three: 1918–1980*, 379.

19 For this volume, Thoreau MacDonald and LP had agreed on what the former described as a "nationalistic & unsentimental" title. See MacDonald to LP, 30 June 1933, repr. in *Thoreau MacDonald: Notebooks* (Penumbra, ON: Moonbeam Press 1980), 137.

20 For a selection of the colophons and marks, see L. Bruce Pierce, *Thoreau MacDonald*, vol. 1, 2nd ed. (Doncaster, ON: Norflex 1973), 43.

21 For Pierce and Thoreau MacDonald's exchange of letters between 1937 and 1954, see "Letters to Lorne Pierce," in *Thoreau MacDonald: Notebooks*, 137–84. Pierce and Thoreau MacDonald discussed papers, ink, production values, thematic content, and many other subjects.

22 Speller, "Book Design in English Canada," 378.

23 Thoreau MacDonald, qtd. in Edison, *Thoreau MacDonald*, 33–4. The book in question was Elsie Pomeroy, *Sir Charles G.D. Roberts* (Toronto: Ryerson 1943), produced at a time of wartime labour and paper shortages at the House. Edison lists MacDonald's important work for Ryerson and other publishers.

24 See Karen McKenzie and Mary F. Williamson, eds., *The Art and Pictorial Press in Canada* (Toronto: Art Gallery of Ontario 1979), particularly Karen McKenzie, "The Nineteenth and Twentieth Centuries," 25–31, as well as their entry on "Art Writing and Criticism" in the *New Canadian Encyclopedia*. In her article, McKenzie discusses the late development of art journals in Canada and the groundbreaking role in the 1940s of the periodical *Canadian Art*, whose editors regularly consulted Pierce.

25 For a discussion of the influence and evolving reputation of the Group of Seven painters, see Dennis Reid, ed., *Tom Thomson* (Vancouver: Douglas and McIntyre 2002), and Catharine M. Mastin, ed., *The Group of Seven in Western Canada* (Toronto: Key Porter 2002). The Tom Thomson exhibition, on display at Ottawa's National Gallery of Canada from June to September 2002, included a display case featuring several Ryerson publications as integral to the nationalistic mythmaking around Thomson.

26 Helen Kemp to Northrop Frye, 26 June 1933, repr. in Robert D. Denham, ed., *The Correspondence of Northrop Frye and Helen Kemp 1932–1939*, vol. 1 (Toronto: University of Toronto Press 1996), 120.

27 Whiteman, *J.E.H. MacDonald*, 83.

28 LP to Lawren Harris, 8 June 1943, file 9, box 9, LPP. Pierce wanted to add a booklet on Harris to the Canadian Art series and asked for suggestions for an author. But he had to drop the idea, with wartime "printing so delayed and prospects so discouraging," for the upcoming year. See Harris to LP, 20 June 1943, and LP to Harris, 30 August 1943, file 9, box 9, LPP.

29 LP, "How to Look at Pictures," in *Our Heritage, Canada Book of Prose and Verse*, 212–16.

30 Ibid., 214–15.

31 Ibid., 213.

32 See Val Seary, "The Brief Summary of the Career of Dr. Lorne Pierce ...," in Seary to BPR, 11 August 1975, in possession of BPR. For Robson's interest in Canadian literature, see Lyn Harrington's history of the Canadian Authors Association, *Syllables of Recorded Time* (Toronto: Simon and Pierre 1981), 182, 183, 252.

33 See C.W. Jefferys, "Albert H. Robson," *Canadian Bookman*, 16 (1939), 4.

34 See Denham, ed., *The Correspondence of Northrop Frye and Helen Kemp 1932–1939*, vol. 2, 875, 876n.1.

35 See Donald Buchanan, *James Wilson Morrice: A Biography* (Toronto: Ryerson 1936), which includes a catalogue raisonné of Morrice's works. Presumably to save costs, there are no colour plates whatsoever in the 187-page book.

36 See W.A. Buchanan, president, Lethbridge *Herald*, to LP, 27 May 1939, file 4, box 7, LPP. Senator Buchanan asked to see Pierce about a financial guarantee he had given for the book.

37 The firm, whose letterhead read "Rous and Mann Ltd. Printed Advertising," was located at 172 Simcoe Street in downtown Toronto. See Albert Robson to LP, 21 April 1937, file 10, box 6, LPP.

38 Ibid.

39 Ibid.

40 See LP to E.K. Brown, 4 May 1938, vol. 3, E.K. Brown Papers, LAC.

41 See Robson to LP, 5 August 1937, 18 September, 21 October, and 2 November 1937, file 10, box 6, LPP.

42 LP, *E. Grace Coombs*, 1.

43 LP, *Thoreau MacDonald*, 8.

44 Arthur Lismer to Northrop Frye, 28 August 1932, qtd. by Helen Kemp, repr. in Denham, ed., *The Correspondence of Northrop Frye and Helen Kemp*, vol. 1, 75.

45 Northrop Frye, reviews of *Clarence Gagnon* (1938) and *Paul Kane* (1938), *Canadian Forum*, December 1938 and February 1939.

46 LP, *A Postscript on J.E.H. MacDonald 1873–1932* (Toronto: Ryerson 1940), 12.

47 Albert Robson, *J.E.H. MacDonald, R.C.A.* (Toronto: Ryerson 1937), 3, 4.

48 William Colgate to LP, 19 April 1948, file 4, box 17, LPP. The book is Colgate, *The Toronto Art Students' League* (Toronto: Ryerson 1954), 33pp. This book, although similar in concept and format, was not designated as part of the now-lapsed Canadian Art series.

49 Robson, *J.E.H. MacDonald, R.C.A.*, 3, 4, 10.

50 Albert Robson, *Paul Kane* (Toronto: Ryerson 1938), 13, 15.

51 There are actually two Krieghoff volumes in the Canadian Art series: Marius Barbeau, who had published *Cornelius Kreighoff: Pioneer Painter of North America* with Macmillan of Canada in 1934, updated the 1937 Robson booklet in a 1948 booklet for the Canadian Art series. Confusingly, both the 1937 Robson booklet and the 1948 Barbeau booklet in the series are entitled *Cornelius Krieghoff*.

52 Donald Buchanan, *James Wilson Morrice* (Toronto: Ryerson 1947), 18.

53 Marius Barbeau, *Painters of Quebec* (Toronto: Ryerson 1946), 6, 42.

54 Thoreau MacDonald, *The Group of Seven* (Toronto: Ryerson, 1952 ed.), 15. Even in the initial 1944 version of the booklet, MacDonald had felt that the arts were "run down" and he hoped for "future interpreters of our Country" to emerge from the "back concessions" or the "armed forces."

55 See LP Diary, 12 March 1939.

56 See LP to Harry McCurry, National Gallery of Canada, 8 and 16 November 1945, file 2, box 13, LPP.

57 Pierce was painted by Wyly Grier and was the subject of two busts sculpted by Randall Wardell Johnston and Bela Janowsky respectively. He was also sketched by Wyndham Lewis, among others. A posthumous crayon portrait of Edith

Chown Pierce was commissioned from Alan Barr by Pierce. The Grier portrait is now at the Art Gallery of Ontario; one bust is at Queen's University and a portrait of Lorne Pierce and C.W. Jefferys is in the historical museum in Saint John, New Brunswick, commissioned from J.R. Tate by Pierce's friend Dr J.C. Webster of Shediac. See Dickinson, *Lorne Pierce: A Profile*, 70–1.

58 See LP to Marius Barbeau, 8 July 1941, file 3, box 8, LPP.

59 A retrospective exhibit, "From the Studio: Selections from the E. Grace Coombs Archive," opened at the Art Gallery of Hamilton on 30 January 1997, featuring the range of her work from landscapes and flower paintings, watercolours to oils. I thank Alison Garwood-Jones, its curator, for information on Pierce and Coombs.

60 LP, *E. Grace Coombs*, 9. LP explains of his booklet: "One of our most competent artists and teachers of art, as well as one of the most reticent of women, Edith Grace Coombs has with great reluctance permitted her husband to issue the present anniversary monograph on herself and her work" (1).

61 Ibid., 3, 2.

62 Other women artists and experts in the field whom Pierce supported often got their entree as family of male friends of his: for example, artist Muriel Newton-White, daughter of an artist-friend; and art historian Muriel Miller Miner, whose book on painter George Reid was published by Ryerson in 1946. See Muriel Miller Miner, *G.A. Reid, Canadian Artist* (Toronto; Ryerson 1946), 230 pp.

63 A.Y. Jackson to LP, 10 October 1939, file 6, box 7, LPP.

64 LP to E.K. Brown, 4 May 1938, vol. 3, Brown Papers. LP got a testimonial from Robson about the plates, so strongly did he feel.

65 Donald MacKay, review of *James Wilson Morrice* by Donald Buchanan and *Walter J. Phillips* by Duncan Campbell Scott, *Dalhousie Review*, undated clipping, Phillips file, mfm. M5473, Scott Papers, LAC. The Scott Fonds also contain another favourable, unidentified review entitled "Appreciation of W.J. Phillips's Art Written by Duncan Campbell Scott."

66 Dr David Farr, telephone interview with author, 18 and 29 March 2003. Farr still has all the booklets with the date and place of purchase written in each. He recalls the 1945 price as having risen to sixty cents. Hardback Canadian art and literary books were beyond his modest budget, so he welcomed the format of the series.

67 See Wallace, *The Ryerson Imprint*, which includes the page length of each booklet in the series.

68 LP to C.W. Jefferys, 23 December 1946, file 8, box 13, LPP.

69 LP to Arthur Lismer, 9 June 1942, file 4, box 9, LPP.

70 Lismer to LP, 12 June 1942, file 4, box 9, LPP. The booklet was never published: LP was also worried about harming sales of the Robson booklet on Jackson by publishing the Lismer speech.

71 See Donald Buchanan to LP, 27 May, 10 July, and 22 July 1939, file 4, box 7, LPP.

72   For example, LP to Marius Barbeau, 20 March 1944, file 5, box 10, LPP. LP wrote: "Our Canadian Art Series is not proving a great publishing success but I think that in spite of that we shall continue to add to it even though we do not make ambitious plans for new titles. When you have your manuscripts on *The First Canadian Silversmiths* and *Haida Carvers of Argillite* [sic], I shall be very glad to see them. Both of them at this distance look like 'musts.'"

73   LP to Marius Barbeau, 11 April 1949, file 1, box 18, LPP. The two had been discussing the book on Emily Carr, which never materialized.

74   LP to W.P. Percival, 10 February 1956, file 5, box 25, LPP.

75   Whiteman, *J.E.H. MacDonald*, 83.

76   William Colgate, *Canadian Art, Its Origin and Development* (Toronto: Ryerson 1943), xi.

77   C.W. Jefferys, Foreword to ibid., vii–viii.

78   Colgate, *Canadian Art*, 76, 255.

79   Helen Kemp to Northrop Frye, 7 May 1934, repr. in Denham, ed., *The Correspondence of Northrop Frye and Helen Kemp 1932–1938*, vol. 1, 230.

80   LP to R.H. Hubbard, 21 February 1945, file 3, box 12, LPP. Hubbard had studied art at McMaster and Wisconsin, and was then working at the National Gallery as an art educator. Where Hubbard published the review is not identified.

81   R.L. McDougall, Introduction to McDougall, ed., *The Poet and the Critic: A Literary Correspondence between D.C. Scott and E.K. Brown* (Ottawa: Carleton University Press 1983), 11.

82   LP to R.H. Hubbard, 21 February 1945, file 3, box 12, LPP.

83   For example, Lawren Harris to LP, 20 March 1948, file 7, box 17, LPP.

84   See Harry McCurry to LP, 8 October 1942, file 4, box 9, LPP. In a letter to LP of 11 September 1945, file 6, box 11, LPP, Martin Baldwin, head of the Art Gallery of Toronto, responds favourably to the idea of collaborating with Ryerson on a series on contemporary art, a project never realized. In Baldwin to LP, 12 September 1941, file 5, box 8, LPP, the two discuss assembling drawings for a show on Thoreau MacDonald.

85   LP Diary, 19 May 1938.

86   LP to BP, 16 March 1948, box 14, PFC. See also Thoreau MacDonald to LP, n.d. [March 1954], file 9, box 23, LPP. MacDonald stoutly refused to share in any profits Pierce might realize on the land because "you stepped in and saved the situation during an emergency." See MacDonald to LP, n.d., file 5, box 12, LPP.

87   For an account of the Foundation, see [Lorne Pierce, ed.,] *Queen's University Art Foundation* (Toronto: Ryerson 1944).

88   See LP to Principal Wallace, 16 April 1942, file 6, box 9, LPP. Bieler was objecting to the Foundation's donation of "Old Ned," a comic genre piece of a rustic grotesque by J.R. Tate. There were ongoing tensions between Bieler, who in 1957 became the first director of Queen's Agnes Etherington Gallery, and the Foundation over art at Queen's.

89 LP to Principal Wallace, 30 October 1939, file 7, box 7, LPP.

CHAPTER EIGHTEEN

1 LP Diary, 31 December 1941.
2 LP to BP, 23 October 1943, box 12, PFC.
3 LP Diary, 3 September 1939.
4 LP to Laura Goodman Salverson, 2 November 1939, file 7, box 7, LPP.
5 LP Diary, 10 and 16 December 1939.
6 Ibid., 1 January 1940.
7 Ibid.
8 Ibid., 28 January 1940. Harriet Pierce died on 9 January.
9 Ibid.
10 LP to Bruce Pierce, 26 February 1944, in possession of BPR.
11 LP Diary, 13 February 1940.
12 See LP to William Kirby, 13 July 1945, file 4, box 12, LPP. Pierce was probably thinking of himself and his mother as well when he commiserated with Kirby: "It will be a great relief to know that your mother is safely 'over.' She has lived a long time and you have no regrets as a son. You were very kind to her. I [have] always thought that life will deal kindly with any child who has been good to his parents."
13 LP Diary, 5 September 1940.
14 LP to BP, 16 May 1945, in possession of BPR. Emphasis added.
15 LP to BP, n.d. [early 1940s], box 16, PFC.
16 LP to BP, n.d. [early Second World War], box 16, PFC. It is useful to recall in this context Hattie Pierce's favourite quotation from John Ruskin: "The constant duty of every man to his fellows is to ascertain his own powers and special gifts, and to strengthen them for the help of others." See LP Diary, 21 November 1915.
17 LP to Bruce Pierce, n.d. [late Second World War], in possession of BPR.
18 Several wartime letters to his children express such sentiments. See, for example, LP to Beth and Bruce Pierce about feeling "burned out before his time," n.d. [late Second World War], in possession of BPR.
19 LP Diary, 6 January 1939.
20 Ibid., 6 January 1939; LP to Lawrence Burpee, 19 December 1940, file 8, box 7, LPP.
21 Frustratingly, financial figures for Pierce's department for both educational and trade titles were combined under an undifferentiated total for the Educational Department in the annual profit-and-loss reports to the Board of Publication, making it impossible to know the relative returns. Generally, of course, profits were made on textbooks, profits that in effect subsidized the general list.
22 LP Diary, 25 March 1940.

23 All profit-and-loss summaries for the 1940s cited in this chapter are taken from the Board of Publication Minutes 1927–1948 [bound volume], box 1, Board of Publication Papers, United Church Archives.

24 The other two 1942 titles were *Anne of Avonlea* and *Anne of the Island*: additional Montgomery titles followed.

25 Anne Marriott to Frank Flemington, 29 July 1942, file 4, box 9, LPP.

26 Textbook losses in 1941/42 had been $4,739.31.

27 Grant Campbell, "William Collins during World War II: Nationalism Meets a Wartime Economy in Canadian Publishing," *Papers of the Bibliographical Society of Canada*, 39, no. 1 (2001): 45–65; and Ruth Panofsky, "'Head of the Publishing Side of the Business': Ellen Elliott of the Macmillan Company of Canada," *Papers of the Bibliographical Society of Canada*, 44, no. 2 (2005): 45–64.

28 LP to Charles G.D. Roberts, 26 April 1943, file 2, box 10, LPP.

29 LP to Pelham Edgar, 24 November 1943, box 1, Canadian Writers' Foundation Papers, LAC.

30 LP to Beth and Bruce Pierce, 10 September 1944, in possession of BPR.

31 Campbell, "William Collins during World War II," 50, 52.

32 LP to Walter McRaye, 22 August 1944, file 1, box 11, LPP.

33 LP to Duncan Campbell Scott, 8 September 1944, file 3, box 11, LPP.

34 LP to Walter McRaye, 26 May 1945, file 7, box 12, LPP. In fact, *Pauline Johnson and Her Friends* was deferred until 1947.

35 LP to Desmond Pacey, 18 May 1945, file 6, box 12, LPP.

36 Educational Department profits were $5,689.18 for 1943/44 and $6,653.18 for 1944/45. They held in the nine-month period ending in November 1945, totalling $6,297.68. See Board of Publication Minutes, box 1, Board of Publication Papers, United Church Archives.

37 LP to Pelham Edgar, n.d. [May 1946], vol. 1, Canadian Writers' Foundation Papers, LAC.

38 LP to W.H. Robb, 28 November 1945, file 1, box 13, LPP.

39 "Hitler's Hero, Siegfried, in Ontario School Readers," editorial, Toronto *Telegram*, undated clipping [September 1944], file 8, box 10, LPP.

40 "Suggests Citation of Deeds of V.C.'s as School Reading," unidentified clipping [September 1944], file 8, box 10, LPP.

41 Lorne Pierce to C.C. Knowles, 18 September 1944, file 8, box 10, LPP. Pierce confided to his children how appalled he was at the "shocking … idiocy" of the charge. LP to Beth and Bruce Pierce, 10 September 1944, in possession of BPR.

42 LP to Anne Hume, 15 May 1945, file 3, box 12, LPP.

43 LP to BP, 9 January 1944, box 13, PFC.

44 According to Pierce's 1943 Report to the House Board of Publication, the novel sold 3,500 copies in one month before Christmas, prompting a second edition of 2,500 copies. See box 21, Board of Publication Papers, United Church Archives. Birney's *David and Other Poems* (1942) went through at least three printings of

500 copies each by June 1943, according to Elspeth Cameron, *Earle Birney: A Life* (Toronto: Viking 1994), 203.

45 LP's frustration is evident in letter and diary references. At one point, a colonel was even writing Pierce about a power problem with a film projector at Camp Borden. On another occasion, Pierce wrote his sister in disgust that "we could fill a library of books with our wasteful talk" as the committee "piddled about." He later wrote that he hoped "soon to shed" chairing a committee of the war libraries council. See LP to Sara and Eldred Chester, n.d. [before September 1942] and 28 September 1942, both box 1, CFP.

46 LP to Sara and Eldred Chester, 28 September 1942, box 1, CFP.

47 G.W. Spinney to LP, 24 February 1942, file 3, box 9, LPP.

48 For an account of the early history of the BSC, see Liana Van der Bellen, "A History of the Bibliographical Society of Canada," *Papers of the Bibliographical Society of Canada*, 34, no. 2 (1996): 117–80. Pierce's role in the founding of the BSC is analyzed in Sandra Campbell, "'The Foundling Has Come a Long Way': Lorne Pierce, Canadiana Collecting, and the Founding of the Bibliographical Society of Canada," *Papers of the Bibliographical Society of Canada*, 43, no. 2 (2005): 67–78.

49 LP, inscription on a book given to Blanche Hume, qtd. in "The Blanche Hume Library 'Comes Home,'" *Douglas Library Notes*, 16, no. 3 (1968): 2. Hume retired on 26 February 1943, having worked at Ryerson since 2 January 1924.

50 LP to Blanche Hume, Christmas 1951, box 1, Hume Papers, QUA.

51 Betsey Jefferys Fee and Eleanor Geagen, interviews with Beth Pierce Robinson, n.d., audiotapes in possession of BPR. Other employees included Norma MacRostie and Mary Paterson.

52 LP Diary, 5 September 1940.

53 E.K. Brown to D.C. Scott, 13 June 1944, and Scott's reply, 30 June/5 July 1944, repr. in R.L. McDougall, ed., *The Poet and the Critic: A Literary Correspondence between D.C. Scott and E.K. Brown* (Ottawa: Carleton University Press 1983), 109, 110.

54 LP to Sara Pierce Chester, n.d. [1940s], box 1, CFP.

55 Pierce's spearheading of projects by his Scottish Rite Masonic lodge, the Toronto Lodge of Perfection, to aid the deaf in Toronto schools in the late 1930s led to wider initiatives with Toronto school inspector Harry Amoss and others to establish a national society to aid the deaf, formally incorporated in 1940 as the National Society of the Deaf and Hard of Hearing. See LP Diary, 31 March 1938, and LP to Brother Harold Young, 26 March 1938, file 3, box 7, LPP. As honorary treasurer of the Society in the 1940s and 1950s, Pierce was to devote many hours to funding and administrative challenges at the Society. See, for example, M. Faircloth to LP, 15 November 1947, file 8, box 14, LPP.

56 See Blanche Hume, n.d. [1942], memo to LP regarding an inquiry from Sir Charles G.D. Roberts about his health: "Because I vowed not to say you were ill, to anyone, I merely said that you were tired and had difficulty in reaching

everything that had to be done." See file 2, box 8, LPP. His convalescence is described in LP to Charles Clay, 19 July 1949, file 1, box 15, LPP.

57 See, for example, Lloyd Roberts to LP, 30 May 1942, and LP to Lloyd Roberts, 3 June 1942, file 5, box 9, LPP. Sir Charles G.D. Roberts had told his son that Pierce, who had had a heart attack weeks before, was "having a bit of a battle physically." Pierce added to his denial: "I have a miserable disposition and that always keeps one tough and going."

58 For example, LP to BP, 9 December 1943, talks of his vertigo: the sleeping remedy taken by both Lorne and Edith is referred to in LP to BP, 9 November and 9 December 1943, in possession of BPR.

59 See the introduction and numerous diary entries in Mary Rubio and Elizabeth Waterston, eds., *The Selected Journals of L.M. Montgomery: Volume V: 1935–1942* (Toronto: Oxford University Press 2004), xiii.

60 LP to BP regarding "Casa Beverley," 4 July 1943, box 12, PFC: "There is something in it after all, this going back in a world all slithery and skiddish, and settling down for a spell in a spot where one's roots go deep, and where one can say, [']One hundred and fifty years ago my people cut a homestead out of these forests and founded my family, and whenever I go back to it I renew my faith in this country, and my feeling of permanence and destiny.[']"

61 LP to Blanche Hume, n.d. [summer 1942], box 1, Hume Papers, QUA.

62 Judge F.C. Howay to LP, 11 August 1942, file 2, box 9, LPP.

63 LP to Bruce Pierce, n.d. [late Second World War], in possession of BPR.

64 Edith's observation is referred to in Percy Comery to LP, 5 June 1946, file 6, box 13, LPP.

65 Thanks to BPR for pointing out this element of Pierce's wartime experience to me in a conversation about LP's wartime letters, Delta, ON, 30 July 1995.

66 LP to Bruce Pierce, 21 August 1943, in possession of BPR. The tunic was labelled "Sgt L.P. No. 3 A.M.C.," Pierce told his son, then stationed in eastern Ontario, as he himself had been two decades earlier.

67 LP Diary, 5 September 1940.

68 LP to Bruce Pierce, n.d. [1944 or 1945], in possession of BPR.

69 LP to BP, 23 October 1943, box 12, PFC. The letter was written after the death of yet another young family friend.

70 LP to Bruce and Beth Pierce, 9 January 1944, box 13, PFC.

71 LP to BP, 5 March 1944, box 13, PFC: "Wrote Dr. Matheson at Quebec re his son. Also Dr. Moxley another [Q]ueen's man who lost his son this week. Also Dr. Kemp of the Nat[ional] Soc[iety] for the Hard of Hearing who lost his son. It is all too much."

72 Hon. John Matheson, interview with author, Rideau Ferry, ON, 1 November 1997.

73 LP to Beth and Bruce Pierce, 11 March 1944, box 13, PFC.

74 LP wrote to Lady Joan Roberts on 26 November 1943: "I am typing this because my hand is becoming more undependable." See file 2, box 10, LPP.

75　The prayer is found in the Appendix.

76　LP, Campbell Crescent guest book, in possession of BPR.

77　ECP, ibid.

78　LP to Beth and Bruce Pierce, n.d. [postmarked 22 June 1945], in possession of BPR.

79　LP to Sara and Eldred Chester, n.d. [April 1940], box 1, CFP.

80　LP to Frederick Philip Grove, 21 May 1940, file 9, box 7, LPP. Pierce wrote: "It is not a question of survival as a people but the growing suspicion in my own mind that … especially as a Canadian people, we are scarcely worth survival."

81　LP, *Unexplored Fields of Canadian Literature* (Toronto: Ryerson 1942), 24.

82　LP Diary, 27 April 1942.

83　All of these are Ryerson titles except *Education in a Democracy*, the text of Pierce's address to the Manitoba Educational Association in May 1933, reprinted by the *Western School Journal*.

84　E.K. Brown to D.C. Scott, 21 November 1944, repr. in R.L. McDougall, ed., *The Poet and the Critic* (Ottawa: Carleton University Press 1983), 124. Brown was then in Chicago, but he had spent some months of the war in Ottawa writing speeches for Prime Minister Mackenzie King.

85　For Pierce's worries at this time, see his notes concerning the *Canadian Spokesman* in December 1941, file 3, box 8, LPP.

86　Russell Harper to LP, 10 March 1941, file 4, box 8, LPP.

87　For example, LP examines in *The Armoury in Our Halls* Spengler's contention that "no people without a soul can have a history" to reinforce his point that Canada urgently needs to develop a "unified living spirit, a civilization, a personality" (7). Spengler was on the minds of many intellectuals in Canada at this troubled period, Northrop Frye among them. See John Ayre, *Northrop Frye* (Toronto: Vintage 1989), 65.

88　LP Diary, 14 February 1941.

89　LP to Sara and Eldred Chester, n.d. [1941], box 1, CFP.

90　Stephen Leacock to Mrs Herbert T. [Fitz] Shaw, 28 April 1942, repr. in David Staines, ed., *The Letters of Stephen Leacock* (Toronto: Oxford University Press 2006), 460. Emphasis in original.

91　LP, *The Armoury in Our Halls*, 1–2.

92　LP to Beth and Bruce Pierce, 7 November 1944, in possession of BPR.

93　LP to Eric Makovksi, 15 November 1945, file 7, box 12, LPP.

94　LP to Beth and Bruce Pierce, n.d. [c. 1944], in possession of BPR.

95　LP, *The Armoury in Our Halls*, 4–5.

96　Ibid., 5–6.

97　Ibid., 19.

98　See Brian McKillop, "Nationalism, Identity and Canadian Intellectual History," *Queen's Quarterly*, 81 (winter 1974): 533–50.

99　LP, *The Armoury in Our Halls*, 6.

100　LP Diary, 10 May 1941.

101 See Rowland Smith, Afterword to Wyndham Lewis, *Self-Condemned* (Santa Barbara, CA: Black Sparrow Press 1983), 411–21. Other sources on Lewis's stormy war sojourn in Canada are Jeffrey Meyers, *The Enemy* (London: Routledge and Kegan Paul 1980); George Woodcock, ed., *Wyndham Lewis in Canada* (Vancouver: University of British Columbia Press 1971); and Catharine Mastin, Robert Stacey, and Thomas Dilworth, *"The Talented Intruder": Wyndham Lewis in Canada, 1939–1945* (Windsor, ON: Art Gallery of Windsor 1993).

102 See Mastin et al., *"The Talented Intruder."*

103 LP, "A Recollection of Wyndham Lewis," *Canadian Literature*, 35 (winter 1968): 62–3. The article appeared posthumously.

104 Wyndham Lewis to LP, 13 October 1941, Lewis Papers, Cornell University Archives.

105 Mastin, "The Talented Intruder," in Mastin et al., *"The Talented Intruder,"* 37.

106 Wyndham Lewis, qtd. in C.H. Dickinson, undated transcript version of "Lorne Pierce" (1964), 10, in possession of BPR.

107 LP, "A Recollection of Wyndham Lewis," 63. One measure of the excellence of the portrait is how aptly the image evokes the qualities in Pierce described by Blanche Hume, his long-time assistant – "graceful, slim, wiry, with a piquant dark face, something elfish about it, something at once shrewd and kindly in the flash of the dark eye and the swift play of features." Blanche Hume, "Lorne Pierce," 4, in possession of BPR.

108 Lewis repeated that "the Canadian school of painting" was "as good in its [field] as anything else on the North American continent": Lewis to LP, 26 May 1941, file 4, box 8, LPP.

109 LP, "A Recollection of Wyndham Lewis," 63.

110 Wyndham Lewis to LP, 26 May 1941, file 4, box 8, LPP.

111 Meyers, *The Enemy*, 263.

112 Wyndham Lewis to LP, 17 June 1941, file 4, box 8, LPP.

113 LP to B.K. Sandwell, 21 August 1941, file 4, box 8, LPP.

114 Wyndham Lewis, *Self Condemned* (London: Methuen 1954).

115 LP to W.K. Rose, 29 April 1960, file 5, box 29, LPP.

116 LP to Wyndham Lewis, 21 August 1941, file 4, box 8, LPP.

117 LP to Beth and Bruce Pierce, n.d. [postmarked 22 June 1945], in possession of BPR.

118 LP, Foreword, *A Canadian People* (Toronto: Ryerson 1945), vii.

119 Ibid., vii.

120 See copyright page of ibid.

121 See LP, reprint of Part IV of *A Canadian People* in *Ontario Public School Argus*, nos. 1 and 2 (January and February 1946): 16–18, 52–4. The condensation in book form of *People* appeared in *Canadian Digest* 1 (April 1946): 81–96. Part IV of *The Armoury in Our Halls* was summarized as "Our Historians: Leaders of the People," *Observer*, 15 May 1944, as part of a series on the future of Canada entitled "The Next Step."

122 LP wrote in his diary at the news of Eayrs's death: "He had been in poor health for some time. Had lunch with him a few weeks ago, and urged him to place himself under a Doctor and submit to a stiff regimen … He came over to see me … and was very bad. His going takes the ablest publisher in Canada and a long-time friend. We have fought many a fight together, from coast to coast." LP Diary, 1 May 1940.

123 See Bruce Whiteman, Introduction to Whiteman et al., *A Bibliography of Macmillan of Canada Imprints 1906–1980*, xii.

124 LP to Desmond Pacey, 18 May 1945, file 6, box 12, LPP.

125 LP to Bruce Pierce, n.d. [postmarked 22 June 1945], in possession of BPR.

126 The effect of his deafness on Pierce's voice was mentioned in several interviews, including the one with Dickinson below.

127 C.H. Dickinson, interview with author, Woodstock, ON, 21 September 1993. See also clipping, "Mencken's Yuletide Tale Banned by Church Press," *Globe and Mail*, 13 December 1946, file 11, box 13, LPP.

128 LP to Sara and Eldred Chester, n.d. [early 1950s], box 1, CFP.

129 Gray, *Fun Tomorrow*, 342.

130 LP to BP, n.d. [Second World War], in possession of BPR.

131 C.H. Dickinson to LP, 30 June 1948, file 5, box 17, LPP.

132 LP to BP, n.d. [late 1943], box 16, PFC.

133 LP to BP, n.d. [c. 1943], box 16, PFC.

134 I am indebted to Beth Pierce Robinson for sharing with me the photographs of the Campbell Crescent house and garden commissioned by her mother during the Second World War.

135 For Macmillan's war cutbacks, see Whiteman, Introduction to Whiteman et al., *A Bibliography of Macmillan of Canada Imprints 1906–1980*, xii.

136 Thanks to Duncan McDowall for this information.

137 LP to Bruce Pierce, n.d. [late Second World War], in possession of BPR.

138 A complete listing of both series year by year is found in Wallace's *The Ryerson Imprint*.

139 LP, Ryerson flyer for the Canada Must Choose series, n.d. [c. 1945], Reserve Collection, LAC. Pierce considered cover and catalogue material so vital in marketing a book that he wrote it himself.

140 LP to Bruce Pierce, 7 November 1944, in possession of BPR.

141 LP to Abbé Arthur Maheux, 3 April 1944, file 1, box 11, LPP. In his reply of 11 April 1944, Maheux reassured Pierce that most of the French press who espoused such views were "fanatics" and "ignorant people" who "do not go very far." See file 1, box 11, LPP. Pierce recounted a similar dinner conversation with littérateur Maurice Hébert in a letter that day to William Colgate, 3 April 1944, file 6, box 10, LPP.

142 LP, *A Canadian People*, 48.

143 Ibid., 50, 51.

144 See, for example, the expressions of amity and goodwill in Arthur Maheux to LP, 26 June 1942, file 4, box 9, LPP, and in G.E. Marquis to LP, 3 October 1945, file 7, box 12, LPP.

145 "Inquiétudes et opinions d'un Anglo-Canadian" (editorial), *Le Droit* (Ottawa), 16 May 1945.

146 A digest of reviews is found on the dust jacket to the second edition of *A Canadian People*.

147 LP Diary, 12 January 1942.

CHAPTER NINETEEN

1 LP uses the phrase in a letter to Ernest Fewster, 12 January 1942, file 1, box 9, LPP.

2 A.J.M. Smith to LP, 1 April 1943, file 3, box 10, LPP.

3 E.K. Brown to LP, 5 July 1943, file 7, box 9, LPP. The two were dickering over revisions to *On Canadian Poetry* in terms of traditional-modernist tensions.

4 LP to Dorothy Livesay, 25 April 1945, file 5, box 12, LPP.

5 LP, "Canadian Literature and the National Ideal," *Canadian Bookman*, 7 (September 1925): 143–4.

6 A.J.M. Smith, "Wanted – Canadian Criticism," *Canadian Forum*, April 1928, 8.

7 LP, epigraph in frontispiece to Makers of Canadian Literature series, in Peter McArthur, *Stephen Leacock* (Toronto: Ryerson [1923]), [iv], and A.J.M. Smith, "Wanted – Canadian Criticism," 8.

8 LP, *A Canadian People*, 11.

9 Of these, only Leo Kennedy had published a book, *The Shrouding* (Toronto: Macmillan 1933).

10 P.K. Page, letter to author, 21 June 1994.

11 LP to Smith, 12 October 1944, file 4, box 11, LPP. See also LP to E.K. Brown, 29 January 1948, vol. 1, Brown Papers, LAC: "If we had [D.C.] Scott on our list I think I could die happy. This would give us everything in the sixties. Sometime this year I hope to publish books by Klein and Kennedy which will give us all the Montreal group."

12 LP to Laura Goodman Salverson, 2 November 1939, file 7, box 7, LPP.

13 LP, *A Canadian People*, 1–2.

14 LP to Dorothy Livesay, 25 April 1945, file 5, box 12, LPP.

15 In these years, Ryerson published three collections of Roberts's poetry – *The Iceberg and Other Poems* (1934), *Selected Poems of Sir Charles G.D. Roberts* (1936), *Canada Speaks of Britain* (1941) – as well as *Flying Colours* (1942), a collection of war poetry edited by Roberts, and Elsie Pomeroy's *Sir Charles G.D. Roberts: A Biography* (1943). Pierce also published a tiny run of a booklet of four poems by Roberts, *Twilight over Shaugamauk* (1937), privately distributed to friends of both that Christmas.

16 See LP Diary, 25 January and 14 February 1925. In the 1920s Pierce launched the Ryerson Chapbook series with Roberts's *The Sweet o' the Year and Other Poems* and also published his *The Vagrant of Time*. Pierce himself wrote the biographical material on Roberts for James Cappon's Makers of Canadian Literature volume *Charles G.D. Roberts*. A letter of warning from L.C. Page to Ryerson Press, 27 June 1925, about publishing Roberts is found in file 2, box 2, LPP.

17 There is a note by Charles G.D. Roberts to his sons, dated 5 September 1925, to the effect that a $500 loan from Pierce has first claim on his estate. See file 3, box 2, LPP.

18 LP to Prime Minister R.B. Bennett, 26 January 1931, file 5, box 4, LPP.

19 Roberts's taste in limericks (and younger women) is detailed in Adams, *Sir Charles God Damn*, 184.

20 See LP Diary, 20 March 1926 and 14 June 1928. Pierce's opinion of Roberts's morals was shared by others, as the latter entry makes clear.

21 LP Diary, 22 January 1941.

22 The 1937 figures are from Adams, *Sir Charles God Damn*, 189, and the 1939 figures are in Roberts to C.H. Dickinson, 18 February 1940, repr. in Laurel Boone, ed., *The Collected Letters of Charles G.D. Roberts* (Fredericton: Goose Lane 1989), 587.

23 Roberts to LP, 9 March 1940, repr. in Boone, ed., *The Collected Letters of Charles G.D. Roberts*, 588–9.

24 Roberts to LP, 9 March 1940, repr. in ibid., 589.

25 Charles G.D. Roberts, "The Empire Speaks of Britain," *Maclean's Magazine*, 1 October 1940. The sonnet was retitled for book publication. Proceeds from the booklet were to go to the War Services Library Council, with whom Pierce was doing volunteer work to supply books to the troops.

26 Roberts to LP, 1 October 1940, repr. in Boone, ed., *The Collected Letters of Charles G.D. Roberts*, 597.

27 It was added at the galley stage. Roberts to LP, 8 June 1942, repr. in ibid., 622. "Resurgant" was his last poem according to Adams, *Sir Charles God Damn*, 199.

28 See Elsie Pomeroy to LP, 12 February 1936, file 6, box 6, LPP.

29 Roberts's motivation is discussed in Adams, *Sir Charles God Damn*, 191–2; Roberts to LP, 3 June 1940, repr. in Boone, ed., *The Collected Letters of Charles G.D. Roberts*, 593.

30 Adams, *Sir Charles God Damn*, 192.

31 Elsie Pomeroy to LP, 12 February 1936, file 6, box 6, LPP. Boone, ed., *The Collected Letters of Charles G.D. Roberts*, charts the troubled evolution of the biography.

32 Frank Flemington, "Phone Memo to Sir Charles," 10 September 1942, file 5, box 9, LPP. Both Pierce's comments and Roberts's reaction are recorded.

33 LP, Introduction to Elsie Pomeroy, *Sir Charles G.D. Roberts: A Biography* (Toronto: Ryerson 1943), xxiii, xxii. Pierce had first been asked to introduce the

volume in 1941, but he did not complete his introduction until March 1943, a month before the official publication date.

34 LP to Charles Clay, 16 October 1944, vol. 1, Canadian Writers' Foundation Papers, LAC. Sales, wrote LP, had "practically stopped."

35 Frank Flemington to Walter McRaye, 14 September 1945, file 7, box 12, LPP.

36 Pelham Edgar, qtd. in Adams, *Sir Charles God Damn*, 196; for Edgar's formal review, see "Sir Charles G.D. Roberts and His Time," in Edgar, *Across My Path*, ed. Northrop Frye (Toronto: Ryerson 1952), 99–108.

37 E.K. Brown to D.C. Scott, 5 Feb 1943, repr. in R.L. McDougall, ed., *The Poet and the Critic* (Ottawa: Carleton University Press 1983), 53. Scott replied on 9 February: "Yes, the advance notice of the Sir Charles book as you say sounds like our national criticism at its worst; L.P. has been one of the chief offenders and I dread to read his contribution to this biography" (54).

38 LP to Sara and Eldred Chester, n.d. [late November 1943], box 1, CFP. For the wedding comment, see LP to BP, n.d. [October 1943], box 16, PFC. He added in the latter that the marriage "did not seem natural or decent."

39 LP to Beth and Bruce Pierce, n.d. [November 1943], box 16, PFC.

40 See Sir Charles G.D. Roberts, *Forest Folk*, ed. Ethel Hume Bennett (Toronto: Ryerson 1949). Pierce found his duties irksome as Roberts's son Lloyd both pressed him about estate revenues and urged him (unsuccessfully) to publish the latter's novel "The Feet of the Years," another of Lloyd's thinly veiled family memoirs. See Lloyd Roberts to LP, 4 July 1947, file 2, box 16, LPP, and LP to Lloyd Roberts, 15 September 1948, file 11, box 17, LPP.

41 For a discussion of Brown and his "Letters in Canada" writings for *University of Toronto Quarterly*, see Laura Smyth Groening, *E.K. Brown: A Study in Conflict* (Toronto: University of Toronto Press 1990), 58–63, 128–9. Brown wrote the supplement until his death in 1951.

42 D.C. Scott to Pelham Edgar, 16 March 1921, Pelham Edgar Papers, Victoria College Library, Toronto.

43 D.C. Scott to E.K. Brown, 24 July 1947, repr. in McDougall, ed., *The Poet and the Critic*, 194.

44 D.C. Scott to E.K. Brown, 12 November 1943, repr. in ibid., 81.

45 See Stan Dragland, *Floating Voice, Troubled Waters: Duncan Campbell Scott and the Literature of Treaty 9* (Concord, ON: Anansi 1994). Dragland quotes Scott's 1929 *cri de cœur* to Elise Aylen: "I know now that I have never fought against anything nor worked for anything but just accepted & drifted from point to point – I have dimly felt that if I worked & protested & resisted I should be wrecked – so maybe you will understand why with some gifts I have done so little" (74).

46 LP, "Duncan Campbell Scott: An Appraisal," 52–3, file 9, box 37, LPP.

47 Pierce's paper with Scott's curt comments is found in file 9, box 37, LPP; see also LP Diary, 27 January 1927.

48 Lorne Pierce to Roderick Kennedy, 13 May 1952, file 4, box 21, LPP.
49 Scott to E.K. Brown, 23 February 1946, repr. in McDougall, ed., *The Poet and the Critic*, 159.
50 LP to Pelham Edgar, 31 January 1943, box 1, Canadian Writers' Foundation Papers, LAC.
51 The titles are *Selected Poems of Archibald Lampman* (1947), *Walter J. Phillips R.C.A.* (1947), and *In the Village of Viger* (1945), originally published in Boston by Copeland and Day, 1896.
52 LP to E.K. Brown, 29 January 1948, vol. 1, Brown Papers, LAC.
53 Pierce's doubts that McClelland and Stewart would sell the rights are discussed in LP to Brown, 29 January 1948, file 3, box 17, LPP, and Brown to LP, 26 October 1949, file 1, box 18, LPP. A formal memo of procedure, apparently drafted by Brown, about the editing of the book is found in file 1, box 19, LPP.
54 See LP to Peggy Brown, n.d., vol. 3, Brown Papers, LAC. Frank Flemington, in a letter of 6 October 1964 in this source, told Brown's widow that the book had finally sold out about two years earlier. Today it is a valuable collector's item.
55 See Groening, *E.K. Brown*.
56 Ibid., 15–16. Pierce was fifteen years Brown's senior, not ten as Groening states.
57 Northrop Frye, diary entry, 31 July 1950, repr. in Robert D. Denham, ed., *The Diaries of Northrop Frye 1942–1955* (Toronto: University of Toronto Press 2001), 422.
58 LP to E.K. Brown, 24 January 1946, file 5, box 13, LPP. In 1946 Ryerson brought out both Page's *As Ten As Twenty* and Anderson's *The White Centre*.
59 Ryerson also published A.J.M. Smith's *News of the Phoenix* in 1943 as well as William Colgate's *Canadian Art, Its Origin and Development*. Both Brown and Smith won Governor General's Awards, although Pierce's ambivalence about Smith's type of poetry – as well as Pierce's lack of baseball expertise – came across in his diary when he described Smith's prize as "Strike Two!" for the Ryerson lists!
60 See Groening, *E.K. Brown*, 84–6.
61 Brown added some material on Roberts's friend Francis Sherman, whose work Pierce had personally edited and published, and included some material on Audrey Alexandra Brown and others. See LP, ed., *The Complete Poems of Francis Sherman* (Toronto: Ryerson 1935).
62 LP to A.S.P. Woodhouse, 6 August 1953, file 15, box 21, LPP. Pierce may have dreamed that Brown would succeed him, but it is difficult to see Brown leaving his congenial post at the University of Chicago for the travails of book publishing on a very modest salary.
63 Brown to D.C. Scott, 17 July 1943, repr. in McDougall, ed., *The Poet and the Critic*, 70.
64 LP to E.K. Brown, 9 July 1943, vol. 1, Brown Papers, LAC.
65 LP to E.K. Brown, 3 July 1943, file 7, box 9, LPP.

66 E.K. Brown to LP, 23 June 1943, file 7, box 9, LPP.

67 LP to Earle Birney, 16 January 1943, file 7, box 9, LPP.

68 A.J.M. Smith to E.K. Brown, 26 January 1939, vol. 3, Brown Papers, LAC.

69 Pierce in fact magnanimously lowered the usual permission fees for Smith's anthology. See Smith to LP, 29 November 1942, file 6, box 9, LPP.

70 See, for example, Smith to LP, 1 April 1943, file 3, box 10, LPP, in which Pierce has underlined the names of a range of young writers praised by Smith.

71 LP to F.R. Scott, 1 December 1944, file 3, box 11, LPP.

72 F.R. Scott to LP, 11 December 1944, file 3, box 11, LPP. Scott was referring to his profile as McGill professor, constitutional lawyer, and Co-operative Commonwealth Federation (CCF) activist.

73 Smith to LP, 29 November 1942, file 6, box 9, LPP.

74 LP to E.K. Brown, 13 January 1944, file 5, box 10, LPP. In the event, Brown became caught up in other projects and no selected edition of Cameron's works ever appeared. Brown did write a brief preface to a reprinted Lampman piece on Cameron. See Brown's prefatory note in Archibald Lampman, "Two Canadian Poets," *University of Toronto Quarterly*, 13 (June 1944): 406–23.

75 Smith to LP, 9 July 1944, file 3, box 11, LPP.

76 LP to Eugenie Perry, n.d. [1947], file 1, box 16, LPP.

77 Louis Dudek to LP, 17 November 1952, file 2, box 21, LPP.

78 Smith, "Wanted – Canadian Criticism," 8.

79 The image is found in LP to Ernest Fewster, 12 January 1942, file 1, box 9, LPP.

80 Smith to LP, 29 June 1943, file 3, box 10, LPP. Smith wrote: "These poems perform a useful function in giving balance and tang to the collection as a whole," which would "win the respect of the younger writers like [Toronto poet Ronald] Hambleton and the *Preview* group." But Smith closed meekly: "I have no wish to be dogmatic or unreasonable ... if your feeling against [the poems] is very strong you may omit them."

81 LP to Louis Dudek, 10 June 1946, file 6, box 13, LPP. In his reply of 14 June, Dudek agreed to the deletions. Pierce asked Anderson to cut lines from the poem "Dancer," which he did, provided other material be added. See Frank Flemington to Patrick Anderson, 19 April 1946, file 5, box 13, LPP. Flemington told Anderson on Pierce's behalf: "We have so much trouble with some of the modern poetry that it is hardly worth the wear and tear to publish certain poems."

82 Layton to LP, 6 December 1954, file 7, box 23, LPP.

83 Layton to LP, 30 December 1954, file 7, box 23, and 22 August 1955, file 6, box 24, LPP. Layton also mailed copies of *Black Mountain Review* to familiarize Pierce with the American poets influencing him and his contemporaries. He promised to dedicate his title poem in *The Cold Green Element* to Pierce – but in the event the book's publisher was Layton, Dudek, and Souster's Contact Press. See

Layton to LP, 21 November 1954, and Layton to LP, 24 October 1954, both in file 7, box 23, LPP.

84 Layton to LP, 22 December 1956, file 8, box 24, LPP.

85 Layton to LP, 6 December 1954, file 7, box 23, LPP. The letter and check are mentioned in Layton to LP, 17 April and 24 March 1955, both file 6, box 24, LPP. For Layton's career at this time, see Elspeth Cameron, *Irving Layton: A Biography* (Toronto: Stoddard 1985), and Brian Trehearne, *Montreal Poetry in the Forties* (Toronto: University of Toronto Press 1999).

86 Malcolm Ross to LP, 6 July 1955, file 8, box 24, LPP, and Fred Cogswell to Irving Layton, August 1955 [no day], Layton Papers, Special Collections, Concordia University Library, Montreal. Ross told Pierce that Layton's work included "a dozen or so really fine poems and a great deal of culch" but that as yet Layton had "little to express and his pugnacious little improvisations are not enough to cover the abyss … There are times when I realize vividly that Tennyson *was* a poet. And so was Carman – I grow old."

87 See Layton to LP, 22 December 1956, file 5, box 25, LPP, and "Poet Attacks Publisher's Attitude," *Globe and Mail*, 14 January 1957, scrapbook, box 67A, LPP.

88 See Layton to LP, 29 June 1957, file 4, box 26, LPP.

89 Louis Dudek to LP, 19 January 1957, file 3, box 25, LPP. Although by his account Dudek had "hard words" with Layton over the telephone on the matter, it is significant that he did not publicly go to bat for Pierce and Ryerson, given their several other very public spats.

90 "Poet Attacks Publisher's Attitude."

91 Layton to LP, 21 October 1957, file 4, box 26, LPP. Layton had earlier visited Pierce's Canadiana collection at Queen's and had written Pierce: "I called down many blessings on you and [Edith Pierce]. Many others besides myself will in future draw comfort and faith there: you have built yourself a monument as enduring as courage and love are." Layton to LP, 22 August 1955, file 6, box 24, LPP.

92 For an account of McClelland's career, see King, *Jack*.

93 LP, *A Canadian Nation* (Toronto: Ryerson 1960), 28.

94 See, for example, Louis Dudek and Michael Gnarowski, eds., *The Making of Modern Poetry in Canada* (Toronto: Ryerson 1967), and Trehearne, *Montreal Poets in the Forties*. A search through Michael Gnarowski, *A Concise Bibliography of English-Canadian Literature* (Toronto: McClelland and Stewart 1973, rev. ed. 1978), makes it clear how ubiquitous the Ryerson imprint became for modernist poets in the 1940s and 1950s.

95 Jack McClelland to Irving Layton, 19 July 1962 (dictated but not mailed), repr. in Sam Solecki, ed., *The Selected Letters of Jack McClelland* (Toronto: Key Porter 1998), 62–3.

96 Groening, *E.K. Brown*, 165.

97 Peggy Deaver Brown to LP, 5 May 1951, file 1, box 20, LPP (emphasis in original); LP to Peggy Deaver Brown, 26 August 1957, vol. 3, Brown Papers, LAC.
98 E.K. Brown to LP, 5 July 1943, file 7, box 9, LPP.

CHAPTER TWENTY

1 LP to A.J.M. Smith, 12 October 1944, file 4, box 11, LPP.
2 E.K. Brown to LP, 23 June 1943, file 7, box 9, LPP.
3 Desmond Pacey to LP, 26 October 1949, file 5, box 18, LPP.
4 LP to Dorothy Livesay, 22 September 1943, file 20, box 2, Livesay Papers, and LP to Desmond Pacey, 28 June 1951, file 10, box 20, LPP.
5 Archibald MacMechan to Andrew Macphail, 27 October 1912, vol. 1, Macphail Papers, LAC. MacMechan added: "There is no one in America that I know writing verse that is comparable to hers. Affectation, violence, vulgarity, cheapness, mechanical effects are the rule [there]."
6 E.J. Pratt, *Dunkirk* (Toronto: Macmillan 1941) and *They Are Returning* (Toronto: Macmillan 1945).
7 LP, Introduction to *The Selected Poems of Marjorie Pickthall*, 19. Pickthall's IQ seems to have deteriorated markedly in Pierce's estimation since he declares that "rapture and intuition are substituted for the discipline of reason" in her poetry, while her body "scarcely sustained the demands of a cloistered life in times of peace" (15, 19).
8 LP, *Marjorie Pickthall: A Memorial Address ...*, 5.
9 Ibid. The address was in conjunction with an exhibition of Pickthall's papers, some of which Pierce had donated to Victoria University after being given them by Pickthall's stepmother after Arthur Pickthall's death. For a similar estimate of Pickthall by Pierce about this time, see LP, "Marjorie Lowry Christie Pickthall," in Charles G.D. Roberts and Arthur Tunnell, eds., *Canadian Who Was Who*, vol. 2 (Toronto: TransCanada 1938), 349–52. Pierce's characterization of Pickthall during the First World War does not seem apt. Pickthall did Land Girl volunteer work for a time in England later in the war, and was much more sophisticated and engaged than Pierce's 1925 account of her suggests.
10 LP, *Marjorie Pickthall: A Memorial Address ...*, 26. This phrase is repeated in his 1957 introduction to *The Selected Poems of Marjorie Pickthall*, 19.
11 LP, *Marjorie Pickthall: A Memorial Address ...*, 9.
12 LP, Introduction to *The Selected Poems of Marjorie Pickthall*, 15.
13 See Dean Irvine, "The Two Giovannis: P.K. Page's Two Modernisms," *Journal of Canadian Studies*, 38, no. 1 (2004): 23–45; Collett Tracey, "The Little Presses That Did: A History of First Statement Press, Contact Press and Delta Canada, and Their Contribution to the Rise and Development of Modernist Poetry in Canada during the Middle Part of the Twentieth Century" (PhD thesis, Université de Montréal, 2001); and Michele Rackham, "Reframing Montreal Mod-

ernisms: A Biographical Study of Betty Sutherland and Her Work with *First Statement*, First Statement Press, *Contact*, Contact Press, and *CIV/n*" (MA thesis, Carleton University, 2006).

14 For this and an overview of Brown's career, see Sandra Campbell, "The Literary Career of Professor Pelham Edgar" (PhD thesis, University of Ottawa, 1983), 241.

15 Carole Gerson, in *Canadian Canons: Essays in Literary Value*, ed. Robert Lecker (Toronto: University of Toronto Press 1991), 47.

16 A.A. Brown to LP, 18 November 1946, file 5, box 13, LPP.

17 D.C. Scott to Pelham Edgar, 15 April 1938, Scott Papers, Victoria College Library, Toronto.

18 Pelham Edgar, Preface to Audrey Alexandra Brown, *A Dryad in Nanaimo*, rev. ed. (Toronto: Macmillan 1934), v.

19 Jean Graham, "Among Those Present, A Sweet Singer ... Audrey Alexandra Brown," *Saturday Night*, 23 July 1933, 8.

20 A.A. Brown to LP, 8 November 1947, file 6, box 14, LPP.

21 Jean Graham, "Among Those Present," 8.

22 Brown's poetry sales fell steadily according to figures in the Macmillan of Canada papers, McMaster University Archives. *The Tree of Resurrection* (Toronto: Macmillan 1937) sold 884 copies while her 1944 volume for Macmillan, *Challenge to Time and Death*, sold 473 copies.

23 Eugenie Perry, 20 January 1946, file 2, box 14, LPP. Brown was by this time living in Victoria, Perry's home.

24 A.J.M. Smith, "Canadian Poetry – A Minority Report [1939]," repr. in Smith, *Towards a View of Canadian Letters* (Vancouver: University of British Columbia Press 1973), 179–80; Earle Birney, "Moon-Wist in Canadian Poesie," review of *The Tree of Resurrection* by A.A. Brown, *Canadian Forum*, August 1937, repr. in Birney, *Spreading Time: Remarks on Canadian Writing and Writers. Book I: 1904–1949* (Montreal: Véhicule 1980), 31–2. Brown refers to Birney's apology in a letter to LP, 8 November 1947, file 6, box 14, LPP.

25 Brian Trehearne, *Aestheticism and the Canadian Modernists* (Montreal & Kingston: McGill-Queen's University Press 1989), 318. See also Trehearne's *The Montreal Forties: Modernism in Transition* (Toronto: University of Toronto Press 1999).

26 See, for example, A.A. Brown to LP, 2 December 1945, and his reply of 5 December 1945, file 7, box 11, LPP. Brown was receiving aid totalling $50 a month at this time. Galloping post-war inflation with a dramatic rise in the cost of living was to make her life even more financially difficult, hardships outlined in Brown to LP, 27 April and 15 May 1946, file 5, box 13, LPP.

27 For LP's payment of Brown's allowance out of his own pocket, see LP to Charles Clay, 5 December 1945, vol. 8, Canadian Writers' Foundation Papers, LAC.

28 LP to Sir Andrew Macphail, 5 November 1930, vol. 3, Macphail Papers, LAC.

29 LP to A.A. Brown, 24 January 1948, file 3, box 17, LPP.

30 E.K. Brown to LP, 26 June 1943, file 3, box 9, LPP.

31 A.A. Brown to LP, 21 May 1947, file 6, box 14, LPP. Emphasis in original.

32 See A.A. Brown to LP, 18 April and 21 May 1947, file 6, box 14, LPP.

33 BPR, telephone interview with author, 18 June 2006.

34 A.A. Brown to LP, 21 May 1947, file 6, box 14, LPP. Brown was responding to a letter in which Pierce had told her that her themes of loss and death had little appeal to the public. She was obviously shaken by the comments, but she concludes gamely: "Your letters are the greatest pleasure to me." What strikes the eye is that the "me" and the signature "Yours, Audrey Alexandra Brown" are cramped and crammed into the corner of the page, in marked contrast to her usual penmanship.

35 A.A. Brown to LP, 3 February 1948, file 3, box 17, LPP.

36 A.A. Brown to LP, 2 December 1945, file 7, box 11, LPP.

37 LP to Eugenie Perry, 24 January 1949, file 5, box 18, LPP, and Brown to Pierce, 1 November 1953, file 2, box 22, LPP. The letters discuss the poor reviews of Brown's book and the fact that 500 copies could not even be sold as remainders.

38 A.A. Brown to LP, 11 September 1955, file 1, box 23, LPP.

39 LP to Teresa Thomson, 21 February 1955, vol. 8, Canadian Writers' Foundation Papers, LAC. To his credit, Pierce, unlike some other former admirers of Brown in the Foundation, supported the continuation of Brown's small pension despite her now-diminished literary output. I wish to thank the Canadian Writers' Foundation for permission to consult this material.

40 LP to E.K. Brown, 21 April 1943, file 7, box 9, LPP.

41 LP to E.K. Brown, 18 August 1944, file 5, box 10, LPP.

42 See Fred Cogswell, "Desmond Pacey," *Dictionary of Literary Biography*, vol. 88, 236–9, and "Desmond Pacey," dust-jacket biography [by LP] in Pacey, *Creative Writing in Canada* (Toronto: Ryerson Press 1952). Pierce wrote the dust-jacket material for Ryerson Press titles himself, since he felt he could not trust such crucial material to anyone else at the House after the dust-jacket errors on Grove's *Settlers of the Marsh* in 1925, according to BPR, interview with author, Kingston, ON, 20 July 2010.

43 LP to Theodore Roberts, 7 November 1947, file 2, box 16, LPP.

44 Cogswell, "Desmond Pacey," 237. Cogswell adds that this approach was accompanied by "the then unusual conviction that the Canadian material examined was worthy of respect."

45 LP to Dorothy Livesay, 22 September 1943, file 20, box 2, Livesay Papers, QUA.

46 Pacey to LP, 9 January 1947, file 1, box 15, LPP.

47 Pacey to LP, 21 March 1945, file 6, box 12, LPP.

48 LP to E.K. Brown, 27 April 1948, file 3, box 17, LPP, and LP to Desmond Pacey, 16 December 1949, file 5, box 18, LPP.

49 Desmond Pacey, *A Book of Canadian Stories* (Toronto: Ryerson 1947). The anthology was revised, enlarged, and reissued in 1950.

50 Desmond Pacey to LP, 11 February 1946, file 2, box 14, LPP. Pacey then sent a plan of the anthology to Pierce in a letter of 7 March.
51 Pacey to LP, 7 October 1946, file 2, box 14, LPP.
52 Pacey to LP, 8 May 1947, file 1, box 16, LPP.
53 Cover text, *Creative Writing in Canada*.
54 Pacey to LP, 8 January and 28 March 1949, file 5, box 18, LPP.
55 Pacey to LP, 26 October 1949, file 5, box 18, LPP.
56 Pacey to LP, 14 November 1949, file 5, box 18, LPP. Pacey did agree that a price increase was "wiser and fairer."
57 LP to Pacey, 16 Dec. 1949, file 5, box 18, LPP.
58 Pacey to LP, 19 December 1949, file 5, box 18, LPP, and 8 December 1950, file 4, box 19, LPP.
59 LP to Pacey, 26 February 1951, file 9, box 20, LPP. Malcolm Ross had published an article on Carman called "Carman by the Sea" in *Dalhousie Review*, 27 (October 1947): 140–4.
60 LP to Pacey, 28 June 1951, file 10, box 20, LPP.
61 LP to Pacey, 26 February 1951, file 10, box 20, LPP.
62 Earle Birney, "Comments on Pacey MS." [1951], file 1, box 20, LPP, and LP to Pacey, 26 February 1951, file 9, box 20, LPP.
63 Pacey to LP, 5 April 1951, file 9, box 20, LPP.
64 Pacey, *Creative Writing in Canada*, 37, 62; LP to Pacey, 26 February 1951, file 10, box 20, LPP.
65 LP to Pacey, 28 June 1951, file 10, box 20, LPP.
66 Ibid.
67 LP to E.K. Brown, n.d. [1943], in 1943–50 correspondence file, vol. 1, Brown Papers, LAC.
68 Pacey, *Creative Writing in Canada*, 36, 92.
69 Desmond Pacey, Introduction, *The Selected Poems of Charles G.D. Roberts*, ed. Desmond Pacey (Toronto: Ryerson 1955), xxii.
70 Pacey to LP, 30 June 1951, file 10, box 20, LPP.
71 Pacey to LP, 15 June 1951, file 10, box 20, LPP.
72 Robert Currie, "Don't Blame This on Bliss," *CIV/n*, 7 [c. April 1954], repr. in Louis Dudek and Michael Gnarowski, eds., *The Making of Modern Poetry in Canada* (Toronto: Ryerson 1967), 149.
73 LP to John E. Robbins, 5 November 1953, file 12, box 22, LPP.
74 LP to Pacey, 12 November 1956, file 5, box 25, LPP.
75 LP to Pacey, 14 February 1955, file 7, box 24, LPP.
76 LP to Pacey, n.d. [1956?], file 7, box 30, LPP.
77 LP to Pacey, 14 February 1955, file 7, box 24, LPP.
78 Bruce Whiteman, Introduction to *The Letters of John Sutherland 1942–1956*, ed. Bruce Whiteman (Toronto: ECW Press 1991), xxv.
79 Pacey to LP, 23 October 1957, file 5, box 26, LPP.

80 Pacey to LP, 1 October 1958, file 6, box 27, LPP.

81 Carl Klinck to LP, n.d. [1959], file 3, box 28, LPP. Pierce died before he could write the chapter.

82 See Klinck, *Giving Canada a Literary History*. LP published Klinck's *Wilfred Campbell: A Study in Late Provincial Victorianism* (1942) and Carl Klinck and Henry Wells, *Edwin J. Pratt: The Man and His Poetry* (1947).

83 See Panofsky, "'Head of the Publishing Side of the Business'"; and King, *Jack*.

84 See Dudek and Gnarowski, eds., *The Making of Modern Poetry in Canada*, and Whiteman, Introduction, *The Letters of John Sutherland 1942–1956*, ix–xxxv.

85 John Sutherland to Dorothy Livesay, 9 April 1943, repr. in Whiteman, ed., *The Letters of John Sutherland*, 7.

86 See John Sutherland, review of *Poems* (1946) by Robert Finch, *Northern Review*, 1, no. 6 (1947).

87 Dudek and Gnarowski, eds., *The Making of Modern Poetry in Canada*, 113.

88 See John Sutherland to LP, 3 January 1946 and 7 February 1946, repr. in Whiteman, ed., *The Letters of John Sutherland*, 33–4, 36.

89 John Sutherland to LP, 8 December 1948, repr. in ibid., 60.

90 LP, *A Canadian People*, 24.

91 John Sutherland to Louis Dudek, n.d. [1949], repr. in Whiteman, ed., *The Letters of John Sutherland*, 84.

92 Louis Dudek to Raymond Souster, 7 June 1951, qtd. in Dudek and Gnarowski, eds., *The Making of Modern Poetry in Canada*, 113.

93 John Sutherland, "The Past Decade in Canadian Poetry," *Northern Review*, 4, no. 2 (1950–1).

94 Meetings are referred to in Sutherland to LP, 28 May 1949 and 10 July 1950, repr. in Whiteman, ed., *The Letters of John Sutherland*, 71, 138. The latter letter also refers to Pierce's efforts with other publishers to raise funds for *Northern Review*.

95 Sutherland to LP, 18 March, 1 May, and 9 June 1951, repr. in ibid., 183, 188, 195.

96 Sutherland to LP, 15 December 1949, repr. in ibid., 99.

97 Sutherland to LP, 14 November 1951, repr. in ibid., 219.

98 Sutherland to Ralph Gustafson, 1 February 1947, repr. in ibid., 51.

99 LP to Sutherland, 30 May 1949, file 6, box 18, LPP. Sutherland was over-optimistic about fall publication: LP only holds out the possibility of later publication and the addition of a couple of chapters at that time.

100 Sutherland to LP, 7 July 1949, repr. in Whiteman, ed., *The Letters of John Sutherland*, 75.

101 Sutherland to LP, 23 August 1949, repr. in ibid., 80. Sutherland was so "sensitive about" his earlier criticism that he asked poet Anne Wilkinson not to read his early *First Statement* editorials when he sent her back issues of the magazine. See Sutherland to Wilkinson, 6 March 1950, repr. in ibid., 111.

102 Sutherland to LP, 15 May 1953, repr. in ibid., 293.

103 Sutherland to W.W.E. Ross, 25 November 1952, repr. in ibid., 269.

104 Sutherland to W.W.E. Ross, 12 February 1953, repr. in ibid., 277.
105 LP, "Report of the Book Editor to the Board of Publication," 27 April 1950, box 21, Board of Publication Papers, United Church Archives.
106 Sutherland to LP, 21 April 1953, repr. in Whiteman, ed., *The Letters of John Sutherland*, 290–1.
107 Sutherland to LP, 16 October 1951, repr. in ibid., 216.
108 Pacey to LP, 19 December 1949, file 5, box 18, LPP.
109 Sutherland to LP, 18 March 1951, repr. in Whiteman, ed., *The Letters of John Sutherland*, 184.
110 Sutherland to LP, 18 March 1951, file 12, box 20, LPP.
111 LP to Pacey, 28 June 1951, file 10, box 20, LPP.
112 Sutherland to LP, 30 March 1954, file 13, box 23, LPP (emphasis in original). This letter is not included in Whiteman, ed., *The Letters of John Sutherland*.
113 Sutherland to LP, 7 July 1949, file 6, box 18, LPP.
114 See John Sutherland, "E.J. Pratt: A Major Contemporary Poet," *Northern Review*, 5, nos. 3/4 (April–May 1952): 36–64.
115 Pitt, *E.J. Pratt: The Master Years*, 438.
116 Ibid., 437.
117 Sutherland to LP, 12 April 1954, repr. in Whiteman, ed., *The Letters of John Sutherland*, 330. He thanks LP for his "warm and understanding" response.
118 Sutherland to LP, 30 March 1954, file 13, box 23, LPP.
119 Sutherland to LP, 22 July 1952, file 8, box 21, LPP.
120 See LP to Pacey, 12 October 1956, file 6 [misfiled], box 26, LPP.
121 Pacey, *Ten Canadian Poets* (Toronto: Ryerson 1958), 167.
122 Pitt, *E.J. Pratt: The Truant Years*, 124. Pitt quotes Pierce's letter to Pacey before questioning Pierce's assertion.
123 Sutherland to John E. Robbins, 6 February 1955, repr. in Whiteman, ed., *The Letters of John Sutherland*, 340.
124 LP to Sutherland, 14 February 1955, file 9, box 24, LPP.
125 LP to Pacey, 19 September 1956, file 5, box 26, LPP.
126 LP to Pacey, 19 September 1957, file 6, box 26, LPP.
127 See Tippett, *Making Culture*, and Litt, *The Muses, the Masses, and the Massey Commission*.
128 Muriel Miller, *Bliss Carman: Quest and Revolt* (St John's: Jesperson 1985), 258.
129 In concert with Mary Perry King, Pierce did manage to bring out a small (forty-five-page) booklet of the poetry after Carman's death, *The Music of Earth* (1931), reissued in 1939 as a Ryerson chapbook. He also secured permission from Boston's L.C. Page to publish a new single-volume edition in 1942 of Carman's *The Pipes of Pan*, originally published by Page in five volumes between 1902 and 1905.
130 LP to Mary Perry King, 9 January 1930, box 40, Mary Perry King Correspondence, LPP. Pierce added ruefully that, even after having made Cappon revise the work, he would "lose money on it as I deserve."

131 LP to Carman, 4 June 1924, file 9, box 21, Bliss Carman Correspondence, LPP.

132 LP to E.C. Kyte, 28 February 1945, file 4, box 12, LPP.

133 LP, "Bliss Carman," *The Canadian Who Was Who*, vol. 1, ed. Charles G.D. Roberts and Arthur Tunnell (Toronto: TransCanada 1934), 98.

134 LP Diary, 21 November 1923.

135 See, for example, LP, *Three Fredericton Poets*, 18–24, and LP, "Bliss Carman," *The Canadian Who Was Who*, vol. 1, 96–101.

136 LP, *An Outline of Canadian Literature*, 74, 75–6.

137 LP, *Three Fredericton Poets*, 22–3.

138 See LP Diary, 5 March and 9 May 1927.

139 Bliss Carman to Morton Fullerton, qtd. in Hermione Lee, *Edith Wharton* (London: Chatto and Windus 2007), 323; see also Marion Mainwaring, *Mysteries of Paris: The Quest for Morton Fullerton* (Boston: University Press of New England 2000), 242.

140 LP Diary, 16 April 1928. On 19 May, Pierce wrote that he sensed "an aloofness" in Carman but that he was resolved to continue. See also Bliss Carman to Margaret Lawrence, 11 July 1928 (emphasis in original), repr. in H. Pearson Gundy, ed., *The Letters of Bliss Carman* (Montreal & Kingston: McGill-Queen's University Press 1981), 361.

141 LP was told of this in Walter McRaye to LP, 3 April 1943, file 1, box 10, LPP.

142 Arthur Stringer to Janet Munro Thompson, 28 July 1936, vol. 2, I.M.C. Thompson Papers, LAC.

143 LP to Carman, 1 April 1928, file 9, box 21, Bliss Carman Correspondence, LPP, and LP to Morris and Mary Perry King, 14 March 1931, file 6, box 40, Mary Perry King Correspondence, LPP.

144 LP to H. Pearson Gundy, 27 March 1961, file 7, box 29, LPP.

145 LP Diary, 9 May 1927.

146 Mary Perry King died on 21 May 1939 and her husband, Dr Morris King, on 13 May 1940. Under the terms of Dr King's will, Pierce became "sole owner of all [Carman's] rights anywhere [to] hold all proceeds in trust until the estate is transferred to the University of New Brunswick." See LP to Roberts, 28 February 1941, file 5, box 8, LPP.

147 A.J.M. Smith to E.K. Brown, 14 June [1942], vol. 3, E.K. Brown Papers, LAC.

148 Mary McGillivary, "The Popular and Critical Reputation and Reception of Bliss Carman," in Gerald Lynch, ed., *Bliss Carman: A Reappraisal* (Ottawa: University of Ottawa Press 1990), 8.

149 A.J.M. Smith to E.K. Brown, 24 July 1942, vol. 3, E.K. Brown Papers, LAC.

150 LP to E.K. Brown, 28 August 1946, file 5, box 13, LPP.

151 Pacey, *Creative Writing in Canada*, 43.

152 See LP, Introduction to *The Selected Poems of Bliss Carman* (Toronto: McClelland and Stewart 1954), 18.

153 *Bliss Carman's Poems* (New York: Dodd, Mead; and Toronto: McClelland and Stewart 1931). Bibliophile and Carman admirer Rufus Hathaway had made the selection from material not under Page's control. See LP to Morris and Mary Perry King, 8 April and 5 August 1931, box 40, Mary Perry King Correspondence, LPP.

154 LP to L.C. Page, 26 November 1949, file 5, box 18, LPP (emphasis in original). Pierce does not mince words: "Whatever rights you claimed have lapsed through non-publication. No court in the civilized world would support any further claim by you to property rights in Bliss Carman ... I fulfil a promise I made him that a great wrong, and one he bitterly resented, would some day be made right." Pierce had written a similar letter to Page on 4 May 1948, file 10, box 17, LPP.

155 L.C. Page to LP, 17 August 1953, file 11, box 22, LPP.

156 LP to L.C. Page, 19 June 1952, file 7, box 21, LPP. Page finally gave permission in L.C. Page to LP, 17 August 1953, file 11, box 22, LPP.

157 LP to L.C. Page, 18 June 1953, file 10, box 22, LPP. Pierce had once thought of publishing a volume of Carman's selected prose, but he told Charles G.D. Roberts that "the more I look at it the less enthusiastic I am." See LP to Roberts, 1 October 1941, file 5, box 8, LPP. He wrote elsewhere that such a volume would "do nothing to strengthen his reputation." See LP to C.B. Chapman of Page and Co., 7 March 1946, file 2, box 14, LPP.

158 LP to John McClelland, n.d. [spring 1951], LPP, and LP to Jack McClelland, 4 January 1952, file 9, box 20, LPP.

159 LP to Teresa Thomson, 21 February 1955, box 8, Canadian Writers' Foundation Papers, LAC.

160 LP to L.C. Page, 26 November 1949, file 5, box 18, LPP.

161 LP, Introduction to *The Selected Poems of Bliss Carman*, 18, 19. The quote about the "endless trailing quatrains" is found in LP, memo regarding "Selected Poems of Bliss Carman," file 43, box 32, Carman Material, LPP.

162 LP, Introduction, *The Selected Poems of Bliss Carman*, 18.

163 See Carman poem typescripts, file 43, box 32, Carman Material, LPP. Notations on the pages in Pierce's handwriting make it clear that the excisions are his.

164 Pacey, *Ten Canadian Poets*, 85.

165 See John Robert Sorfleet, "The NCL Series: An Appraisal Past and Present," *Journal of Canadian Fiction*, 1, no. 2 (1972): 92–6.

166 LP, memo regarding "Selected Poems of Bliss Carman," item 43, box 32, Carman Material, LPP.

167 Malcolm Ross to LP, 5 August [1952?], file 7, box 21, LPP.

168 Ross to John Newlove, 19 March 1973, Ross Papers, box 3, file 12, University of Calgary Archives. I am indebted to Dr Janet Friskney for generously bringing the 1970s Ross letters to my attention.

169 Ross to David Scollard, 22 March 1973, file 12, box 3, Ross Papers, University of Calgary Archives.

170 W.A. Deacon, "Pierce's Summary of Carman a Rare Critical Achievement," *Globe and Mail*, 18 December 1954, 10.

171 Deacon to LP, 17 December 1954, file 43, box 32, Carman material, LPP.

172 Desmond Pacey, "Carman's Verse …," review of *The Selected Poems of Bliss Carman*, Fredericton *Gleaner*, 20 November 1954.

173 Northrop Frye, unidentified 1954 review of *The Selected Poems of Bliss Carman*, qtd. in Fee, "English Canadian Literary Criticism 1890–1950," 194–5.

174 Claire Pratt to LP, 18 May 1960, file 5, box 29, LPP. An editor at McClelland and Stewart, Pratt told LP that although they would not add poems, "we would be pleased to make textual changes."

175 Dorothy Livesay, "Carman and His Editors," in Dean J. Irvine, ed., *Archive for Our Times: Previously Uncollected and Unpublished Poems of Dorothy Livesay* (Vancouver: Arsenal Pulp Press 1998), 170.

176 Sorfleet, "The NCL Series," 94. At this point, however, Sorfleet was not aware that the Ross selections, including two bibliographical misattributions, were drawn from Pierce's *The Selected Poems of Bliss Carman*. In a later article, Sorfleet observed: "I laid the responsibility at Ross's door. I subsequently learned that he had simply ordered the reprinting of many of the poems previously included in Lorne Pierce's anthology, and that it was Pierce who made the silent excisions from Carman's work and who therefore bore the main responsibility." John Robert Sorfleet, "On Analyzing and Editing Bliss Carman's Work: The Critical Question," in Lynch, ed., *Bliss Carman: A Reappraisal*, 59n.1.

177 Ross to David Scollard, 22 March 1973, file 12, box 3, and Ross to John Robert Sorfleet, 3 March 1975, file 1, box 4, both in the Ross Papers, University of Calgary Archives.

178 Laurel Boone, "Bliss Carman's Pageants, Masques and Essays and the Genesis of Modern Dance," in Lynch, ed., *Bliss Carman: A Reappraisal*, 175.

179 Wilson MacDonald, "The World of Beauty Is in Deep Distress (On the Death of Bliss Carman)," *Ontario Library Review*, 14 (August 1929): 5.

180 LP to Carl Klinck, 19 December 1959, qtd. in Klinck, *Giving Canada A Literary History*, 146.

CHAPTER TWENTY-ONE

1 LP, *The House of Ryerson 1829–1954* (Toronto: Ryerson 1954), 52.

2 LP to Carl Klinck, 19 December 1959, qtd. in Klinck, *Giving Canada a Literary History*, 146.

3 BPR, telephone interview with author, 6 January 2003.

4 LP to Beth and Bruce Pierce, 9 January 1944, box 13, PFC.

5 LP to Bruce Pierce, 26 February 1944, in possession of BPR.

6 Frederick Robson to LP, n.d. [summer 1945], file 1, box 13, LPP.

7 LP to Blanche Hume, 17 April 1946, box 1, Hume Papers, QUA.

8 For example, LP to Desmond Pacey, 28 June 1951, file 10, box 20, LPP. He was referring to a weakness in Carman's "Low Tide on Grand Pré."

9 See LP to Blanche Hume, 17 April 1946, box 1, Hume Papers.

10 The alumni reception is mentioned in LP to Eugenie Perry, 20 June 1944, file 2, box 11, LPP. Beth wed on 18 June 1949 and Bruce married Anne Clark in June 1950.

11 Gordon Chown, a Winnipeg physician, died of a heart attack in February 1949; Alice Chown died on 2 March 1949.

12 BPR, telephone interview with author, 6 January 2003.

13 LP to Jack Price, 13 April 1950, file 4, box 19, LPP. An 18 April 1950 letter from LP to Price in this file speaks of her depression and slow recovery after surgery.

14 ECP, 1950, qtd. in Blanche Hume to LP, 1 June 1954, in possession of BPR.

15 Dr Stock was not the physician who had responded without urgency to Edith's discovery of a breast lump.

16 LP to Jack Price, 13 April 1950, file 4, box 19, LPP, and LP to Mildred Thornton, 29 May 1950, file 7, box 19, LPP.

17 LP to Blanche Hume, 13 January 1950, box 1, Hume Papers.

18 Blanche Hume to LP, 1 June 1954, in possession of BPR.

19 Parker, "Trade and Regional Publishing in Central Canada," *History of the Book in Canada Volume Three: 1918–1980*, 172.

20 Pierce was not involved in union negotiations at the House, which were the book steward's responsibility: as Dickinson put it, Pierce was "miles away" from such concerns. C.H. Dickinson, interview with author, Woodstock, ON, 21 September 1993. In the 1940s Pierce was dismayed by the general rancour of attempts to make the House a closed shop. He wrote in the spring of 1944: "The battle is on to make the House a closed shop, and it is a nasty fight. In fact it has gone on since the strike in 1920. I don't know why it is, but in church councils and committees, there is more vanity, more venom, more niggling and nagging and bad manners than in any other group I know." LP to Bruce Pierce, 6 May 1944, in possession of BPR.

21 LP to J.H. Cranston, 16 October 1947, file 7, box 14, LPP.

22 For the cutback, see LP to M.F. Campbell, 19 August 1947, file 7, box 14, LPP. The 1948 and 1949 title lists were some twenty titles shorter than 1947, and the 1950 list shorter still.

23 Profit and Loss Account for the Year Ending February 29, 1948, Board of Publication Minutes, box 1, Board of Publication Papers, United Church Archives. Overall net profits for the House were down to some $69,000 from over $200,000 the year before. Pierce had handed over the business management of

the Educational Department to his employee Victor Seary, now back from military service, on 1 March 1946, but he was still responsible for its performance. See LP to Sir Wyly Grier, 1 March 1946, file 7, box 13, LPP.

24 C.H. Dickinson, interview with author, Woodstock, ON, 21 September 1993.

25 The figures are from C.H. Dickinson, ibid.

26 See "Woods Gordon Review of Operations," January 1964, box 22, Board of Publication Papers.

27 LP, "Report of the Book Editor," April 1954, box 21, Board of Publication Papers.

28 LP, "Report of the Book Editor," April 1952, box 21, Board of Publication Papers.

29 Owen Sheffield [Ryerson educational representative], report of 12 March 1947, Calgary, box 17, LPP. The reader was the Grade 9 textbook.

30 LP, *A Canadian Nation*, 13.

31 Ibid., 16.

32 See Hilda Neatby, *So Little for the Mind* (Toronto: Clarke, Irwin 1953).

33 Vera Lysenko, *Men in Sheepskin Coats: A Study in Assimilation* (Toronto: Ryerson 1947), 205.

34 Laura Goodman Salverson, epigraph to ibid., ii.

35 Lysenko, *Men in Sheepskin Coats*, 252.

36 Kirkconnell became president of Acadia University in 1948, a post he held until 1964. See his memoir, *A Slice of Canada* (Toronto: University of Toronto Press for Acadia University 1967), and W.H. New, "Watson Kirkconnell," *Dictionary of Literary Biography*, vol. 68, 188–93.

37 Gatenby, *Toronto: A Literary Guide*, 43.

38 See Watson Kirkconnell, *Seven Pillars of Freedom* (Toronto: Oxford University Press 1944; rev. ed., Toronto: Burns and MacEachern 1952). For one discussion of Kirkconnell and academe, see Frederick W. Gibson, *Queen's University Volume II 1917–1961: To Serve and Yet Be Free* (Montreal & Kingston: McGill-Queen's University Press 1983), 274ff.

39 Watson Kirkconnell, *Canadian Overtones: An Anthology ...* (Winnipeg: Columbia 1935); *The Ukrainian Canadians and the War* (Toronto: Oxford University Press 1940); and *Our Ukrainian Loyalists (Ukrainian Canadian Committee)* (Winnipeg: Ukrainian Canadian Committee 1943).

40 Lysenko, *Men in Sheepskin Coats*, 118.

41 Ibid., 117–18, 285. She told Pierce that much of the book was written in the period 1943 to 1945. See Lysenko to LP, 11 March 1948, file 8, box 17, LPP.

42 Lysenko, *Men in Sheepskin Coats*, 284. Emphasis in original.

43 Kirkconnell to LP, 12 January 1948, file 7, box 17, LPP. Kirkconnell was referring to the Ukrainian Labour-Farmer Temple Association.

44 The letters were, respectively, Theodore Humeniuk to LP, 8 March 1948, file 7, box 17, LPP; M.I. Mandryka to LP, 19 January 1948, file 9, box 17, LPP; and Paul Yavorsky, Ukrainian Canadian Veterans' Association, to LP, 2 January 1948, file 12, box 17, LPP. The newspaper review in question was written by "Brother" S.

Methodius and appeared in the *Canadian Register*, 21 February 1948, and else-where.

45 LP to Kirkconnell, 28 January 1948, file 7, box 17, LPP.

46 Kirkconnell to LP, 28 February 1948, and Kirkconnell to LP, 7 March 1948, both file 7, box 17, LPP. It is hard to see the relevance of some of the 28 February inclusions, for example, "photostat of proclamation by the Ukrainian Insurrectionary Army (UPA), calling for 'Death to Hitler and Stalin.'"

47 W.A. Deacon [on Canadian Authors Association letterhead], 12 March 1948, file 5, box 17, LPP. Flemington quotes the "crackpot" remark by Deacon in a memorandum for his boss summarizing his telephone conversation with Deacon on his boss's behalf.

48 Frank Flemington, memorandum of phone conversation with W.A. Deacon, attached to LP to Kirkconnell, 28 February 1948, file 7, box 17, LPP.

49 Lysenko to LP, 11 March 1948, file 8, box 17, LPP, and John Murray Gibbon to LP, 19 July 1949, file 2, box 18, LPP; John Murray Gibbon, review of *Men in Sheepskin Coats*, *Canadian Historical Review*, 29, no. 1 (1948): 88.

50 LP to Kirkconnell, 28 January and 15 March 1948, both in file 7, box 17, LPP.

51 Watson Kirkconnell, review of *Men in Sheepskin Coats*, *Opinion* (Winnipeg), July 1948, n.p.

52 Jeann Beattie, *Blaze of Noon* (Toronto: Ryerson 1950).

53 Duncan McDowall, "The Trial and Tribulations of Miss Agatha Chapman: Statistics in a Cold War Climate," *Queen's Quarterly*, 114, no. 3 (2007): 357–73.

54 Paul Yuzyk, *The Ukrainians in Manitoba: A Social History* (Toronto: University of Toronto Press for the Historical and Scientific Society of Manitoba 1953), 110.

55 Ibid., 110n.29.

56 M.I. Mandryka, *History of Ukrainian Literature in Canada* (Ottawa and Winnipeg: Ukrainian Free Academy of Sciences 1958), 111.

57 Eric Thompson, "Prairie Mosaic: The Immigrant Novel in the Canadian West," *Studies in Canadian Literature*, fall 1980, 256n.28.

58 Desmond Pacey to LP, 16 November 1956, file 5, box 25, LPP, and LP to Pacey, 20 November 1956, file 5, box 25, LPP.

59 In the 1950s Ryerson published Livesay's *Call My People Home* (1950) about the internment of the Japanese Canadians during the Second World War, as well as Pacey's edition of her *Selected Poems* (1957). In 1949 Ryerson had brought out Livesay's edition of *Raymond Knister: Collected Poems*, a pet project of Pierce, who, like Livesay, still mourned the early death of Knister in 1932 as a result of suicide.

60 Daniel O'Leary, "Religious Censorship in English Canada," *History of the Book in Canada: Volume Three: 1918–1980*, 473–5.

61 Margaret Laurence, *Dance on the Earth: A Memoir* (Toronto: McClelland and Stewart 1989), 5.

62 LP to Desmond Pacey, 16 November 1956, file 5, box 25, LPP.

63 Desmond Pacey, Introduction to *Selected Poems of Dorothy Livesay 1926–1956* (Toronto: Ryerson 1957), xvi, xvii.

64 LP, "Report of the Book Editor," April 1950, box 21, Board of Publication Papers.

65 Jody Mason, "'Sidown, Brother, Sidown!': The Problem of Commitment and the Publishing History of Irene Baird's *Waste Heritage*," *Papers of the Bibliographical Society of Canada*, 45, no. 2 (2007): 143–61.

66 LP to BP, September 1943 [no day given], box 12, PFC. The two books were Raymond Arthur Davies, *Arctic Eldorado* (1944), and *The Great Mackenzie in Word and Photograph* (1947).

67 LP to Sara and Eldred Chester, 19 April 1942, CFP. Pierce remembered Woodsworth a few days after his death: "He was wrong-headed on some things, but few men of his day counted for so much."

68 LP to Dorothy Livesay, 31 January 1949, file 3, box 18, LPP.

69 LP, "Report of the Book Editor," April 1952, box 21, Board of Publication Papers.

70 LP, *The House of Ryerson 1829–1954*, 51.

71 See Randall Speller, "Arthur Steven at the Ryerson Press: Designing the Post-War Years (1949–1969)," *Papers of the Bibliographical Society of Canada*, 41, no. 2 (2003): 7–44.

72 LP, "Report of the Book Editor," April 1952, box 21, Board of Publication Papers.

73 See Janet Friskney, "McClelland and Stewart and the Quality Paperback," *History of the Book in Canada: Volume. Three: 1918–1980*, 233–7.

74 Pierce's letters to Curry in the period 1945–55 are found in the Correspondence re Publication, Frederick C. Curry Collection, Personal Papers, Brockville Museum Archives. For example, on 23 June 1949, Pierce wrote: "[Your book] should be a lively Baedeker, moving slowly upstream, a book that countless tourists would buy to help through the maze of that section of the river." My thanks to Dr Glenn J Lockwood for kindly bringing this material to my attention.

75 LP, "Report of the Book Editor," April 1952, box 21, Board of Publication Papers.

76 See MacSkimming, *The Perilous Trade*.

77 LP, "Report of the Book Editor," April 1952, box 21, Board of Publication Papers.

78 Blanche Hume to LP, n.d. [spring 1954], in possession of BPR.

79 LP to Blanche Hume, [Christmas 1951], box 1, Hume Papers.

80 Jennie May Hunt, typescript reminiscences for BPR, October 1984, in possession of BPR.

81 See LP's booklet, *Memorial Windows: St George's United Church* (Toronto: St George's United Church 1957), 24pp.

82 LP to BP, n.d. [November 1943], box 16, PFC.

83 LP to Sara and Eldred Chester, n.d. [early 1950s], box 1, CFP.

84 LP, "Presentation," *The Edith Chown Pierce and Gerald Stevens Collection of Early Canadian Glass Presented to the Royal Ontario Museum in Memory of Mrs. Lorne Pierce* (Royal Ontario Museum catalogue: 1957), vi.

85 Evelyn Purvis Earle wrote: "I wish [Edith] would write a book about that [glass] and other articles, china, needlework, shellwork, and furniture used about a hundred years ago in Canada, of which choice specimens can be found here and there. It would be a big help in preserving the culture which is essentially Canadian, and it is sadly needed." Evelyn Purvis Earle to LP, 22 August 1949, file 2, box 18, LPP.

86 ECP, *Canadian Glass: A Footnote to History* (Toronto: privately printed, 1954). There was a second small print run in June 1954.

87 LP to Theresa Thomson, 2 October 1953, vol. 8, Canadian Writers' Foundation Papers, LAC.

88 LP, 1954 Pocket Diary, 1 January 1954, box 35, LPP.

89 C.H. Dickinson to LP, 20 March 1953, file 4, box 22, LPP.

90 LP to Sara and Eldred Chester, 8 February 1959, box 1, CFP.

91 LP to Sara and Eldred Chester, n.d. [spring 1954], box 1, CFP.

92 LP to Sara and Eldred Chester, n.d. [spring 1954], box 1, CFP.

93 See Friskney, "Towards a Canadian 'Cultural Mecca,'" 21.

94 LP to Blanche Hume, 30 August 1954, box 1, Hume Papers.

95 LP, *The House of Ryerson 1829–1954*, 52.

96 LP to Blanche Hume, 17 October 1955, box 1, Hume Papers.

97 LP to Sara and Eldred Chester, June 1954, box 1, CFP. Emphasis in original.

98 LP, 1954 Pocket Diary, 23 April 1954, box 35, LPP.

99 ECP, qtd. in C.H. Dickinson, "A Tribute to Edith Chown Pierce," box 1, CFP.

00 Blanche Hume to LP, n.d. [spring 1954], in possession of BPR. LP used the phrase, for example, in LP to Rev. Marshall Laverty, 23 May 1954, property of Laverty estate, Ottawa.

01 LP to Blanche Hume, n.d. [postmarked 18 October 1954], box 1, Hume Papers.

02 LP to Theresa and Don Thomson, 26 December 1957, vol. 14, Canadian Writers' Foundation Papers, LAC. LP called his association with the Foundation "one of the happiest experiences of my life" despite the workload. Theresa Thomson told a prospective donor that "without [Pierce's] vision and counsel, without the planning and encouragement, without innumerable letters, interviews and introductions – not to mention his continuous financial support – it would have been impossible for me to have attained the present measure of success in my work as [Foundation] Executive Secretary-Treasurer." See LP to Theresa Thomson, 19 January 1957, and Thomson to Douglas McLeod, 2 December 1961, both box 8, Canadian Writers' Foundation Papers, LAC.

03 For example, LP to Blanche Hume, 23 June 1954, box 1, Hume Papers.

04 LP to Rev. Marshall Laverty, 20 September 1954, property of Laverty estate, Ottawa.

05 LP to BPR, 3 August 1954, box 1, CFP.

06 LP to Donald Cameron, 5 February 1956, file 1, box 25, LPP.

107 Pierce was asked by the Canada Council and the University of the West Indies for advice on collecting early prose and verse of the Caribbean. See LP to Sara and Eldred Chester, 9 March 1959, box 1, CFP.

108 LP to Rev. Marshall Laverty, 9 October 1955, property of Laverty estate, Ottawa.

109 LP to Sara and Eldred Chester, 19 October 1958, box 1, CFP.

110 "Canada's Publishing Dean Retires to Write History," unidentified clipping [late 1959 or early 1960], box 1, CFP.

111 LP to Rev. Marshall Laverty, 17 September 1956, property of Laverty estate, Ottawa.

112 LP to Don and Theresa Thomson, 18 August 1959, box 8, Canadian Writers' Foundation Papers, LAC.

113 LP, *The Edith Chown Pierce and Gerald Stevens Collection of Early Canadian Glass*. Pierce also wrote an eighteen-page, privately printed pamphlet, *Early Glass Houses of Nova Scotia* (1958), as a supplement to the above catalogue.

114 LP, "A Substitute for a Memoir," file 8, box 38, LPP. This two-page draft chronology is all that he was able to do at the end of his life.

115 LP, Cottage Diary, 24 May 1953, file 2, box 2, Additions to LPP, QUA.

116 See Don W. Thomson, *The Foundation and the Man* (Ottawa: Penumbra Press 2007), and Campbell, "The Canadian Literary Career of Professor Pelham Edgar."

117 LP to Blanche Hume, 16 August 1954 [postmark], box 1, Hume Papers.

118 Dorothy Livesay, *Call My People Home* (1950) and *Selected Poems 1926–1956* (1957); Miriam Waddington, *The Second Silence* (1955) and *The Seasons' Lovers* (1958). LP had solicited the Purdy chapbook: see LP to Al Purdy, 5 July 1954, file 10, box 23, LPP.

119 Yves Thériault, *Agaguk* (Toronto: McGraw-Hill-Ryerson 1963).

120 See Michelle Thériault (wife of Yves) to LP, 26 April 1948, file 12, box 17, LPP, and Yves Thériault to LP, 28 November 1950, file 7, box 19, LPP. Pierce even tried to obtain a grant for Thériault.

121 John McClelland to LP, 4 January 1957, file 5, box 26, LPP.

122 See Gray, *Fun Tomorrow*.

123 "Lorne Pierce," *Liberty*, 20 September 1947, 17. The *Time* article, "Builder of Books," appeared 28 December 1959, 9.

124 "Persona Grata: The Romantic Puritan," *Saturday Night*, 26 November 1955, 26.

125 LP, "The Modern School and Good Breeding," *Observer*, 1 August 1949, scrapbook 67A, LPP.

126 Eric Nicol, "Lust for Fame," Vancouver *Province*, 10 November 1970, 29. Pierce, who was 5'10" tall, never drove a Cadillac.

127 John Robert Colombo to author, 30 January 2008.

128 For biographical information on Saunders, see Clark Saunders, "Lives Lived: Thomas Saunders," *Globe and Mail*, 17 May 2005, A9.

129 Ryerson published Saunders's chapbook *Horizontal World* (1951). The meeting out west is referred to in Saunders to C.H. Dickinson, 7 March 1951, file 11, box 20, LPP.

130 See Saunders to Dickinson, 5 June 1951; Dickinson marked the error on Thomas Saunders to Dickinson, 24 September 1951. Both are in file 11, box 20, LPP.

131 Memorandum of 24 September 1951 Board of Publication meeting, file 4, box 20, LPP. A search committee – composed of Pierce, H.L. Trueman, and R.C. Wallace – was named, but Pierce was to remain editor for another nine years.

132 LP to Rev. Garth Legg, n.d. [late 1950s], file 4, box 27, LPP.

133 C.H. Dickinson, interview with author, Woodstock, ON, 21 September 1993. Emphasis in original.

134 See King, *Jack*, 357ff.

135 Pierce wrote to his friend Sherwood Fox at Western, for example: "I long to get out of this trap and be free to do a few things I should much rather do than continue as the frayed guide of the Ryerson Press." See LP to Fox, 2 July 1953, file 4, box 22, LPP, as well as LP to Nathan van Patten, 19 June 1951, file 14, box 20, LPP.

136 John Webster Grant, interview with author, Toronto, 22 September 1993. Pierce wrote of the need for the Ryerson editor to have United Church values in a letter to Garth Legg, n.d. [late 1950s], file 4, box 27, LPP.

137 Frye to LP, 8 May 1958, file 2, box 27, LPP.

138 Northrop Frye Diary, 29 June 1950, *The Diaries of Northrop Frye 1942–1955*, ed. Robert Denham (Toronto: University of Toronto Press 2001), 392–3.

139 LP to Pearson Gundy, 2 November 1961, property of the late Pearson Gundy. In the letter, he confirmed with Gundy, Queen's librarian and curator of the Canadiana Collection, their decision not to ask Pacey to take over the still-unwritten Carman biography. Gundy himself published an edition of Carman's letters in lieu of a biography.

140 Desmond Pacey to LP, 23 October 1957, file 5, box 26, LPP.

141 Rev. Garth Legg married my parents in Noranda, my hometown.

142 John Webster Grant, interview with author, Toronto, 22 September 1993.

143 LP to Carl Klinck, 19 December 1959, in Klinck, *Giving Canada a Literary History*, 146.

144 Reta Blair to LP, 17 December 1959, file 2, box 26, LPP.

145 LP to Sara and Eldred Chester, 23 January 1959, box 1, CFP.

146 John Webster Grant to LP, 4 February 1959, file 2, box 28, LPP.

147 LP, Report to the Annual Meeting of the Board of Publication, 27–28 April 1959, scrapbook, box 35, LPP.

148 LP to Blanche Hume, 15 June 1960, box 1, Hume Papers.

149 John Webster Grant, interview with author, Toronto, 22 September 1993.

150 LP to C.H. Dickinson, Confidential Memorandum, 31 July 1959, file 1, box 28, LPP.

151 John Webster Grant, interview with author, Toronto, 22 September 1993. Grant's salary at departure was only $10,000 – academia offered better remuneration and a more congenial working environment, in Grant's view. Years later, Grant recalled his frustration at his inability to get solid information on book costs out of House Accountant Ernie Scott – just like LP.

152 Pearson Gundy to BPR, 2 May 1962, in possession of BPR; and John Webster Grant, interview with author, Toronto, 22 September 1993.

153 LP to Pearson Gundy, 2 November 1961, copy in possession of the author.

154 LP to Sara and Eldred Chester, 10 January 1960, box 1, CFP.

155 LP, qtd. in "Builder of Books," *Time*, 28 December 1959, 9.

156 Frank Flemington, 13 March 1949, file 2, box 28, LPP.

157 Blanche Hume to LP, 29 December 1959, file 3, box 28, LPP. Emphasis in original.

158 LP, 1960 Desk Book, 29 January 1960, box 35, LPP.

159 LP, qtd. in "Canada's Publishing Dean Retires to Write History," unidentified clipping, box 1, CFP.

160 LP to Blanche Hume, 12 September 1961, box 1, Hume Papers.

161 Edith's dying request that Lorne write his memoirs is mentioned in LP to Blanche Hume, 13 June 1955, box 1, Hume Papers. Pierce wrote, somewhat disingenuously: "I may do my memoirs fairly soon, but very private and only two copies for the children. I do that as a promise made to Edith. She wanted them above all else. There will be no biography by [W.S.] Wallace. In time Frank [Flemington] will produce his Lorne Pierce check-list, and will use the Blanche Hume material as best he can, and by then I shall be beyond the sunsets I expect. Nothing important can ever be said about this person. But I have much of importance to say to others."

162 LP to Blanche Hume, 9 November 1961, box 1, Hume Papers.

163 "A Publisher's Papers," *Douglas Library Notes*, 13, no. 3 (1964): 5.

164 LP to Sara and Eldred Chester, 8 April 1961, box 1, CFP.

165 LP to Pearson Gundy, 27 March 1961, copy in possession of the author.

166 See Campbell Hughes to LP, 6 July and 21 July 1960, both in file 2, box 29, LPP.

167 LP to Sara and Eldred Chester, 17 August 1960, box 1, CFP. This was written after the death of Rev. Brewing.

168 LP to Sara and Eldred Chester, 8 April 1961, box 1, CFP. There is an echo here of the Book of Wisdom anthem Edith Pierce had referred to in her last letter to her family: "The souls of those who do right are surely in the hand of God." According to Lorne, Edith added: "I rest on that. Whatever it is, it will be well with me and with you also … in the hand of God. Surely there will be vast surprises of love in the Great Beyond. Therefore we need fear no evil, for we are this day, and every day forever, in His hand." See LP, "In God's Keeping: Meditation," n.d. [after April 1954], file 2, box 26, LPP.

169 LP to Pearson Gundy, 2 November 1961, copy in possession of the author. My thanks to the late Pearson Gundy for kindly sending me a copy after my interview with him.
170 LP to Blanche Hume, 24 November 1961, box 1, Hume Papers.
171 "Obituaries: Dr. Lorne Pierce …," Toronto *Daily Star*, 28 November 1961.
172 "Memorial Service," November 1961, in possession of BPR.
173 Rev. Livingstone to Beth and Bruce Pierce, 1 December 1961, box 15, PFC.
174 [C.H. Dickinson], "Memorial Service, Dr Lorne Pierce, the United Church House, December 6, 1961," box 1, CFP. Emphasis in original.
175 International Brotherhood of Bookbinders, Local 28, *Bindery News*, December 1961, 5, box 1, CFP.

EPILOGUE

1 Robin Farr, interview with author, 10 October 1995, Hamilton, Bermuda.
2 BPR, interview with author, 14 June 2010, Kingston, ON.
3 Finding Aid to the Board of Publication Papers, United Church Archives.
4 "Woods Gordon Review of Operations 1964," box 22, Board of Publication Papers.
5 "1962 Report of Special Committee on Finance," United Church Publishing House, box 22, Board of Publication Papers.
6 Bruce Pierce to author, 29 August 2008.
7 For example, rising young publisher Robin Farr, who briefly succeeded Grant at Ryerson. Robin Farr, interview with author, 10 October 1995, Hamilton, Bermuda.
8 Parker, "Trade and Regional Publishing in Central Canada," *History of the Book in Canada: Volume Three 1918–1980*, 174. See also George Parker, "The Sale of Ryerson Press: The End of the Old Agency System and Conflicts over Domestic and Foreign Ownership in the Canadian Publishing Industry, 1970–1986," *Papers of the Bibliographical Society of Canada*, 40, no. 2 (2002): 7–56.
9 See MacSkimming, *The Perilous Trade*.
10 William C. Heine, "Brief to the Royal Commission on Book Publishing [1971]," LAC.
11 See Scott Symons, "The Meaning of English Canada," repr. in Christopher Elson, ed., *"Dear Reader": Selected Scott Symons* (Toronto: Gutter Press 1998), 31– 8. Not that Pierce's ideas were utterly without influence, and sometimes in unexpected quarters. Scott Symons's controversial 1963 address "The Meaning of English Canada" to the Canadian Centenary Council Symposium shows the influence of his contact with Pierce (both were connoisseurs of Canadian glass) and his reading of LP's *A Canadian Nation*, ironic given Symons's jeremiads against the impact of Methodism on Canadian culture.

12 John Webster Grant, interview with author, 22 September 1993, Toronto.

13 MacSkimming, *The Perilous Trade*, 30.

14 LP to Rev. Garth Legg, n.d. [1958], file 4, box 27, LPP.

15 See King, *Jack*, and MacSkimming, *The Perilous Trade*.

16 C.H. Dickinson, interview with author, 21 September 1993, Woodstock, ON. After retiring from the House, Dickinson moved to Woodstock as associate minister of Chalmers United Church.

17 A copy is in the Edith and Lorne Pierce Collection, Douglas Library, Queen's University.

18 Pearson Gundy to BPR, 17 March 1963, in possession of BPR.

19 LP to Bruce Pierce, 26 February 1944, in possession of BPR.

20 Desmond Pacey, "Romantic of Romantics," review of *Lorne Pierce: A Profile* by C.H. Dickinson, *Canadian Literature*, 28 (spring 1966): 77–8.

INDEX

Crawford, Isabella Valancy, 219, 314, 423, 439, 443
Creighton, Donald, 6, 13, 267, 270, 330–3, 335, 339–40
Creighton, William, 248
Crémazie, Octave, 223
Crosby (Ontario), 17, 386, 387
Crosby Methodist Church, 18
Cullen, Maurice, 367, 371, 377
Curry, Ted, 473
Cutten, Dr, 71

Dalton, Annie Charlotte, 148
Daniells, Roy, 438
Darwin, Charles, 22, 40
Davie, Carolyn, 226
Davies, Blodwen, 271, 365, 367
Davies, Raymond, 471
Davies, Robertson, 358, 444, 483, 500
Davis, R.E.G., 406
Davison, Charles, 30, 37
Deacon, William Arthur, 181, 182–5, 190, 191, 198, 206, 213, 219, 222, 225, 230, 251, 267, 348, 364, 404, 417, 456, 457, 468
Defence of Canada Act, 471
de Gaspé, Philippe Aubert, 222
de la Roche, Mazo, 277, 278
Delta (Ontario) 6, 14–16, 17, 19, 24, 26–7, 30, 83, 503; annual fair, 15, 22, 27; and First World War, 77
Delta Methodist Church (after 1925 Delta United Church), 15, 19, 27, 123, 385, 387, 503
Delta Public School, 29–30
de Montigny, Louvigny, 213, 222
Dent (publisher), 346
Dewart, Edward Hartley, 32, 155, 195
Dewey, John, 299
Dickinson, Clarence Heber, 7, 341–2, 414, 496; relations with LP, 342–4, 404–5, 477, 485, 487–9, 493, 502–4

Dickinson, Emily, 479
Dickinson, Isabelle, 404
Dingle, Della, 180, 245
The Doctrines and Disciplines of the Methodist Church in Canada, 154
Dodd, Frank, 456
Dodd, Mead (publisher), 454
Dolfuss, Englebert, 307
Donaldson, Norman, 333, 335, 338
Doran, George, 249
Dostoevsky, Feodor, 116, 167
Doughty, Arthur, 215
Douglas Methodist Church (Montreal), 133, 147
Dowsley, W.C., 38, 39, 64
Doyle, Arthur Conan, 157
Drummond, William Henry, 420
Dudek, Louis, 264, 409, 412, 423–6, 427, 444–5
Duncan, Norman, 221–2
Duncan, Sara Jeannette, 438
Dundas County Athletic Association, 129
Dupuy, Pierre, 223
Dyde, Samuel, 49

Earle, Evelyn Purvis, 473, 476
Eastman, Kate, 452
Eastman, Samuel, 406
Eaton's department store, 157, 250
Eayrs, Dora Whitefield, 284, 294, 298, 310
Eayrs, Hugh, 5, 6, 7, 13, 142, 168, 187, 202, 267, 271, 366, 403, 471; career and personality, 284–5; joint text-book ventures with LP, 283–90, 291–305, 306, 307–16
Edgar, Pelham, 31, 50, 79, 169, 171, 186, 206, 219, 220, 236–7, 267, 278, 413, 415, 417, 430, 432–7, 481, 486, 492; influence on LP, 81, 183, 202, 418, 422, 423